THE LEE COUNTY LIBRARY
SANFORD, NORTH CAROLINA

— PRESENTED BY —

W. E. Horner, Sr.

THE
RED
BLAIK
STORY

LEE COUNTY LIBRARY
SANFORD, N. C.

THE RED BLAIK STORY

EARL "RED" BLAIK

ARLINGTON HOUSE·PUBLISHERS
NEW ROCHELLE, N. Y.

Copyright © 1960 by Earl H. Blaik and Tim Cohane
You Have To Pay The Price, Part I,
copyright transferred 1973 to Earl H. Blaik
Part II Copyright 1974 by Earl H. Blaik

All rights reserved. No portion of this book may be reproduced without written permission from the publisher, except by a reviewer who may quote brief passages in connection with a review.

MANUFACTURED IN THE UNITED STATES OF AMERICA

Library of Congress Cataloging in Publication Data

Blaik, Earl H 1897-
  The Red Blaik Story.

Part 1, You have to pay the price, written by E. H. Blaik & T. Cohane, was first published separately in 1960.
      1. Blaik, Earl H., 1897- 2. Football.
1. Title.
GV939.B53A37   796.33'2'0924 (B)   74-7266
ISBN 0-87000-267-8

To the men of West Point and Dartmouth

who paid the price

"Fight on, my merry men all,
    I'm a little wounded, but I am not slain;
I will lay me down for to bleed a while,
    Then I'll rise and fight with you again."

"Johnnie Armstrong's Last Goodnight,"
Stanza 18, Anonymous.
From Dryden's *Miscellanies*, 1702

Contents

	PART I *You Have to Pay the Price*	1
I	The Flood and the Game	3
II	The Red Earl of Oxford	15
III	Our Supe, General MacArthur	24
IV	The De-emphasized Cavalry	50
V	The Temporary Avocation	64
VI	The Golden Cutback	79
VII	The Whip	96
VIII	Direct Action in "Heaven"	118
IX	The Big Green and a Stronger Ivy League	143
X	"Uncle Bobby" Goes to Town	167
XI	Storybook Teams	192
XII	The Vindicators	213
XIII	The Break with Notre Dame	231
XIV	The Forgotten Grenadiers	249
XV	The Ninety Scapegoats	279
XVI	College Football's Real Abuse	301
XVII	Where the Black, Gold and Gray Belongs	314
XVIII	You Are My Quarterback	336
XIX	The Lonely End	358
XX	Old Coaches Never Die	391
	PART II *As I Knew Them*	407
XXI	The Decade of the 60's	409
XXII	Assistants Who Became Head Coaches	421
XXIII	Vince Lombardi	434
XXIV	The West Point Scandal Reexamined	444

XXV	The Kennedys: President Jack and Bob	469
XXVI	MacArthur In Action	488
XXVII	MacArthur As I Knew Him	511
XXVIII	Twists and Turns	538
Appendices		555
Index		569

Illustrations

Illustrations follow page 146.

Dad at 70.
Freshman end on the Beta team at Miami, 1914.
At Miami in 1917 I was varsity end and captain-outfielder.
Army football.
Our 1919-'20 basketball team.
Reporting as a new Cadet.
Merle and I go canoeing in 1920.
At Fort Riley Cavalry School in 1920.
My son Bill and I, 1935.
The one and only Harry Ellinger.
Dartmouth golf and fishing pals.
Doc Blanchard cracks Navy in 1945.
Glenn Davis on a 49-yard run.
After the Rice game in 1958.
MacLeod of Dartmouth in 1937.
Pat Uebel in 1953.
Pete Lash, Don Holleder, and Ed Szveteez in 1955.
Bob Anderson of the undefeated Lonely End team.
The Lonely End, Bill Carpenter.
Yale Bowl, 1941.
Congratulations from Navy Coach Oscar Hagberg.
At Notre Dame in '47.
At Northwestern in '53.
We've just beat Navy in '53.
After our '55 upset.
Captain Jim Kernan and General MacArthur.
Pete Dawkins, Assistant Coach Tom Harp, and I.
Andy Gustafson, Herman Hickman, Jabo Jablonsky, and Stu Holcomb.
In Philadelphia's Municipal Stadium in 1946.
Father John Cavanaugh, Coach Frank Leahy, and General Eichelberger.
A young friend, Corky Luke.

Merle and "Lady" in West Point Days.
This is Joe Cahill.
A huddle, of sorts, at the Touchdown Club.
With Grantland Rice and Gen. MacArthur.
The night I was elected to the Football Hall of Fame.
With Attorney General Robert Kennedy.

Foreword

I have known the author intimately ever since he was a cadet at the Military Academy while I was its Superintendent. During the ensuing years I have had the opportunity to observe at first hand his outstanding contributions to the Academy, primarily through his extraordinary influence in the building of character in the members of the Cadet Corps. He has instilled in them a deep devotion to the ideals of the Academy's historic Legend—"Duty, Honor, Country."

As Coach and Director of Athletics his work in the development of strong football teams was dramatic. He never failed to produce the maximum from the material which successive squads had to offer.

Just as football will remain a leading competitive sport in college athletics, so will Earl Blaik be remembered as an outstanding architect of victory on the gridiron. For, apart from his innate grasp of successful strategic and tactical concepts, he possesses those essential attributes of leadership which mold men into a cohesive fighting team and inspire in them an invincible will to victory.

Douglas MacArthur

Publisher's Note

Part I of this book, *You Have To Pay The Price*, was originally published in 1960 and is now out of print. It was co-authored by Earl H. Blaik and Tim Cohane. Part II consists of eight new chapters by Colonel Blaik. The new material covers important experiences of the author since the original volume was written. In addition Part II includes more material on key events in Part I, such as the West Point Scandal of 1951.

Part I

You Have To Pay The Price
Earl H. Blaik with Tim Cohane

Chapter I

The Flood and the Game

I was not much past sixteen years of age, a junior at Steele High School in Dayton, Ohio, when early in the morning of Tuesday, March 25, 1913, I realized there would be no school that day. To me, this fact was the least part of the catastrophe that was upon us.

For five days, steady rains had swollen the Great Miami River until its muddy waters rolled over the levees and caused what was then the most disastrous flood in the history of this country.

At four o'clock in the morning, police and fire alarms awakened us—my parents, my brother and sister, and me—with the prearranged warning signal that the Miami was rampant. As best they could, my parents judged the situation, decided that the flood would not reach our home at 214 Herman Avenue in the Riverdale section, and made plans to stay. About 6:20 A.M. my father went to the grocery store and returned with provisions against the possibility that we might be stranded for a few days by two or three inches of water.

Dad was too realistic to be an optimist, but he was oversanguine that time. At 7:30 A.M., the turbulent Miami broke the levees above the Herman Avenue Bridge and cascaded into a boulevard, formerly a river channel, which crossed Herman Avenue at a point two houses away from ours.

The water swept down the old channel in a wild current. By 8:30 it was two feet deep and lapping ominously at our front steps. When it reached our porch level, we abandoned our home. Dad, Mother, my brother Doug, my sister Mabel, and I linked hands and waded down the front steps into water that was up to our hips and rapidly rising. On all sides, neighbors were seeking the haven of higher ground. Horses and dogs, swimming in the old channel where the water was now well over their heads, were trying to reach a point of refuge. Chickens had fled to the housetops. It was a frightening scene to anyone, terrifying to a youngster.

We waded to the higher ground of the Forest Avenue Presbyterian Church, which provided us and many other families shelter for the next several days. Most of that time my father was separated from us, helping to rescue people and bring them food.

Early on that first morning, communication lines went dead, bridges were washed out. As the waters seethed upward to second-story windows, thousands of people were marooned on roofs. Some houses were torn from their foundations and swept away on the havoc tide. People could be heard moaning and crying for help. At the flood's crest, downtown Dayton lay under fourteen feet of water.

With the first night came the added menace of fire. It started in an upper floor of a downtown office building or warehouse and was fanned by the wind into a blaze that soon enveloped an entire large block and burned buildings down to the water line. When the flames reached a paint company, explosions skyrocketed into the night sky. The blaze grew and lit up the skies like daylight. That night we could see clearly the people stranded on housetops. The fire came within a dozen blocks of us. Then a provident change in wind blew it back over the charred area, where it finally fought itself out.

On Friday morning, the fourth day, the waters began to recede. As if released from the anesthesia of shock, people began to feel the full pain of the devastation. When finally they could get down into the streets and move around, it was in six to eight inches or more of mud. I was one of the first to drive into town and see the desolation. Buildings had been burned or washed completely away. Stocks of stores were scattered shambles. Bloated carcasses of hundreds of dead horses accented the macabre landscape. Over everything was mud, inches of it, thick, black, slimy, and depressing.

If you have not personally known the disaster of a flood, it is impossible to appreciate the depression such a scene evokes, depression that borders on sheer hopelessness. It is most poignant when you see for the first time the destruction visited on your own home. When I first saw ours, I was with my father. He was a man ordinarily unawed by trouble or challenge, but so dour was the prospect of ever making our home livable again that for a time he even considered giving up and returning to Detroit, whence we had come twelve years before. Everything inside and outside our home was buried under a layer of mud, in some places as deep as fourteen inches.

For days, Dad, Doug, and I shoveled it. Moreover, we had laboriously to work all of it off the shovels and sift through every blessed inch of it, faintly hopeful of reclaiming at least part of my mother's cherished silverware, or anything else of some value or utility. We salvaged very little.

Until Mother could get the new furniture she wanted, until carpentry, masonry, and painting were finished, we lived for several months in a house lent to us by a friend. When we did live again in 214 Herman Avenue, it was years before Mother decided that our home was as comfortable as it used to be; years, too, before the stark memories of March, 1913, began to ease.

The Dayton flood was my introduction to catastrophe. Unlike many Daytonians who may have anticipated the disaster a prolonged rainfall might bring, I was too young and inexperienced to be prepared for the shock of Nature suddenly, unexpectedly rising up in terrifying attack and swallowing up before my eyes the safe, ordered, and secure world I had known up to then. Tragedy of a species and magnitude unknown in our personal experience struck us suddenly and hard, frightened, staggered, benumbed us all, and left us desolate.

Thirty-eight years later, I was to know catastrophe and desolation again, of a different sort, but carrying the same kind of shock of a world torn asunder. That was the expulsion from West Point of ninety cadets for a breach of the Honor Code. The ninety included almost my entire football team; among them was my own son.

To the Dayton Flood victims, nothing short of loss by death could have been as personally devastating as the expulsion was to those ninety boys, to myself, and to those close to us. Nor did the flood come as any more of an incredible shock to the nation.

The expulsion, in one sense, was the greater tragedy. In the unique combination of conditions which set the stage for it there was no suspicion of danger. The result was thus the more incomprehensible and chaotic. What had become through a quarter of a century my way of life, my whole world, at once the essence and emblem of all I believed in, shall believe in always, was threatened with inundation.

Mine was a world of West Point and college football and superb young American manhood. A world in which I had known a Charlie Daly, a Pot Graves, a Biff Jones, a Douglas MacArthur, a Red Cagle, a Ralph Sasse, a Harry Ellinger, a Red Reeder, an "Uncle Bobby" Eichelberger, a Tom Doe, a Ray Stecker, a Roland Bevan, a Blanchard, and a Davis.

A world of mighty collisions, off the field as well as on, with the Navy, Notre Dame, Yale, and Michigan.

A world, too, that included Dartmouth, its President Ernest Martin Hopkins, Bob MacLeod, a wild jinx-slaying in Yale Bowl, a "fifth down" game with Cornell that was won after it was lost.

A world of work, pain, valleys, defeat, of accomplishment, exaltation, highlands, and victory.

A world that would emerge slowly, agonizingly from its own receding flood waters and rebuild itself haltingly, laboriously. A world of that never-to-be-forgotten "brave, old Army team" of 1953; of a selfless cadet, Quarterback Don Holleder.

A world of the final, climatic triumphs of 1958; of Bob Anderson, Pete Dawkins, Joe Caldwell, and that mysterious colorful phoenix symbol of it all, Bill Carpenter, The Lonely End.

I was fascinated by this magnificent game, football, almost as far back as I can remember, from Hawthorne grammar-school days in Dayton as a fourth-grader, eight years old, in 1905. I was ten when I formed a neighborhood kids' team and appointed myself coach, captain, and quarterback. We called ourselves the "Riverdale Rovers" after the Rover Boys books we all read.

The Riverdale Rovers played with a round, black, soccer-type ball, rather than the oval rugby kind, and concentrated on the running game. I always did believe that the running game should be paramount, even when, during my last year at the Point, I put in The Lonely End attack. Perhaps my thinking was influenced by my first exposure to the strategy of the game as field general of the Rovers. The forward pass had been legalized in 1906, when I was in the fifth grade, but we Rovers—if we knew about it at all—chose to ignore it.

Riverdale was a neighborhood bounded on the south and east by the Miami River. On the east bank, after its course turned north and before it joined with the Mad River, was another and somewhat more rugged neighborhood, North Dayton. It was connected with Riverdale by the Herman Avenue Bridge. The Riverdale Rovers' schedule consisted almost exclusively of a series of games with a team of North Dayton kids. The contests invariably produced a crescendo of feeling which finally erupted into free-for-alls. Even after the infantry withdrew from the field, artillery elements deployed on opposite ends of the Herman Avenue Bridge and the adjacent banks of the Miami, and cannonaded each other with rocks. It was our only concession to the forward pass.

On Thanksgiving Day morning, 1909, I moved up a bit in football class. Although only an eighth-grader, I was invited to play in the line on a Riverdale team of older boys, including some Steele High players, in a game against Oakwood. I was still a few months shy of thirteen, and I could not have weighed more than 100 pounds. I was somewhat overmatched.

My misadventures that day included a gorgeous black eye, such an unsightly "shiner" that I hesitated to present myself to my father and mother at the Thanksgiving table. Some of the players got me a piece of steak to try to reduce the swelling, and I delayed going home for a couple of hours. Finally, though, I had to face up to it. My parents were not happy, but they didn't say much. I suspect now that they must have felt that a lecture would desecrate the spirit of the holiday.

From earliest childhood, I was, like my mother, a true redhead on the auburn side, and the argumentative traits that supposedly go with this shade of hair were mine. I was usually in minor travail for talking back to my Hawthorne School teachers. The principal of Hawthorne was Emerson L. Horner, who more than once was obliged to summon me to his office and apply the hickory stick. Yet I think we sort of liked each other.

In my youth, school authorities delivered corporal punishment when indicated and truants accepted it, without any great concern on either side. Authority did not fear that the punishment would repress the child's personality and blight his life. The child regarded it as a challenge not to cry.

Mr. Horner once extended me the dubious option of accepting the paddling immediately after school or waiting until the next morning. I chose the next morning, under the illusion that Mr. Horner might relent overnight. He did not. In fact, he compounded the damage with the old saw: "This is going to hurt me more than it hurts you."

The punishment was cut short, however, thanks to some schoolmates. I had told them about my appointment with Principal Horner. They followed me at a distance and peeked through the door, which was slightly ajar. Mr. Horner, sensing the audience, broke off from chastising me, made a sudden rush, and collared my companions. He finished the job on them.

I am afraid I did little studying in grammar school. There were too many more interesting things to do: football, baseball, bicycling, or riding a neighbor's horse around the stable yard. The "horseless carriage" had arrived, but many people regarded it as merely a passing fad. In any event, it was still the day of the horse and my early pleasure in riding had something to do, I am sure, with my choosing the cavalry after I was graduated from West Point.

Like most men looking back to childhood, I am convinced that Mother was the world's most wonderful cook. Perhaps I should be more objective about it and, as in football parlance, merely place her in the top ten. A heel of her homemade bread, still warm and liberally spread with her homemade chili sauce, or buttered and covered with brown sugar—brother, that was living! This I claim in spite of the contention of my old friend Stanley Woodward, the sports editor of the New York *Herald Tribune*, who considers me strictly a Shredded Wheat man. Stanley has even written more than once that I regard food as sinful.

I was fourteen in 1911, when after one year at Parker Junior High as a ninth-grader, I entered Steele High School as a sophomore. The Steele High players were my earliest football heroes. Steele's doors closed for the last time in 1940, but in its day the school enjoyed a fine football tradition. The Lions, as Steele teams were called after the big stone lion at the front of the school, sent such stars as Ed Byrne and Ollie Klee to Ohio State; Jackson Kiefer to Brown; and others to my first college alma mater, the University of Miami at Oxford, Ohio. Kiefer later coached Steele. Roland Bevan, my trainer at Dartmouth and West Point, also coached Steele, but that was after my time there.

The Steele teams practiced at Dayton's old Athletic Park, three miles from the school. They walked to and from the park, and as an eighth-grader at Hawthorne, I frequently tagged along with them. I was awed by their ability in comparison with my own. When they let me hold the kerosene lamp they dressed by, in an old shack at the park after practice, my day was complete and I walked the three miles home on clouds.

Although I was five feet four inches tall and only a few pounds over 100 when I entered Steele, I made quarterback on the scrubs, coached by Alfred McCray, later Judge McCray. His son Latta McCray played guard on my 1935 and 1936 Dartmouth teams. I was shifted to end as a junior in 1912, saw some action, and in my senior year, 1913, made regular end under Coach Jim Mathes. I was then sixteen years old, five feet nine, and weighed 133 pounds. I was not powerful and I had yet to attain the quickness that comes to some athletes only when they mature. I was in there playing, I guess, mainly because I had enthusiasm.

I remember well that we lost our big game to Stivers High, 13–7, in the last fifty-one seconds. I caught a 20-yard pass from fullback Joe Mann on the 2-yard line and went over for our only touchdown. Somewhere between the Riverdale Rovers and the Stivers game, I had found out about the pass. Even though they put me at left end on an All Time Steele Team, selected by the Dayton *Journal* in 1923, I was distinctly not a "blue-chip" high-school athlete. I failed to make the Steele baseball and basketball teams.

In fact, though it may be difficult to believe, I was as successful in high-school dramatics as in athletics. When the Steele High seniors staged a three-act comedy (*His Last Chance*, by Carrie Colburn), I played the part of Sam Buttons, the bellboy. Dayton newspaper reviews the next day included the following:

> Many comic situations admirably acted by the cast kept the audience in laughter from the beginning of the initial act until the final curtain was rung down. The antics of Buttons, the bellboy, were especially amusing. This part was taken by Earl Blaik.

The antics of Blaik as either Thespian or athlete apparently did not amuse his Steele teachers. I believe they realized I had the potential to do well academically, but, as in Hawthorne and Parker days, I was studying only enough to get by.

One of my academic crimes, which I had forgotten, since it had left my conscience so untroubled, was literally unearthed by the Dayton Flood. Miss Alice Hall, my English teacher, had written a letter to my father, suggesting that my application left something to be desired and that he should apply forceful remedies. I had intercepted the dangerous missive and hidden it under the carpet in my parents' bedroom. The flood washed it into the open and Dad eventually found it. He immediately called on Miss Hall to explain that his seeming discourtesy in not answering her several-months-old letter traced to my criminal efforts, which now had been uncovered by an act of God. I remained unforgiven for several days.

The assistant principal of Steele, William B. Werthner, lived in our neighborhood, but we were unenchanted with each other. I have forgotten the precise interplay, but about a week before graduation we came to an impasse. My powers of persuasion proved unavailing. I lost the argument, whatever it was, and was expelled, at least pro tem.

Professor Werthner sent me to Edwin J. Brown, Dayton's superintendent of schools. Mr. Brown told me I would have to come down to Professor Werthner's office with my father and apologize. It was not easy to break this news to Dad. He always had a deep respect for educators and later served as president of the Dayton School Board. In fact he and Superintendent Brown were good friends. But it developed that he was less displeased with me than he was with Mr.

Brown for taking him from his work instead of handling the matter himself.

I recall as if it were yesterday accompanying Dad down Main Street the five blocks from his office to the high school. It was a forced march. Dad always had considered himself a potential sprinter; he often raced me, when I was a small boy, from the corner to our house. Now in his irritation he was really stretching out, in long, rapid strides that were almost a run. Despite my best efforts, I was left some paces to his rear in strictly military fashion. The matter concluded with Dad dressing down Mr. Brown for not taking direct action himself; with me, in turn, apologizing to Mr. Werthner; and with Mr. Werthner restoring me to the graduation rolls.

As I have suggested, my father, William Douglas Blaik, was a strong, sound, forthright individual, a Scotch Presbyterian churchman and a staunch Thirty-third Degree Mason. He was born in Glasgow, Scotland, April 30, 1867. Dad came of seagoing people on both sides, fishermen and freight haulers; one of them was captain of a ship.

Although he seldom referred to the old country and put little stock in a family coat of arms, he was very proud of his Scotch ancestry. He would never abide the change from "Blaik," the true spelling of the name in Scotland, to "Blake," the general Americanization. Whenever he discovered my name written as "Blake," at Steele or thereafter, he would take to the telephone or pen and paper and quickly set the offender straight.

Dad was sixteen when he came to America in 1883. He went first to Thedford, Ontario, where his father's brother, Will Blake, was mayor for many years. Will Blake was a powerful man who ran a blacksmith and carriage shop. For three years Dad worked at learning this trade and saved his money. In 1886, although he was only nineteen, he moved to Detroit and opened his own blacksmith and carriage shop on Twelfth Street. He was not a man to work for anybody else longer than he had to.

Dad's naturally sturdy physique was further developed by labor as a blacksmith. Although a young emigrant seeking to carve out a place for himself found little time for sports, he engaged in some successful amateur swimming competition around Detroit.

It was too bad he never had the opportunity to go to college and play football. With his five feet eleven inches and 220 pounds, he probably would have made a splendid fullback or blocking back; or if not that, perhaps a guard. As it was, he never displayed open enthusiasm for the game, but he certainly was not opposed to it. He did not see me play often, only because he soon discovered that he was the kind of spectator who could not help suffering vicariously from all the pressures of the game.

Dad and other horse and carriage men on Twelfth Street in Detroit were incensed frequently over a man named Henry Ford, who was experimenting with a horseless carriage. When Ford ran his "contraption" down the street, it made so much noise it scared the horses and it was a tough job to keep them from bolting. To the unconcealed satisfaction of the owners of horses he had frightened, Henry's cart broke down frequently. On more than one such occasion he borrowed tools from my father to make repairs.

One of Dad's business neighbors was Henry Purcell, who had a coal and lumber yard on Twelfth Street. Henry's daughter, Margaret Jane, was a bookkeeper in a title and abstract office. The Purcells, who were of Irish extraction, came from Canada, where Margaret's mother had died when she was a little girl. William Blaik had been in Detroit three years when he met Margaret, and the following year, 1890, they were married. Their first child, Douglas Livingston Blaik, was born in Detroit, August 10, 1893. I arrived, also in Detroit, February 15, 1897. My sister Mabel was born in 1907, after we moved to Dayton.

My brother Doug was eight and I was four when we moved from Detroit to Dayton in 1901. Dad sold his business to become Ohio and Kentucky sales representative for the Capwell Horseshoe Company, with headquarters in Dayton. In 1906, he opened his own hardware store. In 1915, he went into real estate and building and remained in it until his death in 1947.

It was in Dayton that Dad became interested in politics. It is one of those interesting twists of fate that he did; otherwise I might never have got to West Point. He was a thoroughgoing Democrat and worked hard to help elect his friend, James M. Cox, to Congress in

1908. This contact with Governor Cox was to help me get my appointment to the Military Academy in 1918.

It happened that after my graduation from West Point in 1920, I was asked to be marshal of the parade of Governor Cox and Franklin D. Roosevelt to the Dayton Fair Grounds, to accept the Democratic presidential and vice-presidential nominations. I turned it down because I felt such an honor belonged to somebody who had been to war. World War I had ended while I was still a cadet.

Our home in the west side of Riverdale bordered the slightly more residential area, Dayton View. Not far from us was Governor Cox's house on Grand Avenue and a few doors away the home of Albert Emanuel, whose son Victor was one of my boyhood friends. Victor is chairman of the AVCO Corporation, where I have been serving as a vice-president and member of the management board since I retired from coaching after the 1958 season.

Our neighborhood also included on Central Avenue such later industrial giants as Hugh Chalmers, Thomas J. Watson, Richard Grant, Edward Andrew Deeds, and Charles Franklin (Boss) Kettering. The Wright brothers, inventors of the airplane, lived on the west side of Dayton and had a little bicycle shop on Third Street.

I remember as a kid peeking into Deeds's garage, one of those old, two-story converted stables, and watching Kettering at work on what was to become the first electric automobile, or "self-starter." Later, I was to meet Kettering often at the Dayton Engineering Club where he lunched. He was creative, imaginative, brilliant, colorful, stimulating. I have often quoted his saying: "It isn't what you don't know that gets you into trouble, but rather what you know—for sure—that isn't so."

Neither Kettering nor any of those other incipient titans, however, loomed as large in my boyhood eyes as Steele High's star back and pitcher, Marvin "Monk" Pierce. Monk lived only six houses away from me, which gave him a special hero's status. I was in the ninth grade at Parker when Monk was a senior at Steele, but he worked for a year after graduation, so that when I entered the University of Miami in 1914, I was only two classes behind him. By example at Steele and more directly later at Miami, Monk exerted considerable influence on my career as an athlete, and has remained a friend through the years. Not long ago he retired as president and publisher of *McCall's* magazine.

Adulation and attempted emulation of Monk Pierce and other local athletic heroes preoccupied my boyhood days. Sports were the center, if not the whole, of my existence. I am not implying, however, that I knew from early Hawthorne days that I wanted to be a football coach and nothing else, and pointed my every step in that direction. Some men, perhaps even some football coaches, may have sensed their goal and begun working toward it that early, but emphatically this was not so with me. My deep love of football was only something normal to thousands of youngsters.

In fact I doubt that any man who made a career of coaching ever got to it so late and so circuitously as I did. I was twenty-nine years old, six years out of West Point, before I became even an assistant coach, and then only temporarily to help out a friend. It was eight years after that, fourteen years after I left college, that I finally decided to become a head coach and make it my life's work. I was thirty-seven years old.

I was to remain a head coach for twenty-five years. I would not have dreamed of trading it for any conceivable peacetime work. I sacrificed everything to it. My late beginning, then, seems all the more strange.

Yet, had it not been for World War I, I would have become a lawyer. Had it not been for the naïve belief of our political leadership at the time that there never would be another war, and a letter that was mailed one day too late, I would have remained a soldier. And had it not been for, of all things, the financial panic of 1893 and its effect on the personal fortunes of a rural Baptist minister in Massachusetts (four years before I was born), I would not, forty-eight years later, have given up the business of building and selling houses.

I think it is stranger still that I ever became a football coach at all.

Chapter II

The Red Earl of Oxford

In my days at the University of Miami in Oxford, Ohio, from September, 1914, to May, 1918, one of the buildings near the campus was a private mental institution known as the Oxford Retreat. It was operated by Dr. George Harvey Cook. As a Beta Theta Pi brother of ours, Dr. Cook let us hold our formal fraternity dances in the Retreat auditorium.

One evening the decorum of a waltz set was broken by the sudden appearance on the floor of one of Dr. Cook's inmates, executing a solo step attired only in long red flannel underdrawers. I took it upon myself with others to usher the old fellow gently out of the hall and back to his quarters, although I can't recall what persuasive arguments I mustered. Afterwards Dr. Cook complimented me on exhibiting the poise of an experienced keeper. He was tempted, he said, to offer me a position on his staff.

Being a keeper in an asylum might be far from the most impractical preparation for coaching football. I should think it would provide invaluable training for coping with some alumni, professors, faculty representatives, undergraduate editors, effigy hangmen, and all other self-appointed experts of the gridiron.

Whether or not helpful experiences with Dr. Cook's patients had anything to do with it, graduates of Old Miami have gone on to success in football coaching at a rate perhaps unmatched by any other college today.

There is Paul Brown, dynamic and consistently successful leader of the professional Cleveland Browns. There is Wilbur (Weeb) Ewbank, a former Paul Brown assistant, who has led the Baltimore Colts to two consecutive world's pro championships. There is Louisiana State's Paul Dietzel, who has delivered outstanding teams. There is the comparably talented Ara Parseghian, who has returned Northwestern to strong contention in the rugged Western Conference. Ara not only learned his undergraduate football at Miami, but later made a fine record there as head coach of the Red and White.

There are still others who are not graduates of Miami, but who acknowledge gratitude for the opportunity of having been head coach there: Stuart Holcomb, former Purdue head coach and now Northwestern athletic director; Sid Gilman, former head coach of the University of Cincinnati and the Los Angeles Rams and now bossing the Los Angeles Chargers of the new American Football League; George Blackburn, head man of Cincinnati; and Woody Hayes, who has turned out several championship teams at Ohio State.

Situated some thirty-five miles northwest of Cincinnati, Miami was founded in 1809, welcomed its first class in 1824, and today has an enrollment of 6,767, including coeds. It is a member of the Mid-American Conference, whose semimajor brand of football approximates that of the Eastern Ivy League and the University Division of the Middle Atlantic Conference. The East had a chance to appraise Miami football when the Redskins played Army at West Point's Michie Stadium October 29, 1960, a game I looked forward to with mixed emotions.

Football at Miami never has been overemphasized, nor has it ever suffered from that even more dangerous malady, deliberate devaluation. The game is conducted within the proper academic framework, and with the will to win.

At Miami, I was challenged for the first time, not only in athletics and other activities, but also in academics. I enrolled in the pre-law course. My father had a respect for that profession, and the prospect of a career that could involve tough, serious debate, with the decision affecting the rights and perhaps even the lives of men, naturally appealed to the strain in me that welcomes argument and action for high stakes.

As a freshman, I studied more than I had at Hawthorne, Parker, or Steele, but the effort was still short of my best. Fortunately, this fact was recognized by Dr. Archie Young, my freshman football coach, who had been an end of All America caliber at Wesleyan in Connecticut. Dr. Young was also Dean of Men at Miami, and taught mathematics. A firm believer in direct action, he wrote my father: "He should be doing 'A' work. If he doesn't do it, you shouldn't be spending money on him." The validity of this argument found a response in Dad's Scots sense of value and Presbyterian sense of right.

Between them, Dr. Young and my father finally got me to speed up academically. In my sophomore year, my marks began to improve. In my senior year, I had all "A's," served as assistant instructor in economics, and occasionally regretted that my freshman effort, or lack of it, was now blocking me from achieving Phi Beta Kappa recognition.

I also became active in extracurricular affairs: student government, class functions, language clubs, the debating team, and dramatics. In my junior year the Miami yearbook, *Recensio*, included a mention of the fact that I was "aloof." There was some discrepancy there, since for my senior year I was elected president of the Student Forum, president of my fraternity, president of the "M" Club, baseball captain, and member of the Senior Honor Society. And I was appointed, in the gag section of one of the *Recensios*, to the "Ancient Order of the Sons of Ursus, for having thrown the bull with profuseness as well as éclat, for various reasons on all occasions."

In dramatics I advanced to roles somewhat more important than that of Buttons, the antic bellhop. In my senior year I was entrusted with the part of Charles Bronson in a drawing-room farce by Roi Cooper Megrue and Walter Hackett, entitled *It Pays to Advertise*. It seems that local reviews were enthusiastic—but very, very local.

They were full, wonderful days at Miami, formative, yet fun. Today I believe it costs an in-state student about $1,500 to get through a year. In my day one could make it on $350. I was able to earn almost that much during summers chauffeuring for the family of Harry Coleman, a prominent Dayton real-estate man with whom my father was associated.

On $350, of course, one lived less like a sultan, more like a soldier. In my sophomore year, for example, John B. Whitlock, today president of the Miami Board of Trustees, three other classmates, and I shared a Beta House two-room "suite," formerly a kitchen and dining room.

It was also in my sophomore year that I first became aware of a charming freshman coed from Piqua, Ohio, named Merle McDowell. The names Earl and Merle go together and so did we. (Years later, while I was coaching at Dartmouth, the Blaiks had a cook named Pearl. You've never really been confused until you've lived in a house with an Earl, a Merle, and a Pearl.)

Merle and I first met at a small party in Bishop Hall, a residence for girls, to which both Beta Theta Pi's and the Delta Zeta sorority brought their pledges. Merle started the evening with somebody else, but ended up with me. We began to date regularly, somewhat to the concern of Jimmy Young, baseball coach, French instructor, a Beta, and a bachelor. Jimmy was more or less my mentor and he feared that my studies, athletics, and extracurricular affairs all would suffer should I become too romantically involved. In later Dartmouth and Army days, whenever I discussed with Merle a promising football player whose development was being arrested by romance, she smilingly reminded me of Jimmy Young and his forebodings.

Actually, Merle and I did not become engaged until the spring of my senior year, 1918, just before I left for West Point. She didn't get my class ring until 1920 and we did not marry until 1923. Our Miami courtship, if that's what it was, was scarcely a blitzkrieg.

Despite Merle, academic improvement, and extracurriculars, athletics continued to hold priority on my interests. I tried out for basketball, made the squad, but did not earn a letter. I did not really begin to develop in that sport until West Point days. But I won three letters in baseball as an outfielder.

Football was my mainspring. I was seventeen when I entered Miami and twenty-one when I graduated, a year younger than the average athlete. In the four years I grew an inch, to six feet even, and added 25 pounds, from 133 to 158. I remained on the lean side, but I was maturing and gaining in speed and strength, and I believe I had a natural toughness. I was knocked out in games, but never injured seriously enough to miss any playing time. I had the speed and maneuverability to handle the defensive end assignments, to get down fast under punts, to block a tackle reasonably well, and to catch passes.

In my freshman year, I played on the Beta team as well as the regular freshman team. I don't think the Betas won more than one game, but the regular frosh team proved excellent cannon fodder for the varsity. In my sophmore year, 1915, I won the regular varsity right-end job and held it for three seasons. The captain of the 1915 team was my old Dayton hero, Monk Pierce. He was Miami's star pitcher as well as backfield ace, a Big Man on Campus and eager to try to ease the way for a fellow Daytonian. In 1914, Monk had been an All Ohio back, and his feats included a 45-yard field goal against Indiana of the Big Ten Conference.

Our 1915 coach was Chester R. Roberts, from Lawrence College, and our record was six wins to two losses. Our two most bitter rivals were the University of Cincinnati and Denison. We beat Cincinnati, 24–12, but lost to Denison, 14–0. Between halves of the Denison game, Coach Roberts tried so hard to exhort us to greater effort that he began pressing. He said if we won the game, he would buy each of us a box of bonbons. We were, if anything, worse on the second half. The experience underlined to me strongly the feeling that in a Spartan game like football the worst possible inducement to a malingering player is, literally or figuratively, any form of sweetening.

In 1916, Roberts was succeeded by George E. Little, former Ohio Wesleyan player, Ohio State line coach, and Cincinnati head coach. Little subsequently was to coach Michigan, Wisconsin, and Rutgers; to serve as athletic director at Rutgers and as executive secretary of the National Football of Fame. He was to exert crucial influence on my career a decade later, when I thought I had put football behind me.

George Little's 1916 team is regarded by Miami as the school's greatest up to that time. We were undefeated, outscored our opponents, 239 to 12, and took the first of three straight Ohio Conference championships. The key to our success was a strong line. Ed Hull, center, later became four-star General John E. Hull, Vice-Chief of Staff, now retired, and president of the Manufacturing Chemists Association, Inc.

After the 1916 season, George Little left Miami to become a captain in the Army, and served overseas with distinction. He was succeeded by George L. Rider, who also coached baseball and is still at Miami as track and cross-country coach. It was under Rider that I did my first actual coaching. He had no assistants, so he asked me to help out with the ends and tackles. For the second straight year, we were undefeated and Ohio Conference champions, scored 202 points, allowed none.

I made All Ohio end that year, and alongside me in the Miami line at right tackle was Ed Sauer, a sophomore. Twenty-seven years later at Army, Ed Sauer's son Johnny was a valuable substitute back on the first of the three Blanchard-Davis teams and pulled off some spectacular pass interceptions in the 1944 victory over Notre Dame. Later Johnny became an assistant on my staff and subsequently head coach at The Citadel.

We had a strong team in 1917, although not quite so powerful as in 1916. There was not the usual all-out enthusiasm for the game. World War I preoccupied our minds. Wilhelm's goose-steppers had stormed through Belgium into France in 1914, there had been the sinking of the *Lusitania*, and now we were in it.

Although the casualty lists from France were setting a fearful record, young men still regarded war with the adventurous, romantic attitudes that had been handed down from Indian campaigns, the victory over Spain, the expedition into Mexico. Besides, this was the war to end all wars. Idealists were pitted against noninterventionists, President Woodrow Wilson against Senator Bob LaFollette. It was no contest. George M. Cohan had written a song called "Over There," and there were few who were not singing it.

Many of my close friends had already joined up. Chief Crawford, Mal Cook, and others were with the French Ambulance Corps and writing me of the excitement. The law career I had envisioned was pushed into the background. Experts estimated that the war in Europe might drag on for eight or ten years. Mine now was to be the life of a soldier, the sooner the better. My first quick urge was to leave college and enlist. Only after parental persuasion did I decide to remain and graduate.

Although football had nothing to do with my ultimate decision to apply for an appointment to West Point, I first got the idea from a football teammate at Miami, the tackle and fellow Beta from Cincinnati, Jackson T. Butterfield. Jack had been a plebe at the Academy in 1912, played in a couple or games for the plebe football team, but was found deficient in mathematics. He transferred to Miami and was graduated in 1916. When we got into the war the following spring, Jack's five months at West Point helped him get a commission as a captain. He suggested that a commission should also be my goal.

My first thought was to enter Officers' Candidate School at Fort Benjamin Harrison in Indianapolis as soon as I completed my degree work at Miami. I put in my application, but before it could be accepted a regulation came out preventing college men from going directly to OCS. It was then that I seriously considered trying for West Point. I was encouraged by Dr. John W. McKemy, a family friend in Dayton, who had served as a regular medical officer in the Spanish War. My father also thought well of the idea. His connection with Governor Cox's campaign for Congress now paid off. Democratic Senator Atlee Pomerene, of Ohio, had one appointment to make from his district for 1918, and I got it as the first alternate. I passed both the validating and physical exams at Columbus, but was advised to have my tonsils removed as soon as possible.

The day I took my physical I looked as if I had already been to war, or maybe had spent three minutes inside the ropes with that rising young heavyweight fighter named Jack Dempsey. I had a tooth knocked out, most of my right eyebrow was missing, there were several stitches above the eye, and my face generally was a patchwork of abrasions. It certainly sounded like "a likely story" when I tried to explain what happened.

I had taken a brief time off from my duties as captain and center fielder of the baseball team to run the hurdles for the Betas in an indoor intramural meet. I was not a very adept hurdler. I tripped over one of the timbers and fell flat. My face scraped along the wooden floor, gathering splinters. It was a worse mishap than any I ever incurred in football. (The accident didn't affect my baseball. I still could cover a lot of ground flagging down flies, and a curve ball was still as great a mystery as ever.)

Graduation at Miami was scheduled for Wednesday, May 29. I had been ordered to report to West Point on Friday, June 14, and I had to undergo a tonsillectomy. I was impatient to have all things in order as soon as possible, so after my last examination in May, I decided not to wait around for commencement. I packed, said hurried good-byes and returned to Dayton to make an appointment with Dr. Horace Bonner, a neighbor. Oddly enough, the appointment was set for the same day as Miami commencement. When my parents left for Oxford that morning, I went downtown to Dr. Bonner's.

I shudder to recall my casual approach to what proved to be an ordeal. I sat on a low stool in Dr. Bonner's surgery. As a titillating preliminary, he reached down my throat and plied the tonsils with the novocain needle. When the stuff began to take effect, Dr. Bonner reached down again and cut around one of the tonsils. He then seized a surgical tool, a long, villainous-looking wire affair with an ugly snare on the end. He managed to work this down my throat and collect the first tonsil.

Before he could tackle the other one, it was necessary to determine how much of a bleeder I was. When it was evident I was just average, Dr. Bonner set out after the second tonsil, but he soon encountered problems. The snare on his demoniac contraption broke not once, but several times. Each time he repaired it with what seemed to me the speed of a grazing horse. By the time he got it to work long enough to snatch the second tonsil, I felt I had spent an eternity on my purgatorial stool.

Dr. Bonner assured me that I would not bleed to death. I walked out of his office, took the elevator to the street, boarded a streetcar for home and sat on the front porch. I was sitting there that night when my parents returned from Oxford with my diploma, and I sat there for several days after. It hurt my throat to talk, so I communicated by notes, the recurrent theme of which was: "It hurts like hell."

Such a tonsillectomy was not an inappropriate warm-up for West Point plebedom. What graduate of the Academy will ever forget that first day he got off the West Shore Railroad train at the little depot. That long, hot, worried walk, heavy bag in hand, up the hill. The greeting by the Beast Detail: "Suck your gut in, mister!" The long period of heckling discipline, exacting academics. If there is any romance to plebe year at West Point, it is strictly in fiction. That first day, and for many, many days thereafter, I asked myself, "Why did I come?"

Yet, I was to revere this beautiful and historic bastion of America. Here, within these somber, tradition-rich walls and battlements, I was to spend twenty-seven of—yes—the best years of my life. I would not be a soldier very long and I would never get to war. But I would command troops in the game that is closest to war, and I would know in this a happiness, as well as a tragedy, that I could not have known in anything else.

Chapter III

Our Supe, General MacArthur

Three times during the Army-Navy baseball game at West Point in June, 1919, the Army cheerleader passed out in the heat. Three times he was revived under the stands by dousings of cold water. Three times he returned weaving to the fray. That such heroic perseverance thrilled the recently appointed Academy Superintendent, Brigadier General Douglas MacArthur, is questionable: Navy beat Army in eleven innings, 10 to 6 (I played left field and got one hit in six times at bat), and General MacArthur, then as always, believed firmly in that philosophy he first expressed in a wire to my 1944 Army team: "There is no substitute for victory."

Shortly after that baseball defeat by Navy, the General found legitimate release for his discontent. The spectators included about two hundred young naval officers, some of them Annapolis graduates, who had come up the Hudson River that morning on a half-dozen destroyers. As the crowd streamed out of the stands onto the field following the final out, one of these officers snatched a uniform cap from the head of a cadet.

This exuberant act started a storm of hat-snatching between naval officers and West Point cadets, most of it near home plate. The scuffle raised a cloud of dust and threatened to become a minor riot. West Point tactical officers strove to separate the combatants, merely complicating the fracas. At this point General MacArthur ordered his guard onto the field. The latter succeeded in prying the fighters apart and restoring some semblance of ragged order. MacArthur ordered the guard to escort the naval officers, many of them hatless, down the hill to their ships. That night the missing naval caps were worn ceremoniously around barracks by cadets.

As an example of the wisdom of direct action, the General's little coup was not lost on the Corps. He had already provided us an even more impressive, if less colorful, lesson. *The Bray,* cadet weekly newspaper, had printed an article criticizing the tactical department. The officer in charge of *The Bray* was Major Archibald V. Arnold, later an outstanding artillery general commanding the Seventh Division, and Military Governor of Korea. (His son, Major Archie Arnold, Jr., was a fine left tackle on our 1944 team.) Major Arnold was supposed to censor *Bray* copy, but he apparently overlooked this incendiary piece against the "tacs." General MacArthur promptly dispatched Major Arnold elsewhere, and silenced *The Bray* forever. This made a tremendous impression on our class, and gave me the first appreciation of the fact that precipitate action, whether right or wrong, will establish command.

I was first introduced to General MacArthur as one of a group summoned to headquarters to meet him as representatives of the first class. This was a formal annual ceremony, calling for full dress, including white gloves, with cadets saluting upon arrival, standing at attention, and saluting before leaving. On this occasion, however, formality was cast aside by the General. "Sit down, gentlemen," he greeted us, and offered us cigarettes—Fatimas or Melachrinos, as I remember.

This was great. We now had a superintendent who either did not know the regulations (no smoking was allowed, except for pipes, and then only in one's own quarters at specified times), or, if he did know them, which was more likely, didn't care. That gesture by MacArthur did more to break the ice and endear him to our class than almost anything else he might have done. It was, as usual, MacArthur doing the unusual.

MacArthur had come to the Superintendent's job with a brilliant World War I record. He had conceived, named, and been largely responsible for organizing and training the celebrated Rainbow Division, so called because it was composed of National Guard units from twenty-seven states. He had been wounded twice, decorated thirteen times and cited seven additional times for extreme bravery under fire.

Although wounded and gassed in March, 1918, he refused to rest from his duties even a day. In October, he added an Oak Leaf cluster to his Distinguished Service Cross, and soon after became the youngest division commander in the Army. French corps reports singled him out for "notably fine judgment."

That MacArthur, at thirty-eight the youngest superintendent in West Point's history, was one of its greatest is indisputable. That he should take over at the time he did was a particular stroke of good fortune for the Academy. Morale was at an ebb tide. The school was moribund, beginning to strangle from some of its traditions, and under attack from without. There was dire need of intelligent, inspiring leadership.

I had arrived with the plebe class that entered on June 14, 1918. Two days before, the class which entered as plebes in 1915 had graduated. The class which entered in 1914 had graduated in August, 1917. The normal four-year course had been telescoped to three years. The class which entered in 1916 was now designated the second class and was scheduled to graduate in 1920. The class which entered in 1917 was designated the third class and listed to graduate in 1921. Our class, designated the fourth class, was due to graduate in 1922. This was the structure of The Corps from June 14 until October 3, 1918, and it is necessary to understand it to appreciate what happened afterwards.

(The terms "plebe," "yearling," "second class" and "first class" are equivalent respectively to a civilian college's freshman, sophomore, junior, and senior. "Plebe" and "yearling" are also synonymous with fourth and third class.)

On October 3, at the noonday meal, which is called dinner at West Point (dinner is referred to as supper), Cadet Adjutant Beverley Saint George Tucker read an order that threw the mess hall into an uproar. The order stated that the second and third classes, originally scheduled to go out in 1920 and '21, were to graduate within a month, on November 1. The order also provided for the admission in November of a new plebe class, to be consolidated with ours, all of us to graduate in June 1919.

It may be that because they were going to get to war faster, the second and third classes cheered more loudly than we plebes, but I doubt it. The way we looked at it, we would be in France ourselves within nine months. Nobody anticipated the imminent collapse of the German Army; military savants estimated several more years of fighting. We plebes realized that this order also meant that within a month, after only five months as plebes, we would be transformed Cinderella-like into the supreme, if only, class at the Academy.

This was also realized by the two upper classes. They decided right then and there in the mess hall to jam eight months of plebe "crawling" we were about to escape into fifteen minutes and then "recognize" us. As *The Howitzer*, the West Point Class Book, for 1920 reports it: "Never did we brace so cheerfully—and forget it so quickly when we shook hands all around with the upperclassmen."

Even by West Point standards that month of October, 1918, was hectic. Intensive drills and lectures pressured the upperclassmen. We plebes worked hard to prepare ourselves to assume the responsibility of Corps customs, traditions, and administration. But despite the stepped-up schedule, it still seemed the longest month of our lives.

November 1 arrived at last. The band played "The Dashing White Sergeant" and the graduating classes marched across the Plain and stood at salute as we passed in review. Two days later, the new plebes arrived. War priorities had left a shortage of the normal cadet-gray material, so the newcomers were issued olive-drab uniforms with leggings and campaign hats circled with orange bands. The orange bands earned them the name of the "Orioles." In an organization that had been clad in gray for 117 years, they were indeed strange-looking birds.

We plebe-upperclassmen could not enjoy the normal prerogative of indoctrinating the Orioles into Beast Barracks, because we were too busy with a stepped-up academic program. Instead the tactical department turned out its own Beast Detail and did the job in three weeks. This made the Orioles the least put-upon plebes in Academy annals, but it did not seem to hurt them. From our "M" company alone came such future generals as Max Taylor, Ben Chidlaw, and Cort Schuyler.

Eight days after the arrival of the Orioles, there came, with shocking suddenness, "the eleventh hour of the eleventh day of the eleventh month." Suddenly, unexpectedly, the German position had deteriorated. The Muese-Argonne offensive had breached Von Hindenberg's line. A quiet, as thunderous in its contrast as the gun roar, enveloped no man's land. A cheer went up around the world. At West Point, a victory bonfire leaped high, as if straining to see its reflection in the waters of the Hudson below Trophy Point.

But there was little rejoicing among the Corps. We were proud of the American Army, yet we also felt almost as if the Plain had been pulled out from under us. War, as I have said, was an adventure to us, and we had chosen it as our profession. We were young men who had been promised a job and were looking forward to it, and now suddenly we realized we were not going to get it. We were let down.

The sudden end of the war brought another rapid reordination of the Corps. The two classes which had graduated on November 1 were taken on a tour of the battlefields of France and then returned to duty as regular officers. It was decided, however, to return the second of those two classes to the Academy early in the winter, to resume study until June. They were known as the "Student Officer Class," and we "Lords of the Plain" had to salute them. With our class, dressed in traditional cadet gray, the Orioles with their atypical garb and the Student Officer Class in regular second-lieutenant uniform, West Point was a strange conglomeration of military tailoring, a sight that would have fascinated Herman Goering.

The closest we and the Orioles got to war was the following March when we paraded up Fifth Avenue as Guard of Honor for the homecoming of the 27th Division. Sometimes now at night, as I look south down Fifth Avenue from our ninth-floor apartment at Eighty-sixth Street, I can see us coming up in column of platoons and taking post in line opposite the reviewing stand at Eighty-second Street.

Cadet Milton Shattuck and I, Sergeants from Company M, carried the colors, he the national, I the West Point flag. Many a hot day on the Plain, Shattuck and I watched ten or twelve cadets topple over on parade, and discussed it out of the sides of our mouths: "What would happen if one of us were to collapse?" Then came a blistering day in July and old Shattuck himself started to weave. With my free hand, I grabbed his standard, and none too soon. He hit the ground face down with a horrendous thud. The next day Shattuck was a private.

On that parade with the 27th up Fifth Avenue, however, it was not Shattuck but I who felt the pressure. Carrying the colors on that long march put severe cramps in my shoulders. If I hadn't changed hands holding the flag every few steps, I might have been busted myself.

Although the victory parades were naturally popular, many people thought that wars were over forever, for had not this been "the war to end all wars"? Many of our political leaders were proclaiming that henceforth there would be no need for an army other than a militia, and the demagogues were saying, why any need for a school like West Point that turned out "war mongers and martinets"?

That the "martinets" charge, though grossly exaggerated, was not entirely without justification is something I believe most West Pointers of and before my time will not refute. Like all wars, World War I had to be fought by civilians. They found West Pointers as a whole extremely competent militarily, in many instances brilliant. They also discovered, through needlessly harsh experience, that a few were also emphatically deficient in human relations.

These deficiencies traced mainly, of course, to the nature of the officer himself. Yet, a real part of the blame must be imputed to the West Point plebe hazing system and the brutalities it could encourage in those with a sadistic streak or those unconditioned by nature to handle authority judiciously when it was thrust upon them.

I have always believed that a rigid form of discipline is indispensable for a cadet, especially the plebe, as the means of teaching him how to give orders by teaching him first how to take them. I have always believed that some plebe hazing, providing humor without detracting from the subject's basic human dignity, is not only harmless but salutary. Even when hazing is essentially petty and silly, I'm not too concerned.

But hazing that is primarily an expression of an ingrained sadistic urge to hurt and humiliate is intolerable and completely unmilitary. When, for instance, it takes the form of depriving a youngster of the food he needs to sustain himself in an already taxing regimen, it is more than asinine, it is utterly unthinkable.

The plebe system at West Point today is far more humane and saner than it was in my days as a cadet. Unfortunately, in the refinement, much of the old humor has been lost. But the new course on the whole is far more salutary, and our Class of 1920 did a lot to help set it. We could not, in one year, eradicate all the abuses of the past, but I feel we made important progress.

National attention and Congressional investigation had first been focused on the plebe system in 1900. Oscar L. Booz, of Bristol, Pennsylvania, who had been a plebe for a short time in 1898, died of tuberculosis. His family insisted the disease took root when he was forced as a plebe to swallow considerable tabasco sauce. Although a Special Congressional Committee decided his death had not been caused by hazing, the case impelled a trend toward badly needed reform.

Hazing was not outlawed, but no upperclassman might lay a hand on a plebe and prearranged fist fights were banned. Penalty for violation of either rule was dismissal. For another twenty years, nevertheless, laying on of hands and prearranged fights were not eliminated. They were merely cut down.

In the winter of 1918-19, my first at the Academy, some members of Congress were handed what they were seeking, a good opportunity to attack West Point through its plebe system. I happened to be in on the beginning of the affair. About nine o'clock on the morning of New Year's Day, I was coming down the stairs by the 27th Division of North Barracks when Cadet Harvey Greenlaw, a classmate, called to me from the door of a nearby room, "Henry, come in here quick! Mr. Bird has passed out!" (Henry is my middle name, and I used to be called that, as well as "Red," when I was a cadet.)

I followed Greenlaw into the room. Cadet Stephen M. Bird was stretched out on the floor, semiconscious and moaning, "Water . . . water. . . ." Blood trickled from a corner of his mouth. Two cadets were applying cold towels to his face from the two buckets of water flanking the washstand. On the study table lay a regular 30.06 caliber Springfield rifle.

I picked up the rifle and out of habit pulled the bolt back and ejected the fired cartridge. One end of several feet of string was tied to the trigger; the other end of the string lay near a chair close to Bird's head. It was plain enough what had happened. He had set the rifle on the table, tied one end of the string to the trigger and worked the other end around the butt of the gun for leverage. Then he had sat himself in a chair close to the table, placed the muzzle of the Springfield against his chest and fired it by pulling the string. The bullet passed through him cleanly and imbedded itself in the wall. We were told later that it missed his heart but pierced a lung.

I told Greenlaw and the others to stand by while I went for help. This was not my first experience with such a tragedy. One snowy night back at Miami, Dr. Cook had asked the Betas to help him find a woman inmate who had escaped from the Oxford Retreat into nearby woods. We tramped those woods half the night to find her— a suicide. Perhaps I thought of that as I rushed down the Barracks stairs. A Ford stood near the Barracks. I requisitioned it and sped to the Post Hospital for a doctor.

Bird died at 6:12 that night. He was an Oriole. Investigation revealed that he had been writing poetry, and had been hazed about it by upperclassmen. That this had disturbed him and that he was probably morose by nature was indicated by the poetry itself.

West Point never has been a comfortable place for poets, including the most sensitive and morose. This fact had been manifested back in 1834 by a cadet named Edgar Allan Poe, the same who later authored "The Raven," "The Telltale Heart," and other somber classics. Cadet Poe once declared despondently that Benny Havens, who conducted a grog dispensary in nearby Buttermilk Falls (now Highland Falls), was "the only congenial soul in this Godforsaken place!" By visiting Benny's, Cadet Poe managed to abide the Academy for a time. He survived it by leaving. Cadet Bird was not so fortunate.

A board of officers and the West Point Board of Overseers made investigations. Many Congressmen were making noises, and criticism of the Academy was heavy when MacArthur arrived.

Even if there had not been a Bird suicide, the General would have taken action because it was natural for a leader of his philosophy to be impatient with the abuses of plebe hazing. In World War I, MacArthur was noted for his insistence that his soldiers go into battle with all possible protection, although he himself made a habit of moving around the front lines without arms, helmet, or gas mask. He carried only the riding crop, that was to become identified with him. In World War II and the Korean War, he continued to take pride in the low casualty rate among his men, something which he always took great pains to insure.

Soon after Commencement Week in 1919, MacArthur appointed seven of us as a Fourth-Class Customs Committee and named me to serve as Chairman. Our job was to root out abuses from plebe hazing, yet retain wholesome traditions. At the start of the work, the General gathered our class in the gym and outlined the objectives. The committee reported to Colonel Robert H. Danford, the Commandant, and to Colonel Charles F. Thompson, Assistant Commandant. We also received valuable help from the Academy Chaplain, the Reverend Clayton E. Wheat. After two months of conscientious work, we came up with a pamphlet outlining the new order.

We reaffirmed that an upperclassman must not lay hands on a plebe, and thenceforth this rule was enforced much more rigidly. An upperclassman must not order a plebe to perform menial tasks. We outlawed such sadism as splits over a bayonet, in which a plebe would be commanded to do a series of squats, each squat bringing his rear end in slight contact with the bayonet point; a miscalculation could be painful and dangerous.

A plebe must not be denied food as punishment for any real or alleged misfeasance, but he could still be made to eat while sitting braced at attention. Although the code drawn up by our committee did not specify it, the custom continued of permitting a plebe to eat unbraced for the rest of the year, if he could qualify on some particular food. To "qualify" meant to eat an enormous amount of the item. One could qualify, for example, on prunes; the prune record, I believe, was well over two hundred.

Most of our classmates supported the new order. But there were still some among our 300-plus who stubbornly resisted anything that eased the burden of the plebes, since it had not been eased in their own plebedom. Some still denied food to an erring plebe.

Let me point out, however, that as late as 1958–59, this abuse was still not eradicated. Pete Dawkins, the leader, scholar, and athlete of whom the country has heard so much, was Brigade Commander and First Captain, the highest military rank in the Corps. Dawkins was forced to report a cadet officer under him for violating his order that no plebe was to be denied food, and the tactical department reduced the offender to private rank. "Such punishment as denying food," said Dawkins, "is appropriate to the training of animals, not men."

Our 1919 Customs Committee also reaffirmed the illegality of prearranged fist fights. It was to be yet a few years before this order would be fully obeyed. To many of us, it was the least of abuses; in fact it could be on occasion, a blessing. Calling out an upperclassman to fight was often the only course left to some plebe against authority not used with discretion and fairness.

Plebes versus upperclassmen were not the only matches. Upperclassmen sometimes called each other out. They would go into the gym ring with gloves or get up before reveille and climb the hill with their seconds to Fort Putnam. The bruises they walked around with afterwards were ignored by the tacs, who gave no official approval, but did not disapprove.

Calling out an upperclassman sometimes served only to compound the plebe's travail. One plebe in my first-class year had an especially rough time. He was John Valentin Grombach, appointed from Louisiana and known as "Frenchy." Today, Colonel Grombach is a business consultant in New York as well as the author of several books on sports, including a history of boxing titled, *The Saga of Sock*.

Frenchy attempted to write his own saga of sock at the Academy. Before entering, he had stoked on a tramp ship, worked as a bouncer, and won an Amateur Athletic Union boxing championship. To use his own words, he considered himself a very rough and tough guy. He rebelled against the plebe system, gave the upperclassmen a bad time and called out a few to fight. Consequently, he was singled out for very harsh treatment.

It was a custom at the time for an upperclassman prematurely to "recognize" a plebe who came from the same Congressional district, to advise and sort of big-brother him through that rigorous first year. But because of Grombach's rebellious attitude, the upperclassman from his Louisiana district refused to recognize him.

The situation reduced Frenchy to low spirits. I felt he was a good man, who needed only a little help to straighten out. In those days, the Corps bivouacked during the summer, until September 1, in the woods behind that section of the Plain now used for football practice. One day I walked into Grombach's tent. He immediately "finned out," the exaggerated position of attention demanded of a plebe.

"At ease," I said. Then I stuck out my hand. "Hello, John," I said, and shook his hand, the traditional form of recognition.

Grombach has often told me that this small act was the turning point in his career at the Academy. It inspired him to be less pugnacious, to make a better effort to fit into the system.

The work of our committee was unsung, but not unappreciated. This was brought home to me some twenty-five years later. Colonel (Thompo) Thompson, the Assistant Com and tac officer, who had worked with our committee, was now Lieutenant General Thompson, with a splendid World War II record behind him. He had returned to the Academy for commencement and I happened to meet him outside the gym. "Red," he said, during our reminiscing, "for years I have wanted to tell you personally what few of our graduates realize: that the action of the Fourth Class Customs Committee did much to save West Point."

This may have been overly high praise, many years after the fact, but it does reflect the seriousness of the adverse Congressional attitude toward the Point in the days when I was a cadet.

Among other things, General Thompo Thompson was an enthusiastic football man. He played right guard on the 1903 team, which beat Navy at Franklin Field, 40–5, the most one-sided score in the series until our 1949 team set a new record against the Midshipmen, 38–0. In the '03 game, Thompson spent much of the afternoon tackling the Navy fullback, one William (Bull) Halsey.

Forty years later, when General Thompson had to confer with Fleet Admiral Halsey in the South Pacific, the Admiral said, "General, the last time I saw you, you were rubbing my nose all over Franklin Field."

"How could I know then, Admiral," replied Thompson, "that you were going to be Commander in the South Pacific?"

Action against plebe hazing abuses was only one of the multifarious improvements at West Point under MacArthur. He modernized the military system. Tactical officers were ordered to keep in direct and constant communication with their cadet companies through the Orderly Room. Not only in company administration but in almost every phase of cadet life, the Orderly Room was to become a fixture.

Against considerable opposition from the Academic Board, MacArthur also broadened and upgraded the academic curriculum. When Congress made gestures toward telescoping the academic course to two years, the General convinced them they should compromise for three. The Academic Board was again critical of him for accepting the three. But he had more understanding of the situation and more foresight than the Board. He realized that if he pressed Congress for an immediate return to four, he might well end up with two. He also anticipated correctly that the three would soon be extended to four.

I believe General MacArthur enjoyed most what he did for West Point's athletics. It was during his tour as Supe, from June 12, 1919, to June 30, 1922, that he delivered the oft-quoted words that are inscribed over the entrance to the Director of Physical Education's office in the South Gymnasium:

> Upon the fields of friendly strife are sown the seeds that, upon other fields, on other days, will bear the fruits of victory.

As a cadet in the class of 1903, MacArthur played left field on the 1901 Army baseball team, the first ever to play Navy. The game was held at Annapolis, and Army won, 4–3. Cadet MacArthur went hitless in three times up, but scored a run, stole a base, and was errorless in the field. He also managed the 1902 football team.

Before, during, and after MacArthur's undergraduate days, West Point's intramural sports program was informal, spasmodic, incomplete. There was a gym in which cadets could wrestle, box, fence, and perform gymnastics. There were also a few intercompany and interclass games.

To replace this inadequate structure, MacArthur instituted thoroughgoing interclass as well as intercompany competition, with the objective of making every cadet an athlete. Under this system, as it developed, every cadet receives expert instruction in many sports, which gives him condition, combativeness, and the ability to supervise the sports as an officer. This comprehensive intramural sports program still serves today as the model for all colleges.

To implement this program, MacArthur was fortunate in having for his Master of the Sword, as the Director of Physical Education at the Academy was known until 1947, Lieutenant Colonel Herman Koehler. Koehler had come to West Point as Master of the Sword on February 1, 1885, and retired on December 14, 1923. From 1897 through 1900, his duties included supervision of the coaching of the football team.

During World War I, he was in charge of the physical training of more than 200,000 troops. He was a Teuton of commanding presence, impressive physique, and wonderful grace of movement. He had a voice that could assert itself to 10,000 doughboys at a time, without the aid of a microphone. When Koehler talked to the cadets, he had the great gift of being able to convince them that what they were doing was the most important thing in their lives.

While MacArthur was determined every cadet should be athletic as a requisite to becoming a well-rounded officer, his interest in sports was keenest at the varsity level. In fact, he hoped that the stepped-up intramurals would develop as a "by-product" some good material for the varsity or, as it is known at the Academy, the Corps squad or "A" squad. The junior varsity is referred to as the "B" squad, the plebe team as the "C" squad.

The "A" squads in all sports were badly in need of any help they could get after World War I. Telescoping of classes and the graduation of four classes within nineteen months, from April, 1917, to November, 1918, had left the Academy woefully short of athletes with any experience at college level. Even MacArthur's program of restoration could move only so fast. In his three years as Supe, MacArthur never saw an Army team win a football game from Navy or, for that matter, from Notre Dame or Yale. But his spade work began to pay off in 1922.

The General's athletic blueprint included plans for a 50,000-seat stadium down by the river, with elaborate yard sidings to accommodate special trains. He did not stay long enough to carry this out, as he probably would have—and how that might have changed the history of Army football! The Notre Dame game might never have left West Point, in which case the series might never have been suspended. The General's stadium plans did stimulate the building of picturesque Michie Stadium, with its 27,500 seats, where the Cadets have played their Academy-site games since 1924.

MacArthur also instituted the policy of Army teams playing teams besides Navy away from West Point. The first such visitation was to Yale Bowl in 1921, and the Corps accompanied the team to New Haven. The groundwork for this game had been prepared by Colonel Danford, the Commandant, in his tour as professor of military science and tactics at Yale.

To appreciate what a wrench with tradition that first football trip to New Haven constituted, let me quote General Jimmy Crawford, who was graduate manager of athletics at the Point from 1916 to 1918:

"Around 1915, Harvard proposed a four-game series with Army, three of the games to be played at West Point and one at Cambridge, but we had to turn them down. At that time, the idea of an Army team leaving the Post for any game but the Navy game was regarded as utter fantasy."

If he could possibly help it, MacArthur never missed an "A" squad practice. During the basketball season, he sat with Captain Louis E. Hibbs, on chairs placed for them on the running track above the west basket. Hibbs, later MacArthur's aide and in 1941 graduate manager of athletics, was officer in charge of basketball and also assisted Joseph (Scrubby) O'Shea in the coaching.

I made regular guard on the 1919-20 team. We had a fair team, I guess, with a 12-2 record. We lost Army's first basketball game with Navy, 24-18, and to City College of New York, 26-20. Our biggest victory was a surprising upset of New York University's National A.A.U. championship team, 17–14, their only loss that year. Their star and captain was Howard Cann, who later coached the sport at N.Y.U. with distinction.

Basketball was a different game in those days: more rugged defense, much lower scoring, far less whistle-tootling. I smile to recall our game with Williams. They had the great football back and all-around athlete, Benny Boynton.

Benny and I played each other like good football players, and before the first half was over we were simultaneously thrown out. This delighted one of my roommates, Lieutenant Willis McDonald, of Company L. Willis had been a classmate of Boynton's at Williams. In fact, Army had tried to get Benny to become a cadet, but had failed, a sad day for the Army. While McDonald got a great kick out of my contretemps with Boynton, it irritated Captain Hibbs.

"Blaik," he informed me, as I left the floor, "you are no gentleman!"

Neither, as I have suggested earlier, was I much of a batter. If I had been able to hit half as well as I could field, the major leagues might have wooed me. In left field, I had range, a sure pair of hands, and I was supposed to be able to throw a ball farther than anybody in the Corps. When we lost at Annapolis in 1920, 11–1, I had probably my busiest afternoon, fielding ground balls that sifted gaily through our rather porous infield. We made eleven errors that day, five by the shortstop alone.

The best catch I ever made, against Penn State in 1919, had a somewhat negative result. The Nittany Lions were at bat in the top of the ninth, trailing by one run, with one out and a man on third. The latter was Henry Luther (Hinky) Haines, who was to win All America halfback honors the following year.

The batter raised a towering foul fly toward left field, perhaps some 45 feet behind third base. I came charging in, made a dive for the ball, grabbed it in my gloved hand and held it. But the force of my dive drove me into a somersault. Before I could recover, the alert Haines tagged up and raced homeward. He beat my throw standing up, to tie the score. Fortunately, we finally won the game in the eleventh inning.

Hans Lobert, our coach, who later managed in the major leagues, has taken great pleasure for years in telling that story. Hans dresses it up a little. He has me making the catch in deepest left—practically on the steps of the Bachelor Building, and Army losing the game. The moral of his story is: How could anybody so dumb as not to drop that foul fly on purpose ever get to be a football coach? I think that the point is well taken.

My batting problem was an inability to follow the parabola of a curve ball. One afternoon at practice, General MacArthur, sympathetic to my plight, tried to give me a personal demonstration of what I was doing wrong. Unloosening his blouse, high collar and Sam Browne belt, he selected a bat and instructed me on how to cope with that bedeviling No. 2 delivery. When the General had concluded his brief seminar, I couldn't even hit a fast ball. This was the one failure in MacArthur's career.

Football always has been the General's favorite sport. When the National Football Foundation and Hall of Fame presented him, on December 1, 1959, with its Gold Medal Award for his contributions to the college game over the years, he said, "Football has become a symbol of courage, stamina, and co-ordinated efficiency. In war and peace, I have found football men to be my greatest reliance."

I must seriously doubt that this great game of ours ever has received a more meaningful testament.

With MacArthur pointing the way, football enthusiasm was high at West Point in 1919. In 1918, we had played only one game, defeating the Mitchell Field Aviators, 20–0. We were coached by Hugh (Mike) Mitchell, halfback on the 1915 team, and captained by Gene Vidal, one of the best backs and all-around athletes in Academy annals. General Leslie Groves, who headed the Manhattan Project, was a center on that squad. I had grown to six feet one and a half inches, weighed 182 pounds, and was able to make the regular right-end job. But with the war on, football interest had been tempered in '18. Now, in '19, the old spirit of the game was in the air.

The 1919 Army coaching staff was one of the ablest and most colorful in Academy history. It was to exert great influence on the game for many years, not only at the Point but all over the country.

It was headed up by Captain Charles Dudley Daley, Field Artillery, and deservedly known as the "Godfather of West Point football."

Daly, a native Bostonian, attended Boston Latin School and then Harvard, where he was an All America quarterback in 1898 and '99. He entered West Point in 1901 and was again named to the All America.

In the 11–5 victory over Navy at Franklin Field, Charlie Daly dominated the field. He got the first five points on a 35-yard field goal, the second five by returning the second-half kick-off 100 yards to a touchdown and the eleventh by drop-kicking the conversion. (A touchdown and field goal were then each worth five points.) He ran the team impeccably, repeatedly drove Navy back with his deadly punting, and twice made open-field tackles to cut off touchdowns. Small wonder one Philadelphia newspaper bore the headline: "Daly 11—Navy 5—Army 0." It is said that Daly's play so excited Theodore Roosevelt that the President leaped over the fence separating the stands from the field and gave out a wild Comanche yell.

Daly was graduated from the Point in 1905, resigned from the Army in 1906, and served briefly as Fire Commissioner of Boston. In 1907, he got back into football, where he belonged, as backfield coach at Harvard under Percy Duncan Haughton.

Haughton introduced organization, dedication, and psychology into football coaching to a degree never known before. In that sense, he was the father of modern coaching. He had the wisdom to absorb the best elements of the techniques, strategy, and tactics which had enabled Yale, mainly through Walter Camp, to dominate the college game up until that time. Haughton was an inspirational, if sometimes brutally tough, leader, and under him, from 1908 through 1915, Harvard enjoyed its football Golden Age. It was also under Haughton that Daly derived most of his theories of football and coaching.

Daly's first assistant, his line coach, his right arm, his "top sergeant" at Army was Ernest (Pot) Graves. They had been classmates and teammates at the Academy on successful West Point elevens. Graves had a brilliant mind. He was graduated second in the Class of 1905 and became known as "Father of the Engineers." During World War II, the Pentagon knew him as "the Colonel who wears civilian clothes." The civvies were a concession to a man whose analytical mind could solve engineering problems that baffled everybody else.

Before entering West Point, Pot Graves had played fullback at North Carolina for three years. At Army, he played some fullback, but mostly tackle. It was in Army's games with Yale on the Plain in 1902, '03, and '04 that Graves absorbed his basic knowledge of line play. His teachers were such Yale All America stars as Tom Shevlin, end; Jim Hogan, tackle; and Ed Glass, guard. The course of study was violent, with an occasional laboratory in fisticuffs, but that suited Graves. He found their psychology in tune with his own, which he was to project as a teacher and which may well be summed up: "Spare the blood and spoil the lineman."

When Graves was commissioned, he thought he had put football behind him. By 1908, he was a most promising young lieutenant of Engineers, doing important work at Washington Barracks. Meanwhile, at Harvard, Haughton was looking for a superior line coach. Daly told him about Graves. Through Teddy Roosevelt, who was President, football enthusiast, and Harvard man all in one, Graves was borrowed from duty to coach the Harvard line in the second half of the 1908 season. In his few weeks at Cambridge, he did much to install the principles of the line play that was the backbone of the Haughton teams.

After the 1908 season, Graves was ordered to the Philippines. By 1912 he was back at West Point as head football coach. The game at the Academy had been in a downcurve since the graduation of Daly and Graves. The officer in charge of football, a former Army center, was Lieutenant Dan Sultan, later a notable lieutenant general in the Far East. Sultan, a shrewd analyst, perceived that the ideal coaching situation at West Point would be Daly as top man, assisted by Graves.

Sultan succeeded in the first step, selling Daly on the prospect. It was then necessary to have Daly recommissioned a first lieutenant, because the Army head coach, until 1940, had to be not only a graduate but in service. After returning to service, Daly was often ordered to far places with the field artillery between football seasons, but from 1913 through 1922, except for World War I years, he was always assigned to the Academy in the fall. The same system was used with Graves, not with Pot's full concurrence. Although he liked football, he preferred engineering.

Daly and Graves confirmed Sultan's analysis. Their Army teams beat Navy every year from 1913 through 1917. Their 1914 and 1916 teams were undefeated and untied. They coached such great players, All America or close to it, as halfback Elmer Oliphant; center John McEwan; end Louis Merillat; quarterback Vernon Prichard; guard Laurence B. (Cowboy) Meacham; tackle Alexander (Babe) Weyand; quarterback Charlie Gerhardt; end Bob Neyland, another outstanding all-around athlete; halfback Gene Vidal, whom I mentioned before; and tackle Lawrence McCeney (Biff) Jones.

Such later Army head coaches as McEwan, Jones, Ralph I. Sasse, Bill Wood, and myself learned much of our football under Daly and Graves. It was from them that General Bob Neyland took and developed the kicking, vertical-field-position and defensive game that made Tennessee a football power and has influenced the game in the Southeastern Conference and elsewhere through this day.

The greatest lesson of strategy that Daly and Graves taught all of us was the value of defense. Football, or any other game, cannot be played successfully without it.

Their psychology also rubbed off on us. I can still see Charlie Daly writing his maxims on the blackboard and reading them off to us in his Boston-Irish and Oxford tones:

"Carry the fight to the enemy and keep it there all afternoon."

"Play for and make the breaks, and when one comes your way, score."

"The team that makes the fewer mistakes wins."

"Press the kicking game. It is here games are won or lost."

"Break any rule to win the game."

This last was not a concession to foul play, but a warning that a desperate situation could justify the unorthodox. It would, however, have to be truly desperate.

Besides his contributions on the field, Daly was founder of the American College Football Coaches Association.

Daly, personally, was a rather aloof, reserved man, who kept people at arm's length and made no attempt to be popular. He could unbend after he got to know you. More important, he had fine character and purpose, and he was a leader.

Behind Daly and Graves on the 1919 staff were Merillat, McEwan, Jones, Oliphant, Meacham, Prichard, Gerhardt, and Benny Hoge, who had captained and played left end on the 1913 team.

McEwan, who had played at Minnesota before his appointment, was captain and star center of the 1916 Army team and later head coach of the Cadets from 1923 through 1925. Big Mac is one of the saltiest characters who ever went through West Point or anyplace else, and worthy of a book all to himself.

Mac might well have become a great writer, had he chosen that career. As the English sections he taught at the Academy will well recall, he has a rich flair for the humorous, off-beat, apt expression. One of his gems that has always tickled me is his reference to Yale as "that small but spirited college in Southern Connecticut." Mac also observed with thundering truth, "You cannot get anywhere in football by going out and exuding an aroma of good fellowship."

Biff Jones had played a standout game at left tackle on the 1916 team. He had been elected captain for 1917, but the wartime telescoping had moved his graduation up from June, 1918, to August, 1917. He served in France as a lieutenant of field artillery.

Lieutenant Ollie Oliphant, of course, had been one of the most remarkable all-around college athletes of all time, first at Purdue, later at Army. He was a tremendous halfback for the Cadets from 1914 through '17. Nobody ever quite put the fear of God in Navy teams the way Ollie did.

Whenever General MacArthur had time for it—and I suspect he made time—he'd call Lieutenant Oliphant over to his office to talk football, and Ollie was not an unwilling collaborator. If Ollie had a chance to pick up two hundred dollars playing a Sunday football game with the Buffalo All Americans, MacArthur would give him special weekend leave.

Daly and Graves and the rest of that fine staff in 1919 did their usual sound, thorough job with what they had. Although there were a record 800 in the Corps, we were far below prewar standards in football. Almost from the time Cadet Dennis Michie formed the first West Point team in 1890 until 1938, when the Academy first observed the three-year rule (restriction of varsity competition to three seasons), Army squads usually included a few men who had played one to three years at other colleges. There were a few such in 1919 on the Plain, but the rest of the squad was far less experienced than that of an average civilian school playing a major schedule.

It was the 1919 fall practice that first convinced me football is war on a limited terrain. There is no question that Graves was an advanced teacher of line play for his time. He wrote a little book titled *The Lineman's Bible,* which was justifiably regarded for years after as the definitive textbook on the subject. Graves did not believe in senseless bellowing. "Don't yell at them," he preached. "Teach them something."

But Graves, like most of the football thinkers of the day, especially in the East, believed that the hard way was not only the best way but the only way. One day, sitting in the Officers Club, he pointed out the window at a steam roller, removed his cigar, and said, "There is my idea of football."

"Pot," said McEwan of Graves, "was a supreme exponent of designed butchery."

The game as he taught it, and as it was taught elsewhere, had elements of brutality long since outlawed. In an attempt to eliminate the brutality by opening up the game, the forward pass had been legal since 1906. But many coaches believed the pass to be effete, perhaps even cowardly. And the rules, though modified, still permitted mayhem. Tackles still wrapped inches of bicycle tape around their hands and belabored the heads of ends who tried to block them until they rang like Chinese gongs.

Major Merillat, our end coach, a star on the battlefield as in football, tried to teach us ends to protect ourselves. But Major Graves was master of the scene. Over and over again, in an ominously controlled monotone, Pot would say, "Let's see some blood." There was just enough blood to prove the tackles were not backward pupils.

The tackles in those days took the high, dominant stance. Yale classicists, like Pudge Heffelfinger, had preached, "Never get down on the prayer rug, boys." We ends assumed a low position of self-preservation. When I threw a block, I ducked my head and rolled with the punch. I knew it was the only way to protect my teeth and the bridge of my nose. If I were quick and lucky enough, I would escape with mere abrasions. They were acceptable as badges of merit.

Today's football is, by comparison, almost gentle and kind. It is just as hard, but the brutality has been expunged. Good rules have contributed. So have changing concepts of strategy and tactics. Movement, maneuver, and possession have supplanted position and stagnation relieved only by a break.

We spent at least an hour a day practicing kicking, receiving kicks, and covering kicks. During September, we rehearsed only three running plays, executing them over and over: a buck, an off-tackle thrust, and an end run. Later we added a fullback smash over the weak-side guard. Graves looked upon the end run as an almost useless frippery. He scorned it as "a forced march in the face of the enemy."

As for the forward pass, the East, especially, considered it somewhat sissified and used it mainly when time was running out at the end of the half of the game and the other team was ahead. I think we had three pass plays. I caught a few passes, but not so many as at Miami.

We lined up in a balanced line, three men to each side of center, with the ends tight to the tackles, the quarterback in the T position over center and the other three backs aligned in tandem to right or left. In modern football terminology, you might call it a tight winged T and not be far off the mark.

We had a strong defense, supported by the excellent kicking of Claude McQuarrie, who had played at Montana, and gave up only five touchdowns all season. Syracuse drove for one; Notre Dame tallied two, principally through the passing of the phenomenal George Gipp; and our second team handed two to Tufts on fumbles.

We were not a great team and not a bad one. We beat Middlebury, 14–0; Holy Cross, 9–0; Maine, 6–0; Boston College, 13–0; Tufts, 24–13; and Villanova, 62–0; and lost to Syracuse, 7–3; Notre Dame, 12–9; and Navy, 6–0.

Syracuse, Notre Dame, and Navy all were strong, especially the Irish. Knute Rockne was in his second year as head coach. His team and his game were built around the legendary Gipp, except Gipp was no legend. He was painfully real. Notre Dame won all nine of its games, scoring two hundred twenty-nine points to forty-seven.

Tufts gave us an unexpected scare. There could have been several reasons for this. The week before, we had taken a tough game from Major Frank Cavanaugh's redoubtable Boston College team, which had earlier won national attention by upsetting Yale in the Bowl, 5–3. The day of the B.C. game, the Corps was host for the first time in Academy history to a reigning monarch: King Albert of Belgium, who was accompanied by Crown Prince Leopold. Elbowing with royalty and Boston College all in one day may have caused us to suffer a letdown. More likely we were looking a week ahead to the game with Notre Dame.

Before a big game in those days, it was customary to order plenty of rest for the best players, who frequently saw no action in the easier game scheduled the week before. This is usually overlooked by those who sing of "the iron men of the good old days." That Tufts game points it up. Charlie Daly not only started a second team but ordered McQuarrie, left halfback Helmer (Abe) Lystad, and myself not to suit up. Since Lystad was president of the first class and I was vice-president, the coach may have thought we needed some free time to confer on class affairs. But when Tufts quickly scored twice after picking up Army fumbles—you could run with a fumble then—we were ordered to hurry to the gym and suit up for the second half. I recall the tension of suiting up and running back across the Plain. Mainly through the work of McQuarrie, Lystad, tackle Maurice Daniel, and end Clovis Byers, we pulled it out.

It rained on the Tufts game, which probably contributed to my catching influenza and landing in the post hospital. Consequently, I regretfully missed the battle with Notre Dame on the Plain, November 8. An orderly brought the score by periods to my bedside. We got a 9–0 lead, but the passing and running of the great Gipp overcame it. Gipp didn't make the All America until 1920. I've often wondered how he missed it in 1919.

I was less concerned with his All America prospects, however, than with regaining my health and strength for the Navy game. I missed the Villanova game on November 15, and we had the customary pre-Navy off Saturday on the twenty-second. I was able to get up for the first time early that week and walk around the hospital.

General MacArthur did his best to speed my recovery. He sent his car and chauffeur to take me for health-restoring rides out Central Valley and around the Hudson Highlands. The post surgeon ordered me to report three times a day for a glass of sherry. The military fashion in which I gulped down this quick builder of strength would have given the miseries to a gourmet.

The Monday before the Navy game, I put on a uniform and got out on the field, but I felt as weak as a tabby cat. I had little hope I could play. I received much encouragement from our trainer, Harry Tuttle, who also trained the Detroit Tigers during the baseball season. Tuttle, and later Roland Bevan, my Dartmouth and Army trainer, influenced my thinking on illness and injuries. They taught me that recovery can be speeded up by positive thinking.

On Thursday night, just before we left for New York and our pre-Navy game bivouac at the Hotel Astor, the coaches held a meeting with the team, and Charlie Daly announced I would start at right end. Several teammates had requested of Daly that he start me. They felt that, regardless of how long I would be able to play, my experience would have a salutary effect.

I felt shaky at the opening kick-off. But as I went along, I seemed to gain strength and confidence. I played fifty-eight and a half minutes.

That 1919 game with Navy at the Polo Grounds was not the most exciting since the beginning of recorded football time. Army was neither overpowering nor imaginative on the offense. Navy Coach Gilmour Dobie, who was to be a respected rival years later in our Dartmouth-Cornell games, worshiped then as always at the shrine of the off-tackle power play. It drizzled rain throughout the game and there was practically no forward passing; not that either team would have darkened the skies with passes, had it been dry and clear.

Navy, which that year lost only to Georgetown, 6–0, had not telescoped its classes during the war, as had West Point, and, consequently, was able to rebuild its football much faster. The Midshipmen pushed us around a bit, 270 yards rushing to 32, but they couldn't push us beyond a point. They got their six points on two field-goal placements of 23 and 15 yards by tackle Clyde King.

The game traced a monotonous pattern. Like all ends at the time, my primary, in fact only, defensive duty against a scrimmage was to turn the play in. Navy would grind off tackle for several first downs. After a while, we'd stop them. We couldn't move the ball on them, so McQuarrie would punt far down the field. Then Navy would start all over again. And so on.

The record shows that I went down the field under eighteen of McQuarrie's punts and that most of the time I was able to drop the receiver in his tracks. This caught the eye of Walter Camp, because he named me third-team end on his All America. That day I also became the first West Point athlete to play against Navy in three sports.

Less welcome recognition was accorded me by some Navy player who stuck a finger in my right eye. An ulcer of the cornea developed and I was returned to the cadet hospital. I had to sit there for days in a dark room with a patch over the eye. I couldn't study. I missed not only the first-semester writs but the turnout (second-chance) exams before Christmas.

General MacArthur sent his aide, Lieutenant Pitt F. Carl, Jr., to the hospital daily to check my condition. One day Lieutenant Carl informed me that the General thought I should take leave and return in the fall of 1920 to redo the year. The patch over my eye had nothing to do with the fact that I couldn't see this. I told the Lieutenant I'd already been to college four years before coming to West Point and I was eager to get my commission in June.

The next day, Lieutenant Carl returned with better news. He told me General MacArthur said that if I would write him a letter asking to be excused from the first semester writs and turnout exams, he would submit it to the Academic Board. I knew what the General submitted would be accepted. The General didn't stop there. He also approved an order for me to take a few days' extra leave.

I don't think missing those first semester exams hurt me very much. I finished 107 in a class of 287. I might have done better, but I hadn't taken any geometry since Steele High. The West Point course covered plain and solid geometry, all in three weeks. I was completely lost in that mathematical maze known as The Theory of Least Squares. My best subjects were history and English. At one time I climbed to sixth in my class in English, even though this work may not show it.

By the same reasoning, I don't think the men of 1918 through 1920, who were commissioned after only two years or less at the Academy, were any the worse for it. Their records as soldiers certainly prove they weren't. I am proud to have been at the Academy in their time. The full four years are ideal and wonderful. But they are not indispensable. In short, you don't need all the stuff and all the guff. It still depends on the man. Our year book says of us:

> We were the link, the frail gray thread, connecting the old with the new. We were of the Corps under the old regime. We were the Corps when peril was near. We survived—when the war clouds lifted, we stood on the other shore.

My father and Merle came on for graduation and saw me receive the Athletic Association Saber, awarded the outstanding athlete in the graduating class. Colonel Koehler made the presentation.

It may be the satisfaction of June Week was dimmed somewhat for my father when for the first time he saw me play baseball, against the Seventh Regiment team. I like to think that what happened may have traced partly to the fact that I had pushed myself hard that morning in defending successfully the Corps 100- and 220-yard championships in an interclass track meet. I know I went into the ball game seeing double from the morning's exertion. I can't believe I was quite that bad a hitter. Nevertheless, I struck out four consecutive times.

My father didn't ask me why; he just looked at me. I know what he was thinking: "And you won the Athletic Saber?"

Chapter IV

The De-emphasized Cavalry

In the Junction City, Kansas, of 1920, the brightest light for young officers from nearby Fort Riley was the drugstore owned by Roy J. Eisenhower, whose older brother Dwight had graduated from West Point five years before. Whenever we had the opportunity, Willis McDonald, Sam Gregory, and myself, lieutenants fresh out of the Academy, would drive the six miles from Riley to Junction City and Eisenhower's in a secondhand Ford we had purchased jointly for $150.

Even when a Kansas freeze blew out an engine plug, we stuck a cork in, filled her with water, and managed our destination just before the radiator started to boil. Riding that old clatter-trap over rocky Kansas roads in all weather provided a training of sorts for the cavalry.

Among the regulars at Eisenhower's was an agent representing the Travelers Insurance Company of Hartford, Connecticut, a persuasive, ingratiating man named Harold Copeland. He got to know all the officers, followed up with visits to the post and soon had sold many of them accident insurance. Considering the hazards indispensable to cavalry training, Mr. Copeland could not have encountered less sales resistance in a scrub football team.

There were so many accidents at Riley that the Travelers sent out on investigator from Hartford, a veritable Sherlock Holmes or Nick Carter among actuaries, to determine whether the Riley officers and doctors were conspiring to defraud the company. The investigator had but to observe one day of riding to be convinced everything was "on the up and up"—in the sense of honest claims.

"Why," the investigator exclaimed to Copeland, "it's a damned lucky thing you didn't sell them life insurance!"

The Travelers people were especially impressed by an officer named West. He had a brother on the post who had been on the 1920 Olympic Equestrian team and was a magnificent rider and instructor. In trying to emulate his brother, perhaps, West was overdoing it. In one fall from a horse, he broke several ribs. Scarcely had he recovered when he tumbled again and fractured a leg. While hobbling around on crutches, he fell downstairs and had to start all over again. Finally, after he was out of the leg cast only two days, he stepped on a cake of soap in a shower and broke his collarbone. In the aggregate, he collected insurance for about thirty of the thirty-nine weeks we were at the school. The Travelers not only paid him off cheerily; when they mailed him the check, they were strongly tempted to enclose a citation.

Risk of limb and life by West and the rest seems somewhat futile in retrospect, when one considers the reigning philosophy of our political leadership of the times that an army of any dimension would be henceforth superfluous. This attitude and the conditions it bred were to prompt many of us to resign within less than two years after we left West Point.

Between commencement and reporting to Riley, I enjoyed a three months' vacation. I haven't had one nearly so long in forty years. Before we left West Point for a summer's relaxation, however, we faced the duty of ushering at the weddings of several classmates. At first, the long walk down the aisle of the beautiful Cadet Chapel was exhilarating. After about six such journeys, however, there developed a certain psychological fatigue. In fact, the stately and somewhat somber strains of Lohengrin's "Wedding March" produced such an accumulatively depressing effect upon my good friend, Sam Gregory, of Company M, that he developed an antipathy toward weddings that became almost a phobia.

Gregory, Willis McDonald, their best girls, Merle, and I had been invited by McDonald's Aunt Emma to her large and beautiful home on Lake Webster, in Massachusetts. The Indian name of the lake is "Chargoggagogmanchaugagogchaubunagungamaug," which means, "You fish on your side, I fish on my side and neither of us shall fish in the middle." (A philosophy all right for fishing but not for football.) I learned how to pronounce that Indian name by the second day. This may have been the reason why I was impatient later on with newspapermen who protested occasional football line-ups of polysyllables and many consonants.

The house party was not an undiluted success. Sam Gregory's aforementioned phobia so overpowered him that an engagement of several years' standing was broken. Almost concurrently, McDonald found out that his girl had been double-dealing with a naval officer and had come to prefer a blue uniform. Speaking of the Navy, I took Merle out in a canoe and promptly capsized it by stepping on the gunwhale. Merle had already been upset by the loss of a suitcase containing her best bib and tucker. We were all young and resilient, however, and even such misadventures failed to dampen our enjoyment of Aunt Emma's warm hospitality.

After returning home to Dayton, I visited old McCook Field one day. A young, daredevil flyer, Captain John A. Macready, whose record would include distinction in both World Wars, altitude, endurance, and distance records, and the first nonstop transcontinental flight, thought it would be a nice thing to take the young fellow fresh from West Point up for a spin and give him the works. I sensed what he was up to and I never had been in a plane before, but I feigned a happy eagerness.

After we had taken off, climbed, and leveled, I actually began to enjoy it. Then Captain Macready suddenly put the plane into a series of stunts. It was an open-cockpit job and I thought repeatedly I was going to fall out. Coming out of the stunt series, Macready shouted, "How do you like it?"

I tried desperately to demonstrate composure. "Just fine!" I hollered back. "Just fine!"

He then went into a second series of stunts. By the time we got on the ground again, I had a greater-than-ever enthusiasm for the cavalry. Also, much to my own as well as Captain Macready's surprise, I held onto my lunch.

The cavalry was my choice because I had always enjoyed riding since kid days in Dayton. At the Academy, we were exposed to enough horsemanship to find out if we liked it. At Riley, there were about 125 of us taking the basic course. As equestrians, we learned how to break, bridle, saddle, and shoe horses. There were about 2,000 of them on the post.

Those we learned to shoe on were big fellows from the artillery, weighing just short of 2000 pounds. They were old hands at being shod. No sooner did you pick up the hoof of one of these old-timers and start to work than he would lean on you. Trimming a hoof of a 2000-pound horse who is leaning on you may be likened to trying, as a junior-high-school end, to block the Baltimore Colt's behemoth tackle, "Big Daddy" Lipscomb.

Shoeing involved paring hoofs and putting nails into the hard places. We neophytes frequently put the nails in the soft places. The botched jobs occasionally perpetrated would have been regarded coldly by the A.S.P.C.A.

More exciting instruction was provided in basic and advanced horsemanship and maneuvers, including jumping and obstacle courses.

The social life at Riley was at once simple but complicated. There were the usual officers' dances. National prohibition was with us (Kansas was a dry state, anyhow), cigarettes were outlawed in Kansas, and we were on a military reservation. Since alcohol never held any attraction for me, the steward at the Riley Officers Club used to concoct me a drink composed of orange juice, syrup, a cherry, and lots of ice. He called it a "Yellow Peril." It tasted fine on a hot day. Yellow Perils had little appeal for my roommates, McDonald, Bill McMillan, and a Kentuckian named John Russell.

Most officers in the basic course were quartered in what had been enlisted-men's barracks, but we were fortunate enough to have a private room. We also had a dandy little colored orderly named Coleman, who took real good care of us. Coleman abetted McDonald and Russell in hiding forty gallons of dried apricot mash in the furnace room until it got well worked up. Then they got hold of an electric stove, a kettle, and a long copper tube, and distilled home-brew. My friends appeared to enjoy the product, although it smelled like the vile belly wash it probably was and our quarters resembled the habitat of a demented chemist.

After graduation from Riley in July, 1921, I was assigned to the Eighth Cavalry Regiment of the First Cavalry Division at Fort Bliss, near El Paso, Texas, just across the Rio Grande from Juarez, Mexico.

Following two months' leave, I arrived at Bliss on a hot Sunday afternoon in August, and reported to the Commanding Officer of the Eighth, Colonel George Tayloe Langhorne, West Point, 1889.

Colonel Langhorne had served as military attaché to Brussels and had fought in the Philippine Insurrection and the Expedition against the Moros. As was quite natural, no doubt, for one who was a brother of Lady Astor, Colonel Langhorne was also rich in the nuances of deportment and the unquestioned cynosure of the El Paso social swirl. By sheer coincidence, for the afternoon I happened to arrive he had scheduled a social gallop over the desert, covering a four-mile course, replete with jumps and other obstacles. It appeared that almost every officer in the Eighth, wives, and several unattached and comely young ladies from El Paso had answered the Colonel's call.

I unwittingly presented myself to Colonel Langhorne about five minutes before the ride was to begin. Nothing would do, he said, but that I join them. I was not properly turned out for a gallop. The Army "pinks" (white riding breeches) I sported were strictly for dress. More to the point, I hadn't been on a horse in two months. However, there was no choice but to accept. The Colonel and his entourage set a fast pace. I was out of practice in taking jumps, but managed them, because it was hardly the time and place to be shown up. The end of the ride found me covered with mud, but socially pristine.

The next day I reported to the Post Commander, Major General Robert Lee Howze, West Point, 1888. General Howze had been Commandant at the Academy from 1905 to '09 and had commanded the American Expeditionary Force's 38th Division; he was a polo enthusiast and the field just south of the Academy's Michie Stadium is named after him.

I had come to Bliss for soldiering, not sports, but General Howze ordered me to play baseball with the Division team. In September, he ordered me to coach and play with the football team. This was my first real head-coaching assignment, although I had handled a team in an interbattalion game back at the Point.

For the first time since Riverdale Rover days, I could choose my own position. I picked quarterback again, where I would have played at Miami and Army also, had the choice been mine. I soon decided to do most of my quarterbacking at Bliss from the bench. I had been away from football for two years, and we were 5500 feet above sea level. Two minutes of scrimmage in that rarefied ozone and I might just as well have been back in the cadet hospital, battling the flu bugs. I couldn't get in shape. That experience with high altitude undoubtedly conditioned my thinking some thirty-five years later, when I questioned the wisdom of allowing an Army team to meet the Air Force Academy at Colorado Springs.

Our Bliss squad numbered forty. Only one besides myself had ever played in college. We did all right against other service teams, but lost to the University of New Mexico, 35-0, at Albuquerque. The defeat was the least painful phase of the expedition. It was roughly 270 miles from Bliss to Albuquerque, and the old-fashioned, side-seated bus we traveled in could grind out an average of 25 miles an hour. The trip up wasn't too bad. We left at six o'clock on a Friday morning and reached Albuquerque about six thirty that night. The return trip, however, was something a Hollywood scenarist might have concocted for Stan Laurel and Oliver Hardy.

We started back Sunday morning at seven, bruised but in tolerable spirits. In my pocket was the $150 guarantee in cash from New Mexico, no small consolation since the Bliss sports program had to be financed independently of government funds. I was figuring out how best to use the $150 when we had our first blowout. We had two spares and two dozen blowout patches, so we took the mishap in stride. We were only 30 miles out of Albuquerque, but better to have done with trouble at the beginning of the journey.

The next 200 miles were unbelievable. We had—and I am not exaggerating in the slightest—twenty-four punctures or blowouts, an average of one every 8⅓ miles. When we had the last blowout, we were still 40 miles from Bliss. It was nine o'clock at night and we had run out of patches. We had one break—an adobe store was within hiking range and it had a phone. I called the officer in charge at the post and asked him to send out a truck for us.

Meanwhile, I faced a problem more acute than blowouts. My men had breakfasted before leaving Albuquerque and had lunched en route—after Blowout No. 10, I believe—on their P.M.E. (Practical Military Engineering) box lunches. These consisted of two sandwiches and an apple. We were supposed to forage for water. Naturally, by nine at night, the men were ravenous.

The inventory of the crossroads store was not lavish. The best I could requisition was two boxes of soda crackers and some vintage baloney, enough for about three. Baloney on top of bruises and blowouts was too much. If my men toyed with thoughts of mutiny, it was understandable. I was relieved when the truck arrived around ten thirty. It was after midnight when we finally pulled into Bliss. By that time the men were beginning to revise their previous opinions of cannibalism. My duties included those of Mess Officer. I woke up the cook and supervised a hasty meal. At breakfast the next morning, the football men were still in sharp appetite.

Even the "Albuquerque Adventure" could not dim the enthusiasm of the enlisted men and noncommissioned officers for sports. One of the finest morale builders was the participation of commissioned officers with the men and the noncoms. In the winter, when I coached the basketball team, I was able to get in more playing time. The officer who is an athlete usually finds he has something extra going for him if he also measures up in other ways, because soldiers always will respect the physical man.

About six weeks after I reported to Bliss, Colonel Langhorne was transferred and replaced as Commanding Officer of the Eighth by Colonel James Haynes (Shorty) Reeves, West Point, 1892. Blunt, humorless but efficient, Shorty Reeves had served in the War with Spain and the Boxer Rebellion and, as Commander of the 353rd Infantry Regiment with the A.E.F., had earned the Distinguished Cross and the Distinguished Service Medal. Reeves was unimpressed with most of the captains in his Bliss command, and assigned troops only to three of them. That was how I came to be put in command of Troop E as a lieutenant.

A young officer out of West Point, if he is wise, will always place great reliance on his top sergeant. In my troop alone, there were five noncommissioned officers who had been decorated for gallantry in France and had risen to captain or major. After the war, they returned by choice to their noncom status, where they felt more at ease. These were soldiers dedicated to the service, but with relatively little education. This had set up a certain intangible barrier, of which they were aware and about which they were sensitive. Furthermore, had they remained commissioned officers, they would have had to forgo such privileges as playing poker with their troopers or drinking tequilla with them on a night's foray for fun across the border in Juarez.

The rapport between young West Point lieutenants and their sergeants was a warm memory. These grizzled old noncoms showed they were proud of you as West Pointers if you rated it, and they took care of you as if you were their own sons. If they saw you heading for a mistake, due to inexperience or impetuousness, they had their own quiet, politic way of steering you right: "Doesn't the Lieutenant think it might be better——"

I was especially lucky to have as my top sergeant, Albert (Pop) Leusche, who later became a member of the Michigan City, Indiana, City Council, and used to write to me regularly until his death on November 25, 1951. With Pop Leusche around, I had no disciplinary problems.

Several nights a week, our troopers would get passes to visit Juarez. They invariably returned well fortified with tequilla, which had a double-barreled effect, guaranteed with the first drink of water before 5:15 reveille formation. Elements of the tequilla troopers were discouraged when Shorty Reeves ordered me to supervise twenty minutes of calisthenics after reveille formation for all men of the Eighth not on duty elsewhere, which meant about 600. The enlisted men and most of the old sergeants thought the calisthenics nonsense, but Pop Leusche thought them a good idea.

Enlisted men and noncoms enjoyed, on the whole, a more satisfying social life than the officers. There were occasional dances and in the late winter of 1922 I got to playing a little polo. I went over to Juarez one Sunday to see a bullfight. One was enough. It did not impress me as sport.

I arrived at Bliss a month earlier than Willis McDonald, who had been assigned from Riley to Fort Ethan Allen in Vermont as an instructor for a couple of months. McDonald sent ahead to Bliss, however, his Dodge roadster, which had replaced the old Ford at Riley, and I had the use of it. When Willis got off the train at El Paso, I greeted him with his roadster and a pretty girl I had met at a post party given by General Howze. Her name was Elizabeth Pfaff and she later became Mrs. McDonald.

I found my greatest outlet in the duties incident to the command of Troop E. I loved everything about cavalry life, from that inimitable flavor of the stables to the gallops across the desert. My mare, Lady, was a beauty in every respect, and the special envy of swashbuckling, swearing, bewhiskered Colonel Tommy Thompson, in command of the Seventh Cavalry, who offered me any two horses in his outfit in trade for her.

It was an exhilarating experience to lead the Troop on maneuvers out on the desert. When you wheeled around and pointed back to El Paso, the city would be 20 miles away, yet, in that rarefied atmosphere, it seemed only about 2 miles. As you galloped toward it, El Paso appeared to recede like some enchanted place out of the Arabian Nights.

With a mount like Lady, I had no need for another, yet I bought one for $40. A first lieutenant's pay was $1800 a year plus quarters and one ration allowance a day. You bought your own uniforms. But an officer was allowed $40 extra a month for his mount, provided he bought the horse himself. It was accepted practice for an officer, whenever he could, to buy a horse, whether he needed one or not. You might even say it was a mild form of chicanery.

Several of us at Bliss chipped in $40 each to buy a carload of remounts that arrived from New Mexico. I shall never forget them. I have had to welcome some unlikely-looking football squads in my time, but I never beheld such a discouraging collection of anything as those horses. Sired on the desert and never before touched by human hands, they were completely wild.

To get those prairie ponies from the unloading pen to the Eighth Cavalry corral was no simple task. I sent two troopers to get mine. It took them a full day to do the job, as the horse refused to be led or driven. Unaccustomed to human persuasion, my prize repeatedly reared and fell back. As a result, by the time it was finally corralled, its neck muscles had been so stretched that it could not lift its head.

The next morning, the animal was a pitiful sight. During the night, the blood had rushed down into the sunken head and the neck bruises had swelled. As a result, the head was twice its normal size. Since the horse never had been shod, its hoofs were as big as pie plates. As I look back on it now, there was an equine only a Dali could have conceived, something even more distorted than a papier-mâché Dobbin you may have observed in such a parade as the Mardi Gras. But at the time, my only reaction was one of pity. The horse finally gave up and keeled over, to remain prone for several weeks. Yet it also remained sufficiently cantankerous to lift a hoof at anyone who came near.

I finally got the horse in apparently good enough shape so that when I resigned I sold it to another officer for $40. I am still waiting for him to pay me, but I wouldn't say he is being unreasonable.

You may have heard of the notorious colt, Pounditout, which millionaire Alfred Gwynne Vanderbilt sold for $300 to thirty members of the New York *World-Telegram* sports staff at $10 a share. Upkeep and training cost another $4800. Pounditout went to the races four times, and managed to finish fourth once, earning $175. Pounditout's mediocre record could have been related to the fact that he was a sway-back. The colt was finally taken off the hands of the *World-Telegram* boys in the fall of its two-year-old season by that kindly restaurateur and sportsman, Gene Leone. Gene put Pounditout to graze on his farm in Central Valley (near West Point), where he also failed dismally as a sire.

Pounditout merely proved that you only get what you pay for. If it is any consolation to Leone and the *World-Telegram* investors, however, my $40 remount out of the New Mexico desert made Pounditout, by comparison, look to be a combination of Man O' War and Alexander the Great's storied white steed, Bucephalus.

Alexander the Great would have found Fort Bliss in my time scarcely a jumping-off-place for magnificent campaigns. Mexican guerilla generals, hangovers from Pancho Villa, occasionally held up a train, but were usually apprehended in due time by the Texas Rangers.

I saw the Rangers ride into Bliss one day with General Juan Merigo and slap him into the guardhouse. (Merigo's chief of staff was a Harvard man, who may have become a soldier of fortune because he sensed the way the Crimson's football policies were shaping.) But as far as we were concerned, it was mostly comic opera. If General Howze heard of a planned uprising by a guerilla general, he would invite the suspect over to review the First Division at Bliss. That usually was enough to quell his ambition.

Once I thought we were going to see a little action. Late in January of 1922, we got the report of an incipient coup by a little guerilla general around Juarez. General Howze ordered the Seventh and Eighth to prepare to cross the Rio the next day, advance into Mexico, and apprehend this guerilla and his men. Troop E was selected to be the advance guard.

Insignificant though it was, the operation promised some fringe of combat. Colonel Reeves determined we would cross the Rio at a narrow shallow upstream and move on Juarez in an enflanking movement from the west. Late in the afternoon before D Day, I reconnoitered Troop E at the point of crossing. I was all anticipation as we galloped back to the post. Whom should I discover there but the would-be insurrectionist himself. He had been turned on by his own men and had given himself up to us for protection. My letdown was thunderous.

More letdowns were due. Not long after, the Army offered enlisted men and noncoms a year's pay to resign. The day that order came out, Troop E had 120 men, including 15 noncoms. The day after the order, resignations left us with 15 men, most of them noncoms. Approximately the same situation obtained with the other troops of the Seventh and Eighth. Each troop still had to exercise and care for 100 horses. We were so shorthanded we pulled their shoes.

Exercising them was a problem that somehow reminded me of

The Theory of Least Squares. A lieutenant and four noncoms from each troop would take their 100 mounts 4 miles out on the desert. Even though we had the horses well separated by troops, when we turned them around, all hell broke loose. One or more lead horses would break into a mad gallop toward the corrals. The others would play follow-the-leader and bolt after them.

The sight of 900 horses stampeding across the desert was truly splendid and awe-inspiring. Our appreciation of the beauty was tempered, however, by our awareness of the chaos it guaranteed. If any horse got in his right corral, it was strictly by accident, and we had to spend hours sorting them out. We finally haltered and led the chronic bolters, and thus brought the insurrections to an end.

We were so shorthanded, we had no time for drilling. We were operating less like soldiers than cowboys. It was necessary to skeletonize the Eighth Regiment from nine troops to three. Troop E was absorbed into C, under Captain George Goodyear. To fill out a troop complement of even 60, it was urgent to ride far and wide around the country to recruit almost anybody we could find.

The persuasive argumentation required to entice such people into the military life no doubt was excellent preparation for that indispensable phase of football coaching known as proselyting. In a *Saturday Evening Post* piece, written when I became head coach at Army in 1941, my old Dartmouth tackle star and now a sportscaster and promising novelist, Dave Camerer, quoted Willis McDonald:

> We'd go carpetbagging for wandering cowboys, hoboes, all manner of floating young men. We'd corral them back to camp, give them a meal and start breaking them in as horse marines. Blaik, I remember, was a pretty shrewd carpetbagger.

The reduction of the United States Army was extending, of course, to the commissioned officers. The aim of the War Department was to cut them from 14,000 to 9,000 by 1923. They got rid of many they considered below par by giving them honorable discharges through "Class B" boards. By the summer of 1922, they were offering even officers they knew to be competent a year's pay to resign.

A West Pointer of the Class of 1920 knew that ahead of him on the promotion list was a hump of 5,000 who had remained in the Army after World War I. Our class had been promoted from second to first lieutenants the day after graduation, there were so many openings then, but by 1923 those who stayed in were reduced back to second lieutenant. They did not achieve their majorities until 1940.

But those words in "Benny Havens, Oh!": "In the Army . . . promotion's very slow," were ignored by many of the men of '20. In fact, this class was to produce over 50 generals. Today, for example, it can point proudly to General Lyman Lemnitzer, Chief of Staff of the Army, and General Tommy White, Chief of Staff of the Air Force. It also included the Dean of West Point's Academic Board, General William W. Bessell, Jr., and three department heads: Colonels Edward C. Gillette, Jr., Physics and Chemistry; Charles W. West, Law; and Lawrence E. Schick, Military Topography and Graphics.

McDonald and I were among those who put in for resignation in February of 1922. We had wanted a career with the horse soldiers—but where was it? We were also disillusioned with the naïve philosophy that there would be no more wars. My resignation was accepted by the War Department on March 15, after having been turned down all the way up to the Secretary of War.

I said my last good-byes that morning and in El Paso boarded the train for Chicago. There was no scheduled stop at Bliss, but the train stopped there that morning. Sergeant Pop Leusche and the men of Troop C were lined up along the tracks at attention. With them, riderless but saddled, was Lady. It was with moist eyes I returned their salute, and the train moved on.

I got home to Dayton on March 17. The next day I received a letter that had been forwarded from Bliss. It had been sent there by General MacArthur. He was concluding his tour as West Point Superintendent in June, and was then to be assigned to the Philippines. He wanted me to go with him as his aide.

The letter had been written and mailed on March 12, and had reached Bliss the same day I left. If the General had written it a day earlier, I would have withdrawn my resignation and stayed in the

Army. No matter what the size of the Army or the philosophy of Congress as to the possibility of any future wars, I knew that where MacArthur was the days would not be dull. If I had become MacArthur's aide and stayed in service, I never would have become a football coach, as I have always held in highest respect the career of a soldier.

Through the years I have often recalled nostalgically those days with the de-emphasized cavalry.

Chapter V

The Temporary Avocation

"If you're not confused," says a consoling modern business adage, "you don't know what's going on." This seeming paradox is just another way of stating that nothing much ever is accomplished without at least one problem that forces even the leading specialist to sweat for a solution. But the adage doesn't apply universally; doesn't fit, for example, the business of firing college football coaches. Alumni and some athletic board members responsible for the firing are almost invariably confused. This by no means implies, however, that they know what is going on.

Modern football has been aptly called "violent chess." It is certainly true that endless study of films, constant changes in offense, compensating diversifications in defense, all make coaching today primarily a thinking job. It requires diligence all around the clock and the calendar. Even then, the game's very best brains confess they are not able to absorb and teach it to the degree they would like, because there is simply not enough time.

Since this is true, how can the layman, who may or may not have visited a locker room once in his life, presume an understanding of the game sufficient to form a sound basis of judgment in appraising the work of a coach? Let us concede the unusual situation where the layman is an ex-player and coach, not too long away from the game and still able to keep up with it reasonably well. Can he profess to know the personnel of a squad, its true potential, strength, and weakness as well as the man and his assistants who practically live with it all the time?

The layman who so presumes and professes is, in the real order of things, ridiculous. His decision that a coach should be fired traces, whether he is conscious of it or not, almost exclusively to an emotional reaction to an unsatisfactory scoreboard or record.

I believe a football coach, like anybody else, must expect to produce reasonable results within reasonable time. That poses an admittedly tough question: Who is truly qualified to pass judgment on the coach? Well, an athletic board, or a majority of its members, should be able to if the college president has selected them judiciously. That is to say, the board members should possess intelligence, integrity, courage, and knowledge of the peculiar problems and atmosphere surrounding football at a given school.

The board should make its decision on substantial evidence: What is the coach permitted in recruiting as compared to opponents? Then there is the question: How does the team look? Most coaches who have stayed long at a school have enjoyed some winning years, probably some big ones, but they have also mastered the subtle art of turning out teams that look good even when losing. I'll admit this is a tough trick, almost as difficult as squaring a circle, especially when the team loses a game it is supposed to win. And no matter how good your teams may look, you still have to have some winning seasons.

The trouble is that the winning season, or lack of it, is usually the *only* evidence that stands up in court when a coach is fired, although I'll allow a striking exception in the case of Steve Sebo and Pennsylvania. Penn held onto Sebo while he was losing and fired him after he won the Ivy League championship. Don't ask me why! I can only repeat that it is possible to be confused and still not know what is going on.

All I know is that ours is a crazy, perilous profession. All I can tell my fellow coaches, all I can advise them is summed up in the following:

If you can, coach at a school where the president and the board of athletic control are not influenced by unrestrained alumni, capable of behaving at times like vicious half-lunatics.

Again, if at all possible, coach at a school where you don't have to report to an athletic director. If his position is strong, he will not jeopardize it trying to save you from strong alumni opposition. If his position is already weak, he will be even less inclined to come to your defense.

If you are one of the majority who have no choice but to coach at schools where the cries of the alumni, authentic or "subway," are heard, and the director of athletics wields first the sword that preserves his status quo, then stuff your ears and fight it out as long as you can.

You knew what you were asking for when you took the job—the midnight phone call from anonymous madman or drunkard or both, the undergraduate editor, the effigy hangman and, worst of all, those suave two-faced, self-appointed saviors of the school. In the end, all you may have left is the belief of your players and your family and the knowledge that you are a braver and a better man than any of your critics—but these are no small things.

Along this line, I offer a quote from President Theodore Roosevelt, which was kindly sent to me by John McKenna, the fine coach of the Virginia Military Institute team:

> It is not the critic who counts; not the man who points out how the strong man stumbled or where the doer of deeds could have done them better. The credit belongs to the man who is actually in the arena; whose face is marred by dust and sweat and blood; who strives valiantly, who errs and comes short again and again; who knows the great enthusiasms, the great devotions, and spends himself in a worthy cause; who, at the best, knows the triumph of high achievement; and who, at the worst, if he fails, at least fails while daring greatly, so that his place shall never be with those cold and timid souls who knew neither victory nor defeat.

No matter where you coach, don't worry because of what is written in the newspapers or said about you over the air. The majority of the writers and broadcasters are fair and reasonably knowledgeable. (It is a strange thing, in fact, that your most ardent supporters among them sometimes unwittingly hurt you and your team by trying to rationalize a defeat for which there is no honest excuse.) As for the minority—the uninformed, the ax-grinders, the professional hatchet men, the locker-room incendiaries and the utter frauds—don't read or hear them. You can't do anything about them. They can't do anything about themselves.

The perilous nature of coaching was brought home to me in my first job as an assistant, when I handled the ends at Wisconsin in 1926 under my old coach at Miami, George Little.

Coaching was far from my mind when I arrived home at Dayton from Fort Bliss on St. Patrick's Day, 1922. I was twenty-five years old. It was time to sit down and take stock. The law career I envisioned at Miami had been knocked in the ears by World War I. Law now would mean three more years of schooling, and I felt it was time I did something productive.

The sudden end of the war and the devaluation of the Army had nipped my ambition to soldier. The MacArthur letter had arrived one day too late.

What to do? Where the road? The pre-law couse at Miami had included business classes. This now suggested real estate and insurance. I had $1500 in the bank, more than enough to open a little office in the Arcade Building on Ludlow Street between Third and Fourth. The sign on the office door read: Earl H. Blaik—Real Estate and Insurance. It was like a lot of other things in life. It looked good and it was harmless—but it didn't mean anything.

The real-estate and insurance business imbued me with what I should imagine to be the sentiments of an underprivileged lion. I was bored and restless. I had a compulsion for action—exciting action. I sought outlets in squash, golf, activity in the Y.M.C.A.

I even served on the Montgomery County Boxing Commssion. I was appointed to this post only because my athletic background at Miami and West Point invested me, in the minds of a surprising number of Daytonians, with a comprehensive knowledge of all sports, which I was far from having.

My duties included paying off the managers of fighters after bouts at North Dayton Park or Lakeside Park. After one fight suspected of not being on the level, I held up the purse, and a taut scene ensued. I have always sympathized with boxing commissioners and wondered how they manage any composure whatsoever.

I borrowed my father's car now and then to drive the 25 miles up the Dixie Highway to 817 West Green Street, Piqua, to visit Merle. Now that I was out of the Army and in business, or what passed for it, propriety demanded that a wedding date be named soon. However, I wanted to hold off until I had $5000 in the bank.

As fall approached, my restlessness increased. Saturdays, I would drive with my friend Dick Israel up to Oxford or wherever Miami was playing, or head for Columbus and the Ohio State game. Sundays and a couple of other nights a week, I'd be up to 817 West Green. I spent the rest of the time wondering what the heck I was doing in real estate and insurance.

One December morning, with my feet up on the desk, I decided that real estate might be all right if it were tied into building. Building might not be as exciting as trying a case or leading a troop, but at least I'd be out in the air and moving around more. My father had been in real estate and building since 1915, and I knew I could go in with him any time I wanted to. We didn't discuss it. It was more or less understood. But if there was going to be a real partnership, even with my father, I felt I should bring some substance to it. So I decided first to become a builder on my own.

I took my savings, still around $1500, and bought a lot (50 by 100 feet) on Highland Avenue in the southwest section of Dayton. I borrowed suitable architectural plans from the company of Harry Coleman, the Dayton real-estate operator I had chauffeured during summer vacations in Miami days.

The plans called for a substantial frame house, with six rooms and bath, cellar, hardwood floors and trim, hot-air heating, and complete inside decorations, including wallpaper. On the outside, I planned some sodding, planting, and landscaping. The house, exclusive of the lot, would cost me $5,000. I was able to borrow that from the Homestead Building and Loan Company, using the lot as collateral, and then hired my carpenters, masons, plumbers, painters, and laborers. I sold the house for $8,000, a $1500 profit.

Before the end of May, 1923, I had built a dozen of them; they are still giving good service today and would bring about $15,000 each. With an $18,000 profit on the twelve houses, I was in a position to go into business with Dad and to get married. We occupied offices on the tenth floor of the Reibold Building at the southwest corner of Main and Fourth.

"Built By Blaik" was the trademark of W. D. and E. H. Blaik, a partnership which flourished, despite my subsequent deviations into football, until the death of my father on January 3, 1947.

Merle and I were married in the First Presbyterian Church in Piqua, Ohio, by the Reverend Edgar Montgomery, on October 20, 1923. The partnership is still going strong. Merle has been the perfect football wife. She always accepted the ceaseless demands of coaching on my time, and took as much interest in my players as if they were her own sons, as one of them was. She aged through the games even more rapidly than I did, and, if it is possible, suffered even more anguish from and was even more intolerant of defeat. She paid the price.

We decided to honeymoon by auto to New York for the Army-Navy game. We had a new Oakland six-cylinder car—it would be called a convertible today. It had big wheels to ride on and an even bigger one, or at least it felt bigger, to steer with. You felt as though you were handling a truck, but we were proud of that Oakland.

Even for such a speed wagon as ours, the 750-mile trip from Dayton to New York, part of it over the Alleghenies, was a three-day haul. We started on a Wednesday, stayed in Greensburg, Pennsylvania, the first night, Philadelphia the second, and pulled into the Bellevue in New York on Friday. It was a big deal, and much more enjoyable than The Albuquerque Adventure.

You could hardly say the same for the Army-Navy game. It was contested in rain and mud on a dark afternoon and ended in a scoreless tie. Both teams missed field-goal attempts. An unusual sequence in the second half saw Army block two successive Navy kicks, both recovered by the Midshipmen, and almost block a third.

Big John McEwan had succeeded Charlie Daly as coach that year and Biff Jones was his first assistant. Both were Army captains, Mac in the Infantry, Biff in the Field Artillery. I visited with them at the Astor after the game. I had not been back to the Academy or seen any of them since graduation three and a half years before. I felt out of touch with things—a stranger.

That honeymoon trip to the Army-Navy game, I realize now, was one of a few telltale tips of a certain direction in which I was facing at least, if not moving. There were those weekend trips to Miami games and to Columbus. There was also a letter (which was still in my portmanteau after I left West Point in March of 1959). When I replied in March, 1922, to General MacArthur's invitation to be his aide, it began a correspondence that has continued for thirty-eight years. On December 30, 1924, the General wrote me from Manila, where he was Military Governor of the Philippines:

> Dear Blake:
> Thank you for sending the clippings with reference to Army football.
> I agree personally with what you say that the system of play at West Point is antiquated, too involved and totally lacking in flexibility and adaptiveness. Had I stayed at West Point, I intended introducing new blood into our coaching staff. Rockne of Notre Dame was the man I had in mind.
> McEwan is more modern than Daly and has had a good year.
> With sincere regards,
> Cordially, DOUGLAS MACARTHUR

(On the envelope, the General spelled the name Blaik.)

The letter which evoked the above reply suggests I had a compulsion to coach, at least from the grandstand. In the fall of 1924 and '25, I actually did get my hand in, when Coach Chet Pittser, of Miami, invited me up to Oxford to work with his ends. In a sense, I was one of those old grads who returned under the illusion that his presence would benefit the cause, a common malady in those days. I was never to accept such gratuitous gestures from old grads when I was a head coach, and I am embarrassed to think there was a time when I myself was guilty.

Late in the winter of 1926, I was given a strong push in the direction in which I was facing. A hobby, as a result, was to become an avocation. George Little came to visit one night in the house Merle and I had built at 1426 Cory Drive in Dayton View. George and I had seen each other occasionally, as our former coach-player relationship developed into friendship, and his wife, Helen Patterson Little, and Merle were girlhood good friends.

After serving in France, Little had resumed coaching as first assistant to Fielding H. Yost, celebrated head man at Michigan since 1901. Yost, known as "Hurry Up," his constant admonition to his players, was a leading coach and a fascinating character. He was an explosive enthusiast of seemingly bottomless energy with self-assurance to match, and he was not a very good listener. Grantland Rice, an old friend of Fielding's, used to love to recall a remark of that gifted sportswriter, author, and humorist, Ring Lardner.

"I asked Ring," said Granny, "if he ever had a conversation with Yost. 'No,' Ring replied. 'My parents taught me never to interrupt.'"

There were few interruptions of Michigan winning streaks in Yost's many prime years. Before he finally did give up coaching for keeps after the 1926 season, he made two false retirements. He actually did not coach the team in 1924, but more or less appointed himself an informal assistant, which he was able to do since he was also athletic director. That year George Little was nominal head coach at Michigan.

Little's 1924 team won six games, including Wisconsin, Minnesota, Northwestern, and Ohio State, and lost to Iowa, 9–2, and Illinois, 39–14. The Illinois game dedicated the new Stadium at Champaign-Urbana on October 18, and that was the day Harold (Red) Grange, the fabulous Illini halfback, made touchdown runs of 95, 75, 60, and 45 yards in the first twelve minutes and another of 11 yards in the last period. According to Little, Yost always claimed that he really coached Michigan that year, except in the Iowa and Illinois games. When Yost decided to become head coach in name again in 1925, Little was naturally glad to accept Wisconsin's offer to become athletic director and head football coach.

To understand what Little was walking into at Wisconsin, it is necessary to scan briefly the history and customs of the game at Madison. Wisconsin won the Western Conference championship outright in 1896 and '97, the first two years of that league's existence. The Badgers shared the title in 1901 and '06 and won it undisputedly again in 1912. When Little took over in 1924, however, as nominal head coach, thirteen years had gone by at Madison without a first place. Wisconsin had come awfully close in 1920, losing out to Ohio State on a pass in the last nine seconds. In 1923, at Madison, an unfortunate decision by an official had turned what probably would have been a 3–0 victory for Wisconsin into a 6–3 loss to Michigan and a post-game riot was narrowly averted.

It was, in sum, a testy, frustrated atmosphere which Little braved. His mandate was clear, total, unqualified. He was supposed to win the Big Ten championship, and the victims en route must include not only the No. 1 and No. 2 traditional rivals, Chicago and Minnesota, but Michigan and Iowa as well.

Little's 1925 Wisconsin team finished in a second-place tie with Northwestern in the Conference, Michigan winning. The Badger record was 6–1–1, their Conference totals, 3–1–1. They defeated Chicago, 20–7; were tied by Minnesota, 12–12; beat Iowa, 6–0; Purdue, 7–0; and lost to Michigan, 21–0.

A long touchdown pass thrown by quarterback Benny Friedman and a touchdown runback of the subsequent kick-off by Benny gave Michigan two of its three touchdowns within about two minutes of play. The third came on Friedman's pass to end Bennie Oosterbaan. The rest of the time Wisconsin outplayed Michigan, made several penetrations inside the Wolverine 20 and missed a touchdown on a pass dropped in the open.

In any event, losing to Michigan was no disgrace that year. Friedman and Oosterbaan were All Americans. The tough Wolverine defense allowed only three points all year, in their only defeat, 3–2, by Northwestern. Yost hailed this Michigan team as "the greatest I ever coached."

But Little had not delivered a championship and he had not beaten Minnesota and Michigan. He knew he would have to do better than that to hang on. He already had an able staff of assistants in Tom Lieb, Irv Uteritz, Edliff (Butch) Slaughter, Guy Sundt, and Glenn Holmes. Lieb was a former Notre Dame tackle, who would later assist Rockne. Uteritz, a brainy fellow, had won All America mention as 1922 Michigan quarterback. Slaughter had been an All America

Michigan guard in '24. Sundt, Wisconsin captain in 1921, later became athletic director and track coach. Holmes coached the freshmen and later carried on the winning tradition established at Oak Park (Illinois) High by Bob Zuppke, who went from that post to Illinois, and by his immediate successor Glenn Thistlethwaite, who moved up to Northwestern.

Little figured he could help himself by bringing me in to coach the ends and also help with the scouting. That was why he had come to see me at Cory Drive.

I wanted to help George out if I could, and I promised him I would talk it over with my father. I pointed out to Dad that I would be at Madison for only two months, beginning September 15, and by that time we would have accomplished our building and selling for the year. The idea did not overplease him, but he didn't stand in my way. He said it might help me get rid of some of my restlessness. So, after Labor Day, I packed a bag and went up to Madison. I lived at the University Club and received a $1500 salary, listed as "expenses."

We had a 5-2-1 record, 3-2-1 in the Conference. Michigan and Northwestern, each 5-0, finished first. We were outclassed by another Friedman-Oosterbaan team, 37-0. We beat Chicago, 14-7; Iowa, 20-10; Indiana, 27-7; and tied Purdue, 0-0.

Doyle Harmon, a hard-nosed halfback, was our team captain. Rollie Barnum, who played both halfback and fullback, was an outstanding all-around athlete in the Big Ten and retired only last fall from an equally fine career as an official. Other standout players were center Earl Wilke; guard Rube Wagner; tackles Austin Straubel, Bob Kasiska, and Lester (Butch) Leitl; quarterback Toad Crofoot, and backs Red Kreuz and Gene Rose.

Straubel, who came from a wealthy Green Bay family, chose to become a flyer rather than go into the family business. As an Air Force major he was shot down in the early days of World War II in the Java Sea area, and Green Bay's Straubel Airport is named in memory of his heroism.

We were hurt by the loss of our versatile senior, Lloyd Larson, who could play end, quarterback, or guard, but who had to sit out the season because of a late-summer knee injury in baseball, the only serious one of his athletic career. Lloyd is well known as the substantial sports editor of the Milwaukee *Sentinel*.

The game that deprived us of a clear claim on second place in the Conference and probably brought about the end of Little as head coach was the defeat by Minnesota at Wisconsin's Camp Randall Stadium.

The year before, the 12–12 tie with the Gophers at Minnesota had been such a rugged affair that it threatened a rupture of the series. Dr. Clarence W. (Fat) Spears, the Minnesota coach (and later coach at Wisconsin), taught strictly Spartan football, which he had first learned as an All America guard at Dartmouth under Major Frank W. Cavanaugh. Dr. Spears was a smart, articulate man, ostensibly cold, yet I later knew him to possess a warmth he revealed to a few. He probably gave his warm side a brief airing after our 1926 game. We had no license to win the game, yet we were sorely distressed over losing it and with strong reason.

We never did make a first down, yet we got ten points. We scored our touchdown peculiarly. Herb Joesting, the Minnesota fullback, fumbled and the ball bounced away crazily and ended up hopping into the hands of our end, Jeff Burrus, who was far from the origin of the play. Burrus, who was anything but fast, managed to beat everybody to the Minnesota goal line 85 yards away. (Burrus, a Rhodes scholar, later wrote an article attacking college football.) Our field goal was a placement from the 40-yard line by Butch Leitl, who only last June rounded out thirty-three years as athletic director at Wisconsin State College in Platteville.

Minnesota, which wound up with something like eighteen first downs, would still have lost, 10–9, except that with four minutes to go, Mally Nydahl, the Gopher right halfback, returned Barnum's longest punt of the day for 60 yards and a touchdown. The final score was Minnesota 16, Wisconsin 10.

From this bitter disappointment, we rallied well to defeat Burt Ingwersen's Iowa team, which had one of the best cutback runners I ever saw in Nick (Cowboy) Kutch. We then went down to Chicago, to finish the season with Mr. Amos Alonzo Stagg's team. There had been a heavy storm, and snow was banked along the sidelines and behind the end zone. I was eager to meet "The Grand Old Man of the Midway," and during pre-game practice managed to strike up a conversation with him. I asked him how he felt before a big game.

"I never worry about football," he replied. "I just take the attitude: 'Let the better team win.'"

Mr. Stagg's announced philosophy seemed to be belied by his obvious emotions in front of his bench as the game unrolled. We scored twice in the first quarter and went on to win, 14–7. Chicago rallied in the third quarter on a pass from Wally Marks to Kyle Anderson. The Maroon completed eleven of twenty-eight passes for 184 yards, something special for those days.

Merle was watching the game with Helen Little. George had told Helen she should never pray for victory, because it was wrong to be bothering God about football when He had so many other more important petitions to consider. Helen got around this by praying, "God give them sense," and included George.

We won, 14–7, but if God gave us the sense to do it, he apparently continued to withhold any from the obstreperous segments of Wisconsin die-hards. The defeat by Minnesota prompted many to write letters to Little. George would have been far better off to ignore them, but he was the type to try to mold the opinions of others to coincide with his own, instead of adopting the view that you are not going to change them, so why bother! He delegated me to answer most of these letters. Since I was representing George, my replies bore no relation to my thoughts.

The Madison papers also were taking a dyspeptic view of George's coaching, which upset him. The sentence fragments, especially, from the curiously droll typewriter of Roundy Coughlan dropped around his ears like literary flak.

George, however, definitely was not fired, although it is logical to assume that he would eventually have been forced to give up the football job. Anyhow, on a winter evening, he informed the athletic board that he was stepping out of coaching and would concentrate on being athletic director. He also recommended and had appointed as his successor Glenn Thistlethwaite, who had lifted Northwestern to the top of the Big Ten, yet was eager to leave there.

Thistlethwaite lasted five years, the longest of any Wisconsin coach from 1903 till 1941, but he could not deliver a championship either. It was not until 1952, under Ivan Williamson, that the Badgers won a share in the Big Ten title, and not until 1959 under Milt Bruhn that they won one outright. So, in far retrospect, Little's removing himself from the job did not materially affect Wisconsin's football fortunes.

While George was worrying his way through the 1925 and '26 seasons at Wisconsin with a precise selection of proper prayers, back at West Point a new coaching regime was beginning under Biff Jones, who had succeeded John McEwan. Two weeks before the Wisconsin-Chicago game, I received a letter from Biff, inviting me to be his guest at the Army-Navy game, which was to be played that year in Chicago's mammoth Soldier Field. The day before the game, I checked in at the Hotel Sherman.

The next morning, I was greatly surprised to see Knute Rockne in the Sherman lobby, because Notre Dame was scheduled to play Carnegie Tech in Pittsburgh that day. Rock had decided Carnegie would not menace his undefeated team. He was also eager to see Army-Navy, especially since he was doing a series of syndicated newspaper articles. So he had left the Irish in charge of his first assistant, Heartley (Hunk) Anderson.

It is not unlikely that Judge Wally Steffen, the Carnegie coach, included some mention of Rockne's absence in his pre-game address to the team. In any event, with Howie Harpster directing at quarterback, Carnegie upset the Irish, 19–0. You can imagine Rock's feelings when the score was relayed to him in his press-box seat at Soldier Field.

I don't know whether Knute's embarrassment was assuaged any by the caliber of game he watched that day, but it was a beauty to thrill the huge crowd of 111,000, who forgot the cold in the spectacle. Biff started Army's second team and Navy got off to a 14–0 lead, while Colonel Koehler, the old Master of the Sword, paced up and down the Army sidelines in a quiet rage. Then Army's first team came in. They had lost only one game, 7–0, to Notre Dame, on a 63-yard run by Christy Flanagan, a perfect "blackboard" off-tackle play. The Cadet first team was more than a match for the undefeated Midshipmen, who had given Michigan its only defeat, 10–0, in an ultrarugged game.

In the third period, with the score tied, 14–14, I saw a plebe halfback, helmet loose on his head, break off tackle, cut to the sidelines and speed 44 yards for the touchdown that put Army ahead. That was Red Cagle. Later, after Navy had scored its third touchdown, I watched a young quarterback calmly place-kick the extra point that earned Navy a 21–21 tie. That was Tom Hamilton.

After the game, I met Biff at his LaSalle Hotel headquarters. I also met for the first time his first assistant, Major Ralph Irvine Sasse. I smile now as I recall my initial reaction to Ralph. I thought him cold, arrogant, uppish, overmilitary. How wrong I was!

Biff took me aside and asked me if I could join his staff at West Point for the next fall. He wanted me to coach the passing game and do some scouting. He said he realized that offensive thinking was more advanced in the West than in the East. I had been exposed to it in the Big Ten and I would be given the chance to offer any ideas I might have.

I explained to Biff that my stint at Wisconsin had been only a temporary gesture to help out George Little, a friend, and that my business was building. He asked me to think it over. I told him that even if I should decide to give it a try, I would have to convince my father, and that would not be easy. It hadn't been too easy the first time. Biff said that if it would help, he would be glad to come out to Dayton and talk to Dad.

Biff did come out to Dayton the following January and huddled with my father. Dad finally concurred, but he told Biff in tones still shaded with a Scots burr, "I cannot understand why Earl would want to take time off from a prosperous and growing business to associate himself with the profession of coaching."

I assured Dad, and myself, too, that I would be going to West Point for one fall only. After what I had seen at Wisconsin, I was convinced football coaching was not so stable a pursuit as building houses, and scarcely a life's work to aspire to. Yet, there was a lot more satisfaction in helping to build a boy into a man than a building a house. Besides, West Point was my school and I owed it to her to accede to Biff's request.

If I was rationalizing, I certainly was not conscious of it. Coaching, I was convinced, was nothing more to me than a temporary avocation.

Chapter VI

The Golden Cutback

When Lawrence McCeney (Biff) Jones was head football coach at Louisiana State University from 1932 through '34, Senator Huey P. Long was "Kingfish." Senator Long's interest in L.S.U. football was normal for him, in other words, proprietary. Since Biff produced good teams, including a Southern Conference champion in 1932, his relations with Long were reasonably placid until the day Huey tried to invade the L.S.U. dressing room at halftime.

It was the final game of the 1934 season at Baton Rouge and L.S.U. was trailing Oregon, 13–0. Long labored under the illusion that what the team needed was the inspiration of a "Kingfish" political-type exhortation. Coach Jones had other ideas and ushered Long out. The next year, Biff was coaching at Oklahoma, but he had made his point.

During the same halftime recess, one of Biff's assistants, who may have been exposed at some time to Long's intemperate, florid oratory, stormed around the room, gesticulating and shouting, "We've got to win! We've got to win!" He even shook a zealous finger in Biff's face. "We've got to win!" he roared. Biff surveyed him dispassionately for a couple of seconds and then inquired, "Yes, my friend, but how?"

Those little halftime tableaux provide keys to the character and personality of Biff Jones and explain his success as coach at L.S.U. and as coach and athletic director at Army, Oklahoma, and Nebraska. The sense of order and organization, which Long failed to breach, was Biff's pre-eminent gift to every job he graced. The soft quietus he cast upon the overwrought assistant reveals the logical analyst. Biff appreciated the coaching verity that what a losing team needs at halftime is not an incendiary pep talk but a quick, keen explanation of why they are being beaten and what they can do about it. Once he had expelled Long and quelled the assistant, Biff went quickly to work with his team and so effectively that they rallied to beat Oregon, 14–13.

Biff's organization and analysis rubbed off on all of us privileged to work under him. He was assigned to the Academy year round as an Instructor of Field Artillery (McEwan had enjoyed the status of English Instructor) so he could keep in constant touch with the football situation. He worked at the job twelve months a year, although in those days there was no spring practice. His 1927 staff included Sasse, Babe Bryan, Johnny Stokes, Corley Hahn, Bill Wood, Roger Wicks, and myself. We held our staff meetings in the North Guardhouse where the west wing of North Barracks now stands. In 1928, we moved into the top floor of the South Gymnasium, our antique, dusty eyrie until the summer of 1958, when we occupied more updated offices in the North Gym.

The walls of the North Guardhouse in Biff's regime echoed many a strong debate. Biff would write FOR and AGAINST on the blackboard and list the arguments under each. We argued the merits of the traditional seven-man line and man-for-man defense on passes against the "newfangled" notion of a six-man line and the zone principle of pass defense. The West had been forced by its more advanced offenses to compensate with the newer defensive concepts, and the East had not yet caught up. But we were making progress. McEwan had broken with the classicism of the past, expressed in Charlie Daly's dictum: "There is only one way to play football, and that is the way we play it here."

Biff was searching for an offense measured to Army's personnel. He had used the Notre Dame shift from a T into a box in 1926. Now, the rules committee had decreed that the backs must come to a complete one-second stop after the shift. Many teams were to go on using this shift successfully for fifteen years after the restriction was written in. But Biff felt that the complete one-second stop had removed a big advantage from the shift in getting the jump on the defense.

I pushed hard to get Biff to install the Warner single-wing unbalanced-line attack, and he seriously considered it, but he finally decided on a short-punt setup behind a balanced line. Red Cagle was the deep back, 6 yards behind center, but he would often fade much deeper as he took the snap. Johnny Murrell, the fullback, was set 3 yards behind the left guard for quick-opening smashes. "Light Horse" Harry Wilson, the right halfback, was posted 3 yards behind the right guard and could be employed on spin plays. The quarterback, William (Spike) Nave, one of the first colonels to be killed in World War II, lined up as wingback a yard behind the right end. The right half and the quarterback could switch positions according to the play called.

This was a practical and exciting formation, calculated to exploit fully the marvelous running and passing ability of Christian Keener Cagle, who must rate with Doc Blanchard and Glenn Davis as the three greatest backs I ever coached. I doubt there was ever a more thrilling back to watch than Red Cagle. He was born in De Ridder, Louisiana, May 1, 1905. Before entering the Academy in 1926, he had been the nation's fifth highest scorer at Southwestern Louisiana Institute.

Those who saw Cagle play can see him just as clearly today, I am certain, across the three decades. He ran with speed, power, elusiveness—and great instinct. He was equally dangerous to right or left. As a cutback artist, he was superb. He ran with long strides, and like all the best cutback runners I've known, he had flat feet. He was dynamic on the option run or pass. He might fake once, twice, three times before throwing the ball or tucking it away and taking off.

If tacklers threatened to inundate him, he broke away from them in backward diagonals until he could enflank or otherwise elude them and turn up the field again. He knew how to spread the defense all over the field, and when he had them spread, how he could cut them up!

Red wore his chin strap hanging loose, a concession to an experience in which a tackler had yanked the helmet off him and he had thought his head was coming with it. That was why, while playing hare and hounds with tacklers, Cagle often lost his helmet. The roaring crowd would roar even louder at the familiar sight of his crisp, curly auburn hair. A handsome lad he was. Not that they needed to see the hair or even his No. 12 to know who it was. From the moment he took the snap and began moving, there could be no mistaking him.

When I say I coached Cagle, it was merely to make the comparison with Blanchard and Davis. There was nothing much I could give him. He had it all. If there was some little point to make to him, I had only to tell him once, because he had a naturally absorbtive football mind.

He also possessed the truly gifted player's instinct for teamwork, and threw his 178 pounds and five feet eleven inches into hard blocking and tackling. I recall a practice turning sour one night because our wingback was permitting the tackle to burst through repeatedly and down Cagle. Red grew increasingly, if quietly, irritated. Finally he switched positions with the wingback and showed him how to block the tackle.

Cagle was a quiet, modest fellow with a fine sense of humor, by preference a listener more than a talker. He must have had an awareness of his truly exceptional ability, but he always kept it to himself. I think it was this genuine modesty, added to his talent, that made him even a bigger man to his teammates and opponents than he was to the sellout crowds and the press that hailed him.

When we beat Navy, 14–9, at the Polo Grounds in 1927, Cagle sparked the drives, but Harry Wilson scored the touchdowns. It was the last game for Wilson, captain of the team, and when the ball got near the goal line, Cagle refused to carry. "Wilson," Red told Spike Nave, "scores the touchdowns today."

In his prime, Light Horse Harry Wilson was just about as great a player as Cagle. He was not exceptionally fast, but he ran with beautiful balance. Before entering West Point in 1924, he was a brilliant halfback at Penn State under Coach Hugo Bezdek, from 1921 through '23. When the Nittany Lions beat Navy's Rose Bowl team, 21–3, in 1923, Wilson scored all three touchdowns, on a 95-yard kick-off return, an 85-yard run from scrimmage, and a 55-yard return of a pass interception. That same year, he also scored all three touchdowns in a 21–0 victory over Pennsylvania on runs of 49, 45, and 25 yards.

The normal attrition of the game and a bad back slowed Wilson down somewhat near the end of his four seasons at Army, but he had already contributed notably to victories over Navy, Notre Dame, and Yale. Like Cagle, Wilson was an all-around natural, a quiet, kindly fellow, liked by everybody. I don't believe any Army backfield had two such men until that time, although some old grads might well argue for Elmer Oliphant and Gene Vidal of the 1916 team.

Since I coached the passing game, both on offense and defense, I spent much time with the ends, Charles Born, Norris (Skippy) Harbold, and Sam Brentnall. Chuck Born had won All America honors as a yearling in 1925. All three were good pass receivers, especially Brentnall.

Biff usually put me on the phones for the big games. I also scouted and, in 1927, I scouted Yale. In those days, Yale could play with anybody and that '27 team, the last coached by Tad Jones, was its best of the 'twenties, excepting only the 1923 team, which most Old Blues regard as the finest in the school's history. Yale's 1927 line, however, may have been even stronger than that of '23. The '27 Yales lost only to Georgia, 14–10, after dominating much of the game. Led by their brilliant halfback, Bruce Caldwell, they beat us, 10–6, in a stirring fight. Cagle's pass to Harbold set up our touchdown on a plunge by Murrell.

As all football enthusiasts are aware, comparative scores can be as misleading as a confidence man. That '27 season offers an interesting example. Notre Dame beat Georgia Tech, 26–7; Georgia Tech beat Georgia, 12–0; Georgia beat Yale, 14–10; Yale beat Army, 10–6; and Army beat Notre Dame, 18–0.

That was a strong Irish team, which lost no other game, but Cagle was never better as he cut them to pieces in Yankee Stadium. He ran 48 yards for one touchdown, caught an 18-yard pass from halfback Dick Hutchinson and ran 15 for another. A third was tallied on an interception and 60-yard runback by Spike Nave.

Our '27 team ended with a 9–1 record, probably was Army's strongest since 1916, and was rated with Yale and Pittsburgh at the top in the East. I believe we would have acquitted ourselves well against the best of any section.

Another strong team was shaping up for 1928 and Biff did not have to be too persuasive to talk me into one more year. It meant another trip to Dayton for Biff. This time it took him three days to crack my father. For all Dad's resistance, I suspect he was aware of the '27 Army record and proud of the part I had in it.

During Biff's visit, we arranged a golf foursome at the Dayton Country Club. Unbeknownst to Biff, we plotted with the club pro to inform us on our arrival that one of the foursome had phoned to say he couldn't make it. Also by prearrangement, an attractive young lady was sitting on the clubhouse veranda. She happened to be Jean Davis, daughter of my friend Jim Davis, and Dayton's Woman Amateur Golf runner-up. Biff, of course, did not know this either.

In what appeared to be a surprising gesture for one who likes to win, I offered to introduce myself to the young lady and ask her to fill out the foursome as my partner if that was all right with Biff. That was fine with Biff. After all, he doubtless concluded, the girl was not only attractive; she probably couldn't play for sour apples. I "introduced" myself to Miss Davis and she accepted our invitation with suitable deprecatory remarks about her game. She then proceeded to play par golf. As Biff's eyes grew wider and wider, so did his slices. By the fourth hole, Biff knew he had been taken, and his powers of analysis correctly deduced the plot.

Practical jokes among coaches are fine after a winning season. After a losing campaign, they are futile and hollow. That off-season we were relaxed and carefree. It was a young and good time in my life. Merle and I were proud parents. Bill, the older of our two boys, had arrived on April 25, 1927.

Bill has considerable interest in football and hockey, but his sports participation has been mainly in hunting and fishing. He is a Dartmouth graduate, a geologist, and now runs his own oil exploration company out of Oklahoma City, the Blaik Oil Co.

It was fun during that visit of Biff to Dayton to relive the 1927 season and look forward to '28. Some of our talk centered around the breakoff of Army-Navy football relations the previous December 3. As it developed, the old rivals would be playing again by 1930, but in '28 the prospect of future games was slim.

The break was caused by Army's refusal to accede to Navy's

demand that participation in the service game be restricted to men who had not played three years of intercollegiate football. Navy did not want us to use players who had already played from one to three years at other colleges. In the last six games with the Cadets, the Midshipmen had done no better than ties in 1923 and 1926. Army victories were owed considerably to Ed Garbisch, outstanding All America center and place-kicker from Washington and Jefferson (his four drop kicks accounted for the 12–0 triumph over the Middies in 1924); to Wilson from Penn State; Cagle from Southwestern Louisiana Institute; Mortimer E. (Bud) Sprague, tackle from Southern Methodist; Nave from Iowa State; and Murrell from Minnesota.

If Army had acceded to Navy's request, Captain-elect Sprague, Cagle, Murrell, and Nave would not have been able to play in the 1928 service game.

This issue had been argued as far back as 1903, with Charlie Daly, who had quarterbacked Harvard for three years before coming to West Point, the reason for it. Army stood fast. Navy set the stage for reopening the question by adopting the three-year rule in June, 1927.

In 1926, Army and Navy signed a general four-year contract. On December 3, 1927, however, Admiral Louis M. Nulton, Annapolis Superintendent, requested that West Point add to the contract for the 1928 game a clause stipulating that "no contestant shall take part in this game on either team who has had three years' experience in intercollegiate football." Admiral Nulton added that Army's refusal to accede to the request would be considered "rejection of the contract and the Naval Academy will consider itself free to schedule another game on November 24, 1928." Major General Edwin B. Winans, Army Superintendent, refused, invoking the position set forth back in 1903 that any cadet not debarred by studies or conduct was eligible to represent the Academy in any contest.

It was not until 1938 that Army accepted the three-year rule, and then it was under an order from the Commander-in-Chief, Franklin D. Roosevelt, who had at one time been Assistant Secretary of the Navy. F.D.R. slipped a penciled note to General Edwin M. (Pa) Watson, West Point 1908, then military aid to the White House, which read, "From now on West Point will abide by the three-year rule." And that was that.

Even without F.D.R.'s action, Army inevitably would have adopted the three-year rule. It should also be understood that there was justification in Army playing these men from other colleges. They were needed to meet Navy, Notre Dame, Yale, Harvard, and other major opponents on approximately even terms. The normal athletic material we had to draw from was below the caliber of the major civilian schools. Our authorized number of cadets from 1927 through 1933 was 1,374. This ranged from 177 to 683 fewer than Navy.

Most important, however, the great majority of these men who played at other colleges wanted the service, stayed in it, and made outstanding records. Many gave their lives. True, they found attractive the prospect of extending their football days at the Point, but the record proves their basic motivation was their desire to become officers.

Although no Army football picture could ever be complete without Navy, the absence of the Midshipmen from the 1928 schedule, paradoxically, contributed to one of the most exciting and, on the whole, satisfying seasons in the annals of the game at the Point.

It exuded a special extravaganza flavor, keyed to the theme of the roaring 'twenties and the golden cutback of Red Cagle.

It also was a perfect fit to the mood and means of a graduate manager of athletics like Major Philip B. Fleming. Shrewd, debonair, expansive, imaginative, Fleming had been appointed to the job two months before the break with Navy. To compensate for the absence of the Midshipmen, he signed a four-year agreement with Harvard, which had been missing from Army's schedule since 1910, arranged home-and-home games with Stanford and Illinois, and brought Southern Methodist and Nebraska to Michie Stadium.

The 1928 schedule included Southern Methodist, Harvard, Yale, Notre Dame, Nebraska, and Stanford. This array was regarded with somber qualm by many West Point traditionalists. Not too many years before, Charlie Daly had expatiated on the impossibility of preparing an Army team to cope successfully with Notre Dame in early October, Yale at a midseason spot, and Navy in the finale. What

Phil Fleming had wrought for '28 was considered to verge on recklessness, if not lunacy.

There was a tendency in some quarters of our coaching staff to underestimate Southern Methodist. The growth of the game in the Southwest Conference had not yet been fully apprehended through the normal fog of seaboard insularism. Biff, however, was not misled, and dispatched me to Dallas to scout S.M.U.

There was no reason for the Mustangs to reveal their hand in winning a warm-up game from Howard Payne, 31-0. Knowledge of my presence may have accounted for their sending the team onto the field for the second half in different-colored jerseys with a new set of numbers. I could still tell they had a fine team, expertly coached by Ray Morrison, fundamentally sound, and dazzling in their staccato passing attack. Their star back, Redman Hume, was just about as dangerous a runner and passer as he claimed to be.

The Mustangs arrived at Michie Stadium with a large support of rooters, their famous jazz band and the first girl cheerleaders, to my knowledge, ever to encroach on the Plain; if the Academy physics department had owned a seismograph station, slight tremors might well have been recorded from the area of the statue of General Sylvanus Thayer, founder of West Point.

We managed to edge the Mustangs, 14-13, in a hair-raiser, with Redman Hume, Cagle, Ed Messinger (who was developing into a star end for the Cadets), Bud Sprague, in fact everybody, putting on a spectacular show. Southern Methodist convinced the East for keeps that they were now playing big-league college football in Texas. Between halves, a Colonel Fred McJunkin from Texas got on the loud-speaker and invited all of us to come down there as his guests, and he did not exclude the plebes. That was the only reciprocal hospitality, however, that was extended to us by our colorful opponents.

Our 15-0 victory at Harvard two weeks later represented Army's first football visit to Cambridge and its first victory in fourteen tries against the school, which, next to Yale, had done most to help condition the early growth of the game at the Point. In our 18-6 triumph in Yale Bowl the next week, Cagle exploded with 51- and 75-yard touchdown runs from scrimmage, one on an end sweep, one on a tackle cutback. Red's flair for the long run and pass was irresistible. We were playing to sellouts every week: 55,000 at Cambridge, 78,000 at New Haven, 85,000 in Yankee Stadium for the Notre Dame game.

We were undefeated and favored to beat the Irish. They were in a formative year and had lost three games: to Wisconsin, Navy, and Georgia Tech. Rockne had not delivered an undefeated season since 1924, and there was some disquietude discernible at South Bend. I was scouting the Irish at old Cartier Field (this was two years before Notre Dame Stadium was opened). Coming down through the stands after the game with Graham McNamee, first of the "name" radio sports announcers, I could not help hearing two Notre Dame fathers discuss Rockne. They appeared to be in agreement that he had been all right in his day, but had lost his touch. Rock disproved this theory emphatically with his undefeated national champions of 1929 and '30, before a Kansas plane crash snuffed out his life on March 31, 1931.

Many of Rockne's 1929 and '30 stars were on that '28 team. They had not reached full development, but, as usual, they played inspirationally against Army. They rallied in the second half, to win, 13–12. Cagle was magnificent. Often the truly great player will achieve some of his finest moments in defeat. After a scoreless first half, Red scored our first touchdown on a 19-yard run and set up the other on a 39-yard pass to Messinger. Then, after Notre Dame took the lead on two valorous drives, Cagle struck back at them furiously. He returned the kick-off from our goal line to their 35, almost getting away. He swept end for 21 yards to their 14. But by then, he had literally played himself into exhaustion and we had to help him from the field. A short pass from Hutchinson to Allan and then a 3-yard smash by Hutchinson brought the ball to Notre Dame's 1-yard line. Before we could line up again, time ran out. What a tough one to lose!

Defeat should always teach us something and we absorbed a valuable lesson from that 1928 Notre Dame game. Like most Eastern teams, Army had clung to the man-for-man pass defense. In the man-for-man, each defensive secondary covers one of the eligible receivers and stays with him no matter where he goes in the pass pattern. The main argument in its favor is that each man will be certain what potential receiver he is responsible for.

The flaw in this argument is that certain knowledge of whom you are to cover is meaningless unless you can cover him. In the zone defense, in which each defender covers an area of the field and plays the ball, the receiver finds it more difficult to maneuver himself into the open, especially on the long, "home run" pass. It is, of course, necessary at times to apply a man-for-man modification to the zone principle when two or more receivers "flood" one area.

In that '28 Notre Dame game, the Irish made the winning touchdown on a fourth-down pass, starting with the ball on our 32-yard line. Halfback Johnny Niemiec threw it to end Johnny O'Brien, who made a tumbling, fumbling grab in the end zone. He was sent in for that one play, was removed immediately afterwards and is thus remembered in Notre Dame lore as "One Play" O'Brien. It is possible that if we had defended with a zone, O'Brien would have continued to be known as just plain Johnny. On the other hand, he might still have become "One Play." The point is, O'Brien taught us painfully that, henceforth, we should use a zone.

All defeats are indigestible. The worst, however, are those which are "upsets" and also spoil a clean record. The 13–12 loss to Notre Dame left us lower than a coal mine in Hades, but our period of mourning was necessarily abbreviated. Nebraska, our next foe, was to win the Big Six title in 1928, first year of the existence of that conference. The week before they engaged us, the big combative Cornhuskers played a scoreless tie with the abrasive Pittsburgh Panthers of Dr. John Bain (Jock) Sutherland. Ralph Sasse scouted the 'Huskers and his report on them scared us half to death.

I don't think any game in the history of Michie Stadium up until that time engendered such enthusiasm. I can look back now and see those Nebraska rooters, marching behind their band up the road to Lusk Reservoir, gay with their red and white pennants, their lunches, their keen anticipation of seeing the team of which they were so proud play the Cadets. I suspect that college football, like all sports of the 'twenties, did, indeed, breed an exuberance perhaps never to be matched—and that's a pity.

What a battle it was! To win it, to hand this Nebraska team its only defeat of the year, Army came up with one of the finest games it has ever played in Michie Stadium. The big 'Husker line, led by guard Dan McMullen, who was built like Tony Galento and was all over the field, begrudged us every yard. In the first half, Cagle's running and his passing to Messinger and wingback Dick O'Keefe repeatedly stormed their redoubts, but we could not crack them.

Nebraska had two excellent backs in Clair Sloan and Edward (Blue) Howell. Sloan was a halfback. Howell was a fullback except for our game, when Coach Ernest Bearg played him at quarterback, presumably for his blocking ability, and had him write the signals on his pants so he could remember them. Near the end of the first half, Howell and Sloan, behind their big line, worked the ball to our 10, and Sloan drop-kicked a field goal to give them a 3–0 lead.

Few teams, however, ever completely contained Cagle. In the third quarter he hit Messinger with a 28-yard pass to their 32. We then called a play we seldom used. From the short punt, Cagle took the snap from center and headed toward Nebraska's left tackle. O'Keefe, from wingback, reversed to his left. As he passed behind Cagle, Red faked to slip him the ball, but kept it and hid it behind his back. The "bootlegging" fooled the Nebraska left side long enough to get them overcommitted and give Cagle the little daylight he needed. He raced down the sidelines for a touchdown that was enough to win. Near the end, with darkness beginning to envelop the field, Hutchinson threw a scoring pass to Charlie Allan and the final was 13–3.

So we carried a solid 8–1 record, that could easily have been 9–0, into our final game with Stanford in Yankee Stadium. The Indians from Palo Alto beat us, 26–0. Not only the score, but everything about that game was anticlimactic from our viewpoint. We had been through the toughest season any Cadet team ever experienced. Nebraska had exacted heavy physical toll. Even if we had been physically primed, however, we could not have handled that Stanford team of Glenn Scobey Warner.

To my mind, Pop Warner was the most creative of all the coaching geniuses. He was a man of few but positive words. His wonderful hands, which made carving seem for him a natural hobby, reflected his probing mind. He liked to tinker and come up with new ideas. He gave football both the single-wing and double-wing attacks. The idea of lining up a back on each wing for an occasional pass had been used by more than one coach, but Warner was the first to put in the fullback-spin element, with the trap series, the reverse, and the double reverse. As he aligned and developed it, the double-wingback formation was something absolutely new.

Eventually, when the defenses learned to crash their men into the running lanes, the double-wing was slowed down and driven out of business. But in its heyday of the late 'twenties and early 'thirties under Warner and the comparably canny Andy Kerr at Colgate, who had once been Pop's assistant at Pittsburgh, the double-wing was effective and beautiful to watch. That day in Yankee Stadium, we simply did not know how to cope with it. Stanford gained 383 yards rushing against us, a truly phenomenal total for those days when ground yardage was far less easily come by.

Even in a show so dominated by Stanford, Cagle could not be eclipsed. On a 65-yard run, he reversed his field and eluded every Stanford player at least once and some twice. It prompted the comment: "Red ran to Newark and back on that one."

We again profited from defeat in that Stanford game. As welcome guests of Pop Warner at Stanford the following spring practice in 1929, Army assistant coaches Ralph Sasse and Harry Ellinger, and Lieutenant Russell P. (Red) Reeder—later an assistant coach but then on tour of duty at the Presidio in San Francisco—studied the double-wing attack. Biff installed it with the 1929 plebe team, and by 1930 the varsity was using it.

The Stanford game also taught a sharp business lesson to the Yankee Stadium management. By playing the Stadium against the Polo Grounds, the enterprising Fleming had negotiated a flat $15,000 rental fee. A jam crowd of 88,000 contributed receipts of $340,000. Army and Stanford each took home $150,000. The division of the receipts left the Stadium people displeased and in a mood to listen to Ray McCarthy, advertising man and promoter. McCarthy sold the

Stadium and Polo Grounds on joining forces as a single lessor for College football with a flat 25-per-cent rental arrangement.

If the Army Athletic Association was making a lot of money, it was also spending it freely. The spirit of the times was freewheeling. Fleming and his public relations officer, the highly regarded and capable Captain Walter (Cappy) Wells, appreciated that in these Army teams sparked by Red Cagle they had something that stood out even in the 'twenties, and they missed no opportunity to publicize it. They entertained the press lavishly. Army never made or got better copy, although the writers as a whole always have been generous in their treatment of us. The sportscasters have been equally kind to us— Ted Husing, Red Barber, Mel Allen, Stan Lomax, Walter Kennedy, now mayor of Stamford, Connecticut, and a host of others.

The freewheeling philosophy carried over somewhat into training, mainly because so many of the players were older than those of later teams. This contributed in part to our mediocre 1929 season. There were other factors. "Senioritis," or "first-class complacency," as it is known at the Point, infected some of our players. Cagle was hindered by a bad shoulder and there were other costly injuries. The breaks, as they usually do in such a season, ran against us. We were also playing some fine teams. September talk had us going undefeated. As it was, our best major-game effort was a 20–20 tie at Harvard. We lost to Yale, 21–13; Illinois, 17–7; Notre Dame, 7–0; and Stanford, 34–14.

Even in defeat, we helped make startling headlines. Harvard tied us on a last-minute pass in the gloaming by the celebrated quarterback, Barry Wood. Cagle, after a hazardous first half, was brilliant in 30- and 45-yard scoring runs.

The next week, in Yale Bowl, Red intercepted a pass and ran 50 yards for a score. Murrell got loose through center for 25 yards and another. We had a 13–0 lead and it looked easy. What happened from then on was no less unbelievable and crushing to us than if nearby West Rock had moved over and fallen on the bowl.

Mal Stevens, the Yale coach, took the blanket off a five-foot-seven, 144-pound New Haven townsman named Albert James Booth, and for that afternoon Little Albie out-Cagled Red. Booth scored three touchdowns, one on a 75-yard punt return that had our tacklers bumping into one another and excusing themselves. He drop-kicked all three extra points. He carried the ball 33 times for 223 yards. He did the punting. He called the plays. If ever one man beat a team all by himself, Albie Booth did it that day, 21–13. Nothing like it ever has been seen in Yale Bowl before or since, nor, I suspect, ever will be again.

Booth was not only a great football player and all-around athlete, but a true competitor and sportsman, an example of the very finest the game can produce. In later years, his work as a football official was equally outstanding.

We were beaten at Illinois on an 8-yard punt that bounced crazily to our rear and a long run of an intercepted lateral. Our touchdown came on Cagle's passes to Messinger and O'Keefe and his running. Red was to make All America for the third straight year, and nobody debated it.

Notre Dame offered us a bright chance to redeem much of the season. Rockne's team had stormed unbeaten through Indiana, Navy, Wisconsin, Carnegie Tech, Georgia Tech, Drake, Southern California, and Northwestern, en route to the national championship.

That Saturday, November 30, 1929, was as bitterly cold and windy a football day as I can recall; it was seven degrees above zero. The Yankee Stadium turf was frozen solid. A congealed sellout crowd sought relief in bottles. There were sufficient empties borne away by garbage trucks after the game to decorate several city dumps, and the way we felt over the outcome, we could well have ridden along with them.

We went the sixty minutes with eleven men: Messinger and Carl Carlmark, ends; George (Buster) Perry and Jack Prince, tackles; Charles (Polly) Humber and Loren Hillsinger, guards; Paul Miller, center; Robert (Rosy) Carver, quarterback; Cagle and Hutchinson, halfbacks; and Murrell, fullback. They were great in by far our best game of the year. Yet we lost it, 7–0.

The Notre Dame score came in the second quarter. Price, a yearling but already a standout tackle, blocked quarterback Frank Carideo's kick and we recovered on their 13. With third and 8 on their

11, Cagle swung out to his right, whirled suddenly and whipped a crossfield pass to Carlmark, who was in the clear. But a gale of wind held up the ball just long enough for it to be picked off by Notre Dame's defensive left halfback. He happened to be Jack Elder, who held the world's sprint record for 60 yards. Elder flew unerringly 95 yards down the field with that ball as if set on establishing another record mark—and with him flew the ball game.

Biff Jones could have said with real justification that he certainly did not get the best of the breaks against Notre Dame. Christy Flanigan's long run beat him in '26, the clock ran out on him in '28, and now there was the Elder interception in '29.

We closed out the season with Army's first cross-country football excursion. The times, to repeat, were liberal and comfortable, even though traditionalists were shaking their heads over Phil Fleming and muttering about commitment papers to some suitable institution. On December 18, at 3:00 P.M., proceeding under Special Orders No. 285, seven Pullmans, packed with varsity, "B" Squad and plebe players, coaches, officers, and newspapermen, left West Point for San Francisco and the Stanford game.

The writers found no dearth of stories on the journey. A snowstorm outside Chicago held us up for several hours. We held one workout at Hutchinson, Kansas, another someplace on the Arizona desert. We were observed there by an inscrutable Indian, perhaps one of Pop Warner's scouts. Cagle almost disappeared from sight chasing a jack rabbit.

Next to the last night on the train, Ralph Sasse tipped the porter to hide the shoes of everybody in the last two cars. When we pulled into Los Angeles, en route to Palo Alto, in the morning, anybody who didn't have an extra pair of shoes with him was in dire straits. One such was Red Reeder, who had been a drop-kick artist and first baseman of major-league potential at the Academy, and was now on the coaching staff. Red was forced to leave the train in a pair of beaded Indian moccasins. This earned him a glacial stare from the Academy Superintendent, General William R. Smith, whose unswerving devotion to the Volstead Act caused him to be known as "Sahara Bill."

There was much less fun in the Stanford game itself. Despite his shoulder, Cagle kept us in it for a half, but we ran out of gas. In the second half, Red's shoulder got so bad he had to leave the game. It was a shock to realize that we were never going to see him carry the ball for the Army again.

After that, it was pretty much downhill for Red. The following May he was forced to resign from the Academy, when it was discovered he had been married since the summer of 1928 to his sweetheart of Southwestern Louisiana days.

Though Red said nothing about it, those who were closest to him agree he remained unhappy because he did not graduate and get his commission. He wanted to be in the Army, and he was restless away from it. When he tried to get into World War II as an officer, the War Department refused him a commission. It was a needless, callous attitude. Cagle had the desire and the qualifications to be a fine leader of troops and he was a decent man. Tragedy continued to pursue and finally to catch him, for on December 23, 1942, at the age of thirty-seven, he died as the result of a skull fracture incurred in a fall down a New York subway stairs.

The 1929 season was my fourth as "temporary" part-time coach. The previous winter, Biff Jones had visited us at Dayton again, to gain my father's acquiescence. That time, Biff was surprised to meet with somewhat less resistance than before.

"I guess you might as well take him and keep him," Dad said. "He doesn't seem to be able to concentrate very well on the construction and real-estate business. Several weeks ago, I gave him a business problem to wrestle with. He retired to the privacy of our conference room for better concentration.

"After several hours, I went back to get the solution. I noticed several sheets covered with X's and O's. They meant nothing to me. 'What's this to do with our business?' I asked him.

" 'It's football,' he said."

Chapter VII

The Whip

The first American combat officer to step on the soil of France in World War I—it was on June 29, 1917—was Lieutenant Ralph Irvine Sasse (pronounced Sass-ee), West Point, Class of 1916. Sasse commanded the 301st Heavy Tank Battalion in the First Infantry Division, operating in the British sector of the Western Front. He was wounded, decorated with the British Distinguished Service Order for gallantry, rose to major, and became recognized as the ranking tank-warfare expert in the United States Army.

Sasse's men not only respected but idolized him to a degree accorded few combat leaders. That was also the way of it with his Army football teams from 1930 through '32. Sasse inspired them to carry the field. Handsome, impressive, dramatic, sincere, Ralph was the equal in dressing-room eloquence of such storied football orators of the era as Princeton's Bill Roper, Knute Rockne, Frank Cavanaugh of Boston College and Fordham, and Bob Zuppke of Illinois. When Sasse took the head-coach job, he told the Corps: "I promise you fireworks!" He made good the promise. He hopped up his teams and kept them that way. They charged down the gridiron with the dash and fire of J. E. B. Stuart's cavalry.

It was as Major Sasse's football chief of staff that I had forcibly brought home to me the first axiom of head-coaching success. If the head coach is a leader, he need not be the comprehensive master of strategy and tactics. He can delegate those responsibilities to others. But unless he can lead, he may know the book by rote and still be nothing.

Sasse came to West Point from his native Wilmington, Delaware. He had been active in hockey, basketball, and polo, as well as football, but it was football he loved best. A knee injury, incurred in leaping a fence, prevented him from winning his letter as an end, but could not keep him out of uniform. So intense was his devotion to the game, he continued to offer himself as a chopping block for the tackles in the Pot Graves "blood drills."

After the Armistice, Sasse served with the Army of Occupation, returned to the United States in March of 1919, took the course at the Fort Riley Cavalry School and was a Distinguished Graduate of the Command and General Staff College at Fort Leavenworth. In 1923, he was assigned to West Point, first as an Instructor for one year and then as an Assistant Professor of Drawing under Colonel Roger Alexander. Colonel Alexander stated that Ralph was his most valuable teacher, because the force of his personality could bring excitement to an essentially dry subject like map-making.

Sasse was even more compelling, and entertaining, too, when he put the trainers and doctors out of the dressing room and talked to the players and the assistant coaches about the Navy. "The boys from Crabtown," he called them. As he declaimed, he would walk around the room, savagely kicking aside stray paper cups or anything else in his path. Then almost invariably at the end of his pep talk, his voice would lower to a sentimental warmth and his head would turn slowly to include everybody.

"There isn't a man in this room," he would say, "that I wouldn't be proud to have for my own son!"

I never knew a man, in football or out, for whom I experienced a stronger feeling of friendship than Ralph Sasse, and he came to regard me as his best friend. Our relationship took root in our common cavalry background and our belief in football as the game closest to warfare.

I was maintaining bachelor quarters in Cullum Hall along with others of the staff. Merle could not be with me at West Point in those years. She was plenty busy at home in Dayton with Bill, now a normal handful as a three-year-old, and our second son, Robert McDowell Blaik, who had arrived on May 22, 1929.

West Point bachelor ranks constituted a far larger company in those days. The football coaching staff alone included Lieutenants Babe Bryan, Johnny Stokes, Emmett (Rosy) O'Donnell, Red Reeder,

Maurice F. (Moe) Daly, Gar Davidson, and civilian grad Harry Ellinger. Our Cullum Hall quarters were adjacent to the Officers Club, where we often played chess, pool, and bridge in the evenings.

The best bridge player on the Post was an Instructor in Chemistry, Lieutenant Al Gruenther, whose skill had him in constant demand to referee national tournaments in New York. Later, General Gruenther was Chief of Staff to General Mark Clark and is now head of the American Red Cross.

We had occasional mild brushes with the punctilio and swank of the old Army. Supper at the Officers Club was quite the apotheosis of militaristic etiquette. The Club was, in those days, as rigidly out of bounds to women as to Hottentots. The bachelors' mess was a long table, of seemly mid-Victorian appointments, seating some fifty, dinner jackets *de rigueur,* and presided over by a dedicated bachelor in his fifties, Colonel Charles P. Echols.

As head of the mathematics department, abode of the West Point academic seraphs, Colonel Echols was ex officio and per se the intellectual colossus of the Post. He was also an iron autocrat, who had been known to challenge even the divinity of Superintendents. Any bachelor who violated the unswerving punctuality of the seven-o'clock supper hour had to march to the head of the table and present himself to Colonel Echols before being permitted to take his seat. When soup was served, the entire group held spoons at the ready, and followed the first dip by the Colonel like captive oarsmen obeying the stern signal of their galley captain.

Early one evening, we stood outside the Officers Club, awaiting the arrival of Colonel Echols in his new Franklin. (He had turned in his old Franklin, which in ten years he probably had not driven over 5,000 miles. He was hardly an automotive Burton Holmes.) Presently, the Colonel drove up. There was a no-traffic sign in the middle of the road, because cars in the area were restricted. For some reason, the Colonel did not drive into the usual parking space, but elected to back the new Franklin against the curb in front of the Club. In so doing, he latched the rear onto the no-traffic sign. The screeching of metal and concrete was hilarious to us onlookers.

To Colonel Echols, however, it was a nightmare compounded of horrible noise and wretched awareness of what was happening to his new Franklin. His state of mind caused him to step on the accelerator instead of the brake. The car shot backwards at startlingly increased speed for what seemed all of 100 yards, and finally scraped to a stop. Mustering what control we could, we approached to watch Colonel Echols emerge and inspect the damage. The car and the no-traffic sign were hopelessly entangled. All Colonel Echols did was cluck his tongue a few times. Then he stalked off into the Club.

The Colonel had taken his place at the head of the bachelors' table and we had seated ourselves after him, when in walked a young lieutenant named Hamilton, who was a congenial, though sometimes argumentative soul. Since his rank placed him below the salt, he had to make the long walk to the head of the table to salute Colonel Echols and make excuse for his tardiness. At that moment, none of us, including the Colonel, realized that Lieutenant Hamilton was slightly in his cups. Soon after he took his place, however, he got into a loud debate with a nearby officer. Just as we were about to dip our soup spoons in time with Colonel Echols, we heard the Lieutenant's raised voice. The Colonel rested his oar and in his high-pitched tones called out to the miscreant, "Mr. Hamilton—Mr. Hamilton. . . ."

At first, the Colonel's voice did not register with the Lieutenant. When it finally did get through, Hamilton stood up, saluted, and said, "Yes sir, Colonel!"

"You have completed your dinner, Mr. Hamilton," said the Colonel. "You have finished! You may be excused!"

With that, the Lieutenant, soup untouched, saluted, executed an about face, and marched out of the mess—perhaps, to a well-earned Scotch and soda.

The Post social bible dictated that an officer or civilian graduate in such positions as Ellinger and myself, pay one formal call a year on the Superintendent. We assistant coaches who were unmarried or did not have our wives with us, usually called in a group. A dress uniform or dinner jacket was required, as well as two calling cards, one for the Supe and one for his wife. The cards were left on the hall tray. If the Superintendent was "at home," a living-room soiree ensued, usually lasting fifteen minutes. If the Supe was not "at home," the cards were eased under the door. In either case, propriety was observed.

Absorption in 1932 fall practice caused us assistant coaches to forget to pay our respects to Major General William D. (Katy) Connor, who had become Superintendent the previous May. A memorandum advised us to rectify the matter. General Connor, who had an outstanding World War I record, also had been an All America halfback for Army in 1896. In fact, he always wore his gold football with his military decorations. He was eager to chat with the assistants on the prospects of the Cadet team.

So, after supper one night, we met in front of Cullum. The group included Lieutenant Gar Davidson, who was later a superintendent himself; Moe Daly and Art Meehan, who gave their lives in World War II; Red Reeder, a much-decorated hero; Emmett (Rosy) O'Donnell, "B" squad coach and later a famous Air Force General; Harley Trice, "B" squad assistant coach; and two civilian grads, Ellinger and myself. We were all properly turned out and armed with the requisite number of calling cards.

We thought it practical to discuss a graceful and synchronized method of social withdrawal, after the prescribed fifteen minutes. Since most of us had played cadet baseball for Coach Hans Lobert, we agreed that the signal for leaving should be Lobert's "steal" or "go" sign, which was the waggling of the fingers of one hand, partially covered by the other hand. Moe Daly was elected to give the sign.

We marched across the Plain to the Supe's, and rang the bell. Duly informed that the Supe was "at home," we were ushered into the splendid living room and received graciously by General and Mrs. Connor. We sat in a large semicircle facing our hosts. One advantage of the chair arrangement was that we could all get a clear view of Moe Daly's "go" sign.

Daly, however, was well known as an imaginative practical joker. We had just seated ourselves, and General Connor had offered his first conversational gambit, when Moe flashed the "go" sign. This threw us into spontaneous and uncontrollable laughter.

General and Mrs. Connor were understandably surprised. Neither had been exposed to Hans Lobert's inside baseball. Here were a group of presumably well-bred young West Point graduates, for no discernible reason suddenly breaking out in idiotic laughter. An uncomfortable impasse might have resulted, had not football talk come to the rescue. Somewhat before the fifteen-minute mark, we arose and thanked our hosts; whether we arose on a signal from Daly, I don't remember. I do recall we laughed all the way back to Cullum. As for the General and Mrs. Connor, they would have been justified to suspect that Major Sasse had unaccountably surrounded himself with a pack of social hyenas.

Although Sasse was married and occupied quarters with his wife, Ralph and I sat late many a night in my monklike Cullum room, or at his house after supper there, talking football and discussing the cavalry exploits of Jeb Stuart, Phil Sheridan, and Nathan Bedford Forrest.

When Biff Jones's four-year tour was up after 1929, Sasse's qualities of leadership and his seven years of experience, three under McEwan and four under Biff, made him the logical successor. By that time, my father was somewhat resigned to my annual fall leave-taking from our business. But I think we both felt that one of these years I would just decide not to return to West Point, and that would be it.

It seemed hardly the time in 1930. First, my friendship with Ralph demanded I stay. Then there was the 1929 season; I was not inclined to leave on a low note. There was the fascination of the game: the constantly changing and improving offensive and defensive concepts and techniques, and Army's part in them. Three years under Biff had strengthened my conviction, first established in Wisconsin, that in every way but monetary, building houses was less rewarding than building men. And, at West Point, we were building men to be professional soldiers.

There was with us another builder of men and professional soldiers, who was a principal reason why Sasse's teams seldom failed to play up to their potential: Harry Oscar (Fats) Ellinger, our line coach.

Ellinger had teamed with Gus Farwick on McEwan's 1923 and '24 teams to give Army some of its most resolute and smartest guard play. Harry graduated with the Class of 1925, but was refused his commission because of a heart condition discovered in his First Class year. He appealed to the Surgeon General's office in Washington, but was again rejected. Lawrence Perry, a leading sports columnist of the day, wrote of this:

> Thereupon Harry turned three or four cart-wheels, walked around the examining room on his hands, offered to wrestle the medical board in turn and, when this was declined, he went to Vermont and swam the 14-mile breadth of Lake Champlain.

That Harry should do all of these things was not at all surprising. Although well aware of his condition, he lived a full, physical life right up until his death on February 11, 1942. He was one of those rare personalities: basically tough, intense, yet ebullient and likable. He possessed a great curiosity and a bright mind.

Harry did not try to remove the drudgery from line play. Nobody can do that. He did succeed in making it more palatable to his gladiators. He preached that line play could and should be raised to a plane of exaltation. "Linemen are not coolies," he told his men. "A mule in the mine could be a lineman, but you have to fuse the mule-in-the-mine philosophy to spirit and brains, to outfighting and outsmarting the other fellows. Then you have the Romance of Line Play."

Few line coaches I've known could package their violent, wearying course of instruction in such a fancy beribboned package and sell it to their men without sounding like snake-oil merchants, but Harry Ellinger was one of them.

With Harry singing of the "Romance of Line Play," and Ralph portraying the role that came so natural to him, that of the demanding, yet understanding and thoroughly lovable parent to all, it developed upon me to play the part of "The Whip."

I drove them and drove them. Seldom on the field did I show them any warmth. I gave no acknowledgment whatsoever to any effort short of superior. I worked behind the second team in signal drill, dummy scrimmage, and live scrimmage. Ralph handled the first team. "Heads! Heads!" was an expression we used to hurry them into the huddle. I was always promising the second team: "You're going to be in better shape than the first team and you're going to carry the load on Saturday." I was always deviling the backs and demanding, "Speed!" I was always keenly aware, from my earliest coaching experience, that speed is the essence of real football.

The players blanched when they knew I was going to put them through the wind sprints. These were all-out ten-yard dashes, with the entire squad taking part. I was always asking them for "one more." I pushed them to the limit, because if they didn't reach their limit one day, they couldn't increase it the next. I insisted that after practice all the backs run across the Plain to the gymnasium. Darkness would be descending on the parade ground by then, but I managed to circulate and jab anybody who was moving slower than at a brisk trot.

When the players turned out their lights at taps and hit the sack, they slept well. Perhaps they dreamed of a demon, cleats coming out of his head like stubby horns, chasing them down an oxygen-rare labyrinth and shouting, "Heads! Heads!" and "Speed! Speed!"

Any violation of the training code evoked severe penalty with no appeal. It was discovered that two players had been smoking in a washroom on the train to Philadelphia for the Navy game. To preclude embarrassing questions, they were allowed to suit up, but they never got in the game—and one of them was important to us. On the train home the next day, I told those two boys that rather than use either of them, Major Sasse would have called for two cadets out of the stands.

My earnestness of purpose was understood and appreciated by the squad. It was anything but aloofness. Actually, by building mutual respect, without which you cannot operate, you bring about the closest imaginable relationship between coach and players. For all my brisk, businesslike, serious approach on the field, I was always available to the men off the field for private talks, "friendly, concerned discussions." I rescued more than one who was harried by the inevitable last-minute request from relatives or friends for "two more Navy tickets." More important, they often came to me with personal problems.

Sasse leaned almost exclusively on Ellinger and myself, so much so that the other members of the staff referred to us as "The Big Three." We worked together in plotting offenses and defenses. Harry and I did some scouting, but we were always with Ralph for the big games, usually in the stands, spotting and working the phones.

It was typical of Ralph that he made no effort to conceal his reliance on us. In fact, he talked about it, and was pleased when such writers as Grantland Rice, George Trevor, and Lawrence Perry gave us considerable credit for the development of his teams. This revealed not only the big-hearted nature of the man, but also his quiet realization that nobody doubted who was the general, the fountainhead of inspiration and victory, the leader.

I also assumed, or, perhaps, had thrust upon me as part of my chief-of-staff duties, the responsibility of stabilizing the social activities of Ralph and Harry—or at least trying to. The many who enjoy gazing upon the wine when it is red are no more numerous, I think, than the compulsions that urge them to the flowing bowl. In the cases of Ralph and Harry, I suspect their intense, taut-wire make-ups found here a way of letting off steam. I chaperoned them on many an escapade, mostly humorous and harmless, but occasionally hectic. They did not always heed the chaperon and then I was left without recourse. After all, I could not threaten to keep them out of the Navy or Notre Dame game.

Ralph seldom visited New York without taking Harry and me to a Greenwich Village restaurant which served his favorite vermicelli soup. While we were spooning it one night, a raucous argument broke out at an adjoining table between a man and wife, climaxed by his slapping her. Harry, a Knight Gallant sporting a cocktail plume on his helmet, would not abide this. He rose up, upbraided the man in threatening tones, and aimed a right. The lady, however, beat Harry to the punch with a lightning left that cut his eye and left him with a shiner of several weeks' duration.

"How dare you threaten my husband!" cried the loyal spouse. Harry wiped the blood away and paid her courtly apology. He always laughed heartily over that skirmish. "If she had only been a man," he chuckled, "we could have worked at getting her an appointment to the Academy."

Ralph always regarded the 1930 team as his best. Harry's linemen included Paul Miller, center; Carl Carlmark, Ed Messinger, Dick King, and John Malloy, ends; Price, Ed Suarez, and Jack Armstrong, tackles; Milt Summerfelt, Harley Trice, and Captain Charles (Polly) Humber, guards. Among our backs were Wendell Bowman, Robert (Rosy) Carver, Cy Letzelter, Fields, Ed Herb, Tom Kilday, Bill Frentzel, and a tall, slim-looking second classman from Hazleton, Pennsylvania, named Ray James Stecker.

In high school, Stecker had been a basketball player. He played his first football as a plebe. As a yearling in 1929, he got into a few minor games. He was eager and quick to learn, the kind of boy it is an adventure to coach. He might well have been overlooked, however, except for his instinctive movements as a runner and his ability to handle a punt—the same two things that were to keep Pete Dawkins from getting lost in the crowd twenty-seven years later. In the early part of the 1930 season, Stecker did not distinguish himself, but kept working hard.

Meanwhile, against Harvard, we unveiled our version of the double-wing for the first time in a major game. We were still novices in the use of Warner's brain child, and Harvard had a good team, which later held Michigan's Big Ten co-champions to 6–3 and defeated Yale. We won, 6–0, on a first-period drive, featured by Bowman's end run and a spinner thrust by Herb. After that, although we came close, we could not score again. This disproved, temporarily at least, Sasse's thesis: "The first touchdown comes hard, the second easier and so on, like a pointer bitch having puppies."

We had to settle for a 7–7 tie with Yale in a rainy Bowl, but this time we stopped Albie Booth. "You put him on a pedestal last year," Sasse roared in the dressing room. "Now, go out there and knock him off it." It happened that when Booth intercepted a Stecker pass near his own goal line, he was hit simultaneously by King, Price, and Trice. Albie was separated from the ball, knocked cold when his head hit the ground, and had to be carried from the game.

Tad Jones, former Yale head coach, and a close friend of the Army coaches, who was then writing articles in the New Haven *Register,* accused us scathingly of dirty play. Fortunately for us, the movies of the game showed clearly that the Army players did not hurt Booth, but that he was knocked out when his head hit the ground. In the end Yale admitted this was the case. The feeling around New Haven, however, reflected what Tad Jones had written, until Phil Fleming drove over there from West Point on Tuesday and placated the Old Blues by showing them the films. Those were the days when to play in Yale Bowl was to be received by royalty.

It was in our 13–0 victory over Illinois that Stecker put on the first of his several big shows on what apparently was his favorite gridiron, Yankee Stadium. Ray sliced off tackle 12 yards for the first touchdown and returned an intercepted pass 50 yards for the second.

We carried a record of eight victories and the Yale tie into the Notre Dame game, scheduled that year for Chicago's Soldier Field. We were, nevertheless, emphatic short-enders. What was to be Rockne's last team was also his greatest. The Irish defeated Southern Methodist, 20–14; Navy, 26–2; Carnegie Tech, 21–6; Pittsburgh, 35–19; Indiana, 27–0; Pennyslvania, 60–20; Drake, 28–7; Northwestern, 14–0; and, after our game, Southern California, 27–0.

Their backfield—Carideo at quarter, Marchy Schwartz and Marty Brill at the halves, and Joe Savoldi at fullback—was brilliant. The line was comparably outstanding, and Rockne had a plenitude of reserves. In fact, it was a third-string fullback, Paul (Bucky) O'Connor, who tore a falsely favored Southern California team to pieces with long runs from the fullback reverse play. This was one of the weapons Rockne had added to his weak-side attack, after legislation slowed down his shift, and with it he could hit and hurt you all along the front. It was an awesome assignment we faced, but we conceded nothing, and went to work with Sasse's words ringing: "Let's roll up our socks and get going!"

The demand for tickets was colossal. Every West Pointer in the Western Hemisphere and a few in the Eastern tried to connive and contrive a way to be in Chicago. Biff Jones was studying at the Fort Sill, Oklahoma, Artillery School that fall. He wrote Ralph and told him he was coming to Chicago for the game. Ralph replied, asking Biff to come to his hotel room upon arrival.

Biff arranged for his Army quarterback of 1926, Lieutenant Neil

(Chick) Harding, then a flying instructor at San Antonio, to pick him up at Sill on Thanksgiving morning in a two-seater, open-cockpit biplane. That day a heavy snowstorm swirled across the Midwest, and as Jones and Harding neared St. Louis, they were flying in the middle of it.

By studying a road map, Harding managed to locate a highway that led directly into Scott Field, St. Louis. In order not to lose the highway, Chick flew at a 300-foot altitude, skimming treetops and telephone poles. He flew this way for thirty minutes. By the time they landed at Scott, Biff felt like a coach who has just watched his team go through sixty minutes of continuous goal-line stands.

Nothing daunted, as soon as they had warmed themselves and the plane was refueled, Harding used his flying instructor's status to prevail on the Scott Field authorities to clear him for another hop through the storm to Chanute Field, Illinois. This leg was not so hair-raising as the jump from Sill to Scott, but when the two intrepid football buffs finally did land at Chanute, they were well frozen. They took a train the rest of the way to Chicago, and at ten o'clock that night, Biff knocked on the door of Sasse's hotel room.

After risking his life to be with us, Biff was in a mood to be greeted with effusive joy and warmth and to recount his hazards. Instead, Ralph and I carried out a "brush-off" cooked up by Ralph on our train ride west. As Biff entered the room, we were seated at a table, our backs to the door, apparently working out a football problem. After a couple of seconds, Ralph turned around, said "Hello" casually, and immediately returned to the problem. I hardly looked up.

Biff stood there flabbergasted. He said afterwards he tried not to feel hurt. He tried to impute our glaring lack of hospitality to coachly preoccupation with the pressures of the Notre Dame game. He was not quite succeeding when Ralph and I suddenly swung around, jumped up, grabbed him and began thumping him on the back. Such simple pleasures can constitute some of life's choicest moments.

The atrocious weather carried over through Saturday. A shivering crowd of 100,000 sat through a rain that poured onto an ice-encrusted field. Until late in the game it was 0–0, as we fought a delaying action.

Then the gifted Schwartz broke loose off our left tackle and ran 46 yards through the messy field for a touchdown, and Carideo converted. On a dry field, we might have headed off Schwartz. Yet, on a dry field, Notre Dame might have scored long before. To paraphrase an old saying, on the road to a losing scoreboard, both gutters are paved with "mights."

We received the kick-off, couldn't move, and Ken Fields got off a long kick to their 19. All day, Carideo had given a masterful exhibition of controlled kicking despite the mud-logged ball. But now Dick King, always dangerous in a critical spot, blocked Carideo's punt. The ball slithered into the end zone. Harley Trice, who had learned about the Romance of Line Play under Professor Ellinger, squirmed through the pack and fell on it for a touchdown. We missed the extra point, and lost the game, 7–6, but we lost it to one of the greatest teams any of us ever saw.

The Notre Dame game had been planned originally to end our season, but the depression of 1929, now a year entrenched, served to bring Army and Navy together again. President Herbert Hoover ordered us to play a game for charity. On December 13, in Yankee Stadium, we beat the Midshipmen, 6–0, when Stecker broke off tackle in the last quarter and ran down the side lines 56 yards.

The 1931 season, Ralph's second in command, brought defeat, numbing tragedy, and final victory. We won promisingly, 20–7, over a strong Michigan State team, well coached by Jimmy Crowley and with a remarkable runner in Bob Monnett. Barry Wood's quarterbacking, passing, and defensive play sparked Harvard to beat us, 14–13, in their first visit to the Academy since 1910. We got to a 13–0 lead on Stecker's running, and we had Harvard down, but we let them get up.

Our second touchdown in that game was scored by right end Dick Sheridan on a recovery of Stecker's goal-line fumble. Richard Brinsley Sheridan, Jr., from Greenville, South Carolina, weighed only 149 pounds and was on the slender side. That couldn't keep him off the football team any more than his failure to obtain a Congressional appointment had been able to keep him out of West Point.

Each year a certain number of men are appointed to the Academy from the regular Army by competitive examination. Sheridan enlisted, served with a howitzer company in the 29th Infantry, took the examination, and topped the list. He entered in 1929 and never was under 2.8, or 90 per cent in any course.

Sheridan did not start the Yale game, but he was in there early in the fourth period. Yale had just tied the score at 6–6 on Dud Parker's 88-yard return of a kick-off. Bob Lassiter, a speedy, high-knee-action halfback, took our kick-off and headed up the field. Sheridan, first man down under the kick, tackled him head on. Lassiter's knee hit him on the back of the head and caused a fracture of the fourth cerebral vertebra and a partial fracture of the fifth.

All action stopped, and suddenly over the roaring crowd there fell a shocking and fearful quiet. Sheridan lay there on the field. Dr. Eddie O'Brien, the referee, the coaches, the team doctors, and the trainers hovered around him. Major Fleming came down out of the stands and conferred with Sasse.

Harry and I were posted as phone spotters in an aisle immediately above a portal in the east stands behind the Army bench. Our phone rang. It was Fleming. He asked me if I thought we should go on with the game. I had realized immediately that Sheridan was grievously hurt and had said so to Harry. We agreed now that there was nothing to be gained, nothing we could do for Sheridan by not carrying on, and that was what I told Fleming. Sheridan was taken from the field on a stretcher and placed in an ambulance. The doctors and the Army chaplain accompanied him to the hospital.

After a ten- or fifteen-minute respite, the game was resumed, but the response of the crowd was not so hearty as before. The word had spread throughout the Bowl that Sheridan was near death. Our players were affected, but they managed to stave off late Yale drives and the game ended in a 6–6 tie. As soon as it was over, Sasse rushed to the hospital and stayed at Sheridan's bedside until the boy passed away two days later. If Dick had lived, he would have been paralyzed. I took the team back to the Academy, and it was a sad journey.

There is no doubt that a contributing factor in the fatal injury to Sheridan was Dick's exceptionally long neck. Thereafter, I would never play a man with that kind of neck conformation. We were also more than ever impelled to stress neck-building exercises as the basis of all proper physical conditioning for football. We also put even more stress on instructing our men to play with their heads up, for the neck can be broken only if the head is down.

The fatality to Sheridan, the subsequent death of Fordham tackle Cornelius J. Murphy, and a considerable list of other casualties and serious injuries brought about salutary rule changes. The flying block and tackle were outlawed; restraining lines prevented flying wedges on kick-off returns; defensive players were penalized for striking opponents on the head, neck or face; and the ball carrier was down when any part of his body, except his hands, touched the ground.

Sheridan's death had its emotional effect on the team, but I doubt this contributed much to the 26–0 thumping we received three weeks later in the Pitt Stadium from one of Jock Sutherland's strong teams. Warren Heller and Paul Reider, the Panther halfbacks, riddled us with passes thrown out of reverse plays as our secondary defense broke down. I could not sleep thinking about it on our train ride back to New York.

We now stood at the season crossroads that so often test the character of a team. One road pointed downward—to another 1929. The other led upward—how far depended on us. We were to face another powerful Notre Dame team, coached by Hunk Anderson, who had succeeded Rockne. The Irish had been tied by Northwestern and were to lose to Southern California, but they had defeated Pitt, 25–12, and every other team they met. And beyond Notre Dame was another presidential-command charity game with the Navy.

Sasse now showed his great leadership. His inspiration and the memory of Sheridan turned up the flame. Before the Notre Dame game, Captain Jack Price told the Corps, "We're going down to New York and take that gang apart to see what makes them go 'round."

Harry and I sat late with Ralph, poring over every footnote on the Irish, preparing our defenses, and plotting our attack to probe and pick at every known or suspected soft spot, however minute, in their defensive fabric. We were more confident now about the double wing, and we were also getting more out of it by mixing in some single wing, which I always regarded as the more substantial formation.

There was no need for us to apply the whip that week. The Cadets were their own whips, and in the Stadium they went to town, uptown and down. The line—King, Price, Summerfelt, Roy Evans at center, Trice, Suarez, and Pete Kopcsak—hustled and harried Notre Dame. "Rosy" Carver at quarterback had a big day.

Stecker led the cavalry charge. He caught a 35-yard pass from Travis Brown, from a fake kick, to set up the first touchdown. He ran 66 yards off tackle for the second. We played with only fourteen men, and did not substitute in the backfield. The final score was 12-0. It would be thirteen years before another Army football team would beat Notre Dame, but nobody dreamt of such a thing that day. We sustained our momentum to beat Navy 17-7. Stecker, in his last game, played well again; as did Brown, Fields, Herb, Kopcsak, and the rest.

For Sasse, the triumphal finish against Notre Dame and Navy did not remove the memory of Sheridan. It stayed with Ralph then, and for long afterwards. After the season, he asked to be relieved of football duty and to be returned to the cavalry. Only on request did he stay on for another year. In the fall of 1932, he again requested that he be transferred after the season, and this time the order was put through.

Ralph tried to forget by plunging into his work or by taking a carefree trip here and there with Ellinger. On April 1, 1932, in Dayton, my old friend Jim Davis (whose golf-gifted daughter had collaborated in the gulling of Biff Jones) received the following telegram from West Point:

WOULD LIKE TO SURPRISE EARL BLAIK STOP ELLINGER AND SELF ARRIVE AT DAYTON 1:35 P.M. YOUR TIME SUNDAY APRIL THIRD VIA NEW YORK CENTRAL STOP CAN WE GO DIRECT TO YOUR CELLAR STOP WILL LUNCH ON TRAIN BEFORE ARRIVAL STOP PLEASE

SHOOT ME A WIRE IF ALL SATISFACTORY AND DO NOT TELL EARL STOP BEST REGARDS

RALPH SASSE

Although the wire was sent on April Fool's Day, Ralph and Harry were in earnest. Jim Davis met them at the train and later gave me an account of the scene. The lunch ordered by Ralph and Harry on the train had been mostly liquid, and they had insisted on sharing it bounteously with the train crew, including the conductors, the porters and, for all I know, the engineer. Attended by conductors and porters in a high state of glow, they alighted from their car like two itinerant rajahs. Their farewells to the train crew were matched in the most acute enthusiasm and sentiment by their greetings of Davis. Later, in Jim's cellar, there were more scenes of fond welcome, mingled on my part with considerable surprise and even more foreboding, which proved completely justified. Ralph and Harry spent three days in Dayton and only occasionally joined me in some buttermilk.

As an antidote to ragged nerves and seething stomachs, buttermilk would have been welcomed by the spectators, coaches, and writers who sat in on the Army-Pittsburgh game early in the 1932 season. The depression held the crowd to only 12,000 but they saw the most exciting game ever played in Michie Stadium.

Jock Sutherland's team was to go undefeated in the regular season and play in the Rose Bowl. But the play that day of their Warren Heller, star end Joe Skladany, and others was matched by such Cadets as Dick King, best end on the field; Captain Milt Summerfelt and Harvey (Jabo) Jablonsky at guards; and Kilday, Felix (Pick) Vidal, and Ken Fields in the backfield.

Fields, an exceptional all-around cadet, stood first in his class of 346 and was awarded seven of nine graduation prizes for academic and military excellence. He later became a general and the manager of the Atomic Energy Commission. Against Pittsburgh in that 1932 game, he had his greatest day as runner, passer, and kicker.

We overcame a 12–0 lead to go ahead 13–12, and, after Pitt stormed back to regain the lead, 18–13, with three minutes left to play we began a march from our own 20 down to their 10. That drive had the writers standing up in the press box, screaming and banging their typewriters—and I mean that literally. With the clock running out on third down, Fields aimed a pass to Vidal in the end zone. The ball was just about to settle into Pick's arms when it was batted away at the last possible split second by defender Joe Tormey.

It was that close—far too close for Dr. Sutherland. Jock and Grantland Rice were both emotionally exhausted by what they had sat through. In fact, Granny was so weary that we had to put him to bed in Cullum Hall that night at what was for him an unusually early hour.

Our showing against Pitt shored us up to win convincingly from Yale, 20–0, and Harvard, 46–0. Jack Buckler, a yearling halfback from Texas, scored twice against Yale, once on a 67-yard run, and Vidal returned a punt 75 yards for another. Buckler had ice water in his emotional stream. He was laughing as he practiced punting before that game, and I criticized him for lack of seriousness. "Don't worry, coach," he assured me, "we'll murder the Yales." Determined not to let Harvard off the floor this time, we handed them their most one-sided defeat since 1884. We gained over 400 yards, but it was a costly victory because Dick King's football was ended by an ankle injury.

The Harvard game was on November 5. Our next major game was Notre Dame on November 26. In between, we were to meet North Dakota State and West Virginia Wesleyan. So Ralph decided to lay the team off after the Harvard game until Thursday. He apprised me of this in Cullum Hall late Sunday afternoon, after our return from Boston.

"Red," he said, "you, and I, and Harry are going to drive to Atlantic City tonight and relax for a few days."

This was an order. We took off at nine that night. Ralph and Harry sat in the rear seat in festive mood, while I chauffeured. Neither Ralph nor Harry knew the road to Atlantic City. I was not up on my geography and thought it was no more than a three-hour drive. I believe we must have approached the resort in some kind of an enflanking movement to its southeast. Ralph said it reminded him of a certain tank operation he had jointly executed with the British in Flanders. Colonel Echols would have been horrified.

It was about three o'clock in the morning and we were still 50 miles away from the city gates, when I suddenly swung the car over to the side of the road, jammed on the hand brake, and turned off the ignition. I was exhausted.

"Listen, you birds," I said. "I'm not driving one more foot."

Harry took over and we made Atlantic City by sunup. On Thursday morning we headed back to West Point. I wouldn't say I found the three days relaxing, but Ralph and Harry enjoyed themselves. Ralph liked to play hide-and-seek with both of us. If we turned our backs, he'd spirit himself out of the room and often it was after many hours of searching in nooks and crannies about the town that we located him. It was after his third such disappearance that we found him in what he said was the accomplishment of his serious objective in the Atlantic City expedition. He was with an old friend who was an Armenian rug weaver.

We could have used that rug weaver on defense in the Notre Dame game. Our defeat by the Irish, 21–0, was the only one of our seven games with them, in my tenure as assistant coach, in which we did not win or make it close. They had another formidable outfit that year, losing only to Pittsburgh and Southern California, yet our showing against Pitt had proved we should have done better against them. We were never in the game. This time they took *us* apart to see what made us go 'round.

The chance for atonement was provided by Navy, and this time the game was not by presidential decree. In August, Rear Admiral Charles Hart, head of Annapolis, and our football-minded Supe General Connor, head of West Point, signed a three-year contract. Annapolis agreed each school could determine its own eligibility standards. Army, in turn, acceded to Navy's request that the game be returned to its old habitat, the University of Pennsylvania's Franklin Field. Navy considered New York to be more our home town than theirs, while Philadelphia was neutral for both. The game was played at Franklin Field until 1936, when it was moved to its site for the last twenty-four years, Philadelphia's Municipal Stadium.

Ralph made his last game as Army coach a memorable one. He did not let the players go on the field until just before the kick-off. He even rejected Harry's plea that the kickers at least be permitted some warm-up.

"And I say," he stated, "that we don't need any practice to beat this crowd!"

It developed he was right. Vidal, Buckler, Frentzel, Joe McWilliam, and Joe Stancook put together our scoring drives and Summerfelt sewed up his All America status in a 20–0 victory.

Ralph returned to coaching later, at Mississippi State, when he was commanding the R.O.T.C. unit there from 1935 through '37. He brought his '35 team to Michie Stadium and beat Army, 13–7. Although Ralph was a Yankee from Delaware, his pep talk to the Mississippi State players before the kick-off at Michie was Confederate to the core.

"We've come one thousand, five hundred miles from State College, Mississippi!" he thundered. "And do you know why? I'll tell you why! We've come to avenge Sherman's march to the sea!"

That same day, November 2, 1935, my Dartmouth team beat Yale for the first time in history. That night, I ran into Ralph in Times Square. He was leading a bulldog on a leash, and he said I should be doing the same.

After Mississippi State, Ralph was assigned to a tank command at Fort Knox and was retired in 1940. Later, he served for a time as Assistant to the President and Director of Athletics at Pennsylvania Military College, but that didn't work out.

Early in 1942, after I had returned to West Point as head coach, I heard that Ralph needed help. I took the train down to Wilmington (Delaware) one Thursday afternoon and phoned his mother's house, where he was living with his wife. He wasn't home, but I left a message for him to look me up at the hotel.

That night, while I was eating, Ralph walked into the dining room. He was much changed from the handsome, dynamic leader I had known. He could only sit down for a couple of minutes, he told me, because he had to make a speech somewhere. I knew he didn't have to make a speech, but I walked with him to his car.

"It's too bad," I said, "that you haven't more time, because I came down here just to see you. Ralph, you need help. That's why I'm here."

He took a long look at me—and I could see some of the well-remembered fire come back into his eyes.

"Red," he said, "you have come down here just to see me? My God, how I need your help!"

"Then let's go up to my room," I said, "and talk about it."

I had come down there with a plan for Ralph. I felt that what he wanted and needed more than anything else was to get back where he belonged—as a tank commander in combat. I had talked this over with the former Graduate Manager of Athletics at West Point and a good friend of Ralph's and mine, Jake Devers, then a general high in the Armored Forces. Jake had promised me he would assign Ralph to duty, if I could guarantee he was cured of drinking.

As Ralph and I sat there talking in that Wilmington hotel room for an hour or more, I became convinced that if he knew assignment to duty was attainable, he would be impelled to fight his problem and lick it. I told him of my plan and he agreed to co-operate. The first step was that he would meet me in New York the following Sunday.

Sunday came and Merle and I went to Pennsylvania Station. Ralph arrived as agreed. He told me he had not taken a drink since he had seen me, and he never did take another one until his death over twelve years later, on October 15, 1954. He went to a sanitarium in Connecticut for a few months. In the summer, he returned to active duty as a colonel to train all replacement troops for the Armored Forces.

It was a great sorrow to Ralph that he was not assigned to action overseas. I merely echo the statement of General Ben Lear and many other generals when I say it was also a distinct loss to the United States. In World War II, Ralph Sasse could have been another George Patton. In fact, it was General Patton who said, "I would rather have Sasse serving under me or serve under him than any other officer in the Army."

After the war, Ralph ran Camp Arrowhead for boys and girls on

Rehoboth Bay near Lewes, Delaware. Just as he inspired soldiers and football players, so did Ralph exert a warm appeal to children. Colonel Red Reeder, who had coached under Ralph at the Academy, sent his son Russell to Camp Arrowhead one summer. When Russell returned home, his father asked him what camp activity he liked best.

"Ralph Sasse," said Russell.

Chapter VIII

Direct Action in "Heaven"

Whenever the chance offered, I was asking other coaches how football affected them. I knew how it affected me. It made my insides churn in ever-increasing tempo as the kick-off neared. Did it do the same to others? When I asked Mr. Stagg at Chicago back in 1926, he said it didn't bother him, and then he behaved otherwise. Now, before Army's 1923 game with Illinois in Cleveland's Municipal Stadium, I asked Bob Zuppke, the picturesque and clever coaching veteran of the Illini.

"You bet!" said Zup. "Why, right now I'm as nervous as an old cat! My stomach is burning up on me! But if it wasn't, I wouldn't be coaching! When you stop burning up inside, then you better quit—because you've had it!"

Zuppke never permitted the fires of tension to destroy his gift for practical psychology. I have always suspected that he went directly from that talk with me to ordering the Illinois Band, one hundred pieces strong, to march onto the field and interfere with Army's pre-game workout. Whether my suspicion was justified or not, the band did bother us. In retribution, Jack Buckler, who was warming up near me, tried to kick the ball into the Illini drum.

The drum was 10 feet in diameter and only 40 yards down the field. Buckler was one of the best control kickers I ever saw, and, as I've mentioned, a cool operator. For some reason, though, he couldn't hit the drum. The best he could do was knock the drummer's hat off his head. Word of what was going on spread around the field and provided our players with a tension-easing laugh they needed. I suspect it helped us win the game, 6–0.

I certainly needed some laughs myself. Football was especially tense for me that season, because I knew I was confronted with a decision. I had to get into football completely—or get out of it completely.

When it was determined in the fall of 1932 that Major Ralph Sasse would be relieved, on his request, of coaching duty at West Point after that season and returned to the cavalry, he endorsed me to succeed him. The Athletic Board also considered me the logical man, but felt compelled to invoke the then unwritten law that only a graduate who was an officer on regular duty could hold the job.

All papers pertaining to the Army Athletic Association and particularly football were handled in those days by the Adjutant General of the Academy, Lieutenant Colonel Robert Lawrence Eichelberger, from Urbana, Ohio. Lieutenant Colonel Eichelberger made all the trips with the football team and got to know the coaches. He worked hard to convince the Athletic Board that they should waive the officer-head-coach rule and recommend me to succeed Sasse, but he failed in his mission.

One evening late in the '32 season, Colonel Roger Alexander, senior member of the Athletic Board, came to my room in Cullum Hall to discuss the situation.

"Red," he said, "you know that Ralph wishes to be relieved and has endorsed you. I want you to know that as much as we all respect your work and contribution to Army football, the A. A. A. Board is agreed our head coach must be an officer on active duty."

"That's all right, Colonel," I assured him. "I haven't had any aspirations or illusions. I can only continue in football so long as it does not interfere with our building business in Dayton, which it would, if I were to become a head coach. I have already been approached by several colleges, including Princeton and Ohio State, but I told them I was not interested."

I believe my reaction not only surprised but relieved Colonel Alexander. He went on to say that the Board was eager for me to go on coaching indefinitely as a continuing force between officer head coaches, whose tour of duty was restricted to four years.

He also told me that Sasse's successor would be either Lieutenant Blackshear M. (Babe) Bryan or Lieutenant Garrison H. Davidson. Bryan, who had been the plebe coach in 1930 and '31, was attending the artillery school at Fort Sill, Oklahoma. Davidson was coaching the 1932 plebe team and was also aide to General Connor, the Superintendent.

Davidson was selected for the job. I decided to accede to the request of the Athletic Board, at least for one more year, and return as first assistant. Harry Ellinger also returned. Not much was expected of the 1933 team by the press, because we had lost so many 1932 regulars by graduation. It was forgotten that the '32 second team had outscored the first, and was ready to move up.

Captain Harvey (Jabo) Jablonsky was an inspirational leader at guard, with worthy running mates in Bob (Moose) Stillman and Stacy Gooch. The tackles were Johnny Hutchison and John (Tiger) Beall. Pete Kopcsak and Paul Burlingame played the regular ends, and the center was Ralph Bucknam. Paul (Beanie) Johnson was the quarterback. The halfbacks were Buckler, Travis Brown, Edward (Whitey) Grove (another very coachable player), Jack Legg, and Henry (Hank) Sebastian. At fullback, Joe Stancook was a solid plunger and blocker. (It is impossible, of course, to include in the body of a work such as this the names of all my players who deserve inclusion. However, I have listed all the lettermen in the appendix.)

Despite few reserves, we mustered an intractable defense, which gave up only four touchdowns in ten games. We also demonstrated a flair for capitalizing on scoring chances. A first-quarter, 60-yard march, with Johnson going over, beat Illinois. A 32-yard pass from Buckler to Brown, another 34-yarder from Grove to Buckler and a Johnson plunge, to cap a 60-yard drive, did for Yale, 21–0. Buckler and Johnson were outstanding again in our defeat of Harvard, 27–0. Johnson's 81-yard punt return and Buckler's 20-yard run-off tackle beat Navy, 12–7, in a game that proved we could come from behind. Buckler, a real triple-threat back, made All America.

By the time we got down to the final game, with Notre Dame, we were expected to go clean, but a sub-par Irish team beat us, 13–12. We had them 12–0, but they climbed back. Their winning touchdown was set up on a 76-yard punt by halfback Nick Lukats to our 6-yard line. When we tried to punt out, end Wayne Milner blocked it and recovered in the end zone for the marker. There had been some talk of the Rose Bowl, but my impression is the Academy was not interested. For one thing, Phil Fleming wasn't graduate manager any more.

As that season wore on, I thought it would be my last as an assistant at West Point—or anyplace else. For one thing, the rapport Harry and I had enjoyed with Sasse was missing. Beyond that, I felt that if I was to stay in football, I owed it to myself and my family to accept a head-coach offer. The debt I owed West Point was paid.

The day before the Notre Dame game, Lynn W. St. John, the Ohio State athletic director, again talked to me about the job. He advised me that Sam Willaman, then the Buckeye coach, would be replaced. Sam's number, in fact, had been up for a couple of years. There was a natural tug to accept St. John's offer. I am a native Ohioan and Ohio State has a rich and compelling football tradition. Yet my observations in one season at Wisconsin had conditioned me to lean away from coaching in a league where I might have to report to a Quarterback Club on Monday. Francis Schmidt eventually replaced Willaman.

I was to be offered many head-coaching jobs through the years. I never believed in advertising such offers, although rumors of them leaked out at times from the other end. I never believed in a "flirtation" with any school unless I meant business. Just for the record, colleges besides Princeton and Ohio State (three times) which contacted me included Michigan, Northwestern, Minnesota, Southern California, California, U.C.L.A., Washington, Texas, Texas A. & M., Nebraska, and Mississippi State. Among the pros, offers came from the Los Angeles Rams, the New York Giants, and the Green Bay Packers.

My name was also linked off and on with the Yale job. It is true that more than once some of my friends among the Old Blues talked to me about the possibility. After the 1933 season, Yale was looking for a successor to Reggie Root. My good friend, the late George Trevor, of the New York *Sun* and Yale, but not necessarily in the order named, practically demanded that Old Eli hire me. Let me quote a wire I received from George in Dayton on December 9, 1933. To me, it is at once amusing and nostalgic, for I always held a deep fondness for George:

WITHIN A WEEK YOU MAY BE APPROACHED BY YALE STOP THE POSITION SEEKS THE MAN STOP THE YALE OF CAMP HOGAN SHEVLIN AND COY LOOKS TO YOU STOP IT IS A MANDATE STOP NO MATTER WHAT YOUR INCLINATION YOU CANNOT REFUSE.

GEORGE TREVOR

Yale was not ready to break with graduate coaching. Raymond (Ducky) Pond, one of her fine halfbacks, coached the team from 1934 through '40. If a firm offer had been made me, I can't say what my reaction would have been. I think it would have been negative. I have always appreciated Yale's tremendous contributions to football as the true fountainhead of the American game, but I sensed that if the Yale coach did not have to report to a formal Quarterback Club, he certainly reported ultimately, if indirectly, to a lot of Old Blues, and not only at the tables down at Mory's.

The truth is that at the age of thirty-six, with eight seasons as an assistant coach behind me, I had seen enough of college football to know that a head coach's job is essentially something on which a man cannot plan a solid future. Sooner or later, too many people who know too little about football have too much to say about it.

The best a coach can possibly hope for is to report directly to a college president, who has not only the authority but the character to support him so long as he justifies it.

And where was I to find such a man?

I have always considered myself extremely fortunate that I did find one in Ernest Martin Hopkins, president of Dartmouth College from 1916 until 1945 and still president emeritus today.

A man of great warmth and charm, with an insatiable intellectual curiosity, completely at home with prince or third-stringer, President Hopkins was an inspiring college leader, who is revered and held in the highest affection by all Dartmouth men.

President Hopkins was born in Dunbarton, New Hampshire, November 6, 1877, the son of a Baptist minister dedicated to work in rural parishes. The elder Hopkins was a graduate of Harvard, Class of 1874. In fact, the family had long been one of Harvard traditions. But Ernest's early New Hampshire environment had instilled in him a lifelong preference for country life over city existence and for Dartmouth over Harvard.

He might still have entered Harvard, however, in deference to his father's wishes, had it not been for the financial panic of 1893. At the time, the Reverend Adoniram Judson Hopkins had a parish in North Uxbridge, Massachusetts. His parishioners, like most, were economizing first by forgoing payment of the minister. As a result the money Reverend Hopkins had set aside to educate his children had to be used to feed and clothe them.

Ernest worked summer vacations and weekends as derrick man in the cutting yard of a North Uxbridge granite quarry to pay his way through Worcester Academy. It was in his junior year at Worcester that he revealed to his father for the first time that he intended to become a renegade and attend Dartmouth.

"My father's reply was typical," he recalls. "He said that he was sorry I felt that way, but that since I was earning my way through Worcester and would have to do the same at Dartmouth, he felt that he had no right to argue against any choice I should make. I graduated at Worcester in 1896, taught grammar school for a year and entered Dartmouth."

How strange that one decision in 1895 should influence another roughly forty-six years later! If Ernest Hopkins had not chosen to enter Dartmouth, I might never have become a head football coach. In 1910, Mr. Hopkins became secretary to the president of Dartmouth, and in 1916, president.

In the business and public-service phases of his multi-faceted career, President Hopkins is today Chairman of the Board of the National Life Insurance Co., and a director of the Northeast Telephone and Telegraph Co.; he has served as an executive of the Rockefeller Foundation and on the President's Committee on Civilian National Honors; he was Assistant Secretary of War under Newton D. Baker. He holds seventeen degrees from various institutions.

Ever since his undergraduate days, he was greatly interested in football. After the 1933 season, he decided that Dartmouth's teams should be held in greater respect by opponents, undergraduates, and alumni alike. This meant parting with old coaching friends and bringing in new ones.

There were 126 candidates for the job. I was not among them. The Dartmouth Athletic Council carefully studied the records and qualifications of over 50 men, including some who had not signified candidacy. Eddie Dooley, former star quarterback for Dartmouth, then a sportswriter for the New York *Sun* and a leading football reporter on radio, today a Congressman from Mamaroneck, was a member of the council, and he argued strongly for me. He was supported by Francis (Red) Lowden, from Minnesota, another former Dartmouth player.

At length, the council resolved their choice to two men. One was Dick Harlow, then coach at Western Maryland and later at Harvard from 1934 through '47—and a real good one. The other was myself. Our names were referred to President Hopkins and he expressed a preference for me. The council then asked him to sell me on the job.

Dooley and Lowden had already half convinced me, in tentative talks, that a good part of heaven was located in Hanover, New Hampshire. But it was my first meeting with Mr. Hopkins at the Plaza Hotel in New York that sold me. Dartmouth, epitomized by him, suddenly became irresistible. I began reasoning that nothing could be finer than to live in a small college community, yet to be saved from complacency by the pressures of being a head coach. Mr. Hopkins talked my language.

"Earl," he said, "always remember that football is incidental to the purpose for which the player is in college." Then he added, "Let's have a winner."

I signed a three-year contract in January, 1941, that specified I should report to him and the athletic council in any matter pertaining to football. At the end of my second year, he insisted I sign a new five-year contract to supersede the old.

Football for the next quarter of a century was to be my profession, business, and hobby. The decision was not an easy one. I did not relish leaving what was a close relationship with my father. Our business was prosperous and stabilized. Dad would soon be sixty-six, but he was to live another thirteen years and much of that time to continue active. He was saddened by my going and yet, in a way, proud.

"I guess I've seen this coming for a long time, Earl," he said. "But it's best a man be in the work he likes best, for there he'll do his best work."

My first move was to acquire the finest possible assistants. For line coach, of course, there could be nobody but Harry. He was as eager as I was for new surroundings and new challenges. He was to be the perfect right arm, the personable foil for my serious approach.

For my backfield and end coaches, I went to Pittsburgh. Andy Gustafson had played fullback at Pitt under both Pop Warner and Jock Sutherland. I had seen and respected the backfields he delivered as an assistant to Jock. Joe Donchess, an All American end at Pitt in 1929, had coached the wings for Jock while studying medicine at Pitt, and now was an interne at the Lahey Clinic in Boston. Joe was to combine coaching and interning successfully for the next three years. For many years now, he has been chief surgeon at the Gary Works of the United States Steel Corporation. After 1936, Joe was succeeded as end coach by Eddie Hirshberg, another oustanding Pitt product, athletically and intellectually, and Frank (Spec) Moore from Louisiana State.

Our first visit to Hanover, in January of 1934, was attended by two feet of powdered snow, a thermometer at 12 below, and a bright sun. It was invigorating as well as inspirational. Although I was Dartmouth's first nongraduate head coach since 1899, we were welcomed by most of the Hanover community as if we were close kin of Eleazer Wheelock. We made that first trip in the private car of Edward S. (Ned) French, then president of the Boston and Maine Railroad and Dartmouth trustee. Ned was always a strong supporter of mine and to this day, he and Mr. Hopkins and I enjoy yearly fishing trips to the north. Harry, before his death, was also one of the party.

Eventually, Merle, Bill, Bob, and I were to move into a beautiful home facing Mount Ascutney, but during that first winter and spring of '34, we coaches took temporary quarters. On our first visit in January, we had been invited by President and Mrs. Hopkins to stay at their home. We occupied their "dormitory," a large room for overflow guests just above the Hopkins bedroom.

On our first night in the "dormitory," we immediately went into a detailed discussion of the type of offense I wanted to install. It combined what I considered the strongest elements of the single-wing attacks used by Army and Pittsburgh: Army's running pass, inside tackle thrust and short reverse, and Pitt's sweep, off-tackle cutback and deep reverse.

We got out paper and pencils, traced the blocking and running routes and leaped up intermittently to demonstrate proper techniques on one another. This caused much scraping and shuffling of feet, punctuated by vigorous thumping and banging. We were so engrossed, we were unaware time was fleeing into early morning hours. We had forgotten, if we ever were aware, that just below us the Hopkins were presumably trying to sleep. I did find out later from Mr. Hopkins that along about 3:00 A.M., Mrs. Hopkins inquired of him, "Do you plan to have all of the season's major games played upstairs?"

We held our first meeting with the squad on an early February night in Davis Field House. I introduced the assistants as the best in America at their jobs. I briefly outlined the system of attack we would use as the most advanced and useful in football. And then I told them:

"We'll be as successful as you men will allow us to be. If there is anybody in this room who is not ready to do some strong sacrificing, I hope we've seen him for the last time tonight. Because we're going to bring home the bacon."

Between our first visit to Hanover and the beginning of spring practice in March, I made a three-week tour, including stops at Atlanta, Tulsa, Denver, and Los Angeles, to talk to alumni groups and prospective players. In our recruiting, we seldom were dealing with the superior type of player like Bob MacLeod, whom other schools were seeking. When we did, my sales talk was the same as for everybody else. It was not quite the same as they heard from most other schools. I believe, however, this made it effective, especially to the kind of boy we were after.

"You have the necessary marks," I would tell him. "It is a privilege to go to Dartmouth. When you finish looking about at other schools and decide that you want to go to Dartmouth, tell us. Then, not before, we will decide to help you in every legitimate way to get your education, which is why you are going to college in the first place. There will be no gold-bricking jobs, no soft touches. Stand up and take your chance with every other student. This is what makes Dartmouth a great college and makes this a great opportunity for you—not because you are a football prospect, but because you do meet the Dartmouth standards."

Dartmouth's aid program was based on the boy's all-around caliber, his personal financial situation, and a job program. It was essentially the same as that practiced by Ivy League schools today.

Our major problem at Dartmouth was to replace the spirit of good fellowship, which is antithetical to successful football, with the Spartanism that is indispensable. I believe there is a place for good-fellowship. I also believe that good fellows are a dime a dozen, but an aggressive leader is priceless.

The successful coach is the one who can sell the Spartan approach, the one who is able to get a willing acceptance from his men that victory or success demands a special price. The play-for-fun approach will lead the player to revolt against the coach and, eventually, even against the game itself, because play-for-fun never can lead to victory.

This does not mean that the Spartan dictates of work, courage, sacrifice, and selflessness turn football into something that is no longer a game. But the essence of the game, the only "fun" of the game, if you will, is the soul-satisfying awareness that comes not only with victory but also with the concurrent realization that victory more than justifies all the communal work and sacrifice that went into it. This savor can also be derived by a losing team to a considerable degree, but only if they know their attempt to win obviously represented their best possible effort.

Interestingly enough, I know of at least one educator who stated that Spartan living becomes the scholar and is conducive to earnest and serious study. This philosophy reflects that of the coach, who knows there is no easy way to learn to play the game of football.

Once Dartmouth players understood what we were getting at, I found them little different from the West Point Cadets. They accepted discipline, sacrifice, and subordination to team effort as a necessary part of success. I have found that young men respect authority and that a football team cannot be coached by committee action.

At the risk of becoming repetitive, let me say that the more you try to soften the approach to this Spartan game, the less the men will respect your coaching. Good players are willing to accept proper discipline and sacrifice to help show that they are better than their teammates or opponents.

I suspect my players, at West Point as well as Dartmouth, considered me not only serious but severe. It may be that some who did not understand what I was trying to do thought me a martinet, and a few may have hated me for it. I also believe that most of them, anyhow, after they left school and assumed more and more of the responsibilities of life, appreciated with increasing clarity what I tried to do—what I had to do. I was not heartless, but any revelation of the slightest sympathy was out of key with the mood I considered urgent if Dartmouth was to regain its lost football respect.

In my first year at Dartmouth, I had occasion to tell a fourth-stringer to turn in his uniform. The next day, the boy's roommate came to see me. He said his roomie was packing up to leave school that night. Would I go over and talk with him?

Merle and I had a dinner date at the Hanover Inn with my old Miami friend and patron, Monk Pierce, Mrs. Pierce, and their friends, Mr. and Mrs. John Sterling. Not only were the Sterlings people Monk wanted me to meet for themselves, but John Sterling, as new president of the Dartmouth Alumni, was also darned important to our football.

That afternoon, I had to go directly from the practice field to a football committee meeting and could not find the time to phone Merle that I would be delayed. The party went through dinner without me. Merle left a message at the Inn that they had gone on to a movie and that I should join them there. Meanwhile, after leaving the committee meeting, I looked up the ex-fourth-stringer, who had packed up to leave.

I drove him around country roads and explained that he must not lose his sense of values. Football, I pointed out, was relatively insignificant, although I don't suppose I completely meant that. Anyhow, I talked him into staying in school. I finally joined our party at the movies around nine thirty.

I'm not suggesting I was wearing my hat inside out each day until I had prevented a non-football player from busting out of school. Acts of kindness are personal matters, not to be publicized for possible acclaim, but we had a reason beyond that for keeping them under cover. They might be misinterpreted as softness, and softness was what we were fighting.

The custom had grown at Dartmouth of holding something of a wake over every fallen gladiator in a scrimmage. Boston newspaper stories every week during the season featured who was in the college infirmary. We had to put a stop to that. We believed that pampering and publicizing injuries were not good for winning morale. Games are not won on the rubbing table.

With coaches of other sports and some athletic officials, our philosophy was not popular. Some of this, I think, traced to lack of understanding. Some of it was due, too, I am sure, to our failure to mingle socially very much. We were motivated here not by choice so much as necessity. We simply did not feel that we could spare the time from our work.

We were not able to establish the conditioning of the men on the proper basis the first year. The resolution of this problem answered the first crucial test of my career as a head coach.

The next to the last game of our first season was at Cornell. We had lost only one game up until then, to Yale, 7–2, and we had beaten Harvard, 10–0. But from midseason, we had been hit heavily by injuries, some real, some slightly fancied. I still thought we could beat Cornell. I guess I never did take a team into a game without the conviction (or delusion) that it could win. Cornell beat us, 21–6, and I did not think we had played up to our potential. I felt like leaping off the cliffs of Ithaca.

On the way home, our special train to Hanover stopped around midnight someplace near Syracuse. I went to bed early, but didn't sleep much. The next morning, as I walked through the train, I sensed something was wrong. I pried the story loose from the team manager by impaling him on the horns of a choice between loyalty to the school or to a few individual players.

It developed that two of the athletic officials and a prominent, sports-minded alumnus had taken three of the players into a railroad saloon and plied them with beer and Scotch. This same group had presided over similar affairs in the two preceding seasons, which accounted in part for the failure of the team to win a major game. They now advised my three players not to worry about that straight-backed soldier, who wouldn't be around next year anyhow.

"These men have had their inning," said one of the elders, "and they've proved exactly nothing. They're through, even if we have to buy up their contracts, and it's back to alumni coaching. At least we won't have to salute them!"

Monday morning found me in the office of President Hopkins. I told him what had happened and what I intended to do, which included relieving the trainer from football duty and action against other athletic officials. This was not an easy task to face, as these men were old residents and I was a somewhat unwelcome intruder.

By eleven that morning, my mission was accomplished, and all without one word to the squad. But the action taken was to the point, and the squad knew it. There was quiet resentment among some officials. This was soon quelled by an "either or" note from President Hopkins, the man who learned as a boy how to crack the toughest granite.

President Hopkins regarded his support of me as merely routine administrative procedure. When he delegated responsibility to an associate, he delegated it. This meant he backed you in whatever you did if he thought you were right—or wrong. In this case, he had no doubt. In the end, those same men who resented me became friendly. The players who broke training developed into three of the most valuable and selfless I coached at Dartmouth.

The following week at Princeton, we trailed at the half, 38–0. In our dressing room, I told the players that what was wrong with them was nothing that coaching could cure. Then I took all the coaches out of the room and left the players by themselves. Inside, I could hear the very devil breaking loose. The men thought I had lost respect for them. Some were recriminating with others and even threatening fisticuffs. But they charged back onto the field like hypoed jaguars and outscored Princeton in the second half, 13–0. In that thirty minutes, the Dartmouth spirit was reborn.

In the spring of 1935, I brought in my new football trainer. He was Roland Bevan, better known to Dartmouth and Army players as "The Beaver." This nickname was born of a mistake. Aren't they all? One of the Dartmouth players, who hadn't got the name straight, asked another shortly after Roland's arrival, "What do you think of Mr. Beaver?"

Bevan, a native of Berne, Ohio, had coached and trained high-school athletic teams at Dayton's Steele, Youngstown's Rayen, and Toledo's Woodward. The conditioning of his teams had won him a wide reputation beyond high-school and state circles. When he passed away on August 16, 1957, our mutual friend, Si Burick, sports editor of the Dayton *News*, wrote of him:

> He built in his athletes an appreciation of the human body and mind. I can think of several dozen doctors of medicine and osteopathy who would admit that early contacts with Bevan touched off the spark. But there are also lawyers, engineers, teachers, ministers, industrialists and merchants, too, who got the original urge for higher education when they were athletes at Steele under Bevan.

I knew Bevan only slightly in 1935, but I recognized that his ideas of conditioning must be identical with mine. Nowhere in his lexicon could be found the word "coddle." He did not drink or smoke, and he watched his weight assiduously. In his sixties, he was still a trim, well-muscled 148 pounds.

Bevan could spot a malingering athlete a mile away. Later, when we were together at West Point, there was a quarterback, a fine player and a good enough boy, yet given to dramatizing injuries that were not too serious. During a game in Michie Stadium, the quarterback lay prone after a play on the far side of the field from our bench.

I was fearful he was badly hurt, even envisioned him lost to us for the season. The Army team physician hurried immediately to the scene, where the Cadet players were gathered concernedly about the prostrate gladiator. Bevan, however, just stood there next to me in front of the bench, an artistic study in cold immobility and indifferent skepticism. His lack of concern irritated me deeply.

"What is the matter with you, Roland?" I upbraided him bitterly. "Why do you stand here doing nothing? Can't you see he may be badly hurt?"

My voice was so loud and angry that spectators in the west stands immediately behind us could not only see but hear the unusual impasse.

"There is nothing the matter with him," said Bevan with sarcasm. "You ought to know him by now. You ought to know he's putting on an act."

"Never mind what you think," I came back at him acidly, "or what I ought to know! You get the hell out there!"

With still some semblance of defiance, The Beaver moved leisurely across the field toward the prostrate Cadet. As he approached, the Army players opened ranks, and the team doctor moved aside to make room. Instead of reaching for restoratives, The Beaver gently applied his toe to the player's ribs.

"You can get up now," he said. "Everybody has seen you. You'll get your applause and be the old school hero."

Sure enough, the player bounced up like an India-rubber acrobat and started to prance toward the center of the field, with Bevan following him. Suddenly the significance of what Bevan had said dawned on him. He stopped, turned, and said to the approaching trainer, "Damn you, Bevan, you've made an ass out of me."

It was the last time, however, the quarterback ever indulged in histrionics, and he was the better player for it. The scorn Bevan visited upon me was nonetheless scathing for its silence.

Bevan never asked of an athlete anything he would not do himself. Even in his last days in a Dayton hospital, one would find him using his good right arm to massage his paralyzed left one. He did it so violently that he was told to take it easy, that he might hurt himself.

"No," said this outwardly hard-bitten, inwardly invincible man. "If anything can get the arm back into shape, it'll be this resistive exercise."

Besides his skill as conditioner and trainer, Roland was an authority on the proper type of equipment to keep injuries at a minimum. In 1942, the Touchdown Club of New York honored him with its annual award for permanent contributions to the game.

If Roland had any weaknesses, it was for snappy sport clothes and garish ties, which he thought set off his bald manliness. Sometimes his attire evoked comparison with the natural scenic beauty of Hanover's Balch Hill when the autumn leaves were turning. He liked occasional ice-cream sundaes and other extravagant desserts. As an admirer of physical culture in all categories, he also saw no harm in attending a burlesque show.

Soon after his arrival at Hanover, Roland sectioned off a corner of the gymnasium and installed all sorts of apparatus for inducing physical fitness. The contraptions and the toll they exacted caused the football players to name Roland's section "The Torture Room."

The philosophy of Bevan and myself on injuries, at Dartmouth and Army, can be simply summed up. First, the team doctor must be the final authority on whether an injured man can play. But the doctor must also understand that a football player is not a layman. Part of a football player's normal development includes a lowering of his pain threshold through will power.

For example, one day halfback Bob MacLeod got his nose broken in a scrimmage. He bled like a stuck hog. A layman would have rushed to a doctor and gone home to bed. Bevan put MacLeod's nose back into shape with one snap, plugged off the bleeding with two wads of cotton and Bob went back into the contact work at top speed.

Ignoring the wounded, removing them, and carrying on, shocked some of the Dartmouth players at first. I well recall the day a player had a nose badly smashed and lay bleeding. The rest of the team, following recent tradition, started to gather around him.

"Move it over," I ordered coldly (meaning the ball), "and keep going! Take care of him, Rollie!"

Later, I got the squad together.

"I want you to understand something," I said. "I was just as concerned about that injured man as you were. But to be consoling an injured man is bad for you and bad for him. It breeds a softness that is inimical to success."

Naturally, we had to practice such preachment, if necessary. While working in the field house one day, I caught my cleats in the cage netting and fell. I tried to break the fall with my hand. Instead, I broke my elbow. It hurt plenty, but I managed to get up right away and go on with the practice. That night the elbow had to be placed in a cast. When the players saw the cast the next day, it helped them buy what we were trying to sell.

I was just as harsh as we had been at West Point on anybody who broke training. A promising lineman was hospitalized with a badly infected leg. Harry went to visit him and found him propped up comfortably in bed, puffing a big cigar. Harry showed no reaction to that or to the youngster's rather airy assurance that he would be back to practice within the week. When he did return, it was to an empty varsity locker. The only way back for him was the rest of the season with the junior varsity as cannon fodder.

We could not, of course, abide injudicious eating habits. Most of our players were enrolled at an eating club for boys conducted by Mary (Ma) Smalley. A goodhearted soul, Ma Smalley probably fed more boys free than anybody in the history of the school. She was always extremely polite with company, but she had on call a vocabulary that would make a pirate tremble. Much to the delight of the players, she occasionally used it in discussing Roland Bevan.

Ma thought that growing boys, football players or not, needed cakes, pies, and ice cream. Bevan was equally sure they did not. In order to catch Ma violating his caloric commandments, Roland found it helpful to conduct subtle espionage campaigns. This, of course, produced more than one comic-opera situation.

Years later, when Roland and I were at West Point, Eddie Chamberlain, who played and coached for me at Dartmouth and is

now Dean of Admissions there, came by to visit us. The talk inevitably got around to the old days and to Ma Smalley. When Eddie returned to Hanover, he told Ma, "I brought back a message from an old friend of yours. He wants to be remembered."
Ma lighted up all over. "Who?" she asked.
"Rollie Bevan," said Chamberlain.
And Ma said, "That little bastard never did!"
One of Bevan's decisive victories over Ma involved Carl (Mutt) Ray, our center, and a fine one. Carl came back one September about 30 pounds overweight at 220 pounds. Bevan immediately relegated him to the select circle at Ma's known as "The Fat Man's Club." This meant Carl was fed mostly lettuce, occasionally relieved by a piece of Ry-Krisp or a carrot, and by the opening game he was down to 190 pounds, where he belonged. Carl's father, a doctor, was somewhat concerned at the rapidity of the weight-shedding and inquired of Bevan if he was trying to reduce Carl to a state of ectoplasm.
Another Bevan weight victory involved fullback John Handrahan, who also reported one fall some 20 to 25 pounds above what we considered his most efficient playing poundage of 180. John and his brother Joe, a 220-pound uninhibited gourmet, who played an agile game at guard, both worked at Gitsis Restaurant in Hanover. Joe, somewhat sympathetic to his undernourished brother, left his shift one night with a bagful of steak sandwiches. En route to their fraternity house, however, he had the misfortune to run into Bevan.
Roland investigated the bag of sandwiches and was aghast. "Who are these for, Joe?" he inquired. Joe admitted that they were for John and tried to convince Bevan his kid brother couldn't exist on lettuce and Ry-Krisp. Joe's efforts were not in vain. Bevan appropriated the sandwiches and walked Joe across the street to Tanzi's Fruit Store, where he bought an apple. "Here, Joe," he said, "take this back to John. It will carry him through the night and I'll see that he gets an extra Ry-Krisp tomorrow."
There will sometimes be an individualist who refuses regimentation even from a Bevan. We had at least one at Dartmouth in Vernon (Moose) Taylor, today a successful Western gas and oil operator.

Taylor had the size, strength, and speed to be a good tackle, but his mental outlook, to understate it, was casual.

The Moose had enough money to afford not only an automobile but an airplane. One spring he declined the invitation to football practice, offering as his reason: "low marks." I don't know how much time he spent studying. I do know he spent a lot of time in his plane, buzzing our practices. He unquestionably irritated us, much to the amusement of the players, but there wasn't very much we could do about it.

We used to mail the players their football shoes for "breaking in" during the summer. Taylor's shoes would never catch up with him until he returned to Hanover in September. They would be in a box postmarked Southhampton, Cannes, and Rome. So we would drop the Moose to the bottom of the tackle list and he would work his way up to the status of "ready reserve." One year he actually got serious enough to win a letter.

Another interesting character was Jack Williams, who played guard and was later my freshman line coach. Jack was a native Vermont farmer and used to sell his apples to Tanzi's. He charged 50 cents extra for the box. Then, late at night, he and Bevan would enter Tanzi's back yard, recover the boxes from the junk pile, and use them for later sales. I don't know the exact terms of the Williams-Bevan partnership, because they kept it to themselves.

Williams used to give us coaches apples that were slightly blemished, yet he took pains to protect us. He would pick up an apple and shake it to hear the seeds rattle. "That's the only way to tell if it's ripe," he'd say. "If you try to pinch it, you bruise it and lose your investment."

For all the seriousness of our approach, there were these and other laughs. I have always welcomed humor and fun in our football setups. It is the necessary leavening to an awfully tough job.

President Hopkins often dropped by practice and would relax with us afterwards in our dressing room. He always got a kick out of Bevan's comments. If Roland knew I was trying to build up a player, he liked to needle me about it. "Why, you know, Blaik," he'd say, "that boy hasn't got it!" And if I inquired about a boy who was really hurt too bad to play, he'd remark with some sarcasm, "I'll have him ready by Thursday."

Old and new friends dropped by Hanover. Moe Daly came over from West Point one winter, and he and Harry bought themselves complete skiing outfits, studied a ski book, practiced a lesson a day and climbed Mount Mousilake. Their plan was to ski down Hell's Highway, then the most terrifying trail in the White Mountains.

Moe was a he-man all the way, a rugged football player and coach, who had lumberjacked, and was later to give his life in World War II. Harry was of the same cut. But when they gazed down Hell's Highway from atop Mousilake—they were both already frozen—they put their skis on their shoulders and walked home. "I've put a plane in a dive for ten thousand feet, ripped the wings off and had to parachute out," said Moe, "but I'll be damned if I'd ski down that thing." As far as I know, Moe and Harry never discussed the venture again.

Arthur Sampson of the Boston *Herald* and Arthur Siegal, of the Boston *Traveler*, were frequent visitors and confidants of mine. Arthur Sampson had been a successful head football coach at Tufts and for the last thirty-two years has been one of the truly ranking sports experts in America. He appreciated our coaching problems. More than one night we drove around the hills of Hanover, while he listened to me moan about trying to get a blocking back who would really knock down an end. Arthur was friend, sounding board, and pillar.

One year, at the annual Dartmouth Winter Carnival, Harry and I were hosts to sporting representatives from the New York *Times* and *Herald Tribune*. After we had returned from the ski-jump events to our rooms in the Hanover Inn on a bitter cold day, our guests began to ply themselves with copious draughts of hot buttered rum. The gentleman from the *Times* was sitting around and imbibing in his bare feet and underdrawers. Before we realized it, the hot rum had warmed him to a degree where he suddenly skipped out of the room and down the four flights of stairs to a lobby well peopled with Carnival visitors. The manager of the Inn promptly phoned my room.

"Come down here and get your friend from the *Times*," he said.

"He's parading around the lobby in his underwear and making a scene."

"I'm not going down there and lead him back," I told the manager. "It's your job to keep peace."

Soon after, the gentleman from the *Times* came traipsing back up the stairs. As he passed a room several doors removed from ours, a beautiful girl came out. The gentleman from the *Times* stopped, turned, and bid her greeting. She went back into her room. It was right after that we heard a tremendous thud. We looked out our door and down at the floor. There lay the gentleman from the *Times*, out colder than the weather. Over him stood a big Dartmouth graduate—a bully, no doubt.

"Is this a friend of yours, Blaik?" he asked.

"No," I said. "He's no friend of mine."

With that, the big bully went into his room and closed the door. The gentleman from the *Tribune*, Ellinger, and I then hauled the exhibit into our room and put him to bed. At eight the next morning, he awoke, put his hand to the side of his head and said, "Somebody put the bee on me. Oh, my jaw!"

We invited Jock Sutherland up one fall, because I admired his fetish for detail and fundamentals. Jock's Pittsburgh teams were never better than at that time, but his relationship with W. Don Harrison, the athletic director, and Chancellor John Gabbert Bowman was not pleasant.

Sutherland stood watching our practice one afternoon with Mr. Hopkins and me. Compared to what he was used to coaching at Pitt, I guess we weren't very much. However when Mr. Hopkins asked him what he thought about our players, "The Great Stone Face" shook his head sadly and burred, "I wish I could coach a squad like this at Pittsburgh just once, Mr. Hopkins. Just once."

Even though it was a good joke, I hastened to change the subject. "Jock," I said, "Mr. Hopkins comes to practice at least two afternoons a week."

"My goodness," said Jock. "You're a lucky man. I've been at Pitt a long time and I can't remember the chancellor ever coming to practice."

"Jock," I said, "I'll make you a trade. I'll give you President Hopkins even up for Marshall Goldberg." Goldberg was Pitt's celebrated All America back.

Jock shook his head. "Much as I would like to have President Hopkins," he said, "I still must have someone to carry the ball."

Mainly because of their exposure to President Hopkins, our football coaches became interested in the philosophy of a liberal arts college like Dartmouth—if there is one quite like Dartmouth, which I doubt. They attended every convocation at which Mr. Hopkins spoke. Harry actually enrolled in a philosophy course. One night, during a staff meeting, he got into a discussion of Hegelianism with Hirshberg.

Hirshberg was a true intellectual, while Harry was somewhat pseudo. When Harry tried to overpower him with loud talk, Eddie remarked, "Ellinger, always remember that as your voice increases your reasoning decreases."

With that, I said, "Let's get to work. Dartmouth pays us for our knowledge of football, not for our erudition."

I suppose that statement might get me tabbed in some quarters as anti-intellectual. My Dartmouth and Army friends know better. We spent much time seeing to it our players hit the books. Even if we had not been disposed to do so, we would have been forced to. A player sidelined by scholastic deficiency is no good to anybody but the opposition. The Dartmouth faculty appreciated our co-operation and returned it. I believe that, to a certain extent, we may have won over even the late Professor of Chemistry, Leon B. Richardson, who was known as "Cheerless."

The nickname referred to Professor Richardson's general mien, not his behavior at football games, which he did not attend. For a time, Cheerless thought I was overemphasizing football and was critical of me. I, in turn, was irritated that he could not be as other professors and occasionally reschedule an hour's examination for a boy, to fit in with a game or a particularly important practice. Cheerless and I hadn't met each other, so the "vendetta" was carried on by third parties and rumor.

Then, one day we were introduced at a cocktail party given by

Mr. Hopkins. It may have been with the help of a Martini or two, but Cheerless brightened up a little. We each at length discovered the other was trying to instill the same lessons in his pupils. We thenceforth enjoyed better understanding. I don't recall whether Cheerless became any more lenient in rescheduling examinations. Probably not. He was a perfectionist and, in his way, dedicated.

Our primary dedication in those early days at Dartmouth was to beat Yale. This was a challenge that obsessed the college. It was something Dartmouth had been unable to accomplish in seventeen games over a period of fifty-two years. The last nine games had been played in Yale Bowl. In several of them Dartmouth had been favored, but the best they had been able to do was three ties. There was supposed to be a jinx.

The challenge became ours and required a studied approach. For one thing, we insisted the so-called jinx was nonsense, that Dartmouth never won because it had played poorly at crucial moments. We also tried to keep the team relaxed. For two years I never mentioned the Yale game. I would refer to it casually as "the game in New Haven."

Nevertheless, we lost the 1934 game in New Haven, 7–2, partly because we were still too tied up fighting the jinx. After the game, while we were sitting in our bus outside the Bowl, ready to leave, we were called on by Yale's Graduate Manager of Athletics, Malcolm Farmer. He had come to say good-bye to us, presumably, but he also looked the length of the bus and gave a little laugh that sounded slightly sarcastic.

If we remembered this, we did not let it prevent us from intensifying the relaxation theme in 1935, a good trick if you can do it. The week of the game, we gave the team as thorough a scouting report as possible. For the usual serious practice and repetition of fundamentals, we substituted in good measure an atmosphere of fun. We played games, with linemen in the backfield and backs in the line. We played touch football. Our attitude was: "Who the heck is Yale? Let's go down there and have a good time."

Does this seem to contradict what I have said about the futility of the play-for-fun approach? It does not, actually. This was no departure from basic Spartanism, which was already ingrained, but a useful psychological modification. Remember that Charlie Daly maxim: "Break any rule to win the game."

I was in poor physical condition leaving for New Haven before that game. I had suffered for some time from an ear ailment that caused a mild vertigo. It had caused me to eliminate speechmaking and forced me to coach much of the time from a kneeling position. I was forced to have the ear opened by a doctor that week and I was in some pain. I forgot it, however, in what took place.

The first time Yale had the ball, Jack Kenny, our captain and fullback, ran over and stuck his head into their huddle, said something and came trotting back with a half-grin on his face.

Our players asked, "What did you say, Jack?"

"I just told them," he said, " 'Let's have a lot of fun today, boys,' and one of them said, 'Get the hell out of here or I'll punch you in the nose!' " Then Kenny laughed. "I think he would, too."

In the second quarter, we marched 47 yards for a score, with Frank (Pop) Nairne, our right halfback, smashing over from the 9. On the play, tackle Dave Camerer put a key wall-out block on Larry Kelley, the Yale right end. John Handrahan converted, and we led, 7–0.

We threatened again in the third quarter, but they stiffened on the goal line. Shortly afterward, Charlie Ewart returned a punt for them 65 yards for a touchdown. They missed the point, so we led, 7–6, but we were not yet home free. That came in the closing minutes, when Carl Ray intercepted a desperate pass on their 8 and ran it over. We again converted and that was it, 14–6.

Unquestionably our relaxed attitude helped us play the game of which we were capable. And it was, like all worth-while victories, a complete team effort.

Three minutes before the end, the goal posts were down. Laughing and crying, old grads and young grads, students, everybody, it seemed, was crowding around our bench and later running over our locker room. It was something none of us who experienced it will ever forget.

President Hopkins had promised me that if we beat Yale, he would make a bonfire of Crosby Hall. (In those days Crosby was an antiquated old wooden-frame dormitory. Today it's a refurbished administration building for alumni affairs.) After we returned to Dartmouth, I asked him what time he was going to set the fire.

"I've decided not to, Earl," he said. "Beating Yale has already given the alumni one shock. I don't think they're quite ready for another."

Chapter IX

The Big Green and a Stronger Ivy League

President A. Whitney Griswold of Yale, in a speech at Johns Hopkins not so long ago, stated that college athletic scholarships are, for the most part, one of the greatest educational swindles ever perpetuated on American youth. He went on to say that they undermine the structure of American education and weaken the educational battle against the Soviet Union. "The cold war continues," said Dr. Griswold, "and so does the athletic-scholarship racket, as if Russia did not exist."

It is nothing new for the front pages of our most prominent newspapers to carry such a speech. Some educators periodically blame everything from the decline of Greek as a popular classics course to the increase of campus panty raids on the evil influences of paying a boy an education in return for his athletic ability. But when a man of Dr. Griswold's stature speaks out, it seems time to take serious notice.

Now, I hold deep respect for Dr. Griswold's erudition and position. But I must say that his collation of the cold war, communism, and the athletic scholarship left me in a daze greater than one induced by the Navy upsetting an Army football team. When the daze had gone away, I decided I should try to answer him, if for no other reason than fairness to legions of football players and coaches, past and present, including those from his own school.

Dr. Griswold was an undergraduate at New Haven from 1925 to 1929. Only a few years before his matriculation, it was not uncommon for Yale, Harvard, Princeton, and other large endowed colleges of the East politely to raid small colleges around the country for transfer students who also happened to be much-needed halfbacks or tackles. And there always seemed to be an influential alumnus of eleemosynary instincts who could not abide seeing the transfer student (or any football player, for that matter) struggle too severely for his education.

In Dr. Griswold's undergraduate days, the selected-transfer raid had become a thing of the past. But aid always has been available to Ivy League football players, and is today, in some form or other, through legitimate alumni help, college grants, or loans to take care of necessary educational and living expenses.

In those earlier eras, the 'twenties and 'thirties, there were far fewer empty seats in Ivy League stadia than you see today. It was considered almost a heresy not to be in Yale Bowl, for example, when Harvard, Princeton, the Army or Dartmouth came to town. Seventy thousand sellouts were frequent. It was almost as difficult to get tickets for a game with Georgia or an occasional Big Ten visitor. This, remember, was when a four-dollar ticket was worth four non-inflated dollars.

Such enthusiasm was ascribable to supercharged old-school-tie rivalries that traced back to the very roots of football at the old Eastern schools which shaped and developed the game. It stemmed also from a rich pride that the Big Three and other Ivy League teams, which had brought the game to the others, could still play the best on even terms.

I recall that Yale's 1923 team handed a 31–10 defeat to an Army team that held Notre Dame's "Four Horsemen" team, in its junior year, to 13–0. The 1927 Yale team, as I mentioned in an earlier chapter, lost only to Georgia after outplaying the Southerners, and imposed the only defeat that year on an Army team which decisively beat Notre Dame, 18–0. As late as 1938, an underdog Yale team, in losing to Michigan, 15–13, all but chased Michigan's Tom Harmon and Forest Evashevski back to Ann Arbor.

Yale wasn't the only one. Harvard's 1931 team, which lost only to Yale, beat Army and Texas, among others. Carl Snavely's Cornell teams of 1939 and '40 upset powerful Ohio State. Pennsylvania's teams had the personnel to play with anybody—and did. The Princeton "Coincidentals" (it was a "coincidence" that so many prep-school captains should show up on one campus) under Coach Herbert

Orrin (Fritz) Crisler in the early 'thirties could have played with the best of any era.

Here, then, was Ivy League football that fitted the concept of "big time": sellout crowds watching teams comparable to the best on the gridiron, with most of the players receiving what was tantamount to an athletic scholarship.

Was all this harmful to the players and the schools? I seriously doubt it. The worst I can say for those spavined old Ivy Leaguers today is that they are doctors, lawyers, statesmen, industrialists, educators, publishers, writers, or just plain, fine American citizens, who somehow managed to get a real education even though their football helped them get it. I see no evidence that these players were swindled by athletic scholarships or, if the semantically squeamish will feel better about it, by need programs.

Dr. Griswold himself indicated why they weren't swindled in that same speech at John Hopkins when he attacked "snap courses." Ivy League men of the 'thirties, and before and since, always have enjoyed the best in education. Therefore, how could any aid they received because of their athletic ability have been harmful to them? Why, then, throw the terms "athletic scholarship" and "snap courses" into the same hopper, when one has no essential relationship to the other?

The Ivy League I was part of at Dartmouth, from 1934 through '40, played an all-out football which provided a stern and stimulating challenge to coach and player.

I have stated that in the 'twenties the West, which had originally received its football from the East, was developing it by more advanced thinking. In the 'thirties, I feel there was a swing back to the East. There was better coaching there, on the whole, than was found in other sections. Others may debate this, but I think it is true.

It was in the East that the potential of the single-wing attack, whether behind balanced or unbalanced line, was exploited to the fullest, just before the arrival on the college scene in 1940 of the modern T formation with man-in-motion and flankers. It was in the East that the concept of multiple and ever-shifting defenses, the compensating offenses they demanded, and exhaustive study of films, all combined in forcing coaches to forgo the development of themselves as personalities and characters and to concentrate on being students of the game in a more authentic sense.

In the Ivy League alone, there were Crisler at Princeton; Carl Snavely at Cornell; Dick Harlow at Harvard; Lou Little at Columbia; DeOrmond (Tuss) McLaughry at Brown; George Munger and his line coach, Rae Crowther, at Penn; and Ducky Pond and his clever aide, Earl (Greasy) Neale, at Yale. Among the major independent coaches, there were Jock Sutherland at Pittsburgh, Jim Crowley at Fordham, Aldo (Buff) Donelli at Duquesne, Dr. Eddie Anderson at Holy Cross and, in the last two years of the decade, Frank Leahy at Boston College.

It wasn't a question of getting up early in the morning to match wits with that group; you weren't even safe if you stayed up all night.

My first two years at Dartmouth coincided with the last two at Cornell of that "Patron Saint" of all of us coachly pessimists, Gilmour (Gloomy Gil) Dobie. Dobie unquestionably was one of the great coaches of his time. He developed many winning teams at Washington, Navy, and Cornell. They all operated the off-tackle play, which was Gil's meat and drink, with a precision and devotion seldom, if ever, matched. As a cadet in 1919, I had played against one of his Navy teams. They reflected their coach all the way: fundamentally sound, conditioned, rugged, dedicated, tough to beat, and unimaginative.

In his later years at Cornell, Dobie's records fell away. Most of this was due to weaker material, but some of it must be charged to Gil's stubbornness. Long after it was proved impractical, he stayed with a seven-man line and a four-man box secondary on pass defense. He predicated everything on rushing the passer. But you can't always get to the passer successfully from a seven, and when you can't, you are vulnerable to the long pass. I am also convinced Gil overdid the preaching of pessimism. You may be able to tell a superior player he's not very good without hurting him, but I must doubt you help

Dad at 70.

I'm fourth from left, 17, freshman end on the Beta team at Miami, 1914.

Above: At Miami in 1917 I was varsity end and captain-outfielder. Below: I got that bad left eye in the 1919 Army-Navy game. I usually played left field.

Our 1919-'20 basketball team. I'm first on left, front row; we upset New York University's national champions.

Reporting as a new Cadet in 1918 (I'm at far left).

Above: Merle and I go canoeing on Lake Webster, Massachusetts, in 1920.
Below: At Fort Riley Cavalry School in 1920.

My son Bill and I looking for eagle eggs in New Hampshire, 1935.

The one and only Harry Ellinger.

Dartmouth golf and fishing pals: Cotty Larman, Ned French, Ellinger, President Ernest Hopkins, Billy Miller, and I.

Doc Blanchard cracks Navy for first score in 1945.

Glenn Davis, in the same game, eludes Clyde Scott on a 49-yard run for the third touchdown.

After the Rice game in 1958 with Rice Coach Jess Neely. We triumphed over the Owls 14–7.

MacLeod of Dartmouth breaks loose against Princeton in 1937.

Pat Uebel, with a pass from Pete Vann, streaks for a touchdown in dramatic victory over Duke in 1953, first big step in the comeback after the expulsions of 1951.

Pete Lash, Don Holleder, and Ed Szvetecz converge on Navy's Guest in 14-6 upset of 1955.

Bob Anderson sweeps Penn State end behind Joe Caldwell, 12, Harry Walters, 33, in '58 triumph of undefeated Lonely End team.

The Lonely End, Bill Carpenter (*far right*) heads downfield against Penn State in 1958.

Above: Yale Bowl, 1941—and a long Eli pass in the air. Below: Congratulations from Navy Coach Oscar Hagberg after our '44 win at Baltimore.

Above: At Notre Dame in '47, with Assistant Coach Johnny Sauer and tackle Bennie Davis. Below: At Northwestern in '53, Pete Vann, on my left, was still "just a boy." On the phone is Paul Amen, later head coach at Wake Forest.

We've just beat Navy in '53. Life has few moments like this.

"Tiny" W. Tomsen

Or like this after our '55 upset. Uebel and Holleder flank the Supe, General Babe Bryan. That's trainer Roland Bevan with the white cap, and on his left, Dick Voris, later head coach at Virginia.

The Philadelphia Inquirer

Captain Jim Kernan and General MacArthur at a September practice game.

Pete Dawkins studies the action as Assistant Coach Tom Harp and I check our spotters at Rice in '58.

Dan Hardy, Houston Post

Photo by Knopf Pix, Inc.

Andy Gustafson, the late Herman Hickman, Jako Jablonsky, and Stu Holcomb at a '45 staff meeting in the old football office.

In Philadelphia's Municipal Stadium, with Tucker, Doc, and Glenn before their last game, Navy, 1946.

Above: Father John Cavanaugh and Coach Frank Leahy of Notre Dame, and General Eichelberger in 1941. Below: A treasured autograph from a young friend, Corky Luke.

Coach Vince Lombardi of the Green Bay Packers was a valued aide in the years '49 through '53.

My son Bob was our 1950 quarterback.

Merle and "Lady" in West Point days.

This is Joe Cahill, Army's irreplaceable sports publicity director, at my desk—a scene almost exactly duplicated shortly afterward when I decided to call it a career.

U.S. Army Photograph

Above: A huddle, of sorts, at the Touchdown Club annual banquet in 1954. Shown with the author are (l. to r.) Speaker of the House Joseph Martin, Clark Griffith, president of Washington Senators, and Henry Tait Rodier, publisher of the *Washington Bulletin*. Below: With Grantland Rice (left) and General Douglas MacArthur.

Above: The night I was elected to the Football Hall of Fame December 8, 1964. Shown with cadets at the Academy table. Dinner was held in the Waldorf-Astoria. Below: With Attorney General Robert Kennedy at the Football Foundation Hall of Fame dinner in 1962. To Bobby Kennedy's left are Dick Diehl, captain of the 1962 Harvard football team and Col. Felix (Doc) Blanchard.

Associated Press Wirephoto

very many average players by downgrading them, privately or publicly, to themselves and others.

Although we had played at Ithaca in 1934, I hadn't met Dobie beyond a perfunctory handshake, because neither of us could be described accurately as "hail fellow well met." I probably would not have got to know him at all, except for Arthur Sampson.

The night before our 1935 game at Hanover, Arthur made a dinner date with each of us at the Hanover Inn, without telling either the other would be present. We both agreed, but both also imposed identical conditions: that we eat in Sampson's room and come into the Inn by a back stairway. Neither Gil nor I had any desire to be waylaid in the lobby or dining room by alumni, glowing or otherwise.

We both enjoyed the evening. That afternoon, during Cornell's practice on Memorial Field, I had observed Dobie take his squad down to each of the 5-yard lines and there deliver them a serious talk. During dinner, I told him I was curious to know why he did this.

"That's simple to explain," he said. "I told them they'd be spending most of tomorrow afternoon there on defense, so I didn't want them to feel strange."

It proved sound preparation. Dobie didn't have much of a squad—the best he could do was a 7–7 tie with Columbia—and we won, 41–6.

It developed he had made another accurate prediction. "You'll probably get beyond midfield once," he told his players. "When you do, I want you to use that special spread play we've put in."

Sure enough, Cornell got beyond midfield once, used the spread play, and scored their only touchdown. Needless to say, he hadn't mentioned the spread play at dinner.

That 1935 victory over Cornell gave us an 8–0 record going into the game at Princeton, but we were by no means favored. I believe the 1935 Tigers under Crisler probably were the strongest in the school's history. Their record was also 8–0. After a 7–6 opener over Pennsylvania, they had not been pressed, nor were they to be. The week after they played us, they trampled Yale, 38–7.

They were far too strong for us, 26–6. The game is remembered as "The Rape in the Snow" and "The Twelfth Man Game."

We were staying at Peddie School in Hightstown, New Jersey, only 11 miles from Princeton. I always tried to sequester my teams away from cities and public hotels.

When we left Peddie by bus around noon on Saturday, the sun was shining. By the time we reached Palmer Stadium, the sky had turned gray and was spitting snow. By game time, the stuff had covered the field. As the game advanced, the storm grew into a blizzard. We had come completely unprepared for anything like this in the way of special cleats, not that it would have made, I suspect, much difference.

The powerful Tiger fullback, Pepper Constable, kept driving over our left side behind superb blocking for 5, 6, 8 yards at a clip. Jack Kenny, our fiery fullback and captain, was backing up that side of the line. Jack kept daring them: "Come on through here again! Come on! You won't make an inch!" The Tigers gleefully accepted all of Jack's invitations. Finally, Dave Camerer, our left tackle, pulled himself off the ground after a foray, and yelled to Kenny, much to the amusement of both sides, "Damn it, Jack, don't forget the bastards are coming through me before they get to you!"

We made the mistake of scoring first and getting Princeton stirred up. That we needed all the help we could get that day was obvious to everybody, even an inebriate who wove down out of the stands, through the blinding storm and onto the snow-covered field, where he lined up between guard Joe Handrahan, Bevan's Tanzi-apple man, and the redoubtable Camerer.

"Kill them Princeton bums," he muttered, and made a wild lunge at Constable. The cops arrived and removed him, but he went echoing down the corridors of football time as "The Twelfth Man." Even if he had been permitted to play, he would not have had enough to stem the tide that day. The next year, however, we were to begin catching up with Princeton.

So far, despite Princeton, the 1935 season had to be accounted successful. (We had not only beaten Yale for the first time, but we had also leveled Harvard by the identical score, 14–6, in what was the second of seven consecutive victories over Dick Harlow's teams. Even when they outplayed us, we managed to win.) But we undid a lot of it by concluding on an emphatically sour symphony in Baker Field, New York. We were upset, 13–7, by a Columbia team, which had been beaten four times and tied. I told the team afterwards how I felt:

"We thought you were a good team despite that Princeton game. You were beaten, badly beaten. So what? So you couldn't forget it and carried it into this one—something a good team doesn't do. That's why I'm horribly disappointed in you!"

Johnny Handrahan, who could play either fullback or halfback for us, suffered a shoulder separation. While the rest of the team scattered around New York and broke training, Bevan worked on the separation with ice and heat pads. Later, Roland took John to dinner and then to a burlesque show, where The Beaver managed front seats. One of the girls in the chorus had undergone an appendectomy sometime in the past. Bevan's background as a trainer gave him a keen appreciation of neat surgery. Here was an example of it which quite overcame him.

"John," he yelled, almost at the top of his voice, "just look at that beautiful scar!"

For the record, our seven seasons at Dartmouth produced forty-five victories, fifteen defeats, four ties. I wish there were room here to salute every single letterman, substitute, and scrub who helped make it possible. I would not pick an All Dartmouth team any more than I would pick an All Army team. It would be unfair. I hesitate to name even a list of our better players at Dartmouth, because differences in ability are often marginal and I'm bound to leave out somebody I shouldn't. I suppose, however, that any list of the superior players would have to include the following:

Merrill Davis and Jim Parks, ends; Camerer and Gordon Bennett, tackles; Lou Young and Gus Zitrides, guards; Carl Ray and Bob Gibson, centers; and Bob MacLeod, Harry Gates, Bill Hutchinson, and Johnny Handrahan, backs. There were players who didn't get the credit they should, like halfbacks Fred Hollingsworth and little 150-pound scat-back Warren King, fullback Colby Howe, and many others.

There is no question that my top player at Dartmouth was Robert

Frederic MacLeod, from Glen Ellyn, Illinois, regular right halfback of the 1936, '37 and '38 teams. It was no coincidence that in Mac's three years, we put together a defeatless string of twenty-two games.

We had just returned from Memorial Field to our dressing room after a mid-September practice in 1936, when MacLeod slammed through the door into our midst. He was still in cleats, a classic picture of determination and controlled anger.

MacLeod, a sophomore, would soon be a great player, we knew, but we had been running him with the second team because his tackling was still uncertain. This traced solely to inexperience, because Mac had sufficient desire for a platoon. He liked to hit hard and, at the moment, looked as if he would sure enjoy hitting something very hard.

His invasion traced to an experiment that day. We had replaced the player who had been running first-string right half with Harry (Heavenly) Gates, the regular quarterback, or blocking back, in our single-wing attack. Gates, a junior, was a more experienced blocker and defensive player than MacLeod. So, for the time being, we had left Mac on the second team. The line-ups had been posted on the bulletin board before practice. Nobody had said anything. The day's work had gone along as usual. Now MacLeod stood before me, self-containment obviously an effort.

"Can I see you a moment, coach?" he asked.

"Sure, Mac," I replied. "Do you want to see me alone or here?"

"Anywhere."

"Right. What can I do for you?"

"What's it take to make this team?"

"First you have to be a tackler, Mac. Strong defensively."

The room, for three or four seconds, was as quiet as before his arrival. Then, MacLeod said, "That's all I wanted to know." He turned and walked out of the room as suddenly as he had come.

In our next few practices, the players MacLeod tackled were never hit harder before or after in their football lives. He not only started the next game but every one of the other twenty-five of his three varsity seasons. He captained the 1938 team, and was an All

American of reality as well as record: a runner, pass receiver, blocker and—underscore it—defensive player.

After graduation in 1939, he played professional football one year with the Chicago Bears, principally to prove to himself that he could play it. George Halas, veteran coach of the Bears, told me that he never saw a finer defensive back than MacLeod. For several years now, Mac has been a success in the magazine business. He was recently promoted from publisher of *Harper's Bazaar* to head of advertising for all Hearst magazines.

I have recalled that tableau in Davis Field House, now almost a quarter of a century in the past, to emphasize that MacLeod didn't complain, didn't rationalize, didn't say he should be on the first team, didn't claim he was a good defensive player. He only wanted to know what he must do to make the first team. He was told, and he did it.

His example epitomizes a truth about college football too seldom appreciated by educators: it is as typically Early American as the founding fathers themselves, because the football player expects and gets no quarter.

Our 1936 team, which lost only to Holy Cross and was tied by Princeton, may have been our strongest, although the 1937 team was undefeated, tied twice. The '36 team was an interesting group and involved in many memorable games. One of these was with Holy Cross at Hanover on Saturday, October 10.

We prepared thoroughly. The Crusaders were then a ranking Eastern power and had gone fifteen games without defeat. They outweighed us in most positions. We relied on quickness more than heft. At the tackles, for example, Camerer was 197 and Gordon Bennett, captain of the team, was actually only 187.

For fear we would not start him, Bennett used to add 10 pounds to his weight when he wrote it on the daily training-room chart. This spirited youngster was to die six years later in the Boston Cocoanut Grove fire. It was the only time in his life he was ever in a night club. He was celebrating his engagement.

Our players went at Holy Cross to win and there was some interesting verbal byplay in the trenches. Carl Ray carried on an exchange much of the afternoon with an opponent playing opposite him. Finally Carl made an unfavorable reference to the opponent's nose, which had been disfigured in some earlier gridiron war. Ray's team mates reported that he was temporarily nonplused when his Crusader target replied, "Who the hell do you think you are, John Barrymore?"

The persiflage, however, was not as good as the game. We outstatisticked the Crusaders but could not capitalize on scoring chances. It was 0–0 in the middle of the fourth period and we were on their 36-yard line when Hollingsworth aimed a pass to MacLeod out to the left. The ace of the Holy Cross team and later a star for the Chicago Bears was fullback "Bullet Bill" Osmanski. Bullet Bill intercepted Hollingsworth's pass and headed up the east sideline for the north end zone, and with him went the ball game; Final score, 7–0.

Some of our players felt they reacted slowly in covering the pass or they might have cut off Osmanski. One of them who felt that way was Carl Ray. Many times in the last twenty-four years, he tells me, people have asked him to name his most vivid football memory. They expect him to name that first-ever Dartmouth victory over Yale, when his interception and run brought the insurance touchdown. They are invariably surprised when he tells them the scene that returns to him most often is Osmanski racing up the east sideline of Memorial Field with that intercepted pass, and his own failure to react quickly enough to get a good shot at him.

"My wife Ruth," says Carl, "on several occasions has considered me slightly touched in the head, when she asked the reason for my faraway look, and I told her I've been reliving those few seconds of indecision which resulted in the Holy Cross touchdown."

I suppose there are intellectuals who would deplore Ray's emphasis on the importance of football as expressed in his often recalling that one play. There are modern psychologists, perhaps, who will argue that such a disappointment as Ray encountered that day, at such an early period in his life, might be harmful to him.

I could agree with the intellectuals only if they could show me how doing anything less than the best you can is worth doing at all; and with the psychologists only if they could show me it is detrimental to be conditioned early to the failures that are part of life. Just for the record, Ray has done as well in life as he did in football.

I would say that, as a whole, the Dartmouth players were more interesting as people than the West Point Cadets, because they had more time to lead a normal life. Our players were interested in everything and argued about everything. This was the result of the stimulating, inquiring atmosphere of the liberal arts college and the all-permeating influence of President Hopkins.

The religious discussions were something. They were usually initiated by Harry Gates, who was called "Heavenly," and had joined The Holy Ghost and Us, a religious society with a farm near Manchester, New Hampshire. The sparks set off by Gates were whipped into a quick flame by MacLeod, a Protestant; halfback Phil Conti, a Catholic; and quarterback Henry (Hank) Whitaker, who said he was an agnostic.

I recall one argument among this group that carried right into the locker room at Harvard and right up until it was time to go onto the field, and the assistants and I had a heck of a time stopping it. However, the boys didn't let their religious debate prevent them from putting together a good enough team game to beat Harvard, 26–7.

The next week we played the first of two hair-raising games with Yale. We had them, 11–0, near the end, when a sub back named Gil Humphrey suddenly went wild passing. He completed one to Larry Kelley for a touchdown that made it 11–7. We seemed safe enough with two minutes to go, but we fumbled on our 19, they recovered and a pass interference call gave them the ball on our 1. They still had time for two plays, but clutch tackling by Camerer, MacLeod, and Lud Pyrtek, our right end, saved us. Brother!

When we got unwound, there was much discussion about the pass interference call that might well have cost us the game. A similar call was to enable Princeton to tie us, 13–13. Other such decisions around the country brought a salutary revision of the pass interference rule, so that a defender was given proper leeway in body contact, provided he was obviously going up after the ball.

Our second straight victory in Yale Bowl convinced even the most superstitious the jinx was dead. We were also getting a lot of publicity mileage out of Bob MacLeod's long runs from our deep reverse. He had torn off several against Yale, almost getting loose all the way more than once.

Yale's assistant coach, Greasy Neale, earned the gratitude of our publicity man, Robert (Whitey) Fuller, by describing the deep reverse as "that play in which the Dartmouth student body comes down out of the stands and gets into the interference." But it was only the old Warner deep reverse, with our own blocking assignments and techniques.

Let me describe the play. Our fullback in the single wing, behind an unbalanced line to the right, took the snap and headed toward their left tackle. Our left end, short-side guard, and inside tackle blocked on the line. Our quarterback, or blocking back, picked off the first defender to penetrate from the defensive left side. As the fullback neared the line with the ball, he eased it off to MacLeod, who reversed in a medium arc aimed at enflanking the defensive right side. Ahead of him were four blockers: the tailback, who had faked to take the snap from center and then had gone after the defensive right end; and the three men who had pulled out of the line, namely, the strong-side guard, the outside tackle and the strong-side end.

Our 1937 prospects were not valued highly in September, but this team, captained by Merrill Davis, worked hard and had tremendous spirit. The Harvard team we beat—20-2, in bad weather, on long runs by sophomore fullback Bill Hutchinson—actually outplayed us. Harvard lost only one other game that year, to Army, 7-6, and by well-conceived defensive line stunting earned a scoreless tie with superior Navy personnel. The Crimson's tricky attack was built around the clever spinning of fullback Vernon Struck, whom George Trevor dubbed "The Magnificent Faker."

We put on a remarkable comeback march in mud and rain to tie Cornell, 6-6. Coach Carl Snavely was just getting the Big Red tuned up for three big seasons ahead. At Columbia's Baker Field, once again in atrocious weather, we played one of our best games in beating a Sid Luckman team, 27–0. Luckman completed his first five passes, but from then on our hard rush and alert secondary foiled him.

It did not seem possible, or at least logical, to have another super-melodrama with Yale back to back. The Elis, captained by Clint Frank, were strong again and were to lose only the finale to Harvard, 13–6.

The story began the Thursday night before the game, when twelve of our players suffered an attack of dysentery from rancid spinach. The ailing included five of the starters, MacLeod among them. The players were still under the weather when we got on the train for New Haven Friday morning. Before practice in Yale Bowl that afternoon, I called MacLeod aside.

"Mac," I said, "the newpapers are all here to watch this practice. Whether we win this game tomorrow or lose, it is going to look bad if these people think we are using illness as a pre-game maneuver to detract from a possible Yale win, or to lull Yale into some sort of security.

"Now, how do you feel? Are you and the others going to be able to do the full job or more? If the answer is no, I have got to re-arrange our pattern. If the answer is yes, I want you to get the other boys who were stricken and tell them individually we are going to put on the darndest practice that has ever been seen in this Bowl! I want those writers to go out of here knowing we are a ready ball club!"

That was the kind of workout we had, and the kind of game we played. Through a brilliant 85-yard runback of an intercepted pass by MacLeod and a field goal by Phil Dostal, we led, 9–2, with little more than a minute to play. We had bottled up Clint Frank, but we couldn't keep the cork in. In the seconds left he engineered a passing attack that took them more than ninety yards. Twice he connected on fourth-down passes. There was time for only one play and the ball on our 35 when he threw the second one to Al Hessberg in our left defensive flat. Hessberg eluded two of our secondaries, who bumped into each other and got into the end zone. Under great pressure, Gil Humphrey kicked the extra point that tied it, 9–9. Two people in the

Bowl suffered heart attacks. "It was a wonder," somebody wrote later, "their names were not Ducky Pond and Red Blaik."

I never saw a morgue to equal our dressing room. Yale's was somewhat happier. They had been favored to win but they were glad to get the tie. As I look back on that game, I think principally of two great players: Clint Frank and Bob MacLeod.

Frank played that day and most of the season with tape covering much of his body. He took a terrific pounding. Moose Taylor, our flying tackle, "crashed" him once without a plane. You would think Frank was through, but somehow he would pick himself up and go on and on. While he could still stand up, he was dangerous.

MacLeod was the same breed. All things considered, both in the blocking and the running, Mac's 85-yard run with that interception of a Frank pass was as fine as any ever seen in the Bowl. Mac played through the game well below par physically. For two nights he had had little, if any, sleep. He came out of the game weighing 169, a drop of 18 pounds since Wednesday. He was a football player.

The wild finish, as spectacular and hair-raising as any Yale team ever engineered, the heroics of MacLeod and Frank, the whole picture had the setting it deserved. The biggest Bowl crowd since before the 1929 depression overflowed into the aisles and the portals. Outside, 10,000 to 20,000 more rioted for tickets. Before the game, Dartmouth people were jumping out of the stands and running up to me with notes from other friends outside who wanted in. I couldn't do anything for them. Besides, I had other things on my mind. There was about the same kind of crowd at our game the following year. What a dreadful display of Ivy League overemphasis!

MacLeod, of course, was elected captain of the 1938 team. It may be that this team, although it lost its two final games, to Cornell and Stanford, got more out of what it had than any I coached at Dartmouth. We had a fine set of backs, but our line was ordinary. They had to make up in quickness and spirit for what they lacked in heft and ability.

They could not afford to let down at any time, which they learned in the Brown game. Brown, well coached by Tuss McLaughry who was to succeed me at Dartmouth in 1941, usually was outmanned by his opponents. That year Tuss had a few boys to work with. It was a frightfully warm Indian summer day at Hanover, the worst I remember. Brown met the challenge of it far better than we did and trailed at the half by only 14–13. We were fortunate they were not ahead of us.

Between halves I told the players that I might have seen at some time a worse-looking football team than they were, but I couldn't remember where. I was concerned as to what I should do.

Sometimes there is nothing you can say that will rouse a tired or indifferent team from its lethargy. If you stay with them, you may lose; probably will. Often, a performance by a second team will wake them up where nothing else will. However, our second team was distinctly a gamble. I talked it over with the coaches and Captain MacLeod, and decided to go with the second team. They came through beautifully in the third period. In the fourth period the first team returned and began to play football. We won, 34–13.

More excitement surrounded "the game in New Haven," but this time of a different mood and texture. I have mentioned Harry Gates, the boy known as "Heavenly" because of his deep religious inclinations. Harry had been our blocking quarterback in 1936 and '37, and the best I had at Dartmouth. In the fall of 1938, however, he did not report for football. His association with The Holy Ghost and Us society apparently had convinced him that his fondness for the game was a form of sinful vanity and exhibitionism, and his violent blocking an example of man's inhumanity to man.

Harry may also have felt that the 72,000 inside the Yale Bowl and the other thousands outside, the autumn before, bespoke much of the spirit of the old Roman arena mobs. Knowing how some alumni are, I must say that he was probably right. Years later, Harry visited an empty Yale Bowl, sat there and pondered the old days. Whether he called them good or bad, I don't know.

Anyhow, the Monday before the '38 Yale game, Harry decided he wanted to come out for the team again. He did not come up to me and say so; there was still a struggle going on within him. But I could see him watching our practices on Memorial Field from a distance. I was also told that when we worked in the field house, he was peeking at us through a window. I knew we needed him badly. We did not have anybody for the position who could block and back up a line like Harry.

On Tuesday evening, Harry came to me and told me he wanted to come back. I put it up to the players, and they were for his return. He suited up on Wednesday and as he called the signals, his high-pitched "One-TWO, One-TWO" never sounded better to me. In New Haven, he did a job backing up the line and eradicating the Yale ends. Finally in the Bowl we won one we could breathe through, 24–6. MacLeod made two long touchdown runs, and Colby Howe was solid at fullback.

We stayed in a Hartford hotel Saturday night until midnight and took a late train to Hanover Sunday. Soon after we left the train at White River Junction Sunday morning, Gates disappeared. He went over the hill to The Holy Ghost and Us people and played no more football. Later, he returned to school and graduated.

Our '38 record was 7–0 going into the game with Cornell at Ithaca. Our defeatless string, which began with the Brown game in '36, had reached twenty-two. But I knew we were up against by far the best team we would play all year. Our backs could match Cornell's, but we were overmatched up front. Snavely said afterwards that his team that day played the game he had been expecting of it all year. Their line simply dominated us. Nevertheless, the final score was only 14–7 and MacLeod's running in the last period threatened to tie it up.

A record crowd of 30,486 sat in Schoellkopf Stadium, and the partisan enthusiasm was most intense. The game was only two minutes old when some Ithacan varlet snipped all the lines connecting our press-box phones with the bench. The who-done-it ranks with such mysteries as the firing of Steve Sebo and why faculty representatives oppose two-platoon football.

The game at Stanford was anticlimactic. The press referred to our small team as "boy scouts," but we won their respect. We presented Stanford an angling defense which bothered them for a while. We trailed, 14–13, going into the last quarter. Then they pushed it up to

23–13. MacLeod was again outstanding and deserved the All America honors accorded him.

Despite the downbeat finish in '38, we could look back on solid progress. Our record from 1935, our second year, through '38 showed twenty-nine victories, five defeats, and three ties; the Yale jinx slain and interred; the twenty-two-game defeatless string; Ivy League championships in 1936 and '37. President Hopkins was happy about it. So were most Dartmouth people. Yet, even in the Ivy League of those days, there was a taint of the philosophy that winning regularly somehow connotes a certain lack of respectability.

Even so good a friend as Dean Lloyd K. Neidlinger, a former Dartmouth tackle (whose brother Newell had been an excellent back on Yale's great '23 team), mentioned one day that it might be a good thing for the series if we lost a game to Harvard. He made the mistake of saying it within earshot of Merle, who upbraided him politely about as follows: "It's never a good thing to lose any game. That was what was the matter when we came here."

Time and affairs somehow invariably contrive sooner or later to trip up or slow down all football dynasties, large, small, and medium. So it was with our medium-size regime. The freshman classes beginning in 1937 were relatively weaker than those of '34 through '36. This began to show up on the scoreboard in '39, although we tied Navy, 0–0, beat Yale and Harvard again, and were beaten resoundingly only by Snavely's undefeated, untied Cornell team. Cornell that year took good care of Ohio State's Western Conference champions at Columbus and had as good a claim on the national championship as anybody.

In 1940, we slipped a little more. Yale beat us, 13–7, for the first time since 1934. We had lost three other games and had no ranking whatsoever as we approached the next to the last game on our schedule: Cornell, at Memorial Field, November 16. Since midway in 1938, Cornell had won eighteen straight, was ranked No. 1 nationally and was at least a 4–1 favorite over us. Snavely himself told Allison Danzig, veteran expert of the New York *Times* and a Cornell alumnus, that of his three powerful teams of 1938 through '40, the '40 team was the best until weakened by injuries, especially on the left side of the line. All but one of these injuries were incurred in the first quarter of our game due to the rugged play.

In preparing for that game, I had two problems: the first technical, the second psychological.

For two years, Cornell's running attack had featured tricky spins, reverses, and traps, with relatively little reliance on straight-ahead power. The year before, we had played into their hands by using a hard-charging line and they had cut us to pieces.

This time, we put together an elaborate defensive pattern, which may well have been as complicated as any devised up until then. We played our ends normally on the line but posted our tackles and guards a yard and a half off the ball. The linebackers, playing shallow, approximated the same depth as the tackles and guards. The plan was for these six men to sit there, forgo early commitment, angle off in the direction of the ball, and by quick reaction and pursuit give up the short gain and no more.

Now, part of the reason why Cornell seldom hit straight ahead was that the fullback, or No. 3 back, in their single wing, Mort Landsberg, was speedy and nifty at darting through a trap hole, rather than powerful. On certain plays, however, Landsberg exchanged places with Captain Walter Matuszczak, Cornell's burly No. 2 or blocking back. This gave them more straight-ahead plunging power and also enabled them to utilize Matuszczak's powerful blocking on sweeps.

They also had a dangerous counterplay from this series, on which Walter Scholl, the tailback, faked a run to the strong side, stopped and tossed a "back diagonal" pass to Landsberg in the weak-side flat. With Landberg's speed, it was a potential long-gainer or gamebreaker if called at the right time, and had proved effective. To cover it, Bob Crego, our weak-side backer-up, who was later to give his life in World War II, was instructed always to play Landsberg, come what may, when he shifted to the No. 2 spot.

So much for the outline of our defensive plan.

We naturally worked at building our men psychologically for a supreme effort. We did not have to sell Cornell's stature. Their record, rank, reputation, and what they had done to us the year before took care of that. There was no problem getting our men keyed up for the game. But as Saturday neared, I thought I detected signs that they might be wound a little too tight. This could be just as harmful as a casual approach. To execute the complex defensive blueprint assigned them and also put on their own offense smoothly, they needed to be dedicated yet relaxed, a finely drawn fusion not always easily attained.

On Friday afternoon, we repaired to our regular pre-game bivouac, the Bonnie Oaks Inn on Lake Fairlee outside Fairlee, Vermont, not too far from Hanover. Saturday morning, we went through our usual routine: an early walk and breakfast. The players were then ordered to rest in their rooms until called by Bevan to have their ankles taped. Any boisterousness was supposed to be out of order. They were supposed to relax.

After breakfast—I guess I had a cup of tea—I went to my room and lay down. I thought about the squad. They looked a little too tight. I thought it over and phoned Captain Lou Young to come up to my room.

When Lou arrived, I tried not to look as white as the bed sheets. I tried to joke with him about the game, but I didn't do a very good job of it. I asked him how he thought the players felt about it. He said he thought they were ready, real ready. I asked him if he understood fully the defensive signals he was to handle, and he said he did.

"Well, Lou," I said, "I think the team is wound a little too tight. Now, there isn't any need for this. We are really a much better team than Cornell expects to meet. We are ready to take them. So, I want the players to relax. After Bevan finishes taping them, I want you to get down in the lobby and turn on the record player. Play some of that hot jazz which seems to be the order of the day. We want to go up to the stadium relaxed."

Lou carried out my instructions and when we boarded the bus, the players seemed to be a little looser. During the ride, I walked up and down the aisle and actually did some clowning, the first time I had done any acting of that type since my role as "Buttons the Bellhop" back at Steele High. Maybe my act wasn't very good, but I believe the players were relaxed the way I wanted them to be when we got to Memorial Field.

I had written in our pre-season football brochure: "the mysterious Indians on one occasion will rise to great play." This was the day. Our defense did the job we wanted. In the first half, we stopped them cold. In the third period, they marched, but we stopped them by an end-zone interception. Then we marched ourselves, and early in the final period we got close enough for end Bob Krieger to place-kick a 27-yard field goal.

With only four and a half minutes to play and the ball on their 48-yard line, Cornell took to the air. Although a light snow had dampened the ball and the field, Scholl was connecting with his receivers. Perhaps they should have begun passing earlier.

One pass was allowed for interference on the 18-yard line, but we were of no mind to complain. It was the "back-diagonal" pass to Landsberg. For once, Crego forgot to pick him up right away. Our phone spotters, sensing it immediately, jumped up and yelled, although Crego couldn't possibly have heard them. Crego, however, realized his mistake as the play developed. He saw that Landsberg was sure to get to the ball before he could, and that would likely spell touchdown and the game. But Crego also saw that he had enough of an angle to tackle Landsberg and take the penalty, which he did. It was quick thinking. In light of what followed, it probably saved the game.

From the 18, another pass from Scholl to right halfback Bill Murphy gave Cornell first down on our 5. There was less than a minute to play as Landsberg hit into the line for two. On second down, Scholl drove to the 1. On third down, Landsberg was piled up for scarcely any gain. The ball rested less than a yard away from our goal line. There was time for two more plays at the most.

Now began a series of events which proved to be a weird prelude to an emotional Donnybrook and an aftermath never duplicated in football history.

To stop the clock, Snavely called time out, so Cornell was penalized 5 yards for delaying the game. This placed the ball on our 6-yard line.

On fourth down, Scholl passed into the end zone. The ball was batted away from Murphy, the intended receiver. William H. (Red) Friesell, a referee of long-proved excellence, put the ball on the 20-yard line, apparently in our possession.

But then, after a consultation requested by Captain Matuszczak, Friesell changed his mind and returned the ball to our 6. For some reason, according to a subsequent quote from Snavely, Matuszczak and other Cornell players thought there had been a double-offside penalty called on the pass which had been batted down in the end zone.

Captain Young protested vigorously to Friesell that there had been no such penalty, and two of the officials backed him up. But Friesell, apparently confused, continued to allow Cornell possession on the 6-yard line and another down.

There were six seconds left—time for Cornell to get off one play. They huddled and decided to go for a touchdown and victory rather than a field goal and a tie. Two seconds remained on the clock when Scholl passed to Murphy in the end zone, and this time Murphy caught it. Nick Drahos, Cornell tackle, kicked the extra point. The game was over and Cornell had won, 7–3.

The coaches on both sides and the fans thought that was it. But our players, two of the officials, and the writers covering the game knew that Cornell had scored on a fifth down. The writers so reported it. The news swept down from the press box, through the crowd, out onto Memorial Field, into Davis Field House and on through Hanover like wildfire. Students began parading, proclaiming a Dartmouth victory. They paraded throughout the weekend, every hour on the hour. One of the parades ended up in front of our house.

When the situation was brought to the attention of Jim Lynah, Cornell's athletic director, he stated that if the officials discovered that there had been five downs, the score would be recorded as Dartmouth 3, Cornell 0. Dr. Ezra Day, president of Cornell, concurred.

President Hopkins and I drove Referee Friesell across the Connecticut River to the White River Junction station. He admitted to us he had apparently made a mistake.

On Monday, after Cornell officials had studied the films, which showed five downs and no evidence of a double-offside, they called Asa Bushnell, Executive Secretary of the Eastern Intercollegiate Association, who then forwarded the information to Friesell.

Friesell issued a statement, expressing his regret. Bushnell then stated that no official had jurisdiction to change the outcome of the game and that any further action would have to come from Dartmouth or Cornell.

When this was reported to Cornell, they sent us two wires. One from Jim Lynah read:

IN VIEW OF THE CONCLUSIONS REACHED BY THE OFFICIALS THAT THE CORNELL TOUCHDOWN WAS SCORED ON A FIFTH DOWN, CORNELL RELINQUISHES CLAIM TO THE VICTORY AND EXTENDS CONGRATULATIONS TO DARTMOUTH.

A second from Coach Snavely read:

I ACCEPT THE FINAL CONCLUSIONS OF THE OFFICIALS AND WITHOUT RESERVATION CONCEDE THE VICTORY TO DARTMOUTH WITH HEARTY CONGRATULATIONS TO YOU AND THE GALLANT DARTMOUTH TEAM.

And we wired Cornell:

DARTMOUTH ACCEPTS THE VICTORY AND CONGRATULATES AND SALUTES THE CORNELL TEAM, THE HONORABLE AND HONORED OPPONENT OF HER LONGEST UNBROKEN RIVALRY.

I had been told almost eight years before, by Eddie Dooley and Red Lowden, that a good part of Heaven was right in Hanover, New Hampshire. I believe they were right. It even included the miracle of a game that was won after it was lost. As I look back down the years, maybe it was a sign that I should not leave Dartmouth.

Even to its supporters, Ivy League football today lacks the appeal that it held in those days before World War II. What has happened? Has the coaching deteriorated? I am convinced that coaching, like all professions, has increased in knowledge and improved in techniques.

Is there a difference in material? Let me quote an Ivy League official:"Overall, there is more talent than there ever was. And it does not arrive unsolicited and unwelcomed. It would make interesting research, as a case in point, to compare the ratio of football players and non-players among Ivy enrollees from certain Western Pennsylvania townships. Even the Big Ten complains Ivy League schools are getting too many of their good boys."

If the coaching and the material are just as good as they ever were, what is the answer? Simply this: the game has been purposely devaluated. It is exactly the kind of game the Ivy League presidents want. Not good enough to create too much enthusiasm. Not bad enough to evoke more than a faint protesting murmur from the alumni.

The devaluation was set in motion by the elimination of spring practice in 1953. There is considerable irony here. There are no restrictions on crewmen, swimmers, lacrosse and baseball players practicing their sports around the calendar. But the Ivy League football player, who usually needs more coaching than players at institutions with less rigid academic requirements, is denied this extra help.

By eliminating spring practice, the presidents downgraded Ivy football. It followed naturally that the incentive of the gifted player to excel was diluted. He soon learned his football ambition was not really important. If it is less important to others, it can hardly be more important to the players.

Therein lies the answer to the question raised by several Ivy officials: "Why do many of our great prospects fail to live up to their promise?" Ivy football has been de-emphasized, as planned, in the mind of the player, undergraduate, and alumnus. And this is a handicap no football player or team can overcome.

Strangely enough, the old spirit of the 'thirties is not dead, merely quiescent. I recall vividly that I was all but maimed in the crush of the Elis who poured down out of the stands to shower approval on their team that beat Army in 1955.

And I recall reading about the tremendous ovation that greeted the late Herman Hickman's 1947 team, returning victorious from Wisconsin. You have only to listen to the Harvard Band playing outside Dillon Field House after a Crimson victory to know the old flame is far from extinguished.

The Ivy League has shown the way in placing football within the proper academic framework. Its standards are unequaled by any other conference and are the same for all undergrads. Any effort to ease the shock of education to athlete or nonathlete would be met with faculty revulsion and firm repulsion.

But by eliminating spring practice, the Ivies have bred a general philosophy that winning is not important. The resultant brand of play fails to enthuse even their own undergraduates.

Ivy League football could be restored to its former stature within three years without a single academic compromise if Dr. Griswold of Yale, Dr. Nathan Marsh Pusey of Harvard, and the other six presidents of the group would exert their undoubted influence to bring about three things:

1. Twenty days of spring practice, at least for freshmen and sophomores.

2. A return to unlimited substitution, to permit two-platoon football—for offense and defense—which would help get the most out of material that is good but limited in depth.

3. Scheduling of several games outside the Ivy League with major teams, some of them from other sections, a Georgia Tech, a Michigan, a Texas, a Stanford. Ivy League football will always be judged as insular and inferior until it again risks outside competition.

These points, I suggest, are the sane contribution the Ivy League can make today to American college football. The way should be led by Yale, Harvard, and Princeton, the schools that gave us the game.

Chapter X

"Uncle Bobby" Goes to Town

During the New Guinea campaign in the South Pacific, World War II, Lieutenant General Robert L. Eichelberger, twice recipient of the Distinguished Service Cross, was inspecting American trenches overlooking Japanese positions in Buna Village.

"I think I see a Jap in one of those trees," Eichelberger said. "Get me a tommy gun."

They gave him the gun, but with trepidation for his safety. "Don't shoot, General," somebody said. "You'll draw fire."

"This is a hell of a war," Eichelberger replied, "if you can't shoot the enemy! Suppose I do draw fire! Then we'll know where they are!"

Whether in battle or on other duty, direct, fearless action always characterized "Uncle Bobby." As West Point Superintendent, from November 18, 1940, to January 12, 1942, he made needed changes, some despite vigorous opposition by the War Department General Staff, others in the face of lean enthusiasm at the Academy.

Eichelberger harbored a deep suspicion that if needed changes were not made at West Point, General George Catlett Marshall, Chief of Staff, might reduce the four-year course to as short a one as all but ruined West Point during World War I. Marshall spoke to him significantly of the short terms which had been initiated in World War II at the Command and General Staff School and the Army War College in Washington. The Chief of Staff sounded not at all enthusiastic over the Academy when he recalled a prank historic at West Point:

"When I was commanding the corps of cadets at Virginia Military Institute under rigid discipline, the cadets at West Point were pointing the reveille guns at the Superintendent's quarters."

Therefore, to justify his resistance to any attempt to telescope the West Point course to less than three years, Eichelberger moved quickly to update the military, physical, and psychological training at the Academy to meet the demands of the impending global war.

There was still some riding and jumping of horses going on at West Point and pictures of it in newspapers. That this might conceivably reflect a belief that there was still a place for the equine in battle irritated powerful men in Congress. So Eichelberger cut it down and kept it out of the papers. He also shut down on publicity pictures featuring cadets with pretty girls.

Instead, he concentrated on training tough combat officers to lead soldiers in modern battle. He had the cadets join with the New Jersey National Guard in rehearsing such practical maneuvers as river crossings under heavy fire.

He ordered that flight training out of nearby Stewart Field be included in the curriculum of some first and second classmen so that they could be graduated with wings. In this way, he tied part of West Point's future in World War II to the Air Force. There was much opposition to this by the General Staff.

I have enumerated some of these principal points in General Eichelberger's program as Superintendent to emphasize that what he ordered for football was merely one step toward his objective that every activity be synchronized with the total effort.

Eichelberger had won his first D.S.C. as a major leading 1918 American operations against the Bolsheviks in the Suchan District of Siberia. Like all general officers who had seen actual combat, he appreciated that football men made fine battle leaders. He also realized that it was poor psychology, especially in such a war as was imminent, to field an Army football team that was a chronic loser.

On Saturday, November 16, 1940, the same day that we were living the wild, weird "Fifth Down" game with Cornell, Uncle Bobby sat in on the nadir of Army's football downcurve. He had taken a short leave of absence with Mrs. Eichelberger, known to friends as "Miss Em," to visit with her relatives in Asheville, North Carolina. En route to West Point to succeed General Jay Benedict as Superintendent the following Monday, he stopped off at Franklin Field to watch Army play Pennsylvania.

The 78,000 seats held only 47,000, as it was understood no contest was in prospect. Pennsylvania won, 48–0, the worst defeat in Army's fifty-one years of football. The Cadets had won their opening game, with Williams, 20–19. The following week, at Michie Stadium, Cornell had beaten them, 45–0, the worst loss in Academy history until then. Army then gained a 6–6 tie with Harvard and lost to Lafayette, 19–0; Notre Dame, 7–0, a strong effort; Brown, 13–9; and would later lose to Navy, 14–0.

The situation had the Army, from top to bottom, very unhappy. On Monday morning, in what may have been his first official act as Supe, General Eichelberger called a meeting of the Athletic Board. It will be recalled that in his earlier tour at the Academy, as Adjutant General, he had worked valiantly, if unsuccessfully, to get the unwritten rule against graduate-officer head coaching rescinded, with the idea of having me named to succeed Ralph Sasse. Now eighteen years later, he had the authority to take action.

"I was impressed Saturday," he told the Board, "by the way the cadets cheered our team right to the end. It looks as if we are developing the finest bunch of losers in the world. By the Gods (a favorite expletive), I believe the cadets deserve a football team which will teach them how to be good winners.

"Our graduate officer-head coaching system has long been outmoded. I propose to ditch it, and, if I can, get Red Blaik back here from Dartmouth."

The Board hesitated. Breaking with tradition in the Army is done slowly, whether it be giving a farewell salute to the last horse on the Post, or to the last graduate-officer head coach. But Uncle Bobby was moving fast. As the door was closing on the last departing member of the Board, he was swinging to his typewriter. This was to be a strictly private letter he would not risk dictating.

"If you have not signed a new contract," he wrote me, "don't sign any until you have talked to me first."

I wrote back: "I understand what you mean. I will see you next week at the Army-Navy game."

The night before the Army-Navy game, I sat with the General in his suite in the Benjamin Franklin Hotel. We talked for a long time. What he said, in sum, was that he wanted me to return to West Point because he felt it urgent that Academy football be restored. I told him this was something I would need some time to think about and to discuss with my family, President Hopkins, and my assistants.

"Take all the time you want, Earl," he said. "But just remember one thing: West Point needs you."

For several weeks I pondered a decision. On one side was the happiness of my family, my assistants, and myself at Hanover. It had been all and more than I could have wanted: the challenge of our job—winning football, within the correct academic framework; our beautiful home; such friends as the Pianes, the Gileses, the Larmans, the Ameses, the Bentleys, the Strongs, the Bowlers, the Neidlingers; the golf games and fishing trips with President Hopkins, Ned French, and the coaches; the over-all stimulating atmosphere. Our roots were deep in Dartmouth. Yes, football had slipped a little in 1939 and '40, but there was the upset of Cornell and there was a fine '40 freshman squad. We were going to get back up at the top of the Ivy League.

But there was another side, more serious, more compelling. The "war to end all wars" had not ended them, of course. World War I had been long and bloody enough, surely, yet it had been only an overture. There had been no mistaking that since Hitler's Panzers started moving. One year, two years, three years, it was going to come. When it did come, I would belong in it.

I reasoned that if I returned to West Point, I would be in a more advantageous position to return to the service I had left twenty-two years before. I also knew what Army football had been once, what it had come to be, what it should be. For that reason also, I had a strong compulsion to answer Eichelberger's call.

There could be no contractual problem. It so happened I had just completed the five-year contract I signed after the 1935 season. Uncle Bobby had known this.

If I did return to West Point, however, with a mandate to restore football, there were at least two basic conditions I knew to be indispensable. First, I would want my entire staff of Dartmouth assistants, and, of course, Bevan, to come with me. General Eichelberger assured me this would be done.

Then there were the age-height-weight restrictions which the

Army had been imposing since 1931 to the considerable hindrance of football recruiting; one of the reasons, though by no means the only one, for the sickness of the game on the Plain. To understand this factor, a background sketch is indicated.

In 1931, a directive had been issued by the Surgeon General, refusing waivers for overweight in a candidate for West Point on the theory that life expectancy is greater for a slender man. Examining boards were instructed to adhere strictly to an age-height-weight chart, by which a seventeen-year-old candidate, six feet tall, should ideally weigh 160 pounds and could weigh no more than 176. If he was six feet four, the Academy height limit, he could weigh no more than 198. A twenty-two-year-old, six-feet-four candidate (men from the regular Army or the National Guard can enter a year older than the twenty-one limit for others) could weigh no more than 208. Under such standards, earlier stars such as tackle Jack Price, who was six feet two, 225 pounds, never could have got into West Point.

In 1937, however, another directive was issued stating that weight in excess of the age-height-weight standard *could* be waived, if it was clearly shown that the excess was due to a robust physique and not obesity or an endocrine disorder. However, the 1937 directive meant nothing because the then Surgeon General reiterated that the slender man lived longer than the heavy man and, therefore, Army weight limits should not be waived, even though the man had an outstanding physique and was, in fact, a fine athlete. The two do not always go together.

Colonel Chauncey L. Fenton, now General Fenton, who was a member of the Athletic Board, had written a memorandum to the West Point Surgeon, criticizing the Surgeon General, and this memo was being used against West Point in Washington. What effort beyond General Fenton's was made by any interested parties at the Academy before Eichelberger's arrival to fight against the senseless restriction, I would not know.

It is ironic that in the same era, on July 1, 1938, the Army adopted the three-year eligibility rule by order of President Franklin D. Roosevelt. This prevented my predecessor, Bill Wood, and myself from using two outstanding players, who entered West Point in 1938 and were graduated in 1942: Carl C. Hinkle, center from Vanderbilt, and John W. Guckeyson, a back from Maryland. Hinkle last winter was ushered into the Football Hall of Fame. Guckeyson was killed in combat.

Now, it was also ironic that the military aide to the President was General Edwin M. (Pa) Watson, West Point '08 and an intense football enthusiast. Pa Watson not only had to relay F.D.R.'s order on the three-year rule, but he had been responsible for getting the Surgeon General appointed.

It was a minor scandal around the Army and Navy Club and Washington in general that Pa Watson was being fleeced by Navy people, who goaded him into betting on Army football teams, which they realized had little chance to beat Navy. Pa had a standing bet on the game of $800 with that staunch man of the sea, F.D.R. The President, not a good winner, was always reminding Watson of his unproductive allegiance, and Pa was getting fed up.

When Eichelberger went to work on the Surgeon General, he had a most eager accomplice in Pa Watson, and since Pa had helped the Surgeon General get his job, he did not go unheeded. Meanwhile, Joe Williams, Scripps-Howard sports columnist and always a trenchant friend, kept hammering at the senselessness of the weight restrictions.

The Surgeon General finally issued a directive, in which he referred to the 1937 directive and emphasized that overweight in a candidate not only could but *should* be waived if it was the result not of obesity but of a robust, athletic build. Weight limits also were liberalized: a six-footer could weigh as much as 201; a six-feet-four man, 226. This meant we could get in some candidates who looked like football players as well as officers.

In mid-December, Merle and I visited Uncle Bobby and Miss Em at the Point. The General took us up to a ridge south of Lusk Reservoir. "I have always thought," he said, "that this would be God's chosen place to live. If you decide to come back, we will build you a home here to your own specifications, to replace the one you have at Dartmouth."

Uncle Bobby was also concerned about our feelings as to how we would be received at the Point as the first graduate head coach not in service. "Go over to the Officers Club," he said, "and get your hair cut by Tom Impel. When you get back, let me know how long he takes." When I reported back that Tom had taken thirty-five minutes, Uncle Bobby said, "You're in. If Tom took that long, you'll be about the second ranking person on the Post."

On the serious side, the General assured me I would report to him and the Athletic Board, which meant I would report to him.

I returned to Hanover for more thought and talks with President Hopkins and Ned French. They wanted me to sign a new five-year contract, yet they were not out of sympathy with either General Eichelberger's or my own motivations. I guess Ned French saw my decision coming the day he said, "Earl, you can't carry on a flirtation like this without getting involved."

On Sunday morning, December 22, I met General Eichelberger at the Ritz Carlton Hotel in New York and told him I had decided to take the job. We quickly settled on contracts and salaries for myself and my assistants: Ellinger, Gustafson, Averell Daniel, former Pitt tackle who had joined us at Hanover, and Spec Moore.

Harry was sleeping at a nearby hotel when I phoned him the news, which he greeted with a large whoop. Uncle Bobby then invited the Athletic Board down from West Point for a luncheon. Harry continued the celebration by going out that night and getting married. When he phoned to tell me about it, he sounded like a sort of prodigal son.

A few days later a press luncheon was held at the Point. Afterwards, the writers were taken on a tour that included the huge new field house down by the Hudson River. One writer remarked, "This must be the greatest thing of its kind ever built."

"I guess so," I replied, "but I've seen some fine football teams that lived out of a suitcase and ate at the corner bean wagon." I was thinking of Sutherland's Pitt players, whose athletic scholarship, regarded patronizingly by the Big Ten, consisted of tuition and enough money for room and board at something less than princely standards.

I was depressed over leaving Dartmouth. Colonel Ollie Danielson, then West Point Adjutant General, was to comment later, "I've never seen a less happy man than Blaik was the morning after the signing. He was a man in a deep fog. All of us, simply by observation, realized how much of a wrench it was for him to leave Dartmouth."

My orders were a "crash" program to restore West Point football. Like President Hopkins, General Eichelberger was a man not afraid to delegate authority in the true sense.

On the subject of football dynasties, let me say that when a team is down, there is little the officials won't do to help a coach raise it up. When he has raised it up, they frequently grow self-conscious about too much success. This is especially true when administrations change, and they change all too frequently at West Point. But there, or anyplace else, so long as academic standards are not compromised, the idea of the game is to win. The philosophy that there can be such a thing as too many victories is a bastard one.

"The field house is yours, when you need it," I was told at West Point in 1941. "We're not interested in other sports." I realized that such an approach was bound to evoke in many quarters an ill will that would detract from the total support necessary to a successful "crash" program. So I also tried to help the other sports as much as I could, although I was not to be named athletic director until 1946.

There had been several reasons for Army's football decline. First, there was the graduate officer-head coach tradition. There had been a lack of organization in recruiting suitable cadet-athlete types, epitomized by the failure to get the age-height-weight restriction waivers applied. A tendency to coddle injuries also had developed. In general, Army's traditional will to make the necessary sacrifice for victory had been diluted. Defeat had become habitual, confidence shaken.

In a talk to the 1941 squad on the importance of strong tackle play, to help make the point I asked suddenly, "Where are most games lost?"

A voice piped up in the rear ranks: "Right here at West Point, sir!"

We put our Spartanism to work, and we began with the training room. It had become overrun with characters to whom training appeared to be merely a side line to their careers as musicians. They actually had a little band along the lines of the "Mississippi Mudcats" of St. Louis Cardinal baseball fame in the days of the "Gashouse Gang."

I decided music at the Point should be left to the unexcelled ministrations of the United States Military Academy Band, made up of talented enlisted men. As far as Bevan was concerned, his love of music centered around that old Negro spiritual, "Dry Bones": ". . . the knee bone is connected to the thigh bone . . . so praise the name of the Lord!"

In preparing boys to become tough combat officers, it is especially important to enforce a rugged, though sane, approach to injuries. In battle, it is fatal for the living to grieve over the dead or wounded. In football, we operated on the assumption that in 70 per cent to 80 per cent of the injuries, the player could carry on. If you got softhearted and gave him two days off, he'd need a lot more than that before he got back into action. To implement our approach, we were fortunate to have, as football medical adviser, Captain Ollie Neiss, now Surgeon General of the Air Force.

On the practice field, that spring and fall of 1941, we scrimmaged the players until they learned some football if for no other reason than self-preservation.

We wrote new rules for games away from the Academy. Players could not go out on a dining permit after the game. They all had to eat together. Bedtime after a game was 12:30. The next morning, we packed up and got them back to West Point instead of letting them walk the streets.

With some players, especially upperclassmen, our ways did not win unqualified popularity. One first-classman (he helped lose us a Navy game by Rip Van Winkle defensive play) wrote Academy officials in 1951 about what an evil man Blaik was. Such an occasional reaction is normal enough.

Our attitude had to be: "Your appearance on the field signifies you accept what we tell you to do. Otherwise, don't show up."

Most of the cadets were glad to take what we dished out. They, too, wanted to win. In selling our philosophy, we were helped tremendously by four officers, former Army players, whom I added to our staff: Colonel Harvey (Jabo) Jablonsky, Colonel Cy Letzelter, and Lieutenants Riggs Sullivan and Emory S. (Hank) Adams. Jablonsky and Sullivan are now generals and Letzelter is deceased. Sullivan is Commandant of the Air Force Academy, and Adams is Graduate Manager of Athletics at West Point.

We did not drive those cadets any harder than we drove ourselves. In my twenty-five years as a head coach, seven at Dartmouth, eighteen at West Point, I seldom took a vacation from the job, and then only when my doctor warned me some relaxation was necessary.

I would arrive at my desk on the top floor of the South Gym around eight o'clock. Our staff meetings began at nine and lasted, except for a very brief lunch period, until midafternoon, when it was time to go onto the field. During fall and spring practice, we worked every night far into the night. Our families saw little of us—a part of the price of our mission, and the steepest part of all. I always drove my assistants as hard as I drove myself, and I never found one who couldn't or wouldn't take it.

The few hours spent on the practice field or in a stadium on Saturday constituted only a minute fraction of the work. There was the book and blackboard detail, the analysis and application of scouting reports, the grinding hours of film study of our practice scrimmages and games and of opponents' games, until our brain lobes felt as worn as the film sprocket holes looked.

Then there was the huge, complicated procedure of recruiting players, getting them appointed, making certain they were prepared adequately for the validating (academic) examination, and seeing to it, after they got in the Academy, that they received tutoring aid, available to all cadets, when they needed it. All these chores and many more were part of the endless wheel of routine, year after year. When you are winning games, it is bad enough. Picture what it is like when you are losing.

How many of the thousands, yes millions, who have thrilled to Army or any college team in a packed stadium on a bright, windswept autumn Saturday, ever stopped to contemplate the years of sweat and worry that went into the production of the inimitable drama unfolding down there below them?

There are no more dedicated, self-punishing men in any endeavor than the college football coaches. The hat of every football lover should be taken off and waved for them.

May I say that the job of coaching at West Point, Annapolis, and the Air Force Academy is particularly tough? True, they have some things going for them: automatic discipline, great natural spirit and dedication, no aid problem (they are on keep and salary by the government), and an intelligent cut of boy who reacts quickly to coaching.

But against those advantages, weigh the handicaps. Of all the colleges playing major football, the Academies are the only ones in which every member of the student body is taking a course comparable to a heavy science major in our best universities. The regimen of the player's life limits the number of hours he is available to the coaches. Much time must be spent in boiling down the instruction so that it can be given to them as completely and as quickly as possible. There is a lot that the coach never has time to give them. He just has to make do, not only with the time available, but with the talent. Not too many good football players also want a service career.

Both times I took over head-coaching jobs, at Dartmouth and West Point, I was fortunate to inherit low-ebb situations. A coach who comes in at the bottom of a curve has a pronounced advantage over one who succeeds to a going or even a half-going operation. In 1941, there was no place to go at West Point but up. We went up at a rate of speed that surprised a lot of people.

With essentially the same squad that had defeated only Williams the year before, we won our first four games: from The Citadel, 19–6; Virginia Military Institute, 27–20; Yale, 20–7; and Columbia, 13–0. V.M.I. had two very fine players in tailback Abisha (Bosh) Pritchard and fullback Joe Muha, both later outstanding as pros.

To the astonishment of all, ourselves included, we were riding undefeated down to Yankee Stadium to meet Notre Dame in Frank Leahy's first year as head coach. The Irish were 3–1 favorite. Their line had an edge in heaviness, and it was quick heaviness. They had a most talented left-halfback passer in Angelo Bertelli. We were perhaps helped some by the mud and rain in containing Bertelli's passes.

Yet, few in the crowd of 76,000 could honestly say we didn't deserve that scoreless tie. Although the Irish reached our 18 and 25 in the second half, we outgained them on the ground, 187 yards to 107, and missed a first down near their 10 by inches. This was a good job against a 3–1 favorite which won every other game that year.

General Eichelberger was so enthused that he vowed: "If we go down to the Navy game undefeated, by the Gods I shall ride the mule myself three times around Municipal Stadium!" That would have been an epic sight! There was no chance the General would have to fulfill that rash vow, however, for we lacked the depth to withstand normal injuries.

Bob Evans, our valiant, sixty-minute center-linebacker, was bruised after the Notre Dame effort and injured early at Harvard the next week; as was Captain Ray Murphy, guard, and an intrepid yearling tackle named Robin Olds. The whole team was downbeat from the battle with the Irish. This cannot detract one whit of credit from Dick Harlow's Harvard team, which beat us thoroughly, 20–6. The Crimson-line, which won a 0–0 tie with Navy, gave us a good licking.

We held Pennsylvania to 14–7, a forty-one-point improvement from the year before, if one was interested in comparative scores, which we weren't particularly.

We even led Navy at the half, 6–0. Although there was not necessarily any cause and effect involved, Mrs. Eleanor Roosevelt sat that first half on our side. At the interim, she was escorted across the field and turned over to the Navy by General Eichelberger. As he returned to our side, Uncle Bobby was greeted by a tremendous roar from the Corps. After recent seasons, they were not averse to a few victories.

Their youthful hopes that we could get one over Navy that day were fated to be splintered. The Midshipmen, who lost only to Notre Dame, 20–13, had halfback Bill Busick, guard Vito Vitucci, and many other fine players. They marched back from the second half kick-off and converted to take the lead, 7–6. We chose to kick off again. Again they marched from the kickoff to another score and conversion, and went on to win, 14–6.

I was criticized for ordering that we kick instead of receive after the first Navy touchdown. My reason was simple enough. Our first-half score had been set up by a long punt return off a reverse. I knew that against such a line as Navy's we could not logically expect to mount a sustained march. I had ordered that we kick after that first score in the hope that we might force them into an error that would give us the ball deep in their territory. I mention this merely to cite a point in strategy. It is a waste of time answering criticism founting from a lack of fundamental knowledge.

Our lack of qualitative reserve strength was to cost us heavily in fourth-period stamina those first three years of my return. It was to be 1944 before we would be able to beat Navy, Notre Dame, or Pennsylvania, but we were moving in on them.

Eight days after that 1941 Navy game, the Japanese attacked Pearl Harbor and our nation went to war. The four-year course at the Academy was telescoped to three years.

On January 12, 1942, General Eichelberger was assigned to organize and train the 77th Division at Fort Jackson, South Carolina, for which he was later awarded the Legion of Merit. He was succeeded as Superintendent by Major General Francis B. Wilby.

This was around the time General Devers and I were working to get Ralph Sasse back in the Army. Early in February, I was back in myself as a colonel. I put in for active duty in the South Pacific, where I would be with old friends. I was eager to serve under General MacArthur.

While awaiting orders, I had a bad shock. Harry Ellinger was in Washington, working on some appointments. During the night of February 12, while in Virginia as a guest of Congressman Eddie Hebert of Louisiana, Harry died in his sleep. He lies in the cemetery at West Point, not far up the road from the football field where in life he knew some of his greatest happiness. Such a friend and comrade is not replaced.

My orders finally came. It had been decided I could serve best by remaining at the Point and carrying out the orders of Uncle Bobby. Testifying before the House Appropriations Committee, General Wilby said, "All of us feel it would be a very sad day if athletics were abandoned at West Point. The body-contact types are one of the finest things in the training of a soldier."

On June 2, Eichelberger was named commanding general of the 11th Army Corps upon its activation. Two weeks later he was given the 1st Army Corps. In October, he was assigned the New Guinea command, but this was not to be revealed until after he won the campaign. The eve of his departure from Camp Blanding, he wrote me on July 5:

> The papers carry no news of West Point, which is understandable, and my mail gets to me so erratically and infrequently that I'm completely out of touch with all those interests which did—and still do—touch me so closely. I *do* know of the clean sweep in sports this spring with the Navy but what there was in the way of football developments I have no idea.
>
> Earl, I must take time to go on record with you that there is *nothing* which we can do in the educational field with our youth which will do more toward winning the war than the production of leadership qualities, courage, initiative, force, and all the other things that go to make up a man. That as a mechanism for this education there is nothing which can touch competitive athletics and, among this group of sports, nothing which can touch football.
>
> Every day that goes by in my immediate job of producing a fighting team—and, believe me, this is a serious and practical job straight 'round the clock—I am constantly running into the crying need for the man who was an athlete, for in him I find the leader, the producer of results, the one who can be relied upon to take action on his own when the emergency arrives, and the one who will carry the others with him. As I tell my people all the time, nicely devised mechanical devices are a great asset but the war is still going to be won by the man who is willing and able to get up front and swap punches. (I told a group the other day that every one wanted to be a climax runner and nobody wants to play in the line—and that as a national trend that sort of thing isn't a sound basis of policy for building a combat team!)
>
> I seem to have got off the track, but what I wanted to emphasize is that competitive athletics in our schools and colleges simply

cannot be allowed to fall by the wayside if we are to go through to a win against the Axis.

Earl, I wish I could go on to express to you how strongly I feel in this matter of development of the leader and how vital a part competitive athletics plays in it as a means at hand for its accomplishment. (The Navy's plan for their pilot production is superb. They are going to put men in planes that are going through to their objectives.)

So boy, keep driving ahead on your job, for it's a top-flight project in our war effort, and don't let anyone tell you anything else. And you can tell 'em I said so—and I'm seeing every day fifteen thousand damn good fighting men who'd be a damn sight better if they'd spent their last year in school under you—and never entered a class room, if that had been necessary.

We certainly kept driving. Beginning in 1942, the program some of those first and second classmen had to handle, combining the regular Academy schedule, flying, and football, was the stiffest in West Point history. Some of our players had to practice after spending most of the previous night in flights up and down the Hudson Valley. I could hear their drone and zoom as I lay awake pondering football problems. There was one for every plane.

There was also reason for hope. Some players of actual or potential above-average talent appeared with the incoming 1942 plebes. Since the freshman rule was suspended for the duration, they began to show up in varsity games: backs Doug Kenna, Tom Lombardo, Dale Hall, Bob St. Onge, and George Troxell; end Ed Rafalko and guard Joe Stanowicz. St. Onge was later shifted to center.

Edgar Douglas Kenna, a halfback, had exceptional ability, but never achieved his full potential as a runner because of injuries. That was one of the reasons I later shifted him to quarterback, where he won All America honors. Doug was also a standout in basketball and tennis. Dale Hall was another exceptional all-around athlete. He delivered many key runs for us in football, and on the basketball court was an All American.

West Point is essentially a serious, often severe, place. It is not without its humorous side, but the humor is mostly of the "situation" type, perhaps funnier in the experiencing than in the telling. But there was among those '42 plebes a strong spirit of humor which provided a welcome relief. More than one laugh was provided us, especially by Ted Halligan, a grand youngster, who played tackle and end and later won a letter.

Ted was full of fire, enthusiasm and excitement, bubbling ever higher as game time approached. In his intensity, he often seemed not to be concentrating on what he was doing. On one occasion, he absent-mindedly put on two sets of shoulder pads and his jersey on top of them and wondered why he felt funny until Bevan discovered the reason for him. Another time, after being shaken up in a game, Ted put his helmet on backwards, so that the neckpiece covered his eyes. Naturally, he could not see anything and he had a momentary fear the collision had caused him to go blind. "My God," he yelled, "I can't see! Beaver, where are you?"

Before the '42 Notre Dame game, in which Bertelli's passes thwarted a strong effort, 13–0, I was telling the squad: "From the starting team to the lowest scrub on the bench, I want you to give all you've got." I pointed suddenly at Ted and barked, "What about you, Halligan?"

In his startled excitement, it took Ted a full ten seconds to speak and then he had lost most of his voice. He retained only enough articulation to manage, in a real bullfrog croak, "Let's get 'em!"

The Wednesday practice before that Notre Dame game was to prove most significant. That year, Frank Leahy had replaced the traditional Notre Dame box with the modern T formation, first popularized in the college game by Clark Shaughnessy at Stanford in 1940. Our plebes were using Notre Dame T plays against the varsity. Despite their unfamiliarity with the formation, they were making them go, frequently for substantial gains. After practice I remarked to my assistants, "If our plebes, with that little experience, can make the T go that way, what would an experienced varsity do with it?"

The idea took deep root and the following spring we adopted the modern T as our formation. I said farewell with respect, thanks and nostalgia to the single wing, for it had severed me well. Like most other coaches, I found the T provided greater deception and quicker hitting and required that a player be, above all things, mobile. As years went on, we were credited with improving the T by new concepts of plays and techniques. For the first year, however, we were feeling our way and stumbling about a bit.

Navy, which was beginning to put together its extraordinarily fine lines of 1943 and '44, beat us, 14–0. Near the end, Kenna sparked two drives that reached their 10, but we could not penetrate beyond.

That game, under presidential order, was played at Annapolis, for the first time since 1893, with an attempt to limit attendance to the regiment of Midshipmen, Annapolis officials, the Army team, Army officials necessary to the playing of the game, newspapermen, and residents within a ten-mile limit of Annapolis. To play an Army-Navy game before such a sparse gathering was a strange feeling.

Even more incongruous was an Annapolis order that half of the Midshipmen brigade must cheer for the Army. This situation was a natural for my old and dear friend, Willard Mullin, whose product as sports cartoonist of the New York *World-Telegram and Sun* admits, for consistent excellence, no superior in any media of journalism, past or present. Willard turned out a typically imaginative and humorous drawing of a group of Middies singing, "On, Brave Old Army Team," but with their fingers most noticeably crossed.

That '42 Navy game also saw tackle Robin Olds give one of the most magnificent demonstrations of fortitude and determination I ever saw on a football field. While crashing through at a first-quarter punt, Olds had four of his teeth dislodged and others loosened, and his lower lip and tongue badly lacerated by the cleats of a Navy blocker. He had to be taken to the dressing room.

Captain Ollie Neiss worked on him for forty-five minutes and put twenty-three stitches in his tongue and lower lip. When Ollie was finished, Robin's face was puffed up almost out of recognition, cotton was jammed up his nose, and he couldn't talk. But by sign language, he insisted to me he was going back in the game. I asked Ollie about it. "He'll be all right," Ollie said, "if he can stand it." Robin signified to me mutely that there was no problem. He played all but one minute of the second half—and he took it out on the Navy.

Grantland Rice named Olds to the All America team and he was elected captain for 1943. Because of the ever-increasing urgency of the war effort, however, the Army directed that the original class of 1944 be graduated in '43, and Robin went with them. In a re-election, the team then named center Cas Myslinski.

On the train home after that '42 Navy game, I said to Olds, "Robin, I am sorry about your losing your teeth."

"That's all right," he said. "I always wondered how I'd look without them."

When they fixed him up, Robin looked as good as he ever did to everybody, including the charming lady who married him, actress Ella Raines.

With the spirit highlighted by Robin Olds, we were carrying out the orders of Uncle Bobby to drive on. We moved on into 1943 and more of the pieces of ultimate success were falling into place.

Since the death of Harry Ellinger, I had been searching for the right man to replace him as line coach. I made long and careful inquiry to find the best in the business. First or second on every list was the name of Herman Michael Hickman, then working under Coach William (Doc) Newton at North Carolina State.

Herman Hickman was born in Johnson City, Tennessee, October 1, 1911, and played guard for Bob Neyland at the University of Tennessee from 1929 through '31. Herman won acclaim as one of the greatest of all time at his position. As a senior, he weighed 225 and stood five feet ten. His tremendous power, likened to that of a gigantic iron beach ball, was matched by his astonishing quickness and speed. After his graduation in 1932, he went on to win All Pro honors as a guard for the Brooklyn Dodgers. He also had five hundred matches in five years of pro wrestling, and was billed as "The Tennessee Terror." "Considering how pro wrestling is run," he used to chuckle, "it is amazing I could be in it that long and escape ever becoming a champion."

A well-rounded man in more ways than one, Hickman early developed a fondness for literature, especially poetry. His prodigious memory enabled him to recite yards of it from such of his favorites as Rudyard Kipling and Edgar Lee Masters. His fine voice, presence, command of English, and delightful sense of humor that flavored his

"Kinfolk" stories made him a sought-after speaker and, after his coaching days, a successful radio and television personality.

Herman had two things in common with Harry Ellinger. He knew how to teach line play, and he had a type of personality that served as a valuable anodyne to my necessarily serious, severe approach. Like myself, Herman was originally a single-wing man, but he went about learning the T like the rest of us.

Part of the legend of Herman Hickman—for it grew to be a legend, though all based on fact—traced to his fondness for food and his feats as a gourmet. In our first interview, at the Vanderbilt Hotel in New York, the summer of '43, to impress me with his seriousness about coaching, Herman said, "Colonel, I have three loves: my wife, football and my belly. And I don't rightfully know which I love the most."

We drove from the Vanderbilt to West Point and in the football office on the top floor of the South Gym, Herman gave his ideas on football to Andy Gustafson and myself. He stood at the blackboard and outlined his concepts of line play. It was a blistering hot summer day, we were right under the roof, and there was no air conditioning. Herman weighed about 270 then. He was eager for the job and, as a consequence, naturally nervous. The nervousness plus the terrific heat caused him to perspire so profusely at that blackboard that actual pools of water formed at his feet. Gus and I finally persuaded him to take off his pants and shirt and continue the dissertation in his shorts.

Several weeks later, Herman, his wife Helen, a fine girl, and their little Chihuahua dog, Tiny, drove up to West Point in Herman's old Packard. He told me that day that he never had bought a new car without transferring the mortgage on the old one. Due greatly to the itinerant nature of pro football and wrestling, it had been difficult for him to save much. I advised him to begin putting away $100 a month as soon as he went on salary with us, and he followed the advice.

In his later days of affluence as a radio personality under the friendly guidance of Dave Driscoll Director of News and Public Affairs for Columbia Broadcasting System radio, Herman owned a beautiful ranch house in the Woodbridge hills west of Yale Bowl and had his own chauffeur, who drove him almost daily to New York for his radio show. Herman lived well, but also provided for his future and Helen's. I believe that it was with us at Army that he first developed the habit of saving.

That first summer of 1943, Herman, Helen, and Tiny lived at Jack Martin's Bear Mountain Inn, where Herman became something of a tourist attraction. It soon was rumored that he had devised a set of signals with the waitresses for various second helpings. "The Hickman Special," his clebrated steak order, was an epic slab of beef that would have made a nice Sunday roast in my house.

Those were good days when Herman was with us. Many a night after supper, after he moved into Quarters 1,000 on the Post, we would drive around the Hudson Highlands discussing our football problems, before returning to the office for late work. I always finished my supper long before Herman did. At first, I used to swing my car down by 1,000 while he was still working into the entree. Not realizing I was disturbing the majesty of his meal, I would toot the horn. Herman put up with this about two nights and then informed me, politely but firmly, that he was dedicated to football and West Point and that he was my man, but he could not let anything interfere with his evening ingestions. After that, I made sure I came by a half hour later.

In his first few years with us, Herman's weight rose from 270 pounds to 330. I became greatly concerned about this, and finally persuaded him to see a doctor. A diet was prescribed and Herman gave it an heroic try. He lost from 25 to 30 pounds in a month. It so happened he also contacted a severe cold in the drafty Highlands, and pneumonia threatened. When he recovered, Herman said with feeling, "I love and respect Colonel Blaik, but if I am going to die, I want to die happy and not from starvation and its complications."

Three days before Herman's death in 1948, I talked to him in a Washington hospital. He confided to me that he realized he spent the happiest years of his life at West Point, from 1943 through '47. He often wondered, he said, if he would not have been better off to have stayed there. I believe he would have been.

Although he was a line coach, one of Herman's joys (as well as Andy Gustafson's) was a back named Glenn Davis, who likewise arrived at the Point in 1943. In fact, everybody liked Glenn, not only as a football player but also as a person.

It was from a Dartmouth friend, Warren Bentley, Professor of Dramatics, that I first heard about Glenn Woodward Davis. Bentley had attended college in Pomona, California, and frequently vacationed there. A relative of his owned a grocery store where Mrs. Davis traded. She asked the grocer if he knew anybody at West Point and this was relayed to Bentley. It was soon after that, early in 1943, that Bentley wrote me:

> Everybody in California talks about a football player at Bonita High School in LaVerne, which is not far from Pomona. They say this kid is the fastest halfback ever seen out there. He's an all-around athlete: baseball, basketball, and track as well as football. Since I am told he is interested in going to West Point, I thought you would want to know about him. His name is Glenn Davis.

Glenn and his twin brother, Ralph, came East in May, visited the Academy, studied for the validating exam, passed it and entered as plebes on July 1.

The plebe mathematics curriculum at West Point is tough: advanced college algebra, solid geometry, plane and solid analytical geometry, plane and spherical trigonometry. The review of solid geometry, a year's course in high school, is covered at the Point in two weeks.

Davis had no natural aptitude for math. Eventually, it was to force him to repeat his plebe year in 1944. But he gave it a real try. In 1943, after every football game away from the Academy, Colonel Francis I. (Buck) Pohl, who was tutoring Glenn, would drive him directly back to the school for a late-Saturday-night session with the math. Many a night, Glenn set his alarm for a 4:00 A.M. bout with the books.

Glenn was an unusually strong boy, far stronger than his 172 pounds, five feet nine suggested. In the ten events of the Academy physical efficiency test, he set a new record of 926½ points out of a possible 1,000. The figures have been topped since, but they were considered astonishing at the time, and are still remarkable enough today.

But even so strong a boy as Davis was severely taxed by the combined drag of his math workouts, the regular Academy regimen, and pressure football. Half the time in '43, he was out on his feet. In a chair at the Knollwood Country Club, in Elmsford, Westchester, where we bivouacked Friday before New York games, or in a movie at nearby White Plains or Scarsdale, regular Friday-night relaxation for the squad on trips, Glenn would nod off to sleep in ten seconds.

Anybody who ever saw Davis carry a football must realize there could not have been a greater, more dangerous running halfback in the entire history of the game, and on this I put no qualifications whatsoever. He was emphatically the fastest halfback I ever knew. He was not so much a dodger and side-stepper as a blazing runner who had a fourth and even a fifth gear in reserve, could change direction at top speed, and fly away from tacklers as if jet-propelled. He could also throw and catch passes and was a superior blocker and tackler. Under pressure, he was a tremendous competitor.

Davis played center field on the baseball team. He had the arm, the base-running and the fielding ability to have made the major leagues. He could hit college pitching and might have learned to hit the big leaguers. Had he been available, Branch Rickey would have signed him for the Brooklyn Dodgers. Several other teams were interested in him.

In the winter, Glenn divided his efforts between basketball and track. He was a standout the spring of 1945, his first-class year, in the 100- and 200-yard dashes. Such were his leg spring and arm and shoulder-girdle strength, he might have been even more remarkable as a pole vaulter, but he discontinued serious vaulting after he left Bonita High.

In his valedictory to Army sports on May 25, 1947, Glenn starred at bat, on the bases, and in the field in a losing baseball game with Navy. After the last out, he was whisked by car from Doubleday Field down to North Field by the river, where Army and Navy were having a track meet. Davis changed from baseball to track togs and with very little warm-up helped Army to victory by winning both the

100- and 220-yard dashes in record times for the East that year, although it was the first time he was in track shoes that spring. The performance made Colonel Biff Jones shake his head.

"The only one I can think of in Army history," said Biff, "who might have done anything like it was Oliphant."

Personally, Davis was a fine boy, with deep affection for family and friends. Much like Light Horse Harry Wilson, Red Cagle, Johnny Murrell, and Ray Stecker, whom I had coached at the Point as an assistant, Glenn was essentially a team man, not only unimpressed with his marvelous ability but truly humble about it.

All great players have had mediocre, even bad days. None I know of had a worse one than Glenn in our 26-0 loss to Notre Dame in 1943. Even though Angelo Bertelli had left for service after the defeat of Navy the week before, The Irish still sent one of the truly great teams of their history against us, one to rank with those of 1924, 1930, 1946, 1947 and 1953. Glenn didn't lose that '43 Notre Dame game for us. He did make the job easier for the Irish by his inexperience on pass defense, his fumbling, and a pass he had intercepted. From that discouraging crucible, Glenn rose to some of the most brilliant days any player ever knew, including two against Notre Dame.

Another great player made it tough for us that day: quarterback Johnny Lujack, of Notre Dame. Lujack had been about ready to come to West Point, the choice of his mother, until his mind was changed by some persuasive emissaries from South Bend.

Davis, though the standout, was not the only fine football player in that 1943 plebe group. There were also Bobby Dobbs, Bob Chabot, Max Minor, Dick Walterhouse, and Johnny Sauer, backs; and Archie Arnold, Jack Green, Bill LaMar, Al Nemetz, Dick Pitzer, Bob Wayne, Bill Webb and Roland Catarinella, linemen.

Despite our unfamiliarity with the T formation, we were flashy at times in making a 7-2-1 record, and were even reduced to pulling our punches against some of our civilian wartime opposition. Between the halves of our 51-0 victory over Temple, I gave explicit instructions that we were not to score again. We were not to pass and if we did not make a first down in two running plays, we were to punt on third down, no matter the distance required.

I soon discovered that not getting a touchdown in one game could be as tough as getting one in another. Charlie Sampson, an ambitious reserve guard, picked off a Temple pass and ran it over half the length of an open field. When Charlie got to the 1-yard line, however, he stopped and put the ball down. This concession to my order was an unintentional insult to Temple, far worse than if he had actually scored, yet Sampson looked over toward me with a self-satisfied smile, as if to say, "Mission accomplished, sir!"

The Army team now gathered in a huddle to decide how not to score. If they tried a running play, they were sure to go over. I had forbidden any passes. A punt was out of the question. They seized on the only alternative, a field-goal attempt, and selected the man least likely to make it, a man who, to my knowledge, never had tried a field goal before, a man named Charlie Sampson. I suppose you can guess what happened. Much to the surprise of the team, myself, and himself, Charlie kicked the field goal. After the game, I hastened to assure Temple's coach, my old friend, Ray Morrison, that Sampson's performance was no preconceived coaching gem, but rather an abortive attempt to exemplify West Point discipline.

Actually, I had offered at the beginning of each period, to shorten the time, but Morrison refused. He explained that these wartime players were as spirited a bunch as he ever coached and totally unbothered by any score that might be run up against them. He told me that on the train ride up from Philadelphia one of the players had asked him, "Coach, will it be all right if we tear down Army's goal posts?"

Ray assured him that it would be O.K., if Temple won.

"Thanks, coach," said the boy. "I just wanted to be sure there would be no penalty for destroying government property."

The Navy game was played at West Point under the same conditions as the '42 game at Annapolis. A group of Cadets were ordered to simulate Midshipmen in singing "Anchors Aweigh." They did so with extraordinary feeling.

Co-Captain Cas Myslinski, center, Ed Murphy, guard, Frank Merritt, tackle, and some of the plebes did well against a superior Navy line. In the second half, however, they wore us down. Lacking a first-class fullback, we tried Davis at that position. He had been effective enough there in earlier games, but what was needed to operate against a line like Navy's was the speed of a Davis at halfback complemented by a powerful fullback. There was one on the way, but we could have used him in that '43 game.

I believe Coach John Esten (Billick) Whelchel's 1943 Navy team should rank with Oscar Hagberg's of '44 as the two best in Annapolis history. The lines were big, strong, quick, and tough. In the first half of that '43 game, five separate fist fights flared up. Somebody remarked afterwards that we could have got by all right without a ball. Whoever won the fights, Navy won the game. One of the Navy players—some said it was Don Whitmire, their big, aggressive tackle—wrote on a blackboard in the South Gym: Navy 13, Army 0.

We didn't need reminding. We were downcast. Navy was dominating us. So was Notre Dame. There wasn't much we could do about it except to remember what Ralph Sasse used to say, "Let's pull up our socks and get going!"

Chapter XI

Storybook Teams

Football ascetism may have reached an apex at West Point, eight o'clock New Year's morning, 1944. Unspeakable hour for a staff meeting though it was, I had ordered one for good reason. I wanted to impress on my assistants that this was the first day of the year in which we were going to beat Navy and we must get to the job without delay. Andy Gustafson arrived in dark glasses. Herman Hickman wore a somewhat weary smile. I had on my usual brown business tweeds.

My assistants were shepherded to the ghastly rendezvous by the post transportation officer, Lieutenant Colonel Leonard (Deadeye) Henry, West Point '31, favorite of our football family and protector of wayward coaches. After depositing the bodies, Deadeye promptly disappeared. He hurried off, I presume, to a long-delayed appointment with Morpheus.

Not only a sleepy hangover or two, but hope and determination sat with us that morning. Hope grew with spring practice down on North Field by the Hudson or, during bad weather, in the big adjoining Field House. The scrimmages gave off blacksmith sparks. Speed began flowing more smoothly out of the T formation. Only July 1, the arriving plebes included a dozen football players who were going to help us. One of them was to become the finest fullback Army or, perhaps, any college team ever had. His name was Felix Anthony (Doc) Blanchard.

Doc Blanchard was the best-built athlete I ever saw: six feet and 208 pounds at his peak, not a suspicion of fat on him, with slim waist, Atlas shoulders, colossal legs. For a big man, Doc was the quickest starter I ever saw, and in the open he ran with the niftiness as well as the speed of a great halfback. He was a terrific tackler and blocker.

He could catch passes, punt, and kick off exceptionally well. Twice in Navy games, I saw him run through a head-on tackle without breaking stride and race on to a touchdown. He had great instinctive football sense, supreme confidence, and deep pride.

If he had been serious about it, Blanchard could have become an Olympic decathlon star. Without too much practice, he put the 16-pound shot 51 feet, 10 and ¾ inches to win the event in the Army-Navy dual meet. He could also run the 100-yard dash in ten seconds flat and won the event in our meet with Cornell. In fact, Doc had the speed, power, and relaxed body control to have excelled in any sport, but he was absorbed in football and took the others casually.

Much of his football ability as well as his nickname, Blanchard inherited from his father, the late Dr. Felix Anthony Blanchard, of Bishopville, South Carolina. For brevity and clarity's sake, let me refer to them as Old Doc and Young Doc. Old Doc played fullback at Tulane under Clark Shaughnessy in 1915 and '16. He was 240 pounds and fast. "When he got mad," says Shaughnessy, "he was one of the best players I ever coached."

Old Doc's marks in medical school tailed off temporarily and he transferred to Wake Forest, where he also did some football playing. He later returned to Tulane, buckled down to serious study and played another year for Shaughnessy in 1920 under the name of Beaulieu. Eligibility rules were loose as ashes in those days, but Tulane didn't wish to appear too flagrant about Old Doc.

Old Doc entered Tulane originally from St. Stanislaus School in Bay St. Louis, Mississippi. Keeping a promise he made to Brother Peter, President of St. Stanislaus, Old Doc enrolled Young Doc there in 1938 at the age of fourteen. By Young Doc's senior year in 1941, there was scarcely a college playing major football which had not heard well of him. Notre Dame, Fordham, and dozen of others approached him, and so did we. En route to the 1941 Sugar Bowl game, Harry Ellinger stopped off at Bishopville to talk to Old Doc. Nothing came of it at that time.

Young Doc narrowed his choice to North Carolina, Duke, and Tulane. He finally chose North Carolina for two reasons. Old Doc wanted him to be nearby, so he could get to see him play. Mrs. Blanchard, born Mary Elizabeth Tatum, was a cousin of the late Jim Tatum, then in his first tour as head coach of the Tar Heels.

As a North Carolina freshman in 1942, Blanchard gave the Tar Heel varsity a hard time. His feats were discussed even by the coaches and players of the Navy Pre-Flight School, stationed on the Chapel Hill campus. After watching Young Doc one day, Glenn Thistlethwaite, former Northwestern and Wisconsin coach, predicted with considerable accuracy: "I have seen all the great fullbacks. This boy will be the greatest."

At the end of his freshman year in 1943, Blanchard tried to get in the Navy V-12 unit, but was turned down for overweight and deficient eyesight. In childhood, a playmate had hit him in the eye with a piece of mud with the result that his vision was less than 20–20. Tatum tried to sweat him down to within V-12 weight limits, but couldn't make it. Later, at West Point, Doc usually played at 207 or 208 as compared to the 215 to 220 he probably would have carried at a civilian school. This made him even more effective. At the end of his playing days as a cadet, he was down to 197.

His eye condition has not prevented Major Blanchard from being a successful jet pilot and instructor, who on May 24 was made commander of the 77th Tactical Fighting Squadron, Wethersfield Air Base, England. On July 2, 1959, Doc landed a burning plane instead of abandoning it with likely peril to a heavily populated area near London. He was cited for this act.

After Blanchard was turned back by the V-12, he enlisted in the Army, took basic training at Miami Beach and served in the chemical warfare division of the Army Air Force ground school at Clovis, New Mexico. In 1943, he was appointed to West Point and was one of 300 studying at Lafayette College for the validating examination.

Doc played no football in 1943. In the spring of '44, he visited the Academy and watched one of our workouts in the Field House. To sound out his enthusiasm, I asked him how he thought the team looked. I guess he wanted to show me he was not awed, and when you look back on it, there certainly was no reason why he should be.

Anyhow, I will never forget his reply: "They don't look so hot to me, Colonel."

Blanchard's early days as a plebe were especially sad ones, because Old Doc had died only a few weeks before. He lived long enough to know his son had passed the exam. There was wonderful rapport between the two, and it was Blanchard's regret, as it was mine, that his dad did not live to see him play fullback for Army.

Blanchard had to be exceptional to stand out in that plebe group, which was probably the strongest in Academy history. We were now deep enough to field two alternate teams, one predominantly plebes. The upper-class unit shared playing time equally with the plebes. Blanchard was always in when we kicked off. The quarterbacks were both first-classmen: Doug Kenna and Tom Lombardo, with Lombardo piloting the predominantly plebe group. They lined up as follows:

Lombardo's Team		Kenna's Team
George (Barney) Poole Tom Hayes	LE	Dick Pitzer
DeWitt (Tex) Coulter	LT	Archie Arnold Bill LaMar
Shelton Biles	LG	Jack Green
Herschel (Ug) Fuson	C	Bob St. Onge
Art Gerometta	RG	Joe Stanowicz
Harold Tavzel	RT	Al Nemetz Bill Webb
Henry (Hank) Foldberg	RE	Ed Rafalko
Tom Lombardo * Young Arnold Tucker	QB	Doug Kenna
Glenn Davis	LH	Dale Hall
Dean Sensanbaugher Dick Walterhouse	RH	Max Minor
Felix (Doc) Blanchard	FB	Bobby Dobbs

* Young was Tucker's real first name, but he was known to everybody as Arnold.

In addition to Blanchard, the plebes on Lombardo's team were Poole, Hayes, Coulter, Biles, Fuson, Gerometta, Tavzel, Foldberg, Tucker, Davis, Sensanbaugher, and West.

When this squad gathered for its first fall practice, I felt I was at last in a position to carry out General Eichelberger's mandate. Possibly, there have been college squads from time to time to compare with that one, but not very many, if any. At that first practice, I told them: "I expect you to be the greatest team in the history of West Point."

They always remembered that.

Much to our satisfaction, our early, one-sided victories over North Carolina, Brown, Pittsburgh, and the Coast Guard were received by press and public with proper reservation. They wanted to see what we would do against Notre Dame, Pennsylvania, and Navy. There was good reason for such skepticism. Army had not defeated Notre Dame since 1931, Navy since 1938.

Duke, an above-average wartime team stocked with some Navy V-12 personnel, gave us just the pre-Notre Dame test we needed at the Polo Grounds. Blazing runs by Davis, Blanchard, Hall, and Minor brought us a 27-7 victory after trailing at the half, 7-6. Between Duke and Notre Dame, we were to meet an old rival, Villanova. The Wildcats had given us many interesting games, but were no match for us that year. So I led a platoon of assistant coaches to Baltimore, to scout Notre Dame vs. Navy, and left the Cadets in charge of Andy Gustafson.

As soon as we got on the Baltimore train at New York Pennsylvania Station, Herman Hickman steered us to the dining car for breakfast. I was about to approach my boiled eggs when Lewis E. Lawes, who had retired as Warden of Sing Sing in 1941, came into the diner and took a table directly across from mine. After greetings, Warden Lawes said; "Earl, I remember another coach who left his team to scout. It was Knute Rockne, and that day Notre Dame lost to Carnegie Tech."

I laid down my spoon quietly. Stu Holcomb, stationed at West Point as Private, First Class, and coaching our ends, was sitting across from me. Stu later became head coach at Purdue and is now Northwestern's athletic director. He still maintains that the Warden's remark made me turn white as the tablecloth.

"I remember, Warden," I said, trying to sound brave. "I was in Chicago for the Army-Navy game Rockne was attending."

I made an effort to resume my breakfast, but it didn't taste very good. It was silly, I suppose, because we defeated Villanova quite easily. Nevertheless, when we reached Baltimore, I arranged to take a portable radio to the stadium, and while I had my eyes on Notre Dame and Navy, my ears were tuned to the broadcast from Michie Stadium.

Notre Dame lost to Navy, 32–13, because it could not handle Navy's exceptionally strong line.

Let me state a few facts about that 1944 Notre Dame team. They came into the Navy game with victories over Pittsburgh, 58–0; Tulane, 26–0; Dartmouth, 64–0; Wisconsin, 28–13; and Illinois, 13–7. Later, they were to defeat Northwestern, 21–0; Georgia Tech, 21–0; and Great Lakes Navy, 28–7.

The Irish had a superior passer in quarterback Frank Dancewicz, a gifted runner in halfback Bob Kelly, and some other good players like fullback Marty Wendell, guards Pat Filley and Frank Mastrangelo, tackle George Sullivan, and center Frank Szymanski.

These Irish certainly were not so strong as their immediate predecessors or the teams to come along beginning in 1946. But they were big physically, spirited, and well coached by Ed McKeever. (Frank Leahy was in service as a Navy Lieutenant during the 1944 and '45 seasons.) They were far from a weak football team.

We were favored to win, but a tough game was expected. Certainly, that was what we looked to and we went hard to work. On Wednesday, our thirty-minute scrimmage on the field in front of Cullum Hall, with the Lombardos against the Kennas, produced what I shall always believe was the best football I ever saw. Neither of the alternate teams could stop the other, as each scored three times. The speed, power, co-ordination, and ferocity were something I have not seen equalled on a gridiron.

Incentive certainly was not lacking. Army's last victory over Notre Dame had been in the time of Ralph Sasse and Ray Stecker thirteen years before. In twelve subsequent attempts, the Cadets had tied two, lost ten. Not since 1938, when end Riggs Sullivan, now the Air Force Academy Commandant, caught Charles (Huey) Long's left-handed pass for a touchdown and Long converted, had Army scored on the Irish.

When we won the toss, we invariably kicked off. We knew Doc's long boot into the end zone—he averaged 56.1 yards on 45 kick-offs that season—precluded any substantial return. We also had confidence our defense could force an immediate return punt, which figured to give us field position for an early foray. We lost the toss to Notre Dame, but it made no difference because they chose to receive. They took Doc's kick-off back to their 18, made 6 yards in three downs and then punted poorly out of bounds on their 44.

Kenna's team marched from there to a touchdown, but it was not easy going. It took fourteen plays, all of them runs, except a fourth-down pass by Doug, which set the ball on their five. Two running plays reached the 1, but on third down they shoved us back to the 5. It was now fourth and 5. Kenna, in a nice bit of faking and hiding, bootlegged around their left end for the score. Walterhouse, who was to set a collegiate record of forty-seven conversions that year, kicked the point and we led, 7–0.

No matter what Notre Dame's strategy, we would have won, because we had the troops and we were emotionally "up" for a peak effort. But if the Irish had elected to play more conservatively, the score would have been something less than 59–0. After the first touchdown by Kenna, however, they "went for broke" with a passing attack that boomeranged to hand us one touchdown after another.

They threw twenty passes and completed ten for 102 yards. We intercepted eight and ran them back for 120 yards. (Our season totals were thirty-six interceptions for 399 yards.) Our second, third, and fourth touchdowns came after interceptions well into their territory. It was this to which I was referring at halftime, with the score 33–0, when I told our players, "This game isn't over."

Of our four second-half touchdowns, one came on a punt return, another after a recovery of a Notre Dame fumble on their 15, and a third after a pass interception on their 4 by plebe tackle Hal Tavzel.

Hal received considerable kidding from his teammates for being referred to in one report of the game as "an obscure Army tackle." When Tavzel and "Little Johnny" Sauer were intercepting passes late in the game, Herman Hickman shook his head at Andy Gustafson.

"My goodness!" said Herman, in deadly earnest. "I never thought we'd ever be sending in subs like this in the Notre Dame game."

We were quite a football organization that day, the best, I think, that West Point ever sent onto a field.

Blanchard uprooted Notre Dame blockers and tacklers. The block he put on John (Tree) Adams, six-feet-seven tackle, was one of the most lethal I ever saw. He even inflicted a dislocated elbow and wrenched knee on head lineman Dr. David Reese, who had the misfortune to get in his way.

Everybody played the game to the hilt, but if I were to single out any individual, it would be Kenna. Hampered by injuries for two years, this great athlete and competitor came into his own that day. In the twenty-six minutes he played, Doug ran the team superbly. He completed four of five passes for 62 yards and two touchdowns. He carried three times for 13 yards and one touchdown. He returned punts and ran back intercepted passes for 104 yards.

Early in the game, when Notre Dame still held some hope, it was Kenna who expunged it. He scored the first touchdown on a run, set up the second with an interception, and threw a pass for the third.

The magnitude of the victory, broadcast by short-wave radio all over the world, was incredible to West Point men at war. Captain Tom Mesereau, who had played a strong tackle and guard for me in 1941 and '42, was with nine other Academy graduates on a ship en route from New Guinea to the invasion of Leyte, when they heard the broadcast in the middle of the night. Gus Farwick, the All America guard who had been Ellinger's running mate, was in the heart of the Appenine Mountains in Italy when he heard the score.

"Just a lot of damned German propaganda," said Gus.

The reverberations continued. Biff Jones, who had come back into service as a colonel and was Athletic Director at the Academy from January 1, 1942, until June 1, 1948, received a letter from his old friend, fellow West Pointer, ex-player, and assistant coach, Colonel

Red Reeder. Red had commanded the 12th Infantry Regiment, 4th Infantry Division in the Invasion of Normandy, and on the sixth day lost a leg. He was now getting well in Walter Reed Hospital in Washington and from there he wrote Colonel Jones:

>Biff, the object of this letter is to tell you and Red Blaik a story. I was told it here last evening.
>Your classmate, Col. "Pop" Goode [Ed. note: former football player, Class of '17] was captured and made C. O. of his prisoner of war camp in Germany. Before the "Battle of the Bulge," German S. S. troopers came to Pop and asked for uniforms from the U. S. Army officers. Pop smelled a rat and told them, "Nutz!" They took the uniforms, anyhow, and at the correct-time-for-them, dropped English-speaking Germans in the uniforms behind our lines to spread confusion. It was difficult to find these Germans as they had up-to-the-minute identification cards and countersigns for the week. With all the confusion and counterorders which developed, it soon became evident that some officers other than ours were giving orders to truck convoys, ammunition trains, etc. We were at a loss as to how to apprehend these ———— until a smart M. P. went up to an officer, suspected of being a phony, and said:
>"Who won the Notre Dame game?"
>The "officer" did not know what the M. P. was talking about, so he was promptly locked up for further questioning, and shooting. This method of checking on phonies spread around and it did the trick.
>I surely got a kick out of this story, and know that you two will also!

In our 62–7 victory over Pennsylvania, their worst defeat since losing to Yale, 60–0, in 1890, we were almost as overpowering as we had been against Notre Dame. Yet we were not a fully accepted football team by many people, including ourselves. For the Navy game lay ahead.

Somehow, the team which most Annapolis people with football background regard as their greatest in history, had lost early-season games to North Carolina Pre-Flight, 21–14, and to Georgia Tech at Grant Field, Atlanta, 17–15. They had demonstrated the power of their single-wing attack and their rugged, resolute defense, however, in trampling Notre Dame, Penn, Purdue, Duke, Penn State, and Cornell.

Their talented backfield included quarterback Dick Duden, fine blocker and field general; halfbacks Hal Hamberg, Bob Jenkins, and Red Barron; and fullbacks Clyde (Smackover) Scott and Vic Finos. Although their backfield was not rated as good as ours, their line was considered better. They had Dick Whitmire, an outstanding tackle; Ben Chase, guard; Jack Martin, center; and Ben Martin, right end.

Ben Martin had played against us as wingback in their victories of 1942 and '43. Ben was subsequently a valued assistant on the Annapolis coaching staff for several years, later was head coach at Virginia, and today holds the job at the Air Force Academy. He is definitely one of the brilliant young coaches of today, with a fine future.

That Navy 1944 team also had good reserves. We regarded them as pretty much our match in over-all personnel. Here was the big test, and we welcomed it.

In many ways, this was the greatest of all Army-Navy games. Since we were ranked No. 1 and Navy No. 2, the service game for the first time was to decide the national championship. Newspapers and radios provided an unprecedented build-up. Service arms all over the world eagerly awaited the short-wave broadcast. It may be there was more interest in this game than in any other ever played, before or since.

For the first time in many years, the Navy game, win or lose, was not being regarded by Army in a sort of anticlimactic sense to another defeat by Notre Dame. Desire to snap the long series of losses to Notre Dame had gradually established priority over the urgency to beat Navy, not only in the Corps but also among many graduates. This had definitely detracted from an all-out approach to the Navy game for several years before 1944.

Originally, the game had been scheduled for Thompson Stadium at Annapolis, as in 1942. However, an opportunity to stimulate war-bond purchases through ticket sales prompted Washington to permit us to play in the old Baltimore Municipal Stadium. Nearly 70,000 were to jam the sprawly wooden horseshoe and foster the sale of $58,637,000 worth of war bonds.

The week of the game, a strange situation developed. I received reports that Navy, the home team that year, was resodding the field. I could appreciate Navy's artistic compulsion to present a pristine turf of sparkling green. I also suspected that new turf, soft and spongy, would slow down Davis, Blanchard, Hall, Minor, and the rest of our fast horses. It may be Navy had considered that also. Certainly, I would be the last to underestimate them.

Our coaching staff included that old Army halfback and cool-potato competitor from Waco, Texas, Captain Jack Buckler. Early Monday morning, I called Buckler up to the football office.

"Jack," I said, "get right down to Baltimore and find out what's going on. If they are resodding the field, stop it!"

When Buckler arrived at Municipal Stadium, he found that almost half the gridiron had been scalped from 40-yard line to goal line. The Navy graduate manager was there. So was the man in charge of the stadium, a retired National Guard General and, according to Buckler, in sympathy with the Navy. Buckler demanded that the sodding work be halted immediately. Sharp words followed between Captain Jack and the Annapolis man.

"It is our home game," said Annapolis, "and we will do what we wish with the field, sir!"

"You may damned well do what you wish with your half of it, sir," replied Buckler, "but we are also going to play in the game, so leave our half alone, sir!"

My recollection is that we lost the argument and most, if not all, of the field was resodded. On Tuesday, rain came and turned the resodded gridiron into a swamp. By Saturday, dry weather had dried it out some, but it was still not conducive to fast footing. We were going to have to lick the sod as well as the Navy.

In the first quarter, the two giants sparred like respectful heavyweights. We won it, however, if for no other reason than their powerful, driving left halfback, Bob Jenkins, who hurt us in 1943, was knocked groggy on a hard tackle by Bobby Dobbs. In the second quarter, "Ug" Fuson picked off a Navy pass on our 32, and we began to move. A grounded fourth-down pass from their 16 halted us temporarily, but when they kicked out, we went all the way, 66 yards in six plays.

Dale Hall, the most underrated back on our team, made the touchdown on a quick-hitting, twisting, 23-yard run, in which he feinted and side-stepped their secondaries. Walterhouse converted and we led, 7–0. That same period, another 1943 tormentor, Don Whitmire, had to leave the scene on a bad ankle. He hurt it on the opening kickoff and the injury was aggravated by the blocking of Foldberg and Coulter. The ankle ballooned and wrecked Whitmire's mobility.

When Joe Stanowicz blocked a kick for a safety and a 9–0 lead in the third quarter, we looked to be on our way again, but then the game turned sloppy. Two penalties and two losses set us back 54 yards, from Navy's 19 to our 27. We had to kick and now Navy staged a beautiful 71-yard scoring drive in sixteen plays. Little Hal Hamberg, talented runner and passer, was the dynamo, assisted by Scott's speedy smashes to the inside and Barron's reverses. Scott went over from the 1 and Finos converted. It was 9–7 and back in the pan.

At this point, I didn't feel so good. I felt worse when Hamberg returned a punt 24 yards to our 46. Jenkins, back in the game briefly, tried a pass, but Davis intercepted it on our 35 and ran it back to our 48.

Blanchard had played a strong game all day. Now he began to take the Navy line apart. Moving like a big, hard, runaway rubber ball, he got around their right end for 20 yards and a first on their 32. It was Blanchard for three, Davis three, and Doc five more to a first on the 21. Minor made a yard. Then it was Blanchard, for three, for four, for three—and first down on their 10. John McEwan was to say the next day, "If I were a Navy man and saw Blanchard coming, I would have resigned from Annapolis immediately."

Lombardo called on Doc once more. This time the big boy roared through Navy's left side and all the way into the end zone. Walterhouse converted, we led, 16–7, and I felt a lot better.

Blanchard had many great days for us, but I have no more potent memory of him than on that 52-yard march: a hungry, 208-pound plebe, wishing his dad was there to see it, carrying the ball seven out of nine times, and gaining 48 of the 52 yards against a Navy line that knew he was coming, and with the most important single game of his three years in the balance.

There was still half a quarter to go, and you can never afford to relax against the Navy. Davis put the crusher on them. We had rigged a fancy play for him which we called "The California Special." Blanchard flanked to the right, Minor went in motion to the left, and Lombardo pitched out to Glenn heading to the left. He broke loose around their right side, and raced 52 yards down the sideline, outdistancing Hal Hamberg, who tried to head him off. Again Walterhouse converted and we were home free, 23–7.

I know there must be a moment in every coach's career which surpasses all the others for him. I suspect that when it comes, he is aware of it, knows it has not come before nor will again. I believe the No. 1 moment for me came in that victory of Army's greatest over Navy's greatest in Baltimore.

General MacArthur wired:

THE GREATEST OF ALL ARMY TEAMS STOP WE HAVE STOPPED THE WAR TO CELEBRATE YOUR MAGNIFICENT SUCCESS.

Wires and letters poured in from Army men all over the world. One letter in particular from Leyte had a special meaning. It read in part:

> Last night I went to bed at 11:30 and at 2:25 this morning the ever faithful Dombroski awakened me with a cup of coffee and with the word that the Navy game would start in five minutes. Yesterday afternoon I had our signal people string a long antenna in front of my house and also requested that they put a very powerful radio here in my office.
>
> I could visualize your excitement, that of the other coaches, team and crowd. Out here we got a big kick out of it, too, and I cannot tell you how proud we all are of you and your fine group of coaches as well as the team that has made a record which will

be talked of the next fifty years in the Army. An air raid alert went on through the middle of the game but we just closed the blackout curtains and kept on listening without ever noticing the raid.

Toward the end of the game this morning, the rain began to drum down on the tin roof and some static developed. I was able, however, to pick up the last quarter of the game again this afternoon at a rebroadcast and it was as clear as a bell. We knew what was going on but we were not sure of the length of the run that Davis made in producing the final touchdown.

ROBERT L. EICHELBERGER

Uncle Bobby was eager to share the good news of the game, especially with Colonel Charles Robert (Monk) Meyer. Monk Meyer had been a celebrated halfback at the Point from 1934 through '36. He never weighed more than 143 pounds and looked as if a strong wind would blow him down the Hudson, but, brother, he was a supercharged competitor, and he had starred in the 28–7 victory over Navy in '36.

At the moment, Monk was leading the 2nd Battalion, 127th Infantry and 32nd Division into the line in the hills at the north end of the Ormoc Valley in Leyte. The trails to his position had been turned into small rivers by the rains. But Uncle Bobby and other officers, including two classmates of mine, Colonels Clovis Byers and Rex Corput, went after Monk in a jeep. When they told him the score, he got as big a kick out of it as they knew he would.

That 1944 team, national champions, won all kinds of honors and set all kinds of statistical records. Blanchard, Davis, Green, Kenna, Stanowicz, and Poole made All America. In a souvenir booklet, restricted to those on the squad or in an official capacity relating to it, I wrote this message to the team:

> Seldom in a lifetime's experience is one permitted the complete satisfaction of being part of a perfect performance.
> To the coaches, the 23–7 is enough.
> To the squad members: by hard work and sacrifice, you su-

perbly combined ability, ambition and the desire to win, thereby leaving a rich athletic heritage for future Academy squads.

From her sons West Point expects the best—you were the best. In truth, you were a story book team.

I feel that the storybook description also fits the 1945 Army team. I have often been asked to compare the two teams.

From the '44 team, we lost Lombardo, Kenna, Hall, Rafalko, Stanowicz, St. Onge, Arnold, Dobbs, Sauer, and Walterhouse.

The incoming plebes of '45 included backs Tom (Shorty) McWilliams, Bobby Jack Stuart, and Elwyn (Rip) Rowan; guard Joe Steffy; and tackle Goble Bryant. Some of these plebes did not begin to fulfill their potentials until after '45.

The '45 team, therefore, did not enjoy quite the qualitative depth of '44. The second team was in reality a second team and not an alternate unit.

But the '45 first team was smoother in execution, more diversified, and even more explosive than either of the '44 alternate units. In '44, we were essentially a running outfit. In '45, we intermixed the pass more effectively. Quarterback Arnold Tucker was a superior passer. Glenn Davis improved as a passer until he, too, was superior. The increased passing threat augmented the running danger of Blanchard, Davis, and our other backs. We scored twenty-three touchdowns on plays that covered 40 yards or more; fourteen on runs, five on passes, two on pass interceptions and two on punt returns.

The seasons of 1944 through '46 are invariably referred to as the Blanchard-Davis era. It was not until 1945, however, that Doc and Glenn were coupled as an entry in an unprecedented public acceptance that also embraced the entire team.

Army teams are traditionally known as the "Cadets." Since 1945, they have also been known as the "Black Knights." This name was hung on us that season by the late Will Wedge of the New York *Sun*. Will based his colorful tag on our home uniform of golden helmet with black band up the middle and dark jersey with golden numbers and arm bands.

Blanchard and Davis were dubbed "Mister Inside" and "Mister

Outside" by George Trevor. Joe Williams referred to them merely as "B." and "D." I doubt whether any football players in history, Jim Thorpe, Red Grange, the Four Horsemen, any of them, were accorded more publicity than Doc and Glenn.

I always was a team maker rather than a star maker, but there was nothing I could do about Blanchard and Davis. Yet we treated them the same as anybody else, on and off the field. In the winter of their first-class year, Doc and Shelton Biles missed a lecture given by a visitor, and got "slugged" for it. This meant that for a two-month period they lost all privileges and had to spend all of their free time walking the barracks area.

As for team effort and team spirit, there never was any problem with Blanchard and Davis. The nature of West Point helps to prevent the individual from being affected by publicity, even if he is susceptible, which these two boys were not.

In the face of a tidal wave of publicity that could have been dangerous, I was able to keep this team from complacency by appealing to their pride.

"You are the champions," I told them many times. "From you people expect only perfect performances. Even to try to approach what they expect, you must remain a team."

They remained a team. At the same time, Blanchard and Davis convinced me—and the conviction, if possible, has strengthened with the years—that they were truly the apotheosis of the one-two punch. With Tucker as quarterback and Shorty McWilliams, a strong blocker as well as a sharp runner, at right half, I would rate that '45 backfield as the best in West Point history and one of the best ever anywhere.

The line that ran in front of them, I also consider Army's best: Pitzer or Poole, Coulter, Green, Fuson, Gerometta, Nemetz, and Foldberg.

So, to answer the question, which was greater, 1944 or 1945, I am not fence-straddling when I say '44 was the greater squad, '45 the greater team.

It was a heavy load those teams carried. The pressure of always being at their best was superimposed on the academic, military, and disciplinary regimen of the Academy, especially rigid and taxing in a souped-up wartime tempo.

The few relaxation periods would come between the time we left the Academy on Friday morning or at noon for a game away from the Post and the time we reached the dressing room on Saturday to suit up.

We traveled in two large, powerful Army Athletic Association buses. They were driven by two loyal, enthusiastic A.A.A. employees, Sam Woodruff and Slim McClain. Sam and Slim drove us, behind a police motorcycle escort, from our pre-game bivouac at the Knollwood Country Club in Westchester or the Manufacturers' Country Club in Oreland, outside Philadelphia, to the stadium. At such times, Sam and Slim handled those big buses with the air of men who believed they were warming up for the Indianapolis 500.

They took the curves, especially the one around City Hall in Philadelphia, in a manner to concern my old friend, Colonel Gerald A. Counts (now General Counts, Retired), Professor of Physics and Chemistry and member of the Athletic Board. But those wild rides relaxed the players (I hope). They cheered Sam and Slim loudly after every hair-raising turn.

In between curves, the players sang. They were led by Fuson and Biles. The harmony was always pretty fair, except for the 1944 attempts at soloing by Rafalko, who couldn't carry a tune in a bucket. Two of our favorites were "The Good Old Mountain Dew" and "I Hear You Knockin' But You Can't Come In." The strains of "I Hear You Knockin'" grew louder and louder and seemed timed to reach fortissimo just as the buses pulled up to the stadium gates. That last "You Can't Come In" always sounded like a song of defiance to the opponent.

Those were great days.

Our '45 schedule included opponents who made good records that year. Navy lost only to us. Michigan, with the first elements of its later great teams of '46 and '47, defeated Great Lakes and finished second in the Big Ten with a 5–1 record; they lost only to the Indiana team coached by Bo McMillin, the Hoosiers' only Conference champion in football. Duke lost only to us and to Navy. Notre Dame tied

Navy, lost to us and the Great Lakes, and defeated all its civilian school opponents.

The Michigan game, played in Yankee Stadium before a 70,000 sellout, may have been our most interesting of the year. The Wolverines were young, but they were talented, spirited and, like all Fritz Crisler teams, precise, deceptive, diversified, and colorful on the attack.

Michigan never would have been able to make the fight of it she did, however, had not Crisler taken advantage of unlimited substitution, permitted by the rules as far back as 1941, to use separate units, or close to it, on offense and defense. This kept fresh men in action, which cut down the edge of superior personnel. It also emphasized the incontrovertible principle that there are always more boys on a squad who can play the game better one way, offensively or defensively, than there are those who can play it both ways.

What I saw that day in Michigan's separate units for offense and defense stayed with me and was to exert a salutary effect on Army football soon after the Blanchard-Davis era.

Michigan fought flashily and spiritedly, but Blanchard and Davis, helped by McWilliams, gradually cut them to pieces with long runs and we won, 28-7. McWilliams' 54-yard scoring run behind a convoy of blockers on the first scrimmage play started us to an impressive 48-13 victory over Duke. While we were beating Villanova the next week, I took Hickman and others of the staff to Cleveland, to see Notre Dame play the 6-6 tie with Navy. The trip was much pleasanter than the similar expedition to Baltimore the year before, since I did not encounter Warden Lawes.

Notre Dame that year was coached by Hugh J. Devore. I have always regarded Hughie as one of the best men in the business. The tie to which he coached his team in the Navy game was no fluke. In fact, the Irish would have won, except for an ill-advised pass which Clyde Scott intercepted and returned for a touchdown.

In losing to us, 48-0, Notre Dame played a more cohesive and saner game than the year before, actually outgained us for much of the first half, but finally succumbed to the lightning thrusts of Glenn and Doc.

"Our team did not fall apart," said Devore later. "We were just up against something we couldn't handle. Red Blaik can be proud of his team."

John Carmichael, of the Chicago *Daily News*, reflected a general opinion when he wrote, "In plain, unvarnished truth, Army's football team doesn't know its own strength."

Our 61–0 victory over Penn at Franklin Field was probably the 1945 team's most impressive handiwork. The blocking and tackling were overpowering, the speed blinding, the timing and deception perfect. Navy scouts leaving Franklin Field made sure the writers heard them say, "Say a few prayers for us. We're going to need them."

They weren't fooling me a bit. After the Notre Dame tie, Commander Hagberg's team had improved and beat Michigan by a larger margin than we did, 33–7. My foreboding about what might happen was well summed up by John McEwan at a rally in the mess hall.

"If you don't win Saturday," said Big Mac, "if you let the Navy upset you after the build-up you've had, you will go down as the greatest flops in the history of sports."

General Eisenhower also addressed that rally by long-distance telephone hooked up to the public-address system.

"I understand," he said, "we're talking on a sort of family line with all the cadets and everyone else at the football rally listening in. How I'd like to be there! It is just thirty-one years since I last participated in a 'beat the Navy' meeting. That year I was cheerleader. I'd like to ask this year's occupant of the same post whether he is any more successful than I was in impressing that gang with his eloquence or in dodging the bombardment of catcalls and insults that was always my portion. Luckily I had a broken leg [Ed. note: this injury had ended a promising varsity career for halfback Eisenhower] and the Corps was gentlemanly enough to abstain from physical violence against a cripple. Anyway, we licked the Navy!"

We were anything but complacent; we went out to sew it up as quickly as we could, and pretty much succeeded. We got three quick ones in the first quarter. We marched 52 yards for the first from the opening kick-off, with Doc blasting in from the 2. Doc also scored the second on a 16-yard burst. Scott had a clean shot at him in the open, but Blanchard went through him as if he were an animated rain cloud. Davis scored the third on a 49-yard run inside tackle. We missed the first conversion, so we led, 20–0.

Navy fought back, as she always will, and scored before the half ended on an impressive 61-yard pass play from Bruce Smith to Scott. That Clyde Scott could fly, and even Davis could not catch him from behind. In the third period, Blanchard picked off one of their passes and ran it back 52 yards. In the fourth period, they stormed back again to make it 26–12. This was far better than anybody, except ourselves, had expected them to do. But when Davis got loose on a 32-yard run to score his eighteenth touchdown of the year (Blanchard had nineteen), we went ahead, 32–13, and that was the final score.

We were again national champions and swamped with other honors, team and individual. Blanchard won the Heisman Trophy, awarded to the nation's outstanding players, with Davis runner-up. Doc also won the Maxwell Cup and the Walter Camp trophy as the player of the year, and became the first football player ever to win the Sullivan Award for being the outstanding amateur athlete in America.

All America honors went to Doc, Glenn, Captain Jack Green (who made his last game the best of his career), Coulter, Nemetz, Foldberg, Poole, and McWilliams.

The Rose Bowl wanted us, but we turned it down. We reasoned there was nothing more for this team to prove. More important, the pre-Christmas examinations lay immediately ahead. The players were disappointed that the bid was turned down. In view of subsequent events, I wish now we had accepted it.

Before Christmas, we had a visitor. General Robert L. Eichelberger came home from the Pacific and back to the Academy he had last seen early in 1942. From game films I sent him, he had seen the great teams for which he was so responsible. Now, one night before the holidays, I brought him up to the quarters he had built for us to meet the 1945 squad in the flesh. Uncle Bobby said he never received a finer Christmas present.

Speaking of holidays, Andy Gustafson never forgot that staff meeting 8:00 A.M., January 1, 1944. Years after, when he was head coach at Miami of Florida, Gus never failed to phone me long distance to West Point on New Year's morning, usually before eight, to inquire whether I was at the office and, if not, why not.

Chapter XII

The Vindicators

One rainy night in the spring of 1946, I was taking a walk before going to bed. My path took me by Lusk Reservoir, which is situated along Mills Road across from Michie Stadium in that especially picturesque area of West Point which spreads below Fort Putnam. Suddenly, from out of the wet shadows surrounding the water-filtration plant, I was apprehended by a military guard.

"Halt!" he ordered militarily, then added unmilitarily, "Who's that?"

Since I was in uniform, I wondered at his challenge.

"Officer of the post," I answered, and waited to hear, "Officer of the post, advance."

Instead, he repeated, "Halt! Who's that?"

"Officer of the post," I came back again, this time somewhat impatiently.

A considerable silence followed. Then, for the third time, he said, "Who's that?"

"Why," I asked, "don't you tell me to advance?"

I sensed he was new to guard duty, and I could observe he was excited. I began to get a little nervous myself when he drew his Colt .45, injected a cartridge, raised the gun aloft, and circled behind me.

"Forward march!" he commanded.

He paraded me some two hundred feet to the guardroom in the filtration plant, and told me to sit down. All the time he was holding the gun not far from my head, three feet, to be accurate. He pointed to the telephone and said, "Call five nine seven."

"Look here," I said, "I am an officer of the post! Why don't you call the sergeant of the guard?"

My captor again pointed to the phone. "Call five nine seven," he repeated. Perspiration was beading his forehead and face. I realized he was even more concerned about me than I was about him—and that was considerably. I decided that even though the war was over, he must think me some manner of spy, who had filched a uniform and come to case the filtration plant preparatory to shutting off the post water supply by a well-placed time bomb.

I dialed 597 and the sergeant of the guard answered. I explained my predicament, but he thought I was some practical joker. "Yeah, sure," he said, "you're Red Blaik and I'm Frank Leahy," and hung up on me.

The guard just stood there staring at me. He was perspiring and holding his gun with a tension that was menacing. I grabbed the phone, dialed the guardhouse again and this time asked for, and got, the officer of the day.

"Listen," I said, "this is no joke! This *is* Blaik and you better get the hell up here right away! This guard has a gun at my head! And he ain't talking!"

The officer of the day arrived within the next five minutes and relieved me of my predicament. The next day, the guard was relieved of his duty. It developed that not only was it his first night on the duty, but the poor fellow was a mental case. Ten minutes more in that filtration plant guardroom with him, and I would have been another one.

The experience, however, while hair-raising, might well be considered a practical part of spring practice that year, because 1946 was to be a season in which I had the feeling much of the time of a man with a gun at his head.

That '46 season, everything considered, was as pressurized and unfunny as any I went through in twenty-five years of head-coaching. I recall only one light note (unless you consider the filtration plant scene was humorous) and that came early in the winter after Herman Hickman returned from addressing a high-school football banquet in nearby Poughkeepsie. As a fee for Herman's oratory, a local shirt manufacturer sent him a half-dozen pastel numbers, cut especially to meet Herman's extraordinary measurements of 20 collar and 33 sleeve. Herman undid the package in front of the staff and took out the shirts, one by one, each with some appropriate comment. From out of one of the shirts, a note fell to the floor. Herman picked it up and read it aloud: "I sure would like to meet the man who could wear this God damn shirt."

That kept us loose for a time, but not for long. Herman could wear the shirt all right. The question was: Could the 1946 team wear the mantle of 1944 and '45 that had been thrust upon it?

I never came across an informed football man who ever tended to devaluate in the slightest the Army teams of 1944 and '45. They were the best, in my opinion, but you don't have to take that. Any critic who counts rates them among the greatest college teams ever assembled.

True, the majority of the civilian college teams they defeated were below par because of the war. Nevertheless, the manner of their victories over the two best Navy teams of all time, two Notre Dame teams which were far from pushovers, Duke in '44 and Michigan in '45, plus the obvious class of our players, individually and as teams, all underscore the caliber of those original Black Knights.

Still, there are always the career carpers. In 1946, they challenged us. The war had been over for more than a year, they argued, and Army was going to meet much tougher opposition from civilian college opponents. Now let's see, they concluded, just how good these Blanchard-Davis teams really are.

As an argument, it was all right as far as it went, but it didn't go far enough. There was no question but that we were taking on one of the toughest schedules in Academy history: Villanova, Oklahoma, Cornell, Michigan, Columbia, Duke, West Virginia, Notre Dame, Pennsylvania, and Navy. Most of these teams were well stocked with returning service personnel. The records of some of them that year place them among the best in the annals of their schools. This was sharply true of Oklahoma, Michigan, Notre Dame, and Pennsylvania.

At Oklahoma, there was a spring practice that saw an unprecedented turnover in material. Jim Tatum, the new Sooner coach, had already coached some of it at the Jacksonville Naval Training Station. Tatum was installing the split-T formation he had learned from its inventor, Don Faurot, at Iowa Pre-Flight. Tatum had taught the formation at Jacksonville.

Coach Fritz Crisler's Michigan squad included most of the men who made up the 1947 Rose Bowl team. Michigan prepared for us from spring practice and reached such a peak for us they suffered a subsequent letdown in a tie by Northwestern and a fumble-ridden upset by Illinois. Those '46 Wolverines won their last four games: from Minnesota, 21–0; Michigan State, 55–7; Wisconsin, 28–6; and Ohio State, 58–6. They rated right up with the '47 team in everything but the over-all record.

The '46 Notre Dame team, with Leahy back as head coach, included service returnees from the teams of 1941, '42, and '43, and some valuable transfers in tackle George Connor and center George Strohmeyer. This was one of the best of all Irish teams. The line was one of the best I have seen, as was their '47 line.

Pennsylvania's personnel was strong. Except for a 17–14 upset by Princeton, Penn lost only to us. Cornell, with a 6–1–1 record under Ed McKeever, was no pushover. Duke, Columbia, and Villanova had winning records, and West Virginia broke even. Navy, which lost heavily by graduation, won only its opening game. But the Midshipmen were to prove, as they have so many times, that when "they sally forth to play the Army," you can ignore their previous record.

Therefore, there can be no argument with that section of the career carpers' thesis that our schedule was going to provide us more testing challenges than in '44 or '45.

The implication, however, that our '46 team was on a level, in first-team talent and qualitative depth, with those of '44 and '45 breaks down under any analysis.

To begin with, from the original regular alternate units of '44, nine men remained: Poole, Hayes, Biles, Fuson, Gerometta, Foldberg, Tucker, Davis, and Blanchard. Injuries to Blanchard, Tucker, and Fuson impaired their effectiveness; Doc for the full season, Arnold and "Ug" in key games.

Part of our reserve problem traced to the return to normal eligibility rules, which prevented us from deriving any help from plebes. As the season progressed, we were thankful that we got increasing help from centers Bill Yeoman and Harvey Livesay, guards Joe Steffy and Ray Drury, tackle Goble Bryant, ends Bobby Folsom and Jim Rawers, and fullback Elwyn (Rip) Rowan. Steffy, Bryant, and Yeoman were especially helpful.

In the line, we were outweighed from tackle to tackle by just about everybody we played. With Coulter, Nemetz, and Green gone, we lacked much of the blocking strength that had opened up those gaping holes for our backs in '44 and '45. I was forced to move Biles, who weighed 183 and had spindly legs, to left tackle. Frank Leahy said later he was amazed at the way Biles could handle himself against bigger men. Shelton did it by outstanding spirit, brains, and quickness.

We were even shorter on reserves in the backfield, Bill Gustafson, Andy's nephew, showed promise at quarterback and Bill West did good work at full and half. But the big load had to be carried by Blanchard, Davis, Tucker, Rowan, and Fuson, and much of the season only Davis and Rowan were in top physical condition.

I have always felt that if Doc and Arnold had been in prime shape all the way, we would have had much easier going.

The nature of the schedule, the loss of so many '44 and '45 aces, the lack of qualitative depth and the injuries added up to plenty of pressure. On top of it all was the challenge thrown us by the "Ranks of Tuscany," a challenge our players refused to ignore.

They knew they were not, as Herman Hickman put it, quoting Tennyson's *Ulysses*, "that strength which in old days moved earth and heaven." They knew they were the No. 1 objectives of some dedicated, loaded teams. They also knew the '44 and '45 teams really needed no vindication. But if there were those who demanded it, then these players of '46 were going to provide it.

That was their challenge, and they never forgot it.

British Field Marshal Viscount Bernard L. Montgomery visited West Point and witnessed one of our scrimmages. He was impressed.

"They worked behind a high canvas screen," he said later, "so that no one could learn what was going on. Their methods and tactics struck me as being very much like those used in battle. I was amazed at the way the players were padded up. I mean, war is a dirty game. What football can be I can't imagine."

The injury to Blanchard, the one thing that hurt us the most, took place in the opening game with Villanova on Michie Stadium turf made relatively spongy and uncertain by rain. We were in front by two touchdowns and moving for a third before giving the subs some much needed experience, Doc broke through Villanova's left side and into a broken field. At their 12, he maneuvered to avoid center Sylvio Yanelli. Right end Frank Kane, pursuing the play, leaped on Doc's back from behind. Just as Kane hit him, Doc's right heel sunk in the turf and bent the knee badly back forcibly.

Ligaments were torn and one of them pulled off a small piece of bone. Doc knelt there on the field, quietly but in great pain. Bevan and our team doctor went out to him. After a minute or so, he hobbled to the sideline. I could tell from his face how badly hurt he was.

Apparently, Doc had an unusually low pain threshold as well as extraordinary fortitude. An injury like that sidelines a player for a long time. We were worried for days after the Villanova game that Doc would never play again. As it was, he missed only the next two games, with Oklahoma and Cornell, and somehow finished the season. His determination and an unusual quadrucep-muscle group enabled him, with a minimum amount of exercise, to stabilize the knee sufficiently to play, but all year long we were harassed by the fear that the knee might go at any time. Doc was never his '44 or '45 self by 40 per cent, although against Navy, for a spell, he looked it. Even at 60 per cent efficiency, however, he was a heck of a football player.

It is worthy of note that X-rays of Doc's injured knee revealed a thigh calcification of earlier years that had hospitalized him for three months at St. Stanislaus. When our doctors studied the plates of that earlier injury, they shook their heads. They wondered how he had overcome it to play any football at all.

Blanchard's missing the Oklahoma game constituted a minor irony. He had looked forward to it with special relish because the Sooners were coached by his second cousin, Jim Tatum. However, Cousin Jim didn't know for sure that Cousin Felix was not going to be in the Army line-up until we actually ran out on the field for the kick-off. Blanchard and Davis were co-captains and Doc suited up and went out with Glenn for the toss.

Our psychology here was to keep Blanchard's playing a possibility as long as possible in the minds of the Sooners. They were already approaching the game with sufficient confidence and dedication.

Five of the players on that Oklahoma team are head coaches today: halfback Darrell Royal (he was shifted to quarterback later that year) at Texas, quarterback Jack Mitchell at Kansas, tackle Wade Walker at Mississippi State, and ends Jim Owens and Warren Giese at Washington and South Carolina. They went on to play for the early teams of the Bud Wilkinson regime. Wilkinson, who replaced Tatum as head coach in '47, after Jim went to Maryland, scouted our '46 team in that Villanova opener, and spotted from the press box in the Oklahoma game.

Since this was the first year with the split T for most of the Oklahoma players, they were having normal growing pains with it, such as we had experienced three years before with the straight T. Nevertheless, they were plenty tough. We were able to resist their terrific bid for victory only through an intrepid team effort, highlighted by the full flowering of Arnold Tucker as a quarterback and the flair of Glenn Davis to murder you one way—this day as a pass receiver—if you stopped him another.

Tucker must rank near the top of all Army quarterbacks. There was nothing to choose between him and that other superior field general of '46, Notre Dame's John Lujack. Natural leadership was a part of Tucker—he was the first man in the Class of '47 to achieve his majority—and a strong will went with it. I remember correcting him at one scrimmage on the execution of a play.

"No, Colonel," Arnold stated. "That play was just right."

"There are coaches here," I felt constrained to inform him, "who have been around longer than you have. Now get in there and do it the way I want it done!"

Arnold had a fine head on his shoulder and a solid sense of strategy. He was also imaginative and inclined to gamble, sometimes too much so for my digestion.

As a competitor, he was simply superb—a fighter who carried on at times with enough injuries to sideline three quarters of a backfield. It was Arnold, more than anybody else, who helped us win that trying game with Oklahoma, 21–7.

After the game, I had to put in a command appearance at a cocktail party given by the Supe, Major General Maxwell D. Taylor. President Harry S. Truman, who had attended the game, was there, and after a time he took me aside.

"Red," he said, "what do you think about your chances with Navy?"

"Reasonably good," I said, with uncommon optimism.

"They've got to be better than that," said the President. "I have twenty bucks riding on the game and I don't want to lose to any Navy so-and-so."

Long runs by Davis and Tucker turned back a stubborn Cornell team, 46–21. We got ready for Michigan, not knowing for sure whether we could start Blanchard. We finally decided to play him and pray the knee would hold up.

That game at Ann Arbor was one of the two or three most memorable of my career. A crowd of 88,000, then capacity for the magnificent quadrangular Michigan Stadium, thrilled to it. The weather was perfect for early October, although near the end there was a sudden overcast and a brief cloudburst. The game, worthy of the setting, was on both sides an impeccably heroic classic in the finest traditions of hard play and invincible spirit.

It began badly for us. A snafued punt that carried only 4 yards gave them early field position on our 41. They moved from there to a score, which came on a 13-yard pass to quarterback Howard Yerges from their talented tailback, Bob Chappuis. Jim Brieske converted and they led, 7–0.

The first few times Blanchard carried the ball, the Wolverines ganged up on him like berserk men, but the knee somehow held up. When we took Doc out for a short breather, he assured Bevan he would be all right.

Meanwhile, we had received another near-mortal wound when Tucker, driven out of bounds while handling a punt, incurred a shoulder separation and a sprained elbow on his right or passing side.

He was in great pain, and could no longer throw a deep pass. Yet, he went on to play the entire game, spinning, handling off the ball, throwing short passes, defending, directing.

Late in the first period, we stormed back at them. From our 19, Rip Rowan chewed off 6 at right guard. Tucker bootlegged their right flank for 16 and a first down on our 41. Davis now demonstrated to that Michigan crowd that what they had read and heard about him as a runner was not overstated in the slightest.

On a well-executed trap play, Glenn sprang through their left guard. As he came through the trap hole, a cluster of Wolverines converged on him. Somehow, he churned and zigzagged his way through them, broke into daylight and set sail down the sidelines like a shaft of light. At the Michigan 15, Paul White, a valiant player that day, tried to close in on him. Glenn, without breaking speed, faked White into a pretzel, veered by him, and shot into the end zone. Jack Ray converted.

It was 7-7 late in the second period, when Davis completed a 44-yard pass to Blanchard. Doc, going up between two Michigan defenders to get the ball, gave a reasonably good imitation of Don Hutson. With fourth and 18 on their 31 and time for only one more play in the half, Tucker called for a pass from Davis to Bob Folsom, a substitute end.

As Tucker took the ball from center and whirled to give it off to Davis, the left side of the Michigan line burst through and harassed the movement. The ball came loose and bounced along the ground. One Michigan lineman grabbed for it and missed. Then, seemingly all in one action, Davis seized the errant ball, pushed off Michigan linemen and fired to Folsom, who made a leaping end-zone catch just inside the back line. On both ends, it was one of the best and maddest pass plays you ever saw. We missed the point and led at the half, 13-7. Everybody in the place knew that the best—or the worst, depending on whose side you were—was yet to come.

Of our dressing room that halftime, I have two dominant memories. I see Doc and Glenn pacing up and down like two caged animals. They felt they had done nothing and were impatient to get going. I can also see myself getting talked into kicking off instead of staying with my original decision to receive.

From that second-half kick-off, Michigan put on a beautiful show. They hit us in a baffling mixture with everything out of their book: spins, traps, buck laterals, reverses, end arounds. They went 83 yards for a touchdown. Biles blocked Brieske's conversion try and it was all tied up again, 13–13.

Now, we threw our book at them. We moved from our 43 to their 14, but they stopped us. Early in the fourth quarter, we started again, this time from our 24. I was wondering how long Blanchard and Davis could go on. If I had to take either of them out of there . . . I did not want to think about it. Even a Davis couldn't carry the attack alone in this kind of thing.

But Tucker and Blanchard were not going to be stopped that day. If anything, the longer Doc played, the stronger he seemed to be getting. He made another leaping catch of a Davis pass, though surrounded by Wolverines on their 24. Tucker snapped a short one to Foldberg for 7 and a first on their 18. Davis hit the middle for 3. Glenn tossed a lateral out to Doc, who circled their right flank for eight and a first in their 7.

Blanchard was hot now and Tucker knew it. He called a fullback counterplay outside their right tackle. The execution was fine, the faking by Arnold and Glenn, the timing by Doc. He hit the hole and headed for home. At the 3, White leaped aboard his back, but for all the good it did him, he was just going along for the ride. Bad knee and all, Blanchard carried both White and the ball into the end zone without breaking stride, Ray converted and that was it, 20–13.

The play of Davis, Blanchard, and Tucker epitomized a colossal team effort. I have emphasized that Blanchrad and Tucker were far from sound physically. Now let me dwell on what Davis did. With the long passing game thrust upon him, he completed seven out of eight for 168 yards, accounting directly for the first touchdown and helping set up the third. His 59-yard run delivered the second.

The effort of our players was so transcendant, an emotional as well as a physical outpouring, they took a long time to unwind and get to sleep that night on our special train. There wasn't much sleeping done by coaches and newspapermen either. It was a game to be played over and over again until the small hours, to the accompaniment of tinkling glasses. I even had a glass of sherry myself.

In moving by Columbia, Duke, and West Virginia the next three weeks, we did not play at peak form. We could not afford to. We played well enough to win without getting into too much pressure. We were looking ahead to the Notre Dame game at Yankee Stadium, November 10, just as the Irish were.

As in '44, I went down to see Notre Dame-Navy at Baltimore, at the head of a scouting contingent, leaving Gus to handle the Cadets against West Virginia. Since I was not scouting officially, I took a seat away from the others of my party high up in the stadium. Who should be sitting two seats away from me but Bob Hope with a friend who had a radio.

Hope relayed the Army-West Virginia situation to me, as he got it from his friend's set. As I say, we were not up for the Mountaineers and we might have been in serious plight, if Tucker had not demonstrated both the sense and courage to throw a 50-yard pass from his own end zone to a speeding Davis. Hope took full advantage of the Michie Stadium drama, my own concern, and his own powers as a comedian to really pour it on in his "rebroadcast." His sense of timing was almost sadistic. The next week Bob spoke at our rally and had the cadets in the aisles.

Notre Dame had one heck of a football team that year. They had begun the season by a 26-6 thumping of the Illinois team which was to win the Big Ten championship and romp over U.C.L.A. in the Rose Bowl. The Irish then went on to grind Pittsburgh, 33-0; Purdue, 49-6; Iowa, 41-6; Navy, 28-0; and, subsequently, Northwestern, 27-0; Tulane, 41-0; and Southern California, 26-6. After a look at the sheer power of them in the Navy game, I felt like calling for a sedative.

We were especially concerned about our ability to meet them from tackle to tackle in a manner to prevent their grinding out, short, inexorable hunks of yardage and thus maintaining ball control.

Their ends were Jim Martin, Jack Zilly, Bob Skoglund, and Frank Kosikowski. George Connor and George Sullivan were the tackles, supported by Jack Fallon and Gasper Urban. Bill Fischer, Joe

Signaigo, and Frank Mastrangelo were the ranking guards. The centers were George Strohmeyer and Marty Wendell.

As I said earlier, I have always considered that Notre Dame line and the one which succeeded it in '47 (which was about the same line, except for Zuggie Czarobski at tackle, Leon Hart at end, and Bill Walsh at center) as two of the best I ever saw.

Their backfield also was rich and deep in talent: Lujack at quarter, Jim Mello and John Panelli at full; and a halfback collection which included Gerald Cowhig, Terry Brennan, Emil (Six Yards) Sitko, Mike Swistowicz, Russell (Pete) Ashbaugh, and Bill Gompers.

Quite an array were "The Lads," as Leahy used to call them.

Army-Notre Dame games always had enjoyed saturation build-ups, we thought, but none of them ever compared with that 1946 game. (Much of the spirit that surrounded it, especially in New York City, was unwholesome, had been for some time. I shall discuss this in detail in the next chapter.) Tickets, always hard to get, were now more exclusive than ever.

"If Yankee Stadium had a million seats," said Biff Jones, who, as our athletic director, bore a major share of the headache, "we would fill it for this game. I have never seen anything like it."

As a spectacular opus, the game did not live up to its billing. The final score was, and deserved to be, 0–0. In our intent on not losing, Leahy and I may have played it too close to the vest. Otherwise, somebody might have scored. After that, it might have been a case of more touchdowns, following Ralph Sasse's "pointer-bitch" philosophy.

The lines dominated the game. From tackle to tackle we stood up well to them. In the second period, they made one devastating drive of 83 yards to our 4. At that point, we dug in to stop Lujack on a sneak and to level off Gompers on a try at our right flank. Except for that march, the longest of the day, they got over midfield only twice.

We were over midfield nine times. We had a fine early opportunity when Goble Bryant recovered a fumble on their 24. Tucker passed to Davis on their 18, but we could penetrate no farther.

In the third period, I thought we might crack them. Tucker picked off a Lujack pass and ran it back to his 32. Then Doc got loose on a counterplay outside their right tackle and took off down the sidelines for 31 yards. For a moment, it looked as if he might go all the way. But up came Lujack, always a great defensive player, and when Doc tried to cut inside him on the 37, the Notre Dame quarterback brought him down. Tucker subsequently passed to Foldberg for a first down on their 20, but Terry Brennan broke up the drive by intercepting our next pass.

If there were relatively few offensive moments, that scoreless tie produced some of the most earth-shaking blocks and tackles anybody ever saw. Freddy Russell, the sports editor and nationally known sports columnist of the Nashville *Banner,* who was among the hundreds of writers from all over covering the game, told afterwards of the reaction of a member of the United Nations Belgian delegation, who was seeing his first American football. After watching ten minutes of the vehement collisions, he remarked with perfect seriousness, "Wouldn't it be simpler if they just gave each team a ball?"

We got off to a slow start in winning from Penn at Franklin Field the next week, 34-7. I recollect that on our second touchdown drive in the first half, Davis got a knee in the head and played on in a fog. When we were informed Glenn didn't recollect scoring the second touchdown, we got him out of there in a hurry. "What are you taking me out for, Colonel?" he wanted to know. "What did I do wrong?" Between halves, Tucker kept asking Glenn questions until we were sure he had snapped out of it. Then he went out and just about matched his Michigan performance.

And so we went down to the finale with Navy, owning a 27-game defeatless string that had begun with the opener against North Carolina in '44. Nobody gave Navy a chance except their coach, Commander Tom Hamilton, the Navy players and the Army coaches. I don't mean the Army players were overconfident, but defeat was not part of their thinking.

We were a weary, used-up ball club. To his bad shoulder and a knee, which he had hurt against Penn, Tucker added a turned ankle a few days before the game. Blanchard, whose normal playing weight for us was 207, had been drained down to 198. In the picture section, there is a shot in Philadelphia's Municipal Stadium the afternoon before the game, which shows how Doc's sunken cheeks made him look thinner than Davis, Tucker, and myself. We took no workout that day. The players just walked up and down the field a couple of times in their cadet-gray overcoats. It was obvious to writers on hand, and even a Navy official remarked, that we looked washed out, peaked, strained. Well, we were.

It would be just hell, I thought, to have this gang come this far with the effort they've made and then have the three-year record spoiled in the last game—and by the Navy. We sure would never hear the end of that.

Get them down fast. Keep them there. That was our plan, as in 1945. We started well. Tucker passed to Davis for 30 yards. Then Glenn took a pitchout from Arnold and snaked his way 14 yards to a score. Jack Ray kicked the extra point. That first conversion was to prove vital, though nobody suspected it at the time. Navy reacted strongly. Sparked by an unsung quarterback, Reaves Baysinger, the Midshipmen marched 81 yards for a touchdown, but missed the point.

Fortunately for us, we were able to play about as well in the second period as we had at any time all year. Blanchard and Davis were in fine form. They alternated in moving the ball from our 19 to our 48. From there, Doc shot over the middle, veered by a linebacker to the outside and outraced all pursuers down the sidelines. On that run, Doc looked more like the Blanchard of '44 and '45 than he had at any time all fall.

Presently, Bill Yeoman intercepted a pass on their 38, and we went on to score on a 26-yard pass play from Davis to Blanchard. This was a deep pass breaking out of a buttonhook fake. Doc executed the fake about 10 yards down field. After luring the defender out of position, he whirled suddenly, broke down field again and took the lead throw from Glenn, who had bluffed the shorter throw. This was the last scoring effort of Blanchard and Davis for Army, but nobody anticipated that at the time. To the stands, it looked as if we could call our shots.

On the bench, however, we were not feeling secure. An early block had aggravated Tucker's knee injury and we had to take him out while we were on defense. To keep the leg from stiffening on him, he had to keep walking up and down the sideline. He was in much pain.

Arnold's condition certainly contributed to our misadventures in the second half. We not only missed him defensively, but his leg prevented him from dropping back to pass. He had all he could do to get the ball away on hand-offs.

That was our side of it, but far from the whole story. Navy caught fire and threatened for a long time to run us out of the stadium and to run off with the game. They ran and blocked like furies and mixed in good passes. They went 79 yards for a second touchdown and 30 yards for a third. They were trailing only 21–18, when they took the ball on their 33-yard line with seven and a half minutes to play.

The crowd of 100,000 had gone hysterical. They had come to sit in on a final Blanchard-Davis walkover. Now they were seeing what threatened to become the most dramatic upset of all the gridiron eras. The day was unseasonably warm and humid. For us now, on the Army bench, it began to turn gray and cold. Navy had been marching without letup. I sensed they would march some more, and I did not know what, if anything, we could do about it. They had wrested the momentum of the game away from us. We were fighting for our lives. Yet, our team, scorched by many fires that year, was concentrating on the job with all the poise the situation demanded. But they were stealing frequent looks at the clock.

It would be just like the Navy, I thought, to spoil everything, to make us swallow a bitter, almost poisonous ending. Then, much of all this courageous Army team had done would be forgotten.

And now they were down on our 24. And now Lynn Chewning, their big fullback came charging around our left side for 23 yards. They were down on our three, and there was a minute and a half left to play.

There was nothing I could do. On top of all else, I had lost phone connection with my press-box spotters, Andy Gustafson and Herman Hickman. I thought something was wrong mechanically. It was not until sometime later, that I learned from Gerry Counts, who was sitting near Gus and Herman, just what happened. There was nothing wrong with the phones. Gus and Herman were ignoring the plaintive ringing. Their emotional state had overcome them. Gus just sat there, staring blankly off into space, afraid to look down on the field, or maybe afraid to miss the space ship he was praying would come and take him away from the awful scene. Herman wasn't looking at the field, either. He had his head down on folded arms and he was softly moaning, "Oh God, don't let it happen! Oh God, please don't let it happen!"

It was here "the brave old Army team," the Vindicators of 1946, stood fast like the Federals of General George Thomas at Chickamauga. Chewning drove at our right side, but Hank Foldberg and Goble Bryant met him head on. Chewning tried the other side. This time Barney Poole hurled him back. Navy was penalized 5 yards for taking a fifth time out for the half, which set them back to the 8. That was a break. But there was still time for one more play. It was third and goal to go.

Fringes of the half-crazed crowd, unable to restrain themselves, had come down out of the stands and pressed against the sidelines at the southwest corner of the field, to see at close hand the climax of the almost unbearable denouement.

Bill Hawkins, a stalwart for the Midshipmen all day, offense and defense both, took the snap from center, faked a buck into the line and flipped a lateral out to halfback Pete Williams. Williams drove 4 yards around our left end, but he was still 4 yards from home when Barney Poole dragged him down. Barney never made a better tackle than that one, or one that meant as much.

There were seven seconds to play when Tom Hamilton sent in a substitute to stop the clock. But before the officials saw the substitute, the clock ran out, and there was considerable argument at the time. Even had the officials seen the sub earlier, the clock would have been stopped only long enough to accept the substitution. It is doubtful there would have been time enough for Navy to run another play.

In the confusion and excitement of the last few seconds, in the traditional American eagerness to salute a gallant underdog which had come so close to achieving a tremendous upset, it was some time before there was full appreciation of what we had done. We had stopped them with the game on the line, after they had been marching unceasingly. We had stopped them twice on our 3-yard line and once on our 4. And that was the season-long story of that Army team of 1946: when the Cadets needed it most, they had it.

Willard Mullin did a typically humorous cartoon on the game. It shows atop the monument, a bronze foot symbolizing the three points difference in our 21-18 victory, the three extra points kicked by Jack Ray. Inscribed on the base of the monument: "To commemorate West Point's great football teams. Unbeaten . . . 1944 . . . 1945 . . . 1946." Walking along, looking up at the bronze foot, are two cadets. One says "Weren't there a couple of other men on that team back there in 1946?"

"Yeah," replies the other cadet. "Couple o' guys named Doc Davison and Glenn Blanchard, or something or other."

For the third straight year, the All America selectors honored Blanchard and Davis, and also acclaimed Foldberg, Poole, Tucker, Steffy, and Gerometta. Tucker received the Sullivan Award as the outstanding amateur athlete of the year.

In the national championship poll, conducted by the Associated Press, Notre Dame was rated No. 1, we were rated No. 2. It is not clear to me, to this day, on what basis the poll majority arrived at that decision. The Army, although tied by Notre Dame, remained an undefeated champion.

The Rose Bowl people wanted us to come out and play U.C.L.A. and this time we were receptive. We felt that the players who had done so much for the Academy and the United States Army deserved the trip. But the exclusive Pasadena pact between the Pacific Coast Conference and the Big Ten had been signed, and the Big Ten did not choose to step aside for one year.

In their annual poll, conducted by the New York *World-Telegram,* my confreres honored me by voting me Coach of the Year.

But the Christmas season, which had brought us so many football gifts in the last few years, was a sad one for me, because my father was dying. He passed away in Dayton on January 3, 1947. Since I was with him, I could not attend the Coach of the Year banquet at Leone's. It was arranged for me, however, to make a brief acceptance speech over a long-distance telephone connected with a loud-speaker.

"As their coach," I said, "I have great pride in the record of the 1944 squad, which was our best squad. I have great pride in the record of the 1945 team, which definitely was our best team. But I reserve the warmest affection and the greatest respect for the 1946 team, which, in the face of adversities, playing the best of college opposition, completely and thoroughly demonstrated its right to be classed as great."

And here again, I salute them: the Vindicators of 1946.

Chapter XIII

The Break with Notre Dame

Through my quarter of a century as a head coach, seven years at Dartmouth and eighteen at West Point, the sports-page streamer headline practically became one of our battle flags.

As a conservative of Scots extraction, I was interested only in finding enough hours around the calendar to coach football properly. I preferred to avoid controversy, and I was never overly impressed by headlines. To me, the winning scoreboard and whatever amount of work would lead to it were the essentials. Yet, if I may paraphrase Shakespeare, controversy was enamored of my parts, and I was wedded to the spectacular and the bizarre.

I suppose the controversy was natural to one of positive viewpoints and the intent to make them work. As for the spectacular and the bizarre, that was luck or fate.

At Dartmouth, they accused me for a while of being a military martinet who was trying to turn the school into an Ivy League version of West Point. I coached Dartmouth teams that smashed the obsession of the Yale jinx, that lined up with The Twelfth Man against Princeton, that lost a quarterback who thought football sinful, that won a "Fifth Down" game from Cornell.

At West Point, I was blessed by the Blanchard-Davis era and would be by the two-platoon era and The Year of The Lonely End. I would also be unblessed by the tragic expulsions of 1951.

For overheated intensity, however, nothing ever matched the reaction to Army's ten-year football break with Notre Dame, from 1947 to 1957. Although not wholly responsible for that decision, I concurred emphatically in it and believe time has proved it a wise one for both schools.

I doubt that the general football public, even Notre Dame and

Army followers, understands to this day why in 1946 we decided not to renew our contract after the 1947 game with such an old and respected rival. Press and public offered many conjectures as to the decision. Some of the theories carried a little weight, others none at all.

It was stated that Army was seeking to avoid inevitable defeats. Yet a real analysis of the series—twenty-four victories for Notre Dame, eight for Army, four ties—reveals that even the games won by the strongest Irish teams were close and bitterly fought. Aside from the years immediately following World War I and for much of the period from 1934 through 1943, when Army football was in decided downcurves, the rivalry was reasonably close.

It is logical to believe that our teams from 1948 through 1950, which lost only the Navy finale in 1950, would also have acquitted themselves well against the Irish, even conceding the latter's great strength in those seasons.

Much more to the point, the twelve consecutive winless years of Army after 1932, the one-sided victories by the Cadets in 1944 and 1945 and the reaction to them, had accumulatively developed an atmosphere in which the Notre Dame game was pre-empting, and would have continued to pre-empt, from Navy the position of traditional No. 1 schedule objective. Still this in itself would not have been nearly enough to impel suspension of the series.

The same is true of the Johnny Lujack incident. When Lujack was a star athlete at Connellsville (Pennsylvania) High, several colleges were after him, including Army and Notre Dame. At the wish of his mother and, apparently, himself, Lujack accepted a principal appointment to West Point, but late in June he was intercepted and rerouted to South Bend by a band of Irish chauvinists. This happened in 1942.

Army's position was simply this: the Cadets had accepted a long series of defeats from Notre Dame without protest. It now seemed to us that if Lujack had settled on West Point, it was the sportsmanlike thing to let him go through with it. Asperities arose which resulted in a conference at the Academy between Father John W. Cavanaugh, then Chairman of the Notre Dame Athletic Board, and Frank Leahy and our Athletic Board, including myself. At this meeting, our position was made clear and supported by documentary evidence.

All this happened four years before it was decided to suspend the series. It was nothing more than a temporary disagreement, something that could crop up in any long, highly competitive relationship. Long before that the series had known discordant notes. Following our victory in 1927, Knute Rockne visited our dressing room. Rock made a habit of such visits, usually to congratulate our players. This time, however, he complained that a tackle by one of our linemen going down under a punt had been overly enthusiastic. We, in turn, considered the behavior of a couple of Notre Dame players in their 1932 victory as distinctly sub-Galahadian.

It is true that a contributing factor to the break was our traditional football schedule problems. These, in the early 'forties, were becoming increasingly acute. The complexity of putting together Army football schedules begins with the necessity of having the football team fulfill its first extrinsic purpose: a supreme rallying point for Corps *esprit*. (The first intrinsic goal is the development of good combat leaders.)

All of the cadets attend the Navy game, of course, and any occasional games played in New York. The first and second classes are each allowed one other football trip. To give the entire Corps the opportunity it deserves to see the team in a majority of its games, it is imperative that at least four games be played at Michie Stadium. Since the seating capacity is limited to 27,500, it is impractical to schedule more than two major games there.

Army schedules until the 'forties had, with few exceptions, consisted of not more than five major games out of the usual total of nine. General Maxwell D. Taylor, who succeeded General Wilby as Superintendent on September 4, 1945, agreed with me that seven major games and two minor games were all that any Cadet team, considering the over-all regimen of Academy life, should be expected to handle. Colonel Dodson Stamps, a board member, held a minority view that seven major games were too much for the Cadets. For one thing, exacting academic demands were already putting the football player at a disadvantage on trips.

West Point always has been under pressure for football games from many sources, some governmental. The demands in the early 'forties, especially as the Blanchard-Davis teams developed, were more clamorous than ever. Old and new opponents wanted intersectional games: Michigan, Illinois, Northwestern, Duke, Georgia Tech, Oklahoma, Rice, Southern California, and Stanford. We also wanted to maintain old sectional rivalries with Yale, Harvard, and Columbia. (Later, as we advanced beyond the Ivy League, mainly because of their own recession, these were replaced with more rugged Penn State, Pittsburgh, and Syracuse.)

To take care of all these demands, retain the Notre Dame game and still restore Navy to its rightful place as No. 1 target, obviously posed a most complicated problem. Yet it was one I believe we could have resolved.

What we were concerned about was the unhealthy atmosphere that had grown up around our game with Notre Dame. The Notre Dame authorities saw it as much as we did and were also concerned about it, yet they were as helpless as we were to combat it.

West Point always has regarded its football team as representative of the service, the country, the people. We were received that way wherever we played, with one exception: the Notre Dame game in Yankee Stadium.

Why?

Thoroughly to understand any such strange phenomenon, it is necessary to inquire fully into the background. A brief study of the roots and growth of the Army-Notre Dame game will be profitable also because it shows that this game itself was a phenomenon born of Army's natural schedule problems.

In 1890 Army fielded its first team, organized, captained, and coached by Cadet Dennis Michie, who was later killed in the charge up San Juan Hill. His memory lives in the beautiful little stadium named for him. From 1890 to 1921, when an Army team went to New Haven to play Yale in the Bowl, the idea of the Cadets playing any team other than the Navy away from the Plain was, as I pointed out in an earlier chapter, regarded as sheer fantasy.

Yale and Army, for example, had played all their games, since the first one in 1891, on the Plain. A dispute about the length of the 1912 game (with blunt Pot Graves drawing figurative blood from Yale Coach Arthur Howe) contributed to the break between Yale and Army from 1912 to 1921. It is also unquestioned that Yale's attitude was conditioned by her weariness with having to come up to West Point to play the game every year. Anyhow, it was the departure of Yale from the schedule that opened the way for Notre Dame.

When Lieutenant Dan Sultan, officer in charge of football, found that Yale was vacating her date of Saturday, November 1, on the 1913 Army schedule, he ordered Cadet Harold Loomis, the football manager, to write some schools about filling it. Loomis wrote almost every college in the East without success. The few who did have the date open did not want to come to West Point for a game. Loomis then extended his quest to the Midwest. One of the places he wrote to was a then little arts college called Notre Dame.

Notre Dame's athletic director and head coach was Jesse Harper. He replied that he had the date open, that he would like to play the game and wanted a guarantee of $1,000. This caused a mild furor at West Point, which never had guaranteed anybody, including Yale and Harvard, more than $350. A special meeting of the Athletic Board was hurriedly called to thrash out this unprecedented fiduciary crisis.

After much red-faced debate, Sultan was authorized to meet Harper's request. (Old Jesse figured his costs well, for Notre Dame netted $83 profit on the trip.) By 1916 and '17, Army not only upped the guarantee to $1500, but was happy to do so. After World War I, the guarantee continued to grow until 1923. From then on, the two schools split the receipts down the middle.

Notre Dame's 35–13 victory on the Plain in that inaugural 1913 game has been sung and resung in every medium, including the cinema, and frequently in distorted tones. The victory was an upset only because the football caliber of the little arts college in South Bend was unknown along the seaboard. The Irish had by no means achieved their later stature. That they were already redoubtable foemen, however, Michigan, Pittsburgh, and other prominent teams knew from firsthand contact.

As to the forward pass, Notre Dame did not introduce it to Army or to the East. What the Irish did demonstrate to the somewhat smug East was how the pass should be used as an integral part of the attack. It was the passing of quarterback Gus Dorais to his ends, Knute Rockne and Gus Gushorst, and to halfback Joe Pliska, intermingled with plunges by fullback Ray Eichenlaub, that beat Army convincingly.

This impressed Army Coach Charlie Daly sufficiently so that he permitted Vernon Prichard, his star quarterback, and Louis Merillat, his star end, more leeway in using the pass. Their use of the weapon played a major part in Army's subsequent 22-9 victory over Navy in the Polo Grounds that season, the first for the Cadets over the Midshipmen since 1905. In that sense, Notre Dame's first victory over Army helped the Cadets.

The rivalry benefited the Irish even more richly. Knute Rockne always acknowledged freely that the Army game was the high springboard from which the Irish rose to Eastern and thence to national acclamation and prestige.

The series falls logically into six eras. The first, 1913 through '17, saw Notre Dame win three, Army two. In the second era, 1919 through '24, Notre Dame won five; Army's best was a scoreless tie in 1922. That was the last year the game was played on the Plain. Crowd appeal demanded that it be transferred to New York. If General MacArthur's plan to build a large stadium down by the river had been carried through, the game probably would have stayed at West Point. If it had stayed at West Point, it is unlikely the series ever would have broken off.

In 1923 the teams met at Ebbets Field in Brooklyn, in 1924 at the Polo Grounds, and in 1925 at Yankee Stadium. The game was played there from 1925 through 1946, with the exception of the '26 and '30 games in Soldier Field, Chicago.

The third era, 1925 through '31, involved good balance, with the Irish winning four, the Cadets three. The fourth era, 1932 through '43, was dominated by Notre Dame. The fifth era, just before the break, saw Army win two, tie one, lose one. It was in the fourth era when Notre Dame won ten and tied two of the twelve games, that the seeds of discord were sown.

Let me emphasize at this point that nobody at West Point that I know of ever objected to that segment of Notre Dame's "Subway Alumni," whose devotion to the school is a spontaneous, natural, healthy thing, not infected by a fanatical demand that the team always be victorious.

What Army did find sharply distasteful was that segment of the Subway Alumni, neither small nor quiet, which had, in the 'thirties and early 'forties, come to regard the Notre Dame-Army game in Yankee Stadium as a sporting event only so long as Notre Dame continued to win it.

It was because of these people that we found ourselves, in ever-mounting degree after 1941, the representatives of an unpopular cause. (With the healthy and unhealthy segments of the Subway Alumni added together, we appeared to have 90 per cent of the Yankee Stadium crowd against us.) This feeling came to a boil after our one-sided victories in 1944 and '45. To these people, apparently, our winning two years in a row by big scores after a twelve-year drought constituted an unpardonable sin.

In its twelve winless years, West Point had maintained a dignified, quiet sportsmanship of acceptance, not always easy in the face of the Yankee Stadium atmosphere. In contrast, our 1944 and '45 teams, leaving the field after victory heard themselves referred to by people as "slackers."

West Point and the United States Army never have made a publicity show out of the deaths in service of former cadets who played football, any more than they have the deaths of former cadets who did not play football.

No matter how long the list, since 1940 alone, of ex-football players who paid the supreme price—Bill Gillis, Tom Lombardo, "Ug" Fuson, Johnny Trent, Lynn Galloway, Ray Drury, Bill Kellum, to name only a few of them—the list of ex-cadet non-football players who paid the same price is obviously much longer.

Let me state, once and for all, that those boys who played football for us in 1944 and '45 and all the others who ever played for us from 1941 on were carrying out the orders of the United States Army as handed down to me by General Robert L. Eichelberger and those who succeeded him as Superintendents of the Military Academy. These boys have proved the wisdom of their selection as officer material, which, while they were still cadets, could also do a job the Army considered worth doing well or not at all.

The shouts of "slacker" were not confined to those who yelled at Yankee Stadium from a safe distance. In the year leading up to the 1946 game, a letter-writing campaign was directed at the Cadets and myself. Some of it was humorous. I used to receive a daily post card from South Bend. The theme of the message was always about the same. For example:

> Dear Coach Blaik:
> This is to remind you that the day of retribution is fast approaching. Might I advise that you make the most of the short time that remains, for as the poem has it, "Gather ye rosebuds while ye may." I trust that you have not severed all affiliations with Dartmouth College—any port in a storm, you know.
> There are but 205 days left until Nov. 9. . . .
> S P A T N C (ND Chapter)

These messages were always signed "S P A T N C." I soon deciphered this as "The Society for the Prevention of Army's Third National Championship."

While some of the letter writing was humorous, most of it was scurrilous.

The slacker-shouters and the poison-penmen, representing a large, loud segment of the Subway Alumni, were deplored by Notre Dame officials and the large majority of students and alumni. Ordinarily, such people and their products would be ignored for what they are. But they were being recognized and stimulated by a few newspapermen, not only in New York but elsewhere around the country.

In sum, the atmosphere of the Army-Notre Dame game in Yankee Stadium and the vitriol that was being injected into what had once been a sportsmanlike as well as a rugged rivalry all the way, were something we considered inimical to relations with a sister college.

Even more serious, the game was generating a form of psychological hate detrimental to the best interests of the United States

Army. The Army could hardly tolerate a condition that bred such ill will for the service and the Military Academy. A long cooling-off period was not only advisable, it was inescapably urgent.

I raised the objection that the absence of the Army-Notre Dame classic would seriously harm college football, especially in New York City where the college game had been retrogressing for several years. But this cogent factor had to be subordinated to even more important motivations.

The decision was wildly unpopular. The animosity that descended on us was heavy and it lingered for at least three years. In that time Army teams were criticized in some areas for almost any reason that could be conceived. Most of the barrage was aimed at me. "Blaik-haters" among the Subway Alumni and their press and radio spokesmen were numerous, thunderous and vicious.

While this campaign was at its height, I feel I coached as well as I ever did in my life.

I am as certain today, as I was then, that the break was a good thing. By coming when it did, it prevented a longer and more serious rift. This was a form of emotional disease that was going to get worse before it got better, unless a vigorous purgative were prescribed.

Any Army-Notre Dame relationship, whether in sports or any other intercollegiate field, deserves no less than the finest framework of sportsmanship. This is especially true today, when discipline as an integral part of education (so flagrantly overlooked at institutions where reports of moral delinquency reflect the overly free thinking of the day) is still the cornerstone of the service academies and of schools like Notre Dame. This is no small thing to have in common.

It is significant that in the break-off game at Notre Dame, which was played, as that gifted Irish alumnus Red Smith put it, "in an atmosphere of studiously courteous assault," the spirit in the crowd was far more salutary for both schools and supported the back-to-the-campus philosophy. No school could have been a more splendid host to us than Notre Dame was in our two games on their campus, in 1947 and '58. The hospitality after the kick-off may have been somewhat overdone, as were our attempts to reciprocate.

Although the renewal game in 1957 was played in Philadelphia's

Municipal Stadium (annual locale of the Army-Navy game, though a non-campus site), the spirit was far different from what it had been in Yankee Stadium. The majority of the crowd was for the Irish, but not in the same percentage as before, and the old acrimony was absent, mainly, I am convinced, because of the ten-year hiatus.

The relationship now seems to have been restored to the healthiness it enjoyed in earlier years. The teams will play again in 1965 and '66 and, I presume, in occasional home-and-home series after that, with the frequency depending on Army's over-all intersectional-game pressures and commitments.

During the suspension both schools developed new, interesting, and profitable rivalries, which might not have been the case had they gone on playing each other. Army's series with Michigan is an example, as is Notre Dame's with Oklahoma. The interim years also gave me the opportunity to develop friendships with Notre Dame's Father Edmund P. Joyce, vice-president and faculty moderator of athletics; Ed (Moose) Krause, athletic director; and Coach Frank Leahy.

I am happy I came to know Leahy better (I seldom fraternized with other coaches while playing them; the Sampson-inspired dinner with Dobie at Hanover Inn was an exception), and have enjoyed visiting his home, where he presides over a delightful family of eight. At golf as in football, I found Frank a great competitor, plenty tough on his own college course, pressing hard when we played on a neutral South Bend course, and completely frustrated on the rugged goat-hill course at West Point.

Leahy and I were scarcely acquainted in the years we sent out teams against each other. Our greetings and conversations, to state it euphemistically, were laconic. For example, when we met outside the Notre Dame Stadium the day before the 1947 game, Frank remarked with the unwarranted pessimism and bland amiability for which he had become notorious, "Red, I think your team is going to be very happy after this game."

"I'll tell you one thing, Frank," I snapped. "The Cadets will give you a battle!"

The Cadets did just that, because that was just the kind of a team they were. They were beaten, 27–7, by a national championship Notre Dame team, but only after playing as well as they could. They were far below their predecessors of 1944 through '46. They were considerably below their successors of 1948 through '50. But they were as vicious in their execution of fundamentals and in their resolution as any Army team I ever had. They failed to play up to their potential only once.

The bulwark of that 1947 team was the line. The core of the line was Captain Bill Yeoman, center; Joe Steffy, one of the best guards in Academy history; and Goble Bryant, tackle. Each year he played for us, Bryant got better. He was typical of those '47 players, who were willing to make every sacrifice.

I have always told my teams: *"You have to pay the price."* Some paid it more fully than others. None paid it more fully, except for one game, than the '47 team.

I smile as I think of encountering Goble Bryant walking from one class to another. The tightness of his schedule required that our talk be brief, conducted almost on the run. I asked him how he was getting along.

"Everything's fine, Colonel," he said, "except I could do with a few more rations at the training table."

Goble was dropping a hint. He was also wasting his time.

"Goble," I said, "I'm glad you could use extra rations. I want all the football players hungry, lean, and mean. When they get fat, they get satisfied, and the results on Saturday are disastrous. Don't ever forget that, Goble."

Goble didn't, either. He kept himself in fine shape, and he was the type who could have easily ballooned up.

Our '47 ends, only fair, improved as the season advanced. Our backfield, on the whole, was ordinary. For much of the season, Bobby Jack Stuart seemed to suffer from the aftereffects of a hernia operation. Our most consistent back was fullback Rip Rowan. Our passing attack was slow to develop, principally because yearling Arnold Galiffa was just breaking in as Bill Gustafson's alternate. (Galiffa's progress as a field general can be charted by his nicknames. In 1948 and '49 he was called "Meister" and "The Pope," but in '47 he had been known as "Musclehead.") Army also had a disquieting habit of dropping touchdown passes in the open.

Notre Dame was hoping fervently, as were we, that our defeatless string, which opened the season at twenty-eight, would extend through the first six games to reach thirty-four by our visit to South Bend for the "divorce" game. When our line fought off Illinois to earn us a scoreless tie in Yankee Stadium, we thought we would still present ourselves unspoiled, though perhaps ripe to be picked, to our Irish friends.

The week of our fifth game, with Columbia at Baker Field, I had a premonition we were in for it. I knew that to get by in any major game we had to be at our best at all times. Columbia, with a 6–2 record that year, had one of Lou Little's best teams. Gene Rossides was at quarterback and Lou Kusserow was at half. (Kusserow had originally intended to go to Army. In fact, he had enrolled at Columbia for one year with the idea of shoring up his math, on lend lease, so to speak, but he became enamored of Morningside Heights.) Bill Swiacki, a remarkable pass catcher, was at end, and Ventan Yablonski at fullback. Swiacki was a transfer from Holy Cross and Yablonski from Fordham.

I tried to warn our players of the danger we would be in, but I could not seem to get through to them. After our Friday afternoon workout in Baker Field, I told my assistants, "This team is not ready, and neither are you coaches."

They were to admit the following Monday how right I was.

In the dressing room before the kick-off, I told the players, "If we don't snap out of it, we're going to get licked. I'm going to give the starting team five minutes to score. Otherwise, they'll be out of there."

We scored after four and a half minutes and led at the half, 20–7. Rowan ran 87 yards off tackle for a touchdown just before the half. They merely complicated my job of arousing them.

The Cadets spent most of the halftime complaining about the officiating, something that occurred only one other time in my twenty-five years. I tried to get them off the subject of the officials. I realized they were rationalizing. They needed a jolt, but nothing seemed to work. In fact, the Army was just ripe to lose.

At the end of the third period, we still led, 20–7. In the fourth quarter, with the ball on our 28-yard line, Rossides hurled a pass down the middle into the end zone. Swiacki dove for it and the field judge called it completed. Careful study of our own and newsreel films the following Monday convinced us no catch was made. But it was called a catch and they trailed us only 20–14.

Columbia now had real momentum. I had sat through the game with a premonition of trouble. Now it was being realized. We had allowed them to take control. To stop Rossides' passes, we pulled an extra man out of the line into the backfield. Rossides was smart enough to counter this by mixing in some runs. They went 61 yards in six plays. Kusserow scored from the 2 and Yablonski kicked the point. Thus ended our defeatless string of thirty-three games, which had begun with the victory over North Carolina in the opener of 1944.

When the defeat of Army was announced in Notre Dame Stadium, where the Irish were hammering Iowa for their fifth straight win, Notre Dame players dashed their helmets disgustedly to the turf. They had wanted us for themselves. If we had to break the string, I guess I would have preferred defeat to come from a Notre Dame triumph rather than from a defeat partially ascribable to an official's error. Not that we played well enough against Columbia to deserve to win. We did not. We could have won only with the kind of effort we made against Illinois, Notre Dame, Pennsylvania, and Navy.

The Notre Dame game began as if the Irish would hand us a shellacking comparable to those they had received in 1944 and '45. We kicked off twice at the beginning. The first went out of bounds. The second was caught on the 3-yard line by halfback Terry Brennan, always a bothersome young man to Army. Brennan came up the west sideline, heading for the north goal, behind power blocking which he used expertly. Key blocks were thrown by tackle George Connor and guard Bill Fischer. Near midfield, Terry was in the clear and went all the way—97 yards, a record for the series.

We received, made one first down, and then kicked. From their 20, the Irish drove impressively 80 yards for a touchdown. Only nine minutes had been played, and they led us, 13–0.

You had only to look at the legs of that Notre Dame line from the knees down to appreciate them: Martin and Hart, ends; Connor and Czarobski, tackles; Wendell and Fischer, guards; Walsh, center. A tremendous line. Yet, our line did not do badly. Their edge lay in their superior ends and backs. Despite the edge, they outscored us only 13–7 in the last fifty-one minutes. We might have had another score if one of our backs had hung onto a pass in the open on their 5-yard line.

Lujack played a strong all-around game at quarterback. He did not pass against us as often as he had in earlier games. Notre Dame opponents, apparently playing to hold the score down, had jammed their defenses to slow down Brennan, Mike Swistowicz, John Panelli, Larry Coutre, and other formidable Irish runners. We were playing to win; we used a balanced defense. Lujack, therefore, hit us with a balanced attack.

In making their twenty-seven points, Notre Dame delivered a complete effort. This was a major reason, I believe, why their margin against Northwestern the next week was 26–19. Something of a letdown was inevitable.

On the train back to West Point that night, I assembled the squad.

"I want you to get the Notre Dame game out of your minds before you get off this train," I told them. "We were defeated by a better team. The question now is one of resolution for the future. We must understand that we face two sure defeats from Pennsylvania and Navy unless we rise to our best effort. You alone have the answer. I believe without reservation that your best effort can turn a bleak-looking future into victory and a great season."

Pennsylvania's '47 team was not Notre Dame, but it probably was the best turned out by Coach George Munger. Led by their great linebacker-center, Charles (Chuck) Bednarik, they were sound and rugged defensively, and gave up more than one touchdown in only one game. Their single-wing attack was well balanced and smoothly executed. They did not lose a game that year and were pressed only by us. Defeated decisively by Army three straight years, they came to our game with flame and ambition, but so did we. A great battle ended in a 7–7 tie. This Army team, rebounding from its effort and disappointment at Notre Dame, had given everything.

"Football is a man's game," I told them in the dressing room, "and you men are my team. You were men today, and I am proud of my team."

One of the players told a friend of mine later: "The Colonel then came in and took his shower with us. He seemed pleased and proud of us to the point of ecstasy."

We now began preparations for the Navy.

I have always believed that fire, determination, fight, proper psychological approach, dedication, being "up," or whatever else you want to call it, is the predominantly decisive factor in a football game only when one team has considerably more of it than the opponent. This was proved in the Penn game of 1947. The Red and Blue were as high as they could be, and so were we. Spirit neutralized spirit, and the outcome had to be reckoned by other factors.

More important, this was also true of our '47 game with Navy.

Navy more than once has defeated or tied Army teams which were favored. The fact that sometimes these Army teams were in degree false favorites, based on the records of the teams rather than their personnel, is not especially germane to the point I want to make. The Navy victory or tie has invariably been ascribed, and usually with sound reason, to the Midshipmen's intense emotional urge.

Yet, I feel there have been just as many times that Army won or tied, whether or not we were supposed to, when Navy was just as supercharged with spirit as in their years of victory or tie. The answer is that we ourselves were also "up."

Proper psychological attitude traces to many things. The main compulsive factor is the importance the team places on the game.

To both Army and Navy, their game is of equal value in that victory to each is indispensable to a successful season. Yet it has always seemed to me that a victory over Army by Navy writes off any previous misadventures by the Midshipmen, while a victory by Army over Navy eradicates earlier setbacks to a lesser degree. I suspect at least part of the reason for this is that Army in most years has been expected to finish higher in both Eastern and national ranking than Navy. In this sense, therefore, the Navy approach to the game has always enjoyed a completeness which Army, consciously or subconsciously, has often been unable to match.

I am not referring only to those years in which the Notre Dame game was in effect the No. 1 target at the Point. This completeness of approach was something the Navy maintained in many of Army's most successful seasons after the Notre Dame series was suspended.

I have raised this psychological angle at this point because the 1947 Army-Navy game proves much of what I am talking about.

Navy had managed only a victory and a tie going into our game, but they had played a rigorous schedule and were rather generally acknowledged to be a much better team than their record. The majority of the men who had almost ruined the Blanchard-Davis finale the year before—sixteen of them by my count—were back. They had lost to us three straight years. They had every incentive to be "up" for us, and they were, about as high "up" as any Navy team we ever faced.

When our soccer team played at Annapolis the week before the football game, the Midshipmen spectators gave them a pretty good verbal going over. Somebody also painted their traveling bus red. All this was reported back to the Point, of course, and contributed to our preparations.

We needed no help from Navy, however, to be ready. Our own season had provided us with all the stimulation we needed. It had been a strange one. Except in the Columbia game, our players had given everything they had, and had improved from week to week. They had earned ties with superior Illinois and Pennsylvania teams and had acquitted themselves well at Notre Dame. Yet we did not have a single big victory to cheer about. This has been true in other years, and Army has gone out and beat Navy.

The 1947 situation, however, was unique in my eighteen years as head coach at the Academy, because it was the only time the Navy game presented us not only the indispensable objective but also the *opportunity to justify a season which had been almost wholly satisfactory in effort yet totally unproductive in major victories.*

In other words, the psychological picture was perfect from our point of view. No matter how high the Navy was, they couldn't possibly be higher than we were. The psychological factor could not be predominantly decisive. The outcome would have to be resolved by other factors. The game bore this out in every respect.

The Midshipmen, taking the opening kick-off, were in a competitive frenzy. They ran it back to their 34-yard line. They then slammed out two first downs and reached our 38-yard line, breathing fire. They would have continued, as they have in some other Army games, if we had been anything but emotionally primed. The turning point came right here. Bill Yeoman, center and linebacker, who had actually outplayed Penn's Bednarik the week before, broke through on two successive running plays to spill Navy for losses that totaled 11 yards.

Navy kept battling, but they had lost dominant momentum, and they could not get it back. Steffy, Bryant, and Yeoman were outstanding as our line threw Navy back and opened up holes. Steffy clinched All America honors and was also to receive the Outland Award from the Football Writers' Association of America as the interior lineman (guard or tackle) of the year. That day against Navy, Joe took out an end with one of the two most devastating blocks in my memory. (The other was thrown by Blanchard against Notre Dame's Adams in 1944.)

On the attack, Rowan had the best day of his career. He threw an 18-yard, special fullback pass to left end Bill Kellum for our first touchdown, followed by the first of Steffy's three extra points. Then, after we had stopped Navy's best effort of the day, a 79-yard drive to our 8, Rip extracted a lot of the cork from them with a 92-yard touchdown run off a burst through their right tackle. Johnny Trent, right end, made our third touchdown when he intercepted a Navy pass and ran it back 18 yards. The final score was 21–0.

For years I showed the film of that game to Army teams as an example of the attitude and execution they should bring to the Navy game, and I still endorse it heartily today.

I suppose somebody is bound to ask why our all-out effort and failure at Notre Dame in 1947 did not detract from our effort and success against Navy. The answer is simple enough. Knowledge that the Notre Dame game (win, lose, or draw at South Bend) had been suspended served to bring home forcibly to the team, the Corps, and the graduates, that Navy should be and was once again Army's No. 1 game.

The primary objective of Army football must be victory over Navy. It cannot be achieved by anything less than complete dedication.

Chapter XIV

The Forgotten Grenadiers

Colonel Gerry Counts and Colonel Orrin C. Krueger, who was Graduate Manager of Athletics, practically steered me by force into the fancy haberdashery on Nob Hill. It was January, 1949, and we were in San Francisco for the annual meeting of the National Collegiate Athletic Association. Gerry and "Ockie" had been imploring me to buy a new necktie to replace my ancient maroon number.

The clerk laid out dozens of ties of varying hues and designs, from grisly grays to ridiculous rainbows. Finally, I pointed to the old stand-by I was wearing and asked the clerk, "Do you have one like this?"

He presented one with the deftness of a conjurer and casually I told him to wrap it up. Then, out of curiosity, I said, "Would you mind showing me one of those ties people pay twenty dollars for?"

"Sir," the clerk replied, "you have just bought one.

I should have said, "No sale!" But I was in an expansive mood. Army football was clicking through another defeatless string. This one began with the 7–7 Penn tie in '47, ended in the '50 upset by Navy and extended through twenty-eight games.

I never coached through seasons more exciting and controversial than those of 1948 through '50. More than one had predicted that after 1946 Army football would relapse into mediocrity. They failed to read correctly the signs of 1947, a transitional though satisfactory season connecting the Blanchard-Davis era with another almost as spectacular. The dour and perhaps sometimes smug pronunciamentos of the seers we accepted as a challenge.

An even more important challenge was the obvious anti-Army climate in some quarters, principally New York City, stemming from our suspension of the Notre Dame series. This situation irritated yet sharpened us.

Strangely, our teams of those years have been to a considerable extent "Forgotten Grenadiers." When The Lonely End team of 1958 was riding high, experts compared it with the Blanchard-Davis teams. Our teams of 1948, '49 and '50 were ignored. Yet, all three would have given The Lonely Enders a hard time. As for the Blanchard-Davis teams, let's just leave them where they belong—in a class by themselves.

The 1949 team, which won nine out of nine, was the best of the 1948-50 era. Next was the '50 team, all victorious until upset by Navy. Then would come the '48 team, also all winning until tied by Navy. There was not much to choose, however, among those three teams. All three were superior. Without any wish to detract in the slightest from Navy's spirited and thoroughly deserved '50 victory and '48 tie, I must state that our teams in those games were far below form. Not to state this would be a distinct disservice to them. Why they were far below par I shall detail later.

The 1948 season marked the beginning of an almost continuous turnover among my assistant coaches, as they went on to take head coaching jobs elsewhere. Herman Hickman was first to go. In '48, he succeeded Howard Odell at Yale. The loss of Herman disturbed me, but I was soon to become inured to the idea of breaking in new men.

Andy Gustafson also left in '48 to take the job at Miami of Florida. Gus was with me from the beginning at Dartmouth and for fourteen consecutive years, the longest of any assistant. He is a very competent coach and as a friend he indeed wears well. For years after he left Army, he never failed to phone us to commiserate after a losing game.

Including Gus and Herman, I was to lose within ten years a total of fourteen assistants to head-man opportunities. The others were Sid Gillman to the University of Cincinnati, subsequently to the Los Angeles Rams and now with the Los Angeles Chargers; Murray Warmath to Mississippi State and Minnesota; Vince Lombardi to the Green Bay Packers after a tour as New York Giants' offensive coach; Clarence (Chief) Boston to New Hampshire; Stuart Holcomb to Purdue; Johnny Sauer to The Citadel; Paul Dietzel to Louisiana State;

Paul Amen to Wake Forest; Bob Woodruff to Baylor and Florida; Bobby Dobbs to Tulsa; George Blackburn to Cincinnati; and Dick Voris to Virginia.

By the standards of typical championship squads in the Big Ten, the South, the Far West, the Southwest, or at Notre Dame, our squads from 1948 through '50 were not outstanding in personnel. After my assistants went on to be head coaches elsewhere, they had a better appreciation of what we had had to work with. They have told me this many times through the years. Each of our squads included six or seven boys who were above average, one or two of them truly superior. The majority, however, were types you could locate in clusters on any campus without looking too hard.

Our championship records traced to hard work, sacrifice, unsurpassed team morale. We were blessed by players almost all of whom lived by my football axioms hung in their locker room:

> There never was a champion who to himself was a good loser. There's a vast difference between a good sport and a good loser.
>
> Physical pressure on the foe is essential. Mental pressure will make him crack.
>
> A relaxed player performs best. A sense of humor and good fun keep one relaxed.
>
> Without ambition and enthusiasm for your work, the parade will pass you by.
>
> Good fellows are a dime a dozen, but an aggressive leader is priceless.
>
> Games are not won on the rubbing table.
>
> The essence of the long gainer is superior downfield blocking.
>
> Inches make the champion, and the champion makes his own luck.
>
> There is no substitute for work. It is the price of success.

I can think of no better examples of Army players who made these axioms pay off than guard Joe Henry and tackle Martin (Tiger)

Howell. Neither was gifted with much natural ability. As a yearling, Henry was buried in the "B" squad, but showed enough desire to get a chance with the varsity in 1947. By hard work he improved himself to the point where in 1948 he was named an All America guard. He weighed 180 pounds.

Howell had played two years of high-school football, but he weighed only 165 when he entered the Academy and failed to make his numerals with the plebe squad. But by 1948 he was the starting right tackle on the defensive platoon at 175 pounds. "I was no All American," said the ineffable Tiger afterwards, "but I started every game and came out with head unbowed." He was the epitome of the spirit we wanted, and the coaches liked to use him as a sounding board, sometimes with humorous overtones.

We had to scramble before we beat Harvard, 20–7, at Michie Stadium in 1948. (The Crimson put up the kind of battle we felt we could expect from all Ivy League opponents when we scheduled them for the postwar years; in '48, of course, the Ivies still had spring practice, which they didn't drop until 1952.) At halftime Harvard was tied with us, 7–7, and had been outhitting us.

"Howell," I said in the dressing room, "did you make a tackle that half?"

The Tiger saw red. Turning to leave the room, he bumped a door slightly.

"Tiger," I commented, "that's the hardest you've hit anything today."

He did much better in the second half, and so did the team.

Speed was our keynote. Speed and more speed. One day I asked the '48 team to run off some new plays at half speed until they got used to their assignments. For the next few minutes they stepped on one another's feet, bumped into one another, and kept fumbling the ball. Finally, I blew the whistle.

"What an idiot I am!" I admitted to them. "I should have realized no Army team could go at half speed."

Our sustained speed and stamina traced in great measure to our adoption in 1948 of the two-platoon system of separate units for offense and defense, permitted by unlimited substitution. Two-platoon football had been possible as early as 1941. The rule that year was amended to read: "A player may be substituted for another at any time, but such player may not be withdrawn from, nor another player returned to, the game until one play has intervened." Before 1941, when a player was removed from the game, he could not return until the succeeding quarter.

As I pointed out, Fritz Crisler was the first to take full advantage of unlimited substitutions, at Michigan, and used it in their '45 game with us in Yankee Stadium. I had seen the value of it that day. Sid Gillman, who succeeded Herman Hickman as our line coach in '48, used two platoons as head coach of Miami of Oxford in '46. This fact further stimulated me to adopt it. Other colleges experimented with it in '47. By '48, it began to take hold widely and was in almost general use from '49 through '52.

It was we at West Point who gave it the name "two-platoon," a natural appellation for an Army man. For this reason, although we were not the originators or earliest developers, the football public associated two-platoon with the Army team.

The majority of my fellow coaches agree with me that two-platoon is the best football the college game has ever known. When the rules committee threw it out after the '52 season, they made a serious mistake. The high schools have kept two-platoon football, because they realize it is better for the players. The professionals have retained it because they appreciate that it makes the most spectacular game for the spectators. Yet the originators, the colleges, gave it up, and cannot seem to get it back.

The reason they cannot get it back is that the rules committee is appointed and influenced by the National Collegiate Athletic Association's faculty group. To my knowledge these people have never appointed to the rules committee any coach who was known to be a strong proponent of unlimited substitution.

The faculty people do not seem to be at grips with the real issues. They also appear to me to be less interested in having the best possible rules for the game than in demonstrating that they, and not the coaches, shall decide what these rules are to be.

I do not mean to devote the rest of this chapter to a thoroughgoing exposition of the arguments for and against two-platoon football. I shall merely outline them briefly.

The arguments in favor of it are that it results in a faster and more exciting game, a chance for more boys to play, fewer injuries, and less practice time. The last two points are the most powerful because they make two-platoon ideally tailored to what should be the objective of the faculty people: keeping football secondary to education. Fewer injuries and less practice mean more time to study.

The arguments against are three: that it demands larger squads and therefore increased recruiting and overhead; that character-building benefits are fewer because the one-way player need not labor to overcome weakness; and that it encourages coaching from the sidelines.

Not one of these arguments can stand up very long under any analysis.

Two-platoon emphatically *does not* require larger squads, more recruiting, greater overhead. It can be played effectively by suiting up as few as thirty-three players, and certainly most college squads suit up at least forty. It can also be coached effectively by the same number of assistants as one platoon.

As for character building, a boy who plays only one way, either offensive or defensive, must still make the sacrifices and work hard. He must still condition himself and learn to block or tackle. He must also spend more time trying to perfect certain phases of the game. So he derives sufficiently deep character benefits. In fact, the character-building argument, carried to its logical conclusion, implies that a boy who does not play football at all must per se be without character.

As to sideline coaching, two-platoon *discourages* it, in two ways: first, the coach does not tend to send in frequent substitutes with plays because this would disrupt the team unity and co-ordination which is of the essence of two-platoon; second, with either the defensive or the offensive platoon always on the sideline for instruction, there is far less reason for the coach to send in advice while they are in action.

If there ever was a rule which encouraged sideline coaching, it is the now *unlimited* "wild-card" substitution rule, which permits and encourages the coach to send in a substitute, with instructions on every play. However, it pleases the N.C.A.A. faculty people, most of whom seldom attack any of college football's real problems, those involving the academic side. More on that later on.

Before leaving the subject of two-platoon football, I should like to quote a letter I received from General MacArthur while he was military governor of Japan in 1948.

26 April

Dear Earl:

Thank you so much for your interesting and comprehensive letter of April 10.

The introduction of the new substitution system opens up a wide range of ramification in the tactical handling of a football team. In effect it makes possible the more or less complete use of specialists in applying the various features of the game.

Specialization under skillful guidance from the bench now will exercise a tremendous influence upon the final results. Heretofore only eleven men could be on the team and each had to represent so much of a general development that specialization was really only incidental to natural ability. All this is now changed. It gives almost unlimited selectivity of an entire squad whose members can from the very beginning be developed for special phases of attack or defense. It makes the game more and more in accord with the development of the tatics of actual combat. In this type of technique, I am convinced the Army will not lag.

It could not have failed to be a great blow to lose simultaneously your line and backfield coaches, both apparently excellent men. However, this again follows the technique of war, for you always lose your best men in the heat of battle.

I will be interested, as always, in your progress, and am deeply appreciative of your taking the time to write me of the general situation. It gives me one of the few bright moments of relaxation that fall to my lot.

With cordial regards and best wishes.

Very faithfully,
DOUGLAS MACARTHUR

We unveiled Army's two platoons in a 28–0 victory over Villanova at Michie Stadium, September 25, 1948. Galiffa's passes to end Danny Foldberg and the running of halfbacks Bobby Jack Stuart and Winfield Scott and fullback Gilbert Stephenson paced our attack. Foldberg and Stephenson, yearlings, were to play outstandingly for three years.

After the games at Michie, it was the custom for Merle and me to hold open house at our quarters for friends and newspapermen. Among those present following the two-platoon inaugural was that energetic and colorful sports editor and columnist of the Newspaper Enterprise Association, Harry Grayson.

Harry is the only newspaperman I know, or can even imagine, who, by the shrill insistence of the telephone, could wake you out of a sound sleep at 3:00 A.M., to provide him esoteric tidbits for his column, yet in some inexplicable way make you feel it would be embarrassing for both parties if you offered any protest.

He would always begin one of these calls by saying, "Earl, I hope I didn't wake you up."

"Harry," I'd say, "you know damned well you woke me up. Now, what do you want?"

He would always end up with a newsworthy point, and would usually develop it into something interesting.

That evening, following the platoon debut, Harry politely elbowed all the other writers out of his path, cocked his cigar in the corner of his mouth at a truculently inquisitive angle, came at me broadside and fired staccato:

"Now, see here, Earl, this two-platoon stuff is fine, see! Fine, see! But what do you do if you have somebody up here like Johnny Lujack? What do you do then, see? A great player, hey? A great player! Play it both ways, terrific, see! What do you do then?"

I doubt that even Frank Leahy, at his most exalted peaks of pessimism, could have bettered my answer.

"Harry," I said, without batting an eye, "we never have that kind of player up here."

(Seriously, I would use a Blanchard, a Davis, a Lujack or a Bob Anderson on both offense and defense, even in two-platoon, as long as the outcome was in doubt. I never have intended to imply that a team should be so exclusively two-platoon minded that the outstanding two-way player should not operate both ways.)

The value of two-platoon in conserving fourth-quarter attacking tempo was underscored in our 26–21 victory at Illinois. We dominated most of it in building a 26–0 margin. Then passes and a couple of breaks enabled Illinois to close up to 26–21. After their third score, however, they never got the ball again, for we marched from the succeeding kickoff all the way to their 1, and would have scored again, most likely, had the clock not run out. We could not have staged such a march that late unless platoon substituting had left the offensive team as fresh, or almost so, as it had been in the first period.

Our lines performed in such a manner as to cause Burt Ingwersen, veteran Illini line coach, to ask us, "How do you get them to charge that way?"

Two weeks later, following the Harvard game, we went up to play Cornell, which was to have an 8–1 won-loss record that year. The game was regarded pretty much as a tossup. Our special train left West Point very early Friday morning, but apparently proceeded to Ithaca by way of Bangkok, Siam. By the time we arrived high above Cayuga's waters, the sun was low in the west and we had to speed through our light Schoellkopf Stadium workout in the twilight.

Fortunately we moved faster than that train the next day in winning 27–6, but it was not easy. That was the hundredth victory of my coaching career. Perhaps in celebration of this record, a couple of our players broke training before returning to the special train that night. I had to set them down.

Between Cornell and the game with Stanford at Yankee Stadium, we had a Michie Stadium date with an old rival and sister military institution, Virginia Polytechnic Institute, called Virginia Tech. V.P.I. has had some strong teams, but that season's was not one of them. However, I sent one of our staff, Major Joel (Dopey) Stephens, down to scout them against Duke. On our return from Cornell on Sunday morning, we gathered in the projection room of the football office to listen to his report.

Major Stephens stood with pointer in hand in front of a blackboard on which Virginia Tech's two-deep personnel had been chalked. I sat in a chair in the middle of the room. I almost fell off it at his opening remarks. He violated the No. 1 precept drummed into our scouts: No matter how mediocre the opposition, drop no hint of this fact to the players. Dopey dropped what was tantamount to a bomb.

"Fellows," he began, "you can name your own score against this team."

I gasped, coughed a couple of times, half choked on the last one, twirled my class ring, almost bit off one end of my glasses and began humming some tune in my off-key monotone. Since I could not for the moment think of anything to say, I walked out of the room.

In thirty seconds I returned and whispered to Dopey, "I think you should confine your remarks to the personnel and the circles and X's. I will be responsible for appraising the strength and weakness of this team."

We probably achieved our season's peak for Stanford. This was not by design; peak form for Navy is always the objective. This Stanford team played 6–7 games with the Southern California team that tied Notre Dame, 14–14 (the first nonvictorious game for a Leahy team since the '46 scoreless tie with us), and with the first of Coach Lynn (Pappy) Waldorf's three straight California Rose Bowl teams. Stanford, however, did not seem physically or mentally attuned to meet our quick, savage-hitting football. We won, 43–0, and our severe blocking and tackling caused them several injuries.

"The Cadets don't mess around," commented the Stanford *Daily* sports columnist. "They play mean, vicious and hungry football, and they play strictly to win."

Is there any other way to play this game?

In analyzing our approach, Bill Leiser, crack veteran sports columnist of the San Francisco *Chronicle,* reported that when one of of our ends missed a tackle, to permit a Stanford back a 4-yard gain, our Captain Bill Yeoman advised that miscreant, "Let that happen again and you're through!"

Our brand of football did not please much of the crowd of 47,000 in Yankee Stadium. As the score mounted and our platoons moved in and out, the Army team, for the only time in history to my knowledge, heard itself booed continually for trying to play the game well. It was obvious, however, that since there was something less than a sellout crowd, not all of the "Subway Alumni" extremists had been willing to invest the price of a ticket to advance their anti-Army campaign.

We had several injuries ourselves going into the game with Pennsylvania at Franklin Field. Penn's team doctor, who had formerly held the same position with Army, came into our dressing room before the game and offered us, if needed, the services of the Penn hospital, which was near the field. His motives may have been good, but our players took his suggestion as an affront. I had the doctor shown out and informed the Cadets that Penn was planning to manhandle them.

A sellout crowd of 73,248 (Army-Penn games from '45 through '50 averaged 71,755) saw a tremendous battle, that included a 103-yard return of a kick-off to a touchdown by Bobby Jack Stuart. Trailing, 20–18, on our own 26 with three minutes to play, we went the distance in seven plays. We were on their 15-yard line with twenty-five seconds to go when Galiffa passed down the middle and Johnny Trent leaped and caught the ball in the end zone, to win the game, 26–20. It was one of the most splendid moments in Army football history.

For the fifth time in five years we came down to the Navy game undefeated. Two days before the game, at the Thanksgiving meal, the players ate rancid turkey gravy. During the night, forty-two of the squad, including most of the twenty-two platoon regulars, became violently ill. At six o'clock Friday morning, not long before our scheduled departure by bus, every medical officer on the post assembled at the gymnasium and turned the training room into a hospital. The cadets were deathly sick. I have a clear memory of doctors walking around with several gallon jugs of paregoric and pouring it out into small bottles.

For the same reasons that had motivated me after the rancid-spinach affair at Dartmouth in 1936, I kept the story from the papers. If anything went wrong, it would sound like a prefabricated alibi. I hoped that we could win despite our condition, and we almost did. After the game we were to be censured for keeping the story quiet. I never have believed, however, that everything that happens to a team is news we are duty-bound to give out. We certainly did not want to improve Navy's normally fine mental attitude for our game by tipping them off to our condition.

President Truman was at the game. He never missed one. His pre-game coin-tossing became a ritual. The secret service men would give the Navy coach and myself precise instructions as to how we were to bring our respective captains to the presidential box. Each year the President would take a brand-new silver dollar out of his pocket and flip it high in the air with the idea of catching it on the back of his hand. Invariably on this first high flip the coin would fall to the ground and the secret service men would take off after it like retriever dogs. On the second try the President would make a lower toss and a successful catch. He would give the toss-winning captain the silver dollar and then reach into his pocket for another one for the losing captain.

When Navy, which had failed to win a game all year, gained a thoroughly earned upset tie with an Army team which had not lost a game all year, the stories likened it to the upset Mr. Truman had won in the presidential race earlier that month. But the President would have been happier without the second upset, because he was a hard-nosed Army rooter.

The 21–21 score was identical to that at Chicago twenty-two years before and just as exciting. Our men had to play up to their full physical potential, to stave off the Midshipmen try for victory, led by Bill Hawkins. Dave Parrish, at end for Danny Foldberg who was out with a shoulder injury, did a fine job catching Galiffa passes. Hal Shultz, at left half in place of Stuart, who had a bad back, did some strong running. Gil Stephenson had a leg calification and I did not use him in the first half. I was forced to use him in the second half and his running helped keep us in the game.

During one of Navy's drives I was advised by Sid Gillman, my line coach, who was observing from the press box, to remove Tiger Howell from tackle.

"They are going through him," said Gillman. "He needs a rest."

Tiger didn't think so, and when I took him out, he came at me like a young bull.

"Why did you take me out of the game?" he demanded.

"Because," I said, "they tell me upstairs that you are smelling out the Stadium!"

With that, Tiger made a beeline to the bench phone, and his end, and probably Sid Gillman's end also, of the ensuing conversation should have been tape-recorded for posterity. It did not seem as funny then as it does now, because we were too upset at developments to really appreciate it. But Tiger managed to talk himself back into the game and then played as he knew how to play.

We were downcast, of course, at the sour ending. Especially so was Sid Gillman. After listening to Sid moan around the lobby of the Benjamin Franklin hotel that evening, Bevan finally growled, "Digging up the body and burying it! Digging up the body and burying it!"

After the '48 season I seriously considered retiring. It was not the disappointment of the Navy tie. We were Eastern Champions for the fourth time in five years, and ranked No. 6 nationally. A promising squad and new challenges lay ahead in 1949.

But I had been a head coach for fifteen seasons and I would soon be fifty-two years old. I had often stated that nobody should coach football after fifty. Beyond that age, it seemed to me, the winning touch too often deserted a man.

I decided it was time to return to business, which I had left almost fifteen years before. Victor Emanuel, chairman of the board of the AVCO Corporation and a friend since Dayton boyhood days, had always followed my football fortunes, both at Dartmouth and Army, with devoted interest. Victor was urging me to give up coaching and join him at AVCO.

I finally decided to stay on at West Point, after General Max Taylor, the Superintendent, convinced me there was still much constructive work I could do for the Cadets. At General Taylor's request I added to my jobs of coach and athletic director that of chairman of the athletic board. I decided to continue only after much deliberation. I unquestionably would have stayed with my earlier decision to resign could I have foreseen what most of the next decade at West Point was to hold for me.

For two more years times continued mostly good. We never worked harder. I seldom took time out even for golf, a game of which I am very fond. My family seldom saw me except at meals. About the only other time I took off was for a week or ten days in late July and early August at a small lake called Bull Pond.

Bull Pond lies atop a mountain 1100 feet above sea level, situated near Central Valley on Military Academy property about eight miles southwest of the Academy complex. The pond, 90,000 square yards in area, never has produced very good fishing, although the late Colonel Jack Coffey did his best to stock it. There is good boating and swimming.

The Pond is vacation quarters for the Academy Superintendents, but they have traditionally made it available for specified periods to senior officers of the Post. There are four cottages on the east shore. "The Superintendent's Cottage," the former clubhouse of the West Point Fishing Club, the boat house, and the caretaker's quarters. In front of these cottages there spreads a sizable beach and a cleared area for outdoor cooking and croquet. All meals except breakfast are served under a large open-ends tent.

For the period each summer that the Supe allotted me Bull Pond, my regular guests were, besides other members of the athletic staff, Colonel Gerry Courts, Willard Mullin, Stanley Woodward, and the co-author of this work.

On the Saturday which usually came about halfway in our vacation, Gene Leone and his son-in-law, Tom Mesereau, my old guard, would come over and cook us a multi-course dinner that would test the imagination of Lucullus. For this night, we would invite as many officers and A.A. personnel from the Post as we could possibly accommodate.

Every night but Sunday, on the screened-in veranda of the clubhouse, overlooking the shore and lake, a Signal Corps projectionist would show movies. The film fare included the latest Hollywood Oscar winners or candidates as well as selected Army seasonal-highlight reels. The audience, strictly amateur movie-goers the rest of the year, delivered highly critical comments on the films, with the superior air of men who had gone through a previous existence of writing reviews for the New York *Times*.

The clubhouse, where the movies were shown was known as the No. 2 cabin, while "The Superintendent's Cottage" was known as the No. 1 cabin. Bull Pond could be a very restful spot with the right guests, but I must have had the wrong ones. It was in the No. 2 cabin that the obstreperous members, who were in the majority, were supposed to sleep in well-appointed dormitories. In the rear of the No. 2 cabin was a room suggestive of a Dodge City deadfall. Here, sarsaparilla, root beer, and other more deadly washes were self-dispensed by those inclined, who were not in the minority.

Gerry Counts, Red Reeder, the Graduate Manager, whoever he happened to be at the time—Ockie Krueger, Phil Draper, Jim Schwenk, Fran Roberts—and I would retire shortly after the movies to the No. 1 cabin. Our sleep, however, was usually shattered by the unearthly cries and calls emanating from the No. 2 cabin as late card games, arguments, and general disorder mounted.

Much of the tumult was contributed by the three nonmilitary and nonathletic guests: Mullin, Woodward, and the co-author. They were known respectively as "The Tycoon," "The Beached Whale" and "The Flower of Fatherhood." Colonel Ockie Krueger, Graduate Manager in the '48–'50 era, was known, in deference to his home town and his spirit at the bridge table, as "The Fevered Buffalonian." The handsome Doug Kenna, my old quarterback star, who was a member of the coaching staff in those days, was hailed as "Chief Douglas, He Who Are the Ugliest."

We had an Army mess sergeant take care of the cooking, except in the summer of 1950. That year I had a brainstorm, possibly induced by overwork, and decreed we should share the kitchen work in daily shifts of two or three. The first day went excellently, as Mullin and Vince Lombardi fed us like good eagle scouts. The next day, it was the turn of Woodward, the co-author, and myself. We soon concocted a culinary chaos.

Breakfast progressed in such a high state of grease that Woodward left camp, seemingly in a huff, and did not return until supper was about to be served. Meanwhile, I had selected for the luncheon entree a jellied omelet. The birth and growth of the omelet recalled an old-fashioned Mack Sennett comedy. When Murray Warmath beheld his portion, he was given to remark, "Am I supposed to eat this, or have I eaten it?" The next year we went back to the Army mess sergeant.

It was also at Bull Pond, along about 1:30 one morning in early August of 1949, that the co-author, seized by a mental typhoon after one too many forays in Dodge City, originated the most authoritative of All America football teams: The Bull Pond.

On that pioneer team, Ugh! of Carlisle was one of the guards; the other was Willie Nutcake, of The Baker School of Creampuffs. Later storied heroes included tackles Yak Blubber of the Igloo Institute of Electrical Appliances and Excalibur Slime of King Arthur's Knight School. Two of the more notable ends of the early days were Chuckles Axmurder of Bedlam Hall and Nero Fiddle of Hook and Ladder Number 7. Two-Star Cementhead of West Point was the 1951 quarterback. Willard Mullin soon began to render annual portraits of the team members. They hang in many a gallery, and there are those who say their creator should hang with them. He feels, however, that they may one day soon be projected in the television medium by Ernie Kovacs.

After a time a Bull Pond Coach of the Year was chosen along with the team. The selection one year was Blaik Von Leahy of South Bend on the Hudson.

We needed lightness, silliness, or madness in those days. It was our only respite from an inexorable grind. Bull Pond still goes on every year, and it is a part of West Point I miss very much.

As we moved into the 1949 season, eleven of the twenty-two platoon regulars from '48 were gone, but we had good replacements, including some first-rate yearling material. From this group emerged the Forgotten Grenadiers of 1949, undefeated, united, Eastern Champions, rated No. 4 nationally. A team of superb speed, co-ordination, and spirit.

The offensive platoon lined up with Galiffa, quarterback; Jimmy Cain and Frank Fischl, halfbacks; Gil Stephenson, fullback; Dan

Foldberg and Bill Kellum, ends; Bennie Davis and either Bill Henn or Bruce Elmblad, tackles; Bob Lunn and Jim Irons, guards; and Ray Maladowitz, center.

The defense platoon deployed with John Trent, team captain, and Hal Loehlein, ends; Charlie (Chuck) Shira and J. D. Kimmel, tackles; Lynn Galloway and Ralph Kaseman, guards; Elmer Stout and Karl Kuckhahn, linebackers; Hal Shultz and Bob Abelman, defensive halfbacks; and Bobby Vinson, safety man.

Our defense was much stronger than in '48, our offense somewhat stronger. Jimmy Cain, fleet-footed halfback, was about as dangerous a runner and pass receiver as you would want. Galiffa reached his peak at quarterback. Foldberg was a tremendous blocking and pass-catching end.

Substitutes who helped us on offense or defense included Charlie Kuyk, Hardy Stone, and Dick Roberts, ends; Bob Haas, tackle; Bruce Ackerson, Gerry Kelley, and Al Thieme, guards; Matt Henrikson and Jack Mackmull, centers; and Jack Martin, Vic Pollock, Tom Brown, Don Beck, Steve Watsey, Herb Johnson, Carl Guess, Al Conway, and my son, Bob Blaik, backs. Many of these boys never would have played in one-platoon ball, but they could play the game well enough one way to be used in the two-platoon system.

In many ways the highlight of the '49 season came at Ann Arbor on October 7, when we played Michigan. The Wolverines went into that game with a proud twenty-five-game winning streak that had begun back in 1946. They were indeed a shining target and since they were the third game on our schedule, we were able to prepare for them almost from the end of the previous season.

We studied films of their games until we felt we knew their strong and weak points and their habits, collectively and individually, in any given situation. We boiled down a huge amount of information to essentials, in order to parcel it out to our platoons within the relatively restricted time they were available. We sent the Cadets into the game thoroughly briefed on what must be done and how it could be done.

For example, Michigan's players were tall with high centers of gravity. We exploited that fact by blocking them so low we got underneath their natural forearm or hand charge. Our success in this maneuver had a profound effect on the game, psychologically as well as physically. We drummed into Galiffa a sequence of plays we felt sure would work, in such a way he could not possibly forget them. This paid off also, for we struck them fiercely at the beginning and rolled them back on a ten-play, 89-yard drive, which Galiffa generaled impeccably.

The week of the game, an aggravation to Stephenson's leg forced us to move Kuckhahn from defensive linebacker to offensive full. For a time I even considered shifting Galiffa to fullback and putting Bob Blaik in at quarter. Bob had looked good throwing touchdown passes in our opening victories against Davidson and Penn State. I finally decided, however, that he did not have sufficient experience for the spot. Kuckhahn's powerful charges set up our first score and he went over from the seven for the third marker that clinched a tremendous 21–7 victory. "A West Pointer Looked West," said one headline, and that was no overstatement. We had been looking West at Michigan for a long time.

It was during the '49 season that the anti-Army and anti-Blaik claques were shrillest. They grabbed eagerly at anything they thought they could twist into criticism. When our hard blocking and tackling injured opponents, we were accused of dirty football. When we won most of our games by conclusive scores, our schedules were criticized. The chorus was inspired and led by the die-hard Subway Alumni, especially the New York chapter. There were a few writers and radio-TV people around the country, some with close Notre Dame affiliations, who joined in.

Yet, paradoxically enough, some of these loud notes were sung by people who presumably would not have been found dead with the bulk of our critics.

On November 1, the University of Michigan *Daily* ran an interview with Professor W. H. Hobbs, then the eighty-five-year-old former head of the university's geology department. Professor Hobbs said that Chuck Ortmann, star Michigan left halfback, who had been forced to leave our game early with a conclussion, had been deliberately kicked between the eyes by Gil Stephenson.

Professor Hobbs went on to state that Army was out to cripple its opponents, and that he had written letters about this to Tommy Devine, then Detroit *Free Press* football writer, to the Commandant at West Point, to the chairman of the Committee on Defense of the House of Representatives and Senate, and to a former player and official at Harvard.

The Michigan *Daily* story further stated that Professor Hobbs had received an answer from his Harvard contact, who agreed that the Army team was the dirtiest he had seen in twenty-two years of playing and officiating.

This story was picked up by wire services and sports columnists and received national attention.

The professor's reference to the Ortmann injury was astonishing. Game films showed clearly how Ortmann was hurt. He was trying to block Trent, our right end, on a reverse play. Trent retreated from the block and Ortmann went to the ground. Don McClelland, Michigan guard who had pulled out to lead the play, inadvertently hit Ortmann in the back of the head with his knee as the halfback started to get up. It was this blow that caused the concussion and his removal from the game.

As for Gil Stephenson, whom Hobbs accused of kicking Ortmann between the eyes, he got in for only four plays at Ann Arbor. Since he played only on offense, he could not have been in contact with Ortmann.

After the Army-Michigan game, Coach Bennie Oosterbaan, Athletic Director Fritz Crisler, and several players, including tackle Al Wistert and back Wally Teninga, visited our dressing room and congratulated our players on their hard, swift football.

"Of course Army plays rough football," Oosterbaan said later. "That's the way to play this game. Don't forget, when they came out here, they were coming into a rough league."

At Harvard nobody was able to learn the identity of the critic who had been playing and officiating for twenty-two years. Art Valpey, Harvard coach, commented on our game: "It was aggressive but not dirty."

But the germ of suspicion had been planted and was nurtured by the Subway Alumni extremists and their press and radio chapters. This was the atmosphere as we approached our game with Fordham at Michie Stadium, Saturday, November 5.

For thirteen years before World War II, Fordham had been a ranking football power. Now her 1949 team seemed to have recaptured some of the old flair. The Rams were undefeated and had recently won impressively over Syracuse and Georgetown. Since we were also undefeated, the build-up was natural. The New York press gave the game about as much publicity as it had ever accorded any of our games with Notre Dame. We suddenly found ourselves with a record demand for tickets for a Michie Stadium game. We could have sold 75,000 if we had them.

Under normal conditions, any game between two such undefeated schools, each with its own football tradition, meeting for the first time, figured to be sharply competitive. But the players on both teams were further influenced by the unhealthy atmosphere growing out of the charges against our rough play. As they lined up for the opening kick-off, they were expecting the worst of each other. Naturally they got what they expected.

By taking firm hold after the first displays of over-roughness, the officials could have prevented what happened, but they let the game get out of hand. It was not dirty football in the sense of surreptitious twistings of ankles and knees. There were some elbows flipped and some fists flung, but they were pretty much flipped and flung in the open. A few teeth were lost on the Army side and three players were put out for fighting.

The climax came near the end of the first half, as we lined up to try to kick the extra point after our second touchdown. Four successive illegal-use-of-hands penalties were called, two against us followed by two against the Rams. The ball was moved from the 3 to the 18 to the 33 back to the 18 and to the 3 again. Finally, on the fifth try, everybody stashed away daggers and blackjacks and we kicked the point. Between halves I vehemently advised the officials to do their jobs. In the second half the carnage was reduced.

We won 35–0, on our superior speed, with Galiffa passing to Cain for three touchdowns and to Foldberg for one. Jack Martin's 50-yard run set up a 5-yard scoring shot by Stephenson. Fordham never gave up, and I believe that, all in all, it was the best 35–0 game I ever saw. Twenty-three penalties were called, twelve against us for 147 yards, eleven against Fordham for 131. As Frank Graham wrote in the New York *Journal-American:* "Boys will be boys."

Pennsylvania, accustomed to rugged football, was unimpressed by either our record or our reputation and we were hard pressed to win another thriller, 14–13, before 72,477 spectators. End Hal Loehlein probably saved the game for us by blocking a field goal attempt.

Two nights before the Navy game the question of our rough football came up again. A New York sports columnist attacked us on his radio and television shows. We attempted to get transcripts of both from the individual himself, but were informed by his secretary that they were ad-libbed. In any event his broadcast points were substantially as follows:

There's an Eastern college coach who teaches dirty football. He doesn't directly order his players to go out and main the opposition's star. He does say, "If that player were not in the game, it would be easier for you to win." Now, I say to you fathers and mothers, this coach must be forced out. Until he is, that institution will be permitted no peace.

And, in almost the next breath:

I hope nothing untoward will happen in the Army-Navy game next Saturday.

As I have earlier stated, our schedules also were under attack much of the season. I finally felt constrained to make a statement:

"We are not making our schedules with a view to the national championship. Much as we appreciate any honors that come our way, we are not developing any neurosis about how we may be ranked. Our type of schedule is sufficiently exacting for the Cadets, who put in a much more rigorous day off the field than any civilian college student."

With the same rigorous off-the-field demands, Navy was attempting an all-major schedule and not doing too well with it. The record of three victories, four defeats and one tie, which they brought to our

'49 game, was their best since 1945. After Eddie Erdelatz became head coach in 1950, they watered down their schedules to more sensible proportions, which contributed to their better records. But in 1949 they scorned our common-sense scheduling. As the Corps paraded into Philadelphia's Municipal Stadium, the Midshipmen gave out with this parody of "On Brave Old Army Team":

> "We don't play Notre Dame,
> We don't play Tulane..
> We just play Davidson,
> For that's the fearless Army way!"

We cared not who composed the doggerel so long as we could win the game. Of all years, the way we looked at it, this was the one to beat the Navy. There was only one answer to all our critics and that was to go out there and take the Midshipmen apart, and that is precisely what the Cadets did, 38–0. It was the most one-sided victory in the history of the series.

It was close to a perfect clinical exposition of two-platoon football. Our defense was so all-encompassing and alert, our pursuit so savagely sharp, Navy never got past midfield. We were always on the march. In addition to the six touchdowns we scored, we were also stopped on their 11, 27 and, just before the end of the first half, on their 3-inch line. It was a great team performance, with many sparkling features, including Bobby Vinson's 92-yard touchdown runback of the second-half kick-off.

A coach does not get many performances like that one in a career. It is one of the good things that make up for a lot of the bad. I tried to explain this at the luncheon where we received the Lambert Trophy, emblematic of the Eastern Championship, for the fifth time in six years.

"You may wonder," I said, "why a man will undergo all the pressures of coaching, which are sure to age him before his time, when he could be doing far less taxing work with much more material return. Well, the answer is here in this 1949 Army team. Once in a while you are lucky enough to have the thrill and satisfaction of working with a group of men who are willing to make every sacrifice to achieve a goal, and then experience the achieving of it with them. In this, believe me, there is a payment that cannot be matched in any other pursuit."

From the beginning of the '49 season, I had been experiencing a special kind of pressure, known to relatively few coaches: that of having my own son on the squad. When I used Bob only sparingly as a substitute for Galiffa in '49, many thought I was leaning backward because his name was Blaik. At the Baseball Writers Dinner in New York the following winter, Ty Cobb said to me, "You have quite a son there. You make a mistake in not using him more."

Actually, I was not leaning backward or forward with Bob. There is nothing that will hurt a promising youngster more than pushing him too fast. In this respect, I handled Bob exactly as I would have handled any youngster of comparable potential.

Bob was a star in football, hockey, and baseball at Highland Falls High School, near West Point. At Exeter Academy, he threw two touchdown passes and made the game's longest run in the 13–0 victory over Andover, Exeter's first over its traditional rival in several years. His 30-foot shot down the center also won the hockey game from Andover, 3–2. At West Point he was the star of the hockey team and a valuable second baseman in baseball. As our 1950 quarterback he was superior as passer, punter, ball-handler, and field general.

Yet Bob was a "manufactured" athlete, a fine example of the boy who makes himself far better than average by work, determination, and brains. He was blessed with a merely good physique, but he developed it by persevering exercise. He did, however, have a naturally strong and accurate passing arm.

As a grammar-school boy on the West Point post, Bob was not sure whether he wanted to be an athlete or a musician. He took lessons on the piano and the cornet. His cornet rendition of an apparent favorite of his, "I Don't Want to Set the World on Fire," might be heard at the most unexpected times from any part of the house, including the bathroom.

Master Sergeant N. E. Fisher, of the West Point Band, his cornet teacher, noticed that Bob's mind was not on his lessons. He'd be staring out the window at the kids playing ball. "The boy is more interested in sports than music," said the sergeant. This confirmed our own suspicions.

During the 1943, '44 and '45 seasons, while Bob was putting in his first three years at Highland Falls High, Glenn Davis was playing for Army, and Glenn was Bob's idol. In 1946, we thought it would be a good idea to have Bill and Bob complete their high-school work at Kimball Union Academy in Meriden, New Hampshire. Bob agreed, but without any great enthusiasm. Bill was enthusiastic. Merle drove them up there; Bill remained, but Bob came back home with her. He wanted to finish at Highland Falls, and on Saturdays watch Glenn Davis. Merle said later that the morning she left for Kimball Union with Bill and Bob, she realized Bob wouldn't stay there long, because he didn't take his football shoes.

Bob has made solid contributions as an assistant coach to Murray Warmath at Minnesota, Andy Gustafson at Miami, and now Bud Wilkinson at Oklahoma. I have tried to talk him out of coaching, because he has a good business career ahead of him any time he wants to move in on it. This far, however, the football bug has bitten him as deeply as it did me. When this virus infects you, you are a goner!

As Bob moved into his second-class year, I felt he was ready to take over the direction of the offensive platoon, which the graduated Galiffa had handled. Our 1950 backfield, with Cain, Vic Pollock, Shultz, Fischl, Martin, and Stephenson returning, had fire power comparable to '49. There were also three exceptional yearling backs in fullback Al Pollard, halfback Gene Filipski, and quarterback Gilbert Reich. Our line, offensively, was not equal to '49. Our defensive platoon was again excellent. Our yearling linemen included a tigerish guard named Ray Malavasi.

We swept impressively through our first eight games, with highlight victories over Michigan, 27–6, in Yankee Stadium and Penn, 28–13, in Franklin Field. Bob's passing and punting, and strong running by Pollard, Filipski, Cain, Fischl, and Martin were supplemented by a vigorous defensive platoon, headed by linebacker Elmer Stout and tackle J. D. Kimmel. Foldberg was again outstanding as an offensive end. Filipski, who ran like an old-fashioned single-wing tailback to delight Jock Sutherland, broke up the Penn game with 29- and 73-yard touchdown runs off tackle.

Between the Penn game and our date at Stanford, we had deliberately scheduled an easy game with the University of New Mexico, and this time we did better than my Fort Bliss team had in the Albuquerque Adventure. But it was the week of the New Mexico game—although we didn't recognize it at the time—that things began to go wrong. We ran into bad weather and had only one practice. As it turned out this was to be our last outdoor practice of the season. The rains continued the following week; we ran into a record downpour during our forty-eight-hour visit in San Francisco's Bay Area and there was more bad weather after our return.

The game at Stanford was played in a downpour and mud. I don't recall ever seeing worse conditions. Cars parked on the campus were so mired that it was days before they could be removed. Considering the conditions we did very well to win, 7–0. Bob set up our score in the third period by punting out of bounds on the Stanford 4. When they kicked out to our 39, we went in for a score. Key smashes by Pollard and Martin got us down to their 17, but we were then penalized 15 for holding. With third and 20 to go on their 27, Bob passed the mud-logged ball to the 5-yard line. Foldberg not only made a leaping catch, but kept his feet in the goo as he ran into the end zone. Pollard converted. On such a day, seven seemed like seventy, and was just as good.

The victory went down in Army football annals as "The Python Game," for an unusual combination of reasons. On Friday, San Francisco front pages carried a story that the remains of a dump fire in the southern part of the city had revealed the body of an eighteen-foot python, apparently burned to death. The story also stated that, two weeks before, a laborer had run in terror to his fellow workers during a lunch hour with the story that he had encountered a giant snake. They ascribed his tale to a hangover, but apparently he had not been "seeing things." How the snake got in the dump was a mystery. Perhaps it had escaped from a circus or zoo. Or it could be it had hidden, when small, in a cargo from the Orient and, still undiscovered, been tossed into the dump with some refuse.

Anyhow the python got into the news again during the half-time portion of the radio broadcast of the Army-Stanford game. A sportswriter from the East was among the guest speakers. Since the rain and mud-ridden game, scoreless at the half, provided little fodder for comment, he discussed the mystery of the python who had been found dead in the dump. Listening to this broadcast 3,000 miles away, while on a hunting trip in the Adirondacks, were Colonel Red Reeder and a friend. Since the reception was faint, Colonel Reeder was using ear phones and relaying the broadcast to his friend. When the sportswriter from the East came on, Reeder's friend wanted to know what he was saying about the game.

"He says," Reeder reported, "there has been so much rain in California that a huge python became depressed and committed suicide by crawling into a dump fire."

The python story got some mileage that night at a little gathering in our suite at the St. Francis Hotel. An honored guest was Colonel Charlie Daly, my old coach. The Godfather of Army football had retired from service. He was living in Orange Grove, California, and painting as a hobby. He came to the game that day and I invited him to say a few words to the team. He was with us again and enjoying himself.

Somebody composed and recited a semi-epic poem, Kiplingesque in scansion and rhyme, but with little else to recommend it. The subject was myself and how I "turned the Lobos [New Mexico] into Hobos in our Hudson Den, but on Monday, by the living God, we'd scrimmage once again." Down in the lobby of the St. Francis, Al Pollard, a Los Angeles boy, was surrounded by about forty people, all relatives. Granny Rice, who was out to see the game, remarked that he never saw such an enthusiastic bunch.

Often I look back on that night at the St. Francis. We did not realize that it would be a long time before we would know another one like it. We were sitting on top. Beginning in 1944 we had enjoyed five out of six undefeated seasons, two national championships, five Eastern titles. We had a record, as we stood, of fifty-seven victories, three defeats, and four ties in sixty-four games. We had put together one defeatless string of thirty-two and we now had another one going which had that day reached twenty-eight. The way it looked, we could go on and on. We fully expected to get by Navy, and another fine squad was in prospect for 1951.

We did not suspect that everything from then on was going to be downhill for a long time. Today, ten years later, Army football never has been able to climb back and to stay on that plateau. We simply did not dream of the shocking, numbing upset by Navy that lay two weeks ahead of us. If any of us had nightmares, they could not have matched the dark valley we were to walk through not many months later.

I have pointed out that the week of the New Mexico game saw our last outdoor practice, and that when we returned to the Academy after the Stanford game, the weather was solidly bad during the two-week interim before the Navy game. We worked out every day in the field house. In my twenty-five years as a head coach, I never made a worse mistake. No matter what the weather, I should have ordered some outdoor work. The lack of it dulled our timing and our precision, and we were a team that relied much on those qualities.

Navy, as deep an underdog as she has ever been in the history of the series, beat our ears off, 14–2. The Midshipmen held us to five first downs, 77 yards on the ground, 60 in the air. They got their two touchdowns in the first half. Quarterback Bobby Zastrow ran for one touchdown and passed for the other, with end Jim Baldinger making a great catch in the end zone. Roger Drew kicked the two conversions.

In the second half, we shut off their attack, and we got to the 21, the 15, the 6, the 3. But we never could turn it into anything. When they most needed to, they put terrific pressure on our runners and so harried Bob's passes that he had five intercepted. It was a great Navy victory, thoroughly earned and deserved, and a fine start for their excellent new head coach, Eddie Erdelatz.

I wrote to a friend before Christmas:

> There is considerable depression about the Navy game and the pictures do not make me feel any better. We were completely sour and the only possible reason could be traced to the indoor work for the month of November.

Some Army people were saying it was a good thing, in a way, that we lost. They were getting a little self-conscious about our constant success. They felt the Navy series had been a little one-sided since 1943. They said that as long as we had to lose sometime, it was best we lose to Navy, which needed the victory. They said this and a lot more silly stuff. I insisted that a Navy football victory over Army, at any time under any conditions, had absolutely nothing to recommend it. In this, I had full suport from Major General Bryant Moore, who had succeeded General Taylor as Superintendent on January 28, 1949.

Let me say a few words about Bryant Moore, one of the finest of the Long Gray Line.

I met him for the first time in Washington, soon after he was named Supe. "You are the athletic director and football coach," were almost his first words. "I don't know anything about football. Tell me something about it." I started to talk, but after only two sentences, he said, "Let's talk about something else." Then he whistled a little tune for about a minute. I left the Pentagon completely bewildered. This bird seemed plenty odd to me. When I found out he was from Ellsworth, Maine, however, I began to recall that in my seven years at Hanover I had met many New Englanders who also seemed strange birds at first flight.

That was the way of it with General Moore. Within two months after he took command at West Point, we were close friends. He was an extremely cultured man, whose love of beauty had been firmly imbedded by the picturesque Maine coast line of his youth. He added to his formal education by much reading, and from 1924 to '29, he taught French at the Academy.

In October, 1942, he commanded the 164th Infantry, and earned the Distinguished Service Medal for actions against the Japanese on Guadalcanal. He later was Assistant Division Commander of the 104th Infantry in the Invasion of Europe, and his leadership in the fighting around Antwerp and in the attack on the Siegfried Line won him command of the Eighth Infantry Division. Its achievements in crossing the Roer River, clearing the Cologne Plain, reducing the Roer Pocket and eliminating the German Army east of the Rhine were so outstanding that General Moore was awarded the Oak Leaf Cluster to his DSM, and promoted to major general. He later won a second Oak Leaf Cluster after the war for his shrewd leadership of the Trieste United States Troops, known as TRUST.

General Moore's military and academic dedication had never permitted him an opportunity to become interested in athletics. His first visits to our football practice were made, I believe, from a sense of obligation. As he observed so many approaches in the training of our squad that were comparable to troop preparation, his curiosity was aroused. He soon developed a keen interest in the game, and was impressed by the dedication of our players.

Early in the afternoon of January 16, 1951, I was in his office discussing the athletic budget when he received a phone call from the Chief of Staff in Washington. His replies were laconic: ". . . Yes, I can be ready. . . . You mean five today? . . . No, five A.M. at La Guardia. . . ." When he hung up, he whistled a few bars, and returned to our budget discussion.

I had been back in my office about an hour, when he phoned me. "Red," he said, "you know where I'm going, don't you?"

"I can make a pretty good guess," I replied.

"Come on over to my quarters," he said, "and sit around with me."

I found him in the beautiful living room, in a turtle-neck sweater and rolling a cigarette, his link to the old Army. "Red," he said, "I've been given a Corps in Korea and I leave La Guardia at five tomorrow morning."

I looked at Mrs. Peggy Moore, whom he had returned to Ellsworth to wed soon after his graduation from the Point in 1917. Outwardly this lovely First Lady of the Post was sharing the Supe's enthusiasm for his new assignment. As she talked about moving their furniture, she put up a cheerful front. I sensed, however, that she must be inwardly sad. General Moore was already packed. He had, in fact, been packed ever since he came to West Point, because he knew that any day he would be recalled to the big game.

Taking command of the ninth corps, first army in Korea, General Moore, typically, was all over the place. On February 24 he was checking progress in the regaining of two important fords that had been lost because of high water, when his helicopter failed and landed in the icy waters of the Han River. He got to shore safely and apparently was all right except for a slight leg injury. He was back on duty making a phone call when he suffered a thrombosis, possibly caused by the leg injury, and died quickly. His body was returned to West Point for the funeral ceremony and burial. The march from the Chapel high on the hill to the cemetery was a sad one. I had missed him since he had left.

I never forgot what he had told me more than once: "I will pattern my next Army corps after the Army team."

Chapter XV

The Ninety Scapegoats

I regret that this work demands inclusion of the 1951 West Point expulsion episode, because I realize the telling of the documented story cannot, in the end, undo what was done, cannot negate the tragedy.

United States Army and West Point archives, however, include only an official and selected version of what took place. I never was permitted to place my own substantiated record of the affair in the library of the Military Academy.

I have omitted many incidents involving persons who perhaps should not be spared. Nine years after the tragedy, I believe much good has come from the soul-searching at West Point which the tragedy demanded. Through it all, and to this day, my respect for the Academy never has wavered.

> There was no real need for the cribbing scandal that wrecked West Point football. It could have been settled quickly, quietly, by a reprimand from the superintendent. That was all that would have been needed except in the case of perhaps two of the boys. And they could have been helped by a kick in the pants.

The above is quoted from an interview with General Douglas MacArthur by the well-known newsman and columnist Bob Considine.

Instead of a quick, quiet, and fair resolution of the problem, however, the Korean War was temporarily reduced to second position on the front pages of America on and for several days after Friday, August 3, 1951. On that day the news was released that ninety cadets were being dismissed from West Point for an infraction of the cadet honor code. It was later revealed that the ninety included sixty varsity athletes, thirty-seven of them members of the football squad.

WEST POINT FIRES 90 BREAKING HONOR CODE . . . . FULLBRIGHT URGES FOOTBALL BAN AT WEST POINT AND ANNAPOLIS . . . . CADETS' KIN PLAN PLEA TO MARSHALL . . . . CRIBBERS GET CHANCE TO QUIT . . . . ACCUSE MORE CADETS! . . . ARMY ATHLETIC APPOINTMENTS UNDER FIRE . . . . ERRING GENERALS FARE FAR BETTER THAN CADETS . . . . SENATORS SET INQUIRY INTO CADET OUSTER . . . .

So screamed the headlines of August 3, 1951, and for weeks afterwards the expulsions were a subject of news and editorial comment all across the nation. Few headline stories ever left the public with such an incomplete, distorted, unfair picture of what actually took place and why.

The infraction of the code did not involve carrying illegal notes or other aids into examinations, or covert classroom exchanges. It involved cadets tipping off one another to the subject matter of identical writs (written tests) given different sections of classes on different days. In most cases, the infraction involved only one subject. Obviously, only those who took the writ on the second day could benefit. The infraction did not involve final examinations. It involved either short daily writs or longer semimonthly writs. The marks therefrom were averaged with the marks from the daily recitations, to give the posted weekly grades.

Some cadets were dismissed who had neither taken nor given unauthorized aid, but merely had knowledge of it and had not reported it.

The ninety cadets had come into the Academy with excellent backgrounds. In order to be appointed and accepted, they had to undergo a rigid academic, physical, and moral screening. They were all recommended as superior all-around boys. Many of them carried the tag: "The finest turned out by our school in years."

The leadership qualities among the expelled football players were at a higher percentage level than in any numerically comparable group that could be selected out of the Corps, not only for that year but for many years back.

Of the thirty-seven football players dismissed, thirty-five had been recruited for their football as well as their officer potential. Of the thirty-five, nine of the first classmen were slated to be high-ranking "makes." One was to be First Captain or Brigade Commander, the highest rank in the Corps. Another was to be Regimental Captain, the second-highest rank. Many of the second classmen involved also were slated to be "makes."

As to their ideals of honor, most of the ninety boys condemned themselves by telling the truth. Since their acts had not involved cheating in the classroom, there was no evidence against most of them. To remain, all they had to do was to refuse to answer or to plead innocence. To them, this would have been dishonorable. Square this alongside their exploitation of the repetitive-writ system and you have, in attitudes, a strange paradox.

Some of the cadets involved were advised by officers not stationed at the Academy to admit nothing. Others involved chose on their own to admit nothing. These stayed on at the Academy.

Dramatic scenes that included the pressure of parents and tearful entreaties not to tell on others were, in the end, revolting to those who had chosen honestly to implicate themselves.

After leaving West Point the expelled cadets entered other colleges and made fine records. Some re-entered service branches in the colleges and held the highest posts of command. One became the outstanding lieutenant of his class at Fort Belvoir, Virginia. He won this distinction in direct competition with young West Point graduates who had been at the Academy with him. He also happened to have been one of the few among the football men who was looked down upon as lacking a few social graces, but to those who appraised him correctly he was "a diamond in the rough," with outstanding leadership potential which he was later to prove at Belvoir.

Conceding that the cadets were involved to varying degrees, it must also be apparent to any objective mind that their dereliction traced in strong measure to a system they encountered—a system that, subsequent investigation established, had been breached before their time—and to an extraordinary combination of circumstances and conditions.

Certainly, ninety fine young Americans of good families and records do not suddenly become "men without honor" unless something basic in a system is wrong and extraordinary conditions and circumstances are affecting them.

First, there was the weakness inherent in the writs system. One regiment was given the identical writs the second day that the other regiment had been given the first day. Until the Corps was divided into two regiments during Reorganization Week in August of 1942, cadets took writs in the same subject *on the same day*.

The system of having cadets tutored, either by an officer or another cadet, involved a freedom of action which was not recognized as inimical to the honor code until the violation, namely, that the tutors sometimes knew what precise subject matter should be covered.

After the erring cadets were dismissed, the repetitive-writs system was abolished and with it, of course, the tutoring weakness. This was an admission, certainly, that the system had been a contributing factor.

The weaknesses of the system were coupled with continuous intermingling of cadets from both regiments at the training tables among the athletes. It was mainly at the training tables among the athletes that the climate was created for a breaching of the system.

Because of our rigid admission standards, only a very few of the ninety were foundering academically and took the illegal aid to stay in the Academy. It was particularly ironic that one such boy, an outstanding football player, was the one I mentioned with the No. 1 military rank in his class and was slated to become First Captain. He had been appointed to the Academy from the battlefield, where he was a lieutenant with forty months of combat.

To pass mathematics and to go on to become a West Point graduate and officer, he succumbed to the temptation to take the illegal aid. Again I say, while one does not condone the mistake, one can understand it, just as one can understand how the boy who helped him was impulsively drawn into the affair.

There is no doubt that some were motivated by friendship and team morale. They were wrong, of course, in placing these things above all else. Yet it is understandable that they might get their thinking mixed up. Certainly I was to blame in part because of the emphasis I put on team morale. The morale of a football team is comparable to the morale of troops in war. Without it, there can be no victory.

None took the aid to gain an advantage over a classmate in rank. In this respect, a subsequent study revealed that the grades of the men while they were taking the aid were approximately the same as their grades when they were not taking it, so that their relative academic rank remained the same.

I am convinced that involvement for many of the boys began with their knowledge that once they were aware that others were taking or giving aid and failed to report it, they were just as guilty of violating the honor code as if they were taking or giving the aid themselves.

To tell or not to tell on the known defectors caused an acute inner conflict. Some of the defectors were upperclassmen. Normal class barrier here constituted a cogent factor to underclassmen with knowledge, as did the natural respect for upperclassmen, especially those prominent in the Corps. Even more impelling was the fact that the defectors were their friends. All this added up to a horrible dilemma. When resolved negatively, it resulted in a personal acceptance of illegal aid by mental association, from which there was no turning back.

A committee report turned in after the expulsions admitted that the exploitation of the repetitive exams dated back to the mid- 'forties, or not long after the time when the Corps was divided into two regiments and the identical exams given on different days. The defectors among the cadets in 1951 knew they were embracing something that had gone on before their time, but the investigatory boards refused to accept this fact.

Some of the cadets involved took the illegal aid to ease their terrific grind. The football player at all the service academies, it should be understood (yet so often is not), carries a load no other undergraduate in this country even begins to approximate. At West Point, he often comes directly from a secondary school, with too little academic preparation. (In contrast, for many years a large percentage of the rest of the Corps came to the Academy after a year at a preparatory school following high school, or as college transfers.) He is saddled with a demanding military regimen and discipline. He has practically no time to relax or reflect. The general load carried by the cadet, football player or non-football player, far exceeds anything required when I was an undergraduate at the Academy.

Even without football, the routine is hardly designed to minister to a cadet's bodily comforts. His day begins at 5:50 A.M., when he is awakened by the field music of the Hell Cats, a select (if demoniac) group from the Army Band. He attends his unit's reveille formation at 6:00, then returns immediately to his room. By 6:30, he must make his bed, complete his personal toilet, change uniforms, and if it is his turn, sweep out the room.

At 6:30, the Corps marches into Washington Hall for breakfast. The Corps marches to all meals, but the cadets leave the dining hall individually. Thirty minutes are authorized for breakfast and dinner (lunch) and thirty-five minutes for supper. Between 7:10 A.M. and his first class at 7:55, the cadet will put the final touches on his room arrangement, take a quick look at the newspaper and, perhaps, have time to review his first hour's lesson.

Each morning, Monday through Saturday, he will attend two classes of an hour and twenty minutes duration each, separated by a study period of approximately one hour. Morning classes terminate at 11:55, which allows the cadet fifteen minutes to return to his room and prepare for dinner formation. At 12:45, he returns from dinner to his room again, to prepare for his afternoon class or classes. Monday through Friday, from 1:00 to 2:00 or from 2:15 to 3:15, he will spend in an academic class. In addition, on Monday and Friday or on Tuesday and Thursday, he will attend a one-hour class in military tactics or drill with his company. Drill periods are scheduled only early in the fall or late in the spring.

On the two days alternate to those on which he attends drills or tactics, a cadet who is not on one of the Academy teams participates in intramural athletics until 4:30 or 5:00. On Wednesday and off-intramural days, he normally is free from 3:15 until 6:20 to study, exercise, or participate in an extracurricular activity.

Exacting as this schedule appears, a football player puts in an even more demanding day. He is excused from drill and intramurals in season but not from military tactics. After class in the afternoon, he must get back to his room, drop off his books, get to the gym, change into uniform, get taped and report to practice by 4:00.

Practice is usually finished at 5:30. This allows the player time to get to the gym, shower, return to his room, change into proper uniform, and arrive in the dining hall by 6:30. Because of their late return to company areas, football players are excused from marching to supper. The only other privilege extended a player is permission to attend 8:00 o'clock instead of 11:00 o'clock service on Sundays, so that he can sit in on a scouting report from 10:30 to 12:00. On Saturday mornings of game days at West Point, he rises with the rest of the Corps at 5:50 and goes to his first class.

Call to Quarters sounds at 7:15, at which time the cadet must be in his room. Unless he has permission to absent himself on official or authorized business, he must remain there until reveille the next morning. At 10:30, taps are sounded and the cadet must extinguish his lights, unless he has permission for late study.

In the days of our finest success, my assistants, my players, and I were certainly not unaware that a few officers and cadets were given to sly remarks that "Blaik's boys," as they called them, were "the chosen cadets." I have already mentioned the two privileges: excused from supper formation and permitted to attend early Sunday service.

Let me add that if the "chosen cadets" were away for a long weekend on a football trip, they made up the academic work and kept up in class with those whose only extracurricular weekend problem frequently was what girl to "drag."

Football tended to irritate some Academy authorities who planned the schedules of visiting potentates. These frequently were officers from foreign countries. More often than not they would break up the planned schedule by requesting to see football practice. The similarity of the game to warfare fascinated them and they would linger on to ask questions. This often vexed some of the Academy rank.

That such an attitude existed among some elements at West Point was not surprising, of course, to myself, nor could it be to anybody with any Army background. Anything even obliquely within the Army chain of command that achieves the degree of success and publicity attained by West Point football in those days invites envy from a type of individual present in every community.

What resentment there was toward football, however, was seldom evidenced against any individual player. For the most part, he was a personality well liked and admired by his classmates. In fact, two of the involved football players were presidents of their respective classes.

Exploitation of the repetitive writs reflected a new atmosphere evident at West Point in the 'forties as an aftermath of World War II. Those were days of change at the Academy. There was a seething among cadets for more freedom, a resentment toward any authority which treated them as boys instead of men. This was especially true of cadets who had already served with distinction in the war.

I had discussed these problems with the Superintendent and some of the Academic Board. They had agreed with me, but admitted these were problems for which they had not found a solution.

A board appointed after the expulsions to study the honor code concluded that service to it was based in large measure on fear of dismissal rather than on any conviction of its deep spiritual significance. Failure here must be imputed in part to inadequate indoctrination by a few in positions of command who measured below average as leaders.

Those responsible for the expulsions repeatedly placed part of the blame on the failure of the football men to be absorbed into the Corps. "They had grown away from the Corps," was the oft-repeated charge. By implication, blame for this was laid at my door. The impression was created, even among our graduates, that the players lived as men apart.

For this there was absolutely no substantiation. Like all other cadets, the football men were integrated into the twenty-four companies, regardless of who or what they were. The selection of the football men for high positions of leadership and class office belies the "group apart" myth.

At West Point or any other college, it has always been a natural thing for varsity teammates to be close friends. Two outstanding examples were cadet football players of the Class of 1915: Eisenhower and Bradley. To state that such friendship represented a "group apart" from the Corps is deduction not only fallacious but juvenile.

I have emphasized that the load carried by the cadet-football player is terrific.

"It's a tough life," Herman Hickman once said. "When I was new around here, some of my linemen were a little slow on the uptake one day. I said to them, 'What's the matter? Out to the corner drugstore last night?' They just stood there and looked at me. They didn't think I was very funny. I was their coach, but that day they taught me something."

I have often wondered how the cadet-football player pays the price. In my last season at the Academy, 1958, Bob Anderson, one of the finest halfbacks West Point or any school ever knew, found the second-class year especially tough because of its courses in mechanics of fluids and mechanics of solids.

Andy had to study long after taps and would average less than seven hours' sleep. To get by on this amount and still play football is a trick nobody can appreciate who has not tried it. Yet Anderson was tremendous in all departments of the game.

Probably the only explanation of how these young men do it is that they somehow call on a physical and emotional reserve they had not suspected they possessed. Sacrifice, to all real college players, seems incidental to the satisfaction they receive from being part of a winning effort, for, I repeat, there are no rewards comparable to it. This spirit always has seemed to me to be especially keen at the service academies because of the generally dedicated and inspirational atmosphere at most times.

Now, if you put it all together, the weaknesses of the system and the extraordinary conditions and circumstances—the repetitive writs and tutorial setup, the intermingling of cadets at training table, the placing of team spirit and friendship above all else, the seething atmosphere of the 'forties, inadequate indoctrination of plebes into the honor system and the super load carried by the football men—you can begin to understand how some of the finest boys in America made the mistake they did.

You can also understand how the other fifty-three equally fine youngsters, even without the extra pressure of football, were likewise caught up in a combination of the system and the extraordinary conditions.

They are boys who would have made fine leaders, because they were good to have around when the going was tough. It is not the least part of their tragedy that they were lost to West Point. As the men they are, they certainly were not lost to the service of the country.

The investigation that sent them on their way was triggered on April 2, 1951, when two cadets reported irregularities. They were urged to try to get more conclusive evidence. This placed them in the role of stool pigeons, in itself a form of conspiracy which violated the spirit of the honor code. By the end of May, evidence was uncovered concerning a limited group. A three-man board of tactical officers was appointed to investigate the alleged violations. The Cadet Honor Committee was told about the matter but never at any time took action.

On May 29, the tactical board began questioning cadets under suspicion. That afternoon, while walking across the Plain to a baseball game, I was informed by one of the football players that an investigation concerning a breach of the honor code was under way. The player said he thought it was not serious. This was my first knowledge of the affair. I assumed it was an individual breach of honor, and did not think much about it.

That night, a few minutes after ten, I received a phone call in my quarters from a football player then in the third, or sophomore class. He asked me if I would meet with a group of his classmates, as something serious had arisen which they wanted to discuss with me. I told them I would meet them in the football-office projection room within fifteen minutes. While driving down to the gym, I thought about what the player had told me that afternoon, and I grew concerned. When I got up to the projection room, twelve players from the third class were awaiting me.

For nearly an hour I heard their stories. Each was anxious to unburden himself. Most of them had yet to go before the board. Of those who had, some had implicated themselves but had not implicated others. A few had not told the truth.

I had no doubt about the seriousness of their acts, yet I knew them to be men of basic integrity. I needed no reflection to advise them.

"You know how we do business in the squad and at the Military Academy," I told them. "Each one of you should state the facts to the board without equivocation."

After the players left, I sat there in the projection room, where we had often gathered for happier purpose. No foreboding could have been greater than my own.

I had been in many a tough game, but this was not a game. It was a catastrophe.

Adjacent to the gymnasium are the Superintendent's quarters. The Superintendent, Major General Frederick A. Irving, and I had known each other for years and our families were close friends. Within a few minutes, I was throwing pebbles at his darkened bedroom window. He came down in his bathrobe and let me in. We sat in his living room, and I gave him an account of my meeting with the twelve third-classmen. I told him that from what I had learned this was a grave situation. We talked for a while and at the end I said, "If I ever gave good advice, this is it: this affair is so serious that you should remove the investigation from the board of young tactical officers and place it in the hands of the Academic Board. This may be a catastrophe and it demands the most mature judgment. I beg you to do so."

The next day, my son Bob and his roommate, who was president of the second (junior) class, came to my office. They told me that their class was involved and that they themselves were involved. I well recall my reaction.

"My God," I said. "How could you? How could you?"

They gave me a complete picture of what had happened. Then and thereafter, they never wavered from their positions.

"Under similar conditions," they said, "we would do it again. We consider ourselves just as honorable as any men in the Corps."

They had not yet been called before the tactical board. They said that when they were called, they intended to tell the board anything it wanted to know about themselves personally, but under no conditions would they involve other cadets. It was up to the other cadets to involve themselves.

After they left, I immediately went to the Superintendent. I was now no longer in an unchallengeable position. I told him of Bob's statement and offered his resignation as a proof of my sincerity.

I realized now, much more acutely than the day before, that without the mature judgment of a professorial board, this investigation could have frightful results.

On Sunday, May 31, the first class, which was about to graduate, returned from a trip to Fort Belvoir, and three of them came to my office seeking advice. They knew of my advice to the men of the second and third classes. But to them I said, "You are to graduate next week. Some of you are to be married. Your parents are here. Either look to them for advice or make your own judgment as I shall not advise you."

I now had a list of those involved from all three upper classes and would soon have a list of the plebes involved. I knew now how deep and terrible was the defection.

The Corps learned formally of the trouble when the Assistant Commandant gave them a very emotional talk. He told them that anyone who had violated the honor code was, in the eyes of West Point, "the same as dead." This was in keeping with Corps tradition that an honor violator should be "silenced" for life, that is, never recognized by a fellow cadet or graduate. To my knowledge, the involved cadets were anything but "silenced" by the Corps.

Most officers, whatever their viewpoint of the affair, were sincere. Days before the true number of defectors was known or suspected, however, the involvement of so many prominent athletes, especially football players, provided a vindictive few on the Post a relished opportunity to whet their blood-axes. From these came fantastic tales almost too grotesque to recite. For example, one officer assisting on the investigatory group said, "They probably threw the Navy game." Dignity went out the window.

Although I had the opportunity to present my views to the Superintendent, at no time during the investigation was I called on to appear before the tactical board. Nor was my request granted to appear before the Academic Board. I had requested that I be permitted to place all the information in my possession before this Board. This I was never permitted to do.

On June 8, the tactical board turned in its report to the Superintendent. The report stated that they had admission of guilt or evidence on ninety cadets, all of whom were in the second and third classes, and that they recommended dismissal. In the meantime, the first class had graduated.

The recommendation of dismissal was devoid of mature thinking. To this tactical board, the violation admitted of no extenuation. In fact, had half or more of the Corps been involved, it still would not have occurred to the board that there was a breakdown in the system.

Any endeavor by those who had been completely forthright to enlarge the scope of involvement was countered with the charge: "By increasing the numbers, you are hopeful of saving yourself." Thus, the case was closed in their minds and labeled "a football conspiracy."

Following the report and recommendation of the tactical board to the Superintendent, the ball was passed on up to the Chief of Staff, Major General J. Lawton Collins, and then to the Secretary of the Army, Mr. Frank Pace, who described himself to me as "a man of warm heart." There were then two months of high-level discussion and action.

With more than required courtesy, the Superintendent permitted me to accompany him on several plane trips to Washington, where I made futile attempts to convert those in high command to a better understanding of what I knew to be true.

At the recommendation of the Chief of Staff upon my request, Secretary Pace appointed a review board, consisting of Learned Hand, retired Judge of the Second United States Court of Appeals; Major General Robert M. Danford, former Commandant at West

Point; and Lieutenant General Troy H. Middleton, President of Louisiana State University.

The Hand Board spent one and a half days at West Point in an examination into the background of the violations and the responsibility of the authorities. The board did not interview any of the violators. They interviewed only cadets selected by the authorities.

I was interviewed by the Hand Board. (This was the first and only time I was interviewed by either of the so-called investigatory boards. In late August, after the expulsions were a *fait accompli*, I appeared before a review board in an attempt to get my views into an official record.)

In order that some viewpoint opposed to the dismissal recommendation other than my own be heard, the Hand Board acquiesced to my request that they interview two senior officers.

The Hand Board reported their findings to Secretary Pace and also recommended dismissal. This came as a severe shock to me and the two members of the Academic Board opposed to expulsion, who had appeared before the Board. The Hand Board gave me strong reason to believe they would recommend a far different solution than expulsion. At the conclusion of their meeting they said to me, "This is the first account we have heard that makes any sense." They said it was evident to them the boys were not callous violators of the honor code. They told me they would do nothing to blight the boys or the Academy.

Years later I called on General Middleton at Louisiana State, and asked him why the Hand Board had changed its mind. He explained to me that the board members were told by a few members of the first class, whom the authorities had arranged for them to interview in New York, that if the erring cadets were not dismissed, *the entire Corps would resign.*

That the Corps would resign was such a far-fetched statement, it is incredible that it carried such weight.

In the first place, it was not possible for anybody at the time to know the attitude of the Corps as a whole. Except for men attached to Beast Detail on the Post or to first-class detail at Camp Buckner, the first class was on leave. The second class was also away from the academy. The only class at hand was the yearling class (sophomores) which had just completed plebe year. They were at Buckner.

I have solid reason to state that not only the cadets interviewed by the Hand Board but those interviewed by newspapermen were carefully selected by some authorities. They no more represented the majority opinion of the Corps as to the handling of the case than the chain of command viewpoint represented a majority opinion of West Point graduates, the Army, or the people of America.

There was definite evidence of a division of opinion among the Corps as to whether expulsion was the correct solution. One cadet was so convinced the action was wrong that he resigned from the Honor Committee. Many cadets strongly opposed to the action maintained silence. They well knew that to speak their minds was not to improve their lot as cadets.

A considerable percentage of our graduates was strongly opposed to the dimissals, but it is not wise for men still in service to express public opposition to the chain-of-command point of view.

It has been argued that if action short of dismissal were taken, the charge would have arisen that the authorities were motivated not for the sake of the individuals but for the sake of football.

To this there is an elementary answer: Where is the relevancy? The point is not what somebody might have thought or said of the action, but was the action right or wrong?

Once the Hand Board made its recommendation of dismissal to Secretary Pace, the next step was from Pace to Secretary of Defense, George C. Marshall. Marshall's services to his country are unquestioned, but his enthusiasm for West Point, on the record, is not. The last transfer was made from Marshall to President Harry S. Truman.

The purpose of having the President ultimately carry the ball was twofold. First, nobody going up the chain of command wanted the formal responsibility for the expulsions attached to him. Secondly, cadets dismissed by presidential decree could not be given the right to appeal for a court-martial. In a court-martial, most of the evidence accepted by the tactical board would have been inadmissible.

A dismissal by presidential directive is known as an administrative or "gray" discharge, "gray" because formally it does not fall into the category of either honorable or dishonorable. I tried with President Truman and others to secure an honorable discharge for the dismissed boys, but I failed. In the final analysis, however, their type of discharge is meaningless. They have written themselves the finest possible character references in the lives they have lived.

After the dismissals I went to Washington for a thirty-five minute meeting with President Truman, arranged through his aide, General Harry Vaughan. The President told me he was not at all satisfied with the way the case had been handled. He said his advice had come from Mr. Pace and the Chief of Staff. He said his sympathy was with the boys, but that it was too late for him now to take any new action, too late for the Army to undo what had been done.

All during the investigation, the cadets were handled in a manner to discredit them. Early in July they were separated and kept in a state of incarceration in barracks. Only after I pointed out to the Superintendent that if they were not allowed to move around, there could well be a breakdown in discipline, were they sent on a five-day leave in July.

The release of the story to the news media, on noon of Friday, August 3, was timed to coincide with the Chief of Staff informing members of Congress. Apparently, no thought was given to permitting the cadets to apprise and consult with their parents before the story was released. I know of only one boy who was able to.

The first-classmen first heard of their expulsion on a Friday radio news report at Camp Buckner. They received no official notice from the authorities until the next day. A Cadet Sergeant of the Guard, ordered to separate the "culprits" and return them to the Academy, told the boys: "Pack up your stuff and move along! And don't try any monkey business!"

When they were returned to the Academy, they were again herded into a section of barracks. They were denied even the use of a telephone until an Academy staff officer, apparently warned by a talk with newspapermen, decided they had better be given the use of one.

"The story," one writer summed it up, "was released to the country attended by fanfare usually reserved for the apprehension by G men of a John Dillinger."

I knew it was urgent, whether I stayed at West Point or not, that I try to place the chaotic picture in something of its true perspective before the country at the earliest possible moment. To this end I invited a group of some forty metropolitan and national-wire-service newspapermen to meet with me for lunch at Gene Leone's Restaurant on West Forty-eighth Street in New York on Thursday, August 9.

Ironically, the day the story was released was our third day at Bull Pond. You can imagine the pall that hung over our usual happy vacation time. I was informed that morning that the announcement would be made by the Chief of Staff at noon. Before I could gather my thoughts, I received a long distance phone call from Asheville, North Carolina. It was General Eichelberger, who was known by the Chief of Staff to be my close friend.

"Red," said Uncle Bobby, "I am distressed beyond words at the action, but the Chief of Staff has asked me to meet you in New York this afternoon. He has asked me to get a commitment from you that when the news is released, you will make no public statement."

I realized immediately that the Chief of Staff's request had been generated by a letter I had written him, which would be in effect, I informed him, my release to the press, if the cadets were discharged.

"Uncle Bobby," I said, "you and I have been friends for years, and I will not allow anything to alter this relationship. Such a meeting could stretch our friendship and would, in the end, achieve no purpose. I would still state to the press what I thought proper."

His reply was typical of my friend.

"Red," he said, "I really didn't want to see you in New York on such a mission. I've only done what was asked of me."

Bull Pond was scheduled to break up on Thursday morning, August 9. The night before I drove down to New York, took a hotel room and remained incommunicado, except to one or two people.

On Thursday morning, about 11:30, I received a phone call from Joe Cahill, who for over seventeen years has done a priceless and often unappreciated job as sports public relations man for the Academy.

"Colonel," Joe said, "I thought I had better warn you. There is a mob scene in front of Leone's."

When I arrived at Gene's, I found Joe had not been exaggerating.

News and newsreel photographers and television cameras were awaiting me. A mob of passers-by stood around curiously and spilled over the curbing into the street, to impede traffic.

My luncheon with those newsmen lasted nearly three hours. At the beginning I sensed in some a certain cynicism, in others an edge of hostility. How could it have been otherwise in view of the news releases that had been coming out of West Point? At the end of my talk and a question-and-answer period, there was an air of friendly understanding and support.

I know that the ninety boys, their families, myself, and many other Americans will always be in the debt of those writers for bringing to the country the first true picture of what had taken place.

I began by saying that I was not sure I had been wise in deciding on the meeting, but that I felt a forthright statement of facts was preferable to the maze of inaccuracies, distortions, opinions, and conjectures that the case had thus far inspired. I said that nobody could challenge my right as a civilian to state my views.

"These young men," I said, "came to West Point as respected, honorable youngsters, many of them the idols of their communities. It would be considered an indictment of leadership at West Point, if after two or three years of Academy character building, they are returned branded in the eyes of the public as no better than common criminals.

"I believe in the youngsters with whom I've been dealing. I know their families. I know them. I know they are men of character. No man in Washington has the right to send them out of West Point with anything other than an honorable discharge. I consider an administrative discharge a gross injustice. My entire endeavor from now on shall be to see that these boys leave West Point with the same reputations they had when they came in."

To document for the writers the caliber of the expelled boys, I quoted high-school principals and teachers from Academy personnel sheets. These quotations were typical of the personnel sheets of all the expelled cadets. They had to be because of the traditionally rigid West Point screening, which I have already mentioned. Let me requote here some of what was read to the writers:

"A brilliant student and an outstanding athlete . . . his type of combination athlete-student crops up only occasionally.

"Considered by many the outstanding boy ever to attend our high school. His achievements, all of us feel, are preliminary to a great career to follow.

"One of the finest all-around boys I have ever known; an outstanding example of American youth, of excellent character and a real leader.

"Has worked hard and conscientiously to secure his education and will rank either at the top of his class or within the top five of a class of 117 . . . a member of the National High School Honor Society.

"A very fine young man, excellent leadership qualities, very well thought of by faculty and students. Ranked 44 from top in class of 266. Member of National High School Honor Society and chosen to represent character at induction of new members.

"A splendid candidate for the Military Academy. He has the physical and mental requirements. He is first of all an outstanding student.

"He is respected for his integrity by teachers and students alike.

"He is refined, modest and highly capable. I consider him to be the best qualified candidate for West Point who has attended our school."

"These reports," I told the writers, "show the character, maturity, and academic ability of these athletes. They came to the Academy with the finest of reputations. There is no moral reason to send them out to other colleges or into other services or endeavors with any other reputation than they had prior to coming to the Academy."

The newsmen had come to Leone's fully expecting me to announce my resignation. Instead, at the conclusion I announced I would remain at West Point. This statement was greeted by cheers.

Afterwards, to relax after what was something of an ordeal, I sat around with Joe Williams of New York *World-Telegram,* and Dan

Parker of the New York *Daily Mirror,* both outstanding sports editors and columnists. It was especially gratifying to me that two such hard-hitting journalists understood the real story behind the expulsions.

Mature men of stature all over the country saw the true picture. This was evidenced in countless letters and wires I received. One wire in particular was especially gratifying and came when most needed, on Saturday, August 4. It was sent by Francis Cardinal Spellman. To this day, I never meet his Eminence without his graciously inquiring how Bob and the other young men are doing.

Many colleges were eager to receive the boys. As I already have pointed out, they made fine records wherever they went. Some played football at the schools to which they transferred. Others did not. Two, interestingly enough, made All America. They graced every campus that welcomed them, not only as students but as men.

When we went down to play Georgia Tech in Atlanta, in 1952, I received a visit from Dr. Jesse W. Mason, dean of their Engineering School, who had one of the expelled players among his students.

"I didn't come to see the game," he said, "so much as to have the opportunity to tell you that this boy is one of the finest characters any of us has ever known. He has inspired all of us by his seriousness of purpose and his fine mind."

I have long since forgotten the horrendous thumping a fine Georgia Tech team handed our depleted squad that day, but I shall always recall the warmth of those words from Dean Mason.

My years of close association with young men gave me an understanding of them denied most educators. I am convinced my knowledge of the cadet was far more intimate than that possessed by officers in uniform. There is an intangible barrier between officer and cadet, which frequently prevents the officer from taking a good look at the cadet, a look that gets beneath the façade thrown up by the system.

My relationship with young men invariably permitted me to catalogue their home life. A boy's reaction to problems traces in large measure to what his parents are like, especially the mother.

Contrary to the often-expressed claim, no service academy or college *makes* basic character. The character of young cadets has been fashioned in their homes, in their formative years of adolescence, by the example of others. The purpose and function of West Point traditionally has been to emphasize integrity and a sense of duty to highly selected young men of basically fine character.

The fact that few colleges make a fetish of honor does not mean there is not a strong sense of integrity among their undergraduates. To believe otherwise is to suggest that integrity in this country is known only to a few.

West Point is a wonderful institution of tried and true values, with a proud and inspiring tradition. It is also an institution with ever-changing leadership that is human and capable of error. In the nine-year period from 1948 through 1956, five general officers served as superintendents. That is comparable to changing a college president oftener than every two years.

The differences I have with the action taken against those cadets do not by any means imply that I do not believe in the Academy's high standards of honor.

My objection is to the inept, callous, and sometimes evasive manner in which some of those in authority handled a most complex problem.

Some West Point professors were strong in their conviction that what happened was a kind of honor breach that required a solution far different from expulsion. But when the dismissal action was taken, there was an immediate closing of the ranks. Consequently an impression was created that those cadets had no internal support. Nothing could be further from the truth.

I shall always believe, and not without good reason, that if football players had not been involved in such wholesale numbers, the violations would have been internally resolved.

For a time I seriously considered resigning. It was General MacArthur who convinced me that I should stay. Other close friends had the same idea. They pointed out that if I left, there would be no one at the Academy in an official position who would defend the expelled boys. They also kindly said that I was the only one who could rebuild a football team from the shambles. But it was General MacArthur's counsel that was decisive.

I drove down to see the General on Saturday morning, August 4.

Merle was with me. We were unavoidably delayed leaving the Academy and about ten miles above Henry Hudson Bridge we had a blowout. I was forced to leave the car in Merle's hands and hitchhike a ride into the city. I arrived at the General's suite in the Waldorf Towers nearly thirty minutes late. He greeted me warmly. His first words were, "They have set the Academy back twenty years. Yes, at least that."

Then he put his arm around my shoulder and led me to his spacious living room.

"Now," he said, "tell me the whole story."

We sat there for several hours and I discussed the sad affair from beginning to end. He was tremendously understanding. At the end, he said, "Earl, you must stay on. Don't leave under fire."

Chapter XVI

College Football's Real Abuse

Not the least irritating by-product of the West Point expulsions of 1951 was the rush of some commentators and educators to cite the tragedy as an example of (1) the abuses that plague college football generally (and are always most acute in immediate postwar years) and (2) the expedient ethics characteristic of modern society.

The expulsion, traceable mainly to a weakness in a system and an extraordinary combination of conditions localized in a single and unique institution, bore no relationship whatsoever to what are defined as the big college game's traditional problems: the abuses of recruiting and subsidies, and a lack of responsibility toward the proper education of the player.

As to ethics, documentation of the characters and records of those ninety young men justifies the unqualified statement that if more like them were peopling our society, we would be the better for it.

Overemphasis of football, too often a threadbare scare-banner of the intellectual, is possible only when the primary purpose of a school, education, suffers from underemphasis. To develop this, let me analyze the problems of a major football program, first as they relate to West Point and then as they apply to college football as a whole.

West Point wants and needs big-time football for several reasons. There is its profound moral value, not only to the individual player and team, but to the Corps of 2,500 as a prime rallying point. There is its showcase value. There is its financial value. The seventeen-sport intercollegiate program, which costs $750,000 now and is ever mounting, would be billed to the taxpayers, were it not underwritten by the football team. To provide that kind of money, the Army team must be able to play the big game against Navy, the Air Force Academy, and several of the most powerful civilian college teams. (Big money in itself, however, does not justify college football.)

It would be impossible to engage such opposition on anything approaching parity if the Army team were selected from the cadets who happened to be appointed. Such a team could play only at the small-college level. It is not that such cadets do not make fine officers and satisfactory physical types. It is simply that they seldom can develop into football players at the major-college level.

Army, therefore, must interest, as do all major college teams, including Annapolis and the Air Force Academy, a certain number of boys who appear to have the potential to play at the major-college level. To get even a reasonable number of such boys, Army and the other service schools must screen more secondary-school players than the big civilian college, because few such boys are eager to test themselves in the regimen of Academy life. Rarely in recent years has a good football player come to West Point as a principal appointee or as a transfer from another college.

In my eighteen years at West Point, I walked the halls of Congress countless miles, asking the men on the Hill to appoint football players and athletes in other sports. I always did this in good conscience. I believe that strong teams in football and other sports, but especially football, are compatible with the highest standards of West Point. I also believe that Army should be represented by a football team the entire country can be proud of.

The athlete is also needed at West Point to balance the Corps, which otherwise would consist almost exclusively of three types: the pluperfect-military, the pluperfect-academic and the pluperfect-social.

In its steep physical, mental, and moral challenges, in its sacrifices, selflessness, and courage, football, beyond any game invented by man, is closest to war. As such, tell me what schools should be more proficient in it than West Point, Annapolis, and the Air Force?

In some educational circles, to recruit an athlete suggests something improper. The recruiting for the Military Academy consists of selling the career of a soldier, and not a football program. The young prospect whose main interest is football is not interested in rising at

5:50 A.M., taking a course comparable to a science major in our best colleges, and being restricted for four years to the disciplined and regimented life of the cadet.

To those still skeptical of the propriety and over-all value of recruiting a cadet-athlete, let me offer some more sparkling evidence. In my last four years at the Academy, three of the four first captains, the highest military rank attainable by a cadet, were recruited cadet-athletes, including the man of whom you have heard so much, Pete Dawkins. In other words, we followed a pattern of raising the standard of the Corps by selecting young cadet-athletes with fine leadership potential.

Service career records prove the ultimate justification for important football at the academies. Every prominent leader of battle forces I ever talked with emphasized that the former Academy football man is a good man to have around when there is a tough job to be done.

It must be obvious to the most lukewarm football fan among the conservative element of West Point graduates and to the public in general that the cadet-athlete is not shortchanged academically.

It is true, as some educators charge, that in some colleges today, though in not nearly so many as they may think, too many football players *are* shortchanged educationally.

It is also true that admission standards and curricula are not the responsibility of the football coach.

I believe, however, that the coaches, athletic directors, faculty representatives, all of us who are directly concerned with the administration of college football, do have a responsibility to the player for his academic welfare. I also believe we have not faced up to it. We have spent too much time debating the nuances of acceptable recruiting and aid. There is still much work to be done in these areas, especially in recruiting, as I will presently point out. But the emphasis has not been where it should be—on the academic side.

As a matter of fact, we had a most ironic situation in 1953 when the National Collegiate Association's faculty committee, which appoints the members of the football rules committee, influenced them to abrogate unlimited substitution, which permits two-platoon football. It was ironic because, as I pointed out in Chapter XIV, the two-platoon game reduces practice and injuries due to fatigue, and, therefore, is particularly tailored to extra study time.

In considering the academic welfare of the player, the entrance requirements should at a minimum insist that the boy have not only the latent ability, but also the desire to do acceptable work in a legitimate course. By "a legitimate course," I mean one that will be of real assistance to him after graduation in some pursuit other than *participation in professional sports.*

I have absolutely no objection to the exceptionally gifted college athlete's playing his sport professionally for a reasonable number of years, especially if it will help him to pay for postgraduate work or to provide the financial springboard for a solid business investment.

My point is that if the college has prepared the boy to do nothing but play a sport professionally—and, sad to say, some of them are still doing only that for some boys—then the college has failed him and has indicted itself as an educational fraud.

Consider two extremes of boys. The honor student who is also an all-state back presents no problems. He can write his own ticket into any college. Then there is the other extreme—the high-school star who has a diploma, but didn't earn it. He had the potential, but nobody—parents, teachers, principal, coaches—made any real effort to develop his scholarship. On the contrary, the way was eased for him because of his hero status. Yet he does have his diploma, and that is all he, or any other student, may need to get into his own or some other state university.

To enable this marginal academic risk, athlete or not, to show progress toward a degree, some state schools, at times under legislative pressure, have tailored the courses to fit the students. That is why we have the snap courses educators deplore.

I believe there is a solution to this situation. If the marginal student, at the end of his sophomore year, has not made sufficient progress in solid major subjects to advance into the junior class, then award him a diploma as a junior-college graduate. This diploma would close out his college career and make him ineligible for further athletic competition.

The president and faculty now may be prevented by law from refusing admission to the marginal academic risk. But the junior-college diploma would enable them to dispose of him after two years, with at least something to show for his time. It would put the needed checkrein on coaches and sophomoric alumni. They would then be able to resist the temptation to recruit the athlete incapable of solid college work, because they would know they could get at most only one varsity season out of him.

And I am also convinced that such a solution would definitely force high schools to toughen their academic standards.

The responsibility of all concerned for the welfare of the player does not end with academic screening. They should see to it that he is integrated, as much as possible, into the rest of the student body. This should be done in two ways. First, don't have him room in an athletic dormitory; mix him with the other students. Second, in between his sport seasons, get the player interested in such extra-curricular activities as debating, the glee club, student government, and the dramatic society.

I appreciate that the growth of football at many schools has made the athletic dormitory the most feasible investment economically, and that not every campus is blessed with a hall or dormitory setup, such as you see at Dartmouth, Notre Dame, or Miami of Ohio. But I believe the athletic dormitory has made the athlete a displaced professional in the eyes of many undergraduates. It should be possible on most campuses to include at least 20 per cent nonathletes in the athletic dormitories and, if need be, spread some of the players elsewhere on the campus.

It is mainly by emphasizing such integration that we can defeat the propaganda of the pseudo-intellectual that football is for those who lack intellect and all-around ability.

The average college-football player receiving aid today has to be of reasonable mentality even to play the game well. Statistics invariably prove he will average up academically with the rest of the student body. He usually has other interests beyond football, which he would like, given the opportunity, to share and develop with others. They would find him to be an interesting and substantial all-around fellow, whose ability to get along with people is not the least lesson football has taught him.

There isn't any truly serious divergence of opinion today on the subject of legitimate aid. All agree you must "interest" a boy of some athletic ability and academic background and make it possible for him to pay for his education and normal living expenses with some type of institutionally controlled aid.

The Ivy League requires that a boy prove he needs aid. Other conferences don't demand this proof. Actually, in most cases, the need factor levels off, because an athlete usually comes from modest circumstances. In other words, he can prove need to those schools that demand proof and get aid from them just as readily as from those schools that do not require such proof.

Some conferences demand a job program; others do not. I am for job programs, because they emphasize to the boy the value of the education he is getting. At the same time, I have always recognized that it is somewhat paradoxical that an athlete should be forced to carry a job program if the hours he spent working could be better used in study.

I see no essential evil in summer jobs and postgraduate jobs as inducements. The summer job should be a real one; the pay honest. Unquestionably, some schools have natural advantages in providing such jobs. But it is not possible to legislate equality in everything.

The two great evils in the area of recruiting and subsidies—and they rank with snap courses as the *real* abuse of college football—are the illegal inducements tendered the star athlete and the attack on his time, as well as his ethics, by the many schools competing for him.

This should be understood: Few blue-chip athletes are given a special "deal" without the coach's being aware of it, usually with acquiescence, tacit or open, if he hasn't actually been the instigator. And if a coach doesn't know what is going on in the recruiting area, he is too naïve to be coaching.

Most of the recruiting turmoil swirls around the three hundred best secondary-school players in the country. As many as thirty or more schools will be in competition for the service of these players. It is here that the climate is created for the type of illegal aid that has cost more than one school dearly the last several years in lengthy probation by the National Collegiate Athletic Association and its own conference.

And even if the bidding for players should abide by aid codes—a somewhat naïve supposition, I agree—the seemingly uninterrupted visits of emissaries to the home and the school of the star athlete, plus the number of visits he makes to various campuses, seriously impede his study schedule at a time when he should be getting up more steam in the stretch drive for his diploma. This situation has become, in the minds of responsible high-school principals, teachers, coaches, parents, and even the kids themselves, an even graver menace than the aid-code violation.

When the N.C.A.A. permitted one college-financed trip to a campus, it invited young athletes to spend every week-end of their high-school senior year traveling hundreds of miles by plane to some far-off college in which they seldom had any interest.

These trips have become a racket, which is resented by other students not so fortunate. Another sorry by-product is that these star athletes are encouraged to adopt a role of self-importance, often shared by their parents, which is only equaled in the business market of short supply.

Frankly, college coaches would be happy to shed the recruiting problem once and for all. They would prefer to have a reasonably even shake in material and then try to outcoach the other fellow. But they often are caught up in the recruiting race, and even the abuses of it, in self-defense.

How can the blue-chip deal and the raid on the academic time of the high-school player be thwarted or controlled? Without any illusions that I am proffering a cure-all, I believe it would be a strong move in the right direction if the N.C.A.A., at least for a four-year test period, adopted approximately the following program:

1. From the close of a player's junior season until the close of his senior season, let as many colleges as wish get in contact with the high-school star. *But* let there be only *one* contact per player made by each school, and *no* sponsored visits by a player to a campus.

2. By January 10 of his senior or graduating year, let the player have selected his top five choices among the schools in which he is interested.

3. Let his principal then notify the five schools, and permit the player one visit to each of the five campuses between January 10 and April 10.

4. By April 15 let him select his school and deliver to his principal a signed letter of intent, which would be honored nationally.

5. Let the number of boys signing such letters of intent for any one college be held within realistic limits.

In such a program, to a far greater extent than before, the boy would choose the school, rather than the school the boy. The intensity of recruiting would be reduced by being spread out. It would be ended well before the high-school academic homestretch and five months before the boy entered college. The letter of intent would preclude the last-minute raid, with its handmaiden, the illegal inducement.

Most important, by reducing the number of schools trying to interest the boy, the area of policing would be so reduced as to make the illegal offer more difficult to hide. Recruiters would then incline more than before to extol educational advantages in trying to sell the boy. And this is a type of competitive bidding I doubt any of us will object to.

This program would not be difficult to sell. The Southeastern and Southwest Conferences have had a satisfactory letter-of-intent program for some time. Many of their leading coaches, like Georgia Tech's Bobby Dodd, have been pushing for a national letter of intent. Although their conferential programs do not fit in with what I have outlined in all specifics, I feel the necessary adjustments would not be difficult.

The N.C.A.A. would not have trouble passing it, I imagine, because most, if not all, of the smaller colleges, which represent the voting majority, would be for it. Such a program might even give them an occasional crack at one of the top three hundred boys.

I suspect that the Ivy League colleges might vote against it. They have an understandable aversion to any restrictions on their contacting at any time a boy who can meet their academic requirements. As one who did his first head-coaching at an Ivy League school and has always believed in academic emphasis, I can appreciate this position.

At the same time, the Ivy League, whether intending to or not, has in recent years given the unfortunate impression of looking down its nose at any standards more liberal than its own. Here would be an opportunity for the Ivies to join the attack on an abuse that is not entirely unknown even within their own most hallowed precincts.

I can anticipate the objection that a school with a great football tradition like Notre Dame would be listed first by many blue-chip players. But the most popular schools can take on only so many players. The rest would be made available immediately to their second and third choices.

There is no essential problem in this area, because there are plenty of good players to go around. There is seldom as great a difference in ability between the first- and second-flight player as is generally supposed. Also, third- and fourth-stringers, now used sparingly on many squads, would play regularly elsewhere.

A program for reducing the abuses of recruiting is not the exclusive responsibility of the American Football Coaches Association. And a junior-college diploma as an answer to the snap course is primarily the consideration of the president and the faculty. Yet I feel both areas challenge the coaches to take the initiative. Too often in the past they have been laggard in constructive attack on problems other than the rules governing the game on the field.

As a result, they have invited the faculty to take action. Very often these people are not at close enough grips with the subject to come up with reasonable programs.

Thus you have seen the chaotic aid code and subsequent death of the Pacific Coast Conference.

You have seen spring practice abolished by the Ivy League, which had least reason for doing so, since its academic standards brought in a type of player who could best use more coaching.

And you have seen, if I may deliberately labor the subject, the abrogation of pure two-platoon football, which so venerable a friend of the game as Amos Alonzo Stagg, for one, has stated was the best football the game has ever known.

My fellow coaches fail year after year to get the rules committee to accept their recommendations for unlimited substitution because the faculty people, who appoint and control the rules committee, go on record against it. One of the main arguments of the faculty people is that two-platoon ball would require more players.

Why, then, in making their pitch, have not the coaches precluded that argument by concurrently proposing that a rule be adopted preventing more than thirty-six players to suit up for a game? No coach is going to recruit a man he can't suit up, be it even, as old Herman Hickman used to say, three-platoon ball, with the third platoon to go to class.

In the drive for unlimited substitution and in all else, the time is ripe now for the coaches to take intelligent, forceful initiative. If they do, it could well lead to the establishment between themselves and the most die-hard faculty people of a rapport that could be translated into a stronger front in resisting the victory-or-else alumni.

Many years ago, the beloved Professor William Lyon Phelps, famous teacher and critic of English Literature at Yale, wrote:

> The football coaches are a fine body of men who are expert teachers. They have unrivaled opportunities for a good influence on character and temperament. Most of them certainly deserve our respect and admiration. And we must remember nowadays, with the relaxation of discipline . . . that the only part of college life where discipline is maintained is in major sports.

Professor Billy Phelps praised us and in the same breath laid down a challenge that was never more timely than it is today.

In dwelling for a time on football's abuses and suggesting some possible cures, I certainly have not intended to put the game in an improper perspective.

Actually, only a small part of this great game is bad and it is far outweighed by the good. That doesn't mean we should not think and fight for ways to conquer the bad part.

College football always has had and always will have its critics. Dr. Henry Steele Commager, the historian, was quoted thus:

> We provide our students with their sports and games, wasting hundreds of thousands of dollars and enormous energy and time on puerile athletic spectacles which do no conceivable good and actually cause harm to education. Why not sweep away the whole absurd paraphernalia of organized intercollegiate sports, with their insatiable demands for money, their fantastic distraction of energy, their immoral emphasis on winning teams and on spectator interest, and let the students manage their own games and sports?

Too many intellectuals today decry our academic system and deplore the fact that Russia's has a seriousness of purpose that will soon outstrip our best efforts. Yet, as I write this, Russia is dedicated to the winning of the Winter Olympics, and this day staked down a heavy claim in the skating events. I suggest that Russia realizes that the devaluation of competitive sports by some of our intellectuals is a philosophy it would be dangerous to emulate.

In answer to Professor Commager it may not be inappropriate again to quote Professor Phelps:

> There is nothing incompatible in an intense interest in athletics and an equally intense interest in intellectual pursuits. In the fifth century before Christ, the Athenians reached the highest stage of intellectual culture. They were so wildly excited about athletics that they always stopped whatever war was going on to permit the Olympian track meets to be held. Over-emphasis?

As recently as February, 1960, a critical fifty-six-page report by a special committee on admission at Harvard included this:

> Athletic ability should be judged as "significant, extracurricular talent," especially since Harvard's winning football and soccer

teams of 1959 were "brighter" in academic performance than previous losing teams.

Many colleges that gave up football have discovered that they lost a valuable rallying point for *undergraduate morale*. I am not against football as a unifying element for the alumni, but its on-campus benefits for the undergraduate are much more important. We see that even the University of Chicago, where Dr. Robert M. Hutchins left a bleak, deserted stadium as a monument to his colossal error, is looking forward to restoring the sport.

I have emphasized the value of football to the service-academy athlete as a preparation for battle. But does it not have equal value in preparing the civilian-school boy for the battle of life?

If it is the game most like war, it is also the game most like life, for it teaches young men that work, sacrifice, courage, perseverance, and selflessness are the price you have to pay to achieve anything worth while. It helps teach that the poet who wrote that life is not "an empty dream" was far closer to home than the modern lyricist who sang that it is "just a bowl of cherries."

I have often said that football is a game in which youngsters from the "wrong side" of the tracks and those from the "right side" can get to know and to respect each other. It is a game in which the violent body contact it is natural to shy from in everyday living teaches a most important lesson of life—the ability to walk through a storm and keep your head high.

It is a game every youngster who is physically qualified should play at some level where the risks of body contact confront him with a challenge he can learn to meet. The showcase of the college game provides the incentive for the youngster to play and to benefit, even if only from the thrill and satisfaction of making a few tackles.

To sum up my philosophy of intercollegiate football, I believe that:

Football should be secondary to the purpose for which the player is in college.

Championship football and good scholarship are entirely compatible.

The purpose of the game of football is to win, and to dilute the will to win is to destroy the purpose of the game.

So long as these three points are understood, football will continue to be a must for American youth.

Chapter XVII

Where the Black, Gold, and Gray Belongs

The last of the ninety expelled cadets left West Point in mid-August, and two weeks later the remnants of a wrecked squad reported for fall practice. The easing off of shock and nightmare only accentuated pain and bitterness. By letter, wire, and phone, hundreds of people from all over the country had conveyed to me their understanding and consternation; others, their outrage at the action. Some were friends; some, Army men; some, football fans; some, men of headline stature; some, just good, thoughtful people. I answered all, among them one of my old Dayton boyhood friends, Mundey Johnston. Because it sums up well my feelings in those bad times, let me quote the letter here:

> Dear Mundey:
> It takes a devil of a catastrophe for you to write me a letter and of course the same goes with an answer.
> The brutal handling which these fine youngsters have received only reflects the confusion which has attended the entire inquiry. It is enough for me to state that in all my dealings with youngsters I have never known a finer group, so you can understand my personal reaction to the drastic action. I would write you at great length but the problem has worn so heavily on me for the last three months I shall be happy when time has erased some of the bitterness.
> Merle and I expect to take a trip through the west after the football season and we shall stop in to see you. In the meantime, my very best to you and again many thanks for your letter.

Our 1951 squad, before the wreckage, had given promise in spring practice of becoming second only to the Blanchard-Davis teams.

A seven-year era from 1944 through '50, unmatched in Army history and geared to continue, was all over.

To build it back would take years. At least ten years was MacArthur's estimate, and the General was not overstating the case. Army football since 1951 never has approached that plateau of constant excellence it enjoyed from '44 through '50. Nor will it again until the traditional conservatives among our graduates, the Pentagon, and Congress understand that the true over-all function and purpose of the game at West Point can be implemented properly only by professional know-how, unharassed by the uninformed.

In the fall of '51, however, the plight of football was insignificant. The important thing was that ninety young Americans had been inordinately punished because they had become enmeshed in a situation too complex for even some men of maturity to evaluate in its full perspective.

Badly shaken by what had happened, I could not, try as I would, coach with my normal enthusiasm, drive, and patience. There can be no such thing as a football coach who is "an easy man to play for," because those are contradictory terms. I certainly was no exception to the rule. That first season after the expulsions, I must have been harder to play for than ever.

When a coach is laboring to restore order to chaos, he is forced to change, to experiment, to reach. But impatience can impel him to overdo it. Those 1951 players did the best they could. I knew they could not possibly do what I wanted them to do. Yet I went on playing a kind of half-make-believe game with myself that they could. I was impatient with them.

I had to suit up "silhouettes," young men who would have been mainly "B" squadders, and a yearling group that was the most unpromising since I returned from Dartmouth. From day to day they would not know, many of them, what group they would practice with, until they opened their lockers and saw either the black jersey of the "A" squad or the gold shirt of the "B." Although I well realized it was as unfair as it was useless, I could not always prevent myself from comparing them with the squad of the previous spring practice.

If they lacked talent, they lacked nothing else. They paid a terrific price of devotion and sacrifice to an almost hopeless cause—a price I could not bring myself to pay. I did not dream, nor did they, that they were exploiting adversity, that this was the stumbling, seemingly pointless, almost ludicrous beginning of a story that two seasons later would end as a football miracle.

That year we lost four more games than we had in the previous seven seasons put together. Our conquerors were Villanova, 21–7; Northwestern, 20–14; Dartmouth, 28–14; Harvard, 22–21; Southern California, 28–6; Pennsylvania, 7–6; and Navy, 42–7. Everything considered, it was downright astonishing that we were able to beat Columbia, 14–9, by a series of goal-line stands, and The Citadel, 27–6, both in Michie Stadium. In fact, we darned near beat Harvard and Pennsylvania. If that Army squad had won four games, it would have called not only for a saliva test but a Congressional investigation.

As for the Navy game—well, I was not the only one in Municipal Stadium that day who sensed that even the Midshipmen were not getting much kick out of it. They knew the situation. They knew what they were beating.

In our straits, we were compelled to embrace the unorthodox. So when we won the toss, I started the defensive platoon with orders to try a short onside kick-off. The theory was to catch Navy off guard, recover in their territory, maybe even turn their shock into a quick touchdown and delay the deluge. However, Navy was not asleep and seized the ball. They then immediately complicated our problem by breaking out a single-wing attack they had not shown before. Our inexperienced players had not faced a single-wing team, so they did not know how to adjust to it, and there was nothing I could do about it. Navy went right down for a score.

I planned, of course, to give our defensive platoon the proper adjustments as soon as they came to the bench after receiving Navy's kick-off. But they fumbled the kick-off, Navy recovered on our 20 and went on promptly to another score. In less than two minutes they had two touchdowns and I had been unable to get the defensive platoon out of the game. I was finally able to after Navy's second kick-off.

A seriocomic touch was contributed by Fred Meyers, our plebe quarterback, who was starting his first Navy game. At one stage I took Meyers out for a consultation. There on the sidelines, in full view of the 100,000 and with millions more watching on television, I talked seriously and Fred listened attentively. I gave him a final pat on the back and he ran toward the Army huddle like a bolting lead horse. When he got there, he suddenly turned around and raced all the way back to me in front of our bench. It looked dramatic, important. Obviously, he wanted to check some very special point of strategy. I never did tell the press afterwards what went on, because it might have been construed as criticism of a boy who scored our only touchdown. What Fred actually said to me on that return trip was, "Coach, what did you tell me to do? I forgot what you said."

The expulsion affair was the kind of thing a man never gets completely out of his system. I believe, however, that I shoved aside much of my bitterness and became imbued with an unshakable determination to build back football at West Point, as a result of unmistakable evidences that developed after the 1951 season.

It was not enough to have dismissed the ninety youngsters. It now became evident to me that nothing would be more pleasing to a small, hard core of Pentagon people and a few Academy authorities than if I resigned. (This attitude was not shared by West Point alumni who, regardless of their views, were warmly considerate of me personally and remained loyal to Academy football.)

Such a resignation, they would see to it, would be misinterpreted as a tacit acknowledgment by me that the expelled boys had been solely to blame, the decision to dismiss them eminently just, and myself and football the ultimate cause of the whole mess.

There never was any direct pressure brought to bear on me to resign. There might have been, had it not been recognized by more than one high authority that I was privy to the bungling and evasion which was characteristic of the inquiry and the action and, more important, was in possession of irrefutable documentary evidence to back up anything I said. Also pertinent, I had signed in January of 1951 a new five-year contract.

Not long after the Navy game, rumor was active in the press that I was on my way out. Much of the rumor was sparked by a story in the Newark *Evening News*, with a Washington date line and under the by-line of a correspondent. The essence of the story was that a "top Pentagon decision" had determined that Blaik must go, to complete a thorough house-cleaning after the cribbing scandal, even though he himself was not involved.

The story also said that Secretary of the Army Pace, General Omar Bradley, an old West Point center and now chairman of the Joint Chiefs of Staff, and General Lawton Collins, Army Chief of Staff, were the men concerned with "what to do about Blaik" since the cribbing scandal. All three denied the story, as did General Irving through his public-relations officer.

Following the Newark *Evening News* story, writers, in locust formation, descended on me in the football office.

"Nobody has told me I am through," I said. "I signed a contract last year for a five-year period and it is still in force. Let me point out, however, that you will notice all of my assistants are around the football office today, although it is the time of year they normally would be away from the Academy trying to recruit some suitable cadet-athletes for next summer's plebe class.

"We have contacted some boys by letter and phone, but we are not going to go beyond that, until I find exactly what kind of a football program is wanted. Do they want the football for which I was brought back here from Dartmouth eleven years ago? Do they want to go back to the small-college brand of the late 'thirties? Or do they want any football at all? I am waiting to find out."

I recall that same afternoon, Len Elliott, sports editor of the Newark *Evening News*, a top-flight football writer and old friend, was with me in my office, when I was suddenly visited by the little seven- and five-year-old daughters of Assistant Coach Paul Amen. The children looked at the relatively modest appointments of my office and one of them said, "Colonel Blaik, you have three telephones on your desk."

"Yes," I said, "I must look just like a broker." To Len Elliott, I added, "You'll probably put your own interpretation on that."

The other little girl then spoke up.

"Colonel Blaik, you have a rug on your floor, a nice rug."

"Oh, yes," I said, "that's a nice rug, isn't it? Of course, they pull it out from under me every once in a while, but it's a nice rug."

At the Touchdown Club Dinner in New York, a few nights later, I discussed the newest developments with General MacArthur, the honored guest. I told him I felt I was in a position to sit tight. He agreed with my plans.

"Timing is of the essence," he said. "Make no move now."

The rumors died off during the holidays. Then, in mid-January, they sprang up again, propelled by a series of three articles in the New York *Times* by its military strategist, Hanson Baldwin, in which he quoted General Irving. Baldwin left the distinct impression that Blaik football was at the bottom of the trouble and that as an antidote the Academy would be much better off without me. In these articles as in his earlier analyses and comments on the expulsions, Baldwin revealed an abysmal ignorance of Academy football.

As a result of the Baldwin trilogy, conferences were held at the Academy involving the Superintendent, the Athletic Board, and myself. The next day's papers carried an announcement from General Irving, in which he said:

> To clear up any doubt arising from speculations concerning Colonel Blaik's status at West Point, I met with him and discussed the reports of his leaving. Colonel Blaik stated that he intended to stay.
>
> In a recent interview I said that the dual position of director of athletics and head football coach was a temporary organization and that I personally felt that these two positions should be separated from a permanent organization.
>
> I should like to emphasize that I meant this statement to apply generally and not to Colonel Blaik in particular. I feel that Colonel Blaik's professional ability as an administrator, as well as a football coach, adequately qualifies him to wear both hats. As I also stated, the question of the future separation of the two positions will be studied.
>
> We will continue not to overemphasize athletics but will see that they have their proper position in the over-all program.

Special privileges are not accorded athletes at West Point. Their athletic activity is considered as additional training which will assist in preparing them for their regular careers in the Regular Army and Regular Air Force. Certain minor changes in time schedule may be necessary to make room for athletic practice. The maximum practice time allowed at West Point, however, is far below that which is normally desirable for varsity athletics.

General Irving had been through many months of emotional turmoil. Although he and I, in our attitudes toward the dismissals, were veritable light years apart, he showed tremendous strength in resisting the determined efforts by some inside and outside West Point to emasculate our football.

It is an ironic fact that when board reports on the honor system, the tutoring system, and our intercollegiate athletics were in, the only report that did not bring changes was that on athletics. The Army Athletic Association continued to do busines precisely as it had before the expulsions. Even the very worth-while Delafield Fund, which supports the tutoring of young candidates for the Academy, continued to receive official sanction. Loyal contributors to the Delafield Fund were my close friends and confidants, Colonel Hayden W. Wagner and his wife, Betty, and Colonel "Deadeye" Henry and his wife, Dodie.

The critics of Army football were searching for a strong indictment. The uninformed had been led to believe that policy revisions were desperately needed. Yet even to those seeking the indictment, the athletic report turned in by a three-man board revealed that the supposed great wrongs of football were disappointingly trivial. Football got the only clear mandate to continue as before. The Superintendent made no changes other than the small time alterations to help practice, already alluded to in his statement and a change in, not the elimination of, the preparatory-school system.

I have never accorded General Irving anything but my highest respect for his decision. If he had acted otherwise, it would not have surprised the uninformed and it would have pleased many who resented the tremendous popularity of Academy football.

A few days following General Irving's statement to the papers after the Baldwin articles, I received the following note from General MacArthur:

Dear Earl:
 I am in entire accord with your decision to remain at West Point. Irrespective of any other consideration, you had been jockeyed into a situation in which any other decision would have subjected you to complete misrepresentation. Your decision is good not only for you but for West Point, for athletics and for the country as a whole.

As we surveyed them in September, the 1952 squad did not appear to be much of an improvement over '51. The sparse yearling group of '51 were now second-classmen with a year of experience. As I look back upon them now, however, I cannot say there was one superior player among them. As for the upcoming plebe group, they were even fewer than the year previous.

It was something of a pleasant surprise to me that our record showed four victories and a tie out of nine games. With quarterback Jerry Hagan providing a most unrealistic keynote in returning the opening kick-off of the season 84 yards to a touchdown, we defeated South Carolina, 28-7; and went on to beat Dartmouth, 37-7; Virginia Military Institute, 42-14; and Pennsylvania, 14-13. We were tied by Columbia, 14-14; and lost to Southern California, 22-0; Pittsburgh, 22-14; Georgia Tech, 45-6; and Navy, 7-0.

Our conquerors were powers. Southern California, Pacific Coast Conference champions, lost only at Notre Dame, 9-0, in their regular-season finale, and had a 10-1 record including a 7-0 Rose Bowl victory over Wisconsin. Pittsburgh's 6-3 record, in a typically murdering Panther schedule, included victories over Iowa, Notre Dame, and Ohio State. Georgia Tech's Southeastern Conference champions had an 11-0 over-all record, including a 24-7 Sugar Bowl triumph over Mississippi. We were so outsquadded in those games, we could not fight anything but a delaying action.

It is a strange thing that in the two immediate postexpulsion seasons, we were still able to do as well as we did against Pennsylvania, losing by 7–6 in '51 and winning in '52, 14–13. That '52 Penn team had a winning record, including a 7–7 tie with Notre Dame.

Our '52 victory over Penn brought into sharp focus the way we were searching the highways and byways of the Corps for anybody who might help us even a little. It was the last season of unlimited substitution. Without two platoons in '51 and '52, our situation would have been impossible instead of merely desperate. Playing as a substitute halfback on the '52 offensive platoon was a boy named Bill Purdue, who has since died.

Although Bill was essentially a track man, he loved football, and he was the fastest sprinter in the Academy. Just before the Penn game, Bill received word in the dressing room that his father had died. Nevertheless, it was his dad's wish that he play, and Bill wrote himself a glowing page of Army football fame. We were trailing, 13–7, late in the game, and Penn had punted out of bounds near midfield, when Bill took over. He swept Penn's left end for 10 yards. He caught a pass for 10 more. And in the last of the eight plays of the 50-yard drive, he raced around left end from the 2-yard line for the score. Rox Shain converted and we won, 14–13.

Navy, which had a six wins, two losses and one tie record that year, beat us 7–0. Why it wasn't far worse I'll never know. We stopped them on our 2, 6, 14, 16, 27, 32, and, with the aid of the clock at the very end, on about our 3-inch line. We never were able to put together any kind of an attack. The unreasonable hope engendered by the upset of Penn was blotted out. I felt as if we had thrust our heads up out of the ashes only to have them shoved back down again.

After our opening victory over South Carolina, I had received this wire:

A GOOD START EARL. THE BEGINNING IS ALWAYS THE HARDEST PART OF THE ROAD BACK. GO ON AND UP TO THE PLACE WHERE THE BLACK, GOLD AND GRAY BELONGS.

MACARTHUR

That wire may have implied a more immediate climb back than was possible. But it bore an inspiration applicable to the season of 1953—and, for that matter, to football at West Point as long as it is played.

When I come to describe the team of 1953, what they meant to me and, far more important, what they meant to West Point, I cannot praise them enough. Of them, Grantland Rice wrote with eloquent simplicity, "They came up the hard way and there probably has never been a squad with a finer spirit."

True, we did look for better things than in 1951 and '52. Players of the classes of '54 and '55 had been to the wars. The upcoming plebes of the class of '56, while as few in numbers as their immediate predecessors, were of high quality and able to give us some badly needed help right away. We did not harbor, however, the faintest dream of even localized empire. Any prognostication that we would win the Lambert Trophy, emblematic of the Eastern Championship, and be rated No. 14 nationally would have been tabbed fantastic.

A normal amount of injuries as the season advanced cost us solid fullback and punter Fred Attaya, hard-nosed right halfback Mike Zeigler, spirited end Godwin "Ski" Ordway, and a few others. By the time we got down to the Penn and Navy games, the starting eleven and about four substitutes carried the full load.

At quarterback, Peter Vann shared the job to some extent with Jerry Hagen early in the season, but improved gradually to indispensable level. Vann, Pat Uebel, and Tommy Bell at the halfbacks and Gerry Lodge at fullback played 60 minutes against Penn and almost all the way in the Navy game.

As a plebe in '51, Vann was an immature youngster, very boyish in his ways and his thinking. On our return trip from Northwestern that year, he missed our plane and had to be flown back in the Superintendent's plane. This I am perfectly willing to offer as a simply horrible example of football privilege.

As a fellow plane passenger of the Supe, Pete gave us all, in a time of grim bitterness, a fleeting grin. I am quite sure it prompted me to say of Pete to newspapermen: "Why, he's just a boy, that's all."

Just a boy." Even after Pete began to arrive in '53, I continued to refer to him as "just a boy," partly from habit, partly to preclude any premature laudation. This latter motivation was recognized by some writers, who needled me about it. Peter Vann always did remain "just a boy," however, in one respect: his invincible compulsion to throw the long, "home-run" pass in the manner of a back-lot strategist.

By diligent effort, however, Pete became a very fine quarterback. He was a more than acceptable passer and field general, a dependable defensive back in a crisis and, in the department of ball-handling and faking, one of the best we ever had at the Academy.

Tommy Bell, the right halfback, was a strong, swift runner from Mt. St. Michael's in the Bronx. Bell ran with the power and speed of a steam engine. In fact, he even sounded like one, snorting and grunting as he hit and was hit, so that his mates referred to him as "Train" or "Locomotive." Tommy also seemed never quite sure in practice scrimmage whether we were to go full or half speed. He provided more than one laugh by stopping halfway from the huddle to the line-up to ask me, "Colonel, is this for real?"

At fullback, after Attaya got hurt, we had a converted guard in Lodge. He enjoyed his new position much more than guard. Lodge certainly did not have the speed and movement of a superior fullback. He did have above-average straightaway power and became a very effective plunger and faker in the "belly series" that became the bread and butter of our attack.

The left halfback, big, fleet, handsome yearling Pat Uebel, must have scored as many key touchdowns in big games for us in '53 as almost any other back in Army history. In '53 and '54 both Uebel and Bell were among the top echelon of all-time West Point halfbacks.

Uebel was especially effective on a play from the "belly series" designated "Number 54." On this play, Vann faked to Lodge up the middle and covertly eased the ball to Uebel heading outside the defensive left tackle. So precise was the faking, ball-handling and timing on "Number 54," that the end, not knowing where the ball was, often was immobilized long enough so that he took himself out of the play and we didn't even bother blocking him.

Mike Zeigler, Bell's alternate until hurt, made notable contributions, especially in his blocking and running against Duke.

Our defense, inexperienced and ragged in spots at the beginning, and for some time after, gradually achieved a tightly knit cohesion and desideratum peak for the Navy.

The heart of the defense was linebacker Bob Farris, a transfer from Vanderbilt, a top man academically and ultimately First Captain of the Corps. The linebacking of Farris against Navy was as fine as I have ever seen in that game. Unfortunately, the abandon with which he played cost him a detached retina that ended his football. To have played him would have risked an aggravation that might have impaired his sight. Nevertheless, Bob captained our '54 team and helped out with the coaching.

Another linebacker who enjoyed his finest day against Navy, after improving steadily all fall, was Norman Stephen.

The regular guards were Ralph Chesnauskas, an above-average yearling, whose talents included extra-point conversions, and Dick Ziegler, no relation to the halfback. The third guard was Captain Roy Lunn.

I think it epitomized the character of this team and Lunn's inspirational leadership that he was able to handle a difficult situation in a manner that increased his stature. It was not an easy thing to walk out there every Saturday for the toss of the coin and then have to return to the bench and not be in for the kick-off. Roy never let this bother his playing when he did get in. He improved so much that he clearly earned the right to start with his team against Navy. Then he went out and played the best game of his career.

Our end play was handled by Bob Mischak, Lowell Sisson, and a yearling of unusual potential named Don Holleder. Sisson was another who kept improving and hit the top in the Navy game. After Attaya's injury, Sisson did the punting. Mischak developed into a fine pass receiver and on defense he delivered the play that was the pivot, in a real sense, of the entire season. Holleder was a naturally talented pass receiver with outstanding speed, hands, and competitive fire. By 1954 he became just about the most dangerous offensive end in college ranks.

At tackle, the starters were two yearlings, Ron Melnik and Howard Glock, with most of the reserve playing by Joe Lapchick, Jr., son of the famous basketball coach of St. John's. The tackles caused us much concern for a while, but down the November stretch they were clicking with the rest.

Our lack of depth, normal injury attrition, and the return to single platoon, forced by abrogation of unlimited substitution, required us to shift people around. Lodge, fullback on offense, played guard on defense, deploying up front in a six-man line and backing up in a five. Farris, linebacker on defense, was tackle on offense. Glock, tackle on defense, moved over to guard on offense.

Tactically, we used in the main a five-four-two or six-three-two alignment with stunting. In the five-four, Pat Uebel operated as defensive cornerman. Our pass defense, incredibly inexperienced and erratic at first, was really good at the end.

I faced a strange psychological problem. For two years these boys had seen the roughest action. They had lived with the coaching lash, dirt, blood, and defeat. They were afraid of nothing, awed by nothing, eager to do anything asked. But in two years they had played in as upperclassmen, or watched as plebes, eleven Army football defeats. They had won one really big game and come gallantly from behind to do it, against Penn in 1952. Yet, the next week, they had been beaten badly by Navy, even though the 7–0 scoreboard did not show it. In that fall of 1953, nobody in the Corps except turnbacks (those who were repeating a year) had ever seen an Army team beat Navy.

I had to convince our team that they not only could be, but should be, winners. I myself was far from convinced for a long, long time that what I was trying to sell them was actually the truth. But I knew I still must try to sell them. The strange thing is, I not only convinced them, but by the end of the season they convinced me.

Each Monday I would set the tempo of thought and work for the upcoming game. I would sum up the scouting report they had heard on Sunday morning. Then I would ask, "Just who the hell are they, anyhow?"

It was in our only defeat, 33–20 at Northeastern, in the second game, that they learned from their mistakes. It was after that they began developing the cohesion they had been slaving for since 1951. Approaching the Northwestern game, our pass defense was problematical, to state it euphemistically. At a staff meeting that week, Vince Lombardi, my backfield coach, suddenly gave a loud and nervous laugh. We stared at him as if he had been bereft of his senses.

"It's all right," Vince said. "I was just thinking about the first time Northwestern throws a pass. All our backs will fall down."

It was not that bad, but it wasn't good. I was somewhat to blame for putting in a new pass defense. It was basically sound, but because it put too much pressure on one of our halfbacks, it caught up with us.

When our flight home from Chicago was delayed Sunday morning, I seized the chance at our hotel to show the players films of the game and go over what we had done wrong. I emphasized to them that if they did not repeat their mistakes, they could become a real fine football team.

They are a great bunch of youngsters, I thought, flying back to the Point. They looked as if they believed what I said. But how can I be sure?

Our pass defense was much improved in our 27–0 victory over Dartmouth at Michie the next week; in fact, sub linebacker Paul Lasley scored our last touchdown on a 42-yard run with an interception. Our other three scores came on Vann passes, two to Mischak, one to Holleder. In the over-all, however, we were not impressive; the score was 0–0 at the half and 7–0 after three periods.

I was just as well pleased there were no television cameras on the game. They had been trained on our quarters the night before as Ed Murrow interviewed Merle and me on "Person to Person." Our quarters, of course, were cluttered with TV equipment. If television had only been invented by 1921, what a show Ed Murrow could have had making a call on me the day after The Albuquerque Adventure. I was told it cost $20,000 just to set up that TV equipment in our quarters. On that amount I could have operated Fort Bliss football in style, including the purchase of a team.

We now got ready for the date of Saturday, October 10, at the Polo Grounds, the opponent an outstanding Duke team. The Blue

Devils were to win seven, lose two, tie one, and take the Atlantic Coast Conference championship. They had a gifted all-round quarterback in Worth Lutz, a speedy halfback in Red Smith and a typically tough line that included Ed Meadows, an All America tackle. They were undefeated with four straight over South Carolina, Wake Forest, Tennessee, and Purdue, and were distinctly favored to beat us.

This was it. An early-October game, yet the crisis of this season and probably of many seasons to come. I knew we must somehow, now, with no more delay, make our stand. We must beat this team we were not supposed to be able to handle. It was the psychological medicine we needed. How else could I get this Army team truly to thinking the way Army teams had thought before the expulsions?

This game linked Army football past, present and future. If ever we were to rise up from the ashes of 1951, this had to be the day of the beginning.

It was a game never to be forgotten.

The heavy humidity of the Indian-summer day compelled frequent substituting, and Duke could substitute with more impunity than we. On a drive quarterbacked by Jerry Hagan, with Uebel, Bell, Attaya, and Mike Zeigler ramming the ball, we went 75 yards to a 7–0 lead. Five passes by Lutz sparked their 93-yard drive to tie it.

In lightning strokes we again took the lead. One was a Ripleyesque pass on which Vann, surrounded by Blue Devils, shifted the ball to his left hand and passed to Attaya, who ran 18 yards to their 43. Then Vann passed 5 yards (with his right hand) to Uebel in the right flat and Pat streaked 43 yards down the sideline. That gave us a 14–7 lead at the half, but the fresher Duke team dominated the third period and, with Lutz again brilliant, scored but missed the point.

So, we led 14–13, but that one point did not look very large then, and all these years later it doesn't look any larger.

After stopping their drive in the fourth quarter, we mounted one of our own that reached their 19-yard line. With fourth down and about five yards to go, I ordered in a substitute with instructions for our team to go for a field goal. If we made it and took a 17–13 lead, we would have precluded at least the possibility of Duke's subsequently making a field goal to win, 16–13, which might, as it developed, easily have been the case.

In an unprecedented action, however, the substitute never got into the game. The assistant manning the bench telephone for me that day was a young graduate officer, who had been our intrepid tackle of Forgotten Grenadier days, none other than Lieutenant Tiger Howell.

Howell, as I have already pointed out in the '48 tie with Navy, was inclined during battle heat to unsurp the command. Now, at this crucial point of the Duke game, Tiger chased after the substitute I had ordered in with the field goal instructions. "No! No!" Tiger yelled, as he ran after him. "Don't! Don't!" The sub stopped 10 yards from the bench and remained rooted. Army tried a running play, failed to gain, and Duke took over the ball.

I was horrified. Howell had countermanded my order. Tiger says I handed him an Army blanket and said, "Take this. You'll need it in Korea." I would have said that, if I had thought of it, because that's the way I felt. But I do remember that as the enormity of his act dawned on the Tiger, he figuratively returned to the bench on his knees. The suffering of the Army side, from that moment until the end of the game, multiplied by X, could not have equaled the agonies that old Tiger went through.

We turned back to the field. There were about three and a half minutes to play. The first 56½ had been enough to wring a crowd emotionally dry. It was a disappointing crowd, 21,000—New York could not comprehend what was on the line in this game—but they were being rewarded by one of the classics of Polo Grounds or Army history. Those first fifty-six and a half minutes had been sustained drama. Yet they were to prove merely a prelude for what was to come.

Worth Lutz knew Duke could not possibly have the energy, and there wasn't the time anyhow, to grind out a long march from their split T. He had to go for broke. He had to call a long-gainer, and he called it. He took the ball from center, handed it off to halfback Bob Pascal, who headed to his right. Pascal then eased it off to Red Smith coming back to his left. The neat faking decoyed our right side into overcommitment. The speeding Smith broke around them and into the secondary, side-stepped a linebacker and took off in a slight diagonal, headed for the southeast corner of the field.

We on the bench and the Corps of gray in the lower stands behind us shot to our feet in sudden silent, stunned consternation. Smith looked home free. I felt our heads were being pushed down once again into the ashes of 1951.

Then from out of the pack pursuing Smith, one white-jerseyed Army player emerged. It was Bob Mischak, our left end. As Smith raced over the 50-yard line, Mischak was cutting down the distance between them. From the Corps and our bench there welled up a roar of hope and encouragement.

As Smith passed the 20-yard line, Mischak had closed the distance to 3 yards. At the 15, to 2 yards. To attempt the tackle too early would be fatal. "Not yet! Not yet!" I mumbled. Smith was passing the 10-yard line. "Now! Now!" Mischak timed his move perfectly. Right on Smith's heels, he took off, high, far, and hard. He landed on Smith's back and brought him to bay on the 7-yard line.

Smith's run covered 73 yards. In somehow catching and collaring him, Mischak displayed heart and a pursuit that for one single play I have never seen matched. Yet his feat, one of the great defensive plays of football, would have been soon forgotten, had it not been for what followed.

There was a time out. Duke was on our 7, first down and goal to go. There was still three minutes left. Plenty of time to get off four plays.

The Corps, boiling with excitement, poured down out of the stands, and crowded along the sidelines and around our bench.

Our scouting reports showed that in such situations, Lutz called plays inside the tackles 95 per cent of the time. Our defense knew this and played accordingly. In three rushes, Duke got to our 2-yard line. Twice before this day, Lutz had scored from the 4 on quarterback sneaks. Now, with fourth down and 2 yards to go for a touchdown, a kicking tee was thrown in from the Duke bench for a field-goal try. Lutz threw it back off the field. He tried the quarterback sneak and a storm of white jerseys converged on him. When the pile was unraveled, the ball rested two inches from the goal line.

A bedlam of noise was cascading around me. I had called over a substitute, but I could not make him hear what I was saying. I finally got it across to him: "We can't risk a running play! It could mean a safety! Tell Vann to have Attaya kick out immediately!"

Suddenly I felt weak. I felt I must sit down, if only for a moment. I chose the nearest thing handy, one of the yard-line markers. I had forgotten it was made of foam rubber. It collapsed under me, of course. I landed right on my butt, with my feet in the air. Players feared I was suffering from a seizure and helped me up.

Nobody was helping Tiger Howell.

Attaya was back in punt formation, close to the back line of the end zone. He got it off all right, but not too far out. Again, they had the ball, this time on our 35. There were thirty seconds left, still time for them to throw some passes, still time for them to win.

Lutz, a calm field general, husbanded his time well. He was able to get off four passes. We watched each one in a seeming eternity of agonizing suspense. Our boys knocked them all down. The last one was batted down in the end zone by Peter Vann. Maybe he was still "just a boy." But he sure did look ready for long pants. Then it was over, and a roar went up that might have been heard all the way to the Pentagon.

The "brave old Army team" had held fast. The Corps, a delirium of gray, carried the team off the field.

"Tiger," Howell says I said, "you don't have to pack your bags."

In the dressing room, I couldn't see any coaches with dry eyes. I had trouble seeing anybody clearly. We knew for the first time since 1951 we were on our way. This was a gang now that was going to be hard to stop. Pennsylvania? Navy?

"Who the hell are they, anyhow?"

The great moment in the dressing room swelled even greater for me when Ralph Sasse walked in. Ralph was not well. A year and five days later, October 15, 1954, he was to pass on. This was the last Army game Ralph ever saw. What an appropriate game for his last. Ralph well knew what we had been through and what this meant.

A victory over Navy must always be the highlight, the *sine qua non* of Army football, but the dramatic apex of 1953 and the turning point in the road that led upward was reached and passed that day in the Polo Grounds in our 14–13 victory over Duke.

Pennsylvania was next. Let me digress briefly here to say that it was a sad thing for both schools and for Eastern football when the Army-Penn series, which had continued without interruption since 1940, ended after the 1955 game.

Although we dominated the Red and Blue in the Blanchard-Davis era, the games from 1947 through '53 were cliff-hanger classics. Consider the scores. Army's is first: 7–7, 26–20, 14–13, 28–13, 6–7, 14–13, 21–14. I challenge anybody to cite seven consecutive years of competition to top that. Sellout or near sellout crowds attended year after year and stood screaming.

Army always played a fine, spirited game in Franklin Field. Invariably, as Coach George Munger and Rae Crowther, his line coach, told me many a time, Penn came up with some of its very best and most-determined football against the Cadets.

The series ended because the formal Ivy League eight-team round robin, which began in 1956, left Penn with only two non-Ivy League dates. Navy had been playing Penn longer than we had and, for this reason I believe, was given the preference. It might have been possible for Army and Penn to play in early October or even late September. This would have been to our advantage, since the Cadets, because of their regimen, achieve top condition earlier than civilian players. But the caliber and the tradition of the game made an early-season date illogical.

I consider the end of the Army-Penn series as the major casualty of the Ivy League round robin. Most of the time these days, there are thousands of empty seats in Franklin Field and other Ivy League stadia. That Ivy League followers prefer a more varied football diet is the inescapable conclusion.

The '53 game with Penn saw us using only three substitutes: Holleder at end, Lapchick at tackle, and Lasley at center. But we enjoyed the perfect condition and the seemingly bottomless stamina that are the handmaidens of the dedicated team.

After three periods of typically slashing Army-Penn play, we were 14–14. In the last period, passes from Vann to Bell, intermingled with smashes by Lodge, carried us to their 9. Uebel had scored our second touchdown with a 5-yard run on the "54" play. Now Vann called it again, and again Pat shot over, this time with the winning marker.

Vann's defensive play that day was also outstanding. He made several clever key tackles, two of them preventing touchdowns. In the dressing room, I evoked stentorian cheers by announcing, "Today, Peter Vann became a man!"

I also told the players that if they beat the Navy, I would sing them a song afterwards. The small part of me that was "Buttons the Bellboy" had not been subordinated completely, not even in 1951 and those years immediately after.

We could not wait to get at the Navy. The Midshipmen had started strongly, tapered off, and then come back by playing a scoreless tie with Duke. We knew they would be typically "up" and tough. So were we.

I made only one special tactical plan. I recalled Rox Shain, our 1952 converter, from the "B" squad and had him practice a short, diagonal kick-off. If we won the toss, we planned to use the short kick-off to force a Navy fumble and recover it. Should it work, we would enjoy a definite psychological advantage. Such strategy works seldom, but this was one of the times. We won the toss. Navy bobbled Shain's deliberately erratic kick-off and Howie Glock fell on the ball on their 31.

We went for the score in seven plays. Bell snorted through tackle for eight. After Vann missed with a pass, Uebel took a pitchout from Peter and skirted their left flank for a first on the 20. Lodge plowed through for eleven and first on their 9. Then he added four more. On second down, they stopped him. On third down, Vann called "54." He faked to Lodge, eased the hidden ball to Uebel, and Pat was home free. Chesnauskas converted and it was 7–0.

A few plays later came a delirious sequence. George Welsh, then a Navy youngster (sophomore) and later one of their great all-time quarterbacks, had a pass intercepted by Uebel on our 33 and Pat began running it back. Just over midfield, however, he had the ball (which he must have been carrying like a loaf of bread) stolen from him by Navy tackle Jack Perkins, who in turn ran it all the way back to our 9-yard line, where Mischak, the indomitable pursuer, knocked him out of bounds. Navy moved to our four, but incurred a 5-yard penalty. On third down, Bell picked off a Welsh pass on our three.

In the second period, Vann did what he dearly loved to do. He fired a gigantic 51-yard pass to Mischak, who was downed on Navy's 18. Uebel picked up 10 yards in two tries. In two more Lodge shoved it to their 3. Once again Vann called old "54" and once again Uebel shot unmolested into the end zone like the handiwork of a magician. Chesnauskas missed the extra point and we led, 13–0.

Before the half we almost scored again. Lodge, the converted guard, refused to behave like one. He intercepted a pass and ran it back 57 yards to Navy's 8. On this run, Gerry actually reversed his field. On our bench coaches and players blinked in astonishment and rubbed their eyes. This was real magic. Navy had now adjusted, however, to "54" and walled off Uebel. We missed a field goal from the 21.

In the third period, the Midshipmen continued to resist fiercely. They stopped us on their 14 and again on their 4. In between those stands, however, Uebel knocked them out of the box. Pat took a punt on his 30 and returned it 70 yards to a touchdown behind blocking that wreaked carnage all over the field. The key blocks were thrown by Farris, Mischak and Glock. Chesnauskas kicked goal and we led, 20–0.

By scoring three touchdowns against Navy, Uebel set an Army record.

Defensively, we were impregnable in the danger zones. We employed mostly a five-man line, with Farris, Stephen, Lodge, and Uebel, the right cornerman, as linebackers. In this way, we were able to harry Welsh, cover the receivers, and stop the long gain. On short-yardage situations, we tightened into a six-three. It was against our substitutes with less than a minute to go that Navy scored. The final was 20–7.

It was the core and fire of our defense, Farris and Stephen, that I first saluted for the newspapermen.

"It was a marvelous all-around exhibition," I said, "and it dates back to September 1, the day we started practice. What makes it all the more marvelous is the fact that many of the boys out there today also played against Navy two years ago when we were trampled, 42-7. We're not out of the woods completely yet, but we're at the point at least where the timber isn't so tall.

"Today we were up a little more than Navy, but believe me, I'm very much surprised at our progress this season, more surprised even than you fellows."

Before the newspapermen arrived, I talked to the players alone.

"I never have coached a team," I told them, "that gave me more than you did. I never have coached a team that has given me as much satisfaction. Considering all the conditions since 1951, you have done more for football at West Point than any other team in the history of the Academy. And now, I'm going to keep my promise. I told you if you beat the Navy, I was going to sing you a song. So here goes:

"Down, Down, Down went the NAYvee——"

That was as far as I got. Their roars drowned me out. Somehow, I didn't mind. I never could carry a tune.

Chapter XVIII

You Are My Quarterback

If you doubt the axiom, "An aggressive leader is priceless," if you think grandstand quarterbacks are few at West Point, if you prefer the air arm to the infantry in football, if you are not convinced we recruited cadet-athletes of superior leadership potential, then you must hear the story of Donald Walter Holleder.

The saga of Holleder stands unique in Army and, perhaps, all college gridiron lore. At the end of his second-class season, Don was ranked the most dangerous offensive end in college. Although he had substituted in 1953 and missed two of the games in '54, his two-season pass-completion totals were thirty-two for 781 yards and nine touchdowns. A quick, competitive, six feet two, 187 pounds, he was also above average defensively and was selected for most of the All America teams.

If Holleder had not been headed for a soldier's career, there is not a professional team which would not have placed his name at or near the top of its draft list. I am by no means overstating it when I say Don had the ability and temperament to have developed into another Don Hutson.

Yet it is not as a great end that we remember Holleder so much as a boy who gladly gave up personal glory for the good of the team. This took place in 1955 when I asked him, although he had never played in the backfield, to become our quarterback.

In the end Holleder won a personal satisfaction that could not be matched if they had ushered him into the Football Hall of Fame. In the end he led a dedicated Army team to a victory few people thought possible in a manner that will always seem incredible.

The Holleder story was born of the dearth of material, especially in key positions, which dogged West Point football for most of the 'fifties. This traced mainly to a self-consciousness in some authorities about successful teams. Among the conservatives of academic preoccupation, this seed of disquietude is always there, and it was nourished by reaction to the expulsions. Consequently, an unrealistic restriction on numbers in our recruiting resulted in an insufficiency of material with ultimate varsity major-game potential in the plebe class each July. This dearth set in with the 1951 plebes (although the expulsions had nothing to do with the paucity that year) and continued through my final six years at the Academy.

From 1951 through '58, we never had enough tools to do the job right; no, not even in the undefeated Lonely End season of '58. The seasons of '55 through '57 especially—and the expulsions by that time were four to six years in the background—found us in predicaments which the average major civilian college coach would chafe at as untenable, if not downright intolerable. My assistants and I realized this acutely at the time. It was re-emphasized later in many letters they wrote me after they became head coaches elsewhere.

"When I compare the personnel we have and we play against," was the theme, "with what we had to work with at West Point for the most part, I shake my head in wonderment how we ever got by with it."

Much of the time we lacked such essentials as quarterbacks and linebackers. Between Pete Vann's last season of '54 and the development of Joe Caldwell in '58, there was nobody in the Corps with the training and potential talent to take over at quarterback. The one or two plebes of ability who did show up were lost by academic failure. We experimented again and again. Finally, we had to take men from other positions and try to remake them into quarterbacks.

It was because I had no alternative that in 1955 I turned to Holleder.

When you are forced to switch personnel around in building a first team and when reserve strength is sparse, injuries are murderous. To make it worse, a fiendish fate decreed that our injured should include just about every "blue-chip" athlete we had.

Bob Kyasky, who entered in '53, could scarcely have missed becoming one of West Point's greatest backs. As it was he played splendidly for us in three different spots: left half, full, and quarterback. All his days at the Point, however, he was plagued by injuries. In plebe season, he broke a collarbone. He rebroke it in the opening '54 game with South Carolina. When the collarbone finally mended, he hurt a knee so severely in '55 fall practice that he ran only a handful of plays late in the season. The knee was operated on the following winter and hampered his effectiveness in '56.

Gene Mikelonis, who entered in '55, promised from plebe year to become one of our finest runners, and he was an honor student as well. Against V.M.I. in his first varsity game, Gene gained 90 yards in eleven carries. On the next one, he tore knee ligaments so badly he never played again.

Bob Anderson, All America left halfback in '57 and '58, suffered a bad knee injury against Illinois last year. Even though he scored twice against the Air Force and once against Navy, Bob actually hobbled through the season.

If Kyasky, Mikelonis, and Anderson had remained whole, it would have made considerable difference to Army football the last six seasons.

The loss of Bob Farris as linebacker for the '54 season, due to the detached retina he suffered in the '53 Navy game, probably kept us out of the national-championship class. Our two losses, to South Carolina, 34–20, in the opener, and to Navy, 27–20, in the finale, traced to the same basic weakness: inability of our linebackers to key the containment of such enflanking maneuvers as pitchouts, options, and screen passes.

Our '54 team, while spirited, also lacked the "hungriness" of those embattled Cadets of 1953.

Between those losses to South Carolina and Navy, our '54 team won seven straight. At the end of the year, the Associated Press actually ranked us No. 7 nationally. For a long time we were able to camouflage our defensive inadequacies by an explosive, spectacular attack. Our line was relatively small, but it was tough and quick-hitting. The passing threat of Vann to Holleder and to our backs coupled with the thunder-and-lightning runs of Bell, Uebel, Kyasky, and Mike Zeigler, when able to play, posed a nightmare to defenses.

Bell became a headline breakaway artist. The "Locomotive" ran for almost 1,200 yards, more than all the rest of the backs combined, and scored 12 touchdowns. Uebel, shifted from left half to full, gained 561 yards. Bell and Uebel each gained over 100 yards and scored a touchdown against Navy, enough to win with a good defense. Zeigler was hampered by a bad back injury, incurred in a fall down a flight of stairs. Yet he was a power for us in the victories over Michigan, Dartmouth, and Duke, until he got his jaw broken in the Duke game.

Despite our defensive problems we went into that '54 season under what were for me the happiest conditions since the superintendency of General Bryant Moore. The new Supe was an old teammate, fellow assistant coach, and friend, Lieutenant General Blackshear M. (Babe) Bryan. The new Commandant was another old football man, fellow assistant coach, and friend, Brigadier General Edwin J. Messinger. Ed Messinger had been an outstanding end under both Biff Jones and Ralph Sasse.

From personal experience, Generals Bryan and Messinger knew the value of the football-trained cadet in combat crisis. Neither, however, would lean forward or backward in treatment of a cadet-athlete. They merely applied justice, fairness, and good old horse sense. They understood the Corps.

The Supe and the Com sweated and suffered with me through our football problems. They gave every help they could and they never second-guessed. They were quietly distraught when the Com was forced in good conscience, much as he disliked doing so, to approve a "slug" imposed on Don Holleder for a summer violation while the second class was visiting the installations at Fort Benning, Georgia.

Holleder's offense was not serious but it was "sluggable." To be "slugged" meant that for thirty days he was confined to his room, except for classes, meals, drills, and one hour's exercise a day; and that, along with other "slugged" cadets, he had to walk off his punishment in the barracks area for a total of twenty-two hours. Don was also reduced to the rank of cadet private. Worst of all from his and our point of view, he could not play football until the thirty-day period was up.

An explanation of Holleder's action which provoked the "slug" is necessary, I think, for two reasons. I have referred more than once to the cadet's severe disciplinary regimen, and this is a striking example. Also I would prefer not to risk a conjecture by the reader that Holleder committed some such heinous offense as surreptitiously peddling packets of marijuana to fellow cadets in the shadows of the statue of General Sylvanus Thayer, Father of the Academy.

Holleder's second class, "The Cows" in cadet parlance, spent the first half of the summer of '54 visiting military installations throughout the country. In the month of July, they were at Fort Benning. These summer trips included a social side cadets looked forward to. On several occasions Holleder dated a girl from nearby Columbus. On their last night at Benning, Holleder's class was restricted to cadet barracks, to pack and prepare for their thirty-day leave, which would begin the next morning.

Earlier in the month many valuable articles belonging to cadets had been stolen from barracks. A cadet guard had been ordered. This last night Holleder was assigned to guard duty in front of the barracks from 10:00 to 12:00. The duty was quiet and there was a public telephone inside the building. Don decided to leave his post long enough to phone his Columbus girl friend and say good-bye.

He put through the call and was awaiting the connection when a tactical officer strode into the barracks. He asked Holleder what he was doing and Don explained. The officer ordered him to hang up the phone and return to duty. The next morning, Holleder left for his home in Rochester, New York, and thought no more of the incident.

The tactical officer reported Holleder for deserting his post. The report, however, was late in arriving at West Point. Otherwise, Holleder might have been able to begin his punishment early enough to work it out before the first game.

As it was, General Messinger processed it as rapidly as possible, but fall practice was already several days under way. When Messinger informed me of the offense and punishment, I called Holleder to my office and asked him what kind of trouble he was in.

I took him completely by surprise. He did not, at first, know what I was talking about. He had placed little importance on the phone-call episode and had obviously forgotten it. When he realized he could not play in the first two games against South Carolina and Michigan, he was a heartbroken youngster.

He felt no worse than the Supe and the Com. More than once the Supe told me Holleder was the type he would like to have as an aide, and the Com felt the same way. Yet, there had been a mild dereliction involved which was "sluggable." To have ameliorated the punishment for Holleder in any degree would have invited charges of favoritism.

General Bryan frequently left his private box in Michie Stadium to sit with Colonel Red Reeder and other friends in the press box, where he perspired and proffered tactical observations. At the South Carolina game, his friends, knowing his true feelings about the Holleder case, needled him gently, even to the extent of the following outlandish doggerel snatch:

> *Blackshear, Blackshear, have you any pull?*
> *Yes sir, yes sir, three stars full.*
> *One for my master and one for my dame,*
> *But none to get Holleder into the game!*

I doubt Holleder's presence would have been enough to turn the South Carolina game our way. We played too poorly on defense to deserve victory. South Carolina had prepared long and well. They came directly from their September training camp to our game before returning to their campus for the opening of school. As happens so often to teams which point for Army, and they all do, the Gamecocks were way down the next week in losing to West Virginia, 26–6.

At our Sunday-morning meeting the Cadets fully expected me to dress them down. I knew it wasn't necessary. I knew they would improve defensively at Michigan the next week, if only out of self-reproach. As a West Point team which had lost its opening game in Michie Stadium, they appraised themselves as pariahs. I also knew that, even with Kyasky out with the collarbone he had reinjured against South Carolina, we could move the ball on anybody.

Yet I faced the trip to Ann Arbor with real trepidation. Our intrinsic defensive instability could be catastrophic against this slick, offensive-minded team. The Wolverines were to write a 6–3 over-all record, including 5–2 in the Big Ten. They were a good team. I knew they would be "up" for us. Their proud football tradition had not accepted four straight defeats from Army with equanimity. The South Carolina game, if it did nothing else for us, at least established us in the quietly happy role of 3–1, 13-point underdogs.

We upset Michigan, 26–7. No outcome that fall caused greater shock. It was basically an offensive-possession victory. We tore into them like wildcats. Our quick line rolled theirs back. With Vann as pilot, Bell, Uebel, and Mike Zeigler slashed and stabbed on short, medium, and long-gainers in an impressive show of infantry. It was a hot muggy day, but we thrived on it. Bell scored twice, on 10 and 48-yard runs. Their only score came on a second-period 46-yard pass.

Although it was a fine team effort, we derived special satisfaction from the work of Mike Zeigler and Ski Ordway. Zeigler spent much of the summer in the hospital with a back injury that threatened to finish his football. Ordway was one of that legion who overcame limited talent by desire. Ski was an offensive center as a plebe and yearling in the dark days of '51 and '52. In '53, he played end until injured. In September of '54, seeking to switch-patch our defensive sieve in spots, we moved him to right tackle. Ordway's sixty-minute job against Michigan was a principal reason why we made our best defensive showing of the year.

That same day we beat Michigan, Saturday, October 2, was also memorable for my former assistants. Stu Holcomb's Purdue team upset Notre Dame, 27–14, to end a thirteen-game Irish streak; Andy Gustafson's Miami took Baylor, 19–13; Bob Woodruff's Florida handled Auburn, 19–13; Murray Warmath's Minnesota ran over Pittsburgh, 46–7; Sid Gillman's Cincinnati topped Tulsa, 40–7; and Clarence (Chief) Boston's New Hampshire triumphed over Rhode Island, 33–7.

We celebrated the return of Holleder the next week by thumping Dartmouth, 60–6, and then went on to defeat Duke, 28–14, and Columbia, 67–12.

The victory over Duke, at Durham, was nearly as impressive as the scotching of Michigan. The Blue Devils, 7–2–1 for the season, were

Atlantic Coast Conference champions and defeated Nebraska in the Orange Bowl. Coming into our game, they had swamped Penn, edged Tennessee, and tied Purdue. Passes from Vann to Holleder and our running attack swept us to three touchdowns in the first quarter. We had the Blue Devils out of the game before they knew what hit them. Hurricane Hazel had torn through Durham only the day before. For all Duke knew, Hazel was still in town.

Although our victory over Virginia the next week was a surprisingly close 21–20, we were given high national rating. We were being generally regarded as the best in the land on attack. We may very well have been that.

On November 6 we played in Yale Bowl for the first time in eleven years. After the expulsions, we had scheduled games with Yale for '54 and '55. I had hopes these games could be the first steps in restoring what had been an old, profitable, and enjoyable rivalry to new permanency. The crowd, I am sure, hoped the same. There were a sellout 73,600 there, the largest Bowl turnout in a quarter of a century.

We were favored, but it was thought Yale would make a battle of it. They had the personnel to do it. They had won their first four games and were to make a 6–2 record for the year. But the Ivy League had banned spring practice, beginning in '52, and had consequently devalued the importance of football in the minds of its players. This was very evident to me in that '54 game in New Haven. On our first play from scrimmage, Bell broke over their left guard on a lightning dive-tackle hand-off from Vann, veered by their linebacker in almost the same motion, and raced 61 yards down the sidelines for a touchdown. Yale never recovered and we went on to bury them, 48–7. It was the highest score in our series and the second highest ever made against a Yale team. Kyasky, though playing with his collarbone strapped up, gave his special rooting section from nearby Ansonia, Connecticut, much to cheer about.

I sat through that Yale game with a 103-degree fever. A heavy bronchial cold had been knifing at me for over a week. When I returned to the Academy immediately after the game, it was discovered I had pneumonia and I was ordered into the post hospital. As a consequence, when we played at Penn the following week, for the first and only time in my twenty-five seasons as a head coach I was not with the team, and not by choice. (I had missed Army games to scout Notre Dame against Navy in 1944, '45 and '46, but that *had been* by choice.)

In my absence Bobby Dobbs, who has been head coach of Tulsa since 1955, handled the Cadets and did well. We won, 35–0. Bell scored twice and contributed runs of 32 and 37 yards. Vann threw two touchdown passes to Holleder. Penn was caught in the switches. Their schedule had been overloaded according to the blueprints of the "Victory for Honor" program of Harold Stassen, Penn president, and Coach Steve Sebo did not have the troops to handle it. The worst thing that can ever happen to any football coach is to get caught without material.

I was out of the hospital the week after the Penn game but feeling wobbly. This was not only because of the aftereffects of pneumonia but also because of the prospect of meeting what was to my mind the finest of the nine Navy football teams coached by Eddie Erdelatz. The '57 Midshipmen may have been tougher on defense, but not by much. The '54 attack was more versatile and dangerous. Quarterback George Welsh was at peak and so was the gifted, fiery Ron Beagle at end. The personnel was deftly balanced, deep and well organized. It was an interesting, pleasing team to watch, unless you were on the other bench.

It is true the Middies lost two games that year, a 6–0 heartbreaker to Notre Dame, in which they fumbled a winning chance on the goal line, and a 21–19 upset by Pittsburgh. Red Dawson, the regular Pitt coach, became ill the week of the Navy game, and the team was taken over by the athletic director, Admiral Tom Hamilton, who had, of course, played and coached at Annapolis with Erdelatz one of his assistants. The Admiral, a very inspirational fellow, inspired the Panthers to beat his alma mater.

Navy, however, won all the rest of their games and manhandled the strong Duke team, 40–7. They later went on to the Sugar Bowl, where, as thoroughly false underdogs, they completely dominated Mississippi, the Southeastern Conference champions, 21–0. I went down to see that game. I kept my own counsel, except to answer, when asked, that it would not be wise to underestimate Navy. I did not wish to destroy their position as underdogs, but I knew their class and was not in the least surprised at what happened.

Consider Navy's performance against Ole Miss in the Sugar Bowl, their decisive defeat of Rice in the Cotton Bowl three years later, Pittsburgh's two drag-out, if losing, battles with Georgia Tech in the Sugar and 'Gator Bowls and the games that Syracuse lost to Texas Christian and won from Texas in the Cotton Bowl. Accumulatively, all this should by this time have convinced our Southern and Texas friends, justifiably proud of their football as they are, that the game played today by the top Eastern independent group is about as effete as a bowie knife or a derringer.

I would say that of the Eastern teams I have named, the best, except for Syracuse of last year, was that '54 Navy team. Good as they were, however, we could have beaten them. Welsh accounted for their four touchdowns, passing for three and running for the other, which he set up with a pass.

We had a chance to get a death grip on the game late in the second period, when we took the lead for the first and last time, on two rapid-fire scores. We recovered a Navy fumble close to their goal line and Uebel smashed over, his fourth touchdown in two Navy games. Then, soon after, Vann connected with Kyasky on a lightning pass-and-run long-gainer and we were ahead, 20–14, with little time left in the half.

At this point, Pete Vann decided to try an onside kick-off. I had instructed the squad that under certain conditions the onside kick-off should be considered useful, but only if I sent in the order. Now, after Kyasky's touchdown gave us the 20–14 lead, there was a line of reasoning to support an onside kick-off. If we could recover and score another quick one, it might well shake Navy's confidence. Furthermore, considering the dangerous Welsh-directed attack and our own known defensive shortcomings, 20–14 was far from a safe margin.

The trouble was that Vann, momentarily forgetful, made two mistakes. First, he acted without orders. Second, he informed Chesnauskas, who was to kick the ball, but did not tell the rest of the team. For that reason, in part, our chances of recovering the kick were not sanguine. Navy fell on the ball and Welsh soon after got off a long scoring pass into the end zone just before the half ended. Navy converted, led, 21–20, added another six points early in the second half and never lost control thereafter. The final was 27–20.

I have detailed the background of the onside kick, certainly not in criticism of Vann, whose place in our football was secure, but to explain for the first time what actually did happen. I did not order the play, but I could not say so at any time after the game. To have said so would have been to criticize Vann. Public criticism of any player cannot be found among my coaching sins.

I repeat, the play in concept was not bad thinking by Vann. His mistake of neglecting to tell nine of our players was one that any boy could make in the heat of battle. Pete was especially unfortunate because the scoring pass that followed was one that not even so talented a tosser as Welsh could have completed more than once in a playing career.

Welsh would be back at quarterback for Navy again in 1955. This problem transcended all others for us. It loomed especially formidable by contrast with our own quarterback situation. Pete Vann would not be back. There were no 1954 reserves for the job. There was nobody up from the plebes to be developed. I experimented with several backs at the position the first week of spring practice. It wasn't working out. It was then that I thought of Holleder.

I knew Don never had played quarterback, never had played in the backfield. He had been an All America end, a great pass receiver, in 1954. Normally, he could be expected to be even more brilliant as a first-classman. Yet, I had nobody to throw the ball to him. He himself threw left-handed. I knew that in the one season of eligibility he had left, he never could possibly develop into a superior passer, but he might do well enough to get by.

On the plus side, Holleder was a natural athlete, big, strong, quick, smart, aggressive, a competitor. I knew he could learn to handle the ball well and to call the plays properly. Most important, I knew he would provide bright, aggressive, inspirational leadership at the key position of the game.

No matter what might happen before the Navy game, I reasoned that we would have no chance to win it, not with Welsh as their quarterback, unless we had a quarterback who could match him at least in dynamic leadership. This was a quality I knew Holleder to be rich in.

On a Sunday afternoon in April, I asked him to come by my office.

"Don," I said, "I am worried about the quarterback position. I have nobody to fill Vann's job. I have looked and looked without success. How would you like to take a shot at it?"

"Colonel," he said, "I never have played in the backfield in my life."

"I am well aware of that," I said. "But I want you to go back to your room and think this over. Then come back to see me tomorrow. One other thing. Do not say a word about this to anyone. Keep it entirely to yourself."

Holleder told me afterwards he did not sleep much that night. He tossed and turned and the problem with him. He wanted morning to come quickly, and he didn't want it to come at all. He looked a little haggard when he came up to see me after his first class Monday morning. He said that if I thought he could do the job, he was willing to make a try at it. I told him if he should become unhappy in the experiment, he could always go back to end. We talked some more. As he left, I said, "Turn in your old end number and get a new one for the quarterback position."

So Don Holleder turned in No. 48 for No. 16. Sixteen is a football number I'll never forget.

From the beginning, the experiment seemed jinxed. Holleder needed every second of practice he could get in his new and taxing assignment. But he was at it only a week when he cracked an ankle in scrimmage and had to wear a cast until the end of May.

That spring and fall, the switch of the All America end to a position he never had played before and, of all places, quarterback, dominated every story written about the Army team. In the past, I had made many switches in personnel without undue questioning or doubt by press, public, and Academy people. The reaction always had seemed to be that they felt I knew what I was doing.

This was different. Admittedly, I never had made so revolutionary a change or taken what seemed to be such a steep gamble. Even such an old friend and patient analyst as Allison Danzig, of the New York *Times,* thought I was making a mistake and said so. Al was far more temperate than others.

It was suggested that four losses in our last five games with Navy (due in considerable measure, of course, to the influence of the expulsions) had driven me into a panic. It was also hinted that since I had passed my fifty-eighth birthday, I might well be approaching the borders of my football second childhood. Maybe they ought to take that football away from Blaik altogether and buy him a nice set of electric trains or an Erector set.

In their preoccupation with the Holleder *cause célèbre,* most people were overlooking our other problems, and, brother, we had them! The injury to Kyasky's knee was a major blow. Mike Zeigler got "slugged" by the tactical department, and after he came off the barracks area, he never did regain his '54 form. Uebel, a fine team captain, was our only returning physically able, experienced back. For our running game, we had to rely on '54 reserves of limited talent and yearlings, and even some of these were injured.

To get a respectable first line, I was compelled to switch men around continuously and to use yearlings. Only end Art Johnson played the position he held down in '54. I switched the '54 guards, Ralph Chesnauskas and Flay Goodwin, to tackle, where we had lost the first three men by graduation. Later, when material became sparse at end, I had to try Chesnauskas there, which, of course, left us short at tackle. Dick Stephenson, a '54 reserve tackle, I shifted to center. Jim Kernan, an outstanding center prospect in the yearling group, suffered a severe neck injury, which sidelined him for the year. Two yearlings move in as regulars: Stan Slater at guard and Bill Saunders at end.

Here, then, was an Army team full of soft spots, any one of which might contribute heavily to a defeat. Yet whenever we lost a game—and we lost three, to Michigan, Syracuse, and Yale—all the blame was placed on Holleder and the "silly old man" who had shifted him from end to quarterback.

It is true that Holleder's seasonal passing record, twenty-two completions out of sixty-five tries, was mediocre. Yet, those twenty-two were good for six touchdowns, only two less than George Welsh's total for the year. The point is, however, that if Holleder's receivers had not been below average, he would have enjoyed a much better percentage of completions. It was argued none of his receivers could compare with himself in that department. How true! But who in the heck was going to throw him the ball?

The heat was off temporarily as we trounced Furman in a warm-up and then beat Penn State, 35–6. Against the Nittany Lions, Holleder passed for one touchdown and ran for another. More comment was excited, however, by our holding Lenny Moore, their brilliant halfback, and later the Baltimore Colts star, to 65 yards and one touchdown on a twelve-yard run.

These two victories did not mislead me into wild optimism, because I appreciated the basic structural weaknesses of our team. Yet, partly from habit, I suppose, I had some hope as we went out to Ann Arbor to play Michigan for the fifth time. They were long overdue and they let us have it good, 26–2. We helped them plenty by fumbling eleven times. They recovered seven, some of them deep in our territory. Holleder completed only one out of eight passes for 15 yards and even that one was ultimately fumbled and recovered by the Wolverines. Don definitely did not resemble Johnny Unitas, but none of us was very good.

Grandstand quarterbacking is something a coach must accept as part of his job. But it is undeniably irritating, especially when the critics are not equipped with an over-all knowledge of the background behind decisions. Grandstand quarterbacking is especially normal to a military school, because the very terms, "field general," "strategy," and "tactics," immediately connote war.

What man in training to be an officer or what commissioned officer, what noncom or private, for that matter, who has a love for football, does not fancy himself a potentially great quarterback? Strange, indeed, then, I could uncover no other quarterback at West Point in '54 but Holleder.

Back at the Academy on Monday following the Michigan game,

I had a visit from the Supe, General Babe Bryan. Our old friendship permitted easy, frank discussion on both sides.

"Red," he commented after a time, "the entire post is critical of the Holleder operation."

"I know it, Babe," I said. "But you tell me. If it's not Holleder, then who?"

"You've got me there," he said.

"Babe," I went on, "much of the blame for the Michigan game is being laid at Holleder's door and mine. Actually, Don had relatively little to do with it. He is not smooth at his job yet, that's for sure, and he will still have some tough times ahead. But I know that he will develop and he is our only hope against Navy.

"I wish you'd do something for me, Babe," I continued. "I wish you would talk it up for Holleder. If you make your support known, the rest won't criticize him so openly. There would be less chance of it then getting back to the boy and, goodness knows, he's under enough pressure as it is."

General Bryan himself never was critical at any time of the Holleder experiment. After the Michigan game, he may have wavered, but I do not know that he did; and if he did, it was not for long and he kept it to himself. His support and that of the Com were a big help right down to the Navy game. With the both of them publicly behind the switch, the rumbling was driven underground for the most part, but it was unmistakably there.

At just about the time General Bryan left the football office that Monday after the Michigan game, Holleder left his quarters to keep a scheduled appointment with me. As he walked to the gymnasium, he could not help hearing a conversation between two cadets who were close on his heels but unaware of his identity.

"I knew even before the Michigan game," said one, "that Colonel Blaik was making a big mistake changing Holleder from end to quarterback."

"You've maxed it" (cadet parlance for a perfect mark), said the other. "Don used to be a pretty good end, but either one of us could play quarterback better than he can."

This dialogue did not tend to alleviate the gloom that hung

heavily around Holleder. He realized their attitude was pretty general on the post. When he arrived at my office, I could see he was downcast.

I sensed he thought I was going to tell him to forget about quarterback and go back to end. This would now have been a bitter disappointment to him. He had the built-in aversion of any real leader to failing to meet any challenge. As a natural athlete he was finding the quarterback position, for all its problems, the most interesting, exhilarating on the field. He had to know not only his own job but all the others, too. He had to probe for enemy weaknesses and exploit them. This enthusiasm he was developing was another reason why I realized that to lose confidence in him would be rank shortsightedness.

I put an arm around his shoulder. "Don," I said, "I thought you played a real fine game against Michigan. The fumbles were not your fault. As far as your passing is concerned, we will keep working on it. I have every confidence in you. It doesn't matter what anybody else thinks or says around this place. I am coaching this Army team, and you are my quarterback."

Holleder was not a boy given to emotionalism, but his eyes filled up. He mentioned the conversation of the two cadets he had just heard.

"Walking up the stairs just now," he said, "I was going to offer to go back to end and fully expected to get my old number back. But I was praying you would say just what you have said. I'll show everybody around here that I can do more for the team at quarterback than I could any place else."

The following Saturday we played Syracuse in Michie Stadium, in one of the heaviest rains in Academy history. The storm blew in on Wednesday and raged for five solid days through Sunday. We were not a very good team under any conditions, but on a wet field we were psychologically impaired before we started. Quick speed, a hallmark of our football, never thrived on a slow terrain. (It had been a clear day at Michigan, but the gridiron, uncovered during a rain, was wet.) Against Syracuse, we could do nothing in the slippery quagmire. Jim Brown, now the Cleveland Browns' paragon of pro running, was approaching stardom as a junior. Jim showed a sure foot in the messy going and set up their two touchdowns with his key gains. The score was 13–0.

On Sunday night it was still raining. As Holleder left the mess hall with his roommate after supper, he heard more cadet conversation critical of his quarterbacking. A brief furlough by the grandstand quarterbacks followed the next two games, however, as we beat Columbia, 45–0, with Pete Lash making a 72-yard touchdown run, and knocked over a good Colgate team, 27–7. In the Colgate game, Holleder threw three touchdown passes, to Chesnauskas for 30 yards, to Art Johnson for 42, to Mike Zeigler for 17, and himself ran for the other score. The Post and the newspapers even chirped a little that maybe Blaik was right after all.

Then we lost to Yale, 14–12, at New Haven. We encountered more miserable weather in the Bowl and we were even sloppier than the rain and mud. We fumbled repeatedly, giving Yale one opportunity after another, and they finally capitalized. The grandstand quarterbacks returned from furlough.

The farewell game with Penn the next week, a 40–0 victory, carried no more meaning than the 35–0 triumph of the year before.

So we were distinct underdogs going into the Navy game. The Midshipmen had a 6–1–1 record, including a thumping victory over Pittsburgh. Their big edge lay in the poised, experienced George Welsh at quarterback, the nation's leader in passing statistics, smooth ball-handler, clever play-caller, fine leader.

As for Army, well that stubborn, half-daffy old man up the Hudson had Holleder, and pretty soon he was going to have to admit, whether he liked it or not, that he was stuck with him.

All season long, I had the impression they were expecting me to return Holleder to end at any moment. When I stayed with him after the losses to Michigan, Syracuse, and Yale, they imputed it to my stubbornness: "Blaik made a mistake and he knows it, but he won't admit it."

They couldn't seem to believe that I believed in Holleder, but he knew I did, and that was all he wanted to know.

The night before the Navy game, we bivouacked as usual at the Manufacturers Country Club outside Philadelphia. Around 9:30, after we returned from the movies, I took the team for our usual pre-taps stroll around the golf course. At one point, I stopped. It was my habit of years to tell the squad a bedtime story.

"I have grown weary," I said, "of walking across the field to offer congratulations this year to Bennie Oosterbaan of Michigan, Ben Schwartzwalder of Syracuse, and Jordan Oliver of Yale. Now I'm not as young as I used to be, and that walk tomorrow, before one hundred thousand people (and fifty million more on television), to congratulate Eddie Erdelatz, would be the longest walk I've ever taken in my coaching life."

There was dead silence for a moment or two, and then Holleder spoke up quietly: "Colonel, you are not going to take that walk tomorrow."

I never saw a more savage-hitting Army-Navy game than that one. At the beginning and for some time afterwards, it appeared they were going to run us right out of the north end of the big horseshoe. From the opening kick-off, they marched 76 yards to a touchdown.

They had prepared especially for us a tricky, double-flanker pattern out of the split T. Welsh directed the drive, one of the best I ever saw a Navy team make, with faultless judgment. He was hitting his receivers, among them the ineffable Beagle, running the ball cleverly on quarterback-keeper numbers and even utilizing a Statue-of-Liberty play. It looked like a long, tough afternoon for us. Even when they missed the extra point, it didn't seem to matter much.

In the first twenty-five minutes of the first half, they so controlled the game that they had thirteen first downs to our one and 208 yards gained to our 39. But they could not crack us. Twice we stopped them at our 20. The first time, Holleder slammed into Beagle so hard, as he caught a fourth-down pass, that Beagle couldn't hold it. The second time Navy fumbled and Holleder fell on the ball.

Early in the second quarter I took Don out of the game. At the time, we had possessed the ball for only nine plays and had only one first down. Holleder had passed once, poorly, and it had been intercepted. When I called Don to the sidelines, the die-hard cynics thought I had finally given up on him, that I had finally admitted the experiment a failure.

Actually I only wanted to check rapidly with him an analysis of what our phone spotters had reported Navy was doing on the attack, and on defense, and what adjustments we should make to meet it. After four plays, I sent Holleder back in.

With five minutes left to play, Navy punted to our 13. From this point, we began to wrest control of the game away from them. Uebel, always at his best against the Navy, began tearing inside and outside their tackles. Holleder called his own number on occasional sneak and keeps. Dick Murtland and Pete Lash, two unsung halfbacks, began biting off useful chunks of yardage.

Without throwing a single pass we marched 86 yards all the way to their 1-yard line; and, then, before we could get off another play, the clock ran out on us and we had to leave the field at the half, trailing, 6–0.

It was enough to take the guts out of a tiger, but not these tigers. With a field leader like Holleder, a team captain like Uebel (Pat gained 125 yards, nine first downs and his fifth touchdown against Navy in three years), and a thoroughly dedicated, game gang behind them, Army this day was not to be stopped.

"Why," said somebody after the game, "it was only the kind of a ball club you could round up at any corner drugstore."

Maybe so, but I would take them, any time.

In the second half, the charge of our line so throttled their running game, Navy was forced to resort almost entirely to passing. Welsh completed eighteen out of twenty-nine passes for 179 yards that day, but all he got out of it was one touchdown.

We threw *two* passes, completed neither.

It was the day of the infantryman. We took them apart on the ground, particularly on their inside right sector, with just enough diversions elsewhere. They deployed in an eight-man front most of the time, and finally all the time when it become evident we were not going to pass. But the charge of our line, the drive of our backs, the cohesion of both and the flaming urge of Quarterback Don Holleder rolled them back and back.

In the third period, we marched 41 yards for our first touchdown. Uebel, appropriately, slammed it over. Chesnauskas converted and we had the hard-won lead, 7–6.

They hove anchor in the last quarter for the last time. The superb Welsh hit his receivers unerringly and they went 72 yards. But they fumbled on our 20, and guard Stan Slater recovered for us.

Soon after we began ramming it down their throats again and we went all the way, 80 yards. The last bite was the fatal one and the big one. Lash, after a fake by Holleder to Uebel up the middle, slanted over their right side, outside their tackle. Their right end was playing so tight, to relieve the beleaguered inside, that Lash's course actually took him outside the end. It was an off-tackle run that looked like a half sweep. When Lash shot into the open, the secondary had lost any decent angles of pursuit on him and he raced 22 yards for the score. Chesnauskas converted again and we had it nailed down, 14–6.

We gained 283 yards on the ground, not a single yard in the air. We did it against a first-class, dedicated football team, against a packed defense that guessed correctly that we would not pass. Without the use of a single completed pass, we beat a team which had proved repeatedly in the past, and for twenty-five minutes that day, that it could both run and pass.

"There hasn't been anything quite like it," wrote Arthur Daley in the New York *Times,* "since the ancient days of the flying wedge."

> Holly's Vindication (wrote Jesse Abramson in the New York *Herald Tribune*). That is the way Army will note and long remember the 1955 Cadet team and the merited, hard-won upset over Navy.
>
> If the Midshipmen had won . . . it might have been called Red Blaik's Folly by those who second-guessed his Great Experiment. Never were a coach and a player subjected to so much criticism on a matter which involves a basic item of coaching: proper appraisal of an individual's ability to handle the job assigned to him.

General MacArthur wired:

NO VICTORY THE ARMY HAS WON IN ITS LONG YEARS OF FIERCE FOOTBALL STRUGGLES HAS EVER REFLECTED A GREATER SPIRIT OF RAW COURAGE, OF INVINCIBLE DETERMINATION, OF MASTERFUL STRATEGIC PLANNING AND RESOLUTE PRACTICAL EXECUTION. TO COME FROM BEHIND IN THE FACE OF APPARENT INSUPERABLE ODDS IS THE TRUE STAMP OF A CHAMPION. YOU AND YOUR TREMENDOUS TEAM HAVE RESTORED FAITH AND BROUGHT JOY AND GRATIFICATION TO MILLIONS OF LOYAL ARMY FANS.

Mainly because Holleder had left his post to make that phone call at Benning and because he exuded self-assurance, there were some officers at West Point as late as the close of Holleder's second-class year in June of 1955 who thought he was something less than a good cadet.

Generals Bryan and Messinger, however, as I have said, realized the latent leadership in this boy. In selecting the "makes," first-classmen to command companies, the Commandant had a problem company to consider. He knew it would require especially strong leadership. He put Holleder in command of that company, and nobody at West Point was ever sorry for it.

After being commissioned in June, 1956, Lieutenant Don Holleder reported to Benning, scene of the "crime," where he attended Infantry Officers School and the Paratroopers School. He then reported to Schofield Barracks in Hawaii, for duty with the 25th Infantry Division. It so happened the commander there was the same who had been forced to "slug" Don for that phone call, none other than the former Commandant at the Academy, General Ed Messinger.

General Messinger had Holleder assigned to duty as a platoon leader. Don also coached the regimental football team to two winning seasons, finishing in a tie the second year for the divisional championship. Holleder's regimental commanders reported to General Messinger that, for a young lieutenant, he was one of the finest officers and best leaders they had ever seen.

General Messinger, General Bryan, and myself were not surprised. Nor would it surprise us if Lieutenant Holleder, now back at West Point on a three-year tour as a member of Dale Hall's coaching staff, goes as far as a military leader as his selflessness, courage, and inspiration led the 1955 Army football team.

Chapter XIX

The Lonely End

The Year of the Lonely End represented a gay and spirited culmination of a long, tough, discouraging, sometimes bitter eight-year return from Army's football ruins of 1951.

An undefeated season, the first in nine years, the Eastern Championship, No. 3 rating nationally, victories over both Navy and Notre Dame in the same season for the first time since 1945 and the eighth time in forty-six years, all combined to provide The Lonely End the fullest dramatic scope and impact. Had we not "gone clean" (the footballism for being undefeated), 1958 might well have become The Year of the Lonely Coach.

The Lonely End was so called because he lined up as a far flanker on either side of the field, some 20 to 30 yards removed from the line, and did not join the huddle between plays. How he got his signals from the quarterback was a question that piqued the normal human interest in mysteries, puzzles, and guessing games.

Propound such a puzzle amid the excitement and fanfare of college football and you have irresistible ingredients of Americana. The Lonely End would have been intriguing on a civilian college team. As a West Point Cadet, he was even more so, because his "loneliness" implied a break with regimentation.

It also helped that the original Lonely End himself, William Stanley Carpenter, a six-feet-two, 205-pound second-classman from Springfield, Pennsylvania, probably was the best offensive wingman in Army history, and also outstanding defensively. In fact there would have been no Lonely End, if there had been no Carpenter. His talents and those of a few other superior players, especially a gifted passer in quarterback Joe Caldwell, sparked the concept and made it practical.

The debut of The Lonely End was also perfectly timed. Professional football has taken the lead over the college game in selling its product through more imaginative and practical presentation. Followers of the college game were looking for something new and colorful. The Lonely End provided it. The press was excited and enthusiastic; a typical comment: "Football hasn't seen anything like him since the invention of the forward pass." Casual fans and some who may not have been fans at all took notice of him. He provoked philosophizing. Ten days after the season was over, the New York *Times* editorial page devoted its "Topics" column to The Lonely End:

> Holding aloof from the huddle, presumably getting the signals by radar or through someone's twitching an ear, Cadet Carpenter came as close to being the nation's dreamboat as is good for an Army man to be.
>
> Did he but know it as he strolled the wings of a Saturday afternoon, Cadet Carpenter did much more than just harass the opposition and catch occasional passes. He represented a good many million family men, a command whose size he is unlikely to surpass in future life. Family men are lonely ends, or think they are, so that it amounts to the same thing. Men are left far outside all family huddles. They are expected to stand a distance away, looking on, when all the major decisions are being made. Signals as to those decisions they must pick up for themselves, often from a sign no more clearly expressed than a twitch of an ear. Once in a while, when the need is desperate indeed, they are thrown the ball. When they catch it, there is little comment, for that is expected of them. When they miss, they get the blame.

We did not, of course, install The Lonely End to spotlight the devaluation of family men. Like most inventions, he was born of necessity. Beneath the thick, tasty frosting of publicity, he had a basic, substantial function. In the spectrum of color, as well as in function, he shared responsibility and acclaim with other leading characters: Caldwell; Bob Anderson and Dawkins, the best pair of college halfbacks on one team in many years; Don Usry, known as "The Sociable —or the Gregarious—End"; and guard Bob Novogratz, sword and flame of a remarkable defensive team.

In the background, totally unpublicized until the very end of the season, was the "Patron Saint" of our dedicated defensive effort each week. I refer to that refugee end and paragon of almost criminally savage tackling from the lists of the All Time Bull Pond All America; Chuckles Axmurder, of Bedlam Hall.

It is something of a paradox that the Lonely End team of 1958, toasted for its dynamic, colorful, "mysterious" attack, was primarily, as all outstanding teams must be, a tough, sound, alert, dedicated defensive unit. We allowed, by running and passing combined, an average of 182 yards to a game. That was the third best statistically in the nation. I believe that when we were in condition, our first team and a few subs put on the *best* defense of that season.

To understand the genesis of The Lonely End, to appreciate the satisfaction it brought us, it is necessary to inspect the contrast of the two preceding seasons of 1956 and '57. They were epics of frustration. They were grisly examples of why coaches keep the strait-jacket industry solvent. In retrospect, both seasons fringed on high tragedy: '56 at least included some low comedy, but there was no relieving humor whatsoever in '57.

We had backfield problems in '56, which we never did solve. We had one talented back in Kyasky. Even slowed down after knee surgery, he was outstanding. As I stated earlier, Gene Mikelonis, the talented yearling runner, hurt his knee in the V.M.I. opener and never played again.

With Holleder gone, the biggest backfield poser was to find a quarterback. For a while, I tried Kyasky there, but later moved him to fullback. I then called on Dave Bourland, who was not a natural quarterback, but was the best we had in '56 and '57 and never gave me less than 100-per-cent effort.

Early in the year, our backs were perilous on pass defense, but they improved and in the Navy game were excellent.

What killed us was our fumbling. We were the fumblingest team I ever coached. We had forty fumbles during the season, and opponents recovered half of them. One reason for the fumbling was lack of sufficient practice time. I concentrated on defense, because I realized if I did not, our backfield deficiencies on offense would get us murdered. This left me relatively little time to devote to offense, and that prevented the development of the cohesion that reduces fumbling. The fumbling, of course, not only broke up our attack continuity but frequently gave the opponent prime field position. This, added to our early-season pass-defense venalities, combined to put terrific pressure on our line. Except at Michigan, the line acquitted itself very well.

In our 14–7 victory over Penn State (which had a 6–2–1 season, including a victory over Ohio State), Kyasky was outstanding, although new to the quarterback post. We made a 55-yard, nine-play march for a touchdown, the first time we got the ball, and Bob's passing and running sparked it. He also scored our other marker on a 24-yard bootleg run. Then, late in the game, while we were fighting to protect the 14–7 lead, Kyasky saved us by fighting off a blocker and knocking halfback Bruce Gilmore out of bounds when he appeared on his way to a touchdown.

In losing, 48–14, at Michigan the next week, we were atrocious. We committed eight fumbles. They recovered six, five of which led directly to touchdowns. We fumbled mainly because we could not make the elementary move of getting the ball back correctly from the center to the quarterback. This had annoyed us in September practice, but we had thought we had corrected it. At Michigan, it cropped up again, and I finally had to take the center and quarterback out of the game to practice snapbacks along the sideline. I mentioned the snapback problem when asked by writers after the game to explain our fumbling. My remark prompted Stanley Woodward to comment in the Newark *Star Ledger*, where he was sports editor at the time:

> Explaining Army's horrendous hosing at Michigan by the failure of the center to snap the ball properly to the quarterback may be likened to blaming the Johnstown Flood on a leaky toilet in Altoona.

From the "Altoona Game," we carried on to another dispiriting involvement at Syracuse. In the early 'fifties, Coach Ben Schwartzwalder used to bring Syracuse down to Army for practice games that benefited both teams. Ben has gone on record more than once that the Orange learned about "hard-nosed" football from Army, and was so quoted, in fact, in a Syracuse paper the week of our '56 game. On the train up there Friday morning, I mentioned this to a writer.

"They say they learned 'hard-nosed' football from us," I mused. "Now we're going up to play them and I'm wondering whether we've got it any more ourselves."

Well, we were "hard-nosed" enough, and I thought we earned and should have had a tie instead of a 7–0 defeat. It seemed to me Vince Barta, our fullback, got over the goal line on fourth down in the second half, before halfback Jim Ridlon hurled him back, but an official ruled otherwise. Except for one long run that set up their touchdown, we kept Jim Brown in reasonable check. Brown saved them once on defense by pursuing and hauling down Gil Roesler, who appeared on his way to a score. It was after the Syracuse game, I decided I would get more out of using Kyasky at full and Bourland at quarter.

Our 60–0 victory at Columbia the next week had no significance, other than it was our farewell, for the foreseeable future, to the Ivy League.

The Colgate game that followed is memorable in Michie Stadium chronicles for odd reasons. The score was Army 55, Colgate 46. We couldn't stop their passing and they couldn't stop our running. There was a total of 939 yards gained and 44 first downs. Only once did as many as six minutes elapse between touchdowns. The crowd, of course, loved it, but I must say it was the worst exhibition of run-sheep-run football I ever saw.

I may be rationalizing, but I suspect the players on both teams were affected by the fact that the guests included Prince Rainier and Princess Grace of Monaco. All that charging up and down the field like Arthurian Knights at Camelot may have been an attempt to impress Princess Grace, and it probably succeeded. But it didn't impress me.

Fumbles again contributed to our 20–7 miseries at Pittsburgh, although the Panthers were stronger than we were. Their fine quarterback, Cornelius Salvaterra, with 138 yards rushing, key passes, and sound generalship, probably played his top game. Our touchdown came on a 14-yard twisting darter by Kyasky.

So we had a 5–3 record and only one decorative victory, Penn State, as we came down to Navy. The Middies had lost only one game and their 7–1–2 record would be their best since 1945. We faced the opportunity, as in 1955, to make it a big year by upsetting them.

Our arrival at Municipal Stadium was a half-slapstick scene, suggestive of the whole season. A traffic accident at Philadelphia's City Hall delayed the two Army A.A. buses bringing us to the battle. By the time we pulled up in front of the northeast gate of the big horseshoe, it was pressing one o'clock. The cadets and midshipmen had paraded in and were seated. Navy was already warming up on the field. The kick-off was only thirty minutes away and we weren't even in the place.

I hurriedly led the players from our buses to the big door which leads into the tunnel and the stairs to the dressing room of the "visiting" team. Unaccountably, the door was locked and there was nobody there awaiting us. I hammered at the door. I kept hammering for what seemed like at least three minutes.

Inside, I learned later, the Pinkerton man in charge finally said to one of his men, "You better tell whoever those wise guys are to stop the racket."

The Pinkerton opened the door a couple of inches and peeked his head out at mine. "You can't come in here," he growled.

"The hell we can't!" I said. "This is the Army football team!"

Unwilling to chance any further delaying debate, I applied shoulder to the door and brushed by the Pinkerton man, the players on my heels. It is a wonder their rush did not knock down the Pinkerton and trample him along with Willard Mullin, who was down there to wish us well. It was, in fact, one of the most authoritative, decisive movements made by the Army team all year, and proved what we could have done had the rules not required us to play with a ball.

In the game, we reverted to form—eight fumbles, five recovered by Navy—and it was a crime, because we outplayed them and should have won. We outgained them on the ground, 200–81, and our defense, sparked by tackle Flay Goodwin and center Jim Kernan, prevented them from getting beyond their 39-yard line on their own power. Kyasky, best back on the field, gained 77 yards and scored our touchdown from the 4 after Bourland intercepted a pass and returned it 27 yards. Bob also punted superbly. But when we fumbled once too often, on our 27-yard line in the last period, they finally capitalized with a scoring drive and got a 7–7 tie.

The tie convinced Rear Admiral W. R. Smedberg, II, Superintendent of Annapolis, that Navy should not accept a bid to the Cotton Bowl, which apparently was still available to the Middies. This was small consolation to us. We felt we had beaten ourselves.

We went into the 1957 season with more hope than in '55 and '56. Not that we were without problems. Our defense was not stable. Except for Captain Kernan and Slater, we had to rebuild a new line. Our reserves were acutely vulnerable against topflight opposition. The "blue-chip" injury jinx made its annual visit. Carpenter, then a yearling but already an outstanding end, suffered a serious leg and ankle injury in a late-summer jeep accident, which also put two other players out for the season. Carpenter got in briefly late in the year, but not enough to win a letter.

Our offensive picture, however, was interesting, even exciting. Our line, while inexperienced, especially at tackle, was our biggest since 1950 and could open up holes. Bourland was improved at quarterback. At fullback, Vince Barta now had two years behind him and was being pushed by a yearling firecat named Harry Walters. Most of all, the spring drills revealed a pair of halfbacks to bring crowds to their feet: Bob Anderson and Pete Dawkins.

Anderson, nineteen, six feet two, 205, from Cocoa, Florida, was the best all-around football player at the Academy since Blanchard and Davis. He did everything well: running, blocking, tackling, passing, catching passes, defending against them, punting. He was also one of the most self-effacing and selfless team players I ever encountered.

While his classic naturalness in every phase of play delighted the connoisseur, Anderson was most exciting as a runner. He had power that blasted through and over tacklers, speed that could outstay pursuit, and a flavor of king-size niftiness. He could break up a game with a long run, a series of 10-to-15 yard intermediate thrusts, or a goal-line ram or hurdle against a packed, expectant mass.

As a yearling in '57, Anderson's 983 yards from scrimmage broke the Academy record of 930, set by Glenn Davis in '45. His eighty-four points were fourth nationally. He was second for the nation in touchdowns with fourteen, and he passed for a fifteenth. As blocker and defender against pass and run, he was equally impressive.

In The Lonely End season, Bob was even more valuable than in '57, although he did not carry the ball as often, because we were in greater need of his blocking. His knee injury against Illinois in '59 was indeed a tragedy, both for the team and himself, because what I had seen of him against Boston College the week before had convinced me that he was going to achieve a new peak. He evidenced the added quickness and power that comes with increasing maturity. It was remarkable that he played at all after the Illinois game, for post-season surgery showed the cartilege hanging in the knee.

Pete Dawkins, as a second-classman in '57, was nineteen, six feet one, and 195. Although his football focused the spotlight on his unique versatility as a cadet, even without the showcase of the gridiron, he would have had to be considered one of the most remarkable cadets in the history of the Academy.

In his first-class year, Dawkins rose to the unprecedented: First Captain or Brigade Commander, the highest military rank in the Corps; Academic star cadet for being in the top 5 per cent of the class, and football captain. He was also outstanding on the hockey team and was president of the class. Despite his onerous schedule, Pete still found time for social activity. His facility with the guitar and other instruments made him a leader of informal barracks musicales.

Dawkins was a leader who inspired fondness with respect. You will recall my mentioning back in Chapter II how a cadet officer was "busted" back to private's rank for violating Dawkins' order that no plebe was to be denied food. I can best show what the Corps thought of Pete by quoting what was written of him in the 1959 *Howitzer*, the West Point class book:

We have stood in awe of this man. But a triumph more enduring promoted him to this singular position: specifically, Pete firmly gripped our hands in deep and understanding friendship. Consequently, never was a task given him not successfully accomplished; for as he cared, so also did we. We were not completely sagacious, but we knew a great friend, a great leader, a great man.

When Dawkins accepted a Rhodes scholarship and went on to Oxford in 1959, he astonished the British as he had us. He assimilated rugby so rapidly that he accomplished the rare feat of an American, in his first year at the game, winning his "blue" by playing, and well, in Oxford's 9–3 victory over Cambridge. Later, Pete starred for Oxford in the 6–5 hockey defeat by Cambridge. While trying to lead a winning charge, he had his jaw cracked by an errant stick and was forced out. When the jaw healed, he played cricket.

"The tea and sociability with opponents after the game," Dawkins was quoted, "is one of the great things about this English rugby football."

I naturally have the deepest respect for Peter and his opinions. I trust, however, he is not implying that Army and Navy should add the British touch to their annual game. I never could imagine Erdelatz and myself exchanging post-game chitchat over a platter of scones and a pot of Oolong.

As a football player, Dawkins came to West Point with average credentials. At Cranbrook, a small preparatory school near his home in Royal Oak, Michigan, he was a good left-handed and passing quarterback in the split-T formation. He applied to and was accepted by Yale and Michigan. His father, Dr. Henry E. Dawkins, and Mrs. Dawkins both were Michigan graduates.

Fred Campbell, Cranbrook's able coach, was eager to have Dawkins attend West Point, and wrote to me about him. The picture of Pete which Campbell enclosed, that of a rather gangly seventeen-year old, did not impress me. I suspected then, and for a long time after, that Dawkins was just another "silk stocking" preparatory-school athlete.

It was my lack of interest, Pete said later, that first made West Point a challenge to him, one he was unwilling to pass up. He had already met and licked tougher challenges. As a seventh-grader, he was hit by polio. It was thought for a time he never would be able to play any sports, much less the rugged, contact type.

In his plebe season of 1955, Dawkins started most of the games at quarterback, but his passing was unimpressive and he was less than mediocre defensively. In 1956 spring practice, he was a third- or fourth-string quarterback, lost far back in the crowd. In a scrimmage during the fall of '56, however, he returned some punts in a way that made me think we might get something out of him as a right halfback. He had the movements of a natural runner. Yet, he played very little that season, only enough to carry six times for 30 yards and score three touchdowns. He got into the abortive 7-7 tie with Navy only briefly.

Pete's big moment in '56 has its retrospective humor, when you consider what was going to happen to him later. We were behind, 48-7, when I put him into the "Altoona Game" at Michigan, and he got our other touchdown. Despite the circumstances, I believe that touchdown was accepted without complaint, in fact with enthusiasm, by his parents and friends who had come from their nearby homes to see the game.

It was in the spring practice of '57 that Dawkins began to take hold. He began to demonstrate the speed, power, elusiveness, and intelligence of a top-flight running halfback and pass receiver. He was also improving on defense and even beginning to block well at times. The poise and confidence, which was to be such a big part of his inspiring leadership of The Lonely End team, first began to shine through that spring.

The best team we met in 1957 definitely was the Navy. The second half of our schedule, however, was not as tough as the first half. On successive Saturdays, we met Penn State at University Park; Notre Dame, in Philadelphia's Municipal Stadium, the first of our home-and-home renewal with the Irish; and the traditionally rugged Pitt Panthers, at Michie.

Penn State was still seeking its first victory over Army, and put up a fierce struggle, leading at the half, 13–6. In the third period, we scored three times on marches of 71, 66, and 40 yards and went on to win, 27–13. That third period was the best fifteen minutes of football played by an Army team since the '55 Navy game.

Our defeat by Notre Dame the next week was the hardest I had to take in twenty-five years as a head coach. This was the Irish team, coached by Terry Brennan, which later snapped Oklahoma's all-time record defeatless string at 47 games. They came back from their 2–8 season of '56 to win seven and lose three. They were a big, deep, fast, talented squad. Their "blue-chip" stars included Nick Pietrosante, one of the all-time top Notre Dame fullbacks; guard Al Ecuyer; Monty Stickles, a pass-catching and field-goal specialist; and a clever quarterback in Bob Williams.

Our problem was a far-below-par second-string situation, which simply would not permit us to substitute with the impunity of Notre Dame. I hoped, however, that while the first team was given relatively short breathers, the reserves would at least give up ground slowly and grudgingly. This formula worked out until near the end of the third period.

To our normal, balanced-line, tight T, we added what we called a "Bazooka" series from an unbalanced line. It put a heavy convoy of blockers in front of Anderson on strong side sweeps and cutbacks. With a runner of his caliber, results could be explosive—and were.

On the second play of scrimmage, from our 19, Bourland called the "Bazooka." Anderson took the pitchout, wheeled wide and sliced back over their left side behind a blocking wave. As Bob veered across the line of scrimmage, linebacker Nick Pietrosante had a shot at him, but Nick got tangled in traffic and taken off his feet. Anderson broke into the open, moved into high gear, and feinted his way gracefully by the last defender. His 81-yard scoring run from scrimmage was a record for the Army-Notre Dame series. We had the lead, 7–0.

Before the period was over, Notre Dame tied it up on an 80-yard march, much of it against our reserves, with Pietrosante blasting over from the 1. But our reserves contested the ground resolutely and well enough to encourage further use of them later on when the first team required a little rest.

For most of the third period, we swept the Irish back on two scoring drives of 72 and 81 yards. Anderson and Dawkins cut and slashed, aided by Bourland, Walters and Barta, behind a fierce line charge. Dawkins scored on a 6-yard sweep of their right end and Anderson smashed over from the one. We converted twice and led, 21–7, with only two minutes left to play in the third period.

At this point, I felt constrained to rest the first team for a few minutes. They had been in there all of the third period. Off our first-half experience, I reasoned that the second team would give up 40 to 50 yards, but in so doing would also use up four or five minutes, and get us over into the fourth quarter. Then, I could return a somewhat rested first team, to get another score, if possible, but at least protect the margin we had established.

That was the theory. It was blasted in one shot when Pietrosante burst loose over guard for a 65-yard touchdown run. Nick had outstanding quickness and power, but was not essentially a breakaway man. His long-gainer traced in good part to an assumption by our deep secondaries that he had been stopped near the line of scrimmage, whereas he had only been slowed down for an instant. They relaxed and when Pietrosante broke away from his temporary entanglement they could not recover quickly enough to establish effective angles of pursuit against him.

Notre Dame, which had trailed, 21–7, and was about to be knocked out of the game, was now right back in it with a 21–14 scoreboard. They had got there, furthermore, with a minimum expenditure of body chemistry.

I got the first team back in there fast, but the Irish, now wheed up psychologically, marched steadily for another score. Yet, they missed the conversion try and still trailed us, 21–20. We had allowed them to wrest momentum away from us, but we might still have protected the one-point lead, if we had not tried an ill-advised pass. We had the ball on our 20, third and 8. Third and 8, with such backs as we had, was not a formidable challenge.

Instead of running, we elected to pass. We did not throw into the sidelines but over the middle, where it was interceptable. A Notre Dame lineman deflected the pass toward the ground. Nick Pietrosante, who had been blocked by Walters, was sitting there. The ball dropped into his lap. On fourth down, Monty Stickles, who had been rejected by West Point because of bad eyes, kicked a 23-yard field goal that won the game, 23–21.

This coach caught merry hell from the newspapers and the grandstand quarterbacks, in and out of the Academy. The West Point high strategic command was heard to proclaim in the market place that I had lost the game by putting in the second team when we were leading, 21–7.

Was this criticism justified? Perhaps. The directing of a game from the bench is one of the most difficult phases of coaching. I have seen great Monday-through-Friday coaches suddenly lose command on Saturday, and become unable to make decisions. There is reason for this, because there is no emotional or mental pressure, short of actual battle, to equal that found on the football bench.

Probably no coach in history ever became more excited on a bench during the heat of battle than the late Francis A. (Shut-the-Gates-of-Mercy) Schmidt, who coached at Ohio State from 1934 through '40. On one occasion, Francis had his two first-string tackles—we shall call them, for the sake of this story, Oxman and Nitro—on the bench. Suddenly, Francis commanded, "Oxman, go in for Nitro!"

"Coach," said Nitro, "I'm right here on the bench."

"Good," said Schmidt, "then you go in for Oxman!"

Another time, Francis bellowed, "Look at Daniell out there, being knocked on his fanny!"

Daniell, who happened to be out of the game and sitting on the bench, heard Schmidt. "You were wrong that time, coach," he said. "I'm not playing!"

"What's the difference?" replied Francis. "That's where you'd be, if you were out there!"

The background to proper bench decisions is experience, homework, good judgment, and action. In the case of the 1957 Army-Notre Dame game, my homework never envisioned a possible 21–7 advantage for the Cadets with only seventeen minutes to go. The obvious fact that another score was needed to put the game on ice and that it might have been better to have kept the tired but dominating Army team in the game to try for another score comes to me today, some three years too late.

But it is such decisions, good or bad, that bring out the great hordes of grandstand quarterbacks, ready to play sixty minutes of sweatless ball.

One of the reasons why defeat in an Army-Navy game or any traditional finale is acutely indigestible is that the defeated have a year to think about it. In contrast, early defeats are cushioned by the urgency of concentrating on the next game.

After such an ulcer-breeder as that 23-21 loss to Notre Dame, the need of getting ready for Pittsburgh was a happy alkaline. An overflow crowd of 27,900 at Michie saw us play our finest game of the year in defeating the Panthers, 29-13. The turn of the game was a 17-play, 83-yard scoring drive in the third period, on which we threw only one pass. Within thirteen minutes of the third and fourth periods, we scored twenty-three points, good going against a team like Pitt. The spark of it was that 83-yard march.

With Pitt overshifted against the "Bazooka" threat, we worked between their left tackle and right end, more from the balanced than the unbalanced T, with Anderson, Dawkins, and Walters slashing and thrusting behind quick, solid blocking. The sixteen running plays were minus a fumble, testament to timing, precision, and poise. In directing this drive, Bourland was at his best as a quarterback.

The victory over Pitt was our biggest since the '55 Navy game, and badly needed, but we were never again the same team that year. We slid downhill, and there was a cogent reason. Since our passing attack was uncertain, we were forced to rely mainly on our strong running game. The execution of the running game and the toll of defense was paid by our starters and only a few reserves. It exacted deep physical attrition. Consequently, we were hard pressed to defeat teams which were not as strong as Penn State, Notre Dame, and Pittsburgh. Desperate rallies and Herculean running feats by Anderson and Dawkins were required to beat Virginia, 20-12, and Tulane, 20-14.

We outscored Jack Curtice's colorful Utah team, 39-33, in a run-sheep-run exhibition comparable to the Colgate game of '56. Anderson's 214 yards from scrimmage and three touchdowns, one on a

54-yard run, were able to neutralize Lee Grosscup, the Utah quarterback, about as fine a college passer as I ever saw. Grosscup completed fourteen of twenty-six passes for 316 yards and two touchdowns, one on the last play of the game. Following an annual custom, 16,000 Boy Scouts sat in Michie Stadium as our guests. Anderson and Grosscup sent them home with enough football lore for several campfires.

The following week, Jack Curtice phoned me from Utah. "Say," he said, "we ought to put that show on the road!"

What with one thing and another, we still had a 7–1 record (which should have been 8–0), going down to play Navy. This strong Navy team, unaccountably defeated by North Carolina, 13–7, and tied by Duke, was to go on to hand Rice a decisive 20–7 beating in the Cotton Bowl. It was a miserable rainy, muddy day in Philadelphia, and Navy's day all the way. They won, 14–0. Ned Oldham, their fine back, climaxed his three years by scoring all their points on a 6-yard run, a 44-yard punt return and two conversions.

Their strong, laterally mobile defense did us in. Anderson, handicapped by a first-period leg injury and not much blocking, was held to 18 yards in 11 carries. Dawkins felt the pressure of his first Navy game as a regular and mussed up several assignments. One of them caused us to fumble on their 9, which we had reached on a 60-yard drive with Pete doing most of the gaining, helped by Anderson's heavy blocking. We also reached their 15 after recovering a fumble, but were stopped by an interception.

Navy's impressive defense was featured by Bob Reifsnyder, a dreadnaught linebacker transplanted from tackle, and right guard Tony Stremic. In this work, I have naturally concentrated on the character lessons taught and learned by Army players in the Navy game. I am sure Navy could provide just as many examples. I am reminded of this by Stremic. As a youngster (sophomore) in '55, Tony had been given a rough afternoon by the Holleder-directed infantry. In '57, he exacted full retribution.

After the Navy game, I was counseled by Colonel Harvey Fraser, Professor of Mechanics, sports enthusiast, humorist, and a wonderful influence for morale at the Academy.

"Don't do anything rash," Harvey advised. "Go for a walk, but stay on the reservation."

The first time I ever saw Colonel Fraser was in 1948 at the annual baseball game on West Point's Doubleday Field (Abner was a cadet at the Academy, even though he never did invent baseball at Cooperstown) with the New York Giants in 1948. The plate umpire was a National League regular, giving his services gratis. Fraser did not know this. If he had, it would have made no difference. He was disturbed by the umpire's decisions and was giving him loud hell. The ump was annoyed, and kept turning around. Fraser happens to have a voice that carries as far south as the Bear Mountain Bridge. Finally, I asked Colonel Red Reeder, "Who is that?"

"I don't know," said Reeder.

"Go find out," I said, "and calm him down."

In a couple of minutes Reeder returned.

"That's a new professor," he said. "Colonel Harvey Fraser, Class of '39. I gave him your message, but he says it's not his fault . . . it's the umpire's!"

I coached through that rainy '57 Navy game, racked by the heavy bronchial cough that had moved in on me each year since 1954 with the raw, cold weather of November. A few days after the season, I went to Florida for a brief vacation. It was on Key Biscayne that I thought out our football problems and decided that the answer to what was ailing us was the far-flanker attack, which was to become known as The Lonely End.

Long study of our game films had demonstrated that the major factor in obstructing our running attack was the corner defense, or the wide linebackers, or cornermen, as they are known, in a 5-4-2 defense.

It was not that we had been wholly unsuccessful in handling them. Our definite slowdown in the second half of the '57 season, however, emphasized that what success we had was demanding an exhaustive physical price for a team seriously limited in replacements.

Let's consider The Lonely End attack, regardless of whether he stays out of the huddle. The basic function of the far flanker is to break up the cornerman defense by forcing either one of the two cornermen into the deep-pass defense. If the cornerman on the side of the far flanker covers him, that breaks it up. If the halfback on the side of the far flanker covers him, this forces a compensating rotation of the deep-pass defense in which the other cornerman must play as a third deep defender; any attempt to cover the eligible pass receivers with only two deep defenders after the ball is snapped concedes defeat.

In other words, the far flanker so spreads the pass defense that it has much more ground to cover. It did something that no other offense in my twenty-five years of coaching had accomplished: it forced a definite weakness in the secondary defense that could not be offset without removing an extra man from the line. And this man could not be spared, because we still had all our backs in close attacking deploy.

I am well aware, of course, that the concept of a far flanker is almost as old as football, although our far flanker lined up farther than far.

To my knowledge, this was the first time a far-flanking alignment constituted the entire attack, with the functions of the far flanker related to every phase of both the running and the passing game.

Needless to state, proper personnel is necessary to make this, or any other, attack perform. I certainly would not have installed it, had I not been blessed, for the first time in four years, with a potentially superior passer, several fine receivers, two extraordinary runners at halfback, a solid fullback, an above-average line, and even a few adequate reserves.

I want to emphasize, however, that The Lonely End attack, given the personnel, will accomplish more, faster and easier, than any other I know.

By 1959, the far-flanker attack had been copied in some degree by scores of teams, with one, two or even three flankers employed. Most of them used it only as a part-time attack.

I believe the way to get the most out of it is to use it as your sole attack and to use only the one flanker.

I believe firmly that its possibilities have only been scratched. In 1958, we were, of necessity, experimenting. After we saw an undefeated season in prospect, we went too conservative.

Conservatism is inimical to a full realization of the possibilities of The Lonely End.

There is a fine point of balance between the proper number of passes and runs. Even in the far-flanking concept, *the running game must dominate,* but not to the same degree as in a tight formation. Our 1958 success was a mixture of runs and passes, with more runs than passes. The threat of the flanker, as receiver or decoy, must help the running game directly or indirectly, if the proper plays are called.

An inordinate series of injuries prevented Army from developing it in 1959. Army, or some team with the correct understanding of the concept and the right personnel, will develop it. Then football will really see something. I often dream of what our Blanchard-Davis teams or our Forgotten Grenadiers would have done with it.

Although we set up the far-flanker attack in spring practice, we did not decide to keep the end out of the huddle at that time. I made that decision in early August. While in Chicago for the All Star Game, I outlined the attack to Andy Gustafson. Gus pointed out that Carpenter's commuting between the huddle and his outpost on every play, added to his game action, would use him up.

"Earl," Gus warned me, "you will run him into the ground!"

This criticism made a lot of sense. On a plane from Chicago to Oklahoma, to visit Bill, I considered what Gus had said. It was then that I thought of keeping the end out of the huddle. I reasoned it would serve three purposes. It would conserve his energy. We would be able to run off more plays. Most important—and this does not seem to be fully appreciated by those who regard his absence from the huddle as merely a gimmick—he would force the defense, or at least a vital part of it, to commit its intentions immediately. This would give the quarterback a chance, much earlier in the twenty-five seconds allotted for getting the ball in play, to assay the defensive alignment and call the proper play to negate it.

As to the "mystery" of how The Lonely End gets his signals, after the '58 season I told the Touchdown Club of New York that he gets them from the positioning of the quarterback's feet. He could, however, get them other ways. The quarterback's feet could at times be a decoy. It is equally interesting, as well as important, how and when

The Lonely End signals the quarterback on how the defense is covering him.

The Lonely End got his name at Bull Pond, in late July of '58, from Stanley Woodward. When I told the Bull Ponders that our new attack would require Carpenter to be a far-flanker on every play, Stanley said, "You ought to call it The Lonely End attack." My subsequent decision to keep him out of the huddle made the pseudonym even more appropriate. Other designations, such as "Lonesome George" and "The Lonesome End," are come-lately misnomers. As Coach Woodward insists, there is a meaningful difference between Lonesome, which suggests mawkishness, and Lonely, which implies a dignified stoicism.

The Chuckles Axmurder Award, given to Army's outstanding defensive "hatchet man" in each 1958 game, was also conceived at Bull Pond that summer, a day or two after The Lonely End was named. Dale Hall, then defensive backfield coach and head scout, and Frank Lauterbur, line coach, were looking for something off-beat to stimulate ever more aggressive defensive line play, something with a humorous touch.

Chuckles Axmurder had recently been ushered into the Bull Pond All Time Hall of Fame. Hall and Lauterbur decided that if Willard Mullin would render a drawing of this fabulous performer, with panel space to write in the recipient of each week's citation, it would be exactly what they were looking for.

Willard came through nobly and the Chuckles Axmurder Award became a big hit with the Cadets. The winner was selected after a close study of game films. Tackling, second effort, pursuit all were considered. At the beginning of each Monday's practice, the winner was announced in a brief ceremony.

The framed Mullin original was presented after the season to Bob Novogratz, who won the citation three times: in the Penn State, Notre Dame, and Villanova games. Other winners were reserve center Bob Oswandel in the September practice game with Syracuse; center Bill Rowe against South Carolina; tackle Ed Bagdonas against Virginia; Bill Carpenter in the Pitt game (imagine being The Lonely End and Charles Axmurder all at once!); guard Charlie (Chuck)

Lytle against Colgate; and tackle Maurice (Monk) Hilliard against Rice. The winner in the Navy game was the Army team. Each member of the squad and coaching staff received framed copies of the Mullin original.

Our '58 line were fine physical specimens, heavier than usual for Army, and rangy, yet they had extraordinary quickness, alertness, and fire. Taking the line as it deployed unbalanced to the right, Usry, shortside end, was six feet three, 212; Lytle, shortside guard, six feet two, 200; Rowe, center, six feet two, 210; Novogratz, strongside guard, six feet two, 210; Bagdonas, inside tackle, six feet two, 220; Hilliard, outside tackle, six feet two, 210, and Carpenter, six feet two, 205. They averaged a streamlined six feet two and 210.

The bigness and ranginess extended through the backfield with king-size Anderson and Dawkins, 205 and 195, and 195-pound fullback Harry Walters.

The eleventh starter, however, was a surprising contrast: quarterback Joe Cadwell, six feet but only 156 pounds. Because he looked scrawny, undernourished, and almost pitiable with his pipestem arms and legs, like a little sandlotter among matured collegians, Joe became known as "The Urchin." I lived in mortal fear all season, and I was not alone, that some big lineman would pick up "The Urchin" and fling him into the trees. Joe, however, proved to have the whipcord toughness of an Uncas.

As a passer, I place him at the head of any I ever coached, and I doubt there was a finer one on college gridirons. In '58, he completed 54 out of 120 for 1,097 yards and eight touchdowns, with only five interceptions—and you must remember that he had no previous varsity experience to speak of. As a field general, Caldwell improved as he went along. He was fortunate in '58 to have Dawkins to advise him. Pete was great for rapid analysis of the defense and what would work against it.

Caldwell had several very fine receivers to throw to. Carpenter was pre-eminent, with twenty-two receptions for 453 yards; followed by Dawkins, with sixteen for 491; Anderson fourteen for 138; Lonely End sub Russ Waters eleven for 146; Usry, ten for 145; and Steve Waldrop, sub for Dawkins, eight for 78.

Waters, Jack Morrison, and Otto Everbach, ends; Steve Waldrop and Gil Roesler at halfbacks; Don Bonko at full; Oswandel at center; and Al Vanderbush at guard, all helped out at critical times in tough games. Except for Vanderbush, a quick, fiery yearling, and Oswandel, there was, however, a discernible fall off from our first to second string. Not as acute as in '57, but still there. We could not, as a result, rest our starting unit as often as our first-flight opposition could.

We were extremely fortunate, therefore, that we were seriously hurt by injuries only in the 14–14 tie with Pittsburgh, which cost us an all-triumphal slate.

We unveiled The Lonely End against South Carolina at Michie Stadium on Saturday, September 27. An inauspicious rain beat across the field. I debated that morning whether I should return to our tight T and delay the inaugural of the new attack until a dry day. I finally decided to go ahead.

Our opponent, which was to make a 7–3 record, was well coached by Warren Giese. They had defeated Duke the week before and were to beat Georgia the week after, and they had definite ideas about beating us. Coach Giese described his team as "the most experienced I've had." We had tried to keep The Lonely End a secret. Judged by the reaction of South Carolina, we had been successful.

They were wholly unable to cope with it. While they were debating how to cover the far-flanking Carpenter on his lightning-quick and diverse downfield patterns as receiver and decoy, Caldwell and Anderson were completing passes not only to The Lonely End but also to Dawkins and Usry. The passing threat and South Carolina's confusion encouraged the running game. We made 344 yards running and 185 passing. We had 38 points before South Carolina ever got across midfield. The final score was 45–8. The crowd and the press were thoroughly dazzled.

Dawkins gained 113 yards in nine rushes and scored four touchdowns. Anderson (whose seasonal passing figures were ten out of fifteen for 141 yards and four touchdowns) completed five out of five from his option sweep, two for touchdowns. On at least two of these options the field opened up and Anderson could have made long runs, probably for touchdowns. I have already mentioned what a selfless team player he was. At times, in fact, he was inclined to overdo it, and these option plays against South Carolina were a prime example. Finally, in some irritation, I called him to the sidelines.

"What's the matter, Bob?" I asked him. "Don't you want to be a hero any more?"

He just half smiled.

"Listen," I said. "Never mind Alphonse and Gaston! When that field opens up for you on that option play, you tuck that ball away and go to town! This good fellowship is a lot of bunk!"

For the first half against Penn State the next week, we must have been as exciting a passing team as anybody ever saw in college. In the thirty minutes, we completed nine out of eleven for 258 yards, and picked up ninety-three on the ground, for twenty-six points.

Our four touchdowns were scored or set up by spectacular pass plays, each one more dazzling than its predecessor. The first came on a 6-yard run by Dawkins to climax a 64-yard drive; Pete set up the finisher on a 19-yard pass from Anderson. The second, bucked over by Anderson from the one, was set up by a sparkling catch of a 33-yard Caldwell pass by Carpenter. The Lonely End went high into the air to steal the ball out of the hands of a defender, a regular trick of his.

On the third touchdown, Caldwell was about to be arrested by a Penn State posse when he got loose a long one which Carpenter snared in stride on their 23-yard line and raced over. For the fourth, Caldwell dropped back to his 18 and cut loose with a medium deep one, which Dawkins grabbed on our 47. Two Penn State men converged on Pete and appeared to have him in chancery, but he somehow extricated himself and ran 53 yards for the score.

In the second half, Penn State adjusted better defensively, and we had a natural letdown. I was not displeased, for we were aiming to reach our early-season peak at Notre Dame the next week.

After the Penn State game, visitors to our quarters included that venerable Notre Dame pillar, my friend Joe Byrne. Joseph seized my lapels and led me away to our cellar laundry. There, for most of an hour, while my other guests wondered what had happened to me, he warned me in the most friendly and detailed fashion that all of Notre Dame had vowed us no mercy. The score, he said, was to be 21–0.

I did not need any help from Joe to be apprehensive. Notre Dame had another strong squad, including Pietrosante, Stickles, Williams, Ecuyer, and other perpetrators of our '57 downfall, plus dangerous sophomores in quarterback George Izo and halfback Red Mack. We knew the Irish were pointing for us, as we were for them, and that they would be typically difficult to handle in Notre Dame Stadium.

Our biggest problem was how to contain such a tireless fullback bulldozer as Pietrosante. We knew we would have to give him a lot of short yardage. We knew we must not give him the long one, as we had at Philadelphia.

We installed a new series of passes with Dawkins in motion to the weak side, and planned to use Carpenter mainly as a decoy. I felt that in the Penn State game we had overstressed the pass to the neglect of the running game. This would not be wise at Notre Dame. If we were to beat the Irish, we must make our running attack go.

As usual, the game dominated the football scene. The Lonely End was now making universal conversation and giving rise to many stories, some real, some apochryphal. Arthur Daley reported one pre-game conversation between Terry Brennan and the late Jack Lavelle, veteran Notre Dame and pro football scout, and a long-time friend of mine.

Brennan asked Lavelle what The Lonely End did when Ed Pillings, who had succeeded Bevan as trainer, came out with the water bucket? Did Carpenter go over for a drink?

"No, siree," replied Lavelle. "He sticks his hand in his pocket and whips out K rations."

It was at Notre Dame that The Lonely End team first impressed me with its tough defense, its unsurpassed stamina, its ability to handle ceaseless pressure, its indomitable spirit.

We might have had a considerably easier time of it, had we been able to capitalize on our first-half thrusts into Irish territory against a slam-bang defense. But we cashed in only once, missed the conversion and, therefore, exposed ourselves to a pressure that relented only after we scored our second touchdown in the last seven seconds of play.

We started on the march early. Dawkins and Anderson slashed

through their abrasive defenses. Caldwell interspersed judicious passes. We moved 54 yards to their 13, but were halted there by an interception. Soon after, Novogratz, a raging terror all day, fell on a fumble on their 21. Anderson charged for five. Then, we tried the new Dawkins-in-motion series. With Pete and Carpenter as decoys, Caldwell found Jack Morrison, Usry's left-end sub, free in the end zone for a scoring pass. We missed the conversion try.

In the second quarter, with Anderson and Dawkins carving out gains, we moved 61 yards to their 5. Now, we tried the same pass that had clicked for us before. Once again, the receiver was open. This time Caldwell delayed a split second too long in getting rid of the ball, just long enough for the Irish to cover.

We had a 6–0 lead at the half, but we were in trouble. Our wasted opportunities meant peril against a team of this caliber. Our peril began right at the start of the second half. We fumbled the kick-off, barely recovered the ball and were forced back by two penalties to our 1-yard line. Caldwell, back to punt, got a high pass from center, couldn't get the kick away, tried to run and was tackled by center Myron Pottios for a safety that made the score, 6–2.

After we kicked out from our 20, following the safety, the Irish had their Stadium in an uproar as they pounded down to our 19. Pietrosante, who gained 87 yards for the day, was hard to handle. We got a breather when a holding penalty set them back from the 19. But it seemed to me they were on the march most of that half.

In the fourth quarter, they staged a 71-yard drive. It was Pietrosante, aided by halfbacks Jim Just and Norman Odyniec. Now, they were down on our 19 again. Our pass defense, tight and alert most of the day, slipped here, but fortune favored us when Bob Williams passed over the head of end Gary Myers in the end zone. They made still another drive, but it foundered on our 30 when we broke up a screen pass.

"And that," said Jack Lavelle, watching up in the press box, "is it."

We now had possession of the ball on our 34-yard line. There were four minutes left in the game. Our first team, with little relief, had borne the weight of one Notre Dame drive after another. They now did something I consider remarkable. They reached down and found enough reserve to go 66 yards for a touchdown.

At the beginning of that march, we on the bench nearly had heart seizures. Caldwell threw a pass intended for Dawkins in the right flat. Williams just barely missed intercepting it right in front of the Irish bench, with a seemingly open road in front of him. Brother! (And, you might add, by that much went Terry Brennan's job.)

Undaunted by this near disaster, The Urchin now wound up and hit Dawkins with a pass down the middle for a 23-yard gain. Dawkins, Anderson, and Walters alternated to bring us to the six. From there, Dawkins cut over their right side and into the end zone. Dawkins passed to Anderson for the two-point conversion. It was only decorative but it was acceptable. It made the final score 14–2.

Our keen '57 disappointment at Philadelphia made this victory especially satisfying. In the dressing room, Captain Dawkins presented me with the ball and made a nice speech—so good, in fact, it was evident he had practiced it for a year. He said the team should have given me the ball the year before. From Pete's looks and aplomb, you would never have suspected he had been in the toughest game of his life.

Tiger Howell, I'm told, used to say of me that I acted as if I thought I was still a first-classman. Well, I felt as young as a first-classman after that game. It was a happy time, a big victory. As I told Dave Condon, who conducts the Chicago *Tribune's* "Wake of the News" column, it is always a great honor for any team to defeat Notre Dame, especially on its home field.

Our 35–6 victory over Virginia at Michie Stadium the next week was noteworthy on two counts. The Cavaliers were coached by Dick Voris, who used to be my line coach, and this was the only time I ever sent a team against a former assistant. Dawkins and Walters were injured, Pete with a severe thigh pull, Harry with a badly sprained ankle.

At Pittsburgh, Walters was used only to kick two extra points, and Dawkins for only one defensive play—and a costly one. I left myself fairly open to the second guess by using Pete at all. Despite a wet field and a rainy, humid day, we led, 14–0, with two minutes left to play in the first half. The Panthers were back on their 13, where Caldwell had angled one of his several fine coffin-corner kicks that day.

Pitt is a team with a devastating habit of breaking loose when about to be penned up, in a game or a season. Now, on a 35-yard pass, they got down to our 43. With time for only one more play, another pass was obvious. I reasoned that Dawkins, even with a lame thigh, wauld be surer on pass defense in such a spot and sent him in. Bill Kaliden, the Pitt quarter, faded and threw a high, deep, lead pass down the middle. John Flara, their second-string left halfback, split our deep defenders, Glen Adams on the left and Dawkins on the right, reached high to take the ball in full stride on our 10, and raced into the end zone. Pitt went on from there to tie the score in the second half. The final score was 14–14.

Dawkins berated himself for allowing the score and took all the blame for the tie game.

"I wouldn't mind it so much, if I missed a block or a tackle," Pete said, "but I just goofed off mentally. I didn't cover Flara properly, because I miscalculated the way they were lined up."

It was the mental error that bothered Dawkins, no doubt of that, but I mention this only to underscore that Pete, among everything else, was a tremendous competitor, a boy who hated to lose.

When we beat Colgate, 68 to 6, at Michie the next week, our guest of honor was President Dwight D. Eisenhower, West Point, Class of 1915. Ike never went to any of the Army-Navy games, and the story got around that he was less interested in the classic than he was in his golf game. Nothing could be further from the truth, and it is about time this canard was brought to heel.

There is no question the President loves his golf. I remember, at one of his several White House stag parties I was asked to come early, and we were discussing a new swing I was enthusiastic about. The President got out a driver and in trying out the swing, endangered the beautiful crystal chandelier hanging in the Red Room.

But he loves football even more. On one occasion, while visiting his old friend, General Harris Jones, then Dean of the West Point Academic Board, General Ike stated that it was the prospect of playing on the Army team that first lured him to the Academy as a plebe from Abilene, Kansas, in 1911.

As a yearling in 1912, he was making strides as a halfback, including a head-on tackle of the great Jim Thorpe in the Army-Carlisle Indian game on the Plain. Then he ruined his knee in the Tufts game and with it a promising football career. He was so discouraged that he seriously considered resigning from the Academy. It was not until he was asked by Charlie Daly to assist in coaching the Cullum Hall team, as the "B" squad was then known, that he again got a lift for cadet life.

Later as a captain in the 3rd Army at Baltimore, where MacArthur was the commanding general, Eisenhower coached the 3rd Army team's backs, and he has stated that this assignment did more than any other to develop his qualities of leadership.

It was precisely his background in football, however, that kept the President away from Army-Navy games. The intense pressure he had known as a competitor and coach returned to him in his partisanship for Army in the service classic, and he knew this would prevent him from attending and enjoying it. That was why he stayed away. (I have known many former coaches who suffered from this same emotional reaction in watching teams they had once coached.)

There was none of this pressure at the Army-Colgate game, so the President could relax and enjoy it.

The President would not have relaxed down in Houston the next week. We made our first visit in history to Texas to meet Jess Neely's Rice team. We won the game, 14–7, in probably the most dramatic finish in all Army football history.

The heat—it must have been close to 95 on the floor of Rice Stadium—added to a peak effort by Coach Neely's well-drilled team came close to undoing us. They went ahead of us, 7–0, on a pass to their brilliant offensive end, Buddy Dial. We tied it on a 70-yard series of air strikes. Caldwell completed seven in a row, two to Carpenter for 18 yards each.

At their 8, The Urchin pitched out to Anderson and Bob, faking the end run, stopped and fired to Carpenter in the end zone. Three Rice players surrounded The Lonely End, but he still went up and made an amazing catch. Although the big Southwest crowd was mainly for Rice, Carpenter's catch thrilled them. Walters converted to tie it, 7–7.

As the second half unwound, the Rice line and the heat gradually rolled us back. We spent most of the last quarter defending in our own half of the field. A pass interception by Glen Adams on the 5 broke up one threat. They stormed back to a first down on our 14. Again, as at Pittsburgh, the weather factor and relatively infrequent substituting had us in a bad way. But we rose up to hold them to 5 yards in three plays. On fourth down, they lined up for a field goal try by halfback Bill Bucek from our 17. Except at Pittsburgh, The Lonely End team all year long was able to make the big play when it had to. With fullback Don Bonko leading the charge, our players swarmed through and over the Rice line and blocked Bucek's kick.

The ball went over to us on our 24-yard line. There was little more than a minute left to play. There was no time for a long march. Even if there had been time, we were not up to it physically. If we were to pull it out, we had to do it with a pass play that would go all the way. Everybody in the stadium knew it. There was time for three more plays. The first two would have to be passes. They would serve three purposes. Either could conceivably bring a score. If incomplete, they would stop the clock. Both would set up a third pass.

On the first one, Caldwell threw to Anderson in their short right outside defensive zone for a 12-yard gain and first down on our 36. On the second, he threw to Dawkins in their short left defensive zone. This one was incomplete. In fact, it was almost intercepted. On the undefeated football journey, luck must ride as postillion.

On the second pass play, however, Dawkins sensed from the way the Rice deep left man was playing him that he could feint him to the outside and veer back to get loose down the middle. In the huddle, he tipped Caldwell, and the play was called. Caldwell faded back to his 25 and cut the ball loose down the middle. Dawkins faked to the outside, reversed sharply to the inside, broke down the middle, took the pass at full speed on the Rice 35, one step beyond the Rice halfback. Then Pete raced for home like one of those old cavalry horses at Fort Bliss, stampeding across the desert toward a corral.

On the 10-yard line, the pursuing Bucek tried to tackle Dawkins from behind. Bucek's arm reached for Pete's heels, found one of them, almost tripped him. For one black instant Pete seemed about to fall. But he managed to keep his feet and get home free. Walters kicked the point.

It was ecstatic for Army, murderous for Rice. It pointed up acutely how football, in one play, in one split second, by one inch, can be at once a peak of exaltation and a ravine of gloom.

Again, I had great reason to be truly proud of this team. That they could turn such a situation into victory again underscored their tenacity and spirit, the destiny-conscious leadership of Dawkins, his flair for the great, the dramatic play. He had been kicking himself for his pass-defense lapse at Pittsburgh. Now he had made up for it.

In our last pre-Navy test, the 26–0 victory over Villanova, Dawkins brewed more magic. The Wildcats were making a strong game of it into the second period. It was 0–0. Then Pete returned a punt 80 yards to a touchdown, a classic of swift, intelligent running behind violent open-field blocking. Soon after, he scored on a 46-yard pass from Caldwell, and on this one he faked and reversed Villanova's deep defenders right out of their shoelaces. He set up the third touchdown on a 48-yard pass play to their six, and on the next play rammed through center for the score.

In writing the story of that game, Stanley Woodward described Dawkins as "the Royal Oak, Michigan, Warlock." I looked up the word "warlock" and found it means a male witch. Not a bad description of Pete that day—and quite a few other days.

Now, for what was to be the last time, I got ready for the big one. It had been a spoiler in the past and could be again. Yet, I knew one thing about The Lonely End team. They would not let anybody down. For the first time in eight years, for the first time since before the expulsions, we were going down to the Navy game undefeated.

We liked this, and so did the Navy. This Navy team, also to be the last coached by Erdelatz, had a 6–2 record, had been upset by Tulane, 14–6, and beaten roundly by Notre Dame, 40–20. A season-long injury to Bob Reifsnyder had hurt their defenses. With Joe Tranchini at quarterback and speedy Joe Bellino at half, however, the ability of the Midshipmen to mount a dangerous attack was unquestioned.

We suspected Navy would install some unorthodox offense for us. A tribute to our defensive stature, yet, at the same time, a problem, because we had no idea what it would be. It turned out to be a strange melange of flankers, double-flankers, double reverses, laterals off double reverses, and even something that looked like the old and hoary Minnesota shift. The Minnesota Shift had first been concocted almost fifty years before by Dr. Harry Williams, who way back in 1891, had been Army's first paid football coach, on a part-time basis. In putting in the Minnesota Shift, I doubt whether Erdelatz had that in mind.

The Navy hash formation, however, was well rehearsed, well executed and gave us a bellyache. Fortunately, Dale Hall, from his spotter's perch in the press box, did such a rapid, expert job of analyzing it, I was able to get our defenses adjusted before it had gone too far.

We prepared some modifications of our own. When The Lonely End flanked to the left, we ran from a balanced instead of the usual unbalanced line. We also installed a new sequence with Anderson in motion toward The Lonely End. We decided we could and should make our running attack go to the inside. We felt Navy's pursuit, even with Reifsnyder in dry dock, would harass our flanking moves. We also knew that the threat of Anderson and Dawkins to the outside, plus the menace of The Lonely End, would give the inside running game that extra shaft of running daylight in the immediate secondary areas. Once our defense got straightened away to give us possession and position, the innovations helped us.

We also hoped to establish early command, so when we won the toss we elected to receive. Dawkins took the kick-off and came up the field with the firm intention of going all the way. His interference was forming and moving well. Peeking from behind it, he sensed daylight opening up to his left, and swerved in that direction. As he made the move, a Navy man came in on him from his right front. Bill Rowe, our center, moved across to block the Navy man. As Rowe made his move, Dawkins' right elbow came in contact with him. The ball squirted loose and Navy fell on it on our 40-yard line.

Had it not been for this fumble, I believe we would have had a far easier day of it. As it was, we had at once presented them with the ideal pad, field-wise and psychologically, from which to launch their weird collection of ancient weapons. That is what they did. They went 40 yards with them, Bellino going over for the score. They missed the extra point.

The second time they got the ball, Bob Novogratz, again our outstanding lineman, made the first of his three fumble-recoveries in their 31. But we promptly fumbled right back to them. Now, against our second team, they went 74 yards to our 13. (We had put back our first team when they reached our 20.) This was our most critical situation. If we could not stop them here, if they went in for another marker, our position would be fringing on the desperate.

Since this was Navy, this was our most important crisis of the year. Typically, The Lonely End team met it. Walters sprang through from his linebacker post, tossed Bellino for a 2-yard loss, and we took over on our 13. We were to be frustrated once more, this time by an interception, after we had moved 54 yards to their 31. The next time we got the ball, however, we finally went all the way, 68 yards, kicked the point and took a 7–6 lead just before the half ended. I felt now that we would go on and handle them.

On that first drive and throughout the afternoon, Bob Anderson was the dominant figure. For some strange reason—the spectacular play of Dawkins, I suppose—it was generally overlooked that the all-around play of Anderson had made him even more valuable than the year before. It should be understood that while Anderson and Dawkins were both great runners, Anderson was emphatically the superior blocker. There was more percentage, therefore, in having Dawkins carry more often. That explains in part why Anderson's running exploits, while still substantial and indispensable, were somewhat overshadowed. Meanwhile, as a supplementary passing threat to Caldwell and as a tower of defensive strength, Anderson was increasing his stature.

In the Navy game, our planned pattern of attack to the inside restored Andy to front stage. He hammered their right side off the dive-tackle play and macerated their left side on a reverse behind the devastating lead blocks of Novogratz.

My old assistants, whenever possible, showed up at Navy games and came around to visit with us afterwards. That day, Vince Lombardi, was present in the stands. I am told he kept standing and shouting, "Give the ball to Anderson! Give the ball to Anderson!"

In twenty-nine carries against defenses that knew he was coming, Anderson totaled 89 yards. The only time he ran to the outside, his eagerness caused him to fumble. He scored our first and second touchdowns at the end of 68- and 58-yard drives. Dawkins, whose poise did not permit his experience on the opening kick-off to affect him, contributed more and more running help as the game advanced. A 29-yard pass he took from Caldwell off the new man-in-motion sequence was a strong factor in our second touchdown march.

We by no means neglected the pass. Caldwell connected on ten of eighteen for 145 yards. With Carpenter used mainly as a decoy, the principal receivers were Usry and Dawkins.

In the second half, with our defenses properly adjusted, we restricted Navy's running to 32 yards and rushed and covered their passes. Chuckles Axmurder was at his best. Yet the possibility of a Navy touchdown and a subsequent two-point conversion left our 14–6 lead unsafe until there was less than two minutes to play.

At that point Usry, "The Gregarious End," mingled advantageously in our pass defense to pick off a Tranchini aerial and return it 38 yards to a score. Then in a most appropriate final fling, Captain Dawkins wrote "The End" to The Year of the Lonely End by pitching, as he had at Notre Dame, a two-point conversion pass to Anderson. That made it 22–6. In fact, that made it.

In the dressing room, Dawkins showed his humility when he remarked to an interviewer, "We got off to a great start, didn't I?"

Anderson, Dawkins, and Novogratz made the All America team, the first time one school had been honored by placing three men since Notre Dame in 1949.

As I look back on The Year of the Lonely End, I think most often of the pressures that were thrown against our team: tough, "up" opposition, injuries, trying weather conditions, lack of any real qualitative depth, and a fumble or interception here and there. No Army team, except the Vindicators of 1946, met and survived such tests of championship mettle as The Lonely End team did against Notre Dame, Pittsburgh, Rice, and Navy.

"It is the hallmark of a fine team," I told the writers after the Navy game, "when it can take adversity and bend but not break. On any given Saturday, when we happened to be playing our game, I do not think any college team in the country could contain us."

Pete Dawkins and The Lonely End team made what was to be the last of my twenty-five seasons as a head coach in many ways the best. Through tremendous first-team talent, brightened with unusual color and favored by good fortune, but most of all through their indomitable spirit, they brought Army football back to the national pre-eminence it enjoyed before the tragedy of 1951.

After the Navy game, General MacArthur wired:

IN THE LONG HISTORY OF WEST POINT ATHLETICS THERE HAS NEVER BEEN A GREATER TRIUMPH. IT HAS BROUGHT PRIDE AND HAPPINESS AND ADMIRATION TO MILLIONS OF ARMY ROOTERS THROUGHOUT THE WORLD. TELL CAPTAIN DAWKINS AND HIS INDOMITABLE TEAM THEY HAVE WRITTEN THEIR NAMES IN GOLDEN LETTERS ON THE TABLETS OF FOOTBALL FAME. FOR YOU, MY DEAR OLD FRIEND, IT MARKS ONE OF THE MOST GLORIOUS MOMENTS OF YOUR PEERLESS CAREER. THERE IS NO SUBSTITUTE FOR VICTORY.

Chapter XX

Old Coaches Never Die

When I resigned as West Point's football coach on Tuesday, January 13, 1959, the announcement caught many by surprise, including my own family. It was natural that many people conjectured as to the reasons. Some said I had disagreed with the Military Academy's Superintendent on athletic policies. My age and health were cited. Army's undefeated Year of The Lonely End also was mentioned as the ideal time to say, "So long."

These three reasons did contribute to my decision, but would not of themselves, singly or collectively, have been enough to impel me to resign. To break away from the fascinating life with the cadets and football was most difficult. The situation finally demanded abrupt action lest it became too late to act with propriety.

The main reason I called it a career after twenty-five years as a head coach was that, at sixty-one years of age, I had received several tempting business offers. One in particular made good sense.

I had seriously contemplated leaving football to return to business as far back as 1948. My retirement in a sense was ten years overdue, therefore, when I accepted the offer in January of 1959 from Victor Emanuel, chairman of the board of the AVCO Corporation, to join that company. Victor had been urging me to join him for several years. The temptation to accept had been strong because of the problems that faced me during my last few years at the Academy. I had not wanted to leave, however, until I felt I had restored Army football, at least within the restrictions that surround it. That time had come, I felt, after our 22–6 victory over Navy provided a soul-satisfying climax to The Lonely End campaign.

The position I accepted from AVCO was that of a vice-president and member of the management group of a corporation doing important and exciting research work in the field of missiles and space exploration.

Mr. Emanuel reasoned that my main work, my life one might say —coaching football—gave me a background in dealing with people that would be valuable to the company. He also felt I had a good business and financial background, having been chairman of the Athletic Board, director of a bank and other enterprises, and partner in the building firm of W. D. and E. H. Blaik.

Shortly after I joined AVCO I attended a meeting of more than nine hundred of the company's stockholders at Wilmington, Massachusetts. For a while this meeting reminded me of my football days. In fact I even suspected somebody had planted a Navy or Notre Dame heckler in the audience when one individual enquired from the floor whether the "athletic director of AVCO" had received stock options.

This "Lonely Questioner" was more than offset, however, by another stockholder who evoked applause by stating that I should be made a six-star general. At length Mr. Emanuel explained to the stockholders just why he was sure I would more than justify the decision to hire me. But to make my position unequivocably clear, I told the stockholders, "If I can't contribute something very material to AVCO, I'll be the first to realize it, and you'll be the first to know when I leave, because I would not want to stay."

Much of my work involves traveling between New York, where we have our head office, and our widely distributed divisional plants, and occasionally to Washington. I am amazed at the amount of paper work. One day's turnover would rival in thickness the sheaf of plays that Francis Schmidt, the old master of razzle-dazzle at Ohio State twenty-five years ago, used to bring onto the field. But I enjoy the work.

As I told Ted Smits, sports editor of the Associated Press, soon after I took the job, you meet the same things in business that you meet in football, but not quite so explosively. There's more give and take in business, more rolling with the punch, more compromise. Business, like football, has its Monday quarterbacks, its sophomore enthusiasts, and its vigilante committees. You could even compare

Congress, in its regulatory functions, to the National Collegiate Athletic Association.

I enjoy my work with AVCO. The fact is, I've been so busy since I left West Point that I haven't had time to sit down and decide whether I miss football—and, if so, how much. However, I am by no means losing contact with the game. I am active in the National Football Foundation and Hall of Fame, and in my spare time I am writing newspaper articles on college football during the season.

Now, about the other reasons given for my retirement. First, my disagreements with Academy athletic policy. For the record, throughout my coaching days at both Dartmouth and Army, I always enjoyed the support of the faculty. Between myself and the rest of the Army Athletic Board, which consisted of three permanent professors and the Commandant, there never was a disagreement on major policy. This fact derived from my belief that football is secondary to the purpose for which the player is in college.

As for my attitude toward West Point football and the profession of soldiering, I always emphasized to the cadet-athlete that a military career, though limited in monetary reward, holds a future of continuous education, travel, and worth-while associations, and provides a personal satisfaction seldom found in any civilian pursuit.

The few disagreements on athletic policy at West Point were with the Superintendent, Lieutenant General Garrison H. Davidson, who succeeded Lieutenant General Blackshear M. Bryan on July 15, 1956. I suppose that, to some extent, it was only natural for a former coach to make athletic policy one of his primary interests and to devote much time to writing athletic directives.

When General Davidson became superintendent I had been head football coach for fifteen years, director of athletics for ten years and chairman of the Athletic Board for seven years. However, the Supe was an old coach, and old coaches never die; they just write directives. In retrospect, though, our differences, except one, were relatively minor.

Let me emphasize here that Army's failure to play in a 1959 Bowl game had absolutely nothing to do with my retirement. The subject of a Bowl game came up yearly at West Point, but happened to be one the Superintendent and I did not discuss.

During most of November in our 1958 season, there was much conjecture in the newspapers about Army and a New Year's Day game, as it was a known fact that, from Pete Dawkins to The Lonely End, our players were eager to be in a Bowl.

Captain Pete Dawkins, who may include clairvoyance among his multiple gifts as a leader, athlete, and student, seemed to sense that we were going to have a great year. He asked me in September if we could go to a Bowl, provided we went undefeated. I promised him I would not oppose the wish of the squad.

For my own part, I am not opposed to Bowl games per se, but rather believe they make New Year's one of the most enjoyable days of the year. Still, the prospect of Army in a Bowl never excited me, because I feel that, after Army-Navy, any game is anticlimactic.

Sure enough, Bowl committees, as in other years, were eager to invite Army. Much to my surprise the Athletic Board voted unanimously to play in the Cotton Bowl. (I abstained from voting.) The Superintendent, however, removed Army from Bowl consideration in a statement ten days before the Navy game. The members of the squad showed their disappointment for several days, but then forgot it in getting ready for the game that had been haunting them for twelve months.

There was, in fact, one major area of difference between the views of the Superintendent and myself, and I refer to it mainly to establish the difficulty of playing topflight football at West Point. This difference was over the number of appointments to the Academy to be apportioned to football men out of the number given to all athletes.

Even with an all-out recruiting effort and the help of Congressmen who appreciated the problem, Army football in my last eight years lacked, and still lacks, sufficient over-all qualitative depth. In 1959 there was a definite shortage from tackle to tackle, and the unusually heavy string of injuries which befell Dale Hall's squad also accentuated the fact that in the positions where there was presumably some reserve power the fall-off from first- to second-string level was still considerable.

Before 1958, however, it was far worse because we were deficient in such essentials as good linebacking and quarterbacking. Lack of qualitative depth can make injuries disastrous. In 1958, we were fortunate, as I have said earlier, that injuries hurt us badly only in the 14–14 tie at Pittsburgh.

This crucial lack of depth traces, of course, to an insufficiency of potentially top-grade players among the incoming plebe class each July. The problem is augmented by the unusually high rate of attrition at West Point.

I hammered at these points to little avail. I argued that if we were to continue to meet successfully not only Navy (which has 1,200 more men than Army's 2,500 and a proportionate, if not greater, edge in football recruitment), but also Oklahoma, Pittsburgh, California, Illinois, Michigan, Syracuse, Duke, the Air Force, and other major college powers, we must increase our qualitative-depth potential by more football appointments.

Let me state the case more specifically. A careful statistical study showed that, of the cadet football players who were appointed to alternate vacancies in the plebe classes of the 'fifties, only 30 per cent were developing to be of ultimate value in a major game. The other 70 per cent were failing to develop major-game caliber, although happily measuring up to West Point standards in other respects.

The reason for this is that the West Point recruiting program seldom brings in a "blue-chip" secondary-school player, like Bob Anderson, because the "blue-chippers" seldom have the ability and/or the inclination to get by the rest of the Academy screening. Dawkins and Bob Novogratz were not exceptional prospects in high school. Yet both won All America honors, along with Anderson. They were examples of boys who developed spectacularly at the Point, largely because of the inspirational atmosphere of the Corps.

Most of our high-school prospects did not develop that way. (A few even chose to play other sports than football; the final decision as to what sport he plays is made by the cadet himself.) Some of course, were injured. Only a few were scholastic casualties, because our recruiting cannot encourage taking the marginal academic risk.

Our study also showed that in the 'fifties the number of plebe football appointments was ranging from eighteen to twenty-four. Applying the average 70-per-cent rate of attrition, we were getting about seven players out of each plebe class who would help us.

Now bear in mind that in 1958, for the first time in my coaching experience at West Point, we had been guaranteed 75 alternate vacancies in sufficient time to establish a definite quota for each sport. Such a positive number of vacancies to be filled held out great hopes for a reasonable replenishing of our depleted football squad.

Early in 1958 I presented our study to the Athletic Board, with the warning that we would soon again be in an untenable position, as we pretty much had been from 1954 through 1957, unless we did something about it. I asked that we be allowed an absolute minimum of thirty-five football appointments among the incoming plebe class of 1958. The Board, as a gesture to show it had not been completely taken in by my plaints, trimmed the number to thirty-three. In the end, however, the Superintendent cut it to twenty-eight.

To the layman, offhand, twenty-eight might seem a sufficient number. It would be if the players could be hand-picked for football ability alone and were not subject to the rigid over-all West Point requirements. But applying the 70-per-cent rate of attrition means you get about eight who will help you. Considering the total and the rate of attrition, twenty-eight doesn't begin to compare with the material recruited by the major schools Army must play. In 1958, for example, the director of athletics at Annapolis stated that Navy brought in over one hundred players.

The Superintendent's policy dictated channeling the extra appointments I asked for into other sports. More than half the baseball, basketball, and hockey appointments in my tenure had come from my work with Congressmen. But the Superintendent's policy was "equality for all sports." I argued that this would be fine—in fact, ideal—if there were enough appointments to go around. But since there were not, football must be first established on a solid footing, if for no other reason than self-preservation.

I pointed out that for eighteen years we had underwritten the school's entire intercollegiate program and that despite a vast expansion program of several million dollars, including a golf course, we had still been able to establish a sound financial position, with $1,500,000 in the bank.

We could only maintain this position, I summed up, by establishing a continuingly realistic football program. Once we had done this, and had somehow arranged for more appointments, we could also improve the other sports. I also pointed out that football schedules had to be drawn up several years in advance, while in other sports they can be made up from year to year to fit the material to be available.

Let me emphasize that the Superintendent's position on this matter was an honest as my own. But I believe his thinking was predicated on the days when the Army football schedule did not compare in toughness with what the cadets take on today.

The disagreements in the final analysis, however, were a minor factor in my resignation, compared with protecting my health. I am in good health today, but I might not have been if I had gone on coaching. Ever since 1954, whenever the raw, cold, rainy fall weather came down the Hudson Valley, I had suffered from that heavy bronchial cough. It was especially aggravated by the normal pressures of coaching, a job that constantly takes something out of one physically, especially as he gets older, whether he is aware of it or not.

After the 1958 season, when I sat down to discuss the business opportunities with Merle and my sons, Bill and Bob, the question of my health came up. But it would not of itself have been enough to make me resign. Nor was our Lonely End record of itself a reason, although admittedly a nice note to leave on.

In short, the principal reason for my resignation was as I have stated it: I had a number of fine business offers and the time had come for me to accept one of them. In football coaching, as in anything else, it is unthinkable to overstay a career.

I had been too preoccupied with the job during the 1958 season to think much about retirement. After the Navy game I realized I must face up to a decision. The first thing I did in early December was to get my assistant coaches signed to new contracts for 1959. This would protect them for a year if I decided to retire and they were not retained in the new regime and the right jobs did not open up for them elsewhere.

I was reasonably certain that graduate coaching would be retained, and if it were, the logical successor would be Dale Hall. In that case, Dale would want to keep intact the staff he had worked with as an assistant—Tom Harp, Frank Lauterbur, Chuck Gottfried, and Bill Gunlock—a young staff and one of the best I ever had: bright, hard-working and loyal. And that was the way it worked out, with Dale, my only recommendation to succeed me, appointed on January 31.

With the assistants signed, I headed for Key Biscayne again to let sun and relaxation work on my bronchial condition. On December 17, I was at Richmond, to receive their first Sportsmen's Club Award from Governor J. Lindsay Almond, Jr. I then returned to the Academy and during the Christmas holidays had more than one talk with my family about retiring. They felt the time had come for me to leave coaching and they sensed that I felt the same. Yet they were not at all sure that I actually would make the break.

Meanwhile I had been conferring regularly with Victor Emanuel, and had discussions also with other companies.

There had been a story by Max Kase in the New York *Journal-American* early in December that I would resign. It was a shrewd guess and forecast, as things developed, but I actually had not made any decision at the time of that story.

As the early days of January passed, the rumors died down, and it was more or less expected that I would stay on. On Sunday, January 11, my son Bill typed the original resignation draft. That was the situation when, late in the afternoon of Monday, January 12, I called in Miss Harriet Demarest, my loyal secretary for eighteen years, and dictated the final letter of resignation to be sent to the Superintendent. Miss Demarest was saddened, I could see, as she took the letter.

"When you've finished it and I've signed it," I said, "put it in an envelope, seal it, and lock it away until tomorrow morning. I want one more night to sleep on it."

The next morning I phoned Joe Cahill, the sports information director, and asked him to come up to my office. Joe, son of an enlisted Army man, had come on the job sixteen years before, in 1943, the same year as Glenn Davis and Herman Hickman. He had been with me through the good times, the bad times, and the other times. I told him I intended to hand in my resignation that morning and wanted to alert him so that he could prepare a press announcement for later in the day. Joe was a little stunned, and I guess I was a little stunned myself. We talked and reminisced for a while. Joe said it would not be the same for him at West Point any more, and I told him my life never would be quite the same any more, either.

Joe said finally, "What time are you figuring on delivering the letter?"

I got up and reached for my hat and overcoat. "Now's as good a time as any, Joe," I said.

I walked across the Plain to the Supe's office. I had never realized it was such a long walk. He was not there, so I left the letter and returned to the football office. Sometime later, he phoned, said he had the letter and was sorry I was leaving. He called a hurried meeting of the Athletic Board and late that afternoon the story was released.

Early in the afternoon I left the Academy and headed for New York, where I had dinner with Merle, Bill, and the McDonalds, who had shared the de-emphasized cavalry days. Before dinner the news of my resignation came over the radio and that was the first Merle knew of it. Although she had suspected I might do it, she wasn't sure; so she was stunned and, I think, a little sad and happy, mostly happy.

I felt that was the way I had to do it. There had been enough talking and discussion. If there had been any more, I might have got argumentative and talked not only my family but also myself into staying on. In the end it had to be my own decision.

The treatment the newspapers, news magazines, radio, and television gave me on my retirement always will be a source of the warmest gratification, as will the hundreds of letters I received from people in all walks of life all over America, in and out of the army, in and out of football. My first phone call came from Secretary of the Army Wilbur M. Brucker, who could not have been more considerate. Since I can't begin to quote even a few of the letters here, I'll quote just one:

The White House,
Jan. 14, 1959

Dear Red:

It was with feelings considerably stronger than astonishment that I learned last evening of your resignation. I hasten to say that although I clearly recognize that your leaving will be an irreparable loss to present and future Army football teams, to West Point, to the Army and, yes, to the public, yet I heartily approve of your action.

Few people, I am persuaded, understand the intensity of the nervous strain under which a coach must live who has to train teams that are engaged in highly competitive athletics. It is no wonder that as the years inevitably creep up on all of us, the man occupying such a demanding position sometimes looks toward an occupation where concentration is less rigorous, the pace a bit slower, and remuneration a bit better. What I am trying to say is that it is high time you thought of yourself—and you have already given more of yourself for the sake of our deeply felt loyalties than have most people.

There was some speculation in my morning's paper that your decision might be based on differences of opinion in the Army as to whether or not West Point should play in post-season bowl games. As for this, I have never heard the matter discussed by any other West Pointer except in terms of "whatever Blaik feels is best, I am for it." For my part I never even turned on the television or the radio to keep track of a bowl game. My interest is in the contests of the season, but possibly this reaction is somewhat affected by my knowledge that West Point has not played in bowl games.

In any event, along with the gratitude that I have always felt for the dedicated, selfless and brilliant services you have rendered at the Academy, I send you also my very best wishes for an even better record in the commercial world. I am quite certain that many thousands, particularly including the Cadets who have played under your tutelage, would like to join in an expression of these sentiments.

Please remember me warmly to Mrs. Blaik, and to both of you my personal regards and Godspeed.

As ever,
DWIGHT D. EISENHOWER

At the annual dinner on January 22 of the Touchdown Club, which presented me its silver-anniversary award for service to football, I quoted from some letters I had received which were rather dissimilar in content and tone to the President's.

For example, one I received after the 14–14 tie with Pitt: "Your dumbness cost the Army a tie. Why didn't you go for a field goal? And you're a coach? You cost me dough. (Signed) A Taxpayer."

Another: "You are to the Army as Durocher was to the Giants. I hope some team knocks your brains out. (Signed) Anti-Blaik."

And this gem: "So you consumed another set-up. Wait till you meet Navy—ya bum. (Signed) Vassar." The word "consumed" made the message authentic Vassar.

I particularly liked this one: "Who ever thought you were a coach? Why did you kick off and where did you get that jerk of a quarterback? You stink. (Signed) Your Friend."

For the first time in my life I got to attending a small round of dinners. The best was a surprise party at Leone's tendered by Bull Ponders, past and present, and attended by General McArthur and his long-time associate, General Courtney Whitney, General Babe Bryan, Victor Emanuel, Biff Jones, Army coaches of all sports, and other Academy friends. Gene said it was the finest party in the entire history of the restaurant. The menu, especially printed, read: "Bull Pond Banquet for BIG BROTHER (The nickname of Big Brother was hung on me at Bull Pond in 1958 by Stan Woodward). Place: The Lonely End Inn. Date: The Ides (Plus 1) of February, 1959. The menu itself was as follows:

Antipasto Novogratz

Fish Cakes a la Notre Dame

Half Baked Goat garnished with Sauce Erdelatz

Chuckles Axmurder Salad

Dawkins Parfait

Hot Cocoa Anderson with Whipped Linebackers

Iced Hemlock . Cashew Nuts . Opium

Thank goodness, there was an optional dinner on request.

These few dinners, however, were oases in a schedule of work and transition that was as exacting as any I ever experienced. There was the sad job of moving out of our West Point quarters, built for us by Uncle Bobby Eichelberger. We took up temporary residence in a New York hotel before moving into a permanent apartment in early summer.

On June 6, Miami of Oxford, first of my two alma maters, presented me with the Honorary Degree of Doctor of Laws at the University's Sesquicentennial Commencement. In my address I mentioned: "It was only yesterday that the mighty sophomores attacked our class in Harrison Hall and were met with a barrage of water that drenched such important targets as Prexy Hughes, Dad Wolfe (the night watchman), and General Ed Hull, then a husky sophomore getting his basic training in warfare. That yesterday, my friends, was over forty years ago."

Much of the glow of my visit to Miami was dimmed soon after when Merle tripped over a telephone cord and suffered a hip fracture that left her hospitalized for many weeks and recuperative for many more.

In addition to the demands of my AVCO job, I had to find time to negotiate with Henry Holt and Company, which was to publish my autobiography; *Look* Magazine, which secured the first serialization rights, and the Associated Press for the semiweekly articles on current football topics, which ran through September, October, and November, of 1959. Ninety-six newspapers across the country carried the articles. I soon discovered some of them had conflicting ideas as to what I should write.

My proceeds from these articles are used to provide postgraduate fellowships, known as the National Football Foundation's scholar-athlete awards. Eight seniors, representing each of the eight districts in college football, are chosen from nominations submitted from district awards committees of the Foundation by a national committee, of which Vincent Draddy is chairman. The 1959 winners were:

District 1 (New England): Paul J. Choquette, Brown University, All Ivy League and All New England first team, Dean's List scholar and Rhodes scholarship nominee, who will study law.

District 2 (Middle Atlantic States): Gerhard H. Schwedes, Syracuse University captain and halfback, Dean's List student, who will study foreign service.

District 3 (Southeastern States): Neyle Sollee, University of Tennessee, fullback and alternate team captain, *magna cum laude* student, who will study dentistry.

District 4 (Middle Western States): Philip G. Roos, Ohio Weslyan University tackle, outstanding lineman for three years and honorary mathematics and physics student, who will study physics.

District 5 (Plains States): Harry R. Tolly, University of Nebraska outstanding quarterback and mathematics student, who will do postgraduate work in education.

District 6 (Southwestern States): Maurice Doke, University of Texas All America guard, outstanding chemical engineering student, and nominated for a Rhodes scholarship; he will study chemical engineering.

District 7 (Mountain States): Pat Smyth, of the University of Wyoming, outstanding guard of the Skyline Conference and honor student in pre-medicine, who will study medicine.

District 8 (Pacific Coast States): Donald P. Newell, outstanding tackle and captain of the University of California and honor student in business administration, who will study law.

In addition to their academic and athletic excellence, these eight boys also met the awards' requisite of campus leadership. They point up my often-reiterated belief that outstanding athletic ability and superior scholarship are altogether compatible.

Although I was too busy to decide how much I missed coaching, when the days of late August and early September arrived and fall practice began, it was indeed a strange feeling not to be doing what I had been doing every fall since 1925, thirty-four years before. I did not appreciate how acutely things had changed for me, however, until the night before Army's opening game with Boston College at Michie Stadium.

An old friend, a coffee merchant whose name I have never found out, phoned me at our new Manhattan home. Ever since the expulsions in 1951, he had called me regularly during the football season, sometimes during the week to cheer me up before a game, sometimes on Sunday to praise or commiserate. He was never critical, so I was always glad to hear from him. He usually phoned during my supper hour and frequently would be interrupted by the operator, asking him to put another coin in the pay phone, which, I always suspected from his invariable mellowness, was located in a pub.

On the eve of my first game as a non-coach, my coffee-merchant friend talked to me in such tearful tones that I was about ready to break down myself.

The next day I drove up to West Point and watched Army beat Boston College in Dale Hall's first game as head coach. It was the first game I ever saw in Michie Stadium as a spectator.

The next week Army played at Illinois. That weekend I had to be at AVCO's New Idea Plant for farm equipment in Coldwater, Ohio. I left Coldwater for New York in a company plane about 3:00 P.M., with Dick Wilson, President of AVCO, and Dr. William Myers, retired Dean of the Cornell School of Agriculture. It was an interesting coincidence that Dick Wilson was statistician of my first team at Dartmouth in 1934.

Dick had a radio and we tuned in on the Army-Illinois game. We heard Illinois take the lead, and we heard of the disastrous injury to Bob Anderson, which began the 1959 Cadet team's long string of misfortunes. It was a helpless feeling to be sitting there in that plane, listening to the Army team in action miles away.

I heard the third quarter of the game in a taxi taking me from the airport to our apartment. Army had struck back and was now trailing only 20–14.

Merle greeted me at the door. "What's the matter?" she asked. "You look as pale as a ghost."

"There is something the matter with me, I guess," I told her, "but I don't know what it is. Have you got the game on? They still have time to pull it out."

They didn't quite pull it out and they went on through an injury-ridden, fumble-plagued fall that ended in the resounding defeat by Navy. All this made my first season away from coaching a hard one to live through.

In September this Army team had been picked to finish among the first five nationally. Stunned Cadet followers, in and out of the Army, were still asking months later, "What happened?"

The answer is obvious. As I have said, lack of qualitative depth can make injuries disastrous. The injuries to Farris, Kyasky, Mikelonis, and others had already proved that through much of the 'fifties. We had been extremely fortunate in 1958. But when an unprecedented string of injuries hit the '59 team, the penalty of insufficient qualitative depth was accentuated as never before.

With Anderson and other key men sidelined or slowed down, a fine coaching staff was unable to mount the running game that is indispensable. Too much reliance was placed on the passing game. Army finally cracked under the strain, and fell apart.

It would be naïve, however, to impute the entire blame to injuries and the consequent fumbling and overemphasis on passing. It is also a fact that the devaluation of football's importance, inherent in the "equality for all sports" philosophy, contributed to what happened, even though the players themselves might not be aware of it.

It is also true that plebe football at the Academy in recent years has been underemphasized.

All of these factors add up to something far short of that complete dedication which is indispensable to achieving the primary objective of Army football: victory over Navy.

I am informed, however, that the Navy debacle has restored to West Point a proper emphasis on regaining football prestige, which reminds me of the "crash program" mandate passed to me back in 1941 by General Eichelberger. "Equality for all sports" has been shelved in favor of "What happened and what can be done to help football?" This augurs well for the future.

The Army team, as it has in the past, will reflect the last words of the Johnnie Armstrong lines by the anonymous author. I quote them here, in finishing this work, because they embody that greatest lesson taught us, young and old, by football, the game closest to life as it is closest to war:

> *Fight on, my merry men all,*
> *I'm a little wounded, but I am not slain;*
> *I will lay me down for to bleed a while,*
> *Then I'll rise and fight with you again.*

Part II

As I Knew Them
Earl H. Blaik

Chapter XXI

The Decade of the 60's

The experiences of the next ten years away from coaching were filled with events that I recall with as much interest as I do the happenings of earlier days, when the scoreboard was the only barometer.

The rewarding 32 years of association as football coach with the young men of West Point and Dartmouth served as my introduction into business and political circles. I can think of no other profession that provides one the opportunity to know on a personal basis such a variety of fine and gracious people. This host of acquaintances and friends has not lessened with retirement, and for this fact I shall be forever grateful.

As a representative of West Point, for years I called on congressmen and senators to solicit appointments for young men to the Academy. This association kept alive the interest kindled in college days in national affairs, a concern that remains paramount in my thoughts. The experiences related in these chapters involve professional and political people whom I knew both during and after my coaching days.

After leaving West Point, I needed only a season to become a fan rather than a coach. Although the game of football changed little, while total attendance moved steadily upward, there was a noticeable downward trend in campus support. As a matter of fact, all is not well with this amateur sport even today.

There is little doubt that undergraduate enthusiasm for football has lessened. The students' seriousness of purpose and concern for world affairs changed the image of Joe College. Lack of interest has replaced the former involvement in all undergraduate affairs. This indifference may be due in part to the fact that this generation was to carry a hated Vietnam war that inspired a break with tradition.

Perhaps the ennui has subconscious roots in the conviction that a welfare state will shelter its people in the future. Certainly, there is less concern for the so-called rainy day. Regardless of reasons, however, the fact remains that the undergraduate attitude toward football, its heroes, and such established institutions as fraternities has eroded.

The open grant of athletic scholarships by colleges emphasizes the view often expressed by faculty members that the football player is an athlete with an incidental scholastic interest. Where football players are housed together and separated from nonplaying classmates, they are inevitably regarded as a group apart, with less dedication to the educational purposes of the college. Thus, the football player has lost his special identity as a man of importance on the campus.

In Chapter XVI of this book, I detailed suggestions that I made to the football coaches' association, the acceptance of which might have encouraged in nonbelievers a greater acceptance of the game. I believe that these suggestions continue to have validity today. For years a vocal college minority has challenged the place of a violent sport in the life of an educational community. It appears that yesterday's minority has increased to a point just short of a majority of undergraduates.

The ever-increasing popularity of professional football, added to the disillusionment fostered by campus unrest, has diminished the interest of the alumnus in his alma mater varsity team. Since college football attendance has risen yearly in the last decade, this may seem paradoxical. Today's mature alumnus has convinced himself of the unimportance of the game to the well-being of his university. The perennial sophomore fan has become a character of the past. Finally, the modern college president is a captive of the undergraduate community and is not inclined to counter the trend.

The names of Stagg, Heisman, Yost, Rockne, Houghton, Warner, winners all, in years past were household names that have few modern counterparts. With the current marked undergraduate indifference to the game few college coaches have the opportunity for leadership on the campus, and just as few are readily recalled by the sporting public. Unfortunately, the college coach and the college game have been submerged in the popular legends that now grow about the professional coach and game. With the sports page emphasis on the professional leagues, the situation would probably be the same even were the great college coaches of yesterday still with us.

A combination of undergraduate reorientation of interests and values; a failure by the coaches' association to recognize the need for change; the high cost of recruiting and fielding a squad; the competition of pro football for prime TV time and newspaper space —all have increasingly forced the college game into a position of secondary importance. What is the future of the college game? The growing lack of undergraduate interest and the burdensome expense of fielding a squad have caused too many colleges to drop varsity football. The fact that this has occurred without strong protest from either students or alumni confirms their indifference to the game. The bottom line of the financial statement of the athletic department in red ink can no longer be balanced by other university funds. There no longer exist other sources to which the college president may turn to alleviate the financial plight of the athletic department.

Even those institutions with huge endowments seem unable to operate with a balanced budget. The stranglehold of the American Association of University Professors, in some ways threatening the life of a university, is as strong as that of any labor union in industry. It is hopeless for university trustees to attempt to gain even a modicum of relief from the featherbedding practices of their faculties. It is no wonder that many colleges are approaching bankruptcy in this day of inflated costs.

Since college football can no longer be underwritten by special funds, coaches must face this fact squarely. Costs must be reduced to stop the trend to reduce the game to intramural status. Too many colleges have already turned to the less expensive popular sport of basketball for national recognition.

Any Monday morning quarterback can pass judgment on conditions about which he knows little. Since there are areas for improvement in college football about which I have some knowledge, I should like to consider the question of how costs may be reduced.

Coaching staffs are much larger than required for efficient planning and field operation. Staffs are too large because the squads are inflated, and squads are unnecessarily large because the coaches recruit too many players. In part, this may be attributed to the two-platoon football system, which I have vigorously endorsed. There is a justified impression that liberal substitution has created specialization and that, to compete with the coach who has team and individual specialists, a large squad is required.

But why let a few coaches of major college teams set the pattern that is forcing the near bankruptcy of college football? Let's take the problems in reverse order. Two-platoon football with specialists can be played well with squads that are smaller in number. The pros, for example, always mindful of the dollar, restrict the number of players to 40. There is ample reason to limit the college varsity squad to 45 and the traveling squad to 36 players.

Once the size of the squads is restricted, it becomes logical to further limit the scholarships given to recruited freshmen and junior college players. This then leads to the coaching staff: if the squads are smaller, there is less need for large staffs both to recruit and to train. The large coaching staffs, heavy recruiting expenses, and the number of scholarships required to field excessively large squads presently are forcing the costs of college teams beyond acceptable limits.

The decrease in the number of squad members and the lowering of attending costs would save thousands of dollars for athletic departments. A smaller coaching staff and fewer players would further the personal relationship of the head coach to his players, a situation that does not exist where large squads make it necessary for the head coach to communicate and delegate through his large staff to his men. Furthermore, the spreading of talent among the colleges would improve the caliber of teams in the small institutions and in no way seriously restrict the performance of the major college teams. There is no justification for overloading with football talent those schools that presently dominate college football.

To further the acceptance of the football player and integrate him into the student body, coaches should encourage their compact group of players to participate in other extracurricular activities. Once this occurs, the term "Jocks" could no longer be applied to the football squad as a separate entity on the college campus.

It is of interest to recall that football was not always big business. In the 1920's the stadiums of this country were filled by college crowds that paid a top price of $3.00. College football came closest to underemphasizing the dollar at the turn of the century when Yale and Harvard came to play the Cadets on the Plain, each for a $300 guarantee. Those games, by the way, were hotly contested, and the interest of the alumni was much greater than it is today.

I recall another example of the game played for its own sake rather than for financial gain. I still have a letter written in 1921 by Knute Rockne to Captain Matthew B. Ridgway, then graduate manager of athletics at West Point and later Army Chief of Staff, agreeing to a game the following November between Army and Notre Dame at West Point for reimbursement of out-of-pocket expenses and no more. The letter lists the cost of railroad fares, berths and meals for a total of $1678.62, an expenditure approved by General MacArthur, then Superintendent of the Academy.

Although the internal problems affecting college football are numerous, many believe that the professional game is the real threat, implying that the college game is inferior and has less spectator appeal. Certainly, the college play in the early sixties was a drab spectacle; during the past several years, however, undergraduate football has given the spectator excitement unsurpassed by the professional game, which has permitted its pattern of play to become stereotyped.

There are also those who believe that college football is merely the farm system for the pros. It has never been more than a source of supply, since only a small percentage of college players are interested in this postgraduate profession or have the ability to engage in it.

It is fortunate for college football that the pro teams are entirely dependent on the teaching of the game and its basic fundamentals by college coaches. Unlike basketball, the pressure from the professional leagues does not involve tampering with college players. The owners of pro franchises are well aware that their game is the beneficiary of years of teaching by dedicated college coaches.

I do not imply that a good college team can compete successfully with a good pro team, but I do believe that good college teams playing opponents of comparable ability generate as much excitement and fascination with their present style of play as do the pros.

The illusion that it takes years for a college player to make the pro team was laid to rest years ago when, through necessity, the pros played recruits who almost immediately became stars. However, the closely knit old pro players are not about to let a come lately college stars jeopardize their positions by making the big time the first year. Thus, there is necessarily a degree of apprenticeship, a period of bench warming before a player becomes a pro. Namath, Plunkett, O. J. Simpson, Butkus and Foreman are necessarily exceptions. There is little difference between the learning span for the two games; to suggest that a pro team employs 300 plays may impress a gullible public, but hardly one closely acquainted with the game.

The professional coach is first an able administrator and organizer of a variety of men, and only then a football tactician. With rare exceptions, the pro coach is not an imaginative innovator, but one who takes the existing excellent college product and the systems long in use in the college game and attempts to improve upon them. The college coach evolves the original thinking and strategy; the process of change in American football flows up to and not down from the pro game.

The threat to college football obviously no longer comes from the professional game; internal problems are the real challenge. Unhappily, these problems may be solved imperfectly by athletic directors with sharp pencils or by educators with scalpels. Logically, however, the future of college football should be determined best by the positive attitude and direct action of the American Association of College Football Coaches.

There is hope, then, that college football will continue to merit the respect movie director Frank Capra, recipient of many Oscars, so eloquently expressed for undergraduate sports:

> A game is a highly concentrated cross section of life itself, with the triumphs and failures, the ups and downs and crisscrosses of life all telescoped into one hour of high-voltage activity. A game is really an unrehearsed form of play before an audience; a play that creates its own plot, its own heroes, villains and fools; where all men start even, but finish staggered; a play that humbles the proud and elevates the meek; a play that X-rays virtues and flaws of character, that not only tests one's moral and physical courage, but builds them as well; a play in which the characters never come out the same as when the curtain went up; a play where growth is the author. Fair play, the will to win, and devotion to team work are American characteristics that are rooted in and nourished by sports.

For some years the National Football Foundation has been the prime force for the advancement of undergraduate football. Through its dedicated leadership of amateurism; through its scholar athlete awards given to deserving senior leaders and scholars who played outstanding varsity football; through its dedication to the building of a shrine and Hall of Fame; and through its endeavor to organize former players and friends of the game to promote college football, the Foundation has become the bulwark of this great American sprot.

I was greatly surprised when, in the summer of 1966, Chester LaRoche, president of the National Football Foundation, and Vincent Draddy, chairman of the Honors Committee, called at my office to inform me that I had been selected as winner of the Foundation's gold medal, to be awarded at the annual dinner in December. Since this award had been made to Presidents Eisenhower, Hoover, Kennedy, and Nixon, as well as to General MacArthur, Justice Byron White, and three distinguished men of business—Roger Blough, Donald Lourie, and Juan Trippe—it occurred to me that I was in company far more distinguished than I deserved. My first impulse was to demur, which I did. Their answer was to the point: "If we've made a mistake, it is too late now." Of course, I thanked them for the honor and told them that I would accept it.

My acceptance speech set forth my philosophy of college football; I like to think that it also shows that I had lost neither my enthusiasm nor my respect for this great American game:

> We are all inspired by the presence here of so many legendary football heroes. As a former coach, I can think of no greater satisfaction than to participate in the honoring of one of my former players. Tonight I have watched with great pride Captain Carpenter, who did the unusual, both on the playing field and on the battlefield. Bill, your old coach is awed by your distinguished record; I am proud of your example of dedication to the service of our country.
>
> It would be fatuous for me to deny that I am overwhelmed by the honor the Foundation accords me tonight. I have no illusion that my credentials qualify me to be included with my predecessors. Perhaps, however, I may stand on the statement that, during 32 years of coaching and eight years of reflection, the respect I hold for the American game of football has never wavered.
>
> One wonders what type of game it is that challenged such distinguished and well-remembered men as Stagg, Yost, Zuppke, Daly, Rockne, Warner, Cavanaugh, Dobie, the Joneses—Tad and Howard—McGugin, Alexander, Neyland, Sutherland, Harlow, and Caldwell, all of whom I knew well.
>
> It is a game played in some form by over a million young Americans, a game uninhibited by social barriers.
>
> It is a game that, in early season, requires exhaustive hard work, often to the point of drudgery.
>
> It is a game of violent body contact that demands a personal discipline seldom found in our modern life.
>
> It is a game of cooperation, wherein the individual's reward is that total satisfaction achieved by being part of successful team play.
>
> It is a game that is 100 per cent fun when you win and that exacts 100 per cent resolution when you lose.
>
> And if it is the game most like war, it is also the game most

like life, for it teaches young men that work, sacrifice, selflessness, competitive drive, perseverance, and respect for authority are the price one pays to achieve worthwhile goals.

It is also a contentious game that has detractors in academic and other circles who enjoy nothing more than their violent verbal attack on the sport. I shall contest the detractors only by observing that, imperfect as it may be, during the past decade college football has been deemphasized to the point where it is now, I believe, in its proper place. Today a solid education is the paramount objective of most college players, as it should be. For my part, so long as the college does not short-change the player on his education, I can not become overly concerned about either athletic scholarships or recruiting.

In essence, then, based on long observation, it is my conviction that the modern approach to the game, as compared with that in years gone by, is more forthright and more sensible and clean. And I suggest that we should not now attempt to over-refine the product.

As a coach, I gave our squads ten axioms to live by. If you don't mind, I shall repeat several of them and relate each to an intimate coaching experience.

AXIOM—*A relaxed player performs best, and a sense of humor and good fun keep one relaxed.* The squads at Dartmouth and West Point had a lot of fun with their trainer, Rollie Bevan, who was a shrewd judge of young players. Bevan was well attuned to any player who courted the attention of the stands. In a hard-hitting Penn State game, a young back went down for the count and was stretched out, seemingly seriously injured. A hush came over the crowd, and there was great anxiety in the stands. Much to my annoyance, Bevan showed a callous disregard of the injured back, and it took considerable prodding on my part before Rollie went onto the field.

This was the scene: Bevan sauntered out to the injured player and, instead of giving the back a whiff of ammonia, jabbed his toe into the player's side; with each jab Rollie said, "Get up, Joe. Get going—the crowd has spotted your number and knows it's you. You're their hero and they'll give you a rousing cheer when you jog around."

At that, Joe jumped up and, sure enough, the relieved crowd

gave him a tremendous cheer. By this time, our players were convulsed with laughter; their trainer had demonstrated that he was a miracle healer. Suddenly, it dawned on Joe that he had been royally taken. Infuriated, he steamed over to Bevan and stammered, "D-d-damn you, Bevan, you made an ass of me."

Coaches, too, supply humor. I enjoy the story on Francis Schmidt, who was the coach of Ohio State in the thirties. The Buckeyes were having great trouble with Michigan, and Schmidt, a wild man on the bench who really needed a keeper on Saturday afternoons, couldn't stand the Wolverine parade through his tackles. After a long gain, Schmidt bellowed, "Look out there! Look at Jim! Just look at our All-American tackle. There he is, knocked flat on his ass." With that, Jim, at the other end of the bench, protested, "No, no, coach. I'm not out there—here's old Jim right here on the bench." Schmidt cocked an eye, measured old Jim, and then said, "Aw, what's the difference, anyway; if you *were* out there, you'd be on your ass."

There is much good fun in football, and certainly a sense of humor keeps the players relaxed.

AXIOM—*Inches make the champion, and the champion makes his own luck.* In the '46 Army-Navy game, the farewell of Blanchard, Davis, and Tucker to Army football, the first half looked like an Army rout of Navy, with the score 21-6. Then came an abrupt change, and for the rest of the game this Cadet team, undefeated in three years, fought the fiercest rear-guard action I have ever seen on a football field. Finally, with the score 21-18, the Cadets stopped the Middies twice on the three-yard line and once on the four, as the game ended in a scene of pandemonium. A half-crazed crowd had come out of the stands and pressed against the sidelines, obliterating my last-minute view of the playing field. I was more isolated than the Lonely End, as my frantic calls to the spotters, Gustafson and Hickman, went unanswered. I later learned that Andy presented a ghostly belligerent stare toward the playing field, while Herman, bless his soul, buried his head and pleaded, "Please, God, don't let them do it— don't let them do it." By all odds, this was the most starkly anxious moment of my coaching career. The Blanchard-Davis Army team prevailed; inches made them champions, and they made their own luck.

AXIOM—*Good fellows are a dime a dozen, but an aggressive leader is priceless.* The 1955 season was most trying for me, as we had a lean squad and no quarterback. A coach has never known trouble unless he has the senseless temerity to change an All-American end into a "T" quarterback in one season. There was hardly an officer or cadet at West Point who didn't believe this switch was a colossal error. Even my friends of the press called the move "Blaik's Folly."

Sunday afternoon, after the Michigan defeat, the Superintendent, my former teammate, came to my office and inquired to whether I was aware of the local sentiment about our quarterback. I told him that the team was aware, the staff was aware, and I was aware but, far more important, they all believed as I did, that our only chance to defeat the Navy was with Don Holleder at quarterback.

A few minutes after the Superintendent left, Holleder came to see me. As he entered the office, I got up, placed my hand on his shoulder, and said, "Holly, you played a good game yesterday, and I'm proud of you. You're making a fine progress as our quarterback." With moisture in his eyes, Holly replied: "I know what the cadets are saying—I have heard the officers' talk—and I came fully prepared to get my old number back, but I want you to know, I prayed all the way here that you would not give up on me."

Now it is many weeks later, the night before the Navy game. As usual, I took the squad for a bedtime walk on the golf course, which ended with a few words about the big game. I recall saying: "Three times this season I've taken the long walk across muddy fields to congratulate, first, Benny Oosterbean, then Ben Schwartzwalder, and then Jordan Oliver. It has been a trying season, and I am a bit weary from those walks. Tomorrow, before 100,000 spectators and 50 million television viewers, I want you men to know it would be the longest walk of my coaching career if I had to congratulate the Navy coach."

There was silence for a moment, then a voice spoke out with resolution. It was Holleder. "Colonel, you're not taking that walk tomorrow."

The Cadets won an upset victory over the Navy. The press stated it was Holly's vindication. It wasn't—it wasn't at all. It was an unforgettable demonstration that an aggressive leader is priceless.

From these remarks you may have sensed that I have fixed opinions on the value of the American game of football. I have, and in summary, simply stated, they are three:

One: Football should be secondary to the purpose for which the player is in college.

Two: Championship football and good scholarship are entirely compatible. We salute our scholar athletes tonight as splendid examples of this fact.

Three: The purpose of the game of football is to win, and to *dilute the will to win is to destroy the purpose of the game.*

This, then, gentlemen, has been my football creed. And I daresay, with the active support and influence of this great Foundation, that college football will not be devalued with the passing of time.

May I repeat that it is an overwhelming honor to receive the gold medal award from the National Football Foundation. I am grateful to the Foundation and to you friends of football, but more especially I am grateful to my former Dartmouth and Army players and to my old coaching associates, many of whom have come far to be with us tonight.

It is to each of you, then, that I give my heartfelt gratitude for this inspiring and memorable evening.

By now, the reader must know that my respect for Don Holleder has no limits. The shock I received when the Department of the Army informed me that Major Holleder had been killed in Vietnam action cannot be described.

Indeed, there are times when strong men are weak, and normal men are not made for such occasions. I am of this latter group. The burial service at Fort Meade Chapel and the interment at Arlington Cemetery aroused my deepest feelings. The sound of taps, the presentation of the American flag to the widow, and the sight of four small daughters without a father will haunt my memory. Nor shall I ever forget that young cadet who said, "Colonel, you're not taking that walk tomorrow."

Chapter XXII

Assistants Who Became Head Coaches

Many encomiums have come my way on my record as a head coach, and I have had immeasurable satisfaction in the professional and business success of my former football players. In retrospect, however, I realize that too little has been written about my one-time assistants.

If I rate my coaching success without any regard for modesty, I regard my intuition in judging and selecting able assistants as at least unusual. To select knowledgeable men of intelligence, ambition, and personality, men with a touch of success who had the desire to be part of a winning combination, was always a challenge because my staff was never unchanging and permanent. I like to think that I had the good sense to allow new coaches uninhibited opportunity to express their views and to encourage them to meet the public by personal appearances and that this permitted them to mature and move toward their goals of becoming head coaches. No assistant was worth his place on my staff unless he had the desire eventually to become a head coach. My staff never operated in a vacuum, and all were encouraged to express independent views; once the decision was made, however, there could be no deviation from it. On the field of play coaches were never permitted to advance individual views and express contrary ideas on techniques. The staff worked in complete harmony, and all were treated as equals. There never was a first assistant; all were regarded as equal associates. I am indeed happy and proud to write about my old colleagues who went on to become head coaches, each with my personal endorsement.

PAUL AMEN

As a University of Nebraska graduate, Amen had a splendid varsity background in football and baseball. During World War II he was assigned as a major to teach English at the Military Academy. He had played for Biff Jones, our athletic director, who persuaded Paul to take on extra duties as head coach of varsity baseball, and I asked him to become a coach on the Plebe football staff. Several seasons later he became the varsity end coach and head of all football scouting.

After the war, Amen continued on our staff as a civilian until 1955, when he was selected as head coach of football at Wake Forest. He did much to rejuvenate their football, and the alumni and faculty regretted his later decision to enter the banking business. Dedicated, serious, a teacher of high intelligence and competence, Amen had a splendid football mind. Paul became president of the $200 million National Bank of Commerce in Lincoln, Nebraska and a highly respected leader in that state.

GEORGE BLACKBURN

George joined the Army staff in 1955 for one season, them left to become head coach of the University of Cincinnati. Later he became varsity football coach at the University of Virginia. George was a knowlegeable backfield coach, completely devoted to the game and to his players. Undoubtedly he was happier as an assistant coach teaching backfield play than he ever was as head coach, with its added chores. Blackburn retired from coaching and in the early 1970's entered business in Cincinnati.

CLARENCE E. BOSTON

Chief Boston, a graduate of Harvard and a back under Harlow, served on the Army staff in 1948 and also was Plebe hockey coach. Well liked by the cadets, Chief went to the University of New Hampshire, where he was a successful head coach of football and later director of athletics.

EDWARD CROWDER

Eddie was assigned to the Army staff while he was a lieutenant in the Army. He had been assistant at Oklahoma and, with this background, in 1955 he joined our varsity staff. Since he had graduated from Oklahoma with a degree in geology, I often suggested to him that, as good as his future was in football, his future career should be with his friends in petroleum in Oklahoma. However, his leadership and dedication to the college game did not allow him to take my advice. Crowder became head coach and director of athletics at Colorado, where he was recognized as one of the leaders in college coaching circles. In December 1973, Crowder hung up his blocking pads. In the future he will serve only as Director of Athletics of Colorado University.

PAUL DIETZEL

In 1953 and 1954 Paul was the offensive line coach of the Army; in 1948 he had been assistant Plebe coach. Dietzel's background in football included playing at Miami (Ohio) and Duke; he was an assistant at Miami and later became a member of Bear Bryant's staff at Kentucky. After serving well on the Army staff as offensive line coach, Paul became head coach at L.S.U. There he gained considerable success and was elected coach of the year. He was lured back to the Army as head coach in 1962, seemingly unaware or perhaps forgetful of how much more difficult the Army assignment is than one in a civilian college. After four years Dietzel left West Point with a record that did not reflect his ability and fully disillusioned with his Academy experience. Dietzel became director of athletics and head coach of football at South Carolina, where his character and fine qualities were properly appreciated.

ROBERT L. DOBBS

Bobby played on the Army team in 1943 – '44 as a fullback and had the respect of his teammates as well as of his opponents. He was a quiet, rugged player who generally left a bruising mark; he was one of those athletes whose physical makeups carry a natural punch that others cannot muster. After serving on the Army staff, Bobby became head coach of Tulsa and later successful coach of the Canadian Stampeders. In the midsixties he was coach of Texas (El Paso), where his teams were regarded as considerably advanced in the passing game. Dobbs was offered the position of head coach of Army when Dietzel left; when he asked to be relieved of his contract at El Paso, however, the ensuing discussion convinced him that he was committed to remain at Texas. Dobbs later retired from coaching and entered business in El Paso.

SIDNEY GILLMAN

Sid joined the Army staff in 1948 when Hickman went to Yale. At the time he was head coach of Miami (Ohio). He took over the coaching of our offensive line and excelled in this work. Not one to remain as assistant, Sid stayed one season, then moved to become head coach of Cincinnati. After several seasons there, Sid got the professional bug and was named head coach of the Los Angeles Rams. Thereafter, he became the manager and head coach of the San Diego Chargers and in 1973 became associated with Houston as manager and coach. In college and professional circles Gillman achieved a reputation as an outstanding football technician. Perhaps because he consumed at least 30 cups of coffee a day, he was a stimulating coach who inspired his men.

JOHN F. GREEN

Jack was captain of the 1945 Davis and Blanchard team. A 180-pound guard, he was a remarkable blocker and strong and quick on defense. He coached either the defensive or the offensive line during the five seasons he was at West Point. Later, when Jack became the first assistant at Tulane, I twice suggested that he rejoin the Army staff. Had he done so, Jack undoubtedly would have been my successor. Instead, Green became the head coach at Vanderbilt, where he was respected as a citizen and coach. His task at Vanderbilt was insurmountably difficult, and success eluded him. In the late 1960's he left coaching and became associated with AVCO's Nashville Division.

ANDREW GUSTAFSON

When the Army played Jock Sutherland's Pittsburgh teams, I was impressed by the precision of the Pitt backfield. When I accepted the Dartmouth coaching position, my first action was to seek out Andy to become my backfield coach. This was my second most important move; the first was to hire Harry Ellinger as line coach. At Dartmouth and the Point, Gustafson was both my friend and my coaching associate. He was with me 14 years, longer than any other staff member. I felt both sadness and elation when he left West Point in 1947 to become head coach of football and later director of athletics at the University of Miami. Extremely able, personable, a favorite of our players, Andy is recalled with affection. After a successful career at Miami, where he did so much to establish that university in top collegiate football circles, Andy retired to serve as a racing commissioner in Miami.

DALE HALL

Dale was a great Army back in the Davis-Blanchard era and was also captain of the basketball team, in which sport he was named to the All-America team. After serving overseas, Dale resigned from the Army to become the backfield coach at Purdue and later at Florida. As a Cadet he was an excellent student; during his assistant years at West Point (1956–58) I regarded him as having one of the best coaching minds I had known. Perhaps he lacked a certain inspirational touch; at any rate, he did not convince General Westmoreland, the Superintendent, that his contract should be renewed by the Military Academy. Time has changed that impression, for no successor has demonstrated a better understanding of cadets and West Point football. After leaving the Academy in 1961, Hall retired from coaching to engage in a successful business career.

TOM HARP

Tom came to West Point from Massillon (Ohio) High School, where he achieved considerable success. As the offensive backfield coach of the Cadets, he served on the staff from 1956 to 1959. Tom's life was geared to football; in 1960 he became the head coach of Cornell. There he did much to rejuvenate the Big Red, but he longed for the so-called big league. He was hired by Duke where, for some inexplicable reason, his career was marked by an indifferent record, with occasional unexpected successes. When he left Duke, he retired from football, but in 1972 the Naval Academy hired him as its backfield coach. At the end of the 1972 season, Harp became head football coach at Indiana State University, and is already on the way to a successful comeback.

HERMAN HICKMAN

In the winter of 1943 Harry Ellinger, my friend and coaching assistant, died of a heart attack in his sleep in the home of Congressman F. Edward Hebert in Washington, D.C. This was an irreplaceable personal and professional loss. Harry and I had served together on the Army staff, and he went with me when I became head coach at Dartmouth. As a line coach he had few equals. His inquisitive mind, restlessness, and naturalness made him a favorite among players and graduates. It was a delight to be in his company. It was no easy task to replace Ellinger, not alone for his coaching ability, but because the war was on and his replacement had to be ineligible for the draft.

From Bob Neyland, coach of Tennessee and soon to become a general, I learned about Hickman, who was then the line coach at North Carolina State. An all-time Tennessee guard, Herman weighed over 300 pounds. To supplement his professional playing and coaching, he had been a professional wrestler and had nearly 500 matches to his credit.

We met in New York at the old Vanderbilt Hotel, and from that afternoon on we became friends. Herman had a sense of humor second to none, was a gifted teller of Southern folk stories, and from early youth had developed a memory that included all the works of Kipling, Service, Masters, and much of Tennyson, which he could recite by the hour. Years later he was a radio panelist on "Information, Please!" with the Fadiman-Levant-Kieran group who trumped each other with instant recall of lines from the classics.

On our drive to West Point from New York, Herman gave me a special introduction to his philosophy when he stated, "I love my wife, my belly, and football, and I'm not sure which I love the most."

As a football coach he did not enjoy the hours of office preparation for outdoor practice; once on the field, however, his knowledge of the game, teaching ability, and carefree rapport with the players made football fundamentals less of a chore, and Herman substituted fun for drudgery. His outgoing personality and droll remarks were good for us all.

Few realized that, with all his chuckles, Herman was a worrier of major magnitude and sweated profusely in many moments of nervousness. Before a Navy game Herman came to me in the locker room to inform me that he was nauseated and much too weak to climb the stairs to the press box. He was in a state of great anxiety as I led him to the door from which an 80-step climb led to the top. I opened the door and said, "Herman, you have half an hour to get up there; take it slowly, and you'll make it to the top." By game time Herman was in full control of his nervous system.

When Herman went to Yale, considerable publicity originated in New Haven to the effect that I had tried to prevent his departure. Hickman's employment by Yale illustrates how attitudes may be misconstrued. One week during spring practice Herman came to me and stated that Yale had approached him to become head coach, but that he wanted me to know that he was not interested in the offer.

A week later on a Monday morning Herman failed to come to the office; when I called his quarters, thinking he might be ill, there was no answer. This absence was not like Herman. I immediately suspected that Hickman was involved with Yale, a fact that Cupe Black later confirmed. Black had taken him in tow in New York to meet with the Yale football committee. Herman was a sucker for big steaks and dollar cigars, and Cupe boasted that he had been a perfect host to the Hickmans.

About noon, that Monday I received a call from the provost of Yale (the president then being in Europe): "We have just hired Herman Hickman as Yale's football coach and want to release the information at once." I replied, "Hickman has a three-year contract with West Point, and I shall not release him. Your approach to Herman has been most un-Ivy-like, to say the least, and I must talk personally with him." The provost was noticeably disturbed by my attitude.

Returning from lunch, I passed the old conference room, where Herman was sitting, having been driven from New York in record time. Heavy beads of sweat had wilted his shirt, and he looked thoroughly depressed. Since I had been his friend, confidant, and advisor for five years, he was more distraught than the time he faced the climb to the Navy press box. The conversation went like this:

HICKMAN: I suppose you think I'm a rat.

BLAIK: What should I think? Now what I want to know is, do you want to go to Yale?

HICKMAN: Yes.

BLAIK: Then why didn't you come direct to me, talk it over, and ask to be relieved of your contract? You may go on one condition. Since we are in spring practice, I want three days before any announcement is made to the press. By that time I shall announce your successor with the news of your release to Yale.

Within two days I had hired Sid Gillman. Although Herman was in New Haven with my blessing, some of the Old Blue thought that Herman was so important to my staff that I had tried to force him to remain. Of course, I hated to see him leave, not because of football, but because life was so pleasant with such a companion.

Years later, when he was in a Washington, D.C. hospital being transfused with quarts of blood because of internal bleeding, I called Herman. He was in good spirits and his voice was still strong. During our conversation he said, "I want you to know that the happiest days of my coaching years were spent at West Point." Several days later my old friend was dead.

EDWARD J. HIRSHBERG

After Joe Douchess left my Dartmouth staff to become surgeon at the U.S. Steel plant in Gary, Ind., I was fortunate to get Eddie Hirshberg to join us as end coach. In every sense of the word he was an intellectual devoted to knowledge. One of my official tasks at Dartmouth was to break up the arguments between Ellinger, moonlighting in areas reserved for the erudite, and Hirshberg, who often reminded Harry, "As your volume increases, your reasoning decreases."

Hirshberg had large business interests in the Pittsburgh area; as a hobby, he later became head coach of Carnegie Tech. There he brought success and an engaging personality to coaching the type of football that he believed was compatible with academic scholarship.

STUART HOLCOMB

Stu came to West Point as a private 3rd class; although Army's football success was great during his time, Stu's only reward was a promotion to private 1st class.

Stu had been head coach at Miami University in Ohio and was assigned to West Point when he enlisted. His coaching ability was never in doubt, and in addition to his other duties he joined my staff. As end coach he contributed much to the success of our team. After the war he became the successful head coach at Purdue and later was director of athletics at Northwestern. He left the college scene to become a top executive with the Chicago White Sox, where he amply demonstrated his leadership.

DOUGLAS KENNA

One of the great players of West Point, Doug Kenna was selected as an All-America by Grantland Rice in 1944. Kenna quarterbacked the '44 backfield of Minor, Hall, and Dobbs. As a Cadet he was second ranking captain of the Corps and stood high in his class academically.

After a tour of duty in Germany, Kenna returned as a backfield coach. As an assistant, he showed all the qualities required of a head coach. His potential was too great for him to remain long as an assistant and his responsibility for four youngsters was also too great to risk the vicissitudes of college coaching. One day I suggested to Kenna that it would be unfair both to himself and to his family to remain in the field of coaching and strongly urged him to leave the field. When he agreed, I wrote my old friend Victor Emanuel that I had a natural for his organization; it was not long before Kenna joined AVCO. Thereafter he became a top executive in several corporations and returned to AVCO when I joined the company. Later he became president of Fuqua Industries. In 1972 he was honored by being selected from a large field to become president of the National Association of Manufacturers, a prestigious and important national position. Although Kenna never became a head football coach, he has quite properly been included in this group as one who is now a head coach of the community of manufacturers.

FRANK LAUTERBUR

Frank had been a coach on the Baltimore Colts' staff when he joined Army as our defensive line coach. Spirited, able, and ambitious, he was with me in 1956–58 and left West Point to become head coach of the University of Toledo several years after I retired. At Toledo he gave the university national prominence when it won over 30 victories without a loss. Not contented with his great success, he wanted a real challenge, which came with his appointment as the coach of Iowa in the Big Ten.

Unfortunately, at the end of the 1973 season Lauterbur ran head-on into the immovable Athletic Board. Like so many coaches who had preceded him, Frank learned that Iowa had dug itself into a deep grave. His talent did not include that of a resurrectionist.

VINCE LOMBARDI

Vince and I were so close professionally and personally for so long a time that, hoping to do justice to his memory and to evoke his spirit for those who did not have the privilege of knowing him, I have devoted a special chapter in this book to our association and his extraordinary career. Here I should like to quote from a letter that he wrote me from Green Bay many years ago. I have always cherished his words, not because I felt that I deserved them, but because of their source and perhaps because I like to feel that I had some influence on his career: "You are the greatest football coach of all time. There has never been anyone your equal—and, more important, you are the finest man it has ever been my pleasure to know. My 'football' is your 'football!' My approach to a problem is the way I think you would approach it. I just hope and pray I can do justice to it and to you."

JOHN E. SAUER

John played halfback with the 1944–45 Army teams; had the times been normal, Sauer would be recalled as an Army great. Although short of stature, he was a strong-legged, intelligent football player whose knowledge of the game was as sound as that of any player I coached. He joined my staff in 1948 and stayed until 1950, when he became head coach of The Citadel. As one of our backfield coaches, John instructed in all punting and kicking and made my son into one of Army's best punters. Probably his one error at The Citadel was to hire Al Davis, later associated with the Oakland pros, as his assistant. The Citadel was hardly large enough to support both this ambitious assistant and Sauer, the able football strategist and teacher. Today Sauer is a broadcaster of professional football and conducts his family business affairs in Dayton.

RICHARD VORIS

Dick came to West Point from a coaching job with several West Coast professional teams. He coached the offensive line for three years (1955–57) and had a thorough knowledge of offensive techniques. Voris soon learned that football was necessarily secondary to a cadet's interest at West Point and was restless because his time was limited with the players. Voris had strong convictions about his football knowledge and unlimited confidence that he would be a success as a head coach. In 1958 he was hired by the University of Virginia, where for several years he coached with decreasing success. I never understood his problems there and was surprised when he returned to coaching on professional staffs. There is no doubt about about his enthusiasm, knowledge of the game, and abilities; with a little luck, Dick Voris should again be a head coach.

MURRAY WARMATH

One of the best coaches I ever had on the Army staff, Murray was the defensive team coach from 1949 to 1951. Strong-willed, with fixed opinions, in the mould of Bob Neyland, his Tennessee coach, Murray was a decided asset to our staff. He readily adjusted to ideas that were not in accord with his own, and thus became a coaches' coach. To Murray, football was a rugged game, a fact that he instilled into the West Point defense. When he left the Point, he became head coach at Mississippi State and later for years coached at Minnesota. There he laid the ghost of Bierman to rest, refused to be cowed, and impressed an initially hostile "M" association with his ability. In every way Murray represented the fighting qualities of the Rebel soldier and the decency of the Southern gentleman. He later retired from coaching, but remained active on the Minnesota athletic staff.

BOB WOODRUFF

Bob was the tackle coach in the days when Hickman was our line coach. Like Herman, Woodruff had played at Tennessee under Neyland and coached there before being assigned as an officer to West Point, where he coached during the seasons of 1944–45. A personable, knowledgeable football teacher, Bob contributed to our fine line play before going on to become head coach at Baylor and then at Florida. He later became the director of athletics at Tennessee.

BILL YEOMAN

Bill was captain of the undefeated 1949 Army team and subsequently was a member of the Plebe staff. As a player he was receptive to coaching, and as a cadet captain in the Corps he was considered strong in leadership. Following overseas service, he resigned from the Army to join the Michigan State staff. The University of Houston tapped him as head coach, and there he made Houston a national name in football. Bright, and energetic, he was bitten early by the football bug, which foreclosed a military and later a legal career. As of this writing, I anticipate that he will have a distinguished career and bring distinction to college football.

In Summary

When I look back to the head coaching careers of my respected assistants, the vagaries of the coaching profession are too evident. Barely one third of this group had extended winning records. Some gave up coaching, while others came to grief occasioned by presidents and alumni of colleges who fit Teddy Roosevelt's apt description. That great Rough Rider noted: "It is not the critic who counts, not the man who points out how the strong man stumbled or where the doer of deeds could have been better. The credit belongs to the man who is actually in the arena. Who, at his best knows the triumph of high achievement, and who, at his worst, if he fails, at least fails while daring greatly, so that his place shall never be with those old and timid souls who knew neither victory nor defeat."

In the uncertainty of personal livelihood, only the profession of football head coaching has the front seat. Today, only four of my former assistants are head coaches.

Chapter XXIII

Vince Lombardi

We stood in front of St. Patrick's Cathedral in two lines through which the heavy casket was carried on the shoulders of the pallbearers to the open hearse. We were the honorary pallbearers, as were 40-odd members of the Green Bay Packers, all of whom, like the deeply saddened Bart Starr and Willie Davis, somehow seemed unlike the old champions whom I remembered.

St. Patrick's had been packed with 3000 of Lombardi's friends from the days of his youth, with dignitaries and the elite of professional football. Along Fifth Avenue stood at least 5000 sympathizers unable to gain entrance to the cathedral to participate in the High Mass conducted by Cardinal Cook. They were not merely curious spectators; in reality, they too were hushed mourners.

Old friends such as Arthur Daley, Tim Cohane, George Halas, Bob Finch and General Hughes representing President Nixon, Jim Farley, Joe Cahill, and General Janarone, dean of West Point, whispered a sad greeting as they passed. Among the honorary pallbearers were Edward Bennett Williams, the attorney; Colonel Orin Krueger, business manager of the Redskins; Richard Bourguignon and Tony Conadeo of the Packers' board of directors; such old friends as Ed Breslin and R. B. Levitas; such former players as Bart Starr, Willie Davis, and Paul Hornung; and myself.

As the casket appeared, we steeled ourselves to the realization that we were to accompany our old friend on his last journey. My own feeling was one of disbelief that such a vibrant, vigorous, and challenging man with his infectious laugh, who had only two months before believed he was in the best of health, should have departed from us. As the casket glided into the hearse and the cortege started its journey to the cemetery in Red Bank, N. J., it still seemed impossible that Vince, who had seemed indestructible, had lost his last game. The limousine in which I rode also carried Colonel Krueger, his wife Doris, Paul Hornung, and my son Bob. It was a long ride, but the time shortened as Hornung, Lombardi's pet player if ever he had one, told of his experiences with the coach.

Hornung, a Heisman Trophy winner, related that after a miserable performance in a Chicago Bears game he didn't have the nerve to face Lombardi in the locker room. However, Vince was on the prowl for him and finally caught Paul as he came out of the showers. "Hornung, for years I've had the greatest respect for the Heisman Trophy Award, but after seeing you play today, it's nothing—absolutely nothing."

Hornung went on to relate one of Vince's favorite stories about Frank Leahy, the Fordham line coach when Lombardi was one of Fordham's Seven Blocks of Granite. In the Army game of 1947 Leahy sent his Notre Dame team on the field with the instructions: "We'll run play 28 the first time we have the ball. Connor, you'll pull out and block the Army end; Ashbaugh, you'll lead the play; and Sitko, you'll take that ball and drive off tackle for a first down." When Notre Dame got the ball, 28 was called and Connor pulled out, but missed the Army end, who smeared Ashbaugh and Sitko for no gain.

As the Irish came off the field, Leahy heard Ashbaugh admonish Connor in this fashion: "Connor, you son-of-a-bitch, why didn't you block that Army end?" With that, Leahy called to Ashbaugh: "My, my Ashbaugh, I'm disappointed that you would use such language. It's not in the tradition of Our Lady. Notre Dame players don't talk that way, especially to our own men."

During the half, Leahy told the team he was giving them another chance. "Run 28 on the first play; and Connor, this time you get that end. Ashbaugh, you lead Sitko off tackle for a long gainer." Play 28 was called, and again Connor missed the end. There was a dead silence as the Irish came toward the bench that Leahy broke with these words: "Ashbaugh, You're right—Connor is a son-of-a-bitch." Lombardi would always break up over that story.

As we rode, my thoughts followed their own course as I remembered the man who had joined the Army coaching staff 20 years before and had become first my respected associate and then my friend.

In 1948, Sid Gilman, an extremely able offensive line coach, left my staff to become head coach at Cincinnati University. Periodically, so many coaches left for better opportunities that the selection of new assistants for the Army staff became an annual affair. Tim Cohane, sports editor of *Look* magazine and a graduate of Fordham, urged me to interview Vince Lombardi, the freshman coach of his alma mater. The Lombardi credentials included several undefeated years at St. Cecilia High School in New Jersey, where he had also taught mathematics and Latin. I had several meetings with Lombardi and, from the first, was increasingly impressed with his enthusiasm, his knowledge of the game, and his personality. Although his record at St. Cecilia as both coach and instructor marked him as a sound teacher, the question arose: Why didn't Fordham make better use of him, especially since its staff was woefully weak? I dismissed this doubt, as Lombardi impressed me, as he did Murray Warmath, our able defensive coach, as one who could learn quickly our required standard of coaching excellence restricted to a minimum time of field instruction.

Lombardi joined the Army staff in January 1949; by spring practice in March, he had studied films and plans until he added confidence to his other qualifications.

The first day of spring practice was an exciting one for Lombardi, whose unbounded enthusiasm and drive were evident. He was coaching the offensive line at one end of the field when I called him away from his group to discuss a technical point. As we stood in conversation, Vince suddenly broke away, bellowing at a player in a tone that reminded me of a first sergeant of the old Army; as he yelled, he started to run toward his group. When I called to him, "Vince, Vince," he abruptly turned and came back to me. I merely said, "Vince, we don't coach that way at West Point." His reply was a rather subdued "Thank you." as he rejoined his group. Never again did I need to challenge his method of coaching; no assistant could have been more able or conscientious.

The season of '49, Army was undefeated. As a matter of interest, Col. Frank Borman, the astronaut, was manager of the '49 team, while Col. Aldrin, later the pilot of Gemini XII and Apollo XI, played on the Plebe squad.

The following spring, I made Lombardi our offensive backfield coach. He was now extremely happy, as this position gave him an opportunity to work with all phases of the offense. His tasks included that of making my son Bob into Army's first-string offensive quarterback, an experience that Vince later used to good effect in grooming Bart Starr. The coaching of an Army son can be very difficult in a community where the officers and the Corps are so close to the training of a varsity team. In 1950 we had another undefeated season until our last game with the Navy, a team that had a miserable season record. Our 14-2 defeat sobered us all, as it ended a winning streak of 26 games. The game was lost in the four weeks of continuous rain prior to the Navy game; although the inevitable indoor practices accounted for the players' loss of timing, as a coaching staff we hardly measured up to the demands of that frustrating day. Certainly, the Middies played as though they were the inspired champions.

We contemplated the '51 season with rare enthusiasm, as the returning squad was easily the best since the 1945 group that included Blanchard, Davis, and Tucker. Our spring workout was successful beyond our expectations, and two unbelievably strong teams gave promise of incomparable success. The Corps and Army fans, however, never got to watch this group in action; in August, 43 of the 44 varsity players left West Point under a cloud, which I have described in Chapter XV, of Book I "The Ninety Scapegoats."

When September came, my staff of Paul Amen, Jack Green, Doug Kenna, Vince Lombardi, and Murry Warmath were emotionally exhausted and depressed as we greeted the '51 squad of former junior varsity and last-year Plebe players. None seemed more disappointed than Lombardi, as he had spent long hours of preparation with those great players who were now scattered about the country.

The Northwestern game, the second of the season, was the tip-off to our fortunes for the season. Army was ahead 14-13, with less than two minutes to play, when Northwestern threw a 50-yard pass over the goal line to beat the Cadets 20-14. So disheartening was this ending to a gallant try by players unaware of their lack of ability that in the dressing room after the game Vince Lombardi stood with tears running down his face. This was the Lombardi I knew; his professional reputation gave no clue to the emotion that was so strong a part of his makeup.

Vince stayed with the Army through two more seasons and had the indescribable satisfaction of seeing those misfits of '51 defeat a strong Navy team two years later, in 1953.

It was after the '53 season that the New York football Giants found themselves in deep trouble. The management had fired Steve Owen, the darling of the New York sports press, and was unable to come up with a name coach. In December of that year, I met with Jack and Wellington Mara three times at the New York Athletic Club. They offered me the Giant coaching position, each time proffering a higher salary. Fantastic as the offer seemed to me, I could not bring myself to leave the Military Academy. At our last meeting Wellington, a Fordham classmate of Lombardi, asked if they could talk to Vince about becoming an assistant on the Giant staff. I told him that I would feel a loss if Vince were to leave West Point, but that I had aided assistants to get head coaching jobs in the past and would not stand in the way of Lombardi's bettering himself. The Maras hired Vince with an attractive financial offer, although they failed to realize that they were getting a man with the potential to become their next head coach.

Several years later, on a Saturday morning in January of 1956, I was in my office, going over a list of possible candidates to fill two vacancies occasioned by the loss of assistants Bobby Dobbs and Paul Dietzel, when I received a call from Lombardi, who asked me to lunch at the Officers Club. During the luncheon, Lombardi asked me if he could return as an assistant on my staff. His contract with the Giants had terminated and he believed that he would be happier coaching at the Military Academy. My reply was that he was immediately hired and that I would do as well financially by him as possible, although I could not match what he was receiving from the Giants.

In deference to Jack and Well Mara, I suggested that I should call to tell them that I was negotiating Lombardi's return. I called the Giant office and broke the news to Wellington, who said, "You can't talk to Lombardi." I replied that Lombardi had no contract, had solicited me to return, and that, when they hired Lombardi, I had cooperated with them. I hung up on Mara and told Vince that Well had forbidden me to talk to him. Vince replied, "I owe nothing to the Giants, and now we have a deal." A few minutes later, Jack Mara called me and stated that he and Well had agreed that it was all right to talk to Vince. Lombardi was set to return to West Point. I was much relieved, for I had no better candidate to fill my vacancy.

Vince was to start Monday morning. Early that day he came to my office. I could read him like a book; the effervescence and enthusiasm were gone. He was a troubled man as he started the conversation. "I have never gone back on my word in my life, and I don't intend to now, but I do think you should know that the Maras were at my house over the weekend and offered a $6000 increase in my salary. This is a big sum of money, and I promised my wife to tell you that she is terribly upset because I'm coming back to West Point."

Never one to stand in the way of a man with such an opportunity, I had no hesitation in saying: "Vince, forget our deal; go back to the Giants as though we had never talked about you returning to West Point." I have no doubt that Vince would have returned to the Academy had I insisted. The fact remains, however, that the Giants had bought him out of our bona fide understanding. I never discussed this incident with anyone until after Lombardi died.

The Maras were too close to Lombardi to realize his potential as a head coach. The Packers, on the other hand, properly assessed his qualities and capacities, and soon he was to make Green Bay the toast of professional football.

Throughout his stay at Green Bay, my relation with Lombardi was an intimate one. Many times during the season he would call to discuss his problems, even when Green Bay was riding the crest of success. After the win over Dallas in subzero weather when Starr, on a sneak, won the game in the last few seconds of play, I listened to the postgame broadcast from the Packers' dressing room. Kramer was asked, "What kind of a man is Lombardi?" "Lombardi is beautiful—just beautiful," answered the all-pro guard. This was at the time when some of the sports writers assessed Lombardi as something akin to an animal. When I heard this remark, I called Vince in the dressing room and, without trouble, got him on the phone. "Vince—a great victory—but greater were the remarks of Kramer, who has stilled those who were skeptical about you as a person."

Toward the end of his stay at Green Bay, we talked for hours about his future, which included a commitment to me to join a syndicate, of which I was a member, to buy the Washington Redskins and later the New York Jets. Vince was to have a share of the club and full managerial and coaching responsibility, comparable to his deal with Green Bay. In each case we were frustrated by owners who backed out of the deals when the chips were down. During his later years with Green Bay, I urged Lombardi to get out of coaching, which was beginning to take its toll. He had reached the heights; there was nowhere to go but down, and this he could not abide. It took him a full year to regain his football vitality, and it was then that he was made a part owner, coach, and manager of the Redskins.

Many stories and books have been written about this great coach. His sayings, such as "The time has come to cheer for the achiever, the doer" and "Winning isn't everything: it's the only thing"—not unlike the MacArthur's, "There is no substitute for victory"—will live as long as his name is remembered.

I sum up my own thoughts about Lombardi with the remarks I delivered before the Fordham alumni on May 8, 1967 on the occassion when Lombardi was honored as the Fordham Man of the Year:

> The pleasure I take in presenting our honored guest is tempered somewhat by the realization that, as he is my respected friend, I may take for granted much that is significant about him.
>
> Perhaps this story from our coaching days together explains my dilemma. In the '51 Army-Navy game the Cadets fielded a wholly inexperienced team quarterbacked by a Plebe. Our pros-

pects in this game were so dreary that, before the Cadets had run one offensive play, the Navy had scored 14 points. Finally, when the Cadets got possession of the ball deep in their territory, I stood on the sideline and gave last-minute instructions to the Plebe quarterback. Then, after a pat on the back, this apprehensive youngster dashed all the way to his huddled teammates and then abruptly turned and ran all the way back to me.

The curiosity of the 100,000 spectators was equaled only by my perplexity. This had to be something serious. It was. Breathlessly the Plebe quarterback gave me this important message: "Coach, what did you tell me to do? I forgot."

We must not forget that your honored guest has been blessed with a father and mother who taught him that the rewards of life are not easy to come by; that hard work, earning his way, tolerance, personal discipline, respect for parental authority, regard for learning, as well as dedication to a family and religious faith, were expected of him. They were parents who gloried in his scholastic success and encouraged his athletic interests.

Vince was a normal youngster of great vitality who was fully capable of disturbing the peace both in and out of his family circle. His high school ambition included going to Fordham, making the football varsity, and achieving academic excellence. He succeeded in these goals far beyond a father's greatest hope for a son.

He then taught mathematics and Latin at St. Cecilia High School, where he coached its football team to 36 straight victories. With this great record, the fascination of coaching football so absorbed his active mind that there was to be no turning back. Later he became Fordham's freshman football coach, but soon thereafter he came to the Plain at West Point, where he served with great distinction as line coach and then coach of the backfield. After six years with the Army staff, another challenge dictated a change.

Certainly the rest of his career is too well known to recite, though I must state that his one coaching ambition was never realized. No graduate of this great university regretted more than he that he could not pass on the inspiration and lessons he learned as a member of the football varsity to the Fordham undergraduates. The paradox of his national prominence as today's most able and successful coach lies in the fact that, to gain this recognition, he was forced to go West. He did not get it here in the East. There, against insuperable odds, he has made Green Bay the acknowledged pattern of national football success.

What is the true measure of Vince Lombardi? Well, it is no easy task to catalogue his virtues, as he is a man of seeming contradictions.

He is volatile and of a temper that he controls like a thermostat. But he is also mellow and rich with an affection that he shares with players, friends, and even on occasion with rivals.

He is a demanding fundamentalist, intolerant of those who fail to meet their own potentials. But he is also a tireless teacher who respects the intellect and spares no effort to make a Bart Starr into the great quarterback he is today.

He is motivated to success, to win if you will, not for personal glory, but rather for the satisfaction that comes with great accomplishment.

He is strong-willed, fearless, of great candor, and on occassion tactless. But he is never one to complain, "I was misquoted."

He is also capable of warm fellowship, but believes strongly that respect is the essential ingredient that cements enduring human relations.

And, with it all, he is strictly a human guy with an infectious personality—moody at times, but always buoyed by proud family ties and by unfailing dedication to his friends, to his church, and to his high principles.

This, then, is the man whose friendship I cherish, who has brought such great distinction to his alma mater, Fordham University. I present your honored guest, Vincent Lombardi.

During his last year at Green Bay, Lombardi made many speeches to organizations of businessmen. There were 1500 guests present at the New York Hilton Hotel when Vince made a challenging address that included what came to be known as the Lombardi Credo. To a man they stood and cheered for minutes after he concluded with these words:

> Leaders are made, they are not born; and they are made just like anything else has ever been made in this country—by hard

effort. And that's the price that we all have to pay to achieve that goal, or any goal.

And despite what we say about being born equal, none of us really are born equal, but rather unequal. And yet the talented are no more responsible for their birthright than the underprivileged. And the measure of each should be what each does in a specific situation.

It is becoming increasingly difficult to be tolerant of a society that has sympathy only for the misfits, only for the criminal, only for the loser. Have sympathy for them, help them, but I think it's also a time for all of us to stand up for and to cheer for the doer, the achiever, the one who recognizes a problem and does something about it, the one who looks for something extra to do for his country, the winner, the leader!

The New York Daily News, in an editorial, summed up what others thought of the great coach:

VINCE LOMBARDI

..... died Thursday morning in Washington's Georgetown University Hospital, and the nationwide outpouring of grief over the passing of the great Washington Redskins coach shows him to have been a national hero.

Mr. Lombardi was a man who believed in playing any game to win, with all you could throw into it, and he inspired his teams with that spirit. In addition, he was a man of honor, integrity, courage, humor, and religious fervor.

You can tell a good deal about any nation from the types it picks as its heroes. As long as most Americans continue to regard such men as Lombardi as heroes, the U.S.A. should continue to be an all-around great and admirable nation.

Chapter XXIV

The West Point Scandal Reexamined

> *It isn't what you don't know that gets you into trouble—but rather what you know for sure, that isn't so.*
> CHARLES "BOSS" KETTERING

I have often been asked what happened to the ninety scapegoats. That's quite a story, and I have often wondered whether I should write a more complete account of those troubled days. It has been 20 years since the tornado hit the Plain and splattered one hundred young cadets on the front pages of most newspapers, domestic and foreign. Perhaps I should recall Bevan saying to Sid Gillman after the unexpected Navy tie in 1948, "Digging up the body and burying it again."

I shall not be the mortician; however, there are some facts that are still of interest, including the question often asked; "What has happened to the discharged men?" Practically to a man, they have gone into business and the professions, including the military, and have acquitted themselves with distinction. They were leaders as cadets, and they established themselves as leaders in their respective communities. I know of only one who carried the scar of separation to the degree that it caused him to suffer a mental breakdown.

My original chapter, "The Ninety Scapegoats," focused on the facts of the investigation and treatment and dismissal of the cadets and also gave the background that set the pattern for the wholesale violation of the honor code. Here, I shall go further to relate incidents, personal opinions, and my conclusions with respect to the honor system.

Perhaps a review of the officers in the chain of command, six in number, whose judgment determined the dismissal is relative.

1. The Secretary of the Army was Frank Pace, a Democrat who for nearly 20 years had served in a variety of important government posts. In 1953, he became president and chairman of General Dynamics, a government contractor. Later he left that company to associate himself as a director with many corporations and to give distinguished service to worthy charitable organizations. As a private citizen, at public gatherings Mr. Pace took considerable credit for his action in dismissing the cadets and saving the Academy honor system. He never admitted that he merely approved the decision of the officer chain of command involving a problem of which he never had any real understanding. His lack of curiosity and his attempt at self-laudation hardly did justice to so distinguished a member of the bar.

2. The Chief-of-Staff of the Army was General J. Lawton Collins of the West Point Class of 1917, who appointed his classmate, Frederick Irving, to be the Superintendent of the Military Academy. During the Collins cadet days the honor code was uncomplicated, and there is no record of resignations for honor violations in the class of 1917.

3. General Maxwell Taylor was the ranking Officer in the Pentagon whose command included the Military Academy section. Taylor had been Superintendent when some of the dismissed cadets were plebes. Even though he had full knowledge of the type of young men involved, General Taylor remained noticeably under cover during the investigation and unavailable when the cadets hoped for his understanding. There is no record of resignations for honor in Taylor's class of 1922.

4. The Superintendent was Major General Frederick Irving. I knew him as the assistant and later commandant under then Supe, General Robert L. Eichelberger. From the early 40's until August, 1951, the Irving family and our own shared a close friendship. After the cadets were dismissed General Irving treated me with consideration and absolute fairness, though seldom did we meet again except in a formal discharge of duty. I never learned when General Irving was informed of the Harkins investigation, although he must have heard the rumor, which surfaced early in June, that the Tactical

Department under Harkins would ask to be relieved if the Supe did not support their recommendation to dismiss the 90 cadets.

5. Colonel Paul Harkins was the Commandant of Cadets; there is evidence that he had knowledge of a limited honor violation early in the spring of 1951. Why he failed to take decisive action then is unknown; it is suggested, however, that he turned sleuth and thus involved many cadets during the following two months. Although his dislike of the success of Army football was known, it was not until early in March of 1951 at a dinner at Leone's Restaurant in New York that the extent of his hostility was revealed. Murray Warmath, our line coach, and the Commandant had an extremely heated argument about several cadet players of Italian background. Harkins had written several books on Army etiquette and customs for the use of officers. The disagreement started when Harkins berated these players, stating they were unworthy of being members of the Corps because they lacked the social graces to become West Pointers. The Commandant thus infuriated Warmath and the football staff. One of these men, later dismissed, became the ranking leader of his class at Fort Belvoir in competition with graduates of West Point.

The Harkins investigation lasted throughout the spring, in late May he selected officer panels or committees from his department that conducted a thoroughly unorthodox inquiry. Despite Harkins' attitude toward varsity football, his department recognized these Army players as individuals and leaders of their respective classes. The early cadet officer "make list" for summer training selected by the Tactical Department included among those dismissed the first and second ranking Corps officers, several company captains, and others of recognized ability. Among the third classmen was a comparably high quota of athletes, including the first ranking corporal. At no time in Academy history did varsity football dominate the selected Corps leadership to such a degree.

6. Early in June, Harkins was reassigned and Colonel John Waters, his assistant, succeeded him as Commandant. As former cavalrymen, they had much in common; more important, Harkins had been chief-of staff to General Patton, and Waters was the son-

in-law of the famous general. Colonel Harkins was the prime mover of the investigation, and Colonel Waters implemented the Harkins action. During his West Point assignment Waters was under constant treatment at the hospital for wounds received in World War II, during which he was captured by the Germans. There is little doubt that Waters was not a well man for much of his West Point tour of duty.

The treatment of the 90 cadets from June until August and the subsequent turmoil during the week of dismissal were in keeping with Waters' determination both to ostracize and to silence these former heroes and leaders. The ordinary citizen will find it difficult, if not impossible, to imagine the thinking that creates such a deeply bred attitude; 20 years later this viewpoint survived to condition a Corps made up of the best of young Americans.

Several years after the 1951 episode the then Superintendent of West Point, his wife and Merle and I were the guests of General Robert Wood at his shooting lodge on Pinkney Island off the coast of Georgia. We had been invited to participate in a turkey shoot. During the second night of our stay the Superintendent asked me to take a walk before retiring. I have had many memorable strolls with squads on a Friday night before a big game, but none was more memorable than the walk that night. No sooner had we left the cottage than the Superintendent remarked; "Red, I am terribly disturbed. There has been another serious breach of the honor code, and I need someone to counsel with me."

My answer was unhesitating: "You came to the right person."

"Several days ago," he said, "I had a cadet in my office who had been asked to resign by the Honor Committee. It is my responsibility to talk with any honor violator before he is discharged. In the course of our conversation, the cadet stated that he was only one of many violators and challenged me to investigate his statement, a challenge that he implied would not be silenced when he left West Point. The young man was too sure of his ground for me lightly to dismiss his accusation. I called in the department head and told him to review all the writ papers [daily tests] of the second class in this subject and to report his findings as soon as possible. The report is unbelievably bad, and now I am confused as to what should be done. There are 174 cadets whose papers indicate that each has falsified his grades. The department gave short writs of a true-or-false nature before each recitation, and each cadet graded his own paper. The department head reported that, although from two to twelve questions were incorrectly answered, the cadets had marked them as correct. The department never reviewed the marked papers. The honor commitee has taken action in this one case, but the cadet whom they have asked to resign knows as we now do that he is only one of nearly several hundred who have done the same as he. Now you know why I am terribly troubled."

I then asked the Supe how many knew about the large number of cadets involved, and he assured me that only four officers had been consulted: the Dean, the Commandant, the head of the department, and his assistant. I remember well giving the Supe my opinion. "Do not appoint a board of inquiry, but immediately give a military order to the four officers who know about the breach not to discuss this subject with anyone. It is obvious that this honor violation is far more serious than the one in 1951. However, as in the case of repetitive writs, so in this case, the system is at fault. I suggest you tell the honor committee head that for special reasons you will handle the case of the guilty cadet. Then I would tell the department head never again to permit the cadets to mark their own papers without a department review of same. In short, change the system in this department."

This suggestion came easily, as it was the same type of advice I had given General Irving in 1951, though he failed to kill the investigation, and it spread throughout the tactical and academic departments. I also stated: "If you dismiss 174 cadets so shortly after the 1951 scandal I dare say you might as well lock the main gate, as the fetish we have made of the word honor before the public will no longer have validity. In fact, there will be no respect for West Point in Congress or among American citizens and a Congressional investigation would make the Academy leadership appear incredibly naive in its judgment of human nature. You and I know that 174 cadets, highly selected as they are with exceptional background records, are not bad, but that the system is. Believe me, don't put this problem in the hands of young officers. Don't repeat the 1951 error. Fortunately for all, this does not involve the football squad, so you should have less difficulty should the violators become known. In this case there can be no claim that this is a conspiracy by the football players to wreck the honor system."

This was the only time I ever discussed the subject with the Supe. Several weeks later the captain of the football team told me that in his capacity as First Captain of the Corps of Cadets he had reported to the Supe's office with the chairman of the honor committee. The Supe had asked them not to pursue further an honor violation, and he was perplexed by the Supe's attitude. I suggested that perhaps the Supe in his wisdom was taking a long-range view, and that it would be wise for them to forget the case. In retrospect, it is fortunate that the Military Academy had a broad-gauged Superintendent in command at that time.

There is no doubt in my mind that the black-or-white-but-no-gray advocates of the honor system would heartily disapprove of my attitude and my suggestion to the Supe as well as his responsive action. In this case, however, they have no scapegoats to blame. It is not easy to answer the question as to what would have happened to West Point if it had become known that the motto of Duty-Honor-Country had been seriously violated a second time.

To restate my views, I believe in the honor code, but I also believe that every reasonable means should be taken to remove inordinate temptation. The black-or-white advocates hold that a solid honor system should present obvious temptation in order to build in the cadet a strong resistance to breaking the code. However, the black-or-white advocates place far too much emphasis on the consequences of breaking the code and too little on an abiding commitment to the moral principle involved. For example, the following is extracted from the *Honor Guide for Officers* used to counsel cadets and issued by the Superintendent, General Davidson, in 1958:

> Honor violators who resign or are separated will be furnished a General Discharge (DD Form 257-A). The only legal disability connected with the 257-A is that it bars a man from becoming a regular officer at any future date. This type of dis-

charge does carry some definite penalties in an extra-legal sense as many large concerns and highly selected colleges will not accept a man who has been given a General Discharge. Other officer programs (OCS—ROTC—Air Cadets) usually will not enroll a man with a General Discharge.

The black-or-white advocates are little concerned that the consequence of breaking the code becomes the important restraining barrier, invoking in the cadets the dreaded fear of dismissal, ostracism, and a type of discharge that may condemn the violator for life. Further, the officers' guide mentions one mitigating situation: "Occasionally a cadet reports himself for an honor violation which otherwise would not be detected. If the Honor Committee feels that the cadet has redeemed himself by his moral courage in reporting himself, they may recommend leniency. In such cases the cadet may receive an honorable discharge." It fails to add that it is basic to the system, however unrealistic, that a cadet report himself for any violation of honor; otherwise, his career will be clouded with a lasting feeling of guilt.

It is obvious, then, from the *Honor Guide for Officers* that the intent of the General Discharge for honor violators is not only to blight the offenders within the Army, but also to extend the blight to such a degree that the dismissed offender becomes morally rejected by society. Thus one concludes that there is a willfulness in the thinking of the black-or-white-but-no-gray adherents and an artificial saintliness to a system that redeems the offender who reports himself by giving him an honorable discharge.

There Are Doubters

No general officer did more to further the career of Fred Irving than General Eichelberger. Like General MacArthur, he believed that the dismissal action taken by the Superintendent, General Irving, and the chain of command represented the judgment of men driven by emotion rather than reason. As a matter of fact, four of eleven Academic Board members, all ranking professors, held this view, and in July Colonel Lawrence Schick, the respected head of the department of Military Topography and Graphics, addressed a letter to the Superintendent pleading for a less drastic course of action because of the obvious responsibility of the Academic Board and the authorities for maintaining the indefensible system that brought about the scandal.

Nearly ten years later General Eichelberger wrote me this letter, from which I have quoted in another connection:

November 4, 1960

Dear Red:

Have been busy with politicking and other things, but I was awake at 2:30 this morning reading the last part of your book and haven't been asleep since. The book to me was extremely interesting and, at time, full of things that made my heartstrings crack.

You know the story of Fred Irving and how I fought to get him another division after Krueger had busted him out in the Pacific. Then out of the fact that I did get him the 38th Division, I was able to win a battle in Washington before the promotion board for general officers. During this, after weeks of struggle, I succeeded in getting him his second star. This was done in spite of a bad efficiency report from Krueger, and from that he went to West Point as a green Superintendent just in time to get mixed up in the scandal. The chapter on that phase of your years at West Point was very well done, and one wonders how the heads at West Point would be willing to ruin so many fine boys. At times I wondered whether Fred had any understanding because he impressed me as being almost owl-like. Certainly your contention that the whole affair should have been shifted to the Academic Board at the highest level cannot be controverted. To let a bunch of young officers commit the Military Academy was entirely wrong. Then, later, the Judge Hand board was apparently designed to save Max Taylor and the Chief of Staff. It certainly didn't go into the affair enough to reach a sound conclusion.

Out of it all, you never made a false step, and you made a record second to none. I just regret that I was not Superintendent at the time this whole affair arose, but for you I can only offer my congratulations again on a book well prepared and superlative work done at the Military Academy.

With all good wishes and affectionate regards to all the Blaiks,

Sincerely,

/s/ Uncle Bobby

Robert L. Eichelberger

One of the basic arguments for dismissing the 90 scapegoats was that an honor violator was unfit to lead men in combat. It is relevant to note that, early in the Vietnam War, President Johnson awarded the Medal of Honor for gallantry and intrepid leadership to a captain who had resigned from West Point. He had allegedly violated the honor code as a cadet.

On numerous occasions I have made the statement that the manner in which we prate the word honor suggests that it is something found in its purest sense only at West Point. Are the graduates of other colleges less informed on the meaning of integrity? The fact is that basic integrity is stamped on young men in their early life and home environment and not after a special indoctrination in honor at either West Point or the Air Force Academy.

In my original chapter, you will recall, there were several cadets whom the Commandant badgered into becoming stool pigeons to obtain for him all the information on the cadets who were giving unauthorized aid. Several years after *You Have to Pay the Price* was published I received the following letter, which I submit without comment, although my answer does reinforce my expressed lack of respect for some of the officers in command when the 1951 episode occurred:

Dear Colonel Blaik:

I have just finished reading your book, an experience which should enrich my life as well as that of my son, who will read it when he is older.

My hopes are that your memory does not place my name immediately. That would cause you unpleasant recollections. Yet, for good reason, I feel I should write to you in reference to comments appearing in your chapter, "The Ninety Scapegoats."

You mention, on page 288, that "two cadets reported irregularities." As I was one of the two, I read your words with great emotion. You have treated my part in the catastrophe very briefly, and my heart thanks you for that. In addition, you have been very generous, implying that the informers were placed in the role of stool Pigeons." I consider this to be the truth, yet it is the first time I have seen it in print.

In December, 1950 I was having difficulty with mathematics and was approached by a close friend in my company who was bearing the same cross. He proceeded to explain how a "large ring" had been established to gather exam data and distribute it to those who needed it. I was invited to join. I immediately refused, dismissing this individual lightly with "Don't be foolish." However, I slept with this episode for several weeks and over the Christmas holidays. I did not mention it to my parents, as the cadet under suspicion had been a guest in our home the previous summer. Additionally, my father would never be convinced that such a thing could ever happen at West Point. After Christmas, the same individual made several additional pleas for me to join the ring. I determined to report him to the Company Honor Representative in the Second Class. I did not trust the First Class Representative. My roommate also reported the same individual, as he too had been invited to the ring. Before submitting this name, I pleaded with him to withdraw from these activities. I told him he was "stupid, crazy" and a few other choice words that young men exchange. He implied that "everyone was in the ring" and that authorities at West Point knew everything that was going on. After all, how could we have such a football team?

Turning this young man in to the Board was not an easy thing to do, Colonel Blaik. On my statement I remember placing the comment, "I regret doing this and I shall remember it for the rest of my life." I certainly have. Regarding the entire affair, I wonder if your life has been made any more miserable than mine. Thank goodness, for my son's sake, that you and others have been decent enough to spare my name. However, one may still hurt. I have been referred to by individuals and the press as a "judicious little prig," a "traitor," a "cheater himself," and the inevitable "stool pigeon." I have been burdened with stories about how a mother died when she heard of her son's dismissal, about ruining the lives of men who "would unquestionably have made better officers than you will make," and I have been threatened. My relatives have been threatened. One graduate wrote to thank me for giving West Point "a great football team in 1952, 1953, and 1954."

Subsequent to my statement reporting the activities of this one cadet I have mentioned, Colonel Harkins requested me to become a member of the ring and gather names, methods, etc. I was very surprised by this request, believe me. At 19 years of age, I was not too young to recognize questionable practices. I telephoned my uncle, a very successful corporation lawyer in New York City, and asked him if he would visit with me that week end, as I had encountered somewhat of a problem. I remember the day of his visit, as I remember most of the events in this episode so well. We walked up to Michie Stadium and then stood by the low wall surrounding Lusk. Outlining the problem without dramatics, I told him that I was prepared to leave West Point myself, if need be. Though I had passed the hurdle of Plebe year, this would have been no supreme sacrifice on my part, frankly. I was happy with the friends I had made at the Academy, and I was well liked—at that time. Yet, academics were hard for me, and I felt my own talents lay in the Arts.

My uncle paused after listening, then said, "You have done nothing wrong. Do not leave under fire. It will involve you. Do as the Colonel says." Respecting him deeply, I accepted his advice and reported back to Colonel Harkins, the Commandant of Cadets.

You have stated that the authorities at West Point handled the episode poorly, though those were not your exact words. I have always considered Colonel Harkins' request to be unfair, unnecessary, and certainly undignified for the Commandant of Cadets. However, is the West Point Yearling privileged to doubt the judgment of the Commandant of Cadets?

Like you, I was very astonished when I learned that the cadets were to be dismissed. My youth did not permit an idea of what might happen to me (by way of personal treatment) had they been permitted to remain. Colonel Harkins had inferred that, "if Cadet _____ tells all the names he knows and other details, then he might be permitted to remain." Upon hearing this, I ran back to South Area and with great joy told

_____ that it was possible for him to remain. _____, who was actually my closest friend, was delighted as his father, a general officer, would probably never learn of the whole mess. I remember we left the room with arms around each others' shoulders! He hurried to the board and told all he knew.

My last two years at the Academy were spent under a cloud of regret and inferiority. I had never wanted the Point. My dad had, and I was fulfilling his lost ambition. I could not hold my head up, nor did it come up right after graduation. At the time of the honor scandal, my mother expressed her extreme disappointment in what I had done, writing to me that "we had taught you as children never to tell on one another."

Will you forgive me for dragging this mess into the open again?

More important is the purpose of my letter. Could not West Point be influenced to modify its honor system? Could it learn from my experience, as well as that of others? My interest is not from the standpoint of the old school tie, but from that of an American. Is the honor system realistic, will it prepare the graduate for life as it exists outside the Highland Falls gate, and is the system what General MacArthur intended it to be? Isn't the kind of young man we want at West Point and in our services the one whose conscience will be wrung for his informing on a fellow classmate? Should the cadet be given the opportunity to intimate through his informing who may, and who may not, continue on a military career? Certainly the Corps can handle the little things such as who may visit the Balcony at the Thayer. What about cheating and stealing and lying? Couldn't the faculty be responsible for this area? Frankly, I am in a teaching situation now (AFROTC), and I would be delighted to shirk the responsibility for addressing those students who cheat by turning it over to the students themselves. However, it is not so simple. I see someone, I lecture him, and that is that. If he repeats his habits, then he is reported to the Dean *by me*. The student is not bitter, for he has been taught in our secondary schools that teachers must act as monitors of honesty. However, let one student come to me to "turn another in" and there is likely to be murder on the campus, honor system or no honor system.

I recall the expressions of the faculty at West Point during the scandal. They were unanimous in stating, "We thought something was going on. We were just about to make a report." Perhaps they were protecting themselves from charges of ignorance, but I believed them. Our system at West Point must be a realistic, beneficial experience for all 2,400 cadets. Further, I submit that, under the present system, they may well be doing damage to the individual who goes by the rules and follows orders and reports his best friend. There will be serious cracks in the armor of that man's character. Using myself as an example, I admit this freely.

In closing, may I mention, with some pride, that my career in the Air Force to this date has been most happy. Recently, upon my return from Europe, I received the Air Force Commendation Medal for my performance as Base Training Officer. The only major criticism of me has been that I "tend to be too easy on subordinates and appear to be reluctant to report individuals who are doing substandard work."

Thank you again for the experience of your fine book and for suffering through this letter. Perhaps one day you will recognize my name as that of a player on West Point's football team. Surely, that is every father's ambition for his son.

Very sincerely,

Captain, USAF

After reading this letter with sympathy and understanding, I sent the following reply:

Dear Captain _____:

Your comprehensive letter covering your conflict of thought both before and after you reported to Colonel Harkins, then Commandant, is appreciated.

I do have some comprehension of the anxiety which you have gone through and understand, as few can, how this episode returns to haunt you.

For my own view, you will find in the book precisely how I feel; the Commandant could have attacked the problem and resolved it with an understanding that befitted a mature mind. Instead, he resorted to using you in a despicable way, which you as a cadet could not evaluate because of the officer-cadet relation, but which marked him as one whose lack of candor made the young calets who openly admitted their involvement comparatively decent men.

It is as useless for me to tell you to forget it as it is to tell Bob the same, but in his case it has haunted him everywhere he has been until those who finally got to know him realize that his sense of integrity and character meet every standard of men of honor.

As far as I know, the many who left West Point remained loyal to the Academy and its concepts and never indicted those who were unfortunately forced to act as stool pigeons. They have never forgiven those who would not listen to their full story or who marked them as a ring dedicated to breaking down West Point ideals. These discharged men were the unfortunate recipients of a system that was passed on to them, and like yourself wondered how it could be, but somehow the respect and affection they held for those upperclassmen who were passing the information allowed them to become enmeshed because they thought it was rampant. Though this was no excuse, as young plebes and third classmen the influence of those above them was stronger than the shallow indoctrination into the honor system of that day.

Again, I hope this letter may tend to alleviate your feelings. Frankly, the book was charitable to many of rank whose derelection before the fact and during the investigation would have turned the stomachs of graduates.

My best wish to you and your fine son who, I hope, will some day make the Army Varsity.

Sincerely,

Earl H. Blaik

A final note on two of the officers involved may be of interest. Colonel Paul Harkins later became the first commander of American troops in Vietnam as a four-star general. At the time his selection concerned me, as I knew from close observation that he could bring only limited military competence to this field command. His experience had been largely limited to that of a staff officer. I was concerned, but hardly surprised by the Harkins assignment. I recalled that Harkins served as Commandant of Cadets under the

Superintendent, General Maxwell Taylor, and later was Taylor's chief of staff in Korea.

As military advisor and later Chairman of the Joint Chiefs of Staff, General Taylor was one of the chief architects of the Kennedy and Johnson commitment in Vietnam. Taylor, who was totally oblivious to the military inadequacies of his protégé, tapped General Harkins for the Vietnam command. There could be little surprise in his selection of Harkins, as General Taylor's Achilles heel was his misreading of men. Dispassionately calculating, with limitless ambition and hardly convivial, the remarkably able, colorful, and distinguished Taylor made a career of impressing others while neglecting to take the full measure of some who impressed him.

The Air Force is an offspring of West Point, and those who were in early command lifted the entire military system from West Point, including the honor code. It is important to know that the Naval Academy has no comparable code; consequently no such honor scandals have troubled Annapolis. The honor code at the Air Force Academy has been seriously breached at least three times in the past decade. An investigation of the breaches of that code showed a strong resemblance to the 1951 episode at West Point.

After the last Air Force scandal, a distinguished panel headed by my late classmate, General Thomas B. White, was charged with making a thorough investigation. Since, at his request, I had two hours before this panel, I wrongly concluded that my views would be included in any impartial and helpful report. Instead, the report did little else than put a whitewash stamp of approval on the Air Force honor system and suggested that there was too much emphasis on football. When I asked the Air Force through Congressman F. Edward Hebert of Louisiana for a transcript of the hearings, the Congressman was told there was no record, as everything had been burned. I recall the military protecting its flanks once before by destroying the record.

I am reminded of the time in September 1951 when the trustees of the Association of Graduates of West Point met for the purpose of endorsing a letter written by General Irving to all graduates, which was to be the final explanation of the scandal. Actually, I never believed that General Irving wrote the letter; rather, it was the work of a special committee dedicated, at any cost, to make the record look good.

As a trustee, I was visited by General Chauncey Fenton, the President of the Association, on the Saturday morning of the meeting day. Chauncey and I were old friends, as we served as directors of several corporations, including the Highland Falls National Bank. General Fenton stated that his mission was to get my word not to challenge the letter or speak during the afternoon session. When I read the letter, I said: "Chauncey, you know me too well to expect me to abide by your request. In fact, in my judgment the letter is full of half truths."

General Fenton's mission failed, and that afternoon I spoke to the point. I concluded by stating that the Supe's letter did not become an institution that parades its honor system. I proceeded to show the lack of candor in many paragraphs and finally recalled the names of several cadets who had changed testimony and lied in order to remain at West Point. Hardly had I mentioned two names before the Superintendent stated; "We will not discuss individual names or cases." "In that case," I replied, "I have nothing further to offer other than to state that I shall not vote to endorse the letter." As I sat down, I turned to the secretary of the Association, Colonel John A. McComsey, who was transcribing the meeting on a record, and requested a transcript of all that had been said. His reply was direct: "You can't have it." I asked, "Why?" "Because I was told to shut off the recorder when you spoke."

The letter went out to the alumni, but its contents were not endorsed by the trustees. In fact, two graduates, Hayden Wagner and Thomas E. Doe, resigned as trustees soon after that meeting because they were disillusioned by what they then "knew for sure" that was not so.

Since the class of 1917 has three ranking officers prominent in the decision to dismiss the cadets—General Lawton Collins, Chief of Staff of the Army; General Frederick Irving, Superintendent of West Point; and General Harris Jones, Dean of the Academic Board of the Academy—it may be of interest to quote the letter of another prominent member of that illustrious class:

Dear Red:

The cadet scandal more than filled a page of the New York *Times*. To me it was stupidly and blunderingly handled. I even doubt the wisdom of the system. Perhaps I am violent because I saw my roommate report a classmate. I lived to see the classmate graduate under a year of silencing. The roommate proved in later life to be a heel and the classmate a good officer.

In fact, as I become more mature and objective in my thinking (I hope), I cannot see where our honor system has produced, in the overall picture, men of higher integrity or spiritual leadership than other schools of equal caliber. The trouble, of course, being that a young man from West Point quickly (or slowly) discovers that he cannot rely on the system in this materialistic world. If he practices it, he is at a disadvantage. He cannot always speak "the truth, the whole truth and nothing but the truth —so help him God." So the young man eventually conforms to the level he finds existing in the world, even as you and I.

Certainly I condemn the staff at West Point that had a system that made possible this condition. In our day, when we took our exams in a matter of hours, the possibility did not exist. Are they not guilty of leaving money on the table?

I've always felt that boys who play football are under a difficult strain at West Point. I tutored a few in the latrine after taps. With the alumni demanding that we produce a winning team at any cost, are they not also guilty?

And these men [the Hand Committee] who with "heavy heart" passed on the verdict! Did they seriously consider that they blasted the lives of 90 young men? Most of them will never fully recover from this type of punishment. There are so many other ways to punish derelictions of this nature. Danford was my Com as a cadet. I was never impressed.

In short, perhaps I have been a civilian too long, but this scandal to me has been handled by men of false pride and colossal egotism. I am very bitter over it.

Sincerely,

/s/ Mac

J. J. McEwan

The above letter brings to mind a recent one, received during the Vietnam War, in which a general officer wrote me: "One thing that impresses me particularly in recent weeks is the behavior of senior officers in Washington. I am not sure what the solution to the problem is, but it seems strange, to say the least, to tolerate false reports and untrue statements from our senior military people in Washington while at the same time we insist on unreasonable standards among the cadets."

The 1951 scandal has never been dormant. Not long ago a most respected retired Major General asked me to have lunch with him. His name is respected by our graduates, and I was stunned by his remarks. He stated that, having read that I had appeared before the General White Committee, he had decided to tell me something he had carried for years and had not before shared with anyone. He said, "Let me preface my words by stating that I do not believe in the honor system." You can understand that I was stunned, for he was one of our most respected graduates. He then told me this story:

> When I was a first classman [senior] and honor representative of my company, a cadet reported a violation of honor by the outstanding man in my company. The man who made the report was ordinary in every sense of the word. For days, I held this information, debating what I should do. Not to report the classmate meant violating the code, but to report him meant sure dismissal and disgrace for this respected cadet. Finally, I rationalized my conscience to the belief that the man to be reported was too good to lose, and the one who reported him was a "slimy cadet." I finally went to the man who had broken the code and told him of the report and that I was not going to turn him in, which meant that I was more guilty of honor violation than he was. The cadet wept, he was so relieved. Mind you, I have carried this guilt all through my career. The one consolation I get from it all is that the cadet whom I should have turned in became a four-star general, and the cadet who reported him was busted out of the Army. Now you can understand me when I say the Academy would be just as effective were there no code.

During the past several years the Corps of Cadets has been increased to 4,400, nearly a 75 per cent increase. Regardless of the effort to get the best prospects, regrettably the Military Academy has been forced to settle for quantity rather than quality. The repetitive or identical writs (tests) given to members of the same class on alternate days were unknown to our graduates prior to the early 1940's, when the Corps was increased to 2,496 cadets. This enlargement required that the Corps be divided into two regiments that recited on alternate days. Thus, classmates were exposed to the identical writ on consecutive days. This led to the tip-off among classmates on what to prepare for. The wholesale violation of the code involved some cadets who failed to report classmates, although they themselves had not accepted the restricted information. In no way did this breach involve cheating in the classroom. Although the repetitive writ is a fault in the system, there has nevertheless been a stubborn resistance to any change.

The genesis of the academic system that more than a century later brought about the identical writ problem may be traced as far back as 1817 when Sylvanus Thayer, the father of the Military Academy, was Superintendent. The writ system was based on the concept that all cadets will recite and be marked daily in all subjects and that the class rank of the individual cadet will be largely determined on this basis. Daily marks are possible, as section classes are restricted to 15 cadets.

The daily writ and the more inclusive monthly and final writs have been identical in order to assure that each cadet is comparably treated. When the Corps was divided into two regiments in the 40's, the tradition of equal treatment required that classmates take identical writs or tests on alternate days. The rationale for the continuation of the repetitive writ is absolute fairness, as the cadet's merit standing determines his precise ranking as an officer of the regular Army.

When the Corps numbered 1200, repetitive writs on the same day could be justified, but with a Corps of 4400 it is absurd to justify them as the only fair method of determining cadet rank. The passing mark is a minimum 2.0 and maximum 3.0—a spread of one unit. How does a department rank cadets of a class numbering 1,300 when each cadet must be structured into one unit? The repetitive writ justified solely by the merit ranking of cadets suggests that tradition has stifled instructor imagination and compromised the common sense of the department heads.

In the spring of 1973, many cadets resigned for honor violation. It was the latest of many honor scandals induced by the system of repetitive writs. Why, I ask, is the yearly attrition for honor violations since the 1940's often greater than the total known violations for the entire decade of either the 1920's or the 1930's? The question is simply answered: the Corps is larger. It is more to the point to ask: Has American youth degenerated or are there faults in the present system? In what way, for example, were the dismissed athletes and presidents of the classes of 1952 and 1953 morally different from the athletes Eisenhower and Bradley of the class of 1915? The superficial answer is: They cheated, didn't they? In passing, it is of interest to note that General Eisenhower in several chapters of his book *At Ease* recalls his cadet days at the Academy, but never once refers to the cadet honor system. In those days a dismissal or resignation for an honor violation was rare, indeed, and the violator had generally established that he was a despicable character. The honor system was not codified until many years after the 1915 class graduated.

While I do not challenge the ideal of an honor system, I suggest that it is time to give the code a maturity and acceptance that remove it from a mid-Victorian indoctrination based on fear of dismissal and fanatic ostracism. Make no mistake about it, the doubters among the graduates are many. I dare say, that, were the cadets not conditioned to respond like parrots, they would be compassionate and view derelictions more dispassionately.

Ostracized

For several years I have deferred publishing this account, and it is with reluctance that I now do so. The Military Academy should not be the focus of controversy occasioned by the decisions of a few in command at any one time. It is to focus on the type of leadership that in 1951 implemented the system that I overcome my reluctance.

In June of 1951, Colonel John Waters, at the time Acting Commandant, with barely controlled emotion read his short paragraph to the Corps. It was to the effect that there has been a serious violation of the honor code by many cadets; no effort will be spared to drive every violator out of the Corps; to us, an honor violator is the same as dead.

In the tradition of earlier military and tribal caste systems, often copied by preparatory schools, violators of certain traditions carry the sentence of ostracism and silence for life. The silence of a violator as described officially to cadets by the honor committee consisted of eight rules:

1. The silence lasts his entire Army career.
2. He is not permitted to wear his class ring.
3. If the silenced man goes to a hop, all other cadets leave the floor as soon as he steps on.
4. If the man goes to the theater, the remainder of the row he sits in is left empty.
5. If he comes into the boodlers, that is vacated.
6. He is addressed only on official business, and then as "Mister."
7. He will not be allowed to have a roommate.
8. The man will eat at a separate table in the dining hall.

In June of 1973, the 19-month silence of Cadet James J. Pelosi by the Corps for known violation surfaced in the press. All forms of the media expressed a revulsion to the silence and to this treatment. The consequence of public pressure and the knowledge that highly critical articles were being written about the West Point honor system forced the announcement in September that the silence was abolished by the honor committee.

In the meantime Pelosi attended the Infantry School at Fort Benning, from which he graduated in October. Although I make no brief whatever for Pelosi as an individual, to their lasting discredit when Lieutenant Pelosi was presented his diploma at Fort Benning he was vulgarly hissed by his Academy classmates. This unforgiveable display of boorish manners reflected the inbreeding of a system they had blindly followed. The action marked these young officers as emotionally immature. Graduates in general must have blanched when they read of this unprecedented affront to a uniformed officer of the Army.

When the silence was abolished in September, it was immaterial whether overwhelming public disapproval of the system showed the Corps the light of day or whether Academy officials realized that West Point was in an untenable position. The fact that the honor committee went on record to end an archaic form of the honor system represents a maturity that is all to the good.

Four years hence the tradition of the silence within the Corps will be thoroughly bred out, although I dare say that for years to come there will be some graduate disapproval and even nonacceptance of the decision to abolish the practice. However, I have great faith in the Corps; as the years pass, I suggest that the cadets will ponder and discuss how officer leadership, yearling in its thinking, could have supported and passed along such ritualistic foolishness.

The Waters statement in 1951 two months before the cadets were discharged was a sorry example of leadership. The young officers of the tactical department who courted recognition were aware that Waters, as the son-in-law of General Patton, had been tapped for high command. He became a four-star general during the 1960's. His decision at the time was meant to influence the thinking of the Corps, though later events established the fact that his actions controlled mainly those cadets whom his department had selected for the cadet top chain of command, a group that went overboard to agree with the thinking of the tactical department under Waters. These were the cadets, nine in number, who met with the Hand board in New York City and told the three board members that, if they did not vote to dismiss the violators, the Corps of Cadets would resign in mass. The pity was that the Hand board believed those cadets, directed by the officers whom they were anxious to impress, and reversed their tentatively agreed position that they would recommend no action that would bring discredit to the Military Academy or the dismissal of the cadets involved.

When the cadets were discharged, every effort I made to get them honorable discharges was thwarted by the military establishment in the Pentagon. The fact that the cadets implicated themselves by telling the truth did not overcome the callous vindictiveness of the military authority. In fact, I was ordered by General Maxwell Taylor to desist in any attempt to help the discharged cadets.

After these many years my recent effort to have those discharged received into the official West Point family, the Association of Graduates, likewise has been unsuccessful. The negative response to me came after the 1973 March meeting of the trustees and ended all hope of a reconciliation of our views. In essence, 23 years after their separation, these men, known by the trustees to be respected citizens, are still ostracized. This decision as reported to me was the consensus of the trustees after a discussion that lasted less than a half hour. The 90 scapegoats are forever condemned by the Academy officialdom.

The Military Academy is not the issue; my reverence for this great institution has never changed. I had postponed including this detailed account in the hope there could be a meeting of the minds, though I had expressed skepticism to several trustees as to any favorable board action. I believe that an inbreeding based on invalid assumptions separates our attitudes.

In no manner, even by inference, do I support the anti-Military Academy critics. The difficulty is that no dispassionate discussion is possible with some graduates on subjects that in any way encroach on tradition. Thus the subject of the honor system is sacrosanct and not open to an in-depth exploration. It is unfortunate that the thinking of a minority of ranking officers, loyal to former command, dominates the many officers whose understanding of human nature imbues them with some compassion. The latter group does not support those in power who would ostracize offenders and forever bar them as untouchables. I recognize, of course, that it takes great courage to challenge entrenched, authority especially when it can affect one's own career.

Nor do I quarrel with the simple code that states that a cadet does not lie, cheat, or steal. However, the added nontoleration clause is the variant that is the weakness of the code: not to turn in your closest friend for a violation makes a cadet equally a violator of the code. To many graduates of understanding, a black-or-white interpretation is ritualistic and unreal in cases where the system is to blame. Such faults in a system encourage seldom detected shades of gray and constitute a stress on the honor code. Incongruous as it may seem, breaches give validity to the code. When a large number of the cadets yearly resign for honor, any public approval of the separation serves as a form of absolution to those who graduate. In this regard, the 1951 episode involving nationally acclaimed athletes was important because their dismissal highlighted in the collegiate world the sanctity of the code. Thus, infractions and resignations serve to emphasize the credibility of the system. The repetitive writ is an obvious fault, but as one Chief of Staff, General McConnell, told me, "If 500 cadets must go, we aren't going to change the system."

The paradox of graduate thinking was evident when many officers later questioned my advice because they knew that the authorities had insufficient ground to discharge the cadets even with the evidence furnished by the stool pigeons. Furthermore, the cadet honor committee was not the judge of its peers; the matter was handled solely by officers in the tactical department. To remain, the cadets had only to refuse to answer or plead innocence; those cadets who did so remained and have been accepted by their classmates and the service as wholly clean. In brief, the 1951 episode could have been solved with as little compromise to the ideals as the later one, forever buried, involving 174 cadets.

Now the question may be properly asked, "Why after all these years should you concern yourself about these men?" The fact is, as the years have passed, I have increasingly doubted the wisdom of the advice I gave those cadets who sought my counsel when I said, "Tell the truth—you know how we do business."

I have checked the officer service careers of many of those involved in passing writ information while cadets in the freshman and senior classes, the two classes not investigated, and also the service records of those men of the two investigated classes, sophomore and junior, who either refused to testify or lied to remain. The sense of doubt that I entertain may be better understood when it is realized that the individual records of both groups support the conclusion that those guilty men who failed to come clean or were not investigated as a group have done remarkably well as officers. Thus, there is reason to believe that their lack of complete adherence to the honor code as cadets in no way adversely affected their Army careers. To be specific, I have always believed that the moral and spiritual values of the scapegoats were no less impressive than those of countless graduates of all ranks whom I have known intimately.

The repeated argument then advanced that the dismissed men lacked integrity, and for that reason could not be military leaders of men, is baseless in this case. This canard is totally dispelled by the service record of those guilty who were not dismissed. As for those who were dismissed, they have been eminently successful in civilian life, where they have demonstrated the same leadership that marked them as outstanding cadets when they were in the Corps. Those dismissed athletes who took the ROTC route to military careers have also been successful; *all five of them rose to become full colonels.*

In my moments of doubt, I am compelled to question the judgment of a small elite group of sanctimonious graduates, traditionalists narrow in their thinking who lack both compassion and understanding of young men. They are certain that their every act as cadets and officers has never been even slightly suspect and that they epitomize men of honor. They assume that the hallmark that differentiates them from graduates of other institutions of learning is not excellence of education, but personal honor. Too many of them have fixed opinions, are unimaginative, and believe they have never been wrong. Their assumed security brooks of no search for the truth with respect to the honor system. Regrettably, as a group they regard their views as above and apart from the mainstream of the services, as well as from that of American society.

Chapter XXV

The Kennedys—President Jack and Bob

It may seem odd that one who supported and worked for the election of President Nixon in 1960 could still have had a close relationship with the late brothers, President Jack and Bob Kennedy. So much has been written about the ruthlessness of the Kennedys that the reader may be surprised to learn that I, who knew them well, never saw any evidence of this quality.

Both Jack and Bob went out for Harvard football as undergraduates. The President was forced to give up the game because of an injury to his back; Bobby was a tiger end who weighed only 150 pounds, but who made the most of his physical talents. He never quite made the first team, though this did not deter him from trying for three years.

After President Kennedy assumed office, I was one of a delegation that called to notify him that he had been selected for the Gold Medal Award by the National Football Foundation. We were no sooner in his oval office in the White House than he turned to me and remarked, "Do you remember the Melville, Rhode Island team that gave Blanchard and Davis such a scare in '45?" I replied that I did and that the score was 13-0 in favor of the PT squad before I sent those two great players into the game. The PT squad was made up of many former college and professional athletes that gave a good account of itself until the players ran out of steam. The President said, "Well, I was there that day with the PT squad; by the way, what was the final score?" I replied, "55-13, Mr. President." He then recalled that he had always enjoyed watching our Dartmouth teams against Harvard and stated that he was present when we lost our only game in my Dartmouth career to Harvard. I replied, "You probably mean the game we should have lost but, won 20-3 when Harvard made great yardage in the mud but no touchdowns, while Dartmouth scored on three long runs." "Well," the President stated, "perhaps I am mistaken; I guess that was the day that Hutchison beat us." His memory of those games was so vivid that I surmised that his assistant, Ken O'Donnell, a former Harvard captain, must have talked a little football with him before we arrived. I had the feeling that President Kennedy, after his gracious demeanor in this casual assembly, could have charmed his way into 1600 Pennsylvania Avenue.

I was in Washington in December 1962 when my secretary informed me that the Attorney General had urgently requested that I call him at the White House. It took me no time to get through to Robert Kennedy, who confided that the President was disturbed by the conflict between the Amateur Athletic Union and the National Collegiate Athletic Association and felt that it was vital to bring these organizations together before our Olympic effort was impaired. He then asked if I knew anyone who could resolve this squabble. My answer was, "Not offhand, but I'll think about it and call you later." No sooner had I hung up than it occurred to me that there was one logical man with the stature to resolve the N.C.A.A.—A.A.U. differences: General Douglas MacArthur. The General had headed the Olympic Committee in 1928, was greatly interested in all sports, and certainly had the presence to command a meeting of the minds of these organizations. I immediately called the Attorney General, suggested the name of MacArthur, and gave the reasons for my selection. Bobby answered, "This is a splendid suggestion" and added that he would talk to the President and call me back within the hour. His return call echoed his first thoughts when he said: "The President is delighted with your recommendation of General MacArthur and asked if you could get him to take on such a difficult task, as neither of us knows him." I replied that I would talk with the General and report the next day.

When I presented the President's request, MacArthur's immediate answer was, "Earl, if the President asks you to do anything within your competence, regardless of your politics, it is your duty as an American citizen to do it. You may tell the President that I shall do it under the condition that you act as my deputy." "Of course, I will," was my answer, "provided no mention is made of my being your deputy, even to the President." I called the Attorney General and told him that General MacArthur would take on the assignment. That night, the President personally called General MacArthur and formally asked him to serve as the arbiter of the N.C.A.A.—A.A.U. dispute.

The N.C.A.A.—A.A.U. feud had been smoldering intermittently for many years, but in the 1960's broke into open fire. It was evident in late 1962 that, unless something was done to check the fight, the United States effort to field a strong team for the 1964 Olympics to be held in Japan would be impaired The spirit of the A.A.U., founded in 1880 "to preserve amateurism or sport for sport's sake in the nation," gradually achieved world-wide adoption; it cooperated with similar organizations abroad to create the International Amateur Federation to set standards for such international athletic competitions as the Olympic games and the Pan-American meets, over which the I.A.F. has full control. The A.A.U. has always had the power of sanction, that is, the right to certify American entrants in these games as amateurs. The I.A.F. recognizes that this power is vital to the existence of the A.A.U. and has never considered allowing any other body to displace it in international councils.

The National Collegiate Athletic Association, founded in 1906, has gradually aquired control of all college sports, the rules for which it formulates, and administers annual championship events in 16 sports. Since the majority of the American athletes who participate in international amateur athletics come from our colleges and since the N.C.A.A. controls collegiate athletic activity, it feels that it is entitled to the sanctioning power possessed by its older rival, the A.A.U., and that it is entitled to select the coaches and administrators for all United States teams participating in international events. In pursuit of this objective, the N.C.A.A. has chosen to concentrate on track and field events and has formed a new organization called the United States Track and Field Federation, inspired by a small group of college track coaches who wish to achieve absolute control of amateur track meets. The contest thus has gone beyond the bounds of certifying amateur athletes for international competition and has degenerated into a struggle for control over amateur athletics in this country between the A.A.U., which draws its support from college graduates who maintain an interest in athletics, the N.C.A.A., which has acquired strength and influence from a treasury inflated by the revenues from televised college football.

Neither side wanted any part of the MacArthur hearings and attended only under pressure from the White House. They met in the General's Waldorf apartment. When nothing was accomplished on Friday, the first day of the conference, the General hardened his approach on Saturday by keeping the groups in continuous session without refreshment from eleven in the morning until seven in the evening. He would force a decision through physical attrition.

At five on Saturday afternoon, the session was hopelessly deadlocked. The General made his final plea based on patriotic duty, forcefully telling the participants that, as individuals representing amateurism, they did not dare leave a conference requested by the President without a compromise solution. When a problem seemed settled and another was under discussion, someone would reopen the first subject. Finally, the General became tired of such stalling tactics and forced each participant to sign the agreed solution before proceeding to the next problem under contention. Between 5:40 and 7:00 o'clock, the entire agenda was forced through, much to the dissatisfaction of the more contentious representatives. The MacArthur agreement provided the temporary peace for our successful 1964 Olympic effort.

The N.C.A.A.—A.A.U. fight still continues, even though several years later the then Vice President Humphrey and a Senate committee tried to ride herd on these organizations. I appeared before Senator Warren Magnusson's Commerce Committee to give my view of the power struggle. I recall stating to the Committee: "Probably the one way to sum up the A.A.U.—N.C.A.A. conflict is to say the one is more pure than able and the other is more able than pure. Until new faces from each group enter the arena, it will continue to be a sorry boxing exhibition of artful dodging."

There is no doubt that the satisfaction of the White House at the disposition of the N.C.A.A.—A.A.U. case and my suggesting and persuading the General to undertake the task made a favorable impression on both the President and his brother.

The next time I heard from the Attorney General was months later. I was playing golf at Blind Brook, a club at Purchase, N.Y., which has been a real source of pleasure and good companionship since I left West Point. I was overtaken on the course by the caddie master, who informed me that Attorney General Kennedy wanted me to call him at once. I was playing a twosome with Gordon Reid, a dedicated conservative in the Goldwater tradition, whose game was ruined when the name of Kennedy was mentioned.

There was a telephone on the course nearby, so I called the Attorney General. This was around 3:00 o'clock in the afternoon on September 19, 1963. Bobby said the President was looking for someone to send to Birmingham, Alabama to bring peace to that community, where the pressure of racial conflict required immediate action. He asked me if I knew anyone who could take on this difficult task: "How about General MacArthur?" I answered immediately, "Bobby, this task is far too physically demanding for the General to consider." At that moment it occurred to me that there was one man eminently qualified for this assignment, so I told him, "If you could get Kenneth Royall, former Secretary of the Army, who integrated that service, a Democrat, a North Carolinian, and an eminent lawyer, I knew of no one with better credentials." The Attorney General thought Royall was an excellent suggestion and said he would call me back. I replied that he need not do so; if the President selected him, they would have a far better chance of getting General Royall than I would.

After this talk, I resumed the game with Gordon Reid, who was not impressed by a call from the administration. We had completed several holes when a courier arrived with a second message to call the White House. I called the Attorney General, who stated that General Royall had agreed to accept the assignment and was delighted with "our" recommendation that I and the General take on this mission together. I stalled for a moment with the rejoinder, "You certainly don't want me; my image is that of a football coach, and neither group in Birmingham will go for me." The answer was; "We have thought of that, and we disagree." So I said, "Let me think it over, and I will call you back." Bobby's answer was a little abrupt: "You have only a half hour to think it over because we have to announce it before 5:00 P.M., when a delegation of Negro leaders will meet with the President. They want him to send troops into Birmingham, and this committee is his answer to them."

I called General Royall, a friend whom I respected and with whom I shared confidences. He did not then, nor to his final day, know that I suggested his name to the President. General Royall stated that the President suggested that his committee should include Allen Dulles and Earl Blaik, but that he had countered by stating that he would take on the assignment only with me as his associate. We were to meet that night and be in the President's office the next day for a briefing. I had already spoken to my associates in management at AVCO, and my decision was determined by my recollection of the MacArthur dictum, "Whenever the President asks you to do something within your competence, it is your duty as an American, regardless of politics, to do it." I therefore called the Attorney General and told him that I had spoken with General Royall and would accept the President's appointment.

Since so many years have passed, it will be necessary to fill in the background of our mission. Birmingham at that time was industrially advanced but politically and socially retarded and had shown in many ways that it would rather wither than submit to integration. Following the end of World War II, the increasing demands of the Negroes were answered with more than 50 bombings of black property; so intense was the violence in one area that it became known as Dynamite Hill. This was but part of a general activity bordering on anarchy then sweeping the South.

Four Negro churches were burned in Georgia in August and September 1962 following a demand for the franchise. These and other demonstrations were dramatized when Gov. George Wallace of Alabama "stood in the schoolhouse door," defying court-ordered school integration, first at the University of Alabama, then in the public schools of Birmingham and other cities. Riots at Birmingham in May 1963 were dramatized when Eugene "Bull" Connor, the Public Safety Commissioner, used dogs and fire hoses on the demonstrators, and the Governor intervened with state troopers. The entire sorry situation came to a head on Sunday, Sept. 15, 1963 when a Negro church was destroyed by a bomb. Four children died in the blast; all were horribly mutilated, and one was decapitated. On the same day a 13-year-old Negro was shot and killed by a white boy. The citizens of Birmingham were distressed and frightened.

The situation caused a group of Negro leaders, headed by Martin Luther King, to visit the President to demand intervention by Federal troops. Kennedy had already sent Burke Marshall, the Assistant Attorney General for Civil Rights, to report on the Birmingham situation. Marshall had reported that, while the Negroes had no confidence in law enforcement, the crux of the problem was a total lack of communication between blacks and whites that had lasted for six months. It has been claimed that Kennedy was reluctant to take decisive action because he had his eye on the 1964 elections, only a year away. My own view is that Kennedy felt that further troop movements could only exacerbate the situation, that moderate elements on both sides had suffered enough, and that an opening of communication might allow their influence to become effective.

General Royall and I departed for Birmingham by government plane with mixed feelings on September 24 after we had been briefed by both Marshall and Kennedy. We were somewhat heartened by the fact that the Negro leaders who had asked for Federal troops withdrew their demand in face of our appointment and that Martin Luther King had reiterated the Negro leadership's unswerving committment to nonviolence. On the positive side was the fact that General Royall's reputation was recognized. As for myself, some Southern papers endorsed my appointment on the ground that the citizenry had more respect for its football coach than it accorded the Governor! A few local bankers checked my standing with their New York correspondents, who knew me well because of my connection with AVCO. My status was further enhanced when they reported that I was a friend of General MacArthur, whom I had consulted about the mission and who had referred me to several Birmingham leaders who had served under him in the Pacific.

On the negative side, a few Negro leaders ignored my industrial connections and said nothing could be expected from a football coach, while Adam Clayton Powell, then a power in Negro circles, called our selection unfortunate and predicted that the mission would be unsuccessful. Perhaps most depressing was our realization that the racial troubles were in great measure economic, the consequence of competition for jobs, and that only a complete revival of business could change the situation. Alabama's per capita income was then only $1538. Business in 1963 had dropped by 20 per cent, and the young people had begun to leave. Executives and trained workers refused to come to what became known as "Bombingham" in Northern liberal circles.

Our arrival in the city was preceded by two bombings—the last in the city—in the Negro section. We were greeted at the airport by Mayor Boutwell and his delegation. Our pleasant lunch at a club high above the city, which followed our arrival, hardly suggested the seriousness of the situation. Our hosts looked at us with gimlet eyes, as though we were a revival of the carpetbaggers, and obviously wanted no part of a committee appointed by Kennedy, whom they disliked almost as much as they had hated Franklin Roosevelt. In all fairness, I must state that many of this luncheon group later gave us their full cooperation.

They were taken back by our announcement that we would hold a short press conference and thereafter would not discuss the Birmingham mission with the press until we were ready to depart from the city. Actually, we never held a formal press conference after the initial meeting. This action proved wise, as it removed our work from political implication and to a marked degree silenced an inquisitive press.

We lived at the hotel and paid our own expenses, thus being obligated to neither the government nor the city. The hearing headquarters was the top floor of the Federal Building. Our staff consisted of my assistant, Don Flodin, and a young lawyer, Robert Larson, from General Royall's Washington office. There were nearly 100 FBI agents in this vicinity and, though we were aware of this fact, we never realized that we were under their constant watch. We walked from the hotel to the Federal Building against the advice of some local citizens.

General Royall was an early riser. By 7:00 o'clock A.M. we were ready for the full day we had planned the previous night.

The first several days were devoted to talking with the Mayor, the City Council, black and white civic and business leaders, educators, spiritual leaders and, in fact, anyone who could helpfully advise us as to the groups with whom we should meet. We discussed the problems and the strategy for attacking them. We then saw any group generally limited to 15 in number and gave each several hours to present its views. In all, we talked to nearly 500 people, though in reality we only listened much of the time, always encouraging the groups to talk themselves out. No group or individual was too unimportant to have our full attention. This demonstrated that we were there to help resolve their problems and not to dictate solutions. The discussions often were trivial and even personal, but important to those who talked. I am sure that the attitude of getting the whole story encouraged the citizens to trust us and to accept the committee as men dedicated to resolving problems without prejudice. As a matter of fact, in less than a week, with rare exceptions, we had broken the freeze which originally was obvious. Leaders on both sides became convinced that we had no preconceived ideas or dictated Washington instructions. Despite this, the meetings often were marked by extreme emotional outbursts. It was evident that both the black and the white leaders were incensed by the intrusion into local affairs by outside agitators.

Two men, Arthur Hayes, the first lawyer for James Earl Ray, the slayer of Martin Luther King, and Eugene "Bull" Connor, the former Birmingham Police Commissioner, were adamant in their negative attitudes. In fact, Connor refused to meet with us and remained the symbol of the uncompromising redneck. On the other hand, we were impressed by the County Sheriff, Mel Bailey, and the Chief of Police, Jammie Moore, both of whom were reasonable and objective in their attitudes and answers to the questions that were raised.

It was apparent from our talks that the wholly white Police Department was woefully understaffed and underpaid. It seemed to us that the patrolmen we interviewed were of average caliber. Except for a few individual cases, the discussions suggested that the claims of general police brutality could not be substantiated. The main exceptions, of course, were the deplorable events that occurred under "Bull" Connor. Even those were perhaps overdramatized because the uncouth Connor was an outspoken braggart and an unreconstructed hater of the Negro community. The only charitable thing that may be said for him is that he never left any doubt as to where he stood on civil rights and the decision of the Supreme Court.

At night General Royall and I made several trips through the Negro community and twice visited in the home of Arthur Shores. He was reputed to be a millionaire, respected by both his own people and the white community. His home was bombed a few weeks prior to our visit with him, as was the motel of A. Y. Gaston, another wealthy Negro businessman, who along with Shores understood the difficulties we faced better than many Birmingham white citizens.

My assignment included the businessmen of Birmingham, whom I called on as individuals or met in small groups. My selling point to these businessmen was that the committee intended to make a fair and factual report of the Birmingham racial problems, regardless of their attitude. If they wished to have Birmingham properly presented to the country, it was only through our report that it could be done. To achieve this end, it was vital that they make every endeavor to present their views as influential citizens of the community and realize that they would have no second chance. I also used the argument that I was a Republican, had not voted for President Kennedy, and could hardly be regarded as a stooge of the White House. Finally, and most important, I stated that the report would be made public regardless of whether they cooperated with our mission. It was no easy task to gain the confidence and support of these men in our undertaking. After all, they were the local respected establishment, and the civil rights movement, inspired and often directed from the North, was anathema to the majority of them.

As I look back to Birmingham in 1963, I realize that many of the important figures in this scenario have died. I recall the political hypocrisy exhibited at times by both the black and white actors. I remember the progress made by the City Council and the Community Relations Committee headed by the Rev. Mr. Carpenter. Several proposals that were agreed upon by this committee composed of black and white members were leaked to Northern papers, with the result that we were plagued by ultimatums from Martin Luther King to the effect that, if the proposals were not precisely implemented, he would return to Birmingham to force action by leading further marches and demonstrations. I felt strongly that King could not abide progress made in his absence and felt that he must force the issue and thus be credited as the leader behind the scene.

This infuriated the Birmingham whites and the Carpenter committee. It took several days to placate them; when we finally achieved further progress, King resorted to the same threats. Toward the end, when King realized we were making great progress, he flew to Birmingham for the express purpose of taking credit for the success of our negotiations. We had broken the impasse, and both groups were talking. We were informed by the Negro leaders who met him at the airport that they were so displeased that they advised him to keep on going to Atlanta and let them resolve their own problems without him. He was finally persuaded to do so. I had definite reservations as to the motives of King, Abernathy, and Shuttlesworth, all of whom were leaders in the Southern Christian Leadership Conference. After dealing either directly or indirectly with them, I believe that they had less concern for the minority group in Birmingham than they had for their own positions of national prominence.

In retrospect, I think our Birmingham mission was more successful than we could have hoped for. First, outside agitators, both black and white, were eliminated from the scene. When Dr. Edward R. Fields was indicted at the time of our arrival for advocating violence to prevent the opening of an integrated school, the community was calmed, as it was by the absense of Martin Luther King. Fields, a leader in the National States Rights Party (a successor to the United White Party), had inflamed feelings through his mimeographed *Birmingham Daily Bulletin* and his 12 page monthly newspaper, *The Thunderbolt*, both anti-Negro and white-oriented. The removal of these and other divisive influences made it possible for us to reestablish communications between the leaders of both sides, all of whom were becoming weary of hate and conflict.

The biracial committee we established found that many issues yielded to discussion and persuasion, although isolated individuals attempted to slow our progress. By March of 1964, several community centers were integrated, four integrated schools were operating smoothly, the city auditorium was open to both races, the department stores were desegregated, the "White Only" signs were removed from public places, and the U. S. Steel plant opened more job opportunities to Negroes. Perhaps most heartening of all was the demand of 63 white Birmingham lawyers for obedience to the relevant decisions of the U. S. Supreme Court. Heartening progress was furthered by the revival of business and by heightening prosperity, confirming my original feeling that much of the racial conflict had an economic basis. The main problem which remained, at that time, was the need to hire black policemen. But the problem was basically economic. Those Negroes who could qualify were making more than the white policemen.

General Royall and I had three meetings with the President, reporting our tentative findings to him. We were never listed as a part of the President's daily calender, but met the Attorney General and entered the White House through the rear garden that led to the porch just outside the oval office. One time we stood on the porch to await the departure of the Russian Ambassador; at the conclusion of the meeting, attended also by Secretary Rusk and

William Bundy, the President saw us outside and invited us to met Mr. Gromyko. On another occasion, Secretary McNamara was there to discuss the tension in Berlin arising from a threat to close the Autobahn. An hour after the Secretary left, McNamara called the President to discuss more serious reports of the closing; Kennedy spoke in a manner that in no way suggested the tremendous tension of the situation. He did not ask us to leave, and thus we were witnesses to his resolve to resist any move the Russians might make.

The next time General Royall and I visited the White House, our unofficial approach was again from the rear. This time, Deputy Attorney General Katzenbach and others were there for a meeting. I was struck by the informality of Katzenbach, who was later to become the Under Secretary of State. He was attired in a sports jacket with patched leather elbows, Ivy fashion, and a pair of loafers that were better suited to a hunting lodge. No sooner had he left than the nurse brought John John and Caroline. John ran to Bobby, and they roughhoused a little, and then he hid under the President's desk, while Caroline, quite ladylike, showed her great affection for her father. This lasted about five minutes until the President showed them out with a command to the nurse to get rid of these marauders.

We got down to a discussion of Birmingham and our progress there. The President sat in his rocking chair until a valet brought in his 6:00 o'clock snack of cream of tomato soup and crackers. General Royall and I sat on adjacent sofas, while Bobby remained in the background, slowly pacing the floor. At one time, I asked the President if he wanted to test his sense of humor and then told him of the hundreds of stickers on the bumpers of automobiles in Birmingham which read: "Kennedy for King, Goldwater for President." For a few moments neither brother understood this couplet until General Royall said; "It means Kennedy for Martin Luther King." They laughed briefly, but immediately saw the political implications of such a sign if it spread over the country. This led to a discussion of the political problems involved in the attempt to enforce the law and simultaneously ease racial tensions. That was the last time we saw the President, as the appointment to submit our formal report was set for the week following the President's assassination.

Our failure to submit a final report is attributable not only to President Kennedy's death. A few days after President Johnson assumed office, he delegated Abe Fortas, later the Associate Justice of the Supreme Court to call on General Royall to say that he wished no further discussion of the Birmingham situation and that he wanted us to issue no report. Thus summarily dismissed, we could nevertheless take satisfaction in the success of our mission, although the only tokens of our assignment were the key to the city of Birmingham that Mayor Boutwell presented to Kenneth Royall and to me in New York many months after we had completed our work. My version of our visit to Birmingham and its results is filed in the records of the Kennedy Library.

Inasmuch as President Kennedy had charged us at our last meeting with the obligation to keep in touch with the Birmingham situation for several months to be certain that it required no further attention, we felt obliged to keep our promise despite the attitude of his successor. When it became evident in December 1963 that the situation was stabilizing and that we need not intervene again, we reported that fact to President Johnson and asked to be relieved of our commission. In return, we received a letter expressing appreciation of our effort "to provide a means whereby communication between the white and Negro communities could be facilitated."

I came to know the Attorney General very well. Several times while on the Birmingham mission, General Royall and I had breakfast at his home in the country. Later I had several luncheons with him at his estate. There we were treated to the rigors of living as a Kennedy and to absolute bedlam, often controlled by a quiet remark from either Ethel or Bobby. Breakfast was frequently interrupted either by one of several dogs wanting a handout or by one of many youngsters, already hungry after a few minutes away from the table. It was in this atmosphere that Bobby must have developed his great degree of concentration as a form of self-defense. I was greatly impressed by the strong interest their parents showed in each youngster. In the house they hung the school drawings the children had made; even in his office, Bobby had many such exhibits, showing his youngster's importance in his eyes and his pride in them. Aside from the children, big black Bruno, the favored dog, had free access to the house and was Bobby's constant companion in his open car and around his office. Such informality in places that called for dignity shows that there was little of pretense about this branch of the Kennedy family.

All the time I knew Bobby Kennedy, he never once assumed that I was anything other than a friend, and he knew that I was not in his political orbit. Nevertheless, he often asked my council, made me chairman of a board to select his service academy appointees, and also invited me to be a trustee of the Kennedy Library, a position that I accepted. At one time, together with others, we were interested in buying the Washington Redskins and later the New York Jets. I suspect that the fact that I had been a football coach first drew us together; the gridiron gave us much in common.

When Justice Byron White of the Supreme Court was awarded the Gold Medal of the National Football Foundation, I had Bobby as my guest; when he was introduced, the boos embarrassed, I am sure, even those who booed. Businessmen always felt that anything Bobby Kennedy did was wrong, especially after his employment of the F.B.I., undoubtedly directed from above, at a time of industrial strife. I do not know that Bobby Kennedy reciprocated this feeling, but I do recall that President Kennedy once said that his father had little respect for businessmen in general, and said that they all were S.O.B.'s.

One day Bobby came into my office, as he often did without notice, sat down, and talked about affairs in general. He said that he had always been a great admirer of General MacArthur and wondered if the General would allow me to set up a meeting. I arranged this for the following week. Bobby and I walked from my office to the Waldorf, where we were joined by Ethel, two of his sisters, and James Symington, Senator Symington's son, now a

Congressman from Missouri. All were a bit fearful that the General might resent the intrusion. On the contrary, it furnished him a forum, and he gave them what Bobby termed the most interesting hour of his life. They formed a circle with General and Mrs. MacArthur. The General told them Civil War stories of his father, General Arthur MacArthur, then a captain, and reminisced about the Washington scene when he was aid to President Teddy Roosevelt and later Chief of Staff under Presidents Hoover and Franklin Roosevelt. It was such an interesting session that Bobby was half an hour late to a luncheon at the Americana Hotel, where he was to address a labor group. Kennedy's admiration and respect for General MacArthur never lessened; although this may have irritated a few intellectuals in the Kennedy camp, their anti-MacArthur attitude in no way modified the feeling of the President and his brother.

When General MacArthur died, Bobby called me to inquire whether there was anything he could do for Mrs. MacArthur and asked whether it would be possible for him and Ethel to board the train in Washington to pay their respects to Mrs. MacArthur. Although the General had died in Walter Reed Hospital outside Washington, his body was returned to New York to lie in state in the Seventh Regiment Armory on Park Avenue, where it was viewed by thousands of mourners. The funeral cortege proceeded to the Pennsylvania Station, where the entire corps of the West Point Military Academy was drawn up as an honor guard; the casket was then placed in the observation car of a special train that bore it back to Washington, slowing down at many towns en route as thousands gathered along the right of way to pay tribute to the General. Before the special train pulled into the Washington station, Bobby and Ethel came aboard and spoke to Mrs. MacArthur, then came over to talk with me just as President and Mrs. Johnson appeared. Bobby, spying the President, nudged me and in an aside whispered, "Wait until he lays an eye on me and you'll see ice." When the train pulled into the station, Bobby asked me to ride in his limousine.

The signal for the cortege to move toward the Capitol had no sooner been given than the chauffeur driving Bobby's car started to move forward before President Johnson's car had started. At that moment Secret Service men jumped in front of the Kennedy car, and we stopped abruptly. The driver's mistake was most embarrassing to the Kennedys, and Bobby was definitely disturbed. He had held the Secret Service in little respect since Dallas and remarked, "I wish they had always been so alert."

After MacArthur's body had lain in state in the rotunda of the Capitol for 24 hours, it was taken by special train to Norfolk, Va. for the final military service. Bobby and Ethel flew down to Norfolk for the funeral. This was no political gesture; the Kennedys wished only to pay homage to a great man whom they admired and respected. After the interment, Bobby came to me and said, "Here is something for the MacArthur Memorial." I suggested he give it to Mr. Duckworth, the president of the Memorial, who was standing nearby. Several months later at a meeting of the board I learned that the check was made out for $10,000. This was certainly not the act of a politician, for he had asked that no mention be made of his gift.

Thereafter, I often called on Senator Kennedy to discuss buying a football team or some other nonpolitical subject. I always felt that we had enough in common of a less serious nature to keep his mind from the tragic memories that haunted him. One morning, as he often did, he came to my office just to talk. The subjects ranged from minority problems to the attitude of businessmen toward him. He remarked, "It is strange that businessmen dislike and even hate me, for in reality I have always been the most conservative and pragmatic member of our family. I just don't know how to make them understand me. What would you suggest?" My offhand reply was that he should cultivate small groups of businessmen— no large forum would be useful—and allow these groups to explore his mind and learn precisely his attitudes on many subjects about which he thought they were misinformed. I suggested that he might start with the boards of directors of large corporations. Although he said little at the time, a week later I received a letter in which he stated that the board of directors idea appealed to him and asked if he might start with AVCO Corporation.

The board of AVCO, like many other boards, was composed of

men who gathered once a month for a quick review of operations. At the next meeing, the chairman told his colleagues of my talk with Senator Kennedy and his desire, as a start, to meet with the AVCO board.

The reaction of some of the directors was violent; some even acted as though a stink bomb had been thrown into the room. One director threatened to resign if Kennedy were invited; another, after uttering a few choice expletives, said frankly, "I hate him, I distrust him, and I want no part of him." On the other hand, several directors spoke up because they were embarrassed by the action of their colleagues and felt they should mollify my feelings. Since I knew the sentiment of the business community, I was not really shocked. I summarized my feeling in this statement: "It really makes no difference to me personally whether you do or do not invite Senator Kennedy. My only thought in suggesting the meeting was that you and Kennedy might exchange opinions and perhaps learn something of each others' viewpoints. After all, some day he might be President of this country." Following the meeting several directors, led by the late Chancellor Litchfield of the University of Pittsburg, suggested that the more amenable members of the board might give the senator a dinner, but this was never held because of my feeling that it was a poor substitute for a board meeting and an obvious evasion of an issue. Paranthetically, I never spoke to any businessman who did not look at me with a jaundiced eye if I spoke well of Bobby Kennedy.

A pragmatist who could adjust his actions to the needs of the time, in this respect he was abler than his brother, the President; unless you knew him intimately, he seemed less personable. Without a trace of arrogance, he sometimes exhibited an abrasive impulsiveness that served to cover a basic shyness. If he sometimes seemed ruthless, this was only a reflection of his determination to carry out his obligations to the President and his administration as he saw them. An extremely knowledgeable politician, he was unfortunately less interested in making friends in the business community than in getting his job done. Very much of a liberal, his devotion to practical politics kept him from becoming too involved with the intellectuals whose liberal thought underlay much of the Kennedy program. Nevertheless, he had the respect of such liberals as McNamara, Schlesinger, Bundy, and Sorensen, to whose deliberations he contributed a sense of reality of action.

It is strange that many businessmen, who would have considered the term ruthlessness as applied to them a badge of success, somehow were frightened when it was mistakenly regarded as one of Bobby's qualities. To their discredit, they never dared meet him with a head-on tackle, preferring to clip him from the rear. I am sometimes moved to speculate on what course this most-talked-about man in the public life of America at that time would have followed had he not, like his brother, suffered the martyrdom of assassination.

Chapter XXVI

MacArthur in Action

From the time in 1918 that General MacArthur was advanced from his post as colonel and chief of staff of the 42nd ("Rainbow") division in Europe to become the youngest brigadier general in the army and to serve with the Army of Occupation in Germany, he was necessarily involved in momentous military and political affairs. While some of these were not to his liking, as a good soldier he followed his concept of duty wherever it led. Since the military and the political were sometimes inextricably involved, it is difficult to separate these two facets of his life. Inasmuch as the political so often controlled the military aspects, however, it will perhaps be best to consider the former first. MacArthur was more or less intimately involved with four successive Presidents—Roosevelt, Truman, Eisenhower, and Kennedy. While these involvements have been thoroughly discussed in military and political histories, a few personal sidelights may be of interest.

From 1951 until his death in 1964, I saw much of General MacArthur, and during the last few years of his life I made a point of visiting him several times a month. The General no longer attended social functions; in fact, he was a recluse who spent considerable time in receiving men of high position in world affairs, keeping abreast of events, and reading avidly history, the classics, and sports. He was acquainted with all periods of history and with the details of every important war. In addition, he had access to many important sources of knowledge regarding national and international affairs. His memory for detail was remarkable; many of his opinions and statements are engraved on my memory. It was a rare experience to listen to the General; at 74, he seemed like a man of 50, vigorous in mind, able to recall the exact wording of forgotten documents, and animatedly recalling in detail scenes long past.

It was in 1944, after General MacArthur had become a national hero in winning the battle of the Coral Sea and the subsequent actions, that he first became aware of his political appeal. President Roosevelt, suspicious of MacArthur's reported White House ambitions, was relieved by the General's forthright statement about the Presidency: "I do not covet it, nor would I accept it." Prime Minister Austin of Australia, a White House guest at the time, told Roosevelt: "In all honesty and sincerity, General MacArthur has no more idea of running against you for President than I have," a statement that Roosevelt relayed to his secretary, Steve Early, with evident relief. It may well be that Roosevelt's suspicions of MacArthur's political ambitions began as far back as 1941, a story to be told later. In any event, in a warm letter to him several years later, the President did express his esteem of MacArthur as a possible President. He wrote to the General: "Personally, I wished much in Honolulu that you and I could swap places, and personally, I have a hunch that you would make more of a go as President than I would as General, in the retaking of the Philippines."

General MacArthur's relations with Roosevelt were neither facilitated nor improved by Mrs. Roosevelt who, in 1944, came to Australia at the beginning of the movement on New Guinea and requested that she be permitted to visit the fighting troops there. Although she insisted, General MacArthur refused to let her go, and she became indignant. She threatened to cable the President if the General did not alter his decision. He respectfully told her there was no place in New Guinea for the wife of the President of the United States, and the subject ended with a mark for the General in command and against MacArthur the man, as far as the First Lady was concerned.

Mrs. MacArthur once told me of an experience she had with Mrs. Roosevelt, with whom she was ushered into a room prior to attending a luncheon. It was such a small room that the women were practically knee to knee when they sat down. While they were in conversation, an Australian diplomat's wife entered and blurted to Mrs. MacArthur, "Isn't it grand? I hear General MacArthur is going to run for President of the United States." Mrs. MacArthur was so taken aback that she actually trembled because the repercussion to such a remark stated so bluntly in front of the President's wife at a time when General MacArthur was having difficulty getting supplies might be disastrous. Mrs. Roosevelt, an experienced trooper, never said a word, and continued the conversation as though she had not heard the remark. It was well that the subject was ignored; the lovely Jean MacArthur was dedicated to "her General," understood war from her experience on Bataan and the harrowing PT boat escape to Australia, and was fully capable of coping with any challenge from the politically oriented First Lady.

MacArthur's next brush with politics came in 1948, when Thomas E. Dewey eventually became the Republican nominee. As the sentiment for drafting MacArthur as the Republican candidate grew, I wrote the General the following resume of his party's position, backed by information from good sources, including the late Senate minority leader, Styles Bridges of New Hampshire:

(1) Sixty days ago, the possibility of a MacArthur nomination was remote. Now a MacArthur boom is regarded as a definite possibility.

(2) Dewey and Taft appear hopelessly deadlocked, neither willing to give ground to the other. Dewey's family is lukewarm to his candidacy, for personal and financial reasons. Contrary to common belief, it would not be an overwhelming disappointment to him if he were not nominated.

(3) Dewey will never make a deal with the Taft camp, and his position on MacArthur is unknown.

(4) Taft will not deal with Dewey, whom he dislikes nearly as much as the New Deal. Taft's position has not been bettered in the last 60 days. Taft's first choice is MacArthur.

(5) Stassen has only nuisance value.

(6) Vandenberg wants the nomination. After himself, Vandenberg's number one choice, as it was several years ago, is MacArthur.

(7) Speaker Martin also wants the nomination. He is most

trusted by politicians. He has no enemies. Martin's first choice after himself is General MacArthur.

(8) As a rule, the endorsement of the Hearst papers generally means the kiss of political death. The MacArthur build-up in the Hearst publications is almost colossal.

(9) McCormick's Chicago *Tribune* has announced for Taft. This is ideal, as it has been a MacArthur booster, and its preconvention endorsement would have been a serious mistake.

(10) The greatest factor in MacArthur's favor is the continued deterioration in relations between Russia and the United States.

Although MacArthur was urged to return to the United States before the convention, he regarded his work in democratizing Japan as Supreme Commander for the Allied Powers too important to abandon for even a short time. At the time I wrote him: "The country knows MacArthur the General, but it does not know MacArthur the statesman and MacArthur the man. You need not campaign, but informed politicians say unless you return you will not be nominated, barring the outside possibility of a convention stalemate." MacArthur did not return to corral delegates, and Dewey won the nomination.

MacArthur's next political encounter occurred with Harry S. Truman, who opposed Dewey in the 1948 election and defeated him. Although Truman was well aware of MacArthur's potentialities as a Republican candidate in the next political campaign, he did not hesitate to acquiesce in his appointment as Commander of United Nations military forces in South Korea when he dispatched United States troops to that beleaguered country in 1950.

When Truman later flew thousands of miles to Wake Island for a conference with his chief field commander and was accompanied by members of the press, the world was led to believe that momentous events were in the making and that the meeting would turn out to have historic significance. I was therefore surprised when I heard the account from the lips of MacArthur, who viewed the Presidential journey as a political junket designed to solidify Truman's domestic support. It was obvious that little was accomplished in this meeting of one and one-half hours—part of it a short private discussion with the President, and part of it a conference attended by General Bradley, Dean Rusk, Admiral Radford, Secretary Pace, and members of the White House staff.

To the discomfiture of those who envied the hero of the Inchon landing, MacArthur's intellect dominated the brief meeting. Admiral Radford told me some years later, "I never saw a man stand as tall as MacArthur at Wake Island at a time when the cards were being stacked against him." All that MacArthur learned from the meeting was the fact that Truman's understanding of the Orient was superficial and that General Omar Bradley's only concern was to determine whether it was possible to have two Korean divisions released for service in Germany.

Undoubtedly the fires were then building for MacArthur's recall and release from duty. In the background there always lurked the great rivalry, abetted by the State Department under Dean Acheson, that had existed between the European and Pacific theaters during World War II. Some of this could be attributed to the competion for men and supplies inherent in a two-front war; another important factor, of course, was the desire of newly elevated generals to nurture and then maintain reputations established in the European theater. During the Korean War, the Department of Defense was dominated by these generals, who could not see beyond the problems of Europe to appreciate the Far Eastern threat and dominated American military thinking to MacArthur's detriment. It is perhaps not generally known that such top commanders of the Navy as Admirals Leahy, Halsey, and Radford respected MacArthur and were aware of the envy that he somehow inspired in the Army brass. Admiral Leahy gave voice to this fact when he stated in *I Was There:* "It was no secret in the Pentagon Building in Washington that there were men who disliked MacArthur."

The Korean situation rapidly came to a head. Determined to end the war with dispatch, MacArthur quickly recaptured Seoul, the South Korean capital, and invaded North Korea across the 38th parallel. When Communist Chinese troops entered the war to save their puppet allies and, by superior numbers, forced the United

Nations troops south of the 38th parallel, MacArthur repeatedly sought permission to attack by air the military bases in Communist China that were supplying the enemy troops. When MacArthur persisted in his opposition to United States and United Nations policies that forced him to fight a war with one hand tied behind his back and warned that "a great nation which enters upon war and does not see it through to victory will ultimately suffer the consequences of defeat," on April 11, 1951 he was dismissed from his command by President Truman. Certainly, the continuing stalemate in Korea makes MacArthur's words seem prophetic; one may go further to contend that our demonstrated fear of the Communists and lack of will to fight to victory encouraged Communist aggression in Indo China, a catastrophe that involved us in disastrous domestic and foreign consequences. In retrospect, it also seems incredible that President Truman, who initially reacted so boldly to the Korean threat, could be forced by timorous and myopic advisers into a policy of compromise.

When MacArthur was relieved, I cabled him immediately: "American public stunned. Time is of the essence to offset Administration hatchetmen. My affection and devotion to you." Because of his conviction that he must alert the American people to a clear danger, he retured to this country immediately. MacArthur acted with a magnanimity that could be expected by those who knew him well. He never disagreed with Truman's right to dismiss him; although he did not respect the President's intellect, he clearly admired his courage. It was inevitable that the General would be hurt by the lack of support he received from such old comrades in arms as Omar Bradley, whom he respected as a military leader, while he expected little from the Chief of Staff, General Lawton Collins, whom he regarded as a man of small abilities, with little to recommend him for his high post.

On April 19 the General addressed a joint session of the Congress, outlining his views on the conduct of the Korean War and then embarked on a speech-making trip about the country to further his views on the dangers of our Eastern policy. It may come as a surprise to some readers to learn that MacArthur soon wearied of the lack of public and administration response that greeted his efforts to make clear what he regarded as the senselessness of our Oriental policy. On July 30, 1951 he wrote me: "Thanks so much for your fine note of July 26th—it is gratifying to know that my lonesome crusade is not perhaps entirely wasted. I have headed many forlorn hopes in my day, and it looks as though I were on my last assignment, but I intend to fight it out on this line to the end."

Inevitably, all this activity thrust him back into the political limelight. In October of 1951, I wrote him my view of the situation: "Your address to the American Legion was a strong, stirring speech and your voice came over the radio with enrapturing vitality. I have a presentiment that the Republican convention will deadlock between Taft and Eisenhower, and from this deadlock I expect that Taft forces to switch eventually to MacArthur. When they do, the Eisenhower delegates will fall like Autumn leaves." As political sentiment hardened, MacArthur was invited to deliver the keynote address to the 1952 Republican National Convention. Although it did not seem to me that this was up to his usual standard, he lost none of the glamour of his position before the convention.

I have always believed that I came very close to calling the turn in predicting a deadlock between Taft and Eisenhower. On Tuesday night of the July Republican convention, at about ten o'clock, I received a call from Victor Emanuel, a devoted friend of Senator Robert Taft. The call came from the Senator's Chicago convention suite. Victor explained that Taft and his staff were convinced that Eisenhower could be stopped only if General MacArthur were to enter the campaign as a dark horse. He stated that MacArthur had the support of Mr. Howard Pew, tacit leader of the Pennsylvania delegation, and that Pew would not release the delegation to Taft. Senator Taft apparently was reconciled to his defeat, but would support the General only if all his delegates agreed to switch. Thus, MacArthur would be nominated only if he could corral all of Taft's delegates and add them to those of the Pennsylvania delegation. Victor asked me to stand by until 2 A.M. and be prepared to go to the General's apartment in the Waldorf Towers to ask him to call Taft in Chicago at once. The call from Victor never came; the

Eisenhower delegates overcame the more conservative elements in the Republican Party, and I was not commissioned to inform MacArthur of a sudden switch in his favor.

Hindsight makes it very clear that MacArthur, who had shown his disinterest in 1948 by refusing to come home to seek delegates, had even less inclination to seek the Presidency in 1952. Immediately after delivering the keynote address, he disappeared, and every effort to reach him on his private telephone and through the Waldorf switchboard was futile. Obviously, he wanted no part of any political maneuvering. This he confirmed to me some time later when I told him of my role as a go-between. He was completely unimpressed. "I did not covet the Presidency if for no other reason than when a man reaches 70 years, his brain is subject to physical change that may take place without his realizing the fact. The decisions the President must take are too important to be made by one who cannot sense an impending mental deterioration. I had no reason to believe I would be an exception to this possibility." Could he have been thinking of Franklin Roosevelt?

To support the fact that MacArthur was not a candidate in 1952, I have several letters from him showing that he gave Taft his full support. In January, 1952, among other things, he wrote: "The political pot is beginning to boil and to me, more and more, it looks like Taft. Eisenhower's absence will be a telling factor against him. It is difficult to build a great scenario with the main actor missing." This MacArthur knew from his 1948 experience. In June of 1952 he wrote: "On the political scene, I am sure Taft is gaining, and I am most hopeful that he will pull through in July. I think if he is nominated we will be able to win with him in November."

There was no love lost between MacArthur and Eisenhower, perhaps because the latter had served as one of the General's subalterns in his earlier days in Washington and in the Philippines. Eisenhower made his feelings clear when I was invited to attend a White House dinner party early in his administration. MacArthur's reaction was, "Go—by all means go," and adding, in support of the President's way of bringing men together and cultivating their good will, "Earl, he was thinking of the football coaches when he asked you; he's also had Leahy." I was therefore nonplussed when Eisenhower said to me, in the course of our predinner conversation, "Red, I think the General is getting senile," a remark that, however I might resent it, I could hardly reject as forthrightly as I might have wished.

MacArthur's views of Eisenhower were more impersonal. He had no great regard for Ike, who he believed was not taking strong positions and had definitely joined the internationalists. MacArthur hoped that the country would eventually become aroused and force the President to take a firmer stand against the "One World" group. When, later in 1953, I asked MacArthur his opinion of Eisenhower as President, he replied: "It is too early to judge him, though Ike has accomplished nothing and will do little else. His popularity is based on the fact that the press is nearly unanimously for him and is even carrying the burden of unselling the public on the campaign promises." General MacArthur did not believe the people would continue to be gullible and that eventually the President's popularity would wane slowly, first in arithmetic and later in geometric proportion. In the end Ike would spend his time trying to salvage the political field for the Republicans.

MacArthur stated that Ike was nominated by the leftwing or liberal Republicans, elected by the conservative wing, and was on the road to becoming a New Dealer. The man closest to the President was his brother Milton, whose intellect Ike always respected. Milton Eisenhower, according to MacArthur, was more of a New Dealer than the Democrats. He was a close follower of Henry Wallace, in whose department he worked. Unlike Wallace, however, he was more practical and had a better mind. General MacArthur believed that Milton Eisenhower would direct the actions and thoughts of Ike more than anyone in the Republican Party, including the members of his cabinet. Incidentally, the General often expressed his fondness for Mamie Eisenhower, whom he credited with astuteness and common sense.

The General was not impressed with such of Ike's displays of religious faith as the opening of cabinet meetings with prayer. MacArthur didn't believe religion should be a part of politics and recalled that the Ike of old would have no part of going to church; "I had my belly full as a Cadet," he told MacArthur on one occasion. MacArthur also stated, "In the old days, General Ike was one of the severest critics of West Point." He was known to be at odds with the Plebe system and the indoctrination of new Cadets into the Military Academy. As a matter of fact, according to classmates, Dwight Eisenhower the Cadet was regarded as a nonconformist, a type which hardly endears itself to academy authority. Often, however, this marked degree of undergraduate indifference as a Cadet reflects an understanding of men and later creates a fellowship with contemporaries that forms the basis for strong future leadership. Thus we find a General Ulysses Grant and a General Robert E. Lee poles apart as models of emulation for Cadets.

General Eisenhower's later endearment to West Point came when his son, John, was a Cadet and he himself had shed the insignia of a lieutenant colonel to become a general officer. He also spoke of the fact that Ike craved adulation, did not enjoy making tough decisions, and was addicted to taking the floor; now that he had an audience, he could ask for nothing better. MacArthur believed that General Ike would end by being a bland President.

Some weeks after President Eisenhower's heart attack in Denver, I asked General MacArthur whether Ike would seek a second term. At that time, the speculation in the press and among the people was that, for reasons of impaired health, he would not run again. This was not MacArthur's view. "Will he run—you mean is he running? He has been subtly campaigning from Denver, and the latest news release from Gettysburg is final assurance that he is, in recuperation, an active candidate. I know him too well not to read his real intention."

It is interesting to note that, as President, Eisenhower never consulted his old commander in chief, whose advice and experience in some areas might have been invaluable. Bob Considine of International News Service was but one of many who noted an omission that could well be construed as a deliberate slight: "But nobody in the administration asks him what to do in our difficult hit-or-miss dealings with that part of the world [the Orient]—at 75 he is spry, alert, surprisingly free of bitterness, supremely self-possessed in a time of epidemic uncertainty, and willing—he is a burning oil well, an abandoned mansion, a neglected book, an untapped reservoir in a drought area. Ah, it's a great pity."

MacArthur's relations with the next President were more pleasant. Bob Kennedy once told me that his brother and he agreed that, of all the men who had visited the White House, MacArthur was both the most impressive and the most interesting.

On one occasion, when MacArthur was invited to the White House, he had nearly an hour before lunch with the President. It was then that he advised Kennedy—as later, when he was dying at Walter Reed Hospital, he vainly advised President Johnson—that no American soldier should be made to fight on Asian soil. He stated his belief that the time might be dangerously near when many Americans might not have the will to fight for their country. About this time, the then Vice Chief of Staff of the Army, General Clyde Eddleman, joined MacArthur and President Kennedy. The President turned to General MacArthur and said, "If you had but one piece of advice to give me, what would it be?" The General told me that he was, for the moment, without words, and then he said, "Mr. President, you are surrounded by men of greater intellect than any President in history. These men are truly intellectuals, and when you ask them for advice, the one on your right gives a plausible reason for action and the one on your left gives a plausible reason for inaction; another gives you some advice of strictly different nature, and a fourth agrees with none, so that by time time you have completed your circle of advisors, you have to be confused. It is my judgment that I would take the advice of those specifically charged with implementing policy, even though they may be less brilliant than the intellectuals. In the end, make your own decision." Following the General's statement, there was a heavy silence and Eddleman, to break the pause, commented, "Of course, Mr. President, that is the way the General governed in Japan."

Then, from the rear of MacArthur came a voice of one of the group of intellectuals who had come into the room unannounced before lunch: "And what did it get the General? Nothing but discredit and dismissal." The General stated that the President was mortified at the lack of the subordinate's courtesy, so General MacArthur said, "Mr. President, I can stand a little lunch, how about you?" And off they went, arm in arm.

MacArthur's relations with President Roosevelt were necessarily so involved and extended over so long a period of time that the General often reverted to them in his conversations with me.

I have mentioned the fact that Roosevelt once harbored suspicions of MacArthur as a presidential contender and that this might well have begun as far back as 1941. At this time MacArthur had served as chief of staff of the Army from 1930 to 1935, when the President appointed him head of the American military mission to the Philippines, then a newly created commonwealth. In 1941 the General had long retired from the Army when Roosevelt, faced by the growing tension in the Far East caused by Japan's rampant expansionist policies, suggested to MacArthur that he return to active duty in the Philippines as commander of our Far East Command. When MacArthur, always ready to answer the call of duty, agreed, he waited four months for the appointment to be announced. Finally, he cabled his friend, Steve Early, Roosevelt's secretary, that unless the appointment were confirmed immediately he would go into final retirement and return to the United States. Aroused to action, Early cabled MacArthur, "Do not do anything until further advised. Break will be coming very soon." Over the weekend Early persuaded the President to issue the order on July 26, 1941 from Hyde Park, where Roosevelt was temporarily insulated from Washington influences.

There are two explanations for the long delay. One is the possible fact that, as early as 1941, Roosevelt foresaw MacArthur's appeal to the Republican politicians and hesitated to add to his stature. A more probable explanation is to be found in the opposition of General George Marshall who, although of the exact age of MacArthur, had seen his rival appointed chief of staff in 1930, a position Marshall did not achieve until the outbreak of World War II forced his advancement in 1939. Certain it is that Marshall never acquiesced in MacArthur's appointment and subsequently held but masked the considerable personal animosity he had toward this great soldier.

On another occasion MacArthur reminisced about his meeting with Roosevelt at Pearl Harbor in August 1944. As he warmed up to telling of this historic event, he made it clear that this meeting of the top Navy command and the Commander in Chief was one of the most dramatic events in the war in the Pacific.

According to MacArthur, General Marshall notified him that he should report immediately for a top secret conference at Pearl Harbor. Since there was no further instruction, the General radioed for more information as to what the meeting was about and what staff he should take. The answer was concise: the meeting was top secret, no prior information could be given, and he needed no staff.

In his own mind, MacArthur had the feeling that the meeting was designed to resolve the question of who should be Supreme Commander of the Pacific. He realized that the Navy was anxious to have either Nimitz or King head the Pacific forces, just as Eisenhower headed the European effort. He himself had come to the conclusion that this was not to be a discussion for him, as he personally believed that the only way to achieve success in the Pacific was to have a unified command of the Army and the Navy under a Supreme Commander.

As he related this story, he strongly emphasized his views by tapping his hand on the arm of the chair. "Now, if the President desired a Navy man as Supreme Commander, I would willingly have accepted the inevitable, as a military victory necessitated such a decision, even though I was a General when Nimitz and King were no more than commanders."

The General stated that he took with him Bonner Fellers, his aide, and made two stops en route to Hawaii. At the last one, Johnson Island, he received a radiogram from his old friend Lt. General "Nellie" Richardson, in command of the Hawaii area, to be prepared for big events. The General realized that any communication he might send to Richardson would be intercepted and probably held up, so he waited until he was in the air to radio Richardson that he would come in at an alternate landing field; he asked Richardson to meet him or, if he was unable to do so, to stay at his quarters until MacArthur arrived. As he suspected, upon arriving over the Army field in Hawaii, he was informed that he could not land; though he pressed his desire to make the landing, word came back that orders had been given not to do so and that he was to land at a designated Navy field. He said that, on landing, he was greeted by a group of Admirals who rather stiffly acknowledged his presence. He finally spotted Admiral Bill Carney, who told him that Admiral Nimitz and all the high Navy brass were on the flagship in the harbor, meeting with President Roosevelt. The General remarked to me that he had had no knowledge that the President was to be there and, of course, had not been asked to meet the Commander-in-Chief. Since therefore there was no reason to go out to the flagship, he followed customary military protocol, signed in at Admiral Nimitz's headquarters, and proceeded to General Richardson's quarters.

General Richardson wasn't there; subsequently MacArthur learned he had not received the radio message off Johnson Island. MacArthur recalled that he went upstairs and made himself at home, took a bath, and again studied the subject of a possible Supreme Commander. Two hours later he was informed that he was to meet the President.

It was agreed that the meeting would be held at ten o'clock the next morning on the battleship *Missouri*. In a very large conference room before a gathering of Navy strength, including the President and Admirals Leahy, Nimitz, and Halsey, as well as Elmer Davis, Judge Samuel Rosenman, and a few others of the Presidential party, General MacArthur alone represented the Army.

The General recounted that he was thrown completely off stride when the President stated that the purpose of the meeting was to discuss the grand strategy of the Pacific and to familiarize MacArthur with the plan that would be used. The President, a Navy buff, was completely at home. For several hours the Navy admirals, who had been briefed for weeks on their part of the program, gave their prearranged presentations, which included talks by Admirals Nimitz, Leahy, and Halsey.

During the time the Navy had the floor, General MacArthur noticed that the President dozed off on two different occasions. The General stated that it was then that he noticed a marked physical and mental difference in the President and that at times his mind seemed to fail him. The General said that he came to the conclusion that the President was a sick man; when MacArthur returned home, he told Mrs. MacArthur that he did not believe the President would live more than six months. The General recalled that time nearly bore out this statement, as within eight months President Roosevelt was dead.

At the end of the completely staged presentation, the President turned to General MacArthur and said, "Douglas (he always called him Douglas, as they had lived in the same quarters in Washington before the first World War and MacArthur had also been the President's Chief of Staff), what do you think?" MacArthur's answer was, "I think we should go to lunch;" the President laughed and said, "I think you are right."

During the lunch hour, MacArthur had occasion to talk with Nimitz, whom he respected, and Halsey, whom he admired. The General related that both of them were aghast that MacArthur had not been informed as to what the meeting was about or that the President was to be there. They could not believe the Army would let MacArthur walk into such a trap. This fact bore out what the General already knew: that neither General Marshall nor his staff was interested in contributing to MacArthur's advancement under any conditions.

After lunch, the group gathered, and MacArthur informed the President that he would like to review the entire subject. He was asked if he would require maps, to which he replied, "No."

Without the advantage of any prior preparation and without especially prepared maps, for 45 minutes General MacArthur proceeded to take the Navy presentation apart and to show the fallacy of the Navy plan as compared to the one he had originally suggested to the Department of Defense.

I asked the General what, in essence, was the Navy strategy. MacArthur replied that it was to bypass the Philippines and go through to Formosa, a plan that he suggested to the President was unsound, as the chance of succeeding in such a venture was not good and gave direct advantage to the Japs. This fact the General believed was borne out by the operation that the Navy later mounted on Okinawa, where the severest losses were recorded. The fact that the Navy was hard pressed in its attacks on Iwo Jima and Okinawa substantiated the fact that the original concept was not sound and that it would have been a risky venture to undertake the Navy's plan of a direct assault on Formosa.

At any rate, at the end of the 45 minutes—which incidentally was later referred to by Halsey as the most brilliant extemporaneous presentation that he had ever heard—MacArthur turned to the President and said that he would like five minutes with him alone. Judge Rosenman spoke up and said, "No, anything to be said should be said in front of us all." The President remarked, "I don't see any reason why I should not speak alone with Douglas," and MacArthur pressed his advantage by adding, "Mr. President, let's go to the corner of the room." MacArthur then proceeded to push the President's chair to the far end of the salon, where for five minutes the General laid it on the line.

The subject of the five-minute discussion was both military and political. He told the President, "You are running again, and if you approve a plan that would bypass the Philippines, leaving those 15 million loyal islanders isolated, you, Mr. President, would be condemned before all the free countries of the world. The United States would lose face in the Orient, and you, Mr. President, would reap the harvest of an intensive anti-Roosevelt drive, which inevitably could lead to your defeat. This, you understand, Mr. President, comes from a Republican." Finally, MacArthur said, "Even you, Mr. President, with your unbounded popularity in the free world, cannot afford to take any course that would bypass those loyal and free people." With that the President nodded, gave no answer, and no more was said about the plan.

MacArthur then told the President that he had given orders for his command to take an island within a couple of days and that he wanted to be there to land with the Sixth Army, as he always desired to be present when his troops attacked. The President urged him to stay another day, as he was to tour the island and expected to appear before six or eight camps, most of which were made up of soldiers. The General replied that he would be glad to stay over.

The following morning he met the President. The caravan of many cars was ready to move out, but no place was reserved for

MacArthur in the President's car; the seat next to the President was intended for Admiral Leahy. When the President realized this, he asked the admiral to give up his place so that MacArthur might sit with him. He took the General's hand and said, "Come with me." Roosevelt and the General toured the camps together; before each stop, the President asked MacArthur what he should say to the soldiers. MacArthur gave him appropriate expressions of greetings, all the while realizing that Roosevelt was truly losing his grip.

At the end of the day, he said good-bye to the President. The only appearance he received that the plan he had earlier suggested to the Department of Defense would take precedence over the Navy plan, of which the admirals seemingly had convinced Roosevelt before he came to Pearl Harbor, came when the President said good-bye: "Don't worry, Douglas, about anything."

With Truman, Roosevelt's successor, MacArthur had relatively little personal contact; certainly, aside from their disagreement over United States and United Nations policy in the Far East and the dismissal of MacArthur that this engendered, there were no dramatic interchanges between them such as occurred between Roosevelt and the General. I can add to what I have previously said about the Truman-MacArthur relationship only my very strong feeling that MacArthur's brilliant mind and towering personality cowed such lesser intellects as Truman, Marshall, Dulles, and Acheson and that his early and deserved promotion and eminence created an envy that is clearly evident in the writings of these contemporaries. Confronting this colorful soldier, lesser intellects could not brook or rise to the challenge of his mind, his personality, his presence, or his achievements. Those to whom the General presented no challenge, those, such as Senators Richard Russell and Robert A. Taft and Presidents Roosevelt, Kennedy and Johnson, who never felt themselves at a loss in any interchange with the General, had nothing but respect and praise for this great leader.

MacArthur was wholeheartedly convinced that Asia, with its boundless physical and human resources, was the area of future contention among the world powers and that our continued focus on the European scene was myopic. In furthering this belief, MacArthur became a lonely and distant voice in the councils of the State Deparment, the Pentagon, and the White House, where his selfless patriotic motives were questioned and ignobly interpreted as bids for personal aggrandizement. It is obvious that he never convinced Truman, and later Eisenhower, of his thesis and that neither of them appreciated his wisdom or evinced an understanding of the fact that his knowledge of world politics was great or that his comprehension of the Orient and the Oriental mind was outstanding. Certainly, the success of his policy in Japan and the devotion that he inspired in the Japaese people should have carried conviction in the mind of even the most untutored.

I cannot help but wonder what course our national destiny would have taken had MacArthur achieved the Presidency. Certainly, the no-win anti-MacArthur policy of Truman and Eisenhower in Korea, as well as Kennedy's and Johnson's failures to accept his "No American soldier on Asian land," have left our position in the Orient in disarray. The withdrawl policy of Nixon attests to the fact that there must have been little reason for our being in Vietnam, Cambodia, and Laos. Today it is difficult for the average citizen to believe that the expenditure of thousands of lives and billions of dollars in Korea and Vietnam has achieved any lasting good either for this country or the world.

MacArthur's brief relation with Eisenhower was more complex and was not facilitated by that President's recollection of his service as a young officer under the General or the fact that MacArthur had once seemed a threat to Eisenhower's political ambitions. Following his dismissal by Truman, as part of his crusade for the reorientation of our Far East policy, MacArthur was the principal speaker at a dinner of the National Association of Manufacturers. He had intended only to repeat his oft-reiterated thesis about returning to the fundamentals that had made this country great, but was persuaded by Jim Rand and some of his associates to include some cordial remarks about General Eisenhower, who had just been elected President, and to discuss the Korean situation.

The reaction to his Korean remarks, which suggested that he had a clear and definite solution to end the war, was far greater than he had expected. The public demanded a meeting between the General and the President-Elect, who was then in the Far East fulfilling his election promise to visit Korea. MacArthur received an immediate invitation from John Foster Dulles to meet with Ike on the latter's return. General MacArthur stated, "It was natural for Dulles to enter the picture, as the new Secretary of State; furthermore, I knew him well, as we had worked together on the Japanese peace treaty."

Prior to the luncheon, MacArthur had some reservations as to how fruitful such a meeting would be. However, he went into it with great hopes of helping the country. The key to the solution was Russia.

After the luncheon, MacArthur outlined his views: "We are bogged down in Korea much as Pershing was in the first World War. Our position, untenable as it is, is the result of inaction, timidity, and lack of imagination among our military thinkers, especially the Joint Chiefs of Staff; in particular, it lies on the shoulders of Collins and Bradley."

MacArthur sensed in Ike a deep feeling of frustration that had come over the President-Elect while he was in Korea. "Ike had never seen this type of warfare in Europe, and had no idea as how best to cope with it."

General MacArthur told Eisenhower that the latter stood in relation to history as no other leader in any country. The faith of our people and the world in his leadership demanded bold and fast action that, in the end, was the only way he could demonstrate his capacity for leadership.

It was MacArthur's belief that never again would the United States have the military superiority to dictate a realistic peace for the world. The Berlin situation required a permanent solution; however, a thorough understanding with Russia with respect to our involvement in Korea and with China was even more vital. Our military position in Korea could then be quickly resolved, with the use of atomic weapons if necessary, combined with full naval and air pressure on China. MacArthur always opposed the commitment of our ground forces to the Asian mainland.

Furthermore, according to the General, our military strength consisted of a trained and tested Army, Air Force, and Navy, power unequaled by any other nation or even the combination of Russia and her satellites. Most important, the United States alone had an arsenal of nuclear weapons. In 1952, Russia was not a threat to the United States. The time was ripe to impose a just and reasonable peace, and end the cold war. "Timing is of the essence," MacArthur stated, "and logic requires a showdown at the height of the President's world popularity. To procrastinate, however, is to give a signal to the Russians to expedite the arms race, eventually nullifying our military advantage." MacArthur emphasized that this was the only way to avoid any third world war involving nuclear weapons.

At the end of the two-hour conference, Mr. Dulles spoke up, contending that such bold action should not be taken at this time, as General Eisenhower needed a year to consolidate his political position. "After all, it has been 20 years since the Republicans were in power," Dulles remarked to MacArthur.

MacArthur then let them have both barrels, reemphasizing the fact that Ike could lead the world to peace or vaccilate and lose the initiative. He further stated: "Today the Russians have such respect for you that strong action will bring them to terms; if you wait, they will no longer follow you as the leader of world opinion. This is the last time I shall call you Ike and speak with you on equal terms. Hereafter you will be Mr. President. So now I say that you have the opportunity to be perhaps the greatest man since Jesus Christ, as only you can dictate peace for the world. I beg of you to take the initiative with bold action."

General MacArthur left the meeting convinced that he had accomplished little other than to help Eisenhower solidify his position with the American public and that this meeting was no more than a political gesture. He never heard from either Dulles or President Eisenhower again. He was told there was some thought that his plan might be followed in part, but even that never came to pass.

MacArthur's foresight about the growing position of Russia as a great power, conceived long before his conference with the President-Elect, may be contrasted with Eisenhower's attitude toward the Russians, as set forth in his book, *Waging Peace*: "The West position in Berlin was the result of political agreements made by the United States, British and Soviet governmental leaders during World

War II, agreements the Soviets never carried out. The arrangements they established for the occupation of Germany were intended to be temporary only. The Allied governments never visualized that the occupation zone of Germany would one day become enduring political boundaries, dividing the population and condemning the millions of unfortunate people to live under dictatorship for decades, possibly generations—but because the West governments undoubtedly looked upon the division of Germany as a temporary arrangement, the exact lines may have seemed, at the time, as of little importance." Eisenhower, in 1944, told President Roosevelt he did not believe that the allies should have sectors in Germany. In 1958 he stated, "But every tick of the clock brought us nearer to the moment when we had to be ready to meet head-on if necessary."

MacArthur could never understand that Eisenhower, after this miscalculation and such threatening consequences as the Berlin blockade, could trust Russia to keep the peace or allow Dulles' parochial political views to nullify the tactical advantages we then possessed and could utilize in the interests of universal peace. In 1974, it seems to me that we are increasingly capitulating to the will of Russia and approaching a time when this military strong power will not hesitate to grasp the opportunity to dominate international affairs that Eisenhower and Dulles so readily relinquished in 1952.

MacArthur's inability to understand that Eisenhower, as a soldier, could be satisfied with anything less than a total Korean victory, without which there could be no lasting peace, led him to deplore the fact that the philosophy of the military was degenerating. Although his immediate reaction was to confess to me, "We shall pay a heavy price for our failure to comprehend the rising power of Communist China," it was obvious that he was looking beyond the realm of immediate peace to the further evolution of the military mind. MacArthur died in 1964 and so was fortunate not to witness the further disintegration of the military spirit of the evolution of the armed service into today's Army.

I can imagine MacArthur's reaction to an article such as "The Case Study of an Army Star," which appeared in the September 25, 1970 issue of *Life*. The author, Lewis Lapham, tells of a young general who attempts to redefine the function of the military in a society increasingly antagonistic to the Army tradition, begins by accepting the idea of "not winning in the traditional MacArthur sense," and proceeds to the belief that such concrete terms such as "glory" and "victory" must be transmuted into some such vague and meaningless phrase as "the successful implementation of national policy." The officer concludes by stating that, while this national policy may require the military to acquiesce in stalemates, it must preserve "such ideals and realities as service, patriotism, subordination of self, American values." Since MacArthur was no longer with us to forthrightly reject the denigration of this philosophy, I undertook to answer the implied slur in these terms: "Such jargon suggests a discussion in a social science class and hardly befits the creed by which company commanders exhort their men to give their all. Let the civilian leadership toy with the polemics of war and the Army leadership follow the words of MacArthur: 'There is no substitute for victory.'"

I venture to believe that the continuing deterioration of the Army ideal does not accurately reflect the view of the American people; it is the inevitable reflection of the permissive attitude that has permeated some sectors of our society. Any number of polls have shown that the American people forthrightly reject any casual acceptance of corruption in government, of disruption of college campuses, and of the travesty of justice—often abetted by radical lawyers—created by the unruly procedures in many of our courts. So much that is undesirable and even disgraceful in today's society is accepted by timorous administrations that do not reflect the will of the majority, but attempt to compromise with loud and vocal minorities in a vain effort to preserve domestic tranquility.

All of this has inevitably had its effect on the Army that, in compromising with those who no longer wish to support their country by military service, has created a disorganized military force less amenable to discipline, with beards and long hair that evince no self-respect. So-called K-P has gone by the board; the new Army is to be composed of men who are wooed to enlist by promises of high pay, reenlistment bonuses, and substantial pensions after a minimum 20 years of service. I fail to see how such a system can be conducted to maintain our international image of military strength, the more so in view of the fact that the Chinese and the Russians still imbue their recruits with nationalistic ideals and devotion to the country's interest. Sadly, many of our younger general officers follow this new approach, however much they may realize that the volunteer army endorsed by the Nixon administration must lack the esprit de corps that can be achieved only by discipline, training, sacrifice, and devotion. They realize that promotion depends on their acceptance of the ruling civilian leadership that trims its sails to every shifting wind of public opinion. One star begets two, and two beget three, and seldom does one gain one's first star by bucking the system.

I have known many football coaches who took the same approach by sugar coating the drudgery and compromising with fundamentals, only in the end to forfeit the respect of their squads. The "New Army" concept suggests a similarly misplaced goodfellow type of leadership.

I am sometimes moved to wonder what would have been the effect had MacArthur been elected to the Presidency, perhaps in Eisenhower's stead. Had he thus been in a position to force the Korean issue to a conclusion, would this example of national resolution have so impressed our adversaries that they would not have dared to challenge us to vicarious battle in Indochina? Russia's withdrawal in the face of our national resolution in the Cuban missile crisis gives point to the question. And had we thus avoided our involvement in that bloody and useless adventure, following MacArthur's injunction that no American soldier should fight on Oriental soil, would we not also have avoided much of the unrest and civil rebellion that followed the consequent disillusionment of our youth that saw no reason for loss of career or sacrifice of life or limb in a war that involved no aspect of our national interest. I always end such speculations with the conviction that we suffered an irreparable loss by allowing our greatest military genius and expert on international affairs to spend his last years on the bench while less capable hands carried—and fumbled—the ball.

Chapter XXVII

MacArthur As I Knew Him

The 1964 Spring edition of *Assembly*, the West Point Association of Graduates' magazine, honored the memory of MacArthur with articles composed by graduates who were selected to write on various segments of the General's life. As one who was an upperclassman during the first year of the General's direction of West Point, I was asked to write of the Corps during his years as Superintendent of the Military Academy.

A Cadet Under MacArthur

On the 11th day of the 11th month in 1918 an armistice was signed, and the first world war ended. The world rejoiced and celebrated, but at the Military Academy the joy was tempered by keen disappointment. All but a few Cadets had missed overseas action in the historic war.

A cold winter and a late spring further depressed the Corps, already chilled as they were by the thought that a military career had been terminated by the then-assumed grand design: we had won the war to end all wars.

For the cadets the winter and spring of 1918–1919 brought gloomy days mixed with hazing, a cadet suicide, personal grudge fights, and a War department investigation. Certainly, an air of melancholy prevailed. Congress was asking the question: Why do we need a military academy? And the pacifists were answering: Abolish West Point. During this time the leadership of West Point was in the hands of retired officers who had returned to duty during the war. In short—a restless Corps, an abbreviated curriculum, and a leadership that was marking time in an attempt to regain the past—all gave further reason to doubt the future of the Military Academy.

June 12, 1919 was a day of dramatic action on the Plain. Brigadier General Douglas MacArthur, age 39, took command of West Point. He replaced the retiring superintendent, Colonel Samuel Tillman, who had been a Cadet during the Civil War. The oldest Supe had been relieved by one of the youngest. There was no ceremony, not even a review of the Corps, when MacArthur took command. We soon learned he was not one to soiree the Corps with unnecessary pomp and ceremony. Perhaps several days passed before the cadets saw this tall, striding officer of casual dignity on Diagonal Walk. But during those days West Point changed. The air was charged with renewed vitality. Days of frustration turned to days of purpose; and so it was to remain for the next three years.

Little was it realized that MacArthur's first meeting with a small group of First Classmen would be prophetic of the changes to come during his tour of duty. The First Classmen were ordered to report to the Superintendent. In proper full dress, white gloves, and with the usual trepidation they were ushered into the General's office. Momentarily they were confused cadets because regulations required a proper salute and the prescribed greeting, "Sir, Cadet So-and so reports to the Superintendent as ordered." But MacArthur wanted none of this, and before the cadets could assume the proper military stance the Supe greeted each with a handshake, a cordial MacArthur pat on the arm, and a suggestion that all should be seated. He then offered cigarettes and, with the military barrier broken, led the cadets in an animated discussion of Corps problems. It was a case of "no contest" for the Supe as he won the enthusiastic loyalty of each Cadet with his surprisingly warm greeting. By Retreat that day it was all over the Corps: "our new Supe was great. He didn't even know the blue-book regs prohibiting the smoking of cigarettes by Cadets." What the Cadets did not realize was that MacArthur knew the regs full well. The meeting had set the stage for a calculated break with parochialism.

When General MacArthur was appointed Superintendent he was told by Chief of Staff General March, "West Point is 40 years behind the times." To Congress and many returned civilian soldiers and officers, West Point Cadets were considered the nation's pampered pets. The all-powerful Academic Board believed that the unwise, early graduation of classes had seriously jeopardized the Academy, and that the only change needed was an immediate return to the pre-World War I conditions that bred the great leaders of that war.

General MacArthur believed his mission at West Point was "to fight for the very life of the Academy." Recognizing that the greatest problems he faced were internal ones, he said later: "It was well understood that it was no light affair to attempt, even in a moderate degree, to modify the status which had proved itself so splendidly for a country at war. It was recognized that reform, to be effective, must be evolutionary and not revolutionary."

The most pressing problem for the new Supe was to ward off further War Department and Congressional investigations into hazing. The report on the suicide of Cadet Stephen Bird had established the fact that harsh and even sadistic treatment was being condoned by upper-classmen in dealing with Fourth Classmen. This had been traditionally accepted practice by the Cadets, who were proud of the fact that to suffer the ordeal of Plebe life carried a badge of distinction outside West Point for "being able to take it." Further, it was the sincere belief of many that the Plebe system, unchanged, was most important to the molding of the future officer. Change would be doggedly resisted.

To meet this serious problem MacArthur did not assemble the Corps to present his view. In fact, he never did formally address the Corps while he was Supe. He did, however, through the Commandant, Lt. Col. Robert Danford, select a group of First Classmen to study cadet life and the Fourth Class system. Captain Charles F. Thompson, of football fame and later a corps commander under MacArthur, was appointed officer-in-charge, and Chaplain Clayton E. Wheat, author of the Cadet Prayer, was their advisor. This group, known as the First Class Committee, for weeks during the summer of 1919 discussed, argued, and finally codified Fourth Class customs in pamphlet form. Bitter feeling arose as the presentation of changes to the Class was vigorously resisted by the traditionalists—supported as they were by some officer sentiment. Several class meetings were held in the gymnasium during August, and finally a definite break with the past was voted by the Class of 1920. In the late 1940's General Thompson told a group of graduates that the action taken by this First Class Committee, to his mind, was the most important single accomplishment of the Corps. Superintendent MacArthur, without directly involving himself, won his first important battle as Supe, for the approved printed pamphlet carried his full endorsement.

The First Class Committee action was followed by the important organization of an Honor Committee and the formal recognition of this group as the supreme court of Cadet judgement on matters involving personal honor. Heretofore, there had been precipitous action on a less formalized basis. This involved either a quick departure of the offender from the post or the alternative to remain and live as a silenced Cadet. The Honor Committee, organized and nurtured by MacArthur, has proved through the years the strength of his design.

With September classes varsity football returned, and the Corps soon learned that the greatest enthusiast for the game was General MacArthur. Never a practice period passed that did not see the Supe, carrying a riding crop, jauntily stride onto the practice field. There was nothing synthetic about the interest of our Supe in sports, and since he was a bachelor, all varsity teams became his family.

I recall a baseball practice session. We were having batting practice at the time and I was having trouble hitting curve balls. As usual, MacArthur had stopped by to watch the team practicing. I knew that he had been a pretty fair ballplayer in his time, so I decided to ask him for a little expert advise on batting. I wasn't too surprised either when the General loosened his stiff collar, took off his Sam Browne belt, and stepped into the batter's box. It must have been the only time that I ever saw him fail to accomplish something he set out to do. When it was my turn to bat again, I not only couldn't hit a curve, I couldn't even hit a straight ball.

He believed in a balanced Corps and openly endorsed the proselyting of athletes, a practice which is now followed on a large scale. Then, as now, there was far from complete acceptance of this policy by the Corps and graduates. He also believed that the Cadet should be broadened by closer associations with civilians, and to accomplish this, varsity teams began to visit sister colleges. Games with Yale in New Haven, Harvard in Boston, and Notre Dame in New York were scheduled, with an all-approving Corps attending these games. Previously, football trips had been limited to the Navy game in New York. MacArthur's Corps gave him no satisfaction in the form of Navy victories, but the program he initiated paid off so well that by the late 'twenties the Navy was growing weary of Army victories, and sued for a cessation of relations.

Varsity teams were only a part of the Supe's interest in sports. The General believed that athletic participation for every Cadet made for better officers. In those days there were few Cadet distractions or extracurricular activities other than sports. The Corps was made up of those who took additional physical exercise voluntarily, those who enjoyed a siesta daily (red comforter boys), and those who studied during every period (thus boning tenths on their less ambitious classmates). In the fall of 1919 the new Supe got the Cadets out of barracks and onto intramural teams. Not long thereafter he had carved on the stone portals of the gymnasium his now famous words:

> Upon the fields of friendly strife,
> Are sown the seeds that,
> Upon other fields, on other days,
> Will bear the fruits of victory.

It is difficult to keep a secret from the Corps, so it was no secret that our Supe was not as warmly received by the Old Line professors as he was by the Cadets. In those days the Academic Board made or interpreted all policy for the Supe. Those omniscient professors—Echols, Carter, Robinson, Wilcox, Stuart, Holt and Fieberger—were as sturdy a lot as the buildings in which they presided. The fact that some of them had taught MacArthur as a Cadet contributed even more to the resentment which they held for the views of this young Supe. Youth meant challenge and change. This they would not willingly or graciously abide.

But MacArthur rode out the storm, and when occasion demanded he acted with finality. The Corps published a weekly paper called *The Bray*. One of the most admired Tacs served as its sole censor. In a facetious moment the editor of *The Bray* wrote an article lampooning some of the changes, including the new Plebe system. *The Bray* was mailed out on Saturday, and that day a football game was to be played. Early in the afternoon General MacArthur was shown a copy of the editorial and before the game was played the Supe had taken the following actions: stopped the mailing of the publications at the post office, relieved the respected Tac from duty at West Point, and issued orders to suspend permanently the publication of *The Bray*. He then took in the football game. Over the weekend a stunned Corps learned the lesson that the MacArthur vision of a better West Point did not include a liberal arts freedom of discussion. West Point was to remain a military academy. (The officer he relieved was later to become one of his divisional commanders in the Far East.)

The fall of 1919 was an exciting one for the Corps. Distinguished visitors such as the King of the Belgians and his Crown Prince, the British Prince of Wales and later King of England, and Marshalls Pétain and Foch came to the Plain. General MacArthur shared these distinguished visitors with the Corps. Many were received as individuals in the old mess hall and barracks with a minimum of ceremony, for MacArthur believed that the opportunity for the Cadets to mingle with great men was no less important than impressing the visitors with the glamor of the Academy.

MacArthur's vision of an evolutionary change included the return of distinguished young officers for assignment either to the tactical or the academic departments. Young officers who had fought with distinction in the war and were proud of the West Point heritage made a profound impression on the Corps.

The breaking up of summer camp at Fort Clinton, the area east of Trophy Point, was one MacArthur action which was accepted with mixed emotion by the upper classes which were to be sent to Camp Dix instead to train with regular troops. This was a drastic break with tradition—a tradition which included the gaiety of summer camp—hops, band concerts, the pranks of guard duty, and only a minimum of military training. It was here that cadets became better acquainted and here that they led a carefree life after the long and stiff session with academics. The disappointment, however, was greater for the officers and wives than for the Cadets who, after all, were getting a chance to get away from West Point. But the social life at West Point became bland when the cadets departed. The resentment by the permanent staff was so great that, shortly after MacArthur's departure, the first change made was the reestablishment of summer camp. It took the Second World War to catch up with MacArthur's thinking, for it was only then that Fort Clinton was permanently dismantled.

It will be 45 years this June since MacArthur took command of West Point. Through all these years no graduate of distinction has spoken more devotedly of his Alma Mater, nor was any prouder of winning his varsity "A." Certainly, this dedication to the Academy must have been sealed during those years of vexation when MacArthur, attuned to the lessons of a great war, prevailed over implacable tradition.

In three short years MacArthur as Supe reared many distinguished officers. Among them were Chairman of the Joint Chiefs of Staff, two Chiefs of Staff of the Army, two Chiefs of Staff of the Air Force, and two Superintedents of West Point.

In a large measure the West Point of today is a reflection of MacArthur, the Supe.

And the Cadets of those transition days under MacArthur understand what Bill Ganoe, his adjutant, so beautifully stated: "If Sylvanus Thayer was the Father of the Military Academy, then Douglas MacArthur was its savior."

General MacArthur had a lifelong interest in sports dating back to the days when he was quarterback of the Texas Military Preparatory School. At West Point he won his "A" as the regular left fielder on the varsity baseball team. Through life he was as proud of his athletic background as he was of his scholastic achievement; even during those final days at Walter Reed Hospital he wore his cadet bathrobe with the attached coveted "A" insignia.

As the bachelor Superintendent, his release from the pressure of those days was to watch the varsity teams practice. He was through life the illustrious West Point graduate whose interest toward varsity sports never dimmed, and especially was he the vicarious coach of football through his long career. In later life, his great joy came from sitting on the player's bench during a practice game scrimmage and returning to his New York apartment to write me his thoughts with respect to personnel and the game in general. His handwritten notes are priceless memoranda of detailed observation that would do credit to a professional coach with the benefit of movies. His keen analytical mind, coupled with his memory of play and players, never ceased to amaze me.

In October 1932, when he was Chief of Staff, he wrote me a letter about Army football, the following paragraph of which is of interest. "I was somewhat startled to see in the papers that Sasse has asked for relief. What is your opinion of Davidson? Write me confidentially!" Major Sasse was then the head coach of football.

My answer to the General included a detailed account of Army football with relation to collegiate athletics. Among other things, I wrote:

>Biff Jones, a smart, farsighted organizer and coach, laid the foundation of the present system. As graduate manager (a post to which he was appointed, but declined, to go to L.S.U. as coach), he would have been a great asset to West Point and the service.
>
>Major Fleming, our graduate manager, has fostered splendid relations, but is leaving.
>
>Sasse, a magnetic, fighting soldier, knows how to lead in action. Army teams under him have had the dash of a Jeb Stuart. Success as a head coach exacts a lot from the individual, and he is no exception. I greatly admire him for desiring to go forward in the service.
>
>With the above background, Davidson comes into the picture. Briefly, he is a fine young officer who may be classed as very popular on the Post. At present, he is aide to the Superintendent. For three years he was the end coach on the Plebe squad; last year he was head coach of the B squad and is now the head coach of the Plebe team. He has never been directly connected

with the varsity. As head coach of the B squad and in scouting assignments he has done excellent work. He possesses neither the drive and personality of a Sasse, nor the football brain of Jones. I would suggest that the big task has been given to him before he is ready, but in justice to Davidson, when he appreciates his task to the full, he may mature overnight, in which case he will do a good job.

During Davidson's first year as head coach, I continued my assignment as first assistant to the Army staff under him. The Army team won all but the last game of the '33 season, losing to Notre Dame 13-12.

In 1940, before I returned to the Academy as head coach, I learned through General Eichelberger, the Superintendent, that Captain Davidson, the former coach, had unsuccessfully petitioned the Superintendent to have him reassigned as head coach. According to Eichelberger, Davidson believed that his many years of association with West Point football had compromised his military future. Ironically in 1959, 25 years after I had left Davidson's staff to go to Dartmouth, it was to Lt. Gen. Davidson, Superintendent of West Point, that I wrote my letter of resignation, a letter, by the way, which he never acknowledged. Football had not damaged his Army career.

While General MacArthur was Chief of Staff, I made personal calls on him without prior appointment and never found him too occupied to see me. He always gave the impression that, at the moment, there was no one more important than his visitor. He worked behind a clean desk—no papers whatever—greeted visitors by coming forward to meet them, and always escorted a visitor to his office door, a gracious gesture that is recalled by many of his friends.

In 1932 on a sizzling hot Fourth of July, I took the nonair-conditioned Pennsylvania Railroad to Washington from Dayton, Ohio to see the General, then the Chief of Staff. As I was out of uniform, there was no protocol to my visit. My mission was to appeal to the General on behalf of a young halfback who had been turned down for insufficient masticating teeth; I had been asked to undertake this task by Sasse, the West Point coach, who knew that I had access to MacArthur. On this occasion, I was greeted by a young Major who sat outside the swinging door to the General's office in the old Army and Navy Building. This young Major was named Eisenhower, an aide to MacArthur.

While the General and I were talking, a prelude to the famous bonus army march was taking place along Pennsylvania Avenue. MacArthur did not allow the great commotion of the marchers to interrupt our conversation. Within a few weeks the order from President Hoover to break up the bonus marcher's camp was to require MacArthur's full attention, an action that haunted his later years. The one picture I have seen of MacArthur looking over the bonus marcher's camp shows Major Dwight Eisenhower about ten feet to his rear.

When I presented the plight of our halfback to the General, he called over a second swinging door, reminiscent of a Western saloon, to his Adjutant, General McKinley: "Mac, the coaches at West Point have a problem for which I know you will have an answer. Blaik says there is a great halfback who needs some teeth fixed. He has been turned down and needs special consideration." The boy had his teeth repaired, and some months later the General inquired how "his boy" with the bridgework was doing. I told him that he was a great back on the Plebe team, but that the Math Department thought little of his ability in algebra, and I was embarrassed to add that the young man had departed at Christmas time.

After the 1933 season, I finally decided to become a head coach and took the position at Dartmouth because I could not resist the challenge presented to me by Dr. Ernest Hopkins, the president of the college. Since General MacArthur knew that Ohio State, Princeton and Yale had shown active interest in inducing me to leave the Army, and I assured him I was not interested in becoming a head coach, it came as a great surprise to him when the news broke that I was going to Dartmouth. It was at this time that I first realized that the General's attachment to the Military Academy could not endorse such changes. Furthermore, I left West Point without a personal discussion with him as to my reasons for leaving the Cadets. Some correspondence between Dr. Hopkins and the General on the subject made me realize that I had made an error in not asking for MacArthur's blessing before I accepted my new position.

In 1941, my return to the Plain occassioned the resumption of our former relations, and from that year on we became closer friends. My files are filled with letters and cables of counsel and blessings. MacArthur's interest in West Point football never diminished during the years of the Japanese war, the occupation of Japan, and the war in Korea. His messages to the Cadets were something they looked forward to as the ultimate in recognition.

In 1948, I lost two assistants from my staff, Herman Hickman to Yale and Andy Gustafson to the University of Miami. In April of the year, the General wrote, "It could not have failed to be a great blow to lose simultaneously your line and backfield coaches, both apparently good men. However, this again follows the technique of war: You always lose your best men in the heat of battle."

In the late 'forties there was a movement in the Pentagon under Louis Johnson, the Secretary of Defense, and in the White House, where General Vaughn had influence, to curtail the course at the Military Academy to two years. It was the plan to make it a graduate school for those men from our universities who contemplated careers as officers. This would, of course, have destroyed the entire competitive athletic system, incluing football, at West Point. When I wrote the General about this effort in August of '49, he replied: "I have noted your concern about the future of the Academy. Many attacks, basic as well as superficial, have been made upon it in the past, but all have failed. I feel sure that such fundamental changes as you suggest will never be successfully promulgated. The people will not permit what would amount to its practical destruction. The stamp of West Point character is too interwoven with our nation's success to be lightly set aside. In case of any real menace you may rest assured I would throw the fullest weight of any influence I possess to prevent it."

In a letter of May, 1950, the General stated: "Your letters and the contacts they bring with West Point are one of the few bright spots which seems to ease the isolation and loneliness of this far-flung outpost—we all enjoyed Mesereau's trip out here very much." I had sent Major Mesereau, a member of the coaching staff, to the Far East to show pictures of the Army games and to talk football with our troops. When Tom went to MacArthur's headquarters, he was shown into the General's office. The first question MacArthur asked Mesereau was: "Why didn't Elmblad start the Navy game?" Tom, a varsity coach, replied: "Sir, I didn't know he hadn't."

From 1951 until his death in 1964 I saw much of General MacArthur, and during the last few years of his life I made a point of visiting him several times a month. This period followed immediately after the General's final retirement from the Army, when he had settled into a very quiet life in New York, going out very little, but reading and following national and international affairs with undiminished interest, and watching television sports broadcasts. His interest in the successes of the West Point football team never waned; I always made it a point to keep him informed of developments in that area, and we often discussed these at length. At one such discussion, he remarked to his wife that we were fortunate not to have lost the Navy game by a heavy score. After reviewing the prospects for the following year, I invited him to attend spring practice and himself see the team in action. He accepted the invitation with pleasure on the condition that I not mention the contemplated visit around the Post so that he might arrive and depart quietly.

During the same discussion the General expressed his disappointment because the Corps seemed indifferent and apathetic in the television showing of the basketball game with Navy. He wanted to know why the Navy seemed to excel in sports while West Point lagged. I could think of nothing better than the lame excuse that these things seemed to run in cycles, but MacArthur refused to accept it; he had a different explanation. With reference to General Irving, the Superintendent of the Academy, he stated, "Our problems would be eased with a winner; the leadership of the Academy needs change." The General was referring to the fact that, although he personally liked General Irving, he had been forced to relieve him of his command during World War II at the request of General

Krueger. MacArthur continued, "I cannot understand why a non-winner, one with his combat record, could ever be selected to head the Military Academy."

My view of General Irving as Superintendent did not coincide with that of MacArthur, and I was more inclined to lay the blame for whatever situation existed elsewhere. In justice to General Irving, it was known that some ranking officers of his division did not share General Krueger's opinion.

When I ventured to differ with General MacArthur over the responsibility for the lack of interest in athletics at West Point, I told him frankly that the former Commandant, Harkins, and his assistant Waters, the succeeding Commandant, Harkins, and his derstanding of the relation of varsity sports to Cadet life. I cited an example to support my belief. Many months before, Field Marshal Montgomery had visited West Point to inspect the Corps, and a schedule for him to watch the cadets in military instruction had been laid out. General Bryant Moore, the Superintendent, decided to show Montgomery football practice before they took in the military functions. The Field Marshal became so absorbed in the practice that he came into the players' huddle as I directed them in full scrimmage. I never saw a man more excited about the game; in consequence, he overstayed and missed much of the military schedule set up by the Commandant. The Marshal's parting remark to me was that, if he were to train a new army, he would use our football methods. As excited over football as Montgomery was, the tactical department was even more furious that football had usurped Montgomery's attention.

"General, the trouble was that Colonel Harkins and Waters viewed our football team's popularity as a challenge to the importance of their personal positions," I said to MacArthur.

"You are a winner, which is not necessarily fashionable," was MacArthur's answer.

Early in 1954 at another meeting, I was accompanied by Doc Blanchard, a member of my staff, who set up a movie projector while General MacArthur and I discussed the prospects of our squad for the coming fall. He was encouraged that we had a small group of likely Plebes to fill the varsity voids created by the many who would graduate. We discussed our difficult scheduling problem. The General thought West Point and Notre Dame were being forced together as football mavericks without a league to support us. We discussed the Notre Dame break, which he had supported, but which he now felt had served its purpose; he agreed that we should play them regularly, although he warned that the game should be scheduled early in the season and never late. This coincided with my view that any return of Notre Dame to our schedule should be on the second Saturday in October.

Doc ran the highlight pictures, and the General was enthusiastically impressed by the seasoned play of the cadets. The General became noticeably animated as he made cogent remarks on an interesting play. Often, as the General spotted action of considerable interest, he would ask Blanchard to rerun a segment of the film. Finally, as the picture ended, he turned to me and stated, "Last season without doubt, Earl, was your finest football hour." Considering the forlorn hopes of two seasons past, he was probably correct.

The discussion moved from football to other areas of interest, the first of which was MacArthur's delight with the selection of General Blackshear "Babe" Bryan as the new Superintendent. The General readily recalled him as a football player when MacArthur was Supe: "Slow lineman—a determined player who was held back by a rheumatic heart condition." He recalled that Babe had graduated with a three-year class and had ranked in the first third. "He'll be a fine Supe and support athletics," was the General's appraisal; his words, as usual, were prophetically true.

I would not wish to leave the reader with the impression that MacArthur's only interest in our conversations centered about football. Since my first contact as a West Point Cadet with MacArthur revolved about athletics and since I had served as coach of the West Point team for so long a period, that was naturally our point of departure for discussions that ranged far and wide. Much of this I have related in my recollections of MacArthur's reflections on his military career and his brief adventures in politics. While it has been possible to prepare much of this in organized fashion, others of my recollections are necessarily more evanescent and perhaps rambling. Nevertheless, they are interesting as showing different facets of the General's mind and recall the impress of his personality.

I recall vividly a visit to the General's apartment in the Waldorf Towers in March of 1953 when I had not seen him for some time. The warrant officer met me at the door an took me into the spacious living room to await the General. The furnishings of the room now included many of the MacArthur personal belongings, and the room no longer was the austere and stately salon formerly reserved for royal dignitaries. It now had the touch of home and Mrs. MacArthur.

In a few minutes the General came through the hallway, pipe in mouth, with the jaunty gait of a young man. He greeted me in his usual friendly way with, "Hello, Earl, how are you?" He shook hands, motioned to the sofa, and asked me to sit down. He started to offer me a cigarette, but then drew back, saying, "Oh, yes, you don't smoke." He took his usual armchair adjacent to the sofa.

My first impression of the General was that he had changed little if at all, and that he appeared even younger than on my last visit. His skin was tight, clear, and unwrinkled. His hair, though threaded with grey, still remained dark and, as usual, parted from the side of his head and carried over to cover an area of baldness. When I remarked how well he appeared he stated that his health was never better. I then asked him about his work at Sperry Rand.

The General talked at some length about his business relations. "I am sure my importance is far overemphasized and bears no relation to my salary. My career in the Army began in the Corps of Engineers, and I have returned to that type of work, except, of course, that now I am occupied with electronics, a very interesting and limitless subject. My contribution to Sperry is more in the nature of advice and at times keeping them from making foolish moves."

I asked the General what he thought of the so-called big businessman. His reply was interesting: "I have known many great financiers in my younger days, including J.P. Morgan and E.T. Stotesbury, my former father-in-law. Today this type of financier has disappeared, and the heads of big banks are in the main nine-to-four men who are administrators and not policymakers. These administrators are the silk-stocking league of Wall Street who are nothing more than puppets for another group of men who sit as interlocking directors of many corporations—men such as Alfred P. Sloan. My respect for this group of financiers is not high; they invariably play angles for position and are not the dominating, creative men of principle such as Morgan and the financiers of former years."

The discussion then turned to our sons. "Don't worry about your boy Bob; he will get his feet on the ground when he goes into the service. He will find that many West Point graduates will go out of their way to encourage him, as not all agreed with the action of the Chief of Staff," who the General believed had showed that he could not think beyond the immediate issue in the case of the dismissed Cadets.

He spoke of his son, Arthur, who was not certain as to what college he should attend. "Arthur is not competitive like me, but rather artistically oriented, as his mother is. He has strong convictions and is completely capable of determining his own future. As a youngster, he saw more of war and death that many soldiers, and I have wondered whether it has left a scar on him. Although Arthur is not a robust athlete, he is an excellent swimmer, is president of his class, and an accomplished musician. I am glad that he is not number one in his class standing, as I believe that brings little reward, though he does rank in the first 10 percent and is especially good in the arts."

Often, when I was with him, the General would sit in his favorite chair, raise his chin, and look into the distance as though visualizing scenes long past, tap his fingers on the arm of the chair for emphasis, and recall some of his difficult hours in the Far East, holding me spellbound. In all our discussions, I never found MacArthur's memory wanting in the slightest detail; never was there anything small or mean in his appraisal of his military colleagues or even the professional, often self-seeking, politicians with whom he came in contact. I recall a case in point in his estrangement from General Robert Eichelberger following the end of World War II. It undoubtedly stemmed from MacArthur's assignment of Eichelberger to the task of taking Buna, which was vital to the initial progress of the Pacific operation against Japan. MacArthur left no doubt as to the importance of success in this mission when he told Eichelberger, "Bob, I expect you to take Buna or not come back alive," a command for which "Miss Em," as Mrs. Eichelberger was known, never forgave the General. The matter went beyond this, however, since the question of promotion and the conflict with General Krueger for seniority of command were constant irritants. Perhaps most important was Eichelberger's feeling that, in accepting assignment to the Pacific, he had lost to Eisenhower the opportunity to become Commander in Chief of the European operation.

In the late '50's, Eichelberger and I had lunch together the day before his departure on a Mediterranean cruise. We discussed General MacArthur, his health following an operation, and the fact that Eichelberger had rather obviously ignored the General for some years, much to the latter's regret. Eichelberger was so convinced that MacArthur had erased him from his list of old friends that he was nonplussed when I told him, "In all my visits with General MacArthur, I have never heard him refer to you except in the highest terms and with a great degree of affection. Why don't you call on him while you are here?"

Eichelberger was taken completely by surprise. Since he was to sail so soon, he could not arrange the suggested visit, but he did send from the Mediterranean a long cablegram full of the warmth and charm so characteristic of him. This pleased MacArthur in the highest degree; once again, he showed his magnanimity by welcoming back to the reservation one who had, as he regarded it, temporarily wandered off.

I recall arranging a visit by Robert Kennedy and his family to General MacArthur. Then a Senator from New York, Kennedy was so entranced by MacArthur's reminiscences that he urged the General to write his autobiography. Although MacArthur was then well past 80, I too had often urged him to write the story of his life, but had always met with an adamant refusal. I was therefore taken completely unaware one day when the General produced his memoirs, written in longhand on hundreds of sheets of yellow pad paper. I took the manuscript and glanced through it; it was a beautiful piece of work, done in perfect handwriting, with no erasures or deletions to mar its appearance. I was moved to say, "General, this is so immaculate in every detail that it must be a corrected copy." His reply surprised me: "No, this is the original; I knew what I wanted to say." When I protested that he had told me that he would never write a book, he confessed that he had done so because he felt that he should be prepared for any financial eventuality if his relation with Sperry Rand should run into difficulties, an event, of course, that never occurred. I treasure a copy of the original manuscript that he gave me. *Life* magazine later published an edited version of those memoirs. The book, good as it is, does not give the true measure of the man, as it might have done had he written it sooner, perhaps in the '50's, when he was closer to events.

In May of '62, General and Mrs. MacArthur motored to West Point for the Thayer Award, given annually by the Association of West Point Graduates to an outstanding citizen whose service and accomplishments to the nation exemplify personal devotion to the ideals expressed in the West Point motto: "Duty, Honor, Country." This was not the usual Thayer Award ceremony, for the name of MacArthur transcended all who had been honored before him. To the Corps the General was West Point's most distinguished graduate, the one through the years who had been the closest to the Corps of Cadets.

After the General had reviewed the Corps, the guests and alumni assembled with the Cadets in the mess hall for lunch, followed by the presentation of the award. The Thayer Award was presented by General Leslie Groves, the President of the Association of Graduates.

When the General received the award, they gave him a wildly enthusiastic greeting. There was some trepidation as to whether this soldier, now thin and frail at 82 years, could live up to the great tradition associated with his name. Mrs. MacArthur, his devoted Jean, and other close friends had reason to be concerned, for the General was no longer physically strong. They could not fail to recall that his father, Lt. General Arthur MacArthur, had died suddenly while he was addressing his comrades in arms of the Civil War.

For this important event, however, the General became his old self. Without a note, never once groping for words, in rhetoric and phrase never heard before in that great hall, the General spoke for 30 minutes. There was not a dry eye in the mess hall when he completed his address. This was his last and greatest day at the Military Academy he revered and loved. The legacy he left that day was a speech that many rank in the tradition of memorable addresses. The speech was delivered extemporaneously and had not been put in written form before it was delivered. This transcript was taken from a recording.

Duty, Honor, Country

No human being could fail to be deeply moved by such a tribute as this. Coming from a profession I have served so long and a people I have loved so well, it fills me with an emotion I cannot express. But this award is not intended primarily to honor a personality, but to symbolize a great moral code—a code of conduct and chivalry of those who guard this beloved land of culture and ancient descent. For all hours and for all time, it is an expression of the ethics of the American soldier. That I should be integrated in this way with so noble an ideal arouses a sense of pride, and yet of humility, which will be with me always.

Duty, Honor, Country: Those three hallowed words reverently dictate what you ought to be, what you can be, what you will be. They are your rallying point to build courage when courage seems to fail, to regain faith when there seems to be little cause for faith, to create hope when hope becomes forlorn.

Unhappily, I possess neither that eloquence to diction, that poetry of imagination, nor that brilliance of metaphor to tell you all that they mean.

The unbelievers will say they are but words, but a slogan, but a flamboyant phrase. Every pedant, every demogogue, every cynic, every hypocrite, every troublemaker, and, I am sorry to say, some others of an entirely different character will try to downgrade them even to the extent of mockery and ridicule.

But these are some of the things they do. They build your

basic character. They mold you for your future roles as the custodians of the nation's defense. They make you strong enough to know when you are weak, and brave enough to face yourself when you are afraid.

They teach you to be proud and unbending in honest failure, but humble and gentle in success; not to substitute words for actions, not to seek the path of comfort, but to face the stress and spur of difficulty and challenge; to learn to stand up in the storm, but to have compassion on those who fall; to master yourself before you seek to master others; to have a heart that is clean, a goal that is high; to learn to laugh, yet never forget how to weep; to reach into the future, yet never neglect the past; to be serious, yet never to take yourself too seriously! to be modest, so that he will remember the simplicity of true greatness, the open mind of true wisdom, the meekness of true strength.

They give you a temperate will, a quality of the imagination, a vigor of the emotions, a freshness of the deep springs of life, a tempermental predominance of courage over timidity, of an appetite for adventure over love of ease.

They create in your heart a sense of wonder, the unfailing hope of what next, and the joy and inspiration of life. They teach you in this way to be an officer and a gentleman.

And what sort of soldiers are those you are to lead? Are they reliable? Are they brave? Are they capable of victory?

Their story is known to all of you. It is the story of the American man-at-arms. My estimate of him was formed on the battlefield many, many years ago, and has never changed. I regarded him then, as I regard him now, as one of the world's noblest figures; not only as one of the finest military characters, but also as one of the most stainless.

His name and fame are the birthright of every American citizen. In his youth and strength, his love and loyalty, he gave all that mortality can give. He needs no eulogy from me, or from any other man. He has written his own history and written it in red on his enemy's breast.

But when I think of his patience in adversity, of his courage under fire, and of his modesty in victory, I am filled with an emotion of admiration I cannot put into words. He belongs to history as furnishing one of the greatest examples of successful patriotism. He belongs to posterity as the instructor of future generations in the principles of liberty and freedom. He belongs to the present, to us, by his virtues and by his achievements.

In twenty campaigns, on a hundred battlefields, around a thousand campfires, I have witnessed that enduring fortitude, that patriotic self-abnegation, and that invincible determination which have carved his statue in the hearts of his people.

From one end of the world to the other, he has drained deep the chalice of courage. As I listened to those songs [of the Cadet Glee Club], in memory's eye I could see those staggering columns of the First World War, bending under soggy packs on many a weary march, from dripping dusk to drizzling dawn, slogging ankle-deep through the mire of shellpocked roads, to form grimly for the attack, blue-lipped, covered with sludge and mud, chilled by the wind and rain, driving home to their objective, and, for many, to the judgment seat of God.

I do not know the dignity of their birth, but I do know the glory of their death. They died, unquestioning, uncomplaining, with faith in their hearts, and on their lips the hope that we would go on to victory.

Always for them: Duty, Honor, Country. Always their blood, and sweat, and tears as we sought the way and the light and the truth. And twenty years after, on the other side of the globe, again the filth of murky foxholes, the stench of ghostly trenches, the slime of dripping dugouts, those boiling suns of relentless heat, those torrential rains of devastating storms, the loneliness and utter desolation of jungle trails, the bitterness of long separation from those they loved and cherished, the deadly pestilence of tropical disease, the horror of stricken areas of war.

Their resolute and determined defense, their swift and sure attack, their indomitable purpose, their complete and decisive victory—always victory, always through the bloody haze of their last reverberating shot, the vision of gaunt, ghostly men, reverently following your passwords of "Duty, Honor, Country."

The code which those words perpetuate embraces the highest moral law and will stand the test of any ethics or philosophies ever promulgated for the uplift of mankind. Its requirements are for the things that are right and its restraints are from the things that are wrong. The soldier, above all other men, is required to practice the greatest act of religious training: sacrifice. In battle, and in the face of danger and death, he discloses those divine attributes which his Maker gave when He created man in His own image. No physical courage and no greater strength can take the place of the divine help which alone can sustain him. However hard the incidents of war may be, the soldier who is called upon to offer and to give his life for his country is the noblest development of mankind.

You now face a new world, a world of change. The thrust into outer space of the satellite spheres and missiles marks a beginning of another epoch in the long story of mankind. In the five billion years or more the scientists tell us it has taken to form the earth, in the three billion years or more of development of the human race, there has never been a more abrupt or staggering evolution.

We deal now, not with things of this world alone, but with the illimitable distances and as yet unfathomed mysteries of the universe. We are reaching out for a new and boundless frontier. We speak in strange terms of harnessing cosmic energy, of making the winds and tides work for us; of creating unheard-of synthetic materials to supplement or even replace our old standard basics; of purifying sea water for our drink; of mining ocean floors for new fields of wealth and food; of disease preventives to expand life into the hundreds of years; of controlling the weather for a more equitable distribution of heat and cold, of rain and shine; of spaceships to the moon; of the primary target in war no longer limited to the armed forces of an enemy, but instead to include his civil populations; of ultimate conflict between a united human race and the sinister forces of some other planetary galaxy; of such dreams and fantasies as to make life the most exciting of all times.

And through all this welter of change and development your mission remains fixed, determined, invincible. It is to win our wars. Everything else in your professional career is but corollary to this vital dedication. All other public purposes, all other public projects, all other public needs, great or small, will find others for their accomplishment; but you are the ones who are trained to fight.

Yours is the profession of arms, the will to win, the sure knowledge that in war there is no substitute for victory, that if you lose, the nation will be destroyed, that the very obsession of your public service must be Duty, Honor, Country.

Others will debate the controversial issues, national and international, which divide men's minds. But serene, calm, aloof, you stand as the nation's war guardians, as its lifeguards from the raging tides of international conflict, as its gladiators in the arena of battle. For a century and a half you have defended, guarded, and protected its hallowed traditions of liberty and freedom, of right and justice.

Let civilian voices argue the merits or demerits of our processes of government: Whether our strength is being sapped by deficit financing indulged in too long, by Federal paternalism grown too mighty, by power groups too arrogant, by morals fallen too low, by taxes grown too high, by extremists become too violent; whether our personal liberties are as thorough and complete as they should be.

These great national problems are not for your professional participation or military solution. Your guidepost stands out like a gleaming beacon in the night: Duty, Honor, Country.

You are the leaven which binds together the entire fabric of our national system of defense. From your ranks come the great captains who hold the nation's destiny in their hands the moment the war tocsin sounds.

The long grey line has never failed us. Were it to do so, a million ghosts in olive drab, in brown khaki, in blue and grey would rise from their white crosses, thundering those magic words: Duty, Honor, Country.

This does not mean that you are warmongers. On the contrary, the soldier above all other people prays for peace, for he must suffer and bear the deepest wounds and scars of war. But always in our ears ring the ominous words of Plato, that wisest of all philosophers: "Only the dead have seen the end of war."

The shadows are lengthening for me. The twilight is here. My days of old have vanished—tone and tint. They have gone glimmering through the dreams of things that were. Their memory is one of wondrous beauty, watered by tears and coaxed and caressed by the smiles of yesterday. I listen vainly, but with eager ear, for the witching melody of faint bugles blowing reveille, of far drums beating the long roll.

In my dreams I hear again the crash of guns, the rattle of

musketry, the strange, mournful mutter of the battlefield. But in the evening of my memory always I come back to West Point. Always there echoes and re-echoes: Duty, Honor, Country.

Today marks my final roll call with you, but I want you to know that, when I cross the river, my last conscious thoughts will be of the Corps, and the Corps, and the Corps.

I bid you farewell.

The week before General MacArthur left for Walter Reed Hospital, I visited with him for an unusually long time, considering his physical condition. He was not anxious for me to leave, though a very apparent jaundice marked him as a very sick man. Somehow, even in grave sickness, his mental and nervous system always remained in balance and completely controlled. When he took me to the door, his parting words were: "Earl, I don't have too many days left." There was no answer to the statement, save a wetting of the eyes.

By the week's end I had a call from General Courtney Whitney, his aide for years, who stated that the General was going to Walter Reed to be operated upon. He asked if I would come to the plane to boost his spirits. The plane was to depart at 11:00 o'clock the next morning.

I was there at 10:45, but too late to catch his accelerated departure time. Other than two officers on official duty, I was alone and thoroughly downcast. The plane had closed its doors, and the engines were being warmed. Never was I more dejected, as I searched in vain to get a glimpse of the General.

Suddenly the engines stopped, the door opend, and the General came out to say good-bye to his old friend. He was appallingly bronze in color. We said a last farewell. When I recall that this desperately ill man on his last journey stopped the plane and delayed his departure, I am moved to wonder that the unknowing could apply to him such unjust adjectives as autocratic, aloof, distant, arrogant, and theatrical. I, who knew him so well, saw the injustice of such terms applied to a man of great dignity, a sometimes seemingly reserved person who never groped for words or used the ordinary phrase, who warmly grasped the proferred hand of friendship, who magnanimously forgave his detractors and lesser men, and who so deeply appreciated every gracious gesture. He was singularly unimpressed by the prevalent struggle for personal aggrandizement, the more so when it was achieved at the expense of others. He cared little for the unsubstantial glory of the moment and for those who pursued it. A born arristocrat in mind and in action, who instinctively followed the rule of noblesse oblige, he remained so to his dying hour.

My old friend, Colonel William Ganoe, knew him well. I close with his words.

MacArthur The Man*

If Sylvanus Thayer was the Father of the Military Academy, then MacArthur was its Savior. A close study of the records will reveal that in many ways he surpassed the Father.

The impression he left on West Point, and the estimate of his worth by many qualified military men, are summed up in a letter from Danford to me:

"When MacArthur knocks at Saint Peter's gate for admission, and Saint Peter's face lights up when he sets eyes on him, the good Saint will leave the gate in charge of an assistant and will himself escort the Soldier-Statesman to the VIP area, and there will say to Caesar, Alexander and Napoleon, 'Move over, gentlemen, here's MacArthur.'"

Other military minds might not be so imaginative as Danford's, but I sense they would arrive at a similar summation.

However, if there be those who would be prejudiced by hearsay, let me ask what other man bolstered one nation to meet a war successfully, rebuilt another militarily and liberated it, conquered another and gave it democratic government, and half saved another—which he would have saved altogether had it not been for faraway powers who were adverse to victory?

If there be those who would question his personal courage, let them find another who has officially won a Medal of Honor,

---

* Ganoe, William, *MacArthur*, (Vantage).

three D.S.C.'s, seven Silver Stars, and Two Purple Hearts. If one wishes, he will find in the files in Washington a recommendation for another Medal of Honor which could not be awarded publicly because of a top-secret deed. Who else in two wars has won twelve separate recognitions for risking his life for his country above and beyond the call of duty? General Menoher said of him that, on the field of battle, where acts of heroism and valor were commonplace, his were outstanding.

If there be those who would look down their noses at medals for heroism, I can furnish them firsthand testimony. As a member of the Medals Board in Europe in the last war, I can vouch for the ceaseless effort to investigate the veriest iota of proof in every recommendation. A general meant no more than a corporal. High and low were refused because of below par qualifications. I can recollect the awarding of only two Medals of Honor, one to a sergeant and another to a private.

If there be those who accuse MacArthur of the crime of showmanship, may I point out a few shrinking violets like King David, Joan of Arc, John Paul Jones, Jeb Stuart, Billy Sunday, and Georgie Patton. Space forbids citing a hundred other successful leaders who did not hesitate to assume striking roles to magnetize their followers.

Yet that crime of showmanship seems for some to eclipse MacArthur's world-wide benefactions. I can think of no commander in all history who performed such far-flung exploits as attacking and attacking over thousands of miles of ocean, often with inadequate forces, island fortresses manned by the fiercest of fighters.

Little men seeing only little things have always been with us. There were those who couldn't see Washington through his wealth and wine, Scott through his fuss and feathers, Lincoln through his mussed hair and dirty stories, Grant through his butcher and bottle, and Cleveland through his duck shooting and trumped-up stories of wife beating. The same types can't see MacArthur through his corncob pipe, embroidered cap, picture poses, aristocratic airs and rumors of a brewery in Manila.

Coming historians will discover in MacArthur a figure whose moral courage was as stout as his physical, whose dignified utterances, unsoiled by profanity, unhalted by hesitancy and unjostled by hot emotions, whose loftiness of purpose, misunderstood at times by those squinting up the heights, lifted him above the smaller passions and meaner impulses of lesser souls. They will look back through the perspective of time to recreate beyond the glory of his triumphs a man of self-denial, whose West Point redemption was met by curtailment, whose domestic fullness came uncommonly late, whose gigantic tasks were undertaken at an age when most men have retired, and whose service ostracized him to rude and royal places in foreign lands, when his stifled yearning was for his own fireside and country. They will see a knight whose shining armor blinded some to the greatness of the heart beneath, the calm reason in the hour of peril and the keen sense of misery over the useless slaughter of his soldiers. They will discern the peculiar patience with which he waited, quickness with which he thrust, hardness with which he struck, doggedness with which he clung, as well as his genius to overcome handicaps. No, this old soldier will never die—much less fade away.

Gradually and imperceptibly, as the decades roll along, generations will discover that no nobler figure ever stood as a bulwark in four nations' lives—any nation's life—and will view him with a reverence which will hush them in the presence of his memory.

Chapter XXVIII

Twists and Turns

Toward the end of my life, already well past the biblical allotment of three score years and ten, all sorts of recollections of a variety of happenings, some of them long forgotten, come unbidden to my mind during my early morning walks under the clear desert skies. Desert quail are in abundance this morning. What a lovely sight! Several hens and strutting cocks are accompanied by 30 or 40 chicks, scurrying about in the fashion of Keystone cops.

Looking back on my life, I recall the maxim that, as a twig is bent, so the tree will grow. Has the truth of that saying ever been more evident than during the last decade? Except for a few examples, children cannot be held to account for their inheritance. Their parents, first, and their communities, second, are responsible for the way they grow.

I was most fortunate in having a mother and father who were anything but permissive. I toed the line on what they believed right or wrong. From them I learned the Scotman's traditional independence of thought. They built in me an adherent dedication to their own high principles, and they helped themselves and me bend that twig by passing on a good genetic endowment, never short of adrenalin.

My good luck has extended into my own family circle. For the past half century all our actions have been guided by Merle, a wife-mother who reared two sons while forming a family bond that created a devotion of all for one and one for all. My, but I'm rich!

Sitting on the sidelines after so full and active a life, I am sometimes moved to wonder that self-centered individuals with little desire to make new friends and diminishing opportunities allow themselves to go to seed. For the lifelong active individual, retirement is a different game with new rules. One not prepared to play it suddenly finds himself standing helplessly deep in his own end zone as the kickoff carries the ball to him. His field of productivity shrinks, withers, and fades away, and he vegetates. He is seen by others, if noticed at all, only as an old man. Then he vanishes entirely, unmissed. For him and his contemporaries, retirement can be destructive.

For those prepared or willing to make an effort to meet new conditions with new routines and habits and for the man with an interesting hobby or an inspiring curiosity on any subject or even merely an appetite for knowledge for its own sake, can the hours and days of the golden years fail to provide opportunities for development and growth?

In my retirement I have had time to develop my golf game and learn how much subtlety and control it requires. In 50 years of desultory devotion to the game I was told repeatedly not to try to "kill" the ball. I did not listen. During the past few years of constant play at the La Quinta Country Club, Dave Evans, our able pro, has often lectured me on the subject, but somehow his advice made little impression on me.

To me, as to many golfers with sufficient muscle tone and timing occasionally to hit a ball well, one of the minor joys of life has been to watch a ball I really belted off a tee soar high and far down the fairway. Another has been to see a long iron shot fly low and true to a trap-guarded green. In comparison, a seldom delicately controlled 20-yard wedge to the pin for a possible birdie aroused but a minor thrill. That tee shot was what I remembered.

But no more. Almost overnight I have been miraculousy changed. The new Red Blaik does not massacre the ball with all his strength, to the detriment of his blood pressure. At long last he believes that easy does it, that a smooth, fluid, rhythmic swing . . . like this . . . somehow makes the ball respond with a more pleasing reaction than when it is whaled at.

Yesterday I shot a three-over-par 39 on the front side at La Quinta and was too satisfied to complete the round. I had learned something. Now I know that the name of the game is Score, not Kill the Ball. Waltz time with a high follow-through is my time, forevermore. But that was yesterday; I forget so easily.

❧ ❧ ❧

Looking back over the manuscript of this book and the throes of composition, I am inclined to ask if there is any greater frustration than having something important to say and being unable to say it? How important to us are words, the ability to use them effectively at the right time clearly to convey our thoughts?

All my adult life has been spent in two different worlds. In many ways the academic and business arenas are poles apart. Yet in both I have observed one essential, a common denominator for high achievement: a sound fundamental background in the understanding and use of words. It is a prime requisite for success.

Thomas Gray's flower wasting its sweetness on the desert air shares its futility with the man with a fine brain who cannot give adequate voice to his thoughts. He is truly an intellectual cripple. Indeed, words being the keys to thought as well as the medium for precise expression, the man without a command of them handicaps his own basic thinking; tragically, he is also unable to reach the minds of others. Regretfully, I speak with some personal experience. I wrote my grandson, a freshman at college, that the acquisition of an education in any discipline depends on an understanding and use of words, spoken and written.

How is a more intriguing, colorful, and effective use of words acquired? I can say with certainty only what has proven useful and helpful to me: reading, writing, and meaningful and stimulating conversations.

Once what is to be said is known approximately, the ability to speak well, or at the very least more effectively, is gained by practice in talking aloud and by repeated rehearsals. A complete failure as a public speaker once subjected himself to a long and rigorous training to correct his weakness. He walked along the beaches, shouting sentences to overcome the crash of breaking waves and to gain a voice and ease of manner that made him the greatest of Greek orators, Demosthenes. Remember those days on the debating team at old Miami?

The parallel thought comes that there is danger in quickly concluding that a man who does not initially say anything during group discussions has nothing to offer. He may be a not unusual type with a fine analytical mind and great oratorical ability. He is self-disciplined. He refrains from offering much more than smiling nods and a few unintelligible grunts during group discussions until almost everyone else has talked. He silently absorbs all that is said, weighing all pros and cons, and then, without being argumentative, says succinctly and clearly what he thinks, covering the field. This man usually becomes the successful dean of his college, president of the company, chairman of the board. Certainly, words facilitate the expression of the well-honed intellect.

❖ ❖ ❖

Twists and turns . . . this morning's path has as many twists and turns as life itself. Where does it lead up this valley-bordering canyon? To a mountain top or a dead end? I am reminded of the twists and turns in the lives of two of my classmates.

Lyman Lemnitzer and Abe Lystad were two members of my class of 1920 at West Point. The upperclassmen told Lemnitzer in his plebe year to resign. "Mr. Dumguard," they said, "get going! You'll never make an Army officer." Lem fooled the yearling wise men. He went on to give his country distinguished service, both on and off the battlefield, and established a remarkable record as Army Chief of Staff.

Abe Lystad was our class president, a leader from whom much was expected. He had great pride in doing well, of being best, and who can be faulted for that? But Abe's pride in accomplishment became so great that, when he failed to be the best in his select group at Fort Leavenworth Staff and Command School, the disappointment consumed him. At least, some of the less gifted plodders thought so when he used his own .45 to destroy himself. Will we ever know the real answer? Can we know what twists and turns lead to such an end?

❖ ❖ ❖

Today's paper states that 64 per cent of Americans favor a year's compulsory national service for all young men. Was I ahead of the time when I visited with President Eisenhower in the White House and told him that all young Americans should be required to give service to the nation? He asked me, "How?" I gave him my proposal for universal service. It consisted of these essential requirements: (1) All youths after graduating from high school or, if not, by the age of 18 should be required to serve. (2) No exemptions, except for extreme medical reason, should be allowed. (3) The period of service should be from May until October, approximately six months, and the trainees should be confined to regional camps. (4) No visitors to be allowed for at least six weeks, and no leaves of absence to be granted except for family emergency. (5) Service to be without pay. (6) Instructors to be selected from high school teachers, coaches, Army, and other service officers. (7) Instruction should be mental and physical, with emphasis on dedication to country.

In essence, this was the plan. The President asked me to submit a detailed paper. This I did. The paper was given high marks by the President and passed on to the department of Health, Education, and Welfare, where it must have run afoul of a paper shredder. Later I suggested the plan to several Congressmen. They thought it was a great idea, "but if we want to be re-elected, forget it." Twenty years later the Gallup Poll states, "Americans support a year's compulsory national service for all young men." The idea is too good; I shall never see it implemented.

❖ ❖ ❖

Oh, no, don't tell me that Dartmouth has gone co-ed; why does the Big Green always ape Yale and Princeton? Could West Point be headed in the same direction? It's difficult for me to see my old "M" Company with cadets and Ms. cadets. "Ms. Dumguard, brace yourself—suck up your gut!" And yet it is not impossible; already some Congressmen have asked for the appointment of girls to the service academies. In the name of all the memories roused by Flirtation Walk and Benny Havens, let the darlings storm the gates on weekends, but why make them full-time boarders? Why all the fuss about women's liberation, anyway? I have yet to know a really winning "libber" who would not be more attractive rearing a closely knit family instead of espousing such a cause. A close look at the liberated Communist Chinese and Russian women should reduce the frantic cries for liberation and equality.

※ ※ ※

Why have I lived in the shadow of such words as "austere" and "aloof" most of my life? They have been used so often in public print to describe me that now they jump off a page at me. I've been conditioned, somewhat like Pavlov's laboratory animals, to see them. Are austerity and aloofness truly my dominant characteristics?

Neither word is entirely incorrect. I have always been abstemious, and my eating habits have been quite temperate. That combination well may be considered austerity in some circles. Also, I shun the ballroom floor. I have two left feet. If that gives me an aura of standing apart, rather than being somewhat dignified, then I have been aloof. It must be added, however, that this did not leave me entirely unsympathetic, which is supposedly a part of being aloof.

How are public criticisms to be valued? In 1940 a one-time Dartmouth football star and then noted Boston sports columnist, Bill Cunningham, openly boosted Boston College's Frank Leahy to succeed me at Hanover. Tuss McLaughry, Brown's talented coach, was appointed. Cunningham thought I had nominated my own successor and, displeased, dissected me. His Boston *Herald* announced to all who might read in New England that the man Army was recalling from Dartmouth was, on his more attractive side, cold, austere, difficult, aloof, brusque, and a prudish teetotaler. That description was so foreign to my image of myself that I sent Cunningham a telegram: "Dear Bill; I don't know the Red Blaik you wrote about. Do you?" The message must have caught the former star lineman in an upright defensive stance and knocked him back a few yards. Within a week he not only published my telegram, but coupled it with words of high praise for that same Red Blaik! A puzzling, most un-Cunninghamlike counterplay.

The shadow persists today; it even darkens. Although I have naturally received little attention from the sports fraternity for years, I recently read a comment in Howard Cosell's Book: "Blaik has been pictured by many as a martinet, a dictator and tyrant, unapproachable and cold." Ordinarily, that demeaning characterization would be pretty strong medicine for a Scotsman to take, but this overkill made me laugh heartily.

Merle thinks the austere-aloof-whatnot shadow has been cast primarily because I did not drink, yet associated freely with those who did. Maybe so. But how could I have done otherwise? For the benefit of all concerned, someone through the years had to steer many pals away from incipient trouble, guide them past open manholes while crossing streets, get them through the gate guard without a call for the corporal and, yes, put them to bed. And who better than their ol' frien', good'n sober, good ol' Red? He did not ask for the assignment. It simply happened that way on occasion. I fear it's too late to change a 50-year-old image now, although let it be known that I do pet stray dogs.

Reflecting on Cunningham and my roles at West Point and Dartmouth brings up memories of football, which occupied so great a part of my existence. A long life has allowed me the satisfaction of following the careers of those who played on my squads. Although the scoreboard was once the major barometer, now the later accomplishments of my old players give me a satisfaction greater than the memory of their feats on the gridiron. The "Blaik Boys," at times derided, have exceeded even my high expectations of them. Well over 30 fought bravely to the end in battles that foreclosed their futures. I remember them with special affection.

Hundreds followed the professions, business, and teaching to become noted surgeons, doctors, astronauts, headmasters, farmers, Congressmen, politicians, writers, corporate heads, soldiers, generals, preachers, publishers, geologists, and good solid family citizens. Most of them are married, a few are divorced, many have sons, and some have grandsons who have played sports in the image of their fathers. Most started from scratch—several became enormously rich in material wealth, others equally rich in their family lives. No man can buy my satisfaction; it has been a colorful parade, and it gives me unmeasured pleasure to have coached these young men.

You ask me who was the best back I ever coached? You have forgotten? Of course, it was 30 years ago. It was Blanchard–Davis, Mr. Inside and Mr. Outside.

⚜ ⚜ ⚜

The National Collegiate Athletic Association has been a burr in my thinking since the time it had the temerity to challenge the Military Academy's policy of offering special academic preparation to athletes to improve their ability to meet West Point's entrance requirements.

Then, as now, the N.C.A.A., strutted importantly. I recall the time that West Point was summoned to appear before the N.C.A.A. faculty board meeting in Chicago. Strengthened by the instructions of the Academy Athletic Board not to yield, I appeared before the faculty representatives then dominated by the Big Ten. It was at the time when Walter Byers, the executive head of the N.C.A.A., was feeling his importance as college football T.V. money gave the N.C.A.A. great influence. The faculty body was not concerned then, nor it is now, about the scholastic excellence of athletes; it was interested only in the politics of control.

After some heated discussion, I stated that the Military Academy would not lower the entrance requirements for a football player and that we would continue to help prospective athletes who were willing to take the more difficult course to an education. We were willing to withdraw from the N.C.A.A. rather than accept a veto of our policy, and it seemed to me that the public would be reluctant to support a faculty committee decision that favored junior college entrance requirements for West Point.

This ended our minor confrontation; it is interesting to note that the faculty representatives who are the N.C.A.A. governing board have never faced the basic problem: far too many athletes do not have the academic credentials to be in college.

⚜ ⚜ ⚜

What was my most satisfying accomplishment as a coach? Two similar experiences come quickly to mind: taking over a Dartmouth and, later, a West Point squad when neither had won a major game in two years and quickly producing 180-degree turnabouts. Dartmouth won its league championship three years later, and after three seasons Army was named national champion.

Neither, however, provided my greatest coaching satisfaction. That came from taking Army's 1951 junior varsity so far so fast that two seasons later I watched them beat a strong Navy team 20-7 and take home the 1953 Lambert Trophy, emblematic of the eastern championship.

Yet, at both Dartmouth and West Point I heard the academic purists say, "We should not win so much!"

❖ ❖ ❖

We went by special train to Ithaca, where the Cadets beat a strong Cornell team to give me my 100th victory. About midnight the squad slowly gathered on the sleepers as their unrelaxed coach greeted them wit hthe enthusiasm reserved for a victorious team.

The train was delayed in moving out, and I soon learned that two important players were unaccounted for. My anxiety was confirmed when belatedly they poured our heroes on the sleeper; they had celebrated the Army victory with the Phi Gams in a thoroughly liberal arts fashion. How unreasonable can a coach be? On Sunday, I told our wayfarers they were on the "B" squad and would not play in the Navy game. No announcement was made to the squad, the press, or the Corps, although the "B" squad on Monday claimed two varsity players.

The parents of one cadet had come from the West Coast to see their only offspring play against the Navy. On learning that his son had been demoted, the father became so desperate that on his last approach to me he asked my price for letting his son play. My only possible reply was, "Come next year, and you'll see him." The following season he was a standout in the Navy game, which the Cadets won 38-0.

The next June after graduation exercises a handsome officer proud in his new uniform came into my office. Before I could congratulate him, he broke into tears and haltingly said, "I didn't come to say good-bye, but to thank you for kicking me off the team. It was the best thing that ever happened to me." Today as I look at his combat record as a career Air Force Colonel, I could not be more proud. "Abe, perhaps I was a heel—you never were."

❖ ❖ ❖

The disastrous record of Army's 1973 team reminds me of the correctness of MacArthur's statement that it would take 20 years or more for the Army to recover from '51. Aside from the 1958 and 1953 seasons, when the cadets ranked nationally third and seventh, the Army record has been spotty.

In 1958 the Superintendent, General Davidson, himself an ex-Army coach, took full charge of West Point sports by initiating the doctrine of equality for all teams. This meant the downgrading of football and the elevation of squash, soccer, and other sports to a parity with the primary sport. With an engineer's precision he spent days working on the football schedule, rating possible Army opponents into three groups according to his view of their strength in competition with the Cadets. He divided the teams into A, B, & C, groups, failing to comprehend that C today could be A or B tomorrow. The 1973 schedule would be rated as 4 A's, 2 B's, and 4 C's as opponents, with all of the A teams being played by the end of October.

As a rule, the difference between a win or loss in football is a thin line, more often than not predicated on the psychological lift given to and reflected by the team. Unfortunately, the Davidson legacy to Army football lowered the importance of the game to the Cadets, a feeling reflected by players. The Corps has been imbued with a form of self-pity, excuses for losses, and a belief that Army can no longer compete with major teams. There is a depression from which the Corps has been unable to rally, try as it may. Many West Point graduates yearn to court and play the Ivy League, not realizing that success would not greatly improve matters and the chagrin of losing be far greater.

Before a resolution of the problems of Army football is possible, the root of the trouble must be understood. The assumption that the Corps as a whole is vitally concerned about football is incorrect; many cadets could not care less. The constant grind of Cadet life takes a heavy toll, and few realize that the load becomes nearly unbearable to the football player already burdened by a demanding academic and training schedule. There are many officers, some stationed at West Point, who believe that the game is a tumor in the Corps. Too many officers do not believe in the MacArthur saying, "There is no substitute for victory." To them this dictum is as outmoded in West Point football as it is in the thinking of some professional leaders of our Army.

A special committee of civilians was appointed by the Chief of Staff, General Westmoreland, to study Corps athletics, particularly football. It was a useless venture, as the committee understood little of the problems of Academy varsity teams.

Football at West Point is still salvagable, can be a tremendous rallying force for the Corps and service, and can be successful despite the difficulties that are little different today than yesterday, but it will require a complete reappraisal of the factors by which success may be achieved. The first question to be resolved is, "Do the Corps and graduates want major football?" If the answer is an affirmative one, then the Secretary of the Army, himself a West Pointer, should take the initiative to restore Army football to a respected position, all within the framework of the high standards of the Academy. Difficult though it may be, it is not impossible.

※ ※ ※

It is not unusual for a head coach to become a school's director of athletics. But why does his successor discover almost immediately that the new director has assumed a wide stance and is most difficult to move in any direction that could help the new coach?

Who was the better Notre Dame Coach, Knute Rockne or Frank Leahy? I knew both men well. Leahy was the better coach, but would most probably lose the contest because Rock would have gathered the better squad. Rockne was a supersalesman.

※ ※ ※

Now, looking back a bit and then as far ahead on the trail as I can see, I worry about my grandchildren and their contemporaries, wonderful as the young always are as children. Are they not being short-changed?

Certainly, they are not exposed to the more difficult days of their fathers. They know nothing of the testing, teaching hard times my father knew, coming across the Atlantic alone at 16 after earning and saving the pitifully small sum that paid his passage.

No one I know wants today's children to duplicate such experiences; quite the contrary. Would they not be better off, however, if they had to earn for themselves many of the things they are now given and take for granted as their just due?

How will today's youths react when banged about in the adult game of life if they have not been toughened mentally by the knowledge that "you have to pay the price" for what you get, sooner or later and one way or another? No one, not even a Frank Merriwell, ever ventured onto a big game field after long enjoying a soft spectator seat without having the whey knocked out of him. It is all too evident that such a destiny is encountered all too often by too many of yesterday's children of both sexes. I do not want one like it for my grandchildren and their friends of the same age.

The answer? The only one that appears effective to me is a complete revision of our archaic elementary school systems. Today's children should be trained to handle the problems of today and tomorrow, not those of yesterday and ages past. The word discipline should be understood and upgraded. This is a community task. The controlling position of the home, even when parents know what they are doing, is becoming completely untenable for more reasons than one, and not the least of these are television and the permissiveness of the elementary schools.

※ ※ ※

For some reason the old man I often pass on my morning walk was less sprightly. His head was lowered, and his eyes seemed to follow a lonely trail.

"What's on your mind this beautiful morning?" I asked.

"Thinking and confused about the low estate of affairs in our great country. As of today, I wonder how the younger generations can be trained to cope with the modern world, the vagaries of our vacillating system, and understand the stop-gap policies of a government which seems to have lost control of many facets of our economy? What are the chances that our democratic government as we have known it will survive into the time of our grandchildren?

"Your pessissism darkens the day," I replied.

"Perhaps; but how does one impress a new generation with a regard for the traditional virtues? How are our grandchildren to maintain the spirit of self-reliance once traditional in this country when government bureaucracy intervenes in every area of their lives? And are the huge corporations any less bureaucratic? Is it any wonder that the younger generations lose hope of personal accomplishment and become impressed with the cradle-to the grave philosophy directed by a government which they expect to solve their social and economic problems? Are they aware that their false sense of security is purchased only at a ruinous cost in taxation? Do they realize that all taxes, Federal and State, now begin to take nearly half of the average income? Is there any limit to taxation? The attempt of Governor Reagan of California to put a ceiling on state taxes by constitutional proviso was defeated by civil servants and bureaucrats who combined with the many lawyers in the California legislature to defeat the Reagan proviso, knowing well that they carefully had set up generous pension plans for their own later years. At what point in history will democracy face a revolutionary change —a dictator—a military take-over?

"My friend, you must be kidding—don't you realize the sun still shines?"

※ ※ ※

Lawyers, lawyers everywhere: should they depart Washington, it would be a ghost town. But have they enriched this country with their efforts and leadership?

By some insidious process lawyers have crept into almost every level of our lives to make themselves indispensable. Masters of the art of misdirection and confusion, their jargon and rituals have repeatedly displaced the authority of common sense and equitable decency.

In every hamlet, city and county, in every one of our 50 supposedly sovereign states, and all through the overriding Federal structure, whenever a bureau, board, committee, commission or legislative group issues a decree to guide and regulate our actions, who decides the final form? Lawyers! And 99.44 per cent of the time they leave in doubt what is actually meant, thus ensuring the employment of many other lawyers to interpret what is written law. Did you ever know a lawyer to form a simple declarative sentence?

Who endorses and perpetuates these barristers? Judges. Who? You know, former lawyers who are retired to positions of awesome power. They judge. Everything. They are the high priests and guardians of the Lawyers Protective Agency, more concerned with the sanctity of procedure than with facts. Thus, a simple trial for murder in California consumes 18 months and costs several million of taxpayers money. This hill is a tough climb this morning!

❧ ❧ ❧

Twists and Turns. It was 1922; I was an officer of the 8th Cavalry stationed at Fort Bliss, Texas. There were only 13,000 officers in the U.S. Army and Congress, totally complacent, reduced funds to limit the number to 9000. It also financially rewarded regular soldiers to resign in order further to reduce our enlisted forces to about 100,000.

World War I was forgotten. President Wilson had declaimed we had fought that war to end all wars. Since then we have fought three major wars, two of which were less than stalemates.

We were instrumental in the destruction of the power of Kaiser Wilhelm and a Hitler. In their place we have erected a still greater threat to world peace by being outwitted by the now colossus of the West, Russia. Are we now about to raise China to a pinnacle of power, hopefully determined that their conflicting interests will limit our exposure?

Do we believe peace has been achieved in Korea, or do we realize that the failure to allow MacArthur to drive through to victory created a stalemate tenuously supported today by thousands of American soldiers in Korea?

Do we for one moment believe we have brought the Vietnamese war to a final conclusion?

Do we realize that the inability of the United States, in all its might and power, to prevail in the Asian misadventures can be attributed to a combination of Chinese manpower and Russian arms abetted by our own inept decisions?

Just how valid then is the Kissinger détente with Russia and China, inwardly disposed as they are to gloat over our dissipation of billions of dollars and countless casualties in Asian wars that shredded our fibre?

Détente is emotionally comforting and prayerfully sought if it does not lull our country into dropping its guard. I am again reminded of 1922; how does our presently depleted volunteer army measure up to those professional forces of Russia and China?

Why are the voices of Congress stentorian on Watergate and muted on preparedness? There is no answer, though assuredly a casually prepared America could cost our great country its freedom.

It's been a long day—few recall 1922.

※ ※ ※

MacArthur, in my opinion our greatest soldier, stood almost alone in his determination to save his country from its Far East blunders. Is it bias to suggest that the General was sacked because the thoughtless politicians and envious high officers within the services subtly worked on President Truman? Was MacArthur prescient or simply a first-rate intelligence making logical, unemotional deductions from facts when he expressed his views? In 1951 he told me: "Russia is moving to the right, and our great country is in retreat to the left. The day may not be too far away when the two will pass; then Russia will succeed in making this the country that was."

I wonder what MacArthur would say to-day about the strange turns our diplomatic maneuvers have taken? Would he applaud our present Secretary of State, bouncing about the globe supposedly in great achievement? How would the General regard the notorious wheat deal of 1973, when the fork-tongued Russians sang us a sad song of crop failures and potential starvation of their people? Would MacArthur have approved of government loans to Russia to finance these purchases that drained our supply and at the time allowed the department of agriculture to pay support subsidies to grain dealers?

The sale caused prices of our daily foodstuffs to rise in leaps worthy of an Irish hunter, and housewives rebelled. Then, lo and behold! Russian ships are reportedly seen unloading wheat at Turkish ports at a price several hundred per cent higher than our prices to the starving Russians. Would not MacArthur have very quickly perceived that the wheat deal was prearranged and was the price we paid to Russia to persuade North Vietnam to cease overt aggression and force her to the peace table?

Finally, would MacArthur have been lulled into a false reliance on Russia's sudden friendship and been surprised by the Arab attack on Israel in October 1973? Would MacArthur fatuously have assumed that Russia would no longer use the Near East crisis to further her ends, would not inspire confrontation, and would warn and join us in a strenuous effort to suppress it? Would the General not have seen that the denial of oil to England and Germany was fomented to drive a wedge between us and our allies?

The life of a nation is replete with twists and turns. Russia soon may rule the Mediterranean, control the Suez Canal, and sail with freedom into the Indian Ocean. In 1952 General MacArthur begged his military comrade to have the showdown with Russia. "Ike, this is the last time I shall call you Ike. Here after you will be Mr. President. You have the opportunity to be the greatest man since Jesus Christ, as only you can dictate peace for the world. I beg of you to take the initiative with bold action." There was no action.

The stage was thus set for us again to test the quicksands of Asia, while a wily Russia, infinitely stronger, encouraged the bloodletting of America, knowing full well that, as in Korea, we had lost our zest for victory. Twists and turns—are we stumbling?

⚜ ⚜ ⚜

Yes, our children and grandchildren will face problems that their parents and grandparents, in default of their ability to solve them, have necessarily learned to live with. I doubt not that many of them will be capable bearers of the torch that falls from our hands, even though many, believing in the futility of achieving the good life in this swirling world of destruction, have refused to participate—a trend that I am sure will be rectified with their emerging maturity. If the world sometimes seems dark, they should know that a smile will brighten the day.

Actuaries may state it has been a long day, but my walk of twists and turns has been all too short. As the sun sinks in the west, the desert quail slowly go to rest; soon they will be replaced by the creatures of the night, scurrying about their business and carrying on the stream of life without regard to the never-ending search for peace by their human counterparts. I shall return to the beauty and the inspiration of the desert tomorrow—and tomorrow—and perhaps tomorrow.

Appendices

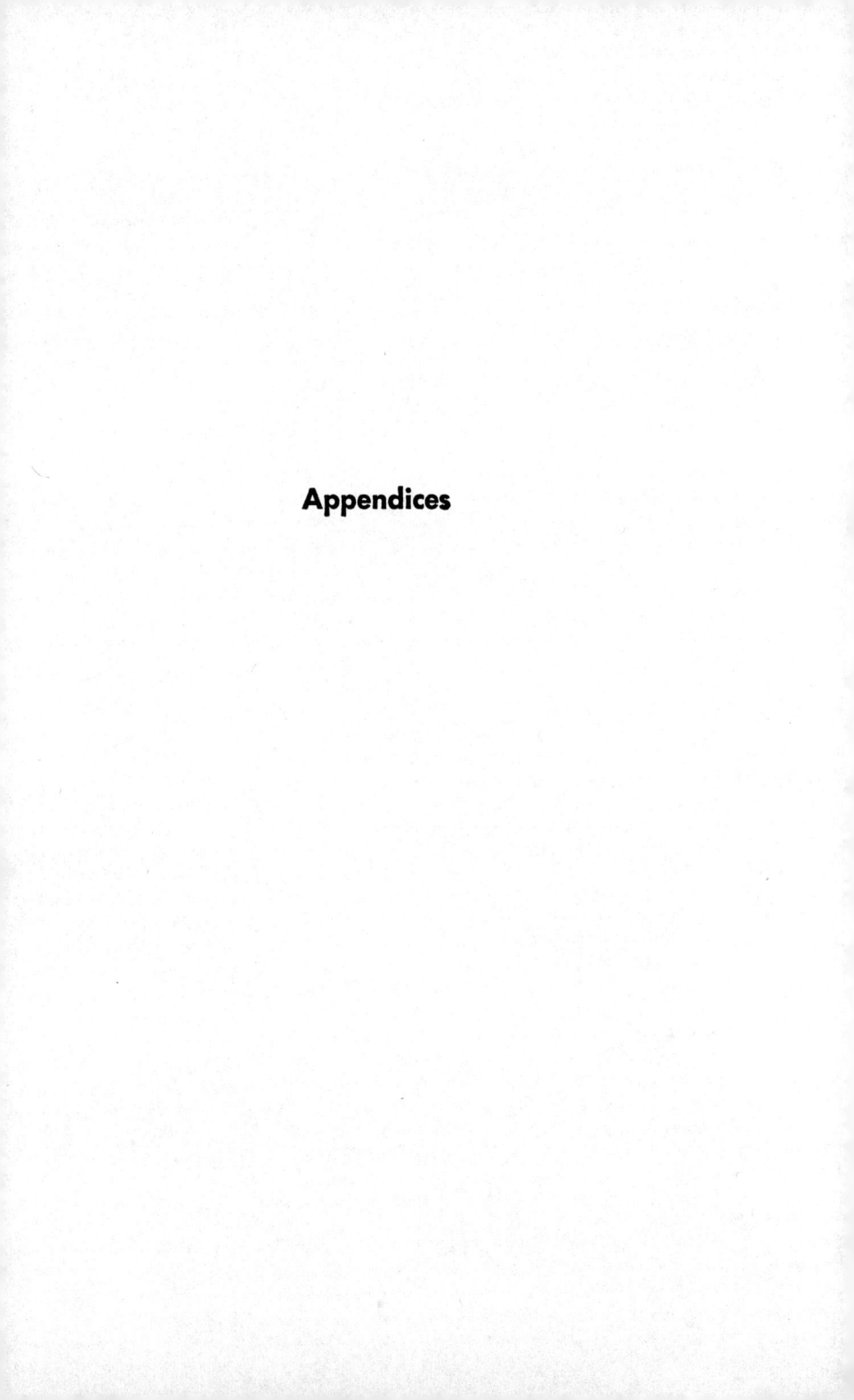

Appendix I

Annual Game Records

From 1927 through 1933 Earl H. Blaik was assistant coach at West Point; from 1933 through 1940 head coach at Dartmouth; from 1941 through 1958 head coach at West Point.

Army		Opponent
	1927	
13	Boston U.	0
6	Detroit	0
21	Marquette	12
27	Davis & Elkins	6
6	Yale	10
34	Bucknell	0
45	Franklin & Marshall	0
18	Notre Dame	0
13	Ursinus	0
14	Navy	9
	1928	
35	Boston U.	0
14	S. Meth.	13
44	Providence	0
15	Harvard	0
18	Yale	6
38	De Pauw	12
6	Notre Dame	12
32	Carleton	7
13	Nebraska	3
0	Stanford	26
	1929	
26	Boston U.	0
33	Gettysburg	7
23	Davidson	7
20	Harvard	20
13	Yale	21
33	S. Dakota	6
7	Illinois	17
89	Dickinson	7
19	Ohio Wesleyan	6
0	Notre Dame	7
13	Stanford	34
	1930	
39	Boston U.	0
54	Furman	0
39	Swarthmore	0
6	Harvard	0
7	Yale	7
33	North Dakota	6
13	Illinois	0
47	Kentucky Wesleyan	2
18	Ursinus	0
6	Notre Dame	7
6	Navy	0
	1931	
60	Ohio Northern	0
67	Knox College	6
20	Michigan State	7
13	Harvard	14
6	Yale	6
27	Colorado Coll.	0
20	LSU	0
0	Pittsburgh	26
54	Ursinus	0
12	Notre Dame	0
17	Navy	7
	1932	
13	Furman U.	0
57	Carleton	0
13	Pittsburgh	18
20	Yale	0
33	William & Mary	0

Army		Opponent
46	Harvard	0
52	N. Dakota State	0
7	W. Va. Wesleyan	0
0	Notre Dame	21
20	Navy	0

1933

19	Mercer	6
32	VMI	0
52	Delaware	0
6	Illinois	0
21	Yale	0
34	Coe College	0
27	Harvard	0
12	Pa. Mil. Coll.	0
12	Navy	7
12	Notre Dame	13

Dartmouth		Opponent

1934

39	Norwich	0
32	Vermont	0
27	Maine	0
27	Virginia	0
10	Harvard	0
2	Yale	7
21	New Hampshire	7
6	Cornell	21
13	Princeton	38

1935

39	Norwich	0
47	Vermont	0
59	Bates	7
41	Brown	0
14	Harvard	6
14	Yale	6
34	William & Mary	0
41	Cornell	6
6	Princeton	26
7	Columbia	13

1936

58	Norwich	0
56	Vermont	0
0	Holy Cross	7
34	Brown	0
26	Harvard	7
11	Yale	7
20	Columbia	13
20	Cornell	6
13	Princeton	13

Ivy League Champions

1937

39	Bates	0
31	Amherst	7
42	Springfield	0
41	Brown	0
20	Harvard	2
9	Yale	9
33	Princeton	9
6	Cornell	6
27	Columbia	0

Ivy League Champions
Ranked No. 7 nationally

1938

46	Bates	0
51	St. Lawrence	0
22	Princeton	0
34	Brown	13
13	Harvard	7
24	Yale	6
44	Dickinson	6
7	Cornell	14
13	Stanford	23

1939

41	St. Lawrence	9
34	Hamp. Syd.	6
0	Navy	0
14	Lafayette	0
16	Harvard	0
33	Yale	0
7	Princeton	9
6	Cornell	35
3	Stanford	14

1940

35	St. Lawrence	0
21	Frank & Marsh	23
6	Columbia	20
7	Yale	13
7	Harvard	6
26	Sewanee	0
9	Princeton	14
3	Cornell	0
20	Brown	6

Army		Opponent

1941

19	Citadel	6

Army		Opponent			
27	VMI	20	48	Notre Dame	0
20	Yale	7	61	Pennsylvania	0
13	Columbia	0	32	Navy	13
0	Notre Dame	0	*National Champions*		
6	Harvard	20			
7	Pennsylvania	14	**1946**		
7	West Virginia	6	35	Villanova	0
6	Navy	14	21	Oklahoma U.	7
			46	Cornell	21
			20	Michigan	13
1942			48	Columbia	14
14	Lafayette	0	19	Duke	0
28	Cornell	8	19	West Virginia	0
34	Columbia	6	0	Notre Dame	0
14	Harvard	0	34	Pennsylvania	7
0	Pennsylvania	19	21	Navy	18
0	Notre Dame	13	*Eastern Champions*		
19	VPI	7	*Ranked No. 2 nationally*		
40	Princeton	7	*Blaik chosen Coach of the Year by the*		
0	Navy	14	*Football Coaches Association of America*		
1943			**1947**		
27	Villanova	0			
42	Colgate	0	13	Villanova	0
51	Temple	0	47	Colorado U.	0
52	Columbia	0	0	Illinois	0
39	Yale	7	40	VPI	0
13	Pennsylvania	13	20	Columbia	21
0	Notre Dame	26	65	Washington & Lee	13
16	USNTS Sampson	7	7	Notre Dame	27
59	Brown	0	7	Pennsylvania	7
0	Navy	13	21	Navy	0
1944			**1948**		
46	North Carolina	0	28	Villanova	0
59	Brown	7	54	Lafayette	7
69	Pittsburgh	7	26	Illinois	21
76	Coast Guard Acad.	0	20	Harvard	7
27	Duke	7	27	Cornell	6
83	Villanova	0	49	VPI	7
59	Notre Dame	0	43	Stanford	0
62	Penn	7	26	Pennsylvania	20
23	Navy	7	21	Navy	21
National Champions			*Ranked No. 6 nationally*		
1945			**1949**		
32	PDC AAF, Louisville, Ky.	0	47	Davidson	7
54	Wake Forest	0	42	Penn State	7
28	Michigan	7	21	Michigan	7
55	MTBS, Melv'e, RI	13	54	Harvard	14
48	Duke	13	63	Columbia	6
54	Villanova	0	40	VMI	14

Army		Opponent
35	Fordham	0
14	Pennsylvania	13
38	Navy	0

Eastern Champions
Ranked No. 4 nationally

1950

28	Colgate	0
41	Penn State	7
27	Michigan	6
49	Harvard	0
34	Columbia	0
28	Pennsylvania	13
51	New Mexico	0
7	Stanford	0
2	Navy	14

Ranked No. 2 nationally

1951

7	Villanova	21
14	Northwestern	20
14	Dartmouth	28
21	Harvard	22
14	Columbia	9
6	So. Calif.	28
27	Citadel	6
6	Penn	7
7	Navy	42

1952

28	South Carolina	7
0	Southern Cal	22
37	Dartmouth	7
14	Pittsburgh	22
14	Columbia	14
42	VMI	14
6	Georgia Tech	45
14	Penn	13
0	Navy	7

1953

41	Furman	0
20	Northwestern	33
27	Dartmouth	0
14	Duke	13
40	Columbia	7
0	Tulane	0
27	North Car. State	7
21	Penn	14
20	Navy	7

Eastern Champions

Blaik chosen Coach of the Year by the Touchdown Club of Washington, D.C.

1954

20	South Carolina	34
26	Michigan	7
60	Dartmouth	6
28	Duke	14
67	Columbia	12
21	Virginia	20
48	Yale	7
35	Penn	0
20	Navy	27

Ranked No. 7 nationally

1955

81	Furman	0
35	Penn State	6
2	Michigan	26
0	Syracuse	13
45	Columbia	0
27	Colgate	7
12	Yale	14
40	Penn	0
14	Navy	6

1956

32	VMI	12
14	Penn State	7
14	Michigan	48
0	Syracuse	7
60	Columbia	0
55	Colgate	46
34	William & Mary	6
7	Pittsburgh	20
7	Navy	7

1957

42	Nebraska	0
27	Penn State	13
21	Notre Dame	23
29	Pittsburgh	13
20	Virginia	12
53	Colgate	7
39	Utah	33
20	Tulane	14
0	Navy	14

1958

45	South Carolina	8
26	Penn State	0

Army		Opponent		
14	Notre Dame	2	14	Rice
35	Virginia	6	26	Villanova
14	Pittsburgh	14	22	Navy
68	Colgate	6	*Eastern Champions*
			Ranked No. 3 nationally

		7
		0
		6

Overall Dartmouth record, 1934 through 1940:
    Won   45
    Lost   15
    Tied   4
    Percentage .750

Overall Army record, 1941 through 1958:
    Won   121
    Lost   32   (11 lost in 1951–1952)
    Tied   10
    Percentage .790

Overall totals, Blaik teams, 1934 through 1958:
    Won   166
    Lost   47   (11 lost in 1951–1952)
    Tied   14
    Percentage .784
    43 first team All-America players

Appendix II

Varsity coaching staffs, West Point, 1927 through 1933

Blaik, Earl H., Assistant Coach, 1927–1933
Born, Lt. Charles F., 1928–1932
Bryan, Lt. Blackshear M., 1927, 1928, 1929
Daly, Lt. Maurice F., 1929, 1931, 1932, 1933
Davidson, Lt. Garrison H., Head Coach, 1933
Ellinger, Harry O., 1929–1933
Farwick, Lt. August W., 1927
Hahn, Lt. Cornman L., 1927, 1928
Harding, Lt. Neil B., 1929
Hewitt, Lt. Orville M., 1927
Johnson, Lt. Edwin L., 1927
Jones, Capt. Lawrence McC., Head Coach, 1927 1928, 1929
Novak, Leo, 1927
Reeder, Lt. Russell P., Jr., 1933
Sasse, Capt. Ralph I., 1927–1929; Head Coach, 1930–1932
Stokes, Lt. John H., Jr., 1927–1930
Trice, Lt. Harley N., 1933
Wicks, Lt. Roger M., 1927, 1928
Wilson, Lt. Harry E., 1930, 1931
Wood, Lt. William H., 1927, 1928, 1932, 1933

Assistant Varsity Coaches, Dartmouth, 1934 through 1940

Chamberlain, Edward T., 1936–1940
Daniell, Averell E., 1939, 1940
Donchess, Joseph C., 1934, 1935, 1936
Ellinger, Harry O., 1934–1940
Gustafson, Andrew F., 1934–1940
Handrahan, Joseph W., 1939, 1940
Hirshberg, Edward J., 1937, 1938, 1939
Holbrook, Caryl F., 1934, 1935
Moore, Frank E., 1940

Assistant Varsity Coaches, West Point, 1941 through 1958

Amen, Paul J., 1947–1955
Antaya, Roger A., 1955, 1956
Blackburn, George E., 1954
Boston, Clarence E., 1948
Buckler, Jack, 1943
Crowder, Edwin B., 1955
Daniell, Averill E., 1941, 1942
Dietzel, Paul F., 1953, 1954
Dobbs, Robert L., 1953, 1954
Ellinger, Harry O., 1941
Gillman, Sidney, 1948
Gottfried, Charles E., 1957, 1958
Green, John F., 1947, 1948, 1950, 1951, 1952
Gunlock, William L., 1958
Gustafson, Andrew F., 1941–1947
Hall, Dale S., 1956, 1957, 1958
Harp, Thomas M., 1956, 1957, 1958
Hickman, Herman, 1943–1947
Hinkle, Carl C., Jr., 1945
Holcomb, Stuart K., 1944, 1945, 1946
Jablonsky, Harvey J., 1946
Kenna, E. Douglas Jr., 1949–1952
Laslie, Carney G., 1952–1956
Lauterbur, Frank X., 1957, 1958
Lombardi, Vincent T., 1949–1953
Moore, Frank E., 1941, 1942, 1943
Oldershaw, Douglas, 1942
St. Onge, Robert J., 1948, 1951
Sauer, John E., 1947, 1948, 1949
Voris, Richard, 1955, 1956, 1957
Warmath, Murray, 1949, 1950, 1951
Woodruff, George R., 1944, 1945

Appendix III

Army Lettermen, 1927 Through 1933

(*The figure in parenthesis indicates selection to 1st, 2nd, or 3rd All-America team during Coach Blaik's years*)

Allan, Charles C. W., 1928
Armstrong, John G., 1930, 1932
Beall, John A., Jr., 1933
Born, Charles F., 1927 (1)
Bowman, Wendell W., 1929, 1930
Brentnall, Samuel R., 1927
Brown, Travis T., 1931, 1932
Buckler, Jack M., 1932, 1933 (1)
Bucknam, Ralph E., Jr., 1932, 1933 (2)
Burlingame, Paul, 1930, 1932, 1933
Cagle, Christian K., 1927 (1), 1928 (1), 1929 (Captain) (1)
Carlmark, Carl W., 1928, 1929, 1930 (2)
Carroll, Paul T., 1932 (Team Manager)
Carver, Robert L., 1929, 1930, 1931
DeLany, Nelson J., 1927 (Team Manager)
Dibb, John, 1928
Edwards, Norman B., 1932, 1933
Elias, Paul, 1927
Elliott, Roland A., Jr., 1932
Evans, Roy T., Jr., 1930, 1931 (1), 1932
Fields, Kenneth E., 1930, 1931, 1932 (2)
Fletcher, George E., 1929
Frentzel, William Y., 1930, 1932
Gibner, Herbert C., 1927, 1928, 1929
Glattly, James E., 1929, 1930
Gooch, Stacy W., 1932, 1933
Hall, William E., 1927, 1928
Hammack, Louis A., 1927, 1928
Harbold, Norris B., 1927
Hays, George R., 1928 (Team Manager)
Herb, Edward G., 1930, 1931
Hillberg, Lauri J., 1931
Hillsinger, Loren B., 1929
Humber, Charles I., Jr., 1928, 1929 (3), 1930 (Captain) (2)
Hutchinson, Richard C., 1927, 1928, 1929
Hutchison, John M., 1932, 1933
Jablonsky, Harvey J., 1931, 1932, 1933 (Captain) (1)
Johnson, Paul E., Jr., 1932, 1933 (2)
Jones, Samuel E., 1929 (Team Manager)
Kenny, Eugene A., 1928
Kilday, Thomas T., 1930, 1931, 1932 (1)
King, Richard T., Jr., 1930, 1931, 1932 (2)
Kopcsak, Peter J., 1931, 1932, 1933
Lankenau, Norman H., 1931
Lawlor, John D., 1932
Lazar, Aaron M., 1929, 1930
Legg, Richard A., 1933
Lincoln, Lawrence J., 1931, 1932
Lynch, Thomas R., 1928
MacLean, Allan D., 1929
MacWilliam, Joseph L., 1930, 1932
Malloy, John T., 1929, 1930
Martz, William V., 1933
Maxwell, Winston R., 1928
McConnell, John P., 1931 (Team Manager)
Meehan, Arthur W., 1927
Messinger, Edwin J., 1928 (2), 1929 (3), 1930
Miller, Carl W., 1933
Miller, Paul G., 1929, 1930
Murrell, John H., 1927, 1928, 1929
Nave, William L., 1927, 1928
Nazarro, Joseph J., 1933
O'Keefe, Richard J., 1928, 1929
Parham, William L., 1928
Pearson, Howard E., 1927
Perry, George W., 1927 (1), 1928, 1929 (1)

Piper, Clark N., 1928
Price, John M., 1929, 1930 (1), 1931 (Captain) (1)
Saunders, LaVerne G., 1927
Sebastian, Henry A., 1930, 1933
Seeman, Lyle E., 1927
Semple, Russell B., 1930 (Team Manager)
Senter, William O., 1931
Simenson, Edwin G., 1931
Simons, Maurice M., 1933
Sprague, Mortimer E., 1927 (1), 1928 (Captain) (1)
Stancook, Joseph C., 1932, 1933
Stecker, Ray J., 1930, 1931 (2)
Stillman, Robert M., 1932, 1933
Stone, William S., 1933 (Team Manager)
Suarez, Edward W., 1929, 1930, 1931
Summerfelt, Milton F., 1930, 1931, (1), 1932 (Captain) (1)
Trice, Harley N., 1929, 1930, 1931
Vidal, Felix L., 1932 (3)
Walsh, Birrell, 1927, 1928
Wilson, Harry E., 1927 (Captain) (3)
Wimer, Benjamin, R., 1928
Winn, James R., 1932, 1933

Dartmouth Lettermen, 1934 Through 1940

Aieta, James V., Jr., 1943
Arico, Joseph F., Jr., 1940
Armanani, Joseph P., 1938, 1939
Bartholomew, Dale E., 1940
Bauman, James C., 1939
Bennett, Gordon P., 1934, 1935, 1936 (Captain)
Billings, Henry, II, 1934, 1935
Boynton, John A., 1938 (Team Manager)
Burnkrant, Eugene G., 1934
Camerer, David M., 1935, 1936 (3)
Camp, Charles F., 1939
Camp, Elbert L., 1934, 1935
Campbell, Richard H., 1937
Carpenter, Richard E., 1934
Chamberlain, Edward T., Jr., 1934, 1935
Christiansan, Herbert P. W., 1937
Clark, P. E. Gordon, 1936
Clark, William B., 1934
Cohen, Arthur J., 1936 (Team Manager)
Cole, William, 1935, 1936
Colton, George H., 1934 (Team Manager)
Conti, Philip S., 1934, 1936
Cottone, Joseph F., 1938
Courter, Sanford T., 1938, 1939
Cowen, John L., 1939 (Team Manager)
Crego, Remsen H. R., 1940
Crowley, Joseph A., 1940
Dacey, Daniel P., Jr., 1939, 1940
Dampier, Maurice S., 1940
Davis, Merrill N., Jr., 1936 (2), 1937 (Captain)
Deckert, Harry C., 1934
Dostal, Philander L., 1938
Duckworth, Roy D., Jr., 1937
Feely, James A., Jr., 1937, 1938
Gates, Harrington K., 1936, 1937
Gerber, Harry G., 1940
Gibson, Robert W., 1937, 1938
Gross, Oliver J., 1939
Guenther, Jack G., 1939, 1940
Hagerman, Donald C., 1934
Hall, Raymond, Jr., 1939, 1940
Handrahan, John B., 1934, 1935
Handrahan, Joseph W., 1934, 1935, 1936 (1)
Hayden, Buford M., Jr., 1939
Hickey, Robert B., 1940
Highmark, Louis A., 1938
Hill, George F., 1934 (Captain)
Hollingworth, Fred W., 1935, 1936, 1937
Howe, Colby D., 1937, 1938
Hull, Lawrence C., III, 1935, 1937
Hutchinson, William D., 1937 (2), 1938, 1939 (3)
Ingersoll, Henry G., 1939
Kast, Edward R., 1940
Kelley, John W., 1939, 1940
Kenny, John J., 1934, 1935 (Captain)
Kiarsis, Victor, 1934
Kiernan, Joseph W., 1934, 1935, 1936
King, Warren, 1936, 1937
Krieger, Robert E., 1938, 1939, 1940
Krumm, Robert R., 1940

Lampke, Robert M., 1939
Lando, Tino, 1935
Lynch, Franklin, II, 1937
MacLeod, Robert F., 1936, 1937 (1), 1938 (Captain) (1)
Mansfield, Alfred B., 1939
Matzinger, John A., Jr., 1934, 1935
May, Stuart L., 1940
McCray, Taylor L., 1934, 1935, 1936
Merrill, John C., 1934, 1935, 1936
Miller, Charles W., 1937, 1938, 1939 (Captain)
Mills, Henry L., 1938
Morris, Robert S., 1935 (Team Manager)
Mudge, George O., 1938
Muello, Anthony G., 1934
Nairne, Frank B., Jr., 1934, 1935
Nissen, Robert W., 1938, 1939
Nopper, Howard A., 1938
Norton, Donald E., 1939, 1940
O'Brien, Robert F., 1939, 1940
Orr, John I., 1938, 1939
Otis, Donald N., 1934
Parks, James M., 1937, 1938
Pearson, Charles M., 1939, 1940

Price, George, 1934
Pyrtek, Ludwig J., 1936
Rand, Norman W., 1934
Ray, Carl P., 1934, 1935 (2), 1936
Reno, Robert H., 1937 (Team Manager)
Ritter, Myron H., 1934
Schildgen, Francis J., 1936, 1937
Smith, Irving F., 1940 (Team Manager)
Sommers, George E., 1938, 1939
Stearns, Charles H., Jr., 1934
Taylor, Vernon F., 1936, 1937
Thompson, Linwood K., 1940
Vulte, Loren J., 1937, 1938 (name changed from Dilkes, Loren J.)
Wakelin, Edmund F., 1938
Whitaker, Henry C., Jr., 1935, 1936
Williams, John L., 1935, 1936
Winship, Granville M., 1939, 1940
Wolfe, George R., 1940
Young, Louis A., Jr., 1938, 1939, 1940 (Captain)
Zitrides, Gregory G., 1937 (3), 1938 (2)

Army Lettermen, 1941 Through 1958

Abelman, Robert M., 1949
Ackerson, Bruce A., 1948, 1949, 1950
Adams, J. Glen, 1958
Anderson, Alfred J., 1946
Anderson, Carl B., 1942, 1943
Anderson, Robert P., 1957 (1), 1958 (1)
Arnold, Archibald V., Jr., 1944
Aton, Bert B., 1947, 1948
Attaya, Freddie A., 1951, 1952, 1953
Bagdonas, Edward, 1957, 1958
Bara, Raymond M., 1950
Barnes, Frank G., 1947, 1948
Barta, Vincent, 1955, 1956, 1957
Beck, Donald A., 1949, 1950
Bell, Thomas J., 1951, 1952, 1953, 1954 (1)
Bergeson, Raymond O., 1951
Biles, Shelton B., 1944, 1945, 1946
Bishop, Joseph A., 1954, 1956
Blaik, Robert M., 1949, 1950
Blanchard, Felix A., 1944 (1), 1945 (1), 1946 (Co-Captain) (1)

Bliss, Charles F., 1954
Bonko, Donald R., 1958
Borman, Frank, 1949 (Team Manager)
Bourland, David W., 1956, 1957
Boyle, Richard D., 1952
Brian, Ben F., 1950
Brown, Thomas E., 1949
Bryant, Goble W., 1945, 1946, 1947 (3)
Bryer, John E., 1958 (Team Manager)
Bullock, Thomas F., 1947, 1948
Burd, Frank A., 1955
Cain, James W., 1948, 1949 (3), 1950
Caldwell, Joseph, 1958
Carley, John W., 1943 (Team Manager)
Carpenter, William S., 1958
Catarinella, Roland S., 1943, 1945
Chabot, Robert A., 1945
Chamberlin, Neil A., 1951, 1952
Chambers, Earl L., 1952 (Team Manager)

Chance, Bill J., 1954
Chesnauskas, Ralph J., 1953, 1954 (1), 1955
Cook, Cline G., 1957 (Team Manager)
Cosentino, Rudolph V., 1947, 1948
Coulter, Dewitt E., 1944 (1), 1945 (1)
Crowell, Dean G., 1942
Cygler, Joseph, 1954, 1956
Daniel, Charles D., 1943
Davis, Bennie L., 1947, 1948, 1949
Davis, Glenn W., 1944 (1), 1945 (1), 1946 (Co-Captain) (1)
Dawkins, Peter M., 1947, 1958 (Captain) (1)
DeLucia, Mario L., 1952
Dielens, August J., 1948
Dobbs, Robert L., 1943, 1944
Doremus, William A., 1952
Drury, Raymond C., 1946, 1947
Elmblad, Bruce E., 1948, 1949, 1950
Enos, James W., 1944, 1945, 1946
Evans, Robert R., 1941
Everbach, Otto G., 1958
Fadel, Richard A., 1956
Farrell, Thomas F., 1941
Farris, Robert G., 1953 (1)
Fastuca, Salvatore E., 1948
Feir, Philip R., 1947, 1948
Filipski, Eugene C., 1950
Fischl, Frank R., 1949, 1950
Foldberg, Henry C., 1945 (1), 1946 (1)
Foldberg, John D., 1948 (2), 1949 (1), 1950 (Captain) (1)
Franklin, Joseph P., 1954
French, Forrest J., 1955 (Team Manager)
Fuqua, Donald G., 1951, 1952
Fuson, Herschel E., 1944, 1945, 1946
Gabriel, Charles A., 1949
Galiffa, Arnold A., 1947, 1948 (3), 1949 (1)
Galloway, Charles L., 1947, 1949
Gelini, Walter C., 1944
Gerometta, Arthur L., 1945, 1946 (2)
Gibson, Francis L., 1958
Gillette, Amos W., 1947
Gillette, Jack W., 1948
Glock, Howard G., 1953, 1954
Goodwin, Flay O., 1954, 1955, 1956

Graf, William S., 1957 (Name changed from Saunders, W. A.)
Green, John F., 1943, 1944 (1), 1945 (Captain) (1)
Greene, LeRoy V., 1958
Gregory, Theodore O., 1951
Gribble, Eugene P., 1950
Guess, Carl B., 1951
Guidera, Robert F., 1951, 1952
Gustafson, William W., 1946, 1947
Haas, Robert J., 1949, 1950
Haff, Wallace Kendall, 1951
Hagan, Jerome F., 1953
Hall, Dale S., 1943, 1944
Halligan, Theodore H., 1943
Harris, James H., 1952
Hart, Gerald E., 1950
Hatch, John E., 1941
Hayes, Robert E., 1943
Hayes, Thomas F., 1945, 1946
Heath, Mark C., 1956 (Team Manager)
Henn, William R., 1949
Hennessey, John J., 1942, 1943
Henrikson, Matthew T., 1948, 1949
Henry, Joseph R., 1947, 1948 (1)
Hill, Ralph J., 1941, 1942
Hilliard, Maurice, 1957, 1958
Holleder, Donald W., 1953, 1954 (1), 1955
Houser, Richard H., 1942 (Team Manager)
Howell, Martin D., 1948
Hynds, Wallace G., Jr., 1944 (Team Manager)
Inman, Richard G., 1951
Irons, James V., 1948, 1949
Jarrell, Herschel A., 1941, 1942
Johnson, Arthur D., 1954, 1955, 1956
Johnson, Herbert L., 1949, 1950
Kaseman, Ralph D., 1949
Keffer, Charles T., 1947, 1948
Kelleher, James E., 1941, 1942 (3)
Kelley, Gerald P., 1949
Kellum, William H., 1947, 1948, 1949
Kemble, Charles R., 1948 (Team Manager)
Kenna, Edgar D., 1942, 1944 (1)
Kennedy, James E., 1958
Kernan, James J., 1955, 1956, 1957 (Captain)
Kimmel, J. D., 1949, 1950 (1)

Knieriem, Fred G., 1954
Kramer, Kenneth R., 1951, 1952
Krause, John E., 1951, 1952, 1953
Krobock, John R., 1950, 1952
Kuckhahn, Karl O., 1948, 1949
Kuick, Stanley J., 1951
Kuyk, Charles F., 1949
Kyasky, Robert A., 1954, 1955, 1956
La Mar, William W., 1945
Ladd, James V. K., 1945 (Team Manager)
Lapchick, Joseph D., 1953
Lash, Peter W., 1954, 1955
Lasley, Paul A., 1953
Lincoln, Ronald H., 1951, 1952
Livesay, Harvey R., 1946, 1947
Lodge, Gerald A., 1951, 1952, 1953
Loehlein, Harold J., 1949, 1950
Lombardo, Thomas A., 1942, 1943, 1944 (Captain)
Lunn, Leroy T., 1951, 1952, 1953 (Captain)
Lunn, Robert J., 1947, 1948, 1949
Lutrey, Theodore T., 1941
Lytle, Charles E., 1957, 1958
Mackinnon, Robert N., 1943
Mackmull, Jack V., 1949
MacPhail, William, 1951
Maladowitz, Raymond, 1949
Malavasi, Raymond J., 1950
Manus, Peter C., 1952
Martin, Jack W., 1949, 1950
Maupin, Jere W., 1941
Maxon, George E., 1943
Mazur, Henry J., 1941 (3), 1942 (Captain) (2)
McCorkle, Alfred S., 1943
McCrane, Joseph M., 1949
McDaniel, Paul B., 1947, 1949
McShulskis, John E., 1950
McWilliams, Thomas E., 1945
Meador, Marion F., 1953 (Team Manager)
Meglen, John D., 1952
Melnik, Ronald P., 1953
Melnik, William C., 1957
Mericle, Russell A., 1954, 1955
Merritt, Francis E., 1942 (1), 1943 (2)
Mesereau, Thomas A., 1941, 1942
Meyers, Frederic D., 1951
Michel, Theodore J., 1941

Minor, John M., 1943, 1944
Mischak, Robert M., 1951, 1952, 1953 (1)
Morales, Michael, 1956, 1957
Morrison, John R., 1957, 1958
Munger, Robert L., 1955, 1956
Murphy, Edward C., 1942, 1943 (2)
Murphy, Raymond P., 1941 (Captain)
Murtland, Richard C., 1954, 1955, 1956
Myslinski, Casimir J., 1942, 1943 (Captain) (1)
Nemetz, Albert M., 1943, 1944, 1945 (1)
Novogratz, Robert, 1957, 1958 (1)
Olds, Robin, 1941, 1942 (1)
Ordway, Godwin, 1952, 1953, 1954
Oswandel, Robert, 1958
Parrish, Davis P., 1948
Paulekas, Alfred E., 1951, 1952 (Captain)
Pearce, Robert McI., 1943
Petruno, Michael J., 1956
Pitzer, Richard J., 1943, 1944, 1945
Pollard, Alfred L., 1950 (1)
Pollock, Victor J., 1949, 1950
Poole, George B., 1944 (1), 1945 (3), 1946 (2)
Purdue, William P., 1953
Quanbeck, Alton H., 1947 (Team Manager)
Rafalko, Edmund A., 1943, 1944
Rawers, James W., 1946, 1947, 1948
Ray, John H., 1946
Reed, Irving B., 1948
Reich, Gilbert M., 1950
Reich, Richard J., 1951
Reid, Donald E., 1954 (Team Manager)
Reid, Loren D., 1955, 1956
Ritchie, John, 1950 (Team Manager)
Roberts, John E., 1941, 1942
Rogers, John C., 1951
Romanek, Henry, 1941, 1942
Roberts, Richard J., 1949, 1950
Roesler, Gilbert E., 1956, 1957, 1958
Rose, Myron W., 1951, 1952
Rowan, Elwyn P., 1945, 1946, 1947 (1)
Rowe, William G., 1956, 1957, 1958
Rowekamp, William H., 1950

Rutte, Robert L., 1951 (Team Manager)
Ryan, John A., 1941 (Team Manager)
St. Onge, Robert J., 1943, 1944 (3)
Salzer, Lester LeR., 1942, 1943
Sampson, Charles W., 1942, 1943
Satterfield, Donald W., 1954, 1955
Sauer, John E., 1945
Saunders, William A., 1955, 1956
Schweikert, Paul, 1952
Scott, Thomas P., 1942
Scott, Winfield W., 1947, 1948
Scowcroft, Brent, 1946 (Team Manager)
Seip, George R., 1941
Seith, Louis T., 1941
Shain, Elwin R., 1953
Shannon, Donald J., 1955
Shelley, John R., 1947, 1948
Shira, Charles N., 1949, 1950 (1)
Shultz, Harold D., 1948, 1949, 1950
Sisson, Lowell E., 151, 1952, 1953
Slater, Stanley A., 1955, 1956 (3), 1957
Stahle, John C., 1942
Stahura, Edward J., 1950
Stanowicz, Joseph J., 1943, 1944 (1)
Steffy, Joseph B., 1945, 1946 (1), 1947 (Captain) (1)
Stephen, Norman F., 1951, 1952, 1953
Stephenson, Floyd Gil, 1948, 1949, 1950
Stephenson, Richard E., 1954, 1955, 1956
Stone, Hardy R., 1949
Stout, Elmer E., 1949, 1950 (1)
Stuart, Robert J., 1945, 1947, 1948 (1)
Szvetecz, Edward, 1954, 1955, 1956 (Captain)
Tavzel, Harold S., 1944, 1946
Tillar, Donaldson P., 1958
Trent, John C., 1947, 1948, 1949 (Captain)

Troxell, George H., 1942, 1943
Tucker, Young Arnold, 1945 (2), 1946 (1)
Uebel, Patrick N., 1953, 1954, 1955 (Captain)
Usry, Donald J., 1957, 1958
Vanderbush, Albert, 1958
Vann, Peter J., 1952, 1953, 1954 (2)
Vinson, Bobby G., 1947, 1948, 1949
Volonnino, Robert L., 1950
Waldrop, Stephen P., 1957, 1958
Walterhouse, Richard G., 1944, 1945
Walters, Harry N., 1956, 1957, 1958
Warner, Richard E., 1955, 1956, 1957
Waters, Russel A., 1958
Watkins, James H., 1941
Wayne, Robert E., 1945
Weaver, John E., 1950, 1952
Webb, William H., 1944, 1945
West, William I., 1946
White, Ernest J., 1941
White, Ralph J., 1941
Whitlow, Robert V., 1941
Wilkerson, Frank S., 1951, 1952
Williams, Lewis A., 1951
Wilmoth, Frederick L., 1956, 1957
Wilson, Willard B., 1941, 1942
Wing, John R., 1951, 1952
Woods, Robert E., 1942
Yeoman, William F., 1946, 1947, 1948 (Captain) (2)
Yost, William D., 1958
Zeigler, Lewis R., 1950
Zeigler, Michael G., 1953, 1954, 1955
Ziegler, Richard G., 1952, 1953

The All-America statistics were assembled with the aid of the football historians, Colonel Alexander M. Weyand of Cornwall-on-Hudson, New York, and Professor Lacy Lockert of Nashville, Tennessee.

Index

Abelman, Bob, 265
Abernathy, Ralph, 479
Abramson, Jesse, 355
Acheson, Dean, 492, 504
Ackerson, Bruce, 265
Adams, Emory S., 176
Adams, Glenn, 383, 385
Adams, John, 199, 247
Albert, King of Belgium, 46
Aldrin, Buzz (Col.), 437
Alexander, Roger (Col.), 97, 119, 416
Allan, Charles, 88, 90
Allen, Mel, 92
Almond, J. Lindsay, Jr., 398
Amateur Athletic Union, 470-3
Amen, Paul, 251, 318, 422, 437
American Association of University Professors, 411
American Football Coaches Association, 42, 309, 410, 411, 414
Anderson, Bob, 6, 256, 287, 404, 405; games, 338, 359, 368-9, 371-2, 377-85, 387-9, 395
Anderson, Dr. Eddie, 146
Anderson, Heartley, 76, 110
Anderson, Kyle, 74
Annapolis: Dartmouth game, 159; West Point games, 82, 108, 114-115, 120, 178-9, 183, 190-1, 201-4, 208, 210-12, 225-9, 245-8, 260-1, 270, 275, 316, 326, 333-5, 338, 344-6, 350, 352-6, 360, 363-4, 367, 372, 386-9, 391, 418, 440-1
Armstrong, Jack, 105
Army Academic Board, 35, 48, 286, 289, 291, 292, 383, 450-1, 459, 513, 515
Army Athletic Association, 92, 119, 208, 320, 362
Army Athletic Association Board, 119-20, 396, 545; chairman, 261, 392, 393-4; meetings, 169, 173, 233,
223-5, 319, 399; members, 171, 208
Arnold, Archibald, Jr. (Maj.), 25, 189, 195, 206
Arnold, Archibald V. (Maj.), 25
Ashbaugh, Russell, 224, 435
Associated Press, 392, 402
Association of Graduates of West Point, 458-9, 466, 511, 528
Attaya, Fred, 323-4, 328, 331
AVCO Corporation, 13, 261, 391-3, 402, 404, 425, 430, 474, 475, 485-6

Bagdonas, Ed, 376-7
Bailey, Mel, 477-8
Baker Field see Columbia University
Baker, Newton D., 123
Baldwin, Hanson, 319, 321
Baltimore Municipal Stadium, 202
Barber, Red, 92
Barnum, Rollie, 74
Barron, Red, 201, 203
Barta, Vince, 362, 364, 369
Beagle, Ron, 344, 353
Beall, John, 120
Bearg, Ernest, 90
Beck, Don, 265
Bell, Tommy, 323-5, 328, 333, 338-9, 342, 343
Bellino, Joe, 386, 388
Benedict, Jay (Gen.), 168
Bennett, Gordon, 149, 151
Bentley, Warren, 187
Bertelli, Angelo, 177, 182, 189
Bessell, William W., Jr. (Gen.), 62
Bevan, Roland, 6, 47, 380, 417-18; at Dartmouth, 131-6, 148, 149; at West Point, 170, 175, 182, 218, 220, 261, 444
Bezdek, Hugo, 82
Biles, Shelton, 195, 196, 207, 208, 216, 217
Bird, Stephen, 30-1, 513
Black, Cupe, 427-8

Blackburn, George, 16, 251, 422
Blaik, Douglas Livingston, 5, 12
Blaik, Earl: childhood and education, 3-49; officer, 50-63; Miami coaching, 64-79; West Point assistant coach, 80-120; games, 82, 83, 87, 89, 90, 92, 93, 105, 106, 108, 109, 110, 112, 113, 114, 115, 118, 120-1; Dartmouth head coach, 121-69; games, 129, 130, 131,˙ 140, 142, 147, 148, 149, 151, 152, 153-8, 159-65, 168, 231; West Point head coach, 170-390; games, 177, 178, 179, 182, 183, 189, 190-1, 196, 197, 198-200, 201-4, 208, 209, 210-11, 216, 218-20, 223, 224, 225-9, 241-4, 245-8, 249, 252, 256, 257-8, 259, 260-1, 266-8, 270, 272-3, 275, 316, 321, 322, 326, 327, 332, 338, 339-42, 343, 344-6, 349, 350, 351-2, 352-6, 360, 361-2, 363, 365, 367-70, 371, 372, 376, 378, 379-82, 383, 384-6, 386-9, 391; civil rights work, 473-82
Blaik, Mabel, 12
Blaik, Margaret Purcell, 7, 8, 12
Blaik, Merle McDowell, 49, 51, 67, 70, 75, 97, 116, 128, 159, 173, 256, 271, 299, 314, 327, 397, 399, 402, 405, 447, 538, 544; marriage, 18, 69
Blaik, Robert McDowell, 5, 289, 298, 397, 435, 437, 457, 526; birth, 97; football, 265, 266, 271-3, 275
Blaik, Will, 11
Blaik, William, 84, 271, 375, 397, 398, 399
Blaik, William Douglas, 10, 16-17, 21, 49, 73, 77, 84, 95, 124, 229; background, 11-13; death, 229
Blanchard, Felix Anthony (Maj.), 6, 20, 81, 82, 231, 234, 246, 247, 249, 250, 256, 314, 332, 364, 424, 425, 437, 544; background, 193, 194, 195, 203; football, 192-6, 198-9, 202-7, 209-11, 215-22, 225-7, 229, 418, 469, 523-4
Blough, Roger, 415
Bonko, Don, 378, 385
Bonner, Dr. Horace, 22
Booth, James Albert, 92-3, 105, 106
Booz, Oscar L., 30

Borman, Frank (Col.), 437
Born, Charles, 83
Boston, Clarence, 250, 342, 422
Boston *Herald*, 137, 543
Boston *Traveler*, 137
Bourguignon, Richard, 434
Bourland, Dave, 360, 362, 364, 368-9, 371
Bowman, John Gabbert, 138
Bowman, Wendell, 105
Boynton, Benny, 38
Bradley, Omar (Gen.), 287, 318, 463, 492, 493, 506
Brennan, Terry, 224, 225, 243, 244, 368, 380, 382
Brentnall, Sam, 83
Breslin, Ed, 434
Bridges, Styles, 490
Brieske, Jim, 220
Brill, Marty, 106
Brown, Edwin J., 10-11
Brown, Jim, 351, 362
Brown, Paul, 15
Brown, Tom, 265
Brown, Travis, 111, 120
Brown University: games, 156-7, 196
Brucker, Wilbur M., 400
Bruhn, Milt, 76
Bryan, Blackshear M. (Gen.), 80, 97, 119, 339, 341, 350, 356-7, 393, 401, 524
Bryant, Bear, 423
Bryant, Goble, 206, 224, 228, 241, 247
Bucek, Bill, 385-6
Buckler, Jack, 113, 115, 118, 202
Bucknam, Ralph, 120
Bull Pond, 262, 264, 360, 376, 401
Bundy, William, 481, 487
Burick, Si, 131
Burlingame, Paul, 120
Burrus, Jeff, 74
Bushnell, Asa, 164
Busick, Bill, 178
Butterfield, Jackson T., 21
Byers, Clovis (Col.), 47, 205
Byers, Walter, 545
Byrne, Ed, 9
Byrne, Joseph, 379-80

Cagle, Christian Keener, 6, 77, 80-3, 85-8, 90-5, 189
Cahill, Joe,2 95, 398, 434

Cain, Jimmy, 264, 265, 268, 272
Caldwell, Bruce, 83
Caldwell, Joe, 6, 337; football, 358-9, 377-9, 381-3, 384-6, 388-9, 416
Camerer, Dave, 61, 141. 148, 149, 151, 153
Camp, Walter, 48
Cann, Howard, 38
Capra, Frank, 415
Carideo, Frank, 93, 106, 108
Carl, Pitt F. (Lieut.), 48
Carlmark, Carl, 93, 94, 105
Carmichael, John, 210
Carney, Bill (Admiral), 501
Carpenter, William Stanley (Lonely End), 6, 358, 364, 375-81, 389, 394, 416, 418
Carter Field, 88; *see* Notre Dame
Carver, Robert, 93, 105, 111
Catarinella, Roland, 189
Cavanaugh, Father John W., 232
Cavanaugh, Frank (Maj.), 46, 74, 96, 416
Chabot, Bob, 189
Chalmers, Hugh, 13
Chamberlain, Eddie, 134
Chappuis, Bob, 220
Chase, Ben, 201
Chesnauskas, Ralph, 325, 333, 334, 345, 348, 352, 355
Chewning, Lynn, 227, 228
Chicago *Daily News*, 210
Chicago *Tribune*, 382, 491
Chidlaw, Ben, 27
Choquette, Paul J., 403
Citadel, The: West Point games, 177, 316
Coast Guard: West Point game, 196
Cobb, Ty, 271
Coffey, Jack (Col.), 262
Cohane, Tim, 434, 436
Colburn, Carrie, 9
Coleman, Harry, 17, 68
Colgate University: West Point games, 352, 362, 371, 383
Collins, Lawton (Gen.), 291, 318, 445, 451, 459, 493, 506
Columbia University: Dartmouth games, 149, 154-5; West Point games, 177, 223, 242-3, 316, 321, 342, 352, 362
Commager, Dr. Henry Steele, 311

Conadeo, Tony, 434
Condon, Dave, 382
Connor, Eugene "Bull", 475, 477, 478
Connor, George, 216, 223, 243, 244, 435
Connor, William D. (Maj. Gen.), 100, 114, 120
Considine, Bob, 279, 497
Constable, Pepper, 148
Conti, Phil, 153
Conway, Al, 265
Cook, George Harvey, 15, 31
Cook, Mal, 20
Cooke, Terence Cardinal, 434
Copeland, Harold, 50
Cornell University: Dartmouth games, 129, 154, 158-9, 165, 168, 231; West Point games, 220, 257
Corput, Rex (Col.), 205
Cosell, Howard, 543-4
Coughlan, Roundy, 75
Coulter, DeWitt, 195, 196, 203, 207, 211, 217
Counts, Gerald A. (Gen.), 208, 249, 262, 263
Coutre, Larry, 244
Cowhig, Gerald, 224
Cox, James M., 12-13, 21
Crawford, Chief, 20
Crawford, James, 37
Crego, Bob, 160, 162
Crisler, Herbert Orrin (Fritz), 144-5, 146, 147, 209, 216, 253, 267
Crofoot, Toad, 73
Crowder, Edward, 423
Crowley, Jimmy, 108, 146
Crowther, Rae, 146, 332
Cunningham, Bill, 543, 544
Curtice, Jack, 372
Czarobski, Zuggie, 224, 244

Daley, Arthur, 355, 380, 434
Dallas Cowboys, 439
Daley, Charles Dudley (Capt.), 6, 70, 80, 86, 141, 416; as coach, 43, 46, 47, 69, 236, 274, 384; player, 40, 41
Daley, Maurice F., 98, 100, 101, 137
Dancewicz, Frank, 97
Danford, Robert H. (Maj. Gen.), 32, 37, 291, 460, 513, 535
Daniel, Averell, 173

Daniel, Maurice, 47
Danielson, Ollie (Col.), 173
Danzig, Allison, 159, 348
Dartmouth College: West Point games, 316, 321, 327, 339-42; see Blaik, Earl
Davidson College, 266
Davidson, Garrison H. (Gen.), 98, 100, 119-20, 393, 396-7, 399, 449-50, 518-19, 547
Davis, Al, 431
Davis, Bennie, 265
Davis, Elmer, 501
Davis, Glenn Woodward, 6, 20, 81, 82, 231, 234, 246, 249, 250, 256, 272, 314, 332, 364-5, 399, 424, 425, 437, 544; football, 186-9, 191, 195, 196, 202-7, 209-11, 215-17, 219-23, 225-7, 229, 418, 469
Davis, Jean, 84, 111
Davis, Jim, 111, 112
Davis, Merrill, 149, 154
Davis, Ralph, 187
Davis, Willie, 434
Dawkins, Dr. Henry E., 366
Dawkins, Mrs. H. E., 366
Dawkins, Pete, 6, 33, 105, 303, 359, 364-7, 369, 371-2, 377-83, 385-90, 394-5
Dawson, Red, 344
Dayton *Journal*, 9
Dayton *News*, 131
Deeds, Edward Andrew, 13
Demarest, Harriet, 398
Detroit *Free Press*, 267
Devers, Jake (Gen.), 116, 179
Devine, Tommy, 367
Devore, Hugh J., 209
Dewey, Thomas E., 490-1
Dial, Buddy, 384
Dietzel, Paul, 15, 250, 423, 424, 438
Dobbs, Bobby, 189, 195, 202, 206, 251, 344, 423-4, 429, 438
Dobie, Gilmour, 47, 147, 240, 416
Dodd, Bobby, 308
Doe, Tom, 6, 459
Doke, Maurice, 403
Donchess, Joe, 125, 429
Donelli, Aldo, 146
Dooley, Eddie, 124, 164
Dorais, Gus, 236
Dostal, Phil, 155

Draddy, Vincent, 403, 415
Drahos, Nick, 163
Draper, Phil, 263
Drew, Roger, 275
Drury, Ray, 237
Duden, Dick, 201
Duke University: West Point games, 196, 209, 223, 327, 339, 342-3
Dulles, Allen, 474
Dulles, John Foster, 504, 506-7, 508

Early, Steve, 489, 499
Ebbets Field, 236
Echols, Charles P. (Col.), 98-9, 114
Ecuyer, Al, 380
Eddleman, Clyde (Gen.), 498
Eichelberger, "Miss Em", 527
Eichelberger, Robert (Gen.), 6, 119, 204-5, 211, 232, 295, 402, 406, 450, 451-2, 526-7; West Point Superintendent, 167-91, 445, 519
Eichenlaub, Ray, 236
Eisenhower, Dwight D., 50, 210, 287, 383-4, 401, 415, 463, 488, 494-7, 500, 505-8, 510, 520, 541-2, 553
Eisenhower, John, 497
Eisenhower, Mamie, 496
Eisenhower, Milton, 496
Eisenhower, Roy J., 50
Elder, Jack, 94
Ellinger, Harry, 6, 193, 199, 425, 429; assistant coach, 91, 97-102, 104, 108-15, 120-1, 125, 134, 137, 138, 139, 173; death, 179, 184, 426
Elliott, Len, 318
Elmblad, Bruce, 265, 522
Emanuel, Albert, 13
Emanuel, Victor, 13, 261, 391-2, 398, 401, 430, 494
Erdelatz, Eddie, 270, 275, 344, 353, 366, 386-7
Evans, Bob, 178
Evans, Dave, 539
Evans, Roy, 11
Evashevski, Forest, 144
Everbach, Otto, 378
Ewart, Charlie, 141
Ewbank, Wilbur, 15

Fallon, Jack, 223
Farley, Jim, 434

Farmer, Malcolm, 140
Farris, Bob, 325, 326, 334-5, 338, 405
Farwick, Gus, 101, 199
Faurot, Don, 216
Fellers, Bonner, 500
Fenton, Chauncey L. (Gen.), 171, 459
Fields, Den, 105, 108, 112, 113
Fields, Dr. Edward R., 480
Filipski, Gene, 2272
Filley, Pat, 197
Finch, Bob, 434
Finos, Vic, 201, 203
Fischer, Bill, 223, 243-4
Fischl, Frank, 264, 272
Fisher, N. E. (Mas. Ser.), 271
Flanagan, Christy, 76, 94
Flara, John, 383
Fleming, Philip B. (Maj.), 86, 87, 91-2, 106, 109, 121, 518
Flodin, Don, 477
Foldberg, Danny, 256, 260, 265, 268, 272-3
Foldberg, Henry, 195-6, 203, 207, 211, 216, 222, 225, 228-9
Folsom, Bobby, 217, 221
Ford, Henry, 12
Fordham University: West Point game, 268
Forrest, Nathan Bedford, 101
Fortas, Abe, 482
"Four Horsemen", 144, 206
Frank, Clint, 155-6
Franklin Field see Annapolis and Pennsylvania
Fraser, Harvey (Col.), 372-3
French, Ned, 170, 173
Frentzel, Bill, 105, 115
Friedman, Benny, 72, 73
Friesell, William H., 163
Fuller, Robert, 154
Fuson, Herschel, 195, 196, 203, 207-8, 216-17, 237

Galiffa, Arnold, 241, 256, 259, 260, 264, 265, 266, 268, 271-2
Galloway, Lynn, 237, 265
Ganoe, Bill, 517, 535-7
Garbisch, Ed, 85
Gaston, A. Y., 478
Gates, Harry, 149, 150, 153, 157, 158
Georgia Institute of Technology, 321

Gerhardt, Charlie, 42-3
Gerometta, Art, 195, 196, 207, 216, 229
Gibson, Bob, 149
Giese, Warren, 219, 378
Gilette, William W. (Gen.), 62
Gillis, Bill, 237
Gillman, Sid, 16, 250, 253, 260-1, 342, 424, 428, 436, 444
Gilmore, Bruce, 361
Gipp, George, 45-6
Glass, Ed, 41
Glock, Howard, 326, 333, 334
Goldberg, Marshall, 139
Goldwater, Barry, 473, 481
Gompers, Bill, 224
Gooch, Stacy, 120
Goodwin, Flay, 348, 364
Goodyear, George (Capt.), 61
Gottfried, Chuck, 398
Grace, Princess of Monaco, 362
Graham, Frank, 269
Grange, Harold, 71, 207
Grant, Richard, 13
Grant, Ulysses S. (Gen.), 497
Graves, Ernest, 6, 40-5, 97, 235
Grayson, Harry, 256
Green Bay Packers, 434, 439-40, 442
Green, Jack, 189, 195, 205, 211, 217, 424-5, 437
Greenlaw, Harvey, 30-1
Gregory, Sam, 50-2
Griswold, A. Whitney, 143-5, 166
Grombach, John Valentin, 33-4
Gromyko, Andrei, 480-1
Grosscup, Lee, 372
Grove, Edward, 120
Groves, Leslie (Gen.), 39, 528
Gruenther, Al (Lieut.), 98
Guckeyson, John W., 172
Guess, Carl, 265
Gunlock, Bill, 398
Gushorst, Gus, 236
Gustafson, Andy, 375, 418, 425, 521; assistant coach, 125, 173, 185, 192, 196, 199, 211-12, 217, 223, 226; head coach, 250, 272, 342
Gustafson, Bill, 217, 241

Haas, Bob, 265
Hagberg, Oscar (Comm.), 191-210
Hagen, Jerry, 321, 323, 328

Hahn, Corley, 80
Haines, Henry Luther, 38
Halas, George, 151, 434
Hall, Alice, 10
Hall, Dale: assistant coach, 357, 376, 387, 394; head coach, 398, 404, 425; player, 181, 195, 196, 202, 203, 206, 429
Halligan, Ted, 182
Halsey, William "Bull" (Admiral), 34, 492, 501-3
Hamberg, Hal, 201, 203
Hamilton, Tom (Admiral), 77, 225, 228, 344
Hand, Learned, 291-3, 451
Handrahan, Joe, 135, 148
Handrahan, John, 135, 141, 149
Harbold, Norris, 83
Harding, Neil, 106-7
Harkins, Paul (Col.), 445-7, 452, 454, 456-8, 523
Harlow, Dick, 124, 145, 148, 178, 416, 422
Harmon, Doyle, 74
Harmon, Tom, 144
Harp, Tom, 398, 426
Harrison, W. Don, 138
Hart, Leon, 224, 244
Harvard University: Dartmouth games, 129, 148, 153, 154, 159; West Point games, 87, 92, 108, 113, 120, 178, 252, 316
Haughton, Percy Duncan, 40-1
Havens, Benny, 31, 542
Hawkins, Bill, 228, 260
Hayes, Arthur, 477
Hayes, Tom, 195-6, 216
Hayes, Woody, 16
Hebert, F. Edward, 179, 426, 458
Heffelfinger, Pudge, 44-5
Heller, Warren, 110-12
Henn, Bill, 265
Henrikson, Matt, 265
Henry, Dodie, 320
Henry, Joe, 251
Henry, Leonard (Lieut. Col.), 192, 320
Herb, Ed, 105
Hibbs, Louis E., 37
Hickman, Herman Michael, 166, 287, 310, 418, 424, 426-8, 432, 521; assistant coach, 184-6, 196, 199, 209, 214-15, 217, 227, 253, 399; death, 428; head coach, 250
Hilliard, Maurice, 377
Hillsinger, Loren, 93
Hinkle, Carl C., 172
Hirshberg, Eddie, 125, 139, 429
Hobbs, W. H. (Prof.), 266-7
Hogan, Jim, 41
Hoge, Benny, 43
Holcomb, Stuart, 16, 196, 250, 342, 429
Holleder, Don, 325, 327, 332, 336-57, 360, 372, 420
Hollingsworth, Fred, 149, 152
Holmes, Burton, 98
Holmes, Glenn, 72, 73
Honor Code, 5, 279-300, 444-68, 514
Hoover, Herbert, 108, 415, 484, 520
Hope, Bob, 223
Hopkins, Rev. Adoniram Judson, 123
Hopkins, Dr. Ernest Martin: with Blaik at Dartmouth, 6, 122-6, 130, 136, 138-9, 141-2, 153, 159, 163, 170, 173, 174, 520
Horner, Emerson L., 8, 9
Hornung, Paul, 434-5
Houston Oilers, 424
Howe, Arthur, 235
Howe, Colby, 149, 158
Howell, Edward, 90
Howell, Martin, 251-2, 260-1, 328, 329, 382
Howze, Robert Lee (Maj. Gen.), 54, 58, 60
Hull, Ed (Gen.), 19, 402
Humber, Charles, 93, 105
Hume, Redman, 87
Humphrey, Gil, 153, 155
Humphrey, Hubert, 472
Husing, Ted, 92
Hutchins, Robert M., 312
Hutchinson, Bill, 149, 154
Hutchinson, Dick, 83, 88, 93
Hutchison, Johnny, 120, 470
Hutson, Don, 221, 336

Illinois, University of: West Point games, 92, 106, 118, 120, 257, 365
Impel, Tom, 173
Ingwersen, Burt, 74, 257
International Amateur Federation, 471
International News Service, 497

Irons, Jim, 265
Irving, Frederick A. (Gen.), 289, 319-21, 445-51, 458-9, 522-3
Israel, Dick, 68
Ivy League, 144-5, 156, 165-6, 170, 231, 234, 252, 306, 309
Izo, George, 380

Jablonsky, Harvey (Gen.), 112, 120, 176
Jenkins, Bob, 201, 202, 203
Joesting, Herb, 74
Johnson, Art, 348, 352
Johnson, Herb, 265
Johnson, Lady Bird, 484
Johnson, Louis, 521
Johnson, Lyndon B., 452, 458, 482, 484-5, 498, 504, 505
Johnson, Paul, 120
Johnston, Mundey, 314
Jones, Harris (Gen.), 383, 459
Jones, Howard, 416
Jones, Lawrence McCeney ("Biff"), 6, 106-7, 111, 189, 199-200, 224, 339, 401, 422; assistant coach, 69; head coach, 76-80, 83-4, 87, 94-5, 101, 518-19; player, 42-3
Jones, Tad, 83, 105-6, 416
Joyce, Father Edmund P., 240
Just, Jim, 381

Kaliden, Bill, 383
Kane, Frank, 218
Kase, Max, 398
Kaseman, Ralph, 265
Kasiska, Bob, 73
Katzenbach, Nicholas, 481
Kelley, Gerry, 265
Kelley, Larry, 141, 153
Kellum, Bill, 237, 247, 265
Kelly, Bob, 197
Kenna, Douglas, 181, 183, 195, 198-9, 205-6, 263, 429-30, 437
Kennedy, Caroline, 481
Kennedy, Ethel, 482-5
Kennedy, John F., 415, 458, 469-82, 483, 484, 486-7, 488, 498-9, 504, 505
Kennedy, John, Jr., 481
Kennedy, Joseph, 483
Kennedy, Robert, 469, 470-1, 473-4, 480, 481, 482-7, 498, 527

Kennedy, Walter, 92
Kenny, Jack, 141, 148
Kernan, Jim, 348, 364
Kerr, Andy, 91
Kettering, Charles Franklin, 13, 444
Kiefer, Jackson, 9
Kilday, Tom, 10J, 112
Kimmel, J. D., 265, 272
King, Clyde, 48
King, Dick, 105, 108, 111-13
King, Martin Luther, 475, 477, 479, 480, 481
King, Warren, 149
Kissinger, Henry, 552
Klee, Ollie, 9
Koehler, Herman, 36, 49, 76
Kopcsak, Pete, 111, 120
Kosikowski, Frank, 223
Krause, Ed, 240
Kreuz, Red, 73
Krieger, Bob, 162
Krueger, Doris, 435
Krueger, Orrin C. (Gen.), 249, 263, 434-5, 522-3
Kuckhahn, Karl, 265, 266
Kusserow, Lou, 242, 243
Kutch, Nick, 74
Kuyk, Charlie, 265
Kyasky, Bob, 337-8, 342, 343, 345, 348, 360-1, 363-4, 405

LaFollette, Robert, 20
LaMar, Bill, 189, 195
Landsberg, Mort, 160, 162
Langhorne, George (Col.), 54, 56
Lapchick, Joe, Jr., 326, 332
Lapham, Lewis, 508-9
Lardner, Ring, 71
LaRoche, Chester, 415
Larson, Lloyd, 73
Larson, Robert, 477
Lash, Pete, 352, 354-5
Lasley, Paul, 327, 332
Lassiter, Bob, 109
Lauterbur, Frank, 376, 398, 430
Lavelle, Jack, 380-1
Lawes, Lewis E., 196, 209
Leahy, Frank, 197, 214, 496; Boston coach, 146, 543; Notre Dame coach, 177, 182, 216, 224, 232, 240, 256, 258, 435, 548
Lear, Ben (Gen.), 116

Lee, Robert E. (Gen.), 497
Legg, Jack, 120
Leiser, Bill, 258
Leitl, Lester, 73, 74
Lemnitzer, Lyman (Gen.), 62, 541
Leone, Gene, 59, 229, 262, 295, 297, 401
Leopold, Crown Prince, 46
Letzelter, Cy (Col.), 105, 176
Leusche, Albert, 57, 62
Levitas, R. B., 434
Lieb, Tom, 72
Life Magazine, 508-9, 528
Lipscomb, "Big Daddy", 53
Little, Lou, 146, 242
Livesay, Harvey, 217
Lobert, Hans, 39, 100
Lodge, Gerry, 323-4, 334
Loehlein, Hal, 265, 269
Lomax, Stan, 92
Lombardi, Vince, 250, 263, 264, 327, 389, 430-1, 435-43; death, 434-5, 443
Lombardo, Tom, 183, 195, 203, 204, 237
Long, Charles, 198
Long, Huey P., 79
Look Magazine, 402, 436
Loomis, Harold, 235
Los Angeles Rams, 424
Lourie, Donald, 415
Lowden, Francis, 124, 164
Luckman, Sid, 154
Lujack, Johnny, 189, 219, 224, 225, 231, 244, 256
Lunn, Bob, 265
Lunn, Roy, 325
Lutz, Worth, 328-31
Lynah, Jim, 163, 164
Lystad, Helmer (Abe), 47, 541
Lytle, Charlie, 376

MacArthur, Arthur, 526
MacArthur, Arthur (Gen.), 484, 528
MacArthur, Douglas (Gen.), 6, 413, 415, 440, 450, 455, 470-3, 476, 483, 488-537, 547, 548, 551, 552-3; association with as undergraduate, 24-49; communications and advice, 63, 67, 70, 179, 204, 236, 255, 279, 299-300, 315, 319, 321, 323, 355, 384, 390, 401, 474; death, 484-5
MacArthur, Jean, 484, 489-90, 502, 522, 525, 526, 528
Mack, Red, 380
Mackmull, Jack, 265
MacLeod, Robert, 6, 126, 133, 149-59
Macready, John A. (Capt.), 52
Magnusson, Warren, 472
Maladowitz, Ray, 265
Malavaski, Ray, 272
Malloy, John, 105
Mann, Joe, 9
Mara, Jack, 438-9
Mara, Wellington, 438-9
Marks, Wally, 75
Marshall, Burke, 475
Marshall, George C. (Gen.), 167, 280, 293, 499, 500, 502, 504
Martin, Ben, 201
Martin, Jack, 186
Martin, Jack (Army), 265, 268, 272, 273
Martin, Jack (Navy), 201
Martin, Jim, 223, 244
Mason, Dr. Jesse W., 298
Mastrangelo, Frank, 197, 223
Mathes, Jim, 9
Matuszczak, Walter, 160, 163
McCall's, 14
McCarthy, Ray, 91
McClain, Slim, 207
McClelland, Don, 267
McComsey, John A. (Col.), 459
McCray, Alfred, 9
McCray, Latta, 9
McDonald, Elizabeth Pfaff, 58, 399
McDonald, Willis, 38, 50, 51, 52, 53, 58, 61, 62, 399
McEwan, John, 42-4, 69-70, 80, 101, 203, 210, 460
McJunkin, Fred (Col.), 87
McKeever, Ed, 197, 216
McKemy, Dr. John W., 21
McKenna, John, 66
McLaughry, DeOrmond, 146, 156-7, 543
McMillan, Bill, 53
McMillin, Bo, 208
McMullen, Dan, 90
McNamara, Robert, 481, 487
McNamee, Graham, 88
McQuarrie, Claude, 45, 46, 48
McWilliam, Joe, 115

McWilliams, Tom, 206, 207, 209, 211
Meacham, Lawrence B., 42-3
Meadows, Ed, 328
Meehan, Art, 100
Mello, Jim, 224
Melnik, Ron, 326
Memorial Field see Dartmouth College
Merigo, Juan, 60
Merillat, Louis, 42, 43, 44, 236
Merritt, Frank, 190
Merriwell, Frank, 549
Mesereau, Tom, 199, 262, 522
Messinger, Ed (Gen.), 87-8, 90, 93, 105, 339, 340, 356-7
Meyer, Charles Robert (Col.), 205
Meyers, Fred, 316-17
Michie, Dennis, 234
Michie Stadium: West Point games, 16, 37, 54, 86-7, 89-90, 112, 115, 131, 169, 197, 213, 218, 223, 233, 253, 256, 257, 268, 316, 327, 341, 351, 362, 367, 371, 372, 378, 382, 383, 403
Michigan Stadium, 220
Michigan, University of: West Point games, 105, 108, 208-9, 220-2, 266-267, 272, 339, 341-2, 349, 361
Middleton, Troy H. (Lieut. Gen.), 292
Mikelonis, Gene, 338, 360, 405
Miller, Paul, 93, 105
Milner, Wayne, 120
Milwaukee *Sentinel*, 74
Minor, Max, 189, 195, 196, 202, 204, 429
Mischak, Bob, 325, 327, 330, 334
Mississippi State University, 115
Mitchell, Hugh, 39
Mitchell, Jack, 219
Monnett, Bob, 108
Montgomery, Bernard L. (Br. Field Marshall Viscount), 217, 523
Montgomery, Rev. Edward, 69
Moore, Bryant (Maj. Gen.), 276-8, 339, 523
Moore, Frank, 125, 173
Moore, Jammie, 478
Moore, Lenny, 349
Morgan, J. P., 525-6
Morrison, Jack, 378, 381
Morrison, Ray, 87, 190
Muha, Joe, 177

Mullin, Willard, 183, 229, 262, 263-4, 363, 376
Munger, George, 146, 332
Municipal Stadium see Annapolis and Notre Dame
Murphy, Bill, 162-3
Murphy, Cornelius J., 110
Murphy, Ed, 190
Murphy, Ray, 178
Murrell, Johnny, 81, 83, 93, 186
Murrow, Ed, 327
Murtland, Dick, 354
Myers, Gary, 381
Myers, Dr. William, 404
Myslinski, Cas, 184, 190

Nairne, Frank, 141
Namath, Joe, 414
Nashville Banner, 225
National Collegiate Athletic Association, 249, 253, 255, 303, 307, 309, 470-3, 545
National Football Foundation, 39, 393, 403, 415-20, 469, 483
Nave, William, 81, 83
Neale, Earl, 146, 154
Nebraska, University of: West Point games, 89-90
Neely, Jess, 384
Neidlinger, Lloyd K., 159, 170
Neiss, Ollie (Sur. Gen.), 175, 183
Nemetz, Al, 189, 195, 207, 211, 217
Newark *Evening News*, 318
Newark *Star Ledger*, 361
Newell, Donald P., 403
New Haven *Register*, 105
New Mexico, University of: West Point game, 273
Newton, William, 184
New York *Daily Mirror*, 291
New York *Daily News*, 443
New York Giants, 438-9
New York *Herald Tribune*, 8, 137-8, 355
New York Jets, 440, 483
New York *Journal American*, 269, 398
New York *Sun*, 121, 124, 206
New York *Times*, 137-8, 159, 263, 319, 348, 355, 359, 460
New York *World-Telegram*, 59, 229, 297

New York *World-Telegram and Sun,* 183
Neyland, Bob (Gen.), 42, 184, 416, 426, 432
Niemiec, Johnny, 89
Nimitz, Chester (Admiral), 500-3
Nixon, Richard M., 415, 434, 469, 505
North Carolina, University of: West Point game, 196
Northwestern University: West Point games, 316, 327, 437-8
Notre Dame Stadium, 240
Notre Dame, University of: West Point games, 83, 87-9, 92-3, 106-8, 113-14, 120-1, 177-8, 182, 189, 197-200, 209-10, 223-4, 241-4, 367-70, 379-82, 435
Novogratz, Bob, 359, 376, 381, 388-9, 395
Nulton, Louis M., 85
Nydahl, Mally, 74

Oakland Raiders, 431
O'Brien, Eddie, 109
O'Brien, Johnny, 89
O'Connor, Paul, 106
Odell, Howard, 250
O'Donnell, Emmett, 97, 100
O'Donnell, Ken, 470
Odyniec, Norman, 381
O'Keefe, Dick, 90, 93
Oklahoma, University of: West Point game, 218-20
Oldham, Ned, 372
Olds, Robin, 178, 183-4
Oliphant, Elmer (Lieut.), 42, 43, 83, 189
Olivar, Jordan, 353, 419
Olympic Committee, 470
Oosterbaan, Bennie, 72, 73, 267, 353, 419
Ordway, Godwin, 323, 342
Ortmann, Chuck, 266-7
O'Shea, Joseph, 37
Osmanski, Bill, 152
Oswandel, Bob, 376, 378
Owen, Steve, 438
Owens, Jim, 219

Pace, Frank (Sec. of the Army), 291-294, 445, 492
Palmer Stadium, 148

Panelli, John, 224, 244
Parker, Dan, 298
Parker, Dud, 109
Parks, Jim, 149
Parrish, Dave, 260
Parseghian, Ara, 16
Patton, George (Gen.), 446, 465, 536
Pelosi, James J., 464
Pennsylvania, University of: West Point games, 178, 200, 210, 216, 225, 244-5, 249, 259, 266, 272-3, 316, 321, 322, 326, 332, 349, 353, 361, 363, 367, 379
Perkins, Jack, 334
Perry, George, 93
Perry, Lawrence, 102, 104
Pew, Howard, 494
Phelps, William Lyon (Prof.), 310, 311
Pierce, Marvin, 13-14, 19, 128
Pietrosante, Nick, 368-70, 380-1
Pillings, Ed, 380
Pittsburgh, University of: West Point games, 110, 112-13, 321, 362, 371, 378, 382-3
Pittser, Chet, 71
Pitzer, Dick, 189, 195, 207
Pliska, Joe, 236
Poe, Edgar Allan, 31
Pohl, Francis I. (Col.), 187
Pollard, Al, 272, 273, 274
Pollock, Vic, 265, 272
Polo Grounds, 82, 91, 236
Pond, Raymond, 122, 146, 156
Poole, George, 195, 196, 205, 207, 211, 216, 228, 229
Pottios, Myron, 381
Powell, Adam Clayton, 476
Price, Jack, 105, 110, 111, 171
Prichard, Vernon, 42-3, 236
Prince, Jack, 93
Princeton University: Dartmouth games, 147, 151, 153
Pritchard, Abisha, 177
Purcell, Henry, 12
Purdue, Bill, 322
Pusey, Dr. Nathan Marsh, 166
Pyrtek, Lud, 153

Radford, (Admiral), 492
Rafalko, Ed, 181, 195, 206, 208
Raines, Ella, 184

Rand, Jim, 505
Ranier, Prince, 362
Rawers, Jim, 217
Ray, Carl, 135, 141, 149, 151-2
Ray, Jack, 221, 226, 229
Ray, James Earl, 477
Reagan, Ronald, 550
Reeder, Russell, Jr., 117
Reeder, Russell P. (Col.), 6, 91, 94, 97, 100, 117, 200, 263, 274, 341, 373
Reese, Dr. David, 199
Reeves, James Haynes (Col.), 56, 57, 60
Reich, Gilbert, 272
Reid, Gordon, 473
Reider, Paul, 110
Reifsnyder, Bob, 372, 386-7
Rice, Grantland, 71, 104, 112, 183, 274, 323, 429
Rice Institute: West Point game, 384-6
Richardson, Leon B. (Prof.), 139
Richardson, "Nellie" (Lt. Gen.), 500-1
Rickey, Branch, 188
Rider, George L., 19
Ridgway, Matthew B. (Capt.), 413
Ridlon, Jim, 362
Roberts, Chester A., 19
Roberts, Dick, 265
Roberts, Fran, 263
Rockne, Knute, 46, 70, 72, 76, 88, 93, 96, 106, 110, 196-7, 233, 236, 410, 413, 416, 548
Roesler, Gil, 362, 378
Roos, Philip G., 403
Roosevelt, Eleanor, 178, 489-90
Roosevelt, Franklin D., 13, 85-6, 171-172, 476, 484, 488, 489-90, 495, 499, 500-4, 508
Roosevelt, Theodore, 40, 41, 66, 433, 484
Root, Reggie, 121
Roper, Bill, 96
Rose, Gene, 73
Rosenman, Judge Samuel, 501-3
Rossides, Gene, 242, 243
Rowan, Elwyn, 206, 217, 221, 241, 242, 247
Rowe, Bill, 376, 387
Royal, Darrell, 219
Royall, Kenneth, 473-82
Rusk, Dean, 480, 492

Russell, Freddy, 225
Russell, John, 53
Russell, Richard, 504
St. John, Lynn W., 121
St. Onge, Bob, 181, 195, 206
Salvaterra, Cornelius, 363
Sampson, Arthur, 137, 147, 240
Sampson, Charlie, 190
San Diego Chargers, 424
San Francisco *Chronicle*, 258
Sasse, Ralph I. (Maj.), 6, 179, 190, 198, 224, 331, 339; active duty, 94, 96, 97; assistant coach, 42, 77, 80, 89, 91; head coach, 103-17, 119, 169, 518-19, 520
Saturday Evening Post, 61
Sauer, Ed, 20
Sauer, John, 20, 189, 199, 206, 250, 431
Saunders, Bill, 348
Savoldi, Joe, 106
Schick, Lawrence E. (Col.), 62, 450-1
Schlesinger, Arthur, 487
Schmidt, Francis, 121, 370, 392, 418
Schoellkopf Stadium, 158, 257
Scholl, Walter, 160, 162, 163
Schuyler, Cort, 27
Schwartz, Marchy, 106, 108
Schwartzwalder, Ben, 353, 361-2, 419
Schwedes, Gerhard H., 403
Schwenk, Jim, 263
Scott, Clyde, 201, 203, 209, 211
Scott, Winfield, 256
Scripps-Howard, 172
Sebastian, Henry, 120
Sebo, Steve, 65, 158, 344
Sensenbaugher, Dean, 195
Shain, Rox, 322, 333
Shattuck, Milton, 28
Shaughnessy, Clark, 182, 193
Sheridan, Phil, 101
Sheridan, Richard Brinsley, Jr., 108-11
Shevlin, Tom, 41
Shira, Charlie, 265
Shores, Arthur, 478
Shultz, Hal, 260, 265, 272
Siegal, Arthur, 137
Signaigo, Joe, 233-4
Simpson, O. J., 414
Sisson, Lowell, 325
Sitko, Emil, 224, 435

Skladany, Joe, 112
Skoglund, Bob, 223
Slater, Stan, 348, 355, 364
Slaughter, Edliff, 72
Sloan, Alfred P., 526
Sloan, Clair, 90
Smalley, Mary, 134
Smedberg, W. R. II (Rear Admiral), 364
Smith, Bruce, 211
Smith, Red, 239, 328-30
Smith, William R. (Gen.), 94
Smits, Ted, 392
Smyth, Pat, 403
Snavely, Carl, 144, 146, 154, 158, 159, 162, 163, 164
Soldier Field, 106, 236
Sollee, Neyle, 403
Sorensen, Ted, 487
South Carolina, University of: West Point games, 321, 338, 341
Southern California, University of: West Point game, 316
Southern Methodist University: West Point game, 87
Spears, Dr. Clarence W., 74
Spellman, Francis Cardinal, 298
Sprague, Mortimer E., 85, 87
Stagg, Amos Alonzo, 74, 119, 310, 410, 416
Stamps, Dodson (Col.), 233
Stancook, Joe, 115, 120
Stanford *Daily*, 258
Stanford University: West Point games, 90, 92, 257-8
Stanowicz, Joe, 181, 195, 203, 205, 206
Starr, Bart, 434, 437, 439, 442
Stassen, Harold, 344, 490
Stecker, Ray James, 6, 105, 106, 108, 111, 189
Steffen, Wally, 76
Steffy, Joe, 206, 217, 229, 241, 247
Stephen, Norman, 325, 334-5
Stephens, Joel (Maj.), 257-8
Stephenson, Dick, 348
Stephenson, Gilbert, 256, 260, 264, 266-7, 269, 272
Sterling, John, 128
Stickles, Monty, 370, 380
Stillman, Bob, 120
Stokes, Johnny, 80, 97

Stone, Hardy, 265
Stotesbury, E. T., 525
Stout, Elmer, 265, 272
Straubel, Austin, 73
Stremic, Tony, 372
Strohmeyer, George, 216, 224
Struck, Vernon, 154
Stuart, Bobby Jack, 206, 241, 256, 259, 260
Stuart, J. E. B., 96, 111, 518, 536
Suarez, Ed, 105, 111
"Subway Alumni," 236-9, 268
Sullivan, George, 197, 223
Sullivan, Riggs (Gen.), 176, 198
Sultan, Dan, 41, 42, 235
Summerfelt, Milt, 105, 112, 115
Sundt, Guy, 72, 73
Sutherland, John Bain, 89, 110, 112-113, 125, 138, 139, 146, 173, 273, 416, 425
Swiacki, Bill, 242-3
Swistowicz, Mike, 224, 244
Symington, James, 483-4
Symington, Stuart, 483
Syracuse University: West Point games, 351-2, 361-2
Szymanski, Frank, 197

Taft, Robert A., 490-1, 494-5, 504
Tatum, Jim, 194, 215-16, 218, 219
Tatum, Mary Elizabeth, 194
Tavzel, Harold, 195, 196, 198
Taylor, Maxwell D. (Gen.), 27, 220, 233, 261, 276, 445, 451, 458, 466
Taylor, Vernon, 135-6, 156
Temple University: West Point game, 189
Teninga, Wally, 267
Thayer, Sylvanus (Gen.), 87, 340, 462, 517, 535
Thieme, Al, 265
Thistlewaite, Glenn, 73, 75-6, 194
Thompson, Charles F., 32, 34-5, 513-514
Thompson Stadium, 201
Thompson, Tommy (Col.), 58
Thorpe, Jim, 207, 384
Tillman, Samuel (Col.), 512
Tolly, Harry R., 403
Tormey, Joe, 113
Touchdown Club of New York, 133, 319, 375, 401

Tranchini, Joe, 386
Trent, Johnny, 237, 247, 259, 265, 267
Trevor, George, 104, 121-2, 154, 206
Trice, Harley, 100, 105, 108, 111
Trippe, Juan, 415
Troxell, George, 181
Truman, Harry S, 220, 260, 294, 295, 488, 491-3, 504-5, 552
Tucker, Beverly Saint George, 26
Tucker, Young Arnold, 195, 196, 206, 207, 216-17, 219-27, 229, 418, 437
Tulane University: West Point game, 371
Tuttle, Harry, 47

Uebel, Pat, 323-4, 326, 328, 333-4, 338-9, 342, 348, 355
Unitas, Johnny, 349
United States Track and Field Federation, 471-2
University of Michigan Daily, 266-7
Urban, Gasper, 223
Usry, Don, 359, 377-8, 381, 389
Utah, University of, 371
Uteritz, Irv, 72

Valpey, Art, 267
Vanderbilt, Alfred Gwynne, 59
Vanderbush, Al, 378
Vann, Peter, 323-4, 327-8, 331, 333, 337-8, 343, 345, 346-7
Vaughan, Harry (Gen.), 294, 521
Vidal, Felix, 112-13, 115
Vidal, Gene, 39, 42, 83
Villanova University: West Point games, 196, 209, 218, 256, 316, 376, 386
Vinson, Bobby, 265, 270
Virginia Military Institute: West Point games, 177, 321
Virginia Polytechnic Institute, 257
Virginia, University of: West Point games, 343, 371, 382
Vitucci, Vito, 178
Voris, Dick, 251, 382, 431-2

Wagner, Betty, 320
Wagner, Hayden W. (Col.), 320, 459
Wagner, Rube, 73
Waldorf, Lynn, 258
Waldrop, Steve, 377-8
Walker, Wade, 219

Wallace, George, 474-5
Wallace, Henry, 496
Walsh, Bill, 224, 244
Walters, Harry, 364, 369, 370, 371, 382, 385-6
Warmath, Murray, 250, 263, 272, 342, 432, 436, 437, 446
Warner, Glenn Scobey, 80, 90-1, 105, 125, 154, 410, 416
Washington Redskins, 434, 440, 443, 483
Waterhouse, Dick, 189, 195, 196, 202, 203, 204, 206
Waters, John (Col.), 446-7, 464, 465, 522
Waters, Russ, 377-8
Watsey, Steve, 265
Watson, Edwin P. (Gen.), 85, 172
Watson, Thomas J., 13
Wayne, Bob, 189
Webb, Bill, 189, 195
Wedge, Will, 206
Wells, Walter (Capt.), 92
Welsh, George, 333-4, 344-7, 349, 352
Wendell, Marty, 197, 224, 244
Werthner, William B., 10-11
West, Bill, 196, 217
West, Charles W., 62
Westmoreland, William (Gen.), 425, 548
West Virginia University: West Point game, 223
Weyand, Alexander, 42
Wheat, Rev. Clayton E., 32, 513
Whelchel, John Esten, 191
Whitaker, Henry, 153
White, Justice Byron, 415, 483
White, Paul, 221-2
White, Thomas (Gen.), 61, 458, 461
Whitlock, John B., 18
Whitmire, Dick, 201
Whitmire, Don, 191, 203
Whitney, Courtney (Gen.), 401, 534
Wicks, Roger, 80
Wilby, Francis B. (Gen.), 179, 233
Wilde, Earl, 73
Wilkinson, Bud, 219, 272
Willaman, Sam, 121
Williams, Bob, 380-1
Williams, Edward Bennett, 434
Williams, Dr. Harry, 387
Williams, Jack, 136

Williams, Joe, 172, 207, 297
Williams, Pete, 228
Williamson, Ivan, 76
Wilson, Dick, 404
Wilson, Harry, 81-2, 85, 189
Wilson, Woodrow, 20, 551
Winans, Edwin B. (Maj. Gen.), 85
Wistert, Al, 267
Wood, Barry, 92, 108
Wood, Bill, 42, 80, 171
Wood, Robert (Gen.), 4477
Woodruff, Bob, 251, 342, 432
Woodruff, Sam, 208
Woodward, Stanley, 8, 262, 263, 361, 376, 386, 401

Yablonski, Ventan, 242, 243
Yale Bowl *see* Yale University
Yale University: Dartmouth games, 129, 140-2, 148, 153, 155-6, 157-8, 159; West Point games, 83, 87, 92-3, 105, 109, 113, 115, 120, 343, 352
Yanelli, Sylvio, 218
Yankee Stadium, 90-2, 106, 208, 242; *see also* Notre Dame
Yeoman, Bill, 217, 226, 241, 247, 258, 433
Yerges, Howard, 220
Yost, Fielding H., 71-2, 410, 416
Young, Archie, 16-17
Young, Jimmy, 18
Young, Lou, 149, 161, 163

Zastrow, Bobby, 275
Zeigler, Mike, 323, 325, 328, 338-9, 342, 348, 352
Ziegler, Dick, 325
Zilly, Jack, 223
Zitrides, Gus, 149
Zuppke, Bob, 73, 96, 118, 416